D0706886

Learning and Expectations in Macroeconomics

FRONTIERS OF ECONOMIC RESEARCH

Series Editors

David M. Kreps   Thomas J. Sargent

Learning and Expectations in Macroeconomics

George W. Evans and Seppo Honkapohja

Princeton University Press
Princeton and Oxford

Copyright © 2001 by Princeton University Press
Published by Princeton University Press, 41 William Street,
Princeton, New Jersey 08540
In the United Kingdom: PrincetonUniversity Press, 3 Market Place, Woodstock,
Oxfordshire OX20 1SY

All Rights Reserved

Library of Congress Cataloging-in-Publication Data

Evans, George W., 1949-
    Learning and expectations in macroeconomics / George W. Evans, Seppo Honkapohja.
        p.cm.—(Frontiers of economic research)
    Includes bibliographical references and index.
    ISBN 0-691-04921-1 (cloth: alk. paper)
      1. Rational expectations (Economic theory) 2. Economics–Methodology.
    3. Economics–Statistical methods. I. Honkapohja, Seppo, 1951- II. Title. III. Series.

    HB172.5.E94 2001
    339—dc21   00-048320

This book has been composed in Baskerville

The paper used in this publication meets the minimum requirements of ANSI/NISO
Z39.48-1992 (R 1997) (*Permanence of Paper*)

www.pup.princeton.edu

Printed in the United States of America

1 3 5 7 9 10 8 6 4 2

*To Pauline and Sirkku
and to our parents*

"Good judgment comes from experience. Experience comes from bad judgment."

(Higdon's Law)

Contents

Part II. Mathematical Background and Tools

Part III. Learning in Linear Models

Part IV. Learning in Nonlinear Models

Part V. Further Topics

Preface

This book provides a systematic treatment of the learning approach to modeling expectations formation in macroeconomics. This approach goes beyond rational expectations, the current standard hypothesis about expectations in macroeconomic theory. We focus on adaptive learning in which, at each moment of time, agents make forecasts using forecast functions formulated on the basis of available data, and these forecast functions are revised over time as new data become available. The body of this book is devoted to the statistical or econometric approach to learning which futher postulates that econometric techniques are used to estimate the parameters of the forecast functions.

Most of the research on adaptive learning within macroeconomics has been in this area, though other approaches have also been studied. While a number of surveys (including two by us) are available, a full treatise has been missing and this book aims to fill the gap.

Models of adaptive learning introduce a specific form of bounded rationality, as economic agents are assumed to maximize utility or profit given their forecasts at each moment of time, and the method used to estimate the forecast parameters is based on standard econometric techniques such as least squares. Rational expectations then becomes an equilibrium or fixed point of the learning dynamics, and in fact some early contributions have informally justified rational expectations as the outcome of a trial-and-error process. One can view the study of adaptive learning as making this justification explicit. In contrast, rational learning retains the rational expectations assumption continuously over time.

The study of adaptive learning offers much more than just a rationale for rational expectations. It provides a check on the robustness of equilibria with respect to expectational errors. It offers a way of selecting among multiple equilibria, which is a major conundrum for many rational expectations models. Another use of learning dynamics is computational, since the recursive algorithms provide a method for numerically computing equilibria. Learning also offers new possibilities for modeling dynamic macroeconomic phenomena. Some of these possible uses of adaptive learning in applied modeling have only recently been explored by researchers.

We have tried to provide a systematic treatment of the econometric approach to adaptive learning in a way that should be accessible and useful to both graduate students and professional economists. After an introductory part, the presentation covers both general techniques and their application to widely used standard frameworks. In several places we extend the state of knowledge in directions that should prove useful in both applied and theoretical macroeconomics. Chapter 10 contains a systematic treatment of adaptive learning for linear multivariate models. Until now this has not been systematically developed in a way that is useful for applications. In Chapter 13 and 14 we provide a discussion of the implications of misspecification in learning, including dynamics of learning with constant-gain algorithms. A further notable feature is Part II, in which the general mathematical techniques are explained in some detail.

Who Should Read This Book and How?

We have intended this book for two audiences. First, the book should be useful for professional economists interested in dynamic macroeconomic theory and applied macroeconomic modeling. This includes practitioners with some previous knowledge but who need a systematic treatment of the subject. It also includes graduate students who encounter the subject for the first time. As explained below, the book is structured so that it contains both an introduction and a systematic treatise of the subject.

The second audience consists of researchers and graduate students in other areas of economics and related fields in which the modeling of expectations is an integral part of their analytical frameworks. A case in point is financial economics in which expectations play a key role. We have not ventured far in this field (or others), though we do discuss the standard present-value model of asset princing.

Part I of the book provides an introduction to adaptive learning. The level of exposition is geared towards first-year graduate students who have some familiarity with modern dynamic macroeconomic theory. It starts with a historical overview and general discussion in Chapter 1, and this is followed by a leisurely introduction of the basic approach and technique in Chapter 2. Chapters 3 and 4 offer, respectively, some variations on the basic approach and an exposition on how to formulate and analyze learning in several standard models.

Part II is devoted to an exposition of the general mathematical technique on which adaptive learning is formally based. After a background chapter on basic mathematical concepts, two main chapters provide a detailed discussion of the methods of stochastic approximation. Chapter 6 is a treatment of the basic stability and instability results for stochastic recursive algorithms. Chapter 7 contains a number of further developments including nonstochastic algorithms, a speed-of-convergence result for the usual algorithms, and some results for algorithms with constant gain. These last results have quite recently found application in economics. It should be noted that this part is technically much more demanding than other parts of the book. However, its detailed reading is not necessary since the formal theorems can be consulted when necessary.

Part III is a systematic discussion of linear models. Chapter 8 contains the most central results for standard univariate frameworks arising from many macroeconomic models. The level of discussion is relatively elementary, and this chapter is accessible to anyone who has read only through Part I. Chapter 9 takes up several further specialized topics for univariate linear models. Chapter 10 is devoted to multivariate linear models. This chapter develops the analysis of learning for general frameworks covering many macroeconomic models that appear frequently in the literature. Two appendices treat the linearization of multivariate models and the Blanchard–Kahn solution technique for both regular and irregular models.

In Part IV attention is directed at nonlinear models with an emphasis on stochastic frameworks that are appropriate when, for example, technology or preference shocks are present. Chapter 11 contains the basic stability and instability results for steady-state equilibria, and these are applied to a number of specific economic models. Chapter 12 takes up nonlinear models of endogenous fluctuations. Both periodic cycles and sunspot equilibria are considered, and these types of equilibria in several models are analyzed for stability under learning. Most of the material in this part should be accessible if the reader is familiar with only Part I.

Part V, the last part of the book, looks at extensions and recent developments. Chapters 13 and 14 consider a number of cases in which learning does not converge to a rational expectations equilibrium. This happens if agents are not using all relevant information or if they use a learning rule that does not fully converge because it allows for recurring structural shifts. Many of these issues have only quite recently been analyzed, and our treatment both introduces and contributes to the literature. Chapter 15 provides an overview of alternative approaches and some further issues. Finally, Chapter 16 offers some perspectives and conclusions on the subject.

Parts of the book are designed so that they can be used during a first-year graduate course in macroeconomics. Familiarity with standard rational expectations modeling is a prerequisite for Part I. This part, by itself or together with

Chapters 8, 11, and 15, would form an attractive introduction to the field for first- or second-year graduate students. Material in the other parts can be added for specialist courses. A web site with problem sets and other supplementary material is available at the address www.valt.helsinki.fi/geshbook/.

Acknowledgments

The book has grown out of our joint research since the late 1980s. The concrete impetus for writing the book came during the Nordic Research Course that we taught in Helsinki in the summer of 1995. Over the years we have given, both together and separately, courses and series of lectures on the subject at the London School of Economics, University of California at Los Angeles, University of Århus, Stockholm School of Economics, Norwegian School of Economics, Hitotsubashi University in Tokyo, Centre for Economic Studies in University of Munich, Bank of Finland, University of Helsinki, and University of Oregon. We have also given a large number of research seminars on our papers in the field. The comments and criticisms from the audiences on these occasions have helped us a great deal. The individuals are too numerous to list.

However, there are persons who have been especially helpful with their comments and suggestions on specific papers, the manuscript for this book, or in our collaboration with them. Their contribution deserves a specific mention: Klaus Adam, Takeshi Amemiya, Jasmina Arifovic, Kenneth J. Arrow, Costas Azariadis, Paul Beaudry, Michele Boldrin, William Brainard, François Bourguignon, Jim Bullard, Pierre-Andre Chiappori, Larry Christiano, In-Koo Cho, Tim Cogley, Birgit Grodal, Peter Howitt, Aaron Jackson, Alan Kirman, Lennart Ljung, Ramon Marimon, Bennett T. McCallum, Bruce McGough, Kaushik Mitra, Mikko Packalen, Marco Pagano, Jouko Paunio, David Romer, Paul Romer, Carolina Sierimo, Ariane Szafarz, Karl Vind, Robert Waldman, Kenneth Wallis, Paul Williamson, and Mike Woodford. We would also like to thank Nina Hauhio for assistance with the index and Katri Uutela for preparation of the theoretical graphs.

We wish to express our very special thanks to Tom Sargent for his encouragement in the writing of the book and for comments on our work over the many years.

We have received financial support from different sources. We gratefully acknowledge this important input from the Academy of Finland, the National Science Foundation, the Yrjö Jahnsson Foundation, the SPES Programme of the European Union, and our Universities.

Learning and Expectations in Macroeconomics

Part I

View of the Landscape

Chapter 1

Expectations and the Learning Approach

1.1 Expectations in Macroeconomics

Modern economic theory recognizes that the central difference between economics and natural sciences lies in the forward-looking decisions made by economic agents. In every segment of macroeconomics expectations play a key role. In consumption theory the paradigm life-cycle and permanent income approaches stress the role of expected future incomes. In investment decisions present-value calculations are conditional on expected future prices and sales. Asset prices (equity prices, interest rates, and exchange rates) clearly depend on expected future prices. Many other examples can be given.

Contemporary macroeconomics gives due weight to the role of expectations. A central aspect is that expectations influence the time path of the economy, and one might reasonably hypothesize that the time path of the economy influences expectations. The current standard methodology for modeling expectations is to assume *rational expectations* (RE), which is in fact an equilibrium in this two-sided relationship. Formally, in dynamic stochastic models, RE is usually defined as the mathematical conditional expectation of the relevant variables. The expectations are conditioned on all of the information available to the decision makers. For reasons that are well known, and which we will later explain, RE implicitly makes some rather strong assumptions.

5

Rational expectations modeling has been the latest step in a very long line of dynamic theories which have emphasized the role of expectations. The earliest references to economic expectations or forecasts date to the ancient Greek philosophers. In Politics (1259a), Aristotle recounts an anecdote concerning the pre-Socratic philosopher Thales of Miletus (c. 636–c. 546 B.C.). Forecasting one winter that there would be a great olive harvest in the coming year, Thales placed deposits for the use of all the olive presses in Chios and Miletus. He then made a large amount of money letting out the presses at high rates when the harvest time arrived.[1] Stories illustrating the importance of expectations in economic decision making can also be found in the Old Testament. In Genesis 41–47 we are told that Joseph (on behalf of the Pharaoh) took actions to store grain from years of good harvest in advance of years in which he forecasted famine. He was then able to sell the stored grains back during the famine years, eventually trading for livestock when the farmers' money ran out.[2]

Systematic economic theories or analyses in which expectations play a major role began as early as Henry Thornton's treatment of paper credit, published in 1802, and Émile Cheysson's 1887 formulation of a framework which had features of the "cobweb" cycle.[3] There is also some discussion of the role of expectations by the Classical Economists, but while they were interested in dynamic issues such as capital accumulation and growth, their method of analysis was essentially static. The economy was thought to be in a stationary state which can be seen as a sequence of static equilibria. A part of this interpretation was the notion of perfect foresight, so that expectations were equated with actual outcomes. This downplayed the significance of expectations.

Alfred Marshall extended the classical approach to incorporate the distinction between the short and the long run. He did not have a full dynamic theory, but he is credited with the notion of "static expectations" of prices. The first explicit analysis of stability in the cobweb model was made by Ezekiel (1938). Hicks (1939) is considered to be the key systematic exposition of the temporary equilibrium approach, initiated by the Stockholm school, in which expectations

---

[1] In giving this story, as well as another about a Sicilian who bought up all the iron from the iron mines, Aristotle also emphasized the advantage of creating a monopoly.

[2] The forecasting methods used in these stories provide an interesting contrast with those analyzed in this book. Thales is said to have relied on his skill in the stars, and Joseph's forecasts were based on the divine interpretation of dreams.

[3] This is pointed out in Schumpeter (1954, pp. 720 and 842, respectively). Hebert (1973) discusses Cheysson's formulation. The bibliographical references are Cheysson (1887) and Thornton (1939).

of future prices influence demands and supplies in a general equilibrium context.[4] Finally, Muth (1961) was the first to formulate explicitly the notion of rational expectations and did so in the context of the cobweb model.[5]

In macroeconomic contexts the importance of the state of long-term expectations of prospective yields for investment and asset prices was emphasized by Keynes in his General Theory.[6] Keynes emphasized the central role of expectations for the determination of investment, output, and employment. However, he often stressed the subjective basis for the state of confidence and did not provide an explicit model of how expectations are formed.[7] In the 1950s and 1960s expectations were introduced into almost every area of macroeconomics, including consumption, investment, money demand, and inflation. Typically, expectations were mechanically incorporated in macroeconomic modeling using adaptive expectations or related lag schemes. Rational expectations then made the decisive appearance in macroeconomics in the papers of Lucas (1972) and Sargent (1973).[8]

We will now illustrate some of these ways of modeling expectations with the aid of two well-known models. The first one is the cobweb model, though it may be noted that a version of the Lucas (1973) macroeconomic model is formally identical to it. The second is the well-known Cagan model of inflation (see Cagan, 1956). Some other models can be put in the same form, in particular versions of the present-value model of asset pricing.

These two examples are chosen for their familiarity and simplicity. This book will analyze a large number of macroeconomic models, including linear as well as nonlinear expectations models and univariate as well as multivariate models. Recent developments in modeling expectations have gone beyond rational expectations in specifying learning mechanisms which describe the evolution of expectation rules over time. The aim of this book is to develop systematically this new view of expectations formation and its implications for macroeconomic theory.

---

[4]Lindahl (1939) is perhaps the clearest discussion of the approach of the Stockholm school. Hicks (1965) has a discussion of the methods of dynamic analysis in the context of capital accumulation and growth. However, Hicks does not consider rational expectations.

[5]Sargent (1993) cites Hurwicz (1946) for the first use of the term "rational expectations."

[6]See Keynes (1936, Chapter 12).

[7]Some passages, particularly in Keynes (1937), suggest that attempting to forecast very distant future events can almost overwhelm rational calculation. For a forceful presentation of this view, see Loasby (1976, Chapter 9).

[8]Most of the early literature on rational expectations is collected in the volumes Lucas and Sargent (1981) and Lucas (1981).

1.2   Two Examples

1.2.1   The Cobweb Model

Consider a single competitive market in which there is a time lag in production. Demand is assumed to depend negatively on the prevailing market price

$$d_t = m_I - m_p p_t + v_{1t},$$

while supply depends positively on the expected price

$$s_t = r_I + r_p p_t^e + v_{2t},$$

where m_p, $r_p > 0$ and m_I and r_I denote the intercepts. We have introduced shocks to both demand and supply. v_{1t} and v_{2t} are unobserved white noise random variables. The interpretation of the supply function is that there is a one-period production lag, so that supply decisions for period t must be based on information available at time $t - 1$. We will typically make the representative agent assumption that all agents have the same expectation, but at some points of the book we explicitly take up the issue of heterogeneous expectations. In the preceding equation p_t^e can be interpreted as the average expectation across firms.

We assume that markets clear, so that $s_t = d_t$. The reduced form for this model is

$$p_t = \mu + \alpha p_t^e + \eta_t, \tag{1.1}$$

where $\mu = (m_I - r_I)/m_p$ and $\alpha = -r_p/m_p$. Note that $\alpha < 0$. $\eta_t = (v_{1t} - v_{2t})/m_p$ so that we can write $\eta_t \sim \text{iid}(0, \sigma_\eta^2)$. Equation (1.1) is an example of a temporary equilibrium relationship in which the current price depends on price expectations.

The well-known Lucas (1973) aggregate supply model can be put in the same form. Suppose that aggregate output is given by

$$q_t = \bar{q} + \pi (p_t - p_t^e) + \zeta_t,$$

where $\pi > 0$, while aggregate demand is given by the quantity theory equation

$$m_t + v_t = p_t + q_t,$$

where v_t is a velocity shock. Here all variables are in logarithmic form. Finally, assume that money supply is random around a constant mean

$$m_t = \bar{m} + u_t.$$

Here u_t, v_t, and ζ_t are white noise shocks. The reduced form for this model is

$$p_t = (1 + \pi)^{-1}(\bar{m} - \bar{q}) + \pi(1 + \pi)^{-1}p_t^e + (1 + \pi)^{-1}(u_t + v_t - \zeta_t).$$

This equation is precisely of the same form as equation (1.1) with $\alpha = \pi(1 + \pi)^{-1}$ and $\eta_t = (1 + \pi)^{-1}(u_t + v_t - \zeta_t)$. Note that in this example $0 < \alpha < 1$.

Our formulation of the cobweb model has been made very simple for illustrative purposes. It can be readily generalized, e.g., to incorporate observable exogenous variables. This will be done in later chapters.

1.2.2 The Cagan Model

In a simple version of the Cagan model of inflation, the demand for money depends linearly on expected inflation,

$$m_t - p_t = -\psi\left(p_{t+1}^e - p_t\right), \qquad \psi > 0,$$

where m_t is the log of the money supply at time t, p_t is the log of the price level at time t, and p_{t+1}^e denotes the expectation of p_{t+1} formed in time t. We assume that m_t is iid with a constant mean. Solving for p_t, we get

$$p_t = \alpha p_{t+1}^e + \beta m_t, \tag{1.2}$$

where $\alpha = \psi(1 + \psi)^{-1}$ and $\beta = (1 + \psi)^{-1}$.

The basic model of asset pricing under risk neutrality takes the same form. Under suitable assumptions all assets earn the expected rate of return $1 + r$, where $r > 0$ is the real net interest rate, assumed constant. If an asset pays dividend d_t at the beginning of period t, then its price p_t at t is given by $p_t = (1 + r)^{-1}p_{t+1}^e + d_t$.[9] This is clearly of the same form as equation (1.2).

1.3 Classical Models of Expectation Formation

The reduced forms (1.1) and (1.2) of the preceding examples clearly illustrate the central role of expectations. Indeed, both of them show how the current

---

[9]See, e.g., Blanchard and Fischer (1989, pp. 215–216).

market-clearing price depends on expected prices. These reduced forms thus describe a temporary equilibrium which is conditioned by the expectations. Developments since the Stockholm School, Keynes, and Hicks can be seen as different theories of expectations formation, i.e., how to close the model so that it constitutes a fully specified dynamic theory. We now briefly describe some of the most widely used schemes with the aid of the examples.

Naive or static expectations were widely used in the early literature. In the context of the cobweb model they take the form of

$$p_t^e = p_{t-1}.$$

Once this is substituted into equation (1.1), one obtains $p_t = \mu + \alpha p_{t-1} + \eta_t$, which is a stochastic process known as an AR(1) process. In the early literature there were no random shocks, yielding a simple difference equation $p_t = \mu + \alpha p_{t-1}$. This immediately led to the question whether the generated sequence of prices converged to the stationary state over time. The convergence condition is, of course, $|\alpha| < 1$. Whether this is satisfied depends on the relative slopes of the demand and supply curves.[10] In the stochastic case this condition determines whether the price converges to a stationary stochastic process.

The origins of the *adaptive expectations* hypothesis can be traced back to Irving Fisher (see Fisher, 1930). It was formally introduced in the 1950s by Cagan (1956), Friedman (1957), and Nerlove (1958). In terms of the price level the hypothesis takes the form

$$p_t^e = p_{t-1}^e + \lambda\left(p_{t-1} - p_{t-1}^e\right),$$

and in the context of the cobweb model one obtains the system

$$p_t^e = (1 - \lambda(1 - \alpha))p_{t-1}^e + \lambda\mu + \lambda\eta_{t-1}.$$

This is again an AR(1) process, now in the expectations p_t^e, which can be analyzed for stability or stationarity in the usual way.

Note that adaptive expectations can also be written in the form

$$p_t^e = \lambda \sum_{i=0}^{\infty} (1 - \lambda)^i p_{t-1-i},$$

which is a distributed lag with exponentially declining weights. Besides adaptive expectations, other distributed lag formulations were used in the litera-

---

[10]In the Lucas model the condition is automatically satisfied.

ture to allow for extrapolative or regressive elements. Adaptive expectations played a prominent role in macroeconomics in the 1960s and 1970s. For example, inflation expectations were often modeled adaptively in the analysis of the expectations-augmented Phillips curve.

The *rational expectations* revolution begins with the observations that adaptive expectations, or any other fixed-weight distributed lag formula, may provide poor forecasts in certain contexts and that better forecast rules may be readily available. The optimal forecast method will in fact depend on the stochastic process which is followed by the variable being forecast, and as can be seen from our examples this implies an interdependency between the forecasting method and the economic model which must be solved explicitly. On this approach we write

$$p_t^e = E_{t-1} p_t \quad \text{and} \quad p_{t+1}^e = E_t p_{t+1}$$

for the cobweb example and for the Cagan model, respectively. Here $E_{t-1} p_t$ denotes the mathematical (statistical) expectation of p_t conditional on variables observable at time $t-1$ (including past data) and similarly $E_t p_{t+1}$ denotes the expectation of p_{t+1} conditional on information at time t.

We emphasize that rational expectations is in fact an equilibrium concept. The actual stochastic process followed by prices depends on the forecast rules used by agents, so that the optimal choice of the forecast rule by any agent is conditional on the choices of others. An RE equilibrium imposes the consistency condition that each agent's choice is a best response to the choices by others. In the simplest models we have representative agents and these choices are identical.

For the cobweb model we now have $p_t = \mu + \alpha E_{t-1} p_t + \eta_t$. Taking conditional expectations E_{t-1} of both sides yields $E_{t-1} p_t = \mu + \alpha E_{t-1} p_t$, so that expectations are given by $E_{t-1} p_t = (1-\alpha)^{-1} \mu$ and we have

$$p_t = (1-\alpha)^{-1} \mu + \eta_t.$$

(This step implicitly imposes the consistency condition described in the previous paragraph.) This is the unique way to form expectations which are "rational" in the model (1.1).

Similarly, in the Cagan model we have $p_t = \alpha E_t p_{t+1} + \beta m_t$ and if m_t is iid with mean $\bar{m}$, a rational expectations solution is $E_t p_{t+1} = (1-\alpha)^{-1} \beta \bar{m}$ and

$$p_t = (1-\alpha)^{-1} \alpha \beta \bar{m} + \beta m_t.$$

For this model there are in fact other rational expectations solutions, a point we will temporarily put aside but which we will discuss at length later in the book.

Two related observations should be made. First, under rational expectations the appropriate way to form expectations depends on the stochastic process followed by the exogenous variables η_t or m_t. If these are not iid processes, then the rational expectations will themselves be random variables, and they often form a complicated stochastic process. Second, it is apparent from our examples that neither static nor adaptive expectations are in general rational. Static or adaptive expectations will be "rational" only in certain special cases.

The rational expectations hypothesis became widely used in the 1970s and 1980s and it is now the benchmark paradigm in macroeconomics. In the 1990s, approaches incorporating learning behavior in expectation formation have been increasingly studied.

Paralleling the rational expectations modeling, there was further work refining the temporary equilibrium approach in general equilibrium theory. Much of this work focused on the existence of a temporary equilibrium for given expectation functions. However, the dynamics of sequences of temporary equilibria were also studied and this latter work is conceptually connected to the learning approach analyzed in this book.[11] The temporary equilibrium modeling was primarily developed using nonstochastic models, whereas the approach taken in this book emphasizes that economies are subject to random shocks.

1.4   Learning: The New View of Expectations

The rational expectations approach presupposes that economic agents have a great deal of knowledge about the economy. Even in our simple examples, in which expectations are constant, computing these constants requires the full knowledge of the structure of the model, the values of the parameters, and that the random shock is iid.[12] In empirical work economists, who postulate rational expectations, do not themselves know the parameter values and must estimate them econometrically. It appears more natural to assume that the agents in the economy face the same limitations on knowledge about the economy. This suggests that a more plausible view of rationality is that the agents act like statisti-

---

[11] Many of the key papers on temporary equilibrium are collected in Grandmont (1988). A recent paper in this tradition, focusing on learning in a nonstochastic context, is Grandmont (1998).

[12] The strong assumptions required in the rational expectations hypothesis were widely discussed in the late 1970s and early 1980s; see, e.g., Blume, Bray, and Easley (1982), Frydman and Phelps (1983), and the references therein. Arrow (1986) has a good discussion of these issues.

cians or econometricians when doing the forecasting about the future state of the economy. This insight is the starting point of the adaptive learning approach to modeling expectations formation. This viewpoint introduces a specific form of "bounded rationality" to macroeconomics as discussed in Sargent (1993, Chapter 2).

More precisely, this viewpoint is called adaptive learning, since agents adjust their forecast rule as new data becomes available over time. There are alternative approaches to modeling learning, and we will explain their main features in Chapter 15. However, adaptive learning is the central focus of the book.

Taking this approach immediately raises the question of its relationship to rational expectations. It turns out that in many cases learning can provide at least an asymptotic justification for the RE hypothesis. For example, in the cobweb model with unobserved iid shocks, if agents estimate a constant expected value by computing the sample mean from past prices, one can show that expectations will converge over time to the RE value. This property turns out to be quite general for the cobweb-type models, provided agents use the appropriate econometric functional form. If the model includes exogenous observable variables or lagged endogenous variables, the agents will need to run regressions in the same way that an econometrician would.[13]

Another major advantage of the learning approach arises in connection with the issue of multiple equilibria. We have briefly alluded to the possibility that under the RE hypothesis the solution will not always be unique. To see this we consider a variation of the Cagan model $p_t = \alpha E_t p_{t+1} + \beta m_t$, where now money supply is assumed to follow a feedback rule $m_t = \bar{m} + \xi p_{t-1} + u_t$. This leads to the equation

$$p_t = \beta \bar{m} + \alpha E_t p_{t+1} + \beta \xi p_{t-1} + \beta u_t.$$

It can be shown that for many parameter values this equation yields two RE solutions of the form

$$p_t = k_1 + k_2 p_{t-1} + k_3 u_t, \tag{1.3}$$

where the k_i depend on the original parameters $\alpha, \beta, \xi, \bar{m}$. In some cases both of these solutions are even stochastically stationary.

---

[13] Bray (1982) was the first to provide a result showing convergence to rational expectations in a model in which expectations influence the economy and agents use an econometric procedure to update their expectations over time. Friedman (1979) and Taylor (1975) considered expectations which are formed using econometric procedures, but in contexts where expectations do not influence the economy. The final section in Chapter 2 provides a guide to the literature on learning.

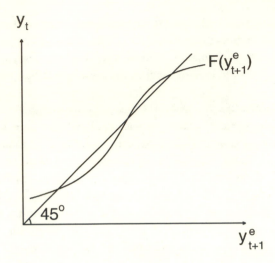

Figure 1.1.

For rational expectations this is a conundrum. Which solution should we and the agents choose? In contrast, in the adaptive learning approach it is supposed that agents start with initial estimates of the parameters of a stochastic process for p_t taking the same functional form as equation (1.3) and revise their estimates, following standard econometric procedures, as new data points are generated. This provides a fully specified dynamical system. For the case at hand it can be shown that only one of the RE solutions can emerge in the long run. Throughout the book the multiplicity issue will recur frequently, and we will pay full attention to this role of adaptive learning as a selection criterion.[14]

In nonlinear models this issue of multiplicity of RE solutions has been frequently encountered. Many nonlinear models can be put in the general form

$$y_t = F\left(y_{t+1}^e\right),$$

where random shocks have here been left out for simplicity. (Note that this is simply a nonlinear generalization of the Cagan model.) Suppose that the graph of $F(\cdot)$ has the S-shape shown in Figure 1.1. The multiple steady states $\bar{y} = F(\bar{y})$ occur at the intersection of the graph and the 45-degree line. We will later give an example in which y refers to output and the low steady states represent coor-

---

[14] Alternative selection criteria have been advanced. The existence of multiple equilibria makes clear the need to go in some way beyond rational expectations.

dination failures. Under learning, a number of interesting questions arise. Which of the steady states are stable under adaptive learning? Are there statistical learning rules for which there can be rational or nearly rational fluctuations between the steady states? We will treat these and other issues for nonlinear models, allowing also for random shocks.

Finally, the transition under learning to rational expectations may itself be of interest. The process of learning adds dynamics which are not present under strict rationality and they may be of empirical importance. In the cases we just described, these dynamics disappear asymptotically. However, there are various situations in which one can expect learning dynamics to remain important over time. As an example, if the economy undergoes structural shifts from time to time, then agents will need periodically to relearn the relevant stochastic processes. Moreover, if agents know that they are misspecifying a model which undergoes recurrent shifts, they may allow for this in their learning in a way which leads to persistent learning dynamics.

1.5   Statistical Approach to Learning

As already discussed, the approach taken in this book views economic agents as behaving like statisticians or econometricians when they make forecasts of future prices and other economic variables needed in their decision making. As an illustration, consider again the cobweb model (1.1).

Assume that agents believe that the stochastic process for the market price takes the form $p_t = \text{constant} + \text{noise}$, i.e., the same functional form as the RE solution. The sample mean is the standard way for estimating an unknown constant, and in this example the estimate is also the forecast for the price. Thus, suppose that agents' expectations are given by

$$p_t^e = \frac{1}{t} \sum_{i=0}^{t-1} p_i.$$

Combining this with equation (1.1) leads to a fully specified stochastic dynamical system. It can be shown that the system under learning converges to the RE solution if $\alpha < 1$. This result holds, too, for the basic Cagan model (1.2) with iid shocks.

It is easy to think of generalizations. If the economic model incorporates exogenous or lagged endogenous variables, it is natural for the agents to estimate the parameters of the perceived process for the relevant variables by means of least squares. As an illustration, suppose that an observable exogenous variable w_{t-1} is introduced into the cobweb model, so that equation (1.1) takes the form

$$p_t = \mu + \alpha p_t^e + \delta w_{t-1} + \eta_t. \tag{1.4}$$

It would now be natural to forecast the price as a linear function of the observable w_{t-1}. In fact, the unique RE solution is of this form.[15] Under learning, agents would forecast according to

$$p_t^e = a_{t-1} + b_{t-1} w_{t-1}, \tag{1.5}$$

where a_{t-1} and b_{t-1} are parameter estimates obtained by a least squares regression of p_t on w_{t-1} and an intercept.[16]

This way of modeling expectations formation has two major parts. First, the economy is taken to be in a temporary equilibrium in which the current state of the economy depends on expectations. Second, the statistical approach to learning makes the forecast functions and the estimation of their parameters fully explicit. A novel feature of this situation is that the expectations and forecast functions influence future data points. Mathematically, this *self-referential* feature makes these systems nonstandard. Analyzing their dynamics is not trivial and requires special techniques. An overview of those techniques is in the next chapter, and they are presented more formally in later chapters.

1.6   A General Framework

The examples described in the previous sections can be placed in a more general framework. As already noted, the approach taken in this book is *adaptive* in the sense that expectation rules are revised over time in response to observed data. We use the phrase "adaptive learning" to contrast the approach with both "eductive learning" and "rational learning." In eductive approaches agents engage in a process of reasoning and the learning takes place in logical or notional time. The central question is whether coordination on an REE (rational expectations equilibrium) can be attained by a mental process of reasoning based on

---

[15]The unique REE is $p_t = \bar{a} + \bar{b} w_{t-1} + \eta_t$, where $\bar{a} = (1 - \alpha)^{-1} \mu$ and $\bar{b} = (1 - \alpha)^{-1} \delta$.

[16]Bray and Savin (1986) and Fourgeaud, Gourieroux, and Pradel (1986) analyzed cobweb and Cagan models for learning.

common knowledge assumptions.[17] Rational learning takes place in real time,[18] but retains the rational expectations equilibrium assumptions, at each point in time, which we do not want to impose *a priori*. The adaptive learning approach instead assumes that agents possess a form of bounded rationality, which may, however, approach rational expectations over time.

To describe our general framework, let y_t be a vector of variables that agents need to forecast and let y_t^e denote the expectations formed by the agents. y_t could include future values of variables of interest as well as unknown current values. (If agents are heterogeneous in the sense that they have differing expectations, then one can treat this by letting $y_t^e(k)$ denote the expectations of agents k. One would then need to examine the evolution of $y_t^e(k)$ for each agent. For simplicity, we continue the discussion under the assumption of homogeneous expectations.) If the optimal actions of agents depend on the second or higher moments as well as the mean of certain variables, then this can be treated by including powers of these variables in y_t. Similarly, expectations of nonlinear functions of several variables may also be included as components of y_t. Thus, at this stage our framework is very general.

Suppose that agents, when they are making their forecasts y_t^e, have observations on a vector of variables X_t. X_t might include a finite number of lags of some or all components of y_t, and could also include lagged values of y_t^e as well as other exogenous and endogenous observables. The forecasts y_t^e are assumed to be a function of the observables so that

$$y_t^e = \Psi(X_t, \theta_{t-1}),$$

where θ_{t-1} is a vector of parameters that may evolve over time. Inclusion of the parameter θ_{t-1} is a crucial aspect of the adaptive learning approach, as we will discuss. However, the framework so far is broad enough to include static expectations, adaptive expectations, and rational expectations as special cases with appropriate fixed values of θ.[19]

Under the statistical approach to learning, the forecast rule $\Psi(X_t, \theta)$ is based on an econometric model specification, i.e., on a perceived law of mo-

---

[17] We briefly discuss the eductive approach in Section 15.4 of Chapter 15. There are close links between the stability analyses of eductive and adaptive learning. For a forceful presentation of the eductive viewpoint see Guesnerie (1999).

[18] An example of fully rational learning is Townsend (1978). See the section on the discussion of the literature in Chapter 2 for further references.

[19] Under rational expectations $y_t^e = \Psi(X_t) \equiv E(y_t \mid X_t)$, the mathematical conditional expectation of y_t given X_t, provided $E(y_t \mid I_t) = E(y_t \mid X_t)$, where $I_t = \{X_t, X_{t-1}, \ldots, X_0\}$ is the information set at time t. This will often hold if X_t is chosen appropriately.

tion for the variables of interest, and the vector θ represents unknown parameters which must be estimated statistically in order to implement the forecast rule. As an example, in the cobweb model the forecast rule (1.5) for $y_t^e = p_t^e$ is a linear function of the observables, where X_t includes the variables 1 and w_t and θ_{t-1} includes the parameters a_{t-1} and b_{t-1}. The forecasting framework is completed by specifying a rule for estimating θ and updating the estimates over time as data is accumulated. We will assume that this takes a recursive form $\theta_t = \mathcal{G}(t, \theta_{t-1}, X_t)$. It is convenient to write this in the equivalent form[20]

$$\theta_t = \theta_{t-1} + \gamma_t Q(t, \theta_{t-1}, X_t),$$

where γ_t is a given deterministic "gain" sequence which governs how responsive estimate revisions are to new data.[21] Recursive estimators are sometimes called "on-line," in contrast to "off-line" estimators in which θ_t could depend on the full history $X_1, \ldots X_t$. However, as we will see, many standard statistical estimators such as least squares can be rewritten in recursive form. A simple special case is that the sample mean $a_t = t^{-1} \sum_{i=1}^{t} p_i$, for $t = 1, 2, 3, \ldots$, can be written in recursive form as $a_t = a_{t-1} + t^{-1}(p_t - a_{t-1})$, where $a_1 = p_1$. Thus, while not completely general, our formulation remains quite general. The recursive version of least squares estimation will be developed in Chapter 2.

The system as a whole is specified once the dynamic process governing the state variables X_t is described. Since the model is self-referential, the dependence of key variables on expectations, manifest in the cobweb model via equations (1.4) and (1.5), will be reflected either in the specification of the process followed by X_t or in the specification of the updating equation $Q(\cdot)$ for the parameter estimates θ_t, or both. This self-referential aspect is what prevents us from analyzing the resulting stochastic dynamic systems using standard econometric tools.

We have thus arrived at a stochastic dynamic system in which economic variables depend through the forecasts of agents on the agents' estimates of key parameters and those parameters are updated over time in response to the evolution of the variables themselves. Analyzing the evolution of this stochastic dynamic system over time is the heart of the adaptive learning approach to expectations formation and the subject of this book.

---

[20] As we will see in the next chapter, in order to make possible a recursive formulation, θ_t must often include auxiliary parameters in addition to the parameters of interest.

[21] The importance of a recursive formulation for obtaining general adaptive learning results was stressed in Marcet and Sargent (1989c).

1.7 Overview of the Book

In the remainder of Part I we describe the adaptive learning approach to expectations formation in some detail and illustrate it with numerous examples from the recent macroeconomic literature. The analysis in Part I is presented in simplified terms to show the key features and applicability of the approach. The level of exposition is aimed at graduate students and other economists with some familiarity of standard macroeconomic theory. In other parts of the book the style of analysis is rigorous and requires familiarity with techniques presented in Part II. However, Chapters 8, 11, 13, and 15 should be by and large accessible after reading Part I.

Chapter 2 spells out the details of the approach in the context of the cobweb model with agents updating their forecast parameters using recursive least squares. This model, in which there is a unique rational expectations equilibrium (REE), is particularly convenient for introducing the technical framework. We show explicitly how to represent the model under learning as a stochastic recursive algorithm (SRA), how to approximate the system with an associated ordinary differential equation (ODE), and how the asymptotic stability of the REE under learning hinges on a stability condition called "expectational stability" or "E-stability." The discussion of the techniques in this chapter is introductory, emphasizing the heuristic aspects. Chapter 3 shows how some simple variations can lead to interesting further results. In particular, we explore the implications of modifying or misspecifying the recursive least squares learning rule. In that chapter we also discuss a simple form of adaptive learning which can be used in nonstochastic models. The standard coordination failure model is used as an illustration of learning in a nonstochastic context.

Chapter 4, the last chapter of Part I, shows how to use the techniques to study adaptive learning in a wide range of frequently encountered models. The examples include the standard overlapping generations model, the Ramsey optimal growth model, simple linear stochastic macro models, the Diamond growth model, and a model with increasing social returns. We give examples of convergence to REEs, and illustrate the possibility of REEs which are not stable under adaptive learning. In this chapter we also provide an illustration of convergence to a "sunspot" solution, i.e., to a solution which depends on extraneous variables because agents learn to coordinate their expectations on these variables.

Part II provides a systematic treatment of the technical tools required for the analysis of SRAs. Chapter 5 provides a summary of standard results on economic dynamics, with an emphasis on stability results. Topics include difference and differential equations, both deterministic and stochastic, as well as a number of specialized results which will be needed. Chapter 6 presents a formal statement of the key technical results on the stability of SRAs which makes possible the systematic study of adaptive learning in macroeconomic models with expectations. Separate local stability, global stability, and instability results are given. As an illustration we obtain the stability conditions for convergence to the unique REE in the multivariate cobweb model. Chapter 7 presents some additional technical results, including speed of convergence and asymptotic approximations for constant-gain algorithms.

In Parts III and IV we apply the techniques systematically to linear and nonlinear economic models. In these parts we continue to focus on the issue of the conditions under which adaptive learning converges to REE. A major emphasis of these two parts is the possibility of multiple equilibria. As we have already stressed, macroeconomic models in which the state of the economy depends on expectations have the potential for "self-fulfilling prophecies," taking the form of multiple REEs. Local stability under learning provides a natural selection principle for assessing these equilibria.

Part III is a systematic treatment of linear models. Chapters 8 and 9 examine univariate linear models, covering many of the standard workhorses of macroeconomics. Part III begins with a full treatment of several special cases in which the full set of REEs can be readily listed. The solutions take the form of one or more minimal state variable (MSV) solutions and one or more continua of ARMA solutions, possibly depending on "sunspot" variables. In some cases there is a unique REE which is nonexplosive, but examples with multiple stationary solutions do arise. In looking at the local stability of these solutions under least squares learning, we emphasize the role of the E-stability conditions, and we distinguish "weak E-stability conditions," which govern local stability when the REE is correctly specified, and "strong E-stability" conditions, which are relevant when the perceived law of motion estimated by the agents overparameterizes the REE solution of interest. We show how to use the tools of Part II to prove that these conditions govern local stability and instability, under least squares learning, for certain classes of solutions, and we provide supporting numerical simulations for other cases where formal proofs are not available.

Economic examples covered in Chapters 8 and 9 include the Sargent–Wallace "ad hoc" model, Taylor's real balance and overlapping contracts models, the Cagan inflation model, asset price models, investment under uncertainty, Muth's inventory model, and a version of Dornbusch's exchange rate model. Recent dynamic general equilibrium models, such as the Real Business Cycle (RBC) model, are inherently multivariate, as are conventional large-scale macroeconometric models. Although the RBC model is nonlinear, a good approximation is often given by linearized versions. In Chapter 10 we take up multivariate linear expectations models. We show how our techniques to assess the local stability of REE under least squares learning can be extended in a straight-forward way to the multivariate setting and we present the E-stability conditions for REE in multivariate linear models. This chapter discusses both "regular" cases, for which there is a unique stationary REE, and "irregular cases" with multiple stationary REE. Economic examples include an IS-LM-new Phillips curve model, the RBC model, and the Farmer–Guo irregular model.

Part IV turns to nonlinear models. From the viewpoint of formal macroeconomic theory these models give rise to the possibility of multiple steady-state REEs, as well as (in nonstochastic models) perfect-foresight cycles and stochastic equilibria which depend on an extraneous variable, a "sunspot." The possibility of multiple steady-state REEs in nonstochastic models is considered in Part I but is more systematically discussed in Chapter 11. This chapter also considers solutions to nonlinear models subject to white noise intrinsic shocks, for example due to random technology, preference, or policy shocks, and we show the existence of "noisy steady states" for nonlinear models with small white noise shocks. We obtain the E-stability conditions and show that they govern local stability under adaptive learning for steady states and noisy steady states. In addition to the overlapping generations (OG) models, with and without stochastic shocks, our examples include the increasing social returns model, the hyperinflation (seignorage) model, and the Evans–Honkapohja–Romer model of growth cycles.

Chapter 12 continues the systematic treatment of nonlinear models. Perfect-foresight cycles can arise in nonlinear models such as the OG model.[22] Chapter 12 shows the possibility of "noisy cycles" in nonlinear models with white noise shocks. We then obtain the E-stability conditions for (perfect-foresight or noisy) cycles and show that these govern the local stability of these cycles under adaptive learning. We derive both weak E-stability conditions, in which the perceived law of motion held by the agents correctly specifies the order of the cycle under consideration, and strong E-stability conditions, which are required for stability when the agents overparameterize the order of the cycle. Sunspot equilibria were originally discovered to exist in nonlinear models, taking the form of Markov chains.[23] Chapter 12 also obtains corresponding weak and strong E-stability conditions and shows that these govern the local stability of stationary sunspot equilibria (and noisy stationary sunspot equilibria) under adaptive

---

[22] See Grandmont (1985).

[23] See Shell (1977), Azariadis (1981), Azariadis and Guesnerie (1982), and Cass and Shell (1983). The possibility of convergence to sunspots under adaptive learning was shown by Woodford (1990).

learning. Particular attention is paid to the E-stability conditions for Markov sunspot solutions which are close to REE cycles or pairs of steady states.

Part V returns to general issues in adaptive learning. We have been modeling the economic agents as making forecasts in the same way as econometricians. This is a weakening of the rational expectations assumption, but one which would appear reasonable since, after all, economists themselves use econometrics as the principal tool for forecasting. As with all bounded rationality assumptions, one can consider further strengthening or weakening of the degree of rationality. The emphasis of much of the book is on the possibility that econometric learning will asymptotically converge to fully rational expectations. Indeed, we have advocated local stability under adaptive learning as a selection criterion when multiple REEs exist. Chapters 13 and 14 consider the possibility that natural econometric learning rules may fail to converge fully to REEs even in the limit.

In Chapter 13 we consider the implications of agents using a misspecified model. When the perceived law of motion estimated by the agents does not nest the REE under consideration, convergence of learning to that REE is, of course, impossible. This does not, however, preclude convergence of the estimators. We give several examples in which underparameterized learning converges to a restricted perceptions equilibrium under least squares learning. This equilibrium, though not rational, may be optimal given the restricted class of perceived laws of motion entertained by the forecasters. In the cobweb model the stability condition is unaffected, but in other examples misspecification can affect the stability condition as well as the asymptotic point of convergence. This chapter and the next also discuss the model of misspecified learning by monetary policy makers recently set forth in Sargent (1999).

If agents have a misspecified model, they may, however, be aware of the possible misspecification and make allowances for this in their learning rule. One way this can be done is to choose the "gain" sequence, which measures the sensitivity of estimates to new data points, so that it is bounded above zero asymptotically. This is in contrast to standard statistical procedures, like least squares, in which the gain shrinks to zero over time as more data is accumulated. Such nondecreasing or constant-gain estimators have the disadvantage in correctly specified models that estimators fluctuate randomly in the limit, precluding convergence to full rationality. But they have the advantage, in some kinds of misspecified models, of being able to track an economic structure which is evolving in some unknown way. Chapter 14 discusses the implications of constant-gain learning in the context of the cobweb model, the increasing social returns model, and Sargent's inflation model. In some cases, dramatic and new persistent learning dynamics can arise because of the incomplete learning.

Chapter 15 contains a discussion of extensions, alternatives, and new approaches to adaptive learning that have been recently employed. Genetic algorithms, classifier systems, and neural networks are alternative forecasting methods available from the computational intelligence literature. We also discuss eductive approaches, as well as extensions which permit agents to use nonparametric methods or to weigh the costs and benefits of improving forecasts. The chapter ends with a discussion of experimental work and recent empirical applications.

Chapter 16 concludes the book with a perspective on what has been achieved and points out some issues for further research.

Chapter **2**

Introduction to the Techniques

2.1 Introduction

In this second introductory chapter we will introduce the main analytical technique which we will use to study convergence under learning dynamics when the economy is subject to stochastic shocks. We will do this in the context of a simple economic model: the cobweb market model introduced in Chapter 1. Our presentation in this chapter will be heuristic and the techniques will be rigorously developed subsequently. Later chapters will also show how to apply these tools to study the dynamics of learning in numerous macroeconomic models.

In the cobweb model there is a unique rational expectations equilibrium (REE). Even if there is a unique REE, convergence under learning is far from obvious since the situation is not analogous to the standard econometric setup. Because in general the economic variables depend on forecasts, they depend on the agents' estimates.[1] Thus the agents are estimating the parameters of a system which in turn depend on the estimates. It is thus possible, and we will see examples, that if agents' estimates deviate from the parameter values of an REE, the actual law of motion under these perceptions will be best described by parameters which are even farther from the REE. In consequence, the estimates will be driven farther and farther from the REE values over time, so that the REE is unstable.

We will develop conditions, called *expectational stability* conditions, which govern whether or not a given REE is stable. When there are multiple REE,

---

[1] This is the sense in which such systems are "self-referential."

these conditions must be interpreted as local stability conditions since then the evolution of the system, and its possible rest points, will depend on the initial perceptions as well as other factors. In fact, it is within models with multiple equilibria that the study of adaptive learning is most fruitful since it provides guidance on what can happen in such models: can the economy become stuck in inefficient steady states? Can it converge to cycles or random fluctuations, even when a deterministic steady state exists? Can the economy begin to track explosive bubble paths? Once we have the technical apparatus in hand, we will consider all of these issues in later parts of the book.

Besides focusing on a version of bounded rationality which makes a minimal deviation from RE, we will also focus, through most of the book, on the asymptotic issue of whether adaptive learning converges to a particular REE in the limit. There are other questions of considerable interest: how fast does convergence take place? What are the properties of the transitional paths en route to the REE? If the economy undergoes frequent structural shifts, will the estimates still converge and how should adaptive agents allow for this? In the last part of the book we will take up these issues. However, we begin with what is clearly the central question: if agents estimate a statistical model which is a correct specification of an REE, under what circumstances will the estimates converge to that REE?

2.2 The Cobweb Model

In this book we will address this issue of stability in the context of a wide variety of stochastic economic models: linear and nonlinear, univariate and multivariate. These will cover a wide range of the macroeconomic models which are currently employed or which have been employed over the last 25 years. In particular, we will be able to study in detail the issue of what solutions emerge under adaptive learning when multiple equilibria are present. However, to present the central techniques it is most convenient to consider a linear univariate model with a unique REE: the cobweb model of supply and demand in an isolated market. This is in fact the model investigated by Muth (1961) in his classic formulation of rational expectations. As noted in the previous chapter, its properties under least squares learning were investigated by Bray and Savin (1986) and Fourgeaud, Gourieroux, and Pradel (1986).

The structural model consists of demand and supply equations:

$$d_t = m_I - m_p p_t + v_{1t},$$
$$s_t = r_I + r_p p_t^e + r_w' w_{t-1} + v_{2t},$$

where m_p, $r_p > 0$ and v_{1t} and v_{2t} are unobserved white noise shocks. The formulation here generalizes the version given in Chapter 1 by permitting supply to depend on a vector of observable shocks w_{t-1}. Bray and Savin (1986) make the assumption that w_t is an iid process. This is much stronger than necessary. One can, for example, permit w_t to follow a stationary exogenous VAR (vector autoregression), driven by a multivariate white noise shock with bounded moments. For convenience we assume that $E w_t = 0$, and we denote the unconditional second moment matrix by $E w_t w_t' = \Omega$.

Assuming market clearing, $s_t = d_t$, yields the reduced form

$$p_t = \mu + \alpha p_t^e + \delta' w_{t-1} + \eta_t, \tag{2.1}$$

where $\mu = (m_I - r_I)/m_p$, $\delta = -m_p^{-1} r_w$, and $\alpha = -r_p/m_p$. Note that $\alpha < 0$. $\eta_t = (v_{1t} - v_{2t})/m_p$, so that we can write $\eta_t \sim \text{iid}(0, \sigma_\eta^2)$. Under rational expectations, $p_t^e = E_{t-1} p_t$, where $E_{t-1} p_t$ denotes the expectation of p_t conditional on information available at time $t - 1$. Operating with E_{t-1} on both sides of equation (2.1) and solving for $E_{t-1} p_t$, we obtain

$$E_{t-1} p_t = (1 - \alpha)^{-1} \mu + (1 - \alpha)^{-1} \delta' w_{t-1}.$$

Since also $p_t - E_{t-1} p_t = \eta_t$, it follows that there is a unique rational expectations equilibrium given by

$$p_t = \bar{a} + \bar{b}' w_{t-1} + \eta_t,$$

where

$$\bar{a} = (1 - \alpha)^{-1} \mu \quad \text{and} \quad \bar{b} = (1 - \alpha)^{-1} \delta.$$

We remark that the reason why this model has a unique REE is that p_t does not depend on expected *future* prices.

2.3 Econometric Learning

Although the REE is unique, we can still ask whether it is *learnable* in the following sense. Suppose that firms believe that prices follow the process

$$p_t = a + b' w_{t-1} + \eta_t, \tag{2.2}$$

corresponding to the REE, but that a and b are unknown to them. There are different possible explanations for this. Firms may be unable to calculate the REE, although they know the form of the economic structure, because the structural parameters are unknown. Alternatively, the form of the structure may be unknown, but firms may reasonably assume that p_t depends linearly on the vector of exogenous observable shocks. In any event, we assume that equation (2.2) is the *perceived law of motion* of the firms and that they attempt to estimate a and b. This is our key bounded rationality assumption: we back away from the rational expectations assumption, replacing it with the assumption that, in forecasting prices, firms act like econometricians.[2]

Under this assumption we have the following model of the evolution of the economy. Suppose that firms have data on the economy from periods $i = 0, \ldots, t - 1$. Thus the time-$(t-1)$ information set is $\{p_i, w_i\}_{i=0}^{t-1}$. We suppose that firms estimate a and b by a least squares regression of p_i on w_{i-1} and an intercept. Their estimates will be updated over time as more information is collected. Letting (a_{t-1}, b_{t-1}) denote the estimates through time $t - 1$, their forecasts at $t - 1$ are given by

$$p_t^e = a_{t-1} + b_{t-1}' w_{t-1}. \tag{2.3}$$

The standard least squares formula gives the equations

$$\binom{a_{t-1}}{b_{t-1}} = \left(\sum_{i=1}^{t-1} z_{i-1} z_{i-1}' \right)^{-1} \left(\sum_{i=1}^{t-1} z_{i-1} p_i \right), \tag{2.4}$$

where

$$z_i' = \left(1 \ \ w_i' \right).$$

We now have a fully specified dynamic system defined by the equations (2.1), (2.3), and (2.4): at time $t - 1$, expectations are formed according to equations (2.3) and (2.4). Given w_{t-1} and the random draw for η_t, the time-t price is determined by equation (2.1). Then parameters can be updated. Adding (p_t, w_{t-1}) to the data set, revised estimates a_t and b_t are computed. Given the random draw for w_t, forecasts p_{t+1}^e are made, which together with the new shock η_{t+1} determine p_{t+1}, and this process is continued over time. The question of interest is whether $a_t \to \bar{a}$ and $b_t \to \bar{b}$ as $t \to \infty$.

In the cobweb model the key parameter satisfies $\alpha < 0$, but there are other structural models with the same reduced form, so we can pose the problem more

---

[2] As indicated in Chapter 1, in making this assumption we are modifying our view of firms to make them behave more like economists who believe the economy is in an REE and use data to estimate the parameters of the REE law of motion.

generally, allowing α to be unrestricted. This is illustrated by the following example.

Example: **Lucas Aggregate Supply Model.** In Chapter 1 we presented the following model, due to Lucas (1973), consisting of aggregate supply function

$$q_t = \bar{q} + \pi(p_t - p_t^e) + \zeta_t,$$

where $\pi > 0$, and aggregate demand function

$$m_t + v_t = p_t + q_t,$$

where v_t is a velocity shock. We now assume that velocity depends in part on exogenous observables w_{t-1} so that

$$v_t = \mu + \gamma' w_{t-1} + \xi_t,$$

and that money supply follows the policy rule

$$m_t = \bar{m} + u_t + \rho' w_{t-1}.$$

Here u_t, ξ_t, and ζ_t are white noise shocks. The reduced form is

$$\begin{aligned}
p_t = {}& (1+\pi)^{-1}(\bar{m} + \mu - \bar{q}) + \pi(1+\pi)^{-1} p_t^e + (1+\pi)^{-1}(\rho + \gamma)' w_{t-1} \\
& + (1+\pi)^{-1}(u_t + \xi_t - \zeta_t).
\end{aligned}$$

This equation is precisely of the form (2.1) with $\alpha = \pi(1+\pi)^{-1}$ and $\eta_t = (1+\pi)^{-1}(u_t + \xi_t - \zeta_t)$. Note that in this example, $0 < \alpha < 1$.

The answer to the question of whether, under least squares learning, the system converges to the unique REE is given by the following result.

Theorem 2.1. *Consider the dynamic system (2.1), (2.3), and (2.4). If $\alpha < 1$, then $\begin{pmatrix} a_t \\ b_t \end{pmatrix} \to \begin{pmatrix} \bar{a} \\ \bar{b} \end{pmatrix}$ with probability 1. If $\alpha > 1$, then convergence occurs with probability* 0.

Thus the REE is stable under least squares learning for both of our examples. An example of an unstable REE would be the cobweb model in which the demand curve is upward sloping and steeper than the supply curve, i.e., $m_p < 0$ with $|m_p| < r_p$.

Theorem 2.1 is an extremely strong global result, both in the positive case and in the negative case. The positive result was proved in Bray and Savin (1986) using direct arguments based on martingale convergence theorems. The negative result, which should be interpreted as stating that when $\alpha > 1$, (a_t, b'_t) converges with probability 0 to *any* point (a, b'), can be shown using the techniques for stochastic recursive algorithms, in particular results from Ljung (1977), as was demonstrated by Marcet and Sargent (1989c). Because in the coming chapters we will develop general techniques suitable for application to a wide range of economic applications, we will not present the proof of Bray and Savin, but instead provide a heuristic development of the techniques we will use throughout the book.

2.4   Expectational Stability

The condition $\alpha < 1$ can be interpreted in terms of a general stability principle, known as "expectational stability" or "E-stability." Since, as we will see, this principle works quite generally to provide the condition for the stability of an REE under adaptive learning, we introduce the concept now.

The basic required concept is the map from the perceived law of motion (PLM) to the actual law of motion (ALM). The *E-stability principle* stated in its most comprehensive form is that the mapping from the PLM to the ALM governs the stability of equilibria under learning. More specifically, E-stability conditions obtained from this mapping provide the conditions for asymptotic stability of an REE under least squares learning. We focus here on obtaining this condition for the cobweb model.

We begin with the assumption that agents have a PLM which they use to make forecasts of the variables of interest. Usually we take the form of the PLM to correspond to the REE of interest. Thus in the current case we take the PLM to be of the form (2.2), $p_t = a + b'w_{t-1} + \eta_t$. For $a = \bar{a}$ and $b = \bar{b}$, the PLM would be the REE, but we allow for the possibility that agents have "nonrational" expectations. For any given values of a and b, the appropriate time-$(t-1)$ forecast of p_t is given by

$$p_t^e = a + b'w_{t-1}. \tag{2.5}$$

Inserting equation (2.5) into equation (2.1), one can solve for the *actual law of motion*, or ALM, implied by the PLM:

$$p_t = (\mu + \alpha a) + (\delta + \alpha b)'w_{t-1} + \eta_t. \tag{2.6}$$

This implicitly defines the *mapping from the PLM to the ALM*

$$T \begin{pmatrix} a \\ b \end{pmatrix} = \begin{pmatrix} \mu + \alpha a \\ \delta + \alpha b \end{pmatrix}. \tag{2.7}$$

The interpretation of the ALM is that it describes the stochastic process followed by the economy if forecasts are made under the fixed rule given by the PLM.

We can now define E-stability in the form appropriate for determining the stability of the REE under least squares learning. Note first that the unique REE for our model is the unique fixed point of the T-map (2.7). Consider the differential equation

$$\frac{d}{d\tau} \begin{pmatrix} a \\ b \end{pmatrix} = T \begin{pmatrix} a \\ b \end{pmatrix} - \begin{pmatrix} a \\ b \end{pmatrix}, \tag{2.8}$$

where τ denotes "notional" or "artificial" time. We say that the REE is expectationally stable, or E-stable, if the REE is locally asymptotically stable under equation (2.8). Intuitively, E-stability determines the stability of the REE under a stylized learning rule in which the PLM parameters a and b are adjusted slowly in the direction of the implied ALM parameters. The REE $(\bar{a}, \bar{b}')'$ is E-stable if small displacements from $(\bar{a}, \bar{b}')'$ are returned to $(\bar{a}, \bar{b}')'$ under this rule.

Expectational stability in this form was introduced in Evans (1989) and Evans and Honkapohja (1992). The closely related notion of iterative expectational stability, which appeared earlier in the literature, will be discussed below.

To determine E-stability in our example, combine equations (2.7) and (2.8) and write the differential equation component by component to obtain

$$\frac{da}{d\tau} = \mu + (\alpha - 1)a,$$
$$\frac{db_i}{d\tau} = \delta_i + (\alpha - 1)b_i, \quad \text{for } i = 1, \dots, n,$$

where n is the dimension of w. It follows that the REE is E-stable if and only if $\alpha < 1$. Note that this is precisely the condition obtained by Bray and Savin for convergence of least squares learning.

The connection between E-stability and the convergence of least squares learning turns out to be quite general, applying in a very wide range of models. This is a great advantage since E-stability conditions are often easy to work out, while the technical analysis of the convergence of econometric learning is substantially more involved.

2.5   Rational vs. Reasonable Learning

Before discussing the analysis of econometric learning, i.e., the justification of
Bray and Savin's result, we briefly note the sense in which we are assuming
bounded rationality. Recall that agents assume that data is being generated by
the process $p_t = a + b'w_{t-1} + \eta_t$, but that they do not know the parameters a and
b. At time t they have estimates (a_t, b_t) which they use to make their forecasts,
so that p_t^e is given by equation (2.3). It follows that under least squares learning,
the true process followed by p_t is given by

$$p_t = \mu + \alpha(a_{t-1} + b'_{t-1}w_{t-1}) + \delta'w_{t-1} + \eta_t,$$

or

$$p_t = (\mu + \alpha a_{t-1}) + (\delta + \alpha b_{t-1})'w_{t-1} + \eta_t,$$

so that the "intercept" and the coefficient on w_{t-1} are not constant but are evolving over time. Agents are thus estimating an econometrically misspecified model
and this is the sense in which they are not fully rational.

However, note that least squares learning may be (in Bray's words) "reasonable" even if it is not fully rational. The first and most important point is
that if $\alpha < 1$, then $(a_t, b'_t)' \rightarrow (\bar{a}, \bar{b}')'$ as $t \rightarrow \infty$. Thus, asymptotically the misspecification is vanishingly small as the coefficients of the process cease to vary
over time. Second, the misspecification may not even be statistically detectable
during the transition. This will depend on the details: the initial deviation from
$(\bar{a}, \bar{b}')'$, the value of $\mathrm{Var}(\eta_t)$, and the size of α. Bray and Savin (1986) investigate this issue and show that in many cases the temporary misspecification dur-
ing the transition to REE would not be detectable by standard good econometric
practice.

2.6   Recursive Least Squares

We now return to the problem of showing convergence under least squares learning. In the remainder of this chapter we will outline the techniques which we will
be using throughout this book to establish whether convergence to an REE takes
place. The crucial first step is to reformulate the dynamic system as a stochastic
recursive algorithm.

We begin by noting that the standard least squares regression formula has
a recursive formulation. In fitting the equation $y_i = c'x_i + e_i$ using data $i = 1, \ldots, T$ on the $k \times 1$ independent vector x_i and the dependent variable y_i, the

value of the $k \times 1$ coefficient vector c which minimizes $\sum_{i=1}^{T} e_i^2$ is given by the least squares formula[3]

$$c = \left(\sum_{i=1}^{T} x_i x_i' \right)^{-1} \left(\sum_{i=1}^{T} x_i y_i \right).$$

c can instead be computed using the *recursive least squares* (RLS) formulas

$$
\begin{aligned}
c_t &= c_{t-1} + t^{-1} R_t^{-1} x_t (y_t - x_t' c_{t-1}), \\
R_t &= R_{t-1} + t^{-1} (x_t x_t' - R_{t-1}).
\end{aligned}
\tag{2.9}
$$

c_t and R_t denote the coefficient vector and the moment matrix for x_t using data $i = 1, \ldots, t$. To generate the least squares values, the initial value for the recursion must be set appropriately.[4] With these initial values, equation (2.9) generates the usual least squares formula for c_t, the least squares coefficient vector using data $i = 1, \ldots, t$, and c above is given by $c = c_T$. This can be verified by induction.[5] Note that $(y_t - x_t' c_{t-1})$ is the most recent forecast error at t.

We now apply the RLS formulas to our learning problem. Our agents are running a least squares regression of p_i on z_{i-1}, where $z_i' = (1 \ w_i')$. For convenience, write

$$\phi_t = \begin{pmatrix} a_t \\ b_t \end{pmatrix}$$

for the vector of coefficients including the intercept. Applying the RLS formulas, we obtain

$$
\begin{aligned}
\phi_t &= \phi_{t-1} + t^{-1} R_t^{-1} z_{t-1} \left(p_t - \phi_{t-1}' z_{t-1} \right), \\
R_t &= R_{t-1} + t^{-1} \left(z_{t-1} z_{t-1}' - R_{t-1} \right).
\end{aligned}
$$

Since p_t is given by equations (2.1) and (2.3), we have

$$p_t = (\mu + \alpha a_{t-1}) + (\delta + \alpha b_{t-1})' w_{t-1} + \eta_t$$

---

[3] Letting y denote the $T \times 1$ column vector with ith component y_i and X denote the $T \times k$ matrix given by $X = (x_1, \ldots, x_T)'$, the formula can be equivalently written in the better known form $c = (X'X)^{-1} X' y$.

[4] Assuming $X_k = (x_1, \ldots, x_k)'$ is of full rank and letting y^k denote $y^k = (y_1, \ldots, y_k)'$, the initial value c_k is given by $c_k = (X_k' X_k)^{-1} X_k' y^k = X_k^{-1} y^k$ and the initial value R_k is given by $R_k = k^{-1} X_k' X_k = k^{-1} \sum_{i=1}^{k} x_i x_i'$.

[5] Using the formulas $R_t = t^{-1} \sum_{i=1}^{t} x_i x_i'$ and $c_t = t^{-1} R_t^{-1} \sum_{i=1}^{t} x_i y_i$, the recursions (2.9) can be seen to lead to the least squares formula.

or

$$p_t = T(\phi_{t-1})'z_{t-1} + \eta_t, \qquad (2.10)$$

where $T(\phi) \equiv T\begin{pmatrix} a \\ b \end{pmatrix}$ is given by equation (2.7). Note that p_t is determined by the ALM generated by the perceptions $\phi'_{t-1} = (a_{t-1}, b'_{t-1})$. Combining equations, we arrive at the stochastic recursive system

$$\phi_t = \phi_{t-1} + t^{-1}R_t^{-1}z_{t-1}\left(z'_{t-1}(T(\phi_{t-1}) - \phi_{t-1}) + \eta_t\right), \qquad (2.11)$$

$$R_t = R_{t-1} + t^{-1}\left(z_{t-1}z'_{t-1} - R_{t-1}\right). \qquad (2.12)$$

We want to know whether equations (2.11)–(2.12) converge as $t \to \infty$. Let $\bar{\phi}' \equiv (\bar{a}, \bar{b}')$. Our claim, following Bray and Savin, is that if $\alpha < 1$, then $\phi_t \to \bar{\phi}$ with probability 1. Since $T(\bar{\phi}) = \bar{\phi}$, it also follows from equation (2.10) that the price process converges to the REE.

To show convergence formally requires results from the stochastic approximation literature.

2.7   Convergence of Stochastic Recursive Algorithms

There is a substantial literature in statistics and engineering which concerns itself precisely with the convergence of stochastic recursive algorithms such as equations (2.11)–(2.12). (This method is also called stochastic approximation.) Marcet and Sargent (1989c) showed how this technique, in particular the results of Ljung (1977), could be applied in economics to the analysis of adaptive learning. In Chapter 6 we will provide the technical details for this tool, and in this section we provide the central technique.

We consider a stochastic recursive algorithm (SRA) of the form

$$\theta_t = \theta_{t-1} + \gamma_t Q(t, \theta_{t-1}, X_t), \qquad (2.13)$$

where θ_t is a vector of parameter estimates, X_t is the state vector, and γ_t is a deterministic sequence of "gains." The function Q expresses the way in which the estimate θ_{t-1} is revised in line with the last period's observations. In our example, θ_{t-1} will include all components of ϕ_{t-1} and R_t, X_t will include the effects of z_{t-1} and η_t, and $\gamma_t = t^{-1}$. In the following section we give the details of how equations (2.11)–(2.12) can be put into the form (2.13). Although, in our example, X_t follows an exogenous process, this is not at all essential. In particular, in the general framework, X_t can be permitted to follow a VAR (vector autoregression) with parameters that may depend on θ_{t-1}. This issue is discussed fully in Chapters 6 and 7.

The stochastic approximation approach associates an ordinary differential equation (ODE) with the SRA,

$$\frac{d\theta}{d\tau} = h(\theta(\tau)),$$

where $h(\theta)$ is obtained as

$$h(\theta) = \lim_{t \to \infty} E Q(t, \theta, X_t), \tag{2.14}$$

provided this limit exists. E denotes the expectation of $Q(t, \theta, X_t)$, for θ fixed, taken over the invariant distribution of the stochastic process X_t. If X_t is not exogenous, but depends on θ_{t-1}, then one needs to use the more general formulation

$$h(\theta) = \lim_{t \to \infty} E Q(t, \theta, \bar{X}_t(\theta)),$$

where $\bar{X}_t(\theta)$ is the stochastic process for X_t obtained by holding θ_{t-1} at the fixed value $\theta_{t-1} = \theta$.

The stochastic approximation results show that the behavior of the SRA is well approximated by the behavior of the ODE for large t. In particular, possible limit points of the SRA correspond to locally stable equilibria of the ODE.

Before elaborating on this statement, it will be helpful to recall some basic stability results for ODEs.[6] $\bar{\theta}$ is an equilibrium point of $d\theta/d\tau = h(\theta)$ if $h(\bar{\theta}) = 0$. $\bar{\theta}$ is said to be locally stable if for every $\varepsilon > 0$, there exists $\delta > 0$ such that $|\theta(\tau) - \bar{\theta}| < \varepsilon$ for all $|\theta(0) - \bar{\theta}| < \delta$. $\bar{\theta}$ is said to be locally asymptotically stable if $\bar{\theta}$ is locally stable and in addition $\theta(\tau) \to \bar{\theta}$ for all $\theta(0)$ in some neighborhood of $\bar{\theta}$. We say that $\bar{\theta}$ is locally unstable if it is not locally stable.

It can be shown that the condition for local stability of $\bar{\theta}$ is based on the derivative matrix (or "Jacobian") $Dh(\bar{\theta})$:

(i) If all eigenvalues of $Dh(\bar{\theta})$ have negative real parts, then $\bar{\theta}$ is a locally stable equilibrium point of $d\theta/d\tau = h(\theta)$.

---

[6]Chapter 5 provides a review of stability results for ODEs.

(ii) If some eigenvalue of $Dh(\bar{\theta})$ has a positive real part, then $\bar{\theta}$ is not a locally
    stable equilibrium point of $d\theta/d\tau = h(\theta)$.

We remark that in the cases not covered (where there are roots with zero real
parts, but no root with a positive real part), more refined techniques are required
to determine stability.

The stochastic approximation results can be stated as follows:

> *Under suitable assumptions, if $\bar{\theta}$ is a locally stable equilibrium point of the
> ODE, then $\bar{\theta}$ is a possible point of convergence of the SRA. If $\bar{\theta}$ is not a
> locally stable equilibrium point of the ODE, then $\bar{\theta}$ is not a possible point of
> convergence of the SRA, i.e., $\theta_t \to \bar{\theta}$ with probability 0.*

Although the above statements appear fairly straightforward, the precise theorems are complex in detail. There are two reasons for this. First, there are various ways to formalize the positive convergence result (when $\bar{\theta}$ is a locally stable
equilibrium point of the ODE). In certain cases, when there is a unique solution
and the ODE is globally stable, it can be shown that under the SRA, $\theta_t \to \bar{\theta}$ with
probability 1 from any starting point. When there are multiple equilibria, however, such a strong result will not be possible, and indeed there may be multiple
stable equilibria. In this case, if one artificially constrains θ_t to an appropriate neighborhood of a locally stable equilibrium $\bar{\theta}$ (using a so-called "projection facility"), one can still obtain convergence with probability 1. Alternatively,
without this device, one can, for example, show convergence with positive probability from appropriate starting points. The different ways of expressing local
stability of $\bar{\theta}$ under the SRA are fully discussed in Chapter 6.

Second, a careful statement is required of the technical assumptions under
which the convergence conditions obtain. There are three broad classes of assumptions:

  (i) regularity assumptions on Q,
 (ii) conditions on the rate at which $\gamma_t \to 0$,
(iii) assumptions on the properties of the stochastic process followed by the
      state variable X_t.

For condition (ii) on the gain sequence, a standard assumption is that $\sum \gamma_t = \infty$
and $\sum \gamma_t^2 < \infty$. This is satisfied in particular by $\gamma_t = t^{-1}$.

The precise statement of the conditions (i)–(iii) depends on the precise version of the stability or instability result, and in some cases, there are alternative sets of assumptions. Again, we will discuss these issues fully in Chapters 6
and 7. Finally, we remark that the formal instability result does not cover the
case in which $Dh(\bar{\theta})$ has roots with zero real parts but no postive roots.

2.8 Application to the Cobweb Model

In this section we show how to apply the results of the previous section to the recursive formulation (2.11)–(2.12) of the cobweb model with learning to obtain the stability and instability results stated in Section 2.3. We begin by showing how equations (2.11)–(2.12) can be rewritten in the standard form (2.13) for the SRA. Then we explicitly compute the associated ODE using equation (2.14) and determine its stability conditions.

To show that the system can be put in standard form, we would like to define θ_t to include all the components of ϕ_t and R_t. However, there is a complication which arises in equation (2.11): on the right-hand side of the equation, the variable R_t rather than R_{t-1} is present, while the standard form allows only the lagged value θ_{t-1}. To deal with this we define $S_{t-1} = R_t$. The system (2.11)–(2.12) can then be rewritten

$$\phi_t = \phi_{t-1} + t^{-1} S_{t-1}^{-1} z_{t-1} \big(z_{t-1}' (T(\phi_{t-1}) - \phi_{t-1}) + \eta_t \big), \qquad (2.15)$$

$$S_t = S_{t-1} + t^{-1} \left(\frac{t}{t+1} \right) (z_t z_t' - S_{t-1}). \qquad (2.16)$$

Note that the second equation has been advanced by one period to accommodate the redating of R_t. This system is now implicitly in standard form with the following definitions of variables:

$$\theta_t = \text{vec} \begin{pmatrix} \phi_t & S_t \end{pmatrix},$$

$$X_t = \begin{pmatrix} 1 \\ w_t \\ w_{t-1} \\ \eta_t \end{pmatrix},$$

$$\gamma_t = t^{-1}.$$

Recall that $z_t' = (1 \; w_t')$. Thus all the components of z_t and z_{t-1} have been included in X_t. Here vec denotes the matrix operator which stacks in order the columns of the matrix $\begin{pmatrix} \phi_t & S_t \end{pmatrix}$ into a column vector. The function $Q(t, \theta_{t-1}, X_t)$ is now fully specified in equations (2.15)–(2.16). The first components of Q, giving the revisions to ϕ_{t-1}, are given by

$$Q_\phi(t, \theta_{t-1}, X_t) = S_{t-1}^{-1} z_{t-1} \big(z_{t-1}' (T(\phi_{t-1}) - \phi_{t-1}) + \eta_t \big),$$

and the remaining components are given by

$$Q_S(t, \theta_{t-1}, X_t) = \text{vec}\left(\left(\frac{t}{t+1}\right)(z_t z_t' - S_{t-1})\right).$$

Having shown that the system can be placed in standard SRA form, the next step is to compute the associated ODE. To do this we fix the value of θ in $Q(t, \theta_{t-1}, X_t)$ and compute the expectation over X_t. Fixing the value of θ means fixing the values of ϕ and S, so that we have

$$h_\phi(\phi, S) = \lim_{t \to \infty} E S^{-1} z_{t-1}(z_{t-1}'(T(\phi) - \phi) + \eta_t),$$

$$h_S(\phi, S) = \lim_{t \to \infty} \frac{t}{t+1} E(z_t z_t' - S).$$

$h(\theta) = \text{vec}(h_\phi(\phi, S), h_S(\phi, S))$, but it is easier to continue to work directly with the separate vector and matrix functions $h_\phi(\phi, S)$ and $h_S(\phi, S)$. Since

$$E z_t z_t' = E z_{t-1} z_{t-1}' = \begin{pmatrix} 1 & 0 \\ 0 & \Omega \end{pmatrix} \equiv M,$$

$E z_{t-1} \eta_t = 0$, and $\lim_{t \to \infty} t/(t+1) = 1$, we obtain

$$h_\phi(\phi, S) = S^{-1} M(T(\phi) - \phi),$$
$$h_S(\phi, S) = M - S.$$

We have therefore arrived at the associated ODE

$$\frac{d\phi}{d\tau} = S^{-1} M(T(\phi) - \phi), \tag{2.17}$$

$$\frac{dS}{d\tau} = M - S. \tag{2.18}$$

This system is recursive and the second set of equations is a globally stable system with $S \to M$ from any starting point. It follows that $S^{-1} M \to I$ from any starting point, provided S is invertible along the path, and hence that the stability of the differential equations (2.17)–(2.18) is determined entirely by the stability of the smaller dimension system

$$\frac{d\phi}{d\tau} = T(\phi) - \phi. \tag{2.19}$$

There are technical details required to establish this equivalence, since one must show that the possibility of a noninvertible S can be sidestepped. The technical arguments on this point are given in Chapter 6.

Recalling that $\phi' = (a \ b')$, note that equation (2.19) is identical to the differential equation (2.8) which defines E-stability. We have already seen that $\bar{\phi}' \equiv (\bar{a}, \bar{b}')$ is stable under equation (2.8) provided $\alpha < 1$. Indeed, using the definition of $T(\phi)$ in equation (2.7), we can write

$$T(\phi) - \phi = \begin{pmatrix} \mu \\ \delta \end{pmatrix} + (\alpha - 1)I\phi,$$

where I is the identity matrix. Equation (2.19) is thus a linear differential equation with coefficient matrix $(\alpha - 1)I$, all of whose eigenvalues are equal to $\alpha - 1$. $\bar{\phi}$ is thus a globally stable equilibrium point of equation (2.19) if $\alpha < 1$, but is unstable if $\alpha > 1$. Applying the stochastic approximation results, it follows that under the SRA (2.15)–(2.16), $(\phi_t, S_t) \to (\bar{\phi}, M)$ with probability 1, from any starting point, if $\alpha < 1$. In particular, $\phi_t \to \bar{\phi}$ if $\alpha < 1$. If $\alpha > 1$, $(\phi_t, S_t) \to (\bar{\phi}, M)$ with probability 0. Since $S_t \to M$ with probability 1[7] even if $\alpha > 1$, it follows that $\phi_t \to \bar{\phi}$ with probability 0 if $\alpha > 1$. Since the dynamic system of least squares learning (2.1), (2.3), and (2.4) can be expressed as the SRA (2.15)–(2.16), we at last obtain the results stated in the theorem of Section 2.3.

To illustrate results for the cobweb model, we exhibit a simulation with reduced form parameters $\mu = 5$, $\delta = 1$, and $\alpha = -0.5$ (recall that in the cobweb model $\alpha < 0$). The observable w_t is a one-dimensional normal white noise process with standard deviation 1, and the unobservable white noise process η_t has standard deviation 0.5. We simulate equations (2.10), (2.11), and (2.12) with initial values $a_0 = 1$, $b_0 = 2$, and R_0 equal to the 2×2 identity matrix. Figure 2.1 shows the trajectories for a_t, b_t, and p_t. Clearly, convergence to the REE values $\bar{a} = 10/3$ and $\bar{b} = 2/3$ occurs quite rapidly.

2.9 The E-Stability Principle

In the remainder of the book we elaborate on the techniques described in this chapter and show how they can be extended to most standard theoretical and applied macroeconomic models. These models can have different types of equilibria such as ARMA or VAR processes, (noisy) k-cycles, or sunspots. It turns out that E-stability will play a central role in determining the stability of the REE under adaptive learning for the different models studied in this book.

---

[7]This is the strong law of large numbers applied to the process $z_t z_t'$, and holds, in particular, if w_t is an exogenous stationary VAR. Alternatively, it follows from applying the stochastic approximation techniques to the subsystem (2.16).

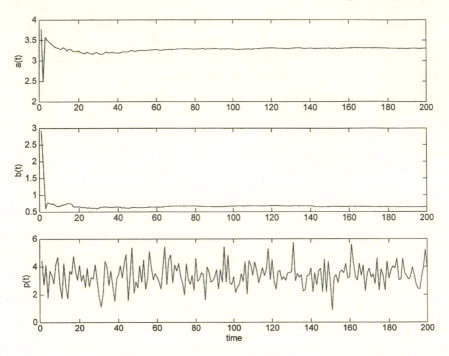

Figure 2.1.

A general definition of E-stability is a straightforward extension of the example in this chapter. Starting with an economic model, we consider its REE solutions. Assume that any particular solution can be described as a stochastic process with particular parameter values $\bar{\phi}$. Here ϕ might be, for example, the parameters of an ARMA process or of a VAR or the mean values at the different points in a k-cycle. Under adaptive learning the agents are assumed not to know $\bar{\phi}$, but try to estimate it using data from the economy. This leads to statistical estimates ϕ_t at time t, and the issue will be whether $\phi_t \to \bar{\phi}$ as $t \to \infty$. We will in each case set up the problem as an SRA in order to examine the stability of the solution $\bar{\phi}$. We will continue to find that stability of $\bar{\phi}$ under learning can be determined by the E-stability equation, i.e., by the stability of

$$\frac{d\phi}{d\tau} = T(\phi) - \phi, \tag{2.20}$$

in a neighborhood of $\bar{\phi}$, where $T(\phi)$ is the mapping from the perceived law of motion ϕ to the implied actual law of motion $T(\phi)$. [Note that REEs correspond to fixed points of $T(\phi)$.] Formally, $\bar{\phi}$ is said to be E-stable if it is locally asymptotically stable under the differential equation (2.20).

The correspondence between E-stability of an REE and its stability under adaptive learning we call the *E-stability principle*. In this book we primarily consider least squares and related statistical learning rules. Here there is strong support for the principle, and it also seems to hold for some non-statistical learning schemes. We regard the validity of the E-stability principle as an operating hypothesis.

It will become clear from the analysis of this book that the validity of the E-stability principle requires restricting attention to the standard case of gain decreasing to zero (in some cases a sufficiently small constant gain can be accommodated). Another assumption that is needed is that the information variables, on which the estimators are based, remain bounded. The general validity of the principle, i.e., general conditions under which the principle holds, remains to be determined.

An issue which will become increasingly important in our development is the precise specification of the learning rule followed by the agents. If we assume that our agents are behaving like econometricians, they will have to face some of the practical difficulties of econometricians, most importantly the issue of specifying the appropriate forecasting model. In our discussion of the cobweb model above, we implicitly assumed that the agents knew the correct asymptotic specification, i.e., they knew the appropriate vector of explanatory variables for forecasting next period's price. We will continue to focus on this case in our analysis of more general economic models. However, it is reasonable to ask how misspecification would alter the results. Suppose agents overparameterize the solution, e.g., suppose the REE being examined follows an ARMA process and the agents fit a process with a higher AR or MA degree. Or suppose the REE being examined is a k-cycle and agents overfit with an *nk*-cycle. Will such overfitting alter the stability conditions? It turns out that this is an important issue to be examined particularly when there are multiple REEs. We can also consider the effect of agents underparameterizing an REEs solution. Here the agents cannot converge to the solution, but we can still ask if they converge and, if so, to what process?

The issue of overparameterization has a simple reflection in terms of E-stability. If agents overparameterize an REE solution, the solution can be represented as a higher-dimensional vector $\tilde{\phi}' = (\phi_1, \phi_2)$ with component values $(\bar{\phi}, 0)$ at the REE in question. We can now look at the stability of

$$\frac{d\tilde{\phi}}{d\tau} = \tilde{T}(\tilde{\phi}) - \tilde{\phi}, \qquad (2.21)$$

where $\tilde{T}$ is the mapping from the perceived to the actual law of motion for this expanded set of parameters. Indeed, it is useful to introduce some terminology to represent this distinction. If the REE $\bar{\phi}$ is locally stable under equation (2.20) but $(\bar{\phi}, 0)$ is not locally stable under equation (2.21), then we say that it is *weakly E-stable*, while if $(\bar{\phi}, 0)$ is also stable under equation (2.21), then we say that the REE is *strongly E-stable*. As we will see, weak and strong E-stability govern whether the corresponding adaptive learning rules are stable. By expanding the dimension of ϕ appropriately, one can also allow for heterogeneous expectations across agents and determine whether allowing for heterogeneity alters the stability conditions for convergence of adaptive learning. In an analogous way, the concept of E-stability can also be adapted to determine conditions for the convergence of underparameterized learning rules by reducing the dimension of ϕ.

One could also consider structural heterogeneity, i.e., models in which individual agents respond differently to expectations. An open question is how E-stability can be adapted to such environments. Throughout the book we implicitly make the assumption of structural homogeneity, so that models such as equation (2.1) arise from a world in which the characteristics of individual agents are identical.

There is one more important conceptual issue that arises in connection with E-stability. In some papers, e.g., DeCanio (1979), Bray (1982), Evans (1983), and Evans (1985), iterations of the T-map are considered and the stability of an REE under these iterations is determined.[8] Formally, this version of E-stability replaces the differential equation (2.20) with the difference equation

$$\phi_{N+1} = T(\phi_N), \quad \text{for } N = 0, 1, 2, \ldots . \tag{2.22}$$

In order to have a clear terminology, we will refer to the notion of stability determined by equation (2.22) as *iterative E-stability*, reserving the unmodified phrase "E-stability" for stability under the differential equation. Thus an REE $\bar{\phi}$ is iteratively E-stable if for all ϕ_0 in a neighborhood of $\bar{\phi}$, we have $\phi_N \to \bar{\phi}$ under equation (2.22).

Formally, there is a simple connection between E-stability and iterative E-stability. The condition for $\bar{\phi}$ to be iteratively E-stable is that all eigenvalues of $DT(\bar{\phi})$ lie inside the unit circle. In contrast, the E-stability condition, based on

---

[8]Iterations of the T-map were also considered in Lucas (1978). The term "expectational stability," and the distinction between weak and strong (iterative) E-stability, were introduced in Evans (1983) and Evans (1985).

equation (2.20), is that all roots of $DT(\bar{\phi}) - I$ have negative real parts; equivalently, the real parts of all eigenvalues of $DT(\bar{\phi})$ must be less than 1. It follows immediately that iterative E-stability is a stricter condition than E-stability. For example, in the model (2.1) the E-stability condition, as we have shown, is that $\alpha < 1$, while the iterative E-stability condition is $|\alpha| < 1$.

We have seen that E-stability provides the condition for stability under adaptive learning rules such as least squares. What, therefore, do we learn from iterative E-stability? One rationale given in the papers cited was that it gave the condition for stability if agents kept fixed their perceived law of motion until a large amount of data was collected, revising their estimates infrequently rather than at each point in time. An alternative "eductive" rationale, also suggested in these papers, was that it described a process of learning taking place in "mental time," as each agent considered the possible forecasts of other agents, iteratively eliminating those that correspond to dominated strategies. Using the game-theoretic notions of rationalizability and common knowledge, this approach was developed in Guesnerie (1992). It is discussed in Section 15.4 of Chapter 15. It has also been recently shown that iterative E-stability plays an important role for learning dynamics based on finite-memory rules in stochastic frameworks (see Honkapohja and Mitra, 1999).

Since this book focuses on adaptive learning, the appropriate stability conditions required are in almost all cases the E-stability conditions provided by the differential equation formulation.

2.10 Discussion of the Literature

In addition to the cobweb model, which we discussed throughout this chapter, the overlapping generations model and various linear models were the most frequently used frameworks in the early literature on learning.

Lucas (1986) is an early analysis of the stability of steady states under learning in an OG model. Grandmont (1985) considered the existence of deterministic cycles for the basic OG model. He also examined learning using the generalizations of adaptive expectations to nonlinear finite-memory forecast functions. Guesnerie and Woodford (1991) proposed a generalization to adaptive expectations by allowing possible convergence to deterministic cycles. Convergence of learning to sunspot equilibria in the basic OG model was first discovered by Woodford (1990).

Linear models more general than the cobweb model were considered under learning in the early literature. As already noted, Marcet and Sargent (1989c)

proposed a general stochastic framework and the use of stochastic approximation techniques for the analysis of adaptive learning. Their paper includes several
applications to well-known models. Margaritis (1987) applied Ljung's method
to the model of Bray (1982). Grandmont and Laroque (1991) examined learning
in a deterministic linear model with a lagged endogenous variable for classes of
finite-memory rules. Evans and Honkapohja (1994b) considered extensions of
adaptive learning to stochastic linear models with multiple equilibria.

The more recent literature on adaptive learning will be referenced in the
appropriate parts of this book. See also the surveys Evans and Honkapohja
(1995a, 1999). The comments below provide references to approaches and literature that will not be covered in detail in later sections.

For Bayesian learning the first papers include Turnovsky (1969), Townsend
(1978), Townsend (1983), and McLennan (1984). Bray and Kreps (1987) discussed rational learning and compared it to adaptive approaches. Nyarko (1991)
showed in a monopoly model that Bayesian learning may fail to converge if the
true parameters are outside the set of possible prior beliefs. Papers studying the
implications of Bayesian learning include Feldman (1987b), Feldman (1987a),
Vives (1993), Jun and Vives (1996), Bertocchi and Yong (1996), and Nyarko
(1997). The collection Kurz (1997) contains central papers on a related notion
of rational beliefs.

The study of finite-memory learning rules in nonstochastic models was initiated in Fuchs (1977), Fuchs (1979), Fuchs and Laroque (1976), and Tillmann
(1983), and it was extended in Grandmont (1985) and Grandmont and Laroque
(1986). These models can be viewed as a generalization of adaptive expectations. We remark that the finite-memory learning rules cannot converge to an
REE in stochastic models, as noted by Evans and Honkapohja (1995c) and studied further by Honkapohja and Mitra (1999). Further references of expectations
formation and learning in nonstochastic models are given in Section 7.2 of Chapter 7.

Learning in games has been subject to extensive work in recent years. Surveys are given in Marimon (1997) and Fudenberg and Levine (1998). Carton
(1999) applied these techniques to the cobweb model. Kirman (1995) reviewed
the closely related literature on learning in oligopoly models. Another related
recent topic is social learning, see, e.g., Ellison and Fudenberg (1995) and Gale
(1996).

Chapter **3**

Variations on a Theme

3.1 Introduction

In this chapter we discuss some extensions and variations of econometric learning. Several issues arise naturally. So far we have assumed representative agent learning, although diversity of expectations should surely be treated. One can also consider alternative adaptive learning schemes and the possibility that the agents do not know the true model. In this chapter we show how such issues can be readily addressed in the context of the basic cobweb and asset pricing models.

We also take up learning in nonstochastic frameworks and obtain the key conditions for local stability under adaptive learning of perfect-foresight steady states. Since some standard textbook models are often presented in a nonstochastic setting, we will occasionally draw on these results in later chapters. In this chapter we show how the technique can be applied directly to assess local stability of equilibria in simple nonstochastic coordination games.

3.2 Heterogeneous Expectations

For expository purposes we simplify the cobweb model of the previous chapter. Dropping the intercept and assuming a scalar stationary shock w_{t-1}, the model becomes[1]

$$p_t = \alpha p_t^e + \delta w_{t-1} + \eta_t. \tag{3.1}$$

Recall that the RE solution is given by

$$p_t = \bar{b} w_{t-1} + \eta_t, \quad \text{where } \bar{b} = (1-\alpha)^{-1} \delta.$$

We allow for $i = 1, \dots, N$ different groups of agents who may have different expectations $p_{i,t}^e$, but assume that the average expectations

$$p_t^e = N^{-1} \sum_{i=1}^{N} p_{i,t}^e$$

influence the market price in equation (3.1). Each group of agents forecasts according to the linear rule

$$p_{i,t}^e = b_{i,t-1} w_{t-1}.$$

Thus the agents are forecasting in the same way, but they are allowed to have different parameter estimates.

We continue to assume that agents learn from the data on past prices and the exogenous variables and use a variation of least squares learning to update their estimates. In fact, we allow for a slight generalization of recursive least squares as follows:

$$
\begin{aligned}
b_{i,t} &= b_{i,t-1} + \gamma_t R_{i,t}^{-1} w_{t-1} (p_t - b_{i,t-1} w_{t-1}), \\
R_{i,t} &= R_{i,t-1} + \gamma_t \left(w_{t-1}^2 - R_{i,t-1} \right).
\end{aligned} \tag{3.2}
$$

In the previous chapter the least squares formula set $\gamma_t = t^{-1}$. We have now introduced a more general gain parameter γ_t, as discussed in Section 2.7 of that chapter.

Combining the earlier equations for the individual expectations with equation (3.1) leads to

$$p_t = N^{-1} \alpha \left(\sum_{i=1}^{N} b_{i,t-1} \right) w_{t-1} + \delta w_{t-1} + \eta_t.$$

---

[1] The argument can be readily generalized to allow for an intercept and a vector stationary shock w_t. In fact, one can also allow for p_t to be a vector. Details are provided in Evans and Honkapohja (1997).

This equation and the updating rule (3.2) define a standard stochastic recursive algorithm as introduced in Section 2.7. As pointed out there, the analysis of convergence in these algorithms is carried out by deriving the associated ODE. Following the same steps as in Section 2.8 of Chapter 2, we obtain

$$
\frac{db_i}{d\tau} = R_i^{-1} M\left[\delta + N^{-1}\alpha \sum_{i=1}^{N} b_i - b_i\right], \qquad i = 1, \dots, N,
$$
$$
\frac{dR_i}{d\tau} = M - R_i, \qquad i = 1, \dots, N,
$$

where $M = E(w_t^2)$.

Since $R_i \to M$ globally for $i = 1, \dots, N$, stability of this differential equation system is governed by stability of

$$
\frac{db_i}{d\tau} = \delta + N^{-1}\alpha \sum_{i=1}^{N} b_i - b_i, \qquad i = 1, \dots, N.
$$

This system can be written in the matrix form

$$
\frac{db}{d\tau} = \begin{pmatrix} \delta \\ \vdots \\ \delta \end{pmatrix} + \left[N^{-1}\alpha \begin{pmatrix} 1 & \cdots & 1 \\ \vdots & \ddots & \vdots \\ 1 & \cdots & 1 \end{pmatrix} - I_N \right] b.
$$

The coefficient matrix of this linear system has one eigenvalue of $\alpha - 1$ and $N - 1$ eigenvalues of -1 and is therefore globally asymptotically stable with each b_i converging to $\bar{b}$, provided $\alpha < 1$.

Appealing to the results on convergence of stochastic recursive algorithms as in the previous chapter, we have the striking result that the convergence condition under heterogeneous expectations is the same as that for the case of a representative agent. That is, provided $\alpha < 1$, all agents learn asymptotically the rational expectations equilibrium.

We remark that the preceding argument implicitly makes the "representative agent" assumption of structural homogeneity. Thus equation (3.1) is assumed to arise from an economy in which the cost functions of individual suppliers are identical. In principle structural heterogeneity could be tackled by the same techniques.

3.3   Learning with Constant Gain

So far we have considered cases where there is asymptotic convergence to the rational expectations equilibrium. In models with stochastic shocks, this can only happen if the learning algorithm is of the "decreasing-gain" type, i.e., $\gamma_t \to 0$. We now briefly analyze the case of a constant gain, i.e., $\gamma_t = \gamma$, a small positive constant.

For our example we pick the model

$$p_t = \alpha + \beta E_t^* p_{t+1} + v_t,$$

where v_t is iid with mean zero and $E_t^* p_{t+1}$ denotes the (rational or nonrational) expectation of the next period price. We here use $E_t^* p_{t+1}$ in place of p_{t+1}^e to emphasize that the expectations are formed at time t. This model was introduced in Chapter 1 as the "Cagan Model" and it was noted there that it could also be interpreted as the standard asset pricing model with risk neutrality.[2] For both cases we have $0 < \beta < 1$.

We focus on learning of the market fundamental rational expectations solution. This is a stochastic steady state $p_t = \bar{a} + v_t$, where $\bar{a} = (1 - \beta)^{-1}\alpha$. We first begin with the standard decreasing-gain learning rule which does converge to the REE. We assume that forecasts take the form $E_t^* p_{t+1} = a_t$, where a_t is the estimated mean which is updated according to

$$a_t = a_{t-1} + t^{-1}(p_{t-1} - a_{t-1}).$$

Since $p_{t-1} = \alpha + \beta a_{t-1} + v_{t-1}$, we have

$$a_t = a_{t-1} + t^{-1}(\alpha + (\beta - 1)a_{t-1} + v_{t-1}).$$

The associated ODE takes the form

$$\frac{da}{d\tau} = \alpha + (\beta - 1)a.$$

Applying the stochastic approximation results, it follows that $a_t \to \bar{a}$ provided $\beta < 1$. (Using the global convergence results of Chapter 6, it can in fact be shown that convergence occurs with probability 1.) The condition $\beta < 1$ can easily be seen to be the E-stability condition, so that we obtain the expected result that when this condition is satisfied there is convergence to the REE.

---

[2]For further discussion of this model see Section 8.6 of Chapter 8.

Now we consider the implications of replacing t^{-1} by a constant parameter γ. The forecasts still take the form $E_t^* p_{t+1} = a_t$, but now a_t is updated using the constant-gain learning rule

$$a_t = a_{t-1} + \gamma(p_{t-1} - a_{t-1}), \quad \text{where } 0 < \gamma \leq 1. \tag{3.3}$$

We remark that this learning rule is equivalent to the traditional adaptive expectations formula. Note also that it can be expressed as an exponentially weighted average of lagged prices since $a_t = \gamma \sum_{i=0}^{\infty} (1 - \gamma)^i p_{t-1-i}$.

Since $p_t = \alpha + \beta a_t + v_t$, we have

$$a_t = \alpha\gamma + \left(1 - \gamma(1 - \beta)\right)a_{t-1} + \gamma v_{t-1}. \tag{3.4}$$

This is an AR(1) process which is stationary if $|1 - \gamma(1 - \beta)| < 1$ or equivalently, $2 > \gamma(1 - \beta) > 0$. A necessary condition for stationarity is that $\beta < 1$, which is also the weak E-stability condition for this model. In the limit $\gamma \to 0$, the E-stability condition $\beta < 1$ is also sufficient for stationarity.

The price process takes the form

$$p_t = \left(1 - \gamma(1 - \beta)\right)p_{t-1} + \alpha\gamma + v_t - (1 - \gamma)v_{t-1}.$$

This is an ARMA(1,1) process. Assuming $|1 - \gamma(1 - \beta)| < 1$ so that both a_t and p_t are (asymptotically) stationary, it is easily verified that the (asymptotic) mean of both p_t and a_t are equal to the RE value $\bar{a} = (1 - \beta)^{-1}\alpha$. Thus the forecast a_t is asymptotically unbiased. It is also possible to compute the (asymptotic) variance of p_t.[3] This is given by

$$\text{var}(p_t) = \left(\frac{1 + (1 - \gamma)(1 - 2\beta)}{1 + (1 - \gamma)(1 - 2\beta) - \gamma\beta^2}\right)\text{var}(v_t).$$

For $\gamma > 0$ the variance is higher than the RE value of $\text{var}(v_t)$, though it approaches this as $\gamma \to 0$. This illustrates the phenomenon of excess volatility induced by the fixed-gain learning rule.

---

[3]For a stationary ARMA(1,1) process

$$y_t = \phi y_{t-1} + \varepsilon_t + \theta\varepsilon_{t-1},$$

where $|\phi| < 1$ and ε_t is white noise with variance σ^2, it can be shown that

$$\text{var}(y_t) = \frac{(1 + \theta^2 + 2\phi\theta)}{1 - \phi^2}\sigma^2.$$

See, for example, Harvey (1981).

Although, as just demonstrated, fixed-gain learning rules do not generally converge to rational expectations, they can do so if the model is nonstochastic. Thus suppose that $v_t \equiv 0$, so that

$$p_t = \alpha + \beta E_t^* p_{t+1}.$$

With forecasts $E_t^* p_{t+1} = a_t$ and learning rule (3.3), we have convergence to the perfect-foresight steady state $p_t = \alpha/(1 - \beta)$ if and only if $|1 - \gamma(1 - \beta)| < 1$, i.e.,

$$1 - 2/\gamma < \beta < 1.$$

Note that if $|\beta| < 1$, this holds for all $0 < \gamma \leq 1$, whereas for $\beta < -1$ we need $\gamma < 2(1 - \beta)^{-1}$. Thus, if the expectational stability condition $\beta < 1$ holds, in the nonstochastic model there is always convergence to the RE under the constant-gain learning rule if the gain parameter γ is sufficiently small.

3.4   Learning in Nonstochastic Models

We now take up the issue of learning steady states in nonstochastic models in a more general setting. Consider models of the form

$$p_t = f(E_t^* p_{t+1}).$$

One natural adaptive learning rule is to forecast p_{t+1} as the average of past observed values, i.e.,

$$E_t^* p_{t+1} = a_t,$$

where $a_t = t^{-1} \sum_{i=0}^{t-1} p_i$, for $t = 1, 2, 3, \dots$. This can be written recursively as

$$a_t = a_{t-1} + t^{-1}(p_{t-1} - a_{t-1}).$$

As discussed for a linear model in the previous section, in nonstochastic models the constant-gain version also has the potential to converge to a perfect-foresight steady state. This remains true for local analysis of nonlinear models. Both of these cases are covered by the following recursive formulation:

$$a_t = a_{t-1} + \gamma_t(p_{t-1} - a_{t-1}), \tag{3.5}$$

where the gain sequence γ_t satisfies

$$0 < \gamma_t \le 1 \quad \text{and} \quad \sum_{t=1}^{\infty} \gamma_t = +\infty.$$

The choice $\gamma_t = t^{-1}$ is an example of a "decreasing-gain" algorithm (i.e., an algorithm in which $\lim_{t \to \infty} \gamma_t = 0$).

The formulation (3.5) reflects the common practice of assuming that the parameter estimate a_t depends only on data through $t - 1$. This has the advantage of avoiding simultaneity between p_t and a_t. However, we also briefly consider the implications of an alternative assumption in which

$$a_t = a_{t-1} + \gamma_t (p_t - a_{t-1}). \tag{3.6}$$

We will see that the choice of assumptions can matter in the fixed-gain case, but is not important if $\gamma_t = t^{-1}$ or if $\gamma_t = \gamma > 0$ is sufficiently small.

Standard timing assumption: We consider first the case (3.5), which we will refer to as the standard timing assumption. Combining equations, we have $p_t = f(a_t)$ so that

$$a_t = a_{t-1} + \gamma_t (f(a_{t-1}) - a_{t-1}).$$

In a perfect-foresight steady state, $p_t = \bar{p} = a$, where $a = f(a)$. In the constant-gain case, we have $a_t = (1 - \gamma)a_{t-1} + \gamma f(a_{t-1})$. To analyze stability we apply standard results on nonlinear difference equations.[4] Using these, it is easily established that a steady state $a = \bar{p}$ is locally stable if and only if $|1 + \gamma(f'(a) - 1)| < 1$, i.e., iff $1 - 2/\gamma < f'(a) < 1$. Note that $1 - 2/\gamma \to -\infty$ as $\gamma \to 0$.

Under the decreasing-gain assumption $\lim_{t \to \infty} \gamma_t = 0$, it can be shown that a steady state $a = \bar{p}$ is locally stable if and only if $f'(a) < 1$.[5] We here present a proof of this for the case $0 < f'(a) < 1$. [For $f'(a) < 0$, the argument is more involved.] Without loss of generality we suppose the initial point $a_0 < a$. We assume that a_0 is sufficiently close to a so that f is monotonically increasing

---

[4] See Chapter 5 for a review of the stability results. The key result is that a steady state $\bar{y}$ of a multivariate difference equation $y_t = F(y_{t-1})$ is locally stable if the derivative matrix $DF(\bar{y})$ has all eigenvalues inside the unit circle. In the case at hand we have a univariate difference equation, and so the condition is just that the derivative is less than 1 in absolute value.

[5] The results for the decreasing-gain case in this section can be shown formally by using the implicit function theorem and applying Evans and Honkapohja (2000). Details are given in Chapter 7.

between a_0 and a. Then at each time t one has $f(a_t) > a_t$, implying $a_{t+1} > a_t$. Since $\gamma_t < 1$, it follows that $a_{t+1} \le a$. To show that $a_t \to a$, suppose to the contrary that $\lim a_t = \hat{a} < a$.[6] Let $d = f(\hat{a}) - \hat{a} > 0$. For t sufficiently large, $a_{t+1} \ge a_t + \gamma_t(d/2)$, so that $a_{t+s} \ge a_t + (d/2) \sum_{i=t}^{t+s} \gamma_i$, yielding a contradiction since $\sum_{t=1}^{\infty} \gamma_t = \infty$.

Alternative timing assumption: Under equation (3.6) we instead have the implicit equation

$$a_t = a_{t-1} + \gamma_t(f(a_t) - a_{t-1}).$$

In general, there need not be a unique solution for a_t given a_{t-1}, though this will be assured if γ_t is sufficiently small and if $f'(a)$ is bounded. Assuming uniqueness and focusing on local stability near a, we can approximate this equation by

$$a_t - a = \left(1 - \gamma_t f'(a)\right)^{-1}(1 - \gamma_t)(a_{t-1} - a).$$

Under the fixed-gain assumption this leads to the stability condition that either $f'(a) < 1$ or $f'(a) > 2/\gamma - 1$ (these possibilities correspond to the cases $\gamma f'(a) < 1$ and $\gamma f'(a) > 1$). Under decreasing gain the condition is again simply $f'(a) < 1$.

The results of this section can be summarized as follows. Fixed-gain learning can converge to perfect-foresight steady states in nonstochastic models and such rules have somewhat different stability conditions than the decreasing-gain rules which are standard for stochastic models. The stability conditions also depend on assumptions made concerning the timing of information. However, for the small gain case, i.e., decreasing gain or a sufficiently small constant gain, the condition for local stability under adaptive learning is not affected by the timing assumption and is simply $f'(a) < 1$, generalizing our earlier results for linear models. This stability condition has a straightforward interpretation in terms of E-stability: For a PLM $y_t = a$, the corresponding ALM is $y_t = f(a)$. The E-stability differential equation is then $da/d\tau = f(a) - a$ with stability condition $f'(a) < 1$.

The methods of this section can also be easily applied equally to models of the form $p_t = f(E_{t-1}^* p_t)$. For this setup, the expectation $E_{t-1}^* p_t$ cannot depend on p_t and the timing assumption appears clear. Supposing that $E_{t-1}^* p_t = a_{t-1}$ with $a_t = a_{t-1} + \gamma_t(p_t - a_{t-1})$ leads to the recursive algorithm

---

[6]Recall that a bounded monotonic sequence always has a limit.

$a_t = a_{t-1} + \gamma_t (f(a_{t-1}) - a_{t-1})$ as with the preceding model under the standard timing assumption. It follows that a perfect-foresight steady state $p_t = \bar{p}$, where $\bar{p} = f(\bar{p})$, is locally stable under decreasing gain if $f'(a) < 1$ and under constant gain $\gamma_t = \gamma$ provided $1 - 2/\gamma < f'(a) < 1$.

3.4.1 Application: Coordination Problems

The general methods of this section can be applied to study adaptive learning in certain nonstochastic macroeconomic models formulated as games. In this section we consider coordination games involving strategic complementarities along the lines of Cooper and John (1988) and Cooper (1999). A large finite number of agents $i = 1, \ldots, I$, each choose an action $x_i \in [0, 1]$. We consider a representative agent model in which the payoff for agent i is given by $U(x_i, Y(x_{-i}))$, where x_{-i} denotes the vector of actions by other agents and $Y(x_{-i})$ is an aggregate statistic. $U(x_i, Y(x_{-i}))$ is assumed to be twice continuously differentiable and strictly concave in the first argument. We focus on symmetric outcomes in which each agent chooses action x and we adopt the notation $Y(x)$ for $Y(x_{-i})$. We assume that $Y(x)$ is twice continuously differentiable and that $Y'(x) > 0$ for all $x \in [0, 1]$.

A symmetric Nash equilibrium is an action x which maximizes $U(x, Y)$ with respect to x, given Y, and where $Y = Y(x)$. In general, there may be multiple equilibria. For this game, a necessary condition for this is strategic complementarity, defined by $\partial^2 U / \partial x \partial Y > 0$. Let $\phi(Y)$ denote the best response of the representative agent to Y. In the case of strategic complementarity we obtain an increasing function $\phi(Y(x))$ as in Figure 3.1.

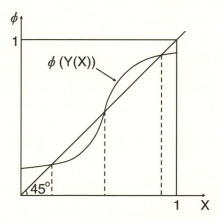

Figure 3.1.

We illustrate the common case of three steady states, given by the fixed points $x = \phi(Y(x))$. Obviously, the number of equilibria could be larger or smaller than three in the case of strategic complementarity. Note that $\bar{x} = \phi(Y(\bar{x}))$ is a fixed point of $\phi(Y(x))$ if and only if $\bar{a} = Y(\bar{x})$ is a fixed point of $Y(\phi(a))$.

The above description is presented as a static game, but is often used in the context of repeated games. We continue to focus on the static Nash equilibria. Agents now have available information on past outcomes which they can use to forecast the behavior of other agents and in particular the value of the key aggregate statistic Y.

Let x_t be the action of the representative agent at time t and Y_t be the value of $Y(x_t)$ at t. Stability under learning can be treated following the general techniques developed in this section. At each time t, agents forecast the aggregate statistic Y and choose the optimal action conditioned on this forecast. Letting a_t denote the expectation of Y_t, we assume

$$a_t = a_{t-1} + \gamma_t(Y_{t-1} - a_{t-1}),$$

where γ_t is the gain sequence. Here we use the standard timing assumption.[7] Given this expectation for Y_t, the representative agent chooses action $x_t = \phi(a_t)$ so that

$$Y_t = Y(\phi(a_t)).$$

From the general analysis of this section we immediately conclude that a fixed point $\bar{a}$ of $Y(\phi(a))$ is locally stable under this learning rule for a_t if and only if $dY(\phi(\bar{a}))/da < 1$. It follows[8] that an equilibrium $\bar{x}$ is locally stable if and only if $d\phi(Y(\bar{x}))/dx < 1$. In Figure 3.1, the lowest and highest steady states are thus stable, while the middle one is unstable. Since $d\phi(Y(\bar{x}))/dx > 0$ in the case of strategic complementarities, this stability condition holds both for decreasing-gain sequences and also for all constant gains $0 < \gamma \le 1$.

There are many economic settings that fit into the framework of strategic complementarities. The underlying economic mechanisms rely on diverse phenomena such as technological complementarities, imperfect competition, demand spillovers, and search externalities.[9] Cooper (1999) gives an up-to-date

[7]The alternative timing assumption of contemporaneous information seems particularly unnatural in this model.

[8]Use $dY(\phi(\bar{a}))/da = Y'(\phi(\bar{a}))\phi'(\bar{a}) = Y'(\bar{x})\phi'(Y(\bar{x}))$.

[9]Early papers in the extensive literature on coordination problems include Bryant (1983), Bryant (1987), Diamond (1982), Hart (1982), Schleifer (1986), and Weitzman (1982).

discussion of the different types of models in which complementarities arise. A number of the models presented in this book incorporate complementarities into a dynamic framework. A simple example is given in Section 4.6. Howitt and McAfee (1992) study learning in a dynamic search model with complementarities.

3.5 Stochastic Gradient Learning

We return to the cobweb model of Chapter 2 which we repeat for convenience:

$$p_t = \mu + \alpha p_t^e + \delta' w_{t-1} + \eta_t.$$

Various alternatives to least squares learning have been proposed in the literature. These include neural networks and genetic algorithms, which we will discuss in Chapter 15.[10] Another learning scheme which has been proposed is the stochastic gradient method, and using our techniques it is possible to give formal results.[11]

Agents are assumed to use the linear forecast rule

$$p_t^e = a_{t-1} + b_{t-1}' w_{t-1} = \phi_{t-1}' z_{t-1},$$

where $\phi_{t-1}' = (a_{t-1}, b_{t-1}')$ and $z_{t-1}' = (1, w_{t-1}')$.

The stochastic gradient algorithm adjusts the parameter estimates in accordance with the following scheme:

$$\phi_t = \phi_{t-1} + \gamma_t z_{t-1} (p_t - \phi_{t-1}' z_{t-1}). \tag{3.7}$$

This algorithm differs from least squares by neglecting the R_t^{-1} term. It is thus a gradient algorithm rather than a Newton-type algorithm, since the latter also uses information on second moments (as does least squares). Stochastic gradient algorithms have been proposed as a simple alternative to least squares.

Substituting the forecast function into the original model yields

$$p_t = (\mu + \alpha a_{t-1}) + (\delta + \alpha b_{t-1})' w_{t-1} + \eta_t$$

---

[10]Time-varying parameter methods have also been suggested. For the cobweb model this has recently been examined by McGough (1999). See also Bullard (1992) and Margaritis (1990).

[11]See Sargent (1993), Kuan and White (1994), Heinemann (2000b), Barucci and Landi (1997), and Evans and Honkapohja (1998c).

or

$$p_t = T(\phi_{t-1})' z_{t-1} + \eta_t. \tag{3.8}$$

The system (3.7), (3.8) can be combined to yield a stochastic recursive algorithm

$$\phi_t = \phi_{t-1} + \gamma_t z_{t-1} \left[(T(\phi_{t-1})' - \phi'_{t-1}) z_{t-1} + \eta_t \right].$$

Following the methods of Chapter 2, the associated ODE can be computed as

$$\frac{d\phi}{d\tau} = \begin{pmatrix} \mu \\ \delta \end{pmatrix} + (\alpha - 1) M \phi,$$

where $M = E(z_t z_t')$ is assumed to be positive definite. This is a linear system of differential equations in ϕ with constant coefficients. Its coefficient matrix $(\alpha - 1)M$ of the ODE is negative definite iff $\alpha < 1$, and under this condition the ODE is (globally) asymptotically stable.

It follows from the results on stochastic recursive algorithms that under the E-stability condition $\alpha < 1$, stochastic gradient learning converges to the RE solution. Thus, for this model the convergence conditions for least squares and stochastic gradient learning are identical. For models of the cobweb type this holds more generally (see Evans and Honkapohja, 1998c), but there appear to be examples in which least squares and stochastic gradient learning do not have identical stability conditions (see Heinemann, 2000b).

3.6   Learning with Misspecification

So far it has been assumed that agents learn using a PLM (perceived law of motion) that is well specified, i.e., nests an REE of interest. However, economic agents, like econometricians, may fail to correctly specify the actual law of motion, even asymptotically. It may still be possible to analyze the resulting learning dynamics.

As an illustration, consider the Muth model with the reduced form

$$p_t = \mu + \alpha E^*_{t-1} p_t + \delta' w_{t-1} + \eta_t,$$

where we use the alternative notation $E^*_{t-1} p_t$ for p_t^e. For simplicity we assume that w_{t-1} is an iid vector of exogenous variables and η_t is an unobservable white noise shock. In the treatment in Chapter 2, agents were assumed to have a

PLM of the form $p_t = a + b'w_{t-1} + \eta_t$, corresponding to the REE. Suppose that instead their PLM is $p_t = a + \eta_t$, so that agents do not recognize the dependence of price on w_{t-1}, and that they estimate a by least squares. Then

$$a_t = a_{t-1} + t^{-1}(p_t - a_{t-1}),$$

and the PLM at time $t - 1$ is $p_t = a_{t-1} + \eta_t$ with corresponding forecasts $E^*_{t-1}p_t = a_{t-1}$. Thus the ALM is

$$p_t = \mu + \alpha a_{t-1} + \delta' w_{t-1} + \eta_t$$

and the corresponding stochastic recursive algorithm is

$$a_t = a_{t-1} + t^{-1}(\mu + (\alpha - 1)a_{t-1} + \delta' w_{t-1} + \eta_t).$$

The associated ODE is $da/d\tau = \mu + (\alpha - 1)a$, and it follows that $a_t \to \bar{a} = (1 - \alpha)^{-1}\mu$ almost surely.[12]

In this case we have convergence, but it is not to the unique REE which is $p_t = (1 - \alpha)^{-1}\mu + (1 - \alpha)^{-1}\delta' w_{t-1} + \eta_t$. Agents make systematic forecast errors since their forecast errors are correlated with w_{t-1} and they would do better to condition their forecasts on this variable. However, we have ruled this out by assumption: we have restricted PLMs to those which do not depend on w_{t-1}. Within the restricted class of PLMs we consider, agents in fact converge to one which is rational given this restriction. The resulting solution when the forecasts are $E^*_{t-1}p_t = \bar{a}$ is

$$p_t = (1 - \alpha)^{-1}\mu + \delta' w_{t-1} + \eta_t.$$

We might describe this as a *restricted perceptions equilibrium* since it is generated by expectations which are optimal within a limited class of PLMs.[13] The basic idea of a restricted perceptions equilibrium is that we permit agents to fall short of rationality specifically in failing to recognize certain patterns or correlations in the data.

It is apparent that there are many forms of misspecification that may be of interest. For example, the agents may include only a subset of w_{t-1} in their forecast rule. Similarly, the model might be nonlinear, while agents forecast using a linear model. We will explore some of these possibilities and others in Part V.

---

[12] The ODE $da/d\tau$ can also be interpreted as the E-stability equation for the underparameterized class of PLMs here considered.

[13] The term *self-confirming equilibrium* is also used in the literature, see Sargent (1999).

Chapter 4

Applications

4.1 Introduction

In this last introductory chapter we consider adaptive learning in several well-known macroeconomic models, including some standard models which appear in graduate-level textbooks. Stability under learning is of interest even in models with a unique equilibrium, such as the Ramsey growth model and the Real Business Cycle model. Here expectations play a central role in the structure of the model, but they have no independent influence on the paths of the economy. That is, given the current state of the economy, there is a single way to forecast the future under RE: expectations are fully determinate. Still, rational expectations remains a strong assumption, and showing that the rational expectations equilibrium is stable under learning lends support to this solution concept in these models.

Recently, macroeconomists have increasingly developed models with multiple rational expectations equilibria (REEs). Coordination failures, bubbles, sunspots, endogenous fluctuations, and indeterminacy of equilibria are all phrases which reflect this phenomenon in various ways. In this context it is natural to look at the issue of how a particular REE might be arrived at and whether all solutions should be taken equally seriously. In these situations the study of adaptive learning acts as a selection criterion, i.e., it reduces the number of attainable REEs. In some cases it may even single out a unique equilibrium as the stable outcome of a learning process. In some other important cases there are multiple learnable equilibria. Models with multiple equilibria have been used in particular for explaining business cycles as endogenous macroeconomic fluctuations. In these models expectations play an independent role in addition to fundamentals such as preference and technology shocks.

59

As discussed in the first chapter, our basic approach in this book is to model economic agents as econometricians who estimate the stochastic process of relevant variables and use these estimates to make forecasts. We adopt this approach because it treats the agents as having a degree of rationality comparable to that of the economic analyst: when making forecasts, economists use econometrics and statistical inference. In this chapter we sometimes use simplified versions of the forecast rules in order to avoid technical complications which we will later treat carefully.

4.2   The Overlapping Generations Model

Various overlapping generations models have been popular frameworks for macroeconomic analysis. The basic overlapping generations model, the so-called Samuelson model, provides a simple dynamic model in which expectations play a crucial role and it provides a convenient example to illustrate some basic ideas of adaptive learning in a nonlinear context. We here develop a simple version of the model which we will later extend in various ways. In this version there is production of a single perishable good, using labor alone, under constant returns to scale.

The economy consists of overlapping generations of identical agents each of whom lives for two periods. Population is constant, as the old agents who die at the end of the second period of life are replaced by an equal number of young agents at the start of the next period. Agents work when they are young and consume when old. The utility function of an agent in generation t takes the form $U(c_{t+1}) - V(n_t)$, where c_{t+1} is consumption at old age and n_t is labor supply. We assume that $U(\cdot)$ is concave and $V(\cdot)$ is convex. Moreover, both $U(\cdot)$ and $V(\cdot)$ are taken to be twice continuously differentiable.

Trade is intertemporal, since in each period t, the output produced by the young is sold to the old in a competitive market. In the basic model there is a constant stock of money M which is the only means of saving the revenue obtained from working. There are no capital goods. In the simplest model the production function depends only on labor input and is linear, so that $c_t = n_t$ after a normalization by choice of units of measurement. With this production function, the wage earned is equal to the price of the consumption good in the same period.

The budget constraints faced by generation t are

$$p_t n_t = m_t,$$
$$p_{t+1} c_{t+1} = m_t.$$

Here m_t denotes the nominal saving by the representative agent, and p_t denotes the prevailing price in period t. At time t when the agent is deciding on its choice of n_t, the current price p_t is known, but next period's price p_{t+1} is unknown. The agent's optimization problem is thus

$$\max E_t^* U(c_{t+1}) - V(n_t) \quad \text{subject to } p_{t+1}c_{t+1} = p_t n_t,$$

where E_t^* denotes the (subjective) expectations of the agent at time t. Substituting in the constraint for c_{t+1}, differentiating with respect to n_t, and interchanging the order of expectations and derivatives, leads to the first-order condition for interior points

$$E_t^* \left(\frac{p_t}{p_{t+1}} U' \left(\frac{p_t n_t}{p_{t+1}} \right) \right) = V'(n_t).$$

Since this model can have equilibria in which money becomes worthless, it is convenient to reformulate the analysis in terms of the price of money $q_t = 1/p_t$, so that we have

$$E_t^* \left(\frac{q_{t+1}}{q_t} U' \left(\frac{q_{t+1} n_t}{q_t} \right) \right) = V'(n_t).$$

The market-clearing condition is $M = m_t$ or equivalently $q_t M = n_t$ at each period t.

For simplicity we postulate parametric forms for the utility functions

$$U(c) = \frac{c^{1-\sigma}}{1-\sigma}, \qquad V(n) = \frac{n^{1+\varepsilon}}{1+\varepsilon},$$

where $\sigma, \varepsilon > 0$. We also assume point expectations of the price level, i.e., that agents treat as certain their expectations of the price of money $E_t^* q_{t+1}$, which for convenience we will denote q_{t+1}^e. The assumption of point expectations allows us to bring the expectation operator E_t^* inside the (possibly) nonlinear function, so that the first-order condition can be written as

$$n_t = q_t^{(\sigma-1)/(\sigma+\varepsilon)} \left(q_{t+1}^e \right)^{(1-\sigma)/(\sigma+\varepsilon)}.$$

Combining this with market clearing yields

$$q_t = M^{-(\sigma+\varepsilon)/(1+\varepsilon)} \left(q_{t+1}^e \right)^{(1-\sigma)/(1+\varepsilon)} \equiv \mathcal{F}\left(q_{t+1}^e \right). \tag{4.1}$$

This relationship is graphed in Figure 4.1 for the case of $\sigma < 1$. With perfect foresight, $q_{t+1}^e = q_{t+1}$, and it can be seen that there are two steady states. There

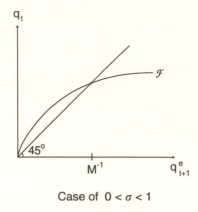

Case of $0 < \sigma < 1$

Figure 4.1.

is an interior steady state at $q_t = M^{-1}$ and an "autarkic" steady state at $q_t = 0$. It can also be seen that there exists a continuum of perfect-foresight paths converging toward the autarky solution, indexed by the initial value of q_t which can be chosen arbitrarily provided $0 < q_0 < M^{-1}$.[1]

We now posit the forecast rule for q_{t+1}^e. Suppose people form expectations adaptively from past data in the following way:

$$q_{t+1}^e = q_t^e + \gamma_t(q_{t-1} - q_t^e), \tag{4.2}$$

where $0 < \gamma_t < 1$ is the gain sequence. Two main cases of interest are $\gamma_t = t^{-1}$ and $\gamma_t = \gamma$, a constant.

The first case corresponds to agents taking the average of prices q_i, $i = 0, \ldots, t-1$, i.e.,

$$q_{t+1}^e = t^{-1} \sum_{i=0}^{t-1} q_i,$$

as can be verified by substitution into equation (4.2) with $\gamma_t = t^{-1}$. Thus this forecast method corresponds to a learning rule in which agents estimate an unknown constant by updating the sample mean. Note that in this kind of learning rule, each new data point has a smaller weight with $\lim_{t \to \infty} \gamma_t = 0$. Such gain

---

[1] Note that for $q_0 > M^{-1}$, there appear to be dynamic perfect-foresight paths with $q_t \to \infty$. However, if an upper bound on labor supply is imposed, these paths are not feasible.

sequences are known as "decreasing gain." The second case $\gamma_t = \gamma$ is a version of the traditional adaptive expectations assumption, but can also be viewed as a constant-gain learning rule.

Substituting equation (4.1) into equation (4.2) yields the difference equation

$$q_{t+1}^e = q_t^e + \gamma_t \left(\mathcal{F}(q_t^e) - q_t^e \right),$$

and q_0^e is treated as an arbitrary initial expectation. This fits the framework of Section 3.4 of Chapter 3. Since $\mathcal{F}'(M^{-1}) < 1$, it follows that the steady state $q_t = M^{-1}$ is stable under learning for decreasing gain or small constant gain.[2] If $\sigma < 1$, the autarky solution $q_t = 0$ also exists, but, since $\mathcal{F}'(0) > 1$, it is not stable under learning. Thus we have shown that learning dynamics will converge always to the monetary steady state, not to autarky. [This point was first noted by Lucas (1986).] In the case $\sigma > 1$, only the monetary steady state exists, and the above argument shows its stability under learning.

We remark that the model with learning could instead be formulated in terms of employment n_t. Using $n_t = Mq_t$ and $n_{t+1}^e = Mq_{t+1}^e$, equation (4.1) is equivalent to $n_t = (n_{t+1}^e)^{(1-\sigma)/(1+\varepsilon)}$. This formulation, which we will often use below, leads to the same stability result. Overlapping generations models are further discussed in Chapters 11 and 12. In Section 4.6 of this chapter we develop and study a version of this model that has multiple interior steady states.

4.3 A Linear Stochastic Macroeconomic Model

Many macroeconomic models are linear or log-linear and allow for random shocks to the structural equations. The analysis of learning in such models can be studied using the stochastic approximation techniques introduced in Chapter 2. As an example, we consider the well-known Sargent and Wallace (1975) "ad hoc" model. This consists of three equations. The aggregate supply curve is of standard form and postulates that output depends positively on unexpected inflation (or price surprises)

$$q_t = a_I + a_p \left(p_t - E_{t-1}^* p_t \right) + u_{1t}, \quad \text{where } a_p > 0,$$

and where q_t denotes the logarithm of output and p_t is the logarithm of the price level. The "IS curve" postulates that aggregate demand depends negatively on

---

[2]For $0 < \mathcal{F}'(M^{-1}) < 1$, stability holds for all $0 < \gamma \leq 1$.

the ex ante real interest rate

$$q_t = b_I + b_r\left(r_t - (E^*_{t-1}p_{t+1} - E^*_{t-1}p_t)\right) + u_{2t}, \quad \text{where } b_r < 0,$$

and where r_t denotes the nominal interest rate. Finally, the "LM curve" describes the money market equilibrium, in which the demand for real balances is assumed to depend positively on output and negatively on the nominal interest rate

$$m = c_I + p_t + c_q q_t + c_r r_t + u_{3t}, \quad \text{where } c_q > 0, \ c_r < 0.$$

Here m is the logarithm of the money supply, assumed constant. u_{1t}, u_{2t}, u_{3t} are white noise shocks to output supply, output demand, and money demand, respectively.

The model can be solved to yield the reduced form of the price level

$$p_t = \alpha + \beta_0 E^*_{t-1} p_t + \beta_1 E^*_{t-1} p_{t+1} + v_t, \tag{4.3}$$

where v_t is a linear combination of the shocks and therefore satisfies

$$E_{t-1} v_t = 0.$$

The reduced form parameters are functions of the structural parameters and the key ones are given by

$$\beta_0 = \left(a_p(1 + b_r c_q c_r^{-1}) + b_r\right)\big/\left(a_p(1 + b_r c_q c_r^{-1}) + b_r c_r^{-1}\right)$$

and

$$\beta_1 = (1 - \beta_0)\big/\left(1 - c_r^{-1}\right).$$

These satisfy the restrictions $\beta_1 > 0$ and $\beta_0 + \beta_1 < 1$. Equation (4.3) has the stochastic steady-state solution

$$p_t = \frac{\alpha}{1 - \beta_0 - \beta_1} + v_t. \tag{4.4}$$

There are other solutions to the model, but these are stochastically explosive and equation (4.4) is the solution usually chosen in applied work.

To model the learning we suppose that agents perceive the economy to be in a stochastic steady state, i.e., that prices follow the process $p_t = a + v_t$, but that the mean a is unknown. In this case the natural statistical estimate of a is the sample mean,

$$a_t = t^{-1} \sum_{i=0}^{t-1} p_{t-i}.$$

Agents form the expectations accordingly, i.e., $E_{t-1}^* p_t = E_{t-1}^* p_{t+1} = a_{t-1}$. Inserting these into the reduced form, we obtain

$$p_t = \alpha + (\beta_0 + \beta_1)a_{t-1} + v_t. \tag{4.5}$$

This is the law of motion for prices under the learning rule. Notice that if a_t converges to $\alpha/(1 - \beta_0 - \beta_1)$, then the price process converges to the stochastic steady state (4.4). We want to study whether this will in fact happen.

As was seen in the preceding example, the sample mean can be written in recursive form $a_t = a_{t-1} + t^{-1}(p_t - a_{t-1})$. Inserting equation (4.5) into the recursive form, we obtain the dynamic equation

$$a_t = a_{t-1} + t^{-1}\left(\alpha + (\beta_0 + \beta_1)a_{t-1} - a_{t-1} + v_t\right). \tag{4.6}$$

This is a stochastic recursive algorithm that can be analyzed using stochastic approximation techniques. The basic technique was introduced in Chapter 2. The formal tools presented in Chapter 6 are applied to models of this type in Chapter 8.

We here outline the result that for this model, learning converges globally to the solution (4.4).[3] Applying the stochastic approximation technique, we obtain the associated ODE

$$\frac{da}{d\tau} = T(a) - a,$$

where $T(a) = \alpha + (\beta_0 + \beta_1 - 1)a$. It follows that $a_t \to \alpha/(1 - \beta_0 - \beta_1)$, i.e., we have convergence to the stationary REE, provided $\beta_0 + \beta_1 < 1$, a condition which is satisfied by the model. Indeed, the global convergence theorem of Chapter 6 applies and there is convergence to this REE with probability 1.

To illustrate these results, we provide an example simulation of equations (4.5)–(4.6). We set $a_2 = 1$, $b_2 = -0.4$, $c_1 = 1$, and $c_2 = -.5$. This leads

---

[3]The same techniques can be used to study whether the explosive solutions mentioned earlier can be attained as a result of a learning process. See Chapters 8 and 9.

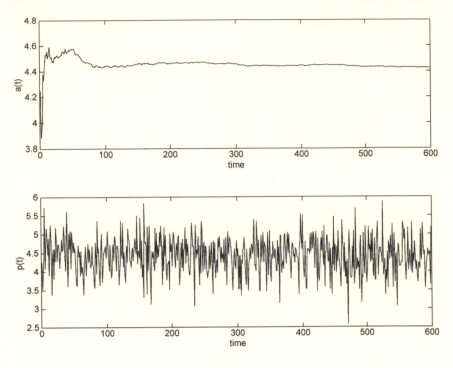

Figure 4.2.

to $\beta_0 = 0.6667$ and $\beta_1 = 0.1111$, and we also set $\alpha = 1$. v_t was assumed iid normal with standard deviation of 0.5. The initial value of a_t was set at $a_0 = 4$. The top panel of Figure 4.2 illustrates convergence of the parameter estimate a_t to its RE value. The bottom panel shows the corresponding path for the market price p_t. Of course, because of the intrinsic random shocks v_t, the price path p_t remains random in the limit, i.e., even after a_t has converged to $\alpha/(1 - \beta_0 - \beta_1)$.

Numerous extensions to this analysis are of interest. First, the assumption of iid unobserved shocks is unnecessary. One could, for example, allow for observable shocks to any or all of the structural equations and the shocks could be allowed to follow specified exogenous processes. Agents would then use recursive least squares, as in Chapter 2, to estimate the dependence of p_t on available information, and they would use their estimates to make appropriate forecasts. These issues are taken up in Chapter 8, where we show that there is convergence to the REE under slightly strengthened stability conditions.

As another extension, suppose that the previous assumption of a constant money supply m is replaced by a policy feedback rule in which money supply depends on the lagged price level

$$m_t = d_I + d_p p_{t-1} + u_{4t}.$$

The reduced form now becomes

$$p_t = \alpha + \delta p_{t-1} + \beta_0 E_{t-1}^* p_t + \beta_1 E_{t-1}^* p_{t+1} + v_t. \qquad (4.7)$$

There are now two rational expectations solutions of the form

$$p_t = a + b p_{t-1} + v_t,$$

where b is a solution to the quadratic equation $\beta_1 b^2 + (\beta_0 - 1)b + \delta = 0$.[4] Provided $|d_p|$ is not too large, only one of the solutions will satisfy the stationarity condition $|b| < 1$.

Is this solution stable under learning? Again, it is now natural to assume that agents will recognize the dependence of price on lagged price in their "perceived law of motion." In particular, suppose that agents have a perceived law of motion (PLM) of the same form as this REE, but do not know the RE values of a and b. Modeling the agents as econometricians, we can assume that they estimate the unknown parameters by least squares, regressing prices on lagged prices and an intercept, using the data that has been generated by the economy up to that point in time. Thus supposing that at time $t - 1$ their estimates are a_{t-1}, b_{t-1}, they will make their forecasts of $E_{t-1}^* p_t$ and $E_{t-1}^* p_{t+1}$ accordingly. Will their parameter estimates converge over time to the RE values? The results on the convergence of SRAs introduced in Chapter 2 can again be applied, even though the regressors are no longer exogenous, and the results are discussed in Chapters 8 and 9.

Finally, the inclusion of future expectations $E_{t-1}^* p_{t+1}$ in equation (4.3) leads to a crucial difference from the cobweb model of Chapter 2, namely that formally there are now multiple RE solutions. Although it can be shown that in the Sargent–Wallace "ad hoc" model of this section there is a unique stationary solution, there are other examples of the form (4.3) which have multiple stationary RE solutions. In such cases we will therefore want to examine systematically the stability under learning of the various solutions. This issue will be studied at length in Chapters 8 and 9.

---

[4]This is easily verified by computing $E_{t-1} p_t = a + b p_{t-1}$ and $E_{t-1} p_{t+1} = a(1+b) + b^2 p_{t-1}$ and substituting into equation (4.7) and equating coefficients. We are assuming real solutions to the quadratic.

4.4 The Ramsey Model

The Ramsey growth model is widely used in macroeconomics. For simplicity we give a version which ignores population growth, technological progress, and depreciation.

An infinitely lived representative consumer maximizes intertemporal expected utility

$$E_t \sum_{i=0}^{\infty} \beta^{t+i} u(C_{t+i})$$

subject to the budget constraints

$$C_{t+i} + K_{t+1+i} = w_{t+i} + (1 + r_{t+i}) K_{t+i}$$

for $i = 0, \ldots, \infty$. Here C_{t+i}, K_{t+i}, w_{t+i}, and r_{t+i} denote consumption, capital, real wages, and interest rate in period $t + i$, respectively. $0 < \beta < 1$ is the subjective discount factor. Labor supply is normalized at unity. We assume the household maximizes expected utility (rather than realized utility) because our households will not usually be assumed to have perfect foresight (also in later models random shocks will often be present).

The firm maximizes its profit

$$F(K_{t+i}, N_{t+i}) - r_{t+i} K_{t+i} - w_{t+i} N_{t+i}$$

in each period. Here $F(\cdot, \cdot)$ is the production function with constant returns to scale and N_{t+i} denotes the labor input. Assuming perfect competition and market clearing, the first-order conditions for the firm yield the usual conditions that factors are paid their marginal products. These relations can be written

$$
\begin{aligned}
r_{t+i} &= f'(K_{t+i}), \\
w_{t+i} &= f(K_{t+i}) - K_{t+i} f'(K_{t+i}),
\end{aligned}
$$

where $f(K/N) \equiv F(K/N, 1)$ and we have used the labor market clearing condition $N_{t+i} = 1$.[5]

---

[5] $F(K, N) = N f(K/N)$ because of constant returns to scale. Differentiating with respect to K yields $\partial F / \partial K = f'(K/N)$ and differentiating with respect to N yields $\partial F / \partial N = f(K/N) - (K/N) f'(K/N)$. Note that constant returns to scale also implies that $f(K/N)$ is equal to output per worker.

To maximize utility we substitute the household budget constraints into the objective function. By differentiation with respect to K_t, one obtains

$$u'(C_t) = \beta E_t[(1 + f'(K_{t+1}))u'(C_{t+1})],$$
$$C_t = K_t + f(K_t) - K_{t+1},$$

as the dynamical system. In the standard textbook analysis perfect foresight is assumed and we obtain a pair of nonlinear difference equations in K_t, C_t. For example, under the parametric assumptions $F(K, N) = K^\alpha N^{1-\alpha}$ and $U(C) = C^{1-\sigma}/(1 - \sigma)$, we obtain

$$C_{t+1} = C_t \left[\beta \left(1 + \alpha (K_t + K_t^\alpha - C_t)^{\alpha-1} \right) \right]^{1/\sigma},$$
$$K_{t+1} = K_t + K_t^\alpha - C_t.$$

To illustrate the system we write it in the form

$$C_{t+1} - C_t = C_t \left[\beta \left(1 + \alpha (K_t + K_t^\alpha - C_t)^{\alpha-1} \right) \right]^{1/\sigma} - C_t, \qquad (4.8)$$
$$K_{t+1} - K_t = K_t^\alpha - C_t,$$

which is shown in Figure 4.3 and exhibits the familiar saddle point feature. It is easily verified that there is a unique steady state $(\bar{K}, \bar{C})$. The saddle point properties of the steady state can be verified formally by computing the Jacobian of equation (4.8) at $(\bar{K}, \bar{C})$ and noting that the eigenvalues λ_1 and λ_2 satisfy $0 < \lambda_1 < 1 < \lambda_2$. See, e.g., Azariadis (1993, pp. 72–75).

As seen in Figure 4.3, given K_0, there is a unique choice of C_0 such that the path (K_t, C_t) converges to $(\bar{K}, \bar{C})$. Other paths explode, as illustrated in the figure. These paths can be ruled out as perfect-foresight equilibria because they eventually violate nonnegativity or transversality conditions.

But suppose we drop the perfect-foresight assumption? The saddle path might then appear delicate, since agents would then be making forecasting errors. Formally, if agents form one-step-ahead expectations at each time t, we have the system

$$u'(C_t) = \beta E_t^*[(1 + f'(K_{t+1}))u'(C_{t+1})], \qquad (4.9)$$
$$C_t = K_t + f(K_t) - K_{t+1},$$

where $E_t^*(\cdot)$ denotes the (in general nonrational) expectations of the households. This system defines a temporary equilibrium in which C_t and K_{t+1} are determined, given these expectations and K_t. A reasonable learning rule will, of

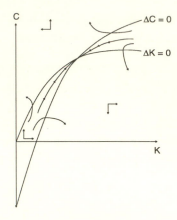

Figure 4.3.

course, respond to forecast errors and attempt to eliminate them, but it is not obvious whether such behavior will eventually lead the economy to the perfect-foresight path or whether even small errors will drive the economy onto some unstable trajectory.

To analyze this question we will endow the agents with a forecast rule which determines $E_t^*(\cdot)$ as a function of the observables. The forecast rule depends on parameters which will be updated each period on the basis of new observations. Such a system defines the economic dynamics under learning.

Perhaps surprisingly, it can be shown that the perfect-foresight saddle path for this economy is indeed locally learnable, i.e., is attained under a natural specification of the learning dynamics. We put off the demonstration of this result because of the relative complexity of this model, giving the formal details for the Ramsey model in the appendix at the end of this chapter. In Chapter 10 we show how to extend these results to the standard Real Business Cycle model, which is a well-known and widely used generalization of the Ramsey model incorporating variable labor supply and random productivity shocks.

More generally, realistic contemporary applied macroeconomic models are usually formulated as multivariate models in which the variables depend on their lags, on expectations of future variables, and on exogenous stochastic processes. In a neighborhood of a steady state these can be approximated by linear multivariate models, the solutions to which can be written as vector autoregressions. In Chapter 10 we show how to extend the techniques for studying least squares learning to multivariate frameworks and we apply the tools developed there to several models, including models with sunspot solutions as well as "regular" models like the Real Business Cycle model.

4.5 The Diamond Growth Model

This model introduces physical capital goods into the overlapping generations structure. For an exposition of this model, known as the "Diamond model," see, for example, Blanchard and Fischer (1989) or Romer (1995). To simplify the model we assume that the labor supply is held fixed and there is no monetary asset so that all saving is in the form of capital. Households supply (one unit of) labor when young and consume in both periods of their two-period lifetime. We also simplify by assuming that there is neither technical progress nor population growth.

Households born in period t maximize the utility function

$$U_t = \frac{C_{1t}^{1-\theta}}{1-\theta} + \beta \frac{C_{2,t+1}^{1-\theta}}{1-\theta}$$

subject to the budget constraint

$$C_{2,t+1} = (1 + r_{t+1})(w_t - C_{1t}),$$

where r_{t+1} is the interest rate in period $t+1$ and w_t is the real wage. Assuming perfect foresight, one can show that saving depends on the interest rate and is proportional to w_t. Let $s(r_{t+1})$ denote saving as a fraction of income w_t (recall that there is a labor supply of 1). Note that $s(r)$ is increasing or decreasing in r as θ is less than or greater than 1.

Since the old consume all of their income, the capital stock in period $t+1$ is given by $K_{t+1} = s(r_{t+1})w_t$. Output is produced from capital and labor in the same way as in the Ramsey model, i.e., $Y_t = F(K_t, 1) \equiv f(K_t)$. Under perfect competition, factors are paid their marginal products, so that $r_t = f'(K_t)$ and $w_t = f(K_t) - K_t f'(K_t)$. We thus arrive at the key dynamic equation

$$K_{t+1} = s(f'(K_{t+1}))\big[f(K_t) - K_t f'(K_t)\big].$$

The system starts at time $t = 0$ with an initial capital stock K_0 owned by an initial old generation.

Under perfect foresight, there are various possible cases depending on the utility and production functions. For example, if the utility is logarithmic and the production function is Cobb–Douglas, there is a unique interior steady state to which the system converges from any initial capital stock $K_0 > 0$. However, as is well known, for some choices of the utility and production functions, multiple interior steady states can exist, as illustrated in Figure 4.4. In fact, this figure shows a case where multiple K_{t+1} can exist for a certain range of K_t. Under

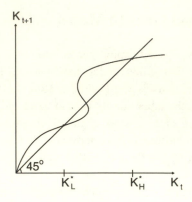

Figure 4.4.

perfect foresight, there would be no way to select between two alternative paths for an initial K_0 in that range.

   In contrast, consider the situation under learning. If households have an expected interest rate r_{t+1}^e and save according to $s(r_{t+1}^e)$, then the law of motion is instead

$$K_{t+1} = s(r_{t+1}^e)\big[f(K_t) - K_t f'(K_t)\big]. \qquad (4.10)$$

To complete the model under learning we postulate a simple adaptive learning rule

$$r_{t+1}^e = r_t^e + \gamma_t(r_t - r_t^e). \qquad (4.11)$$

Substituting $r_t = f'(K_t)$, this leads to a two-dimensional dynamical system which will be analyzed in the appendix to this chapter. We state the result here: K_L^* and K_H^* are both stable under learning, though stability is only local and the eventual rest point will depend on the initial K_0 and initial expectations r_1^e. The middle steady state is not stable.

4.6   A Model with Increasing Social Returns

A model with multiple steady states that are stable under adaptive learning can be developed using a simple extension of the OG production model introduced in Section 4.2. We develop this model at some length since it can also be used to illustrate the possibility of sunspot equilibria and the role of policy in models with multiple equilibria. This model will also be used to illustrate extensions and further phenomena in Parts IV and V.

4.6.1 The Basic Framework

We return to the overlapping generations model discussed in Section 4.2. However, we replace the simple production function $Q_t = n_t$ by the function

$$Q_t = f(n_t, N_t),$$

where N_t denotes aggregate labor effort and represents a positive production externality. We assume $f_1 > 0$, $f_2 > 0$, and $f_{11} < 0$. Here $N_t = \ell n_t$, where ℓ is the total number of agents in the economy. ℓ is assumed large enough so that each agent has a negligible effect on N_t.

A specific formulation of $f(n_t, N_t)$, given in Evans and Honkapohja (1995b) is as follows. The output Q_t of an individual agent is assumed to depend on the individual's labor input, which is partly mental, and on available complementary "ideas" for designs. There is a base level of standard design ideas I^* that always exist, but if aggregate output is sufficiently high, then the number of complementary ideas I_t, assumed generated in proportion to total labor effort and publicly available, exceeds I^*. If the dependence takes a Cobb–Douglas form, we have $Q_t = A n_t^\alpha I_t^\beta$ if $I_t \geq I^*$ and $Q_t = A n_t^\alpha I^{*\beta}$ otherwise, with $0 < \alpha < 1$.

Suppose that agents have a unit endowment of time available to scan and absorb ideas, that the number of suitable ideas generated is λN_t, and that it takes a units of time to receive and absorb a suitable idea. Then $I_t = 1/(a + (\lambda N_t)^{-1})$ and we have

$$f(n, N) = A n^\alpha \left\{ \max\left(I^*, \lambda N/(1 + a\lambda N) \right) \right\}^\beta.$$

Convenient features of this technology are that the externality is not present at low levels of N and that it is bounded as $N \to \infty$.

Returning to the general formulation $f(n_t, N_t)$, we can obtain the equilibrium equation as in the basic OG model. Agents are again assumed to maximize expected utility and the budget constraint is now that $p_t Q_t = p_{t+1} c_{t+1}$. Since each agent treats aggregate N_t as given, the first-order condition becomes

$$V'(n_t) = E_t^* \frac{p_t}{p_{t+1}} f_1(n_t, \ell n_t) U'(c_{t+1}).$$

In the basic overlapping generations model we analyzed expectations and learning in terms of the price of money. It is more convenient here to choose average employment n_t as the variable to be forecast. (Since n_t is in 1–1 correspondence with the price level, this is an innocuous assumption.) We therefore reformulate the model entirely in terms of n_t.

With a constant money supply M, we have $p_t Q_t = M$ and $p_t/p_{t+1} = Q_{t+1}/Q_t$. Using also $c_{t+1} = Q_{t+1}$, we have

$$V'(n_t) f(n_t, \ell n_t)/f_1(n_t, \ell n_t) = E_t^* f(n_{t+1}, \ell n_{t+1}) U'\big(f(n_{t+1}, \ell n_{t+1})\big),$$

or

$$\mathcal{W}(n_t) = E_t^* G(n_{t+1}). \tag{4.12}$$

It can be verified that $\mathcal{W}(n_t)$ is a strictly increasing function of n_t. Solving for n_t and assuming point expectations yields $n_t = \mathcal{F}(n_{t+1}^e)$ for a suitable $\mathcal{F}$. For our examples we will assume utility functions of the form

$$U(c) = c^{1-\sigma}/(1-\sigma), \qquad V(n) = n^{1+\varepsilon}/(1+\varepsilon).$$

For appropriate σ and ε and parameter values for the production function above, one can obtain reduced form functions $\mathcal{F}$ which yield three interior steady states, as in the graph labeled $\mathcal{F}$ in Figure 4.5. Examples are given in Evans and Honkapohja (1995b) and below.

Employment levels $n_L < n_U < n_H$ correspond to low, medium, and high output levels. The steady states n_L and n_U can be interpreted as coordination failures since the steady states can be Pareto ranked and welfare is higher in n_H than in either n_L or n_U. [For a proof see Evans and Honkapohja (1995b, Proposition 3).]

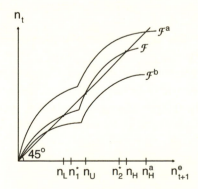

Figure 4.5.

Learning of a steady state is formally identical to that in Section 4.2, equations (4.1) and (4.2) with q_t replaced by n_t. The argument given in Section 3.4 of Chapter 3 can again be applied here to show that a steady state $n^* = \mathcal{F}(n^*)$ is locally stable under learning if $\mathcal{F}'(n^*) < 1$. It follows that n_L and n_H are locally stable, while n_U is unstable. In this model it is therefore possible for the economy to become stuck in a low-activity, low-welfare steady state.

4.6.2   Adaptive Learning and Economic Policy

The possibility of the economy becoming trapped in a low-level steady state raises the issue of whether economic policy can be effective in dislodging it from such inefficient equilibria. In the context of a positive production externality, it is natural to consider the effects of a proportional subsidy ρ to the price of output financed by a lump-sum tax $T = \rho p_t f(n_t, \ell n_{t+1})$. Here p_t is now the producer price, so that the price paid by the consumer is $(1 - \rho)p_t$. If $\rho < 0$, this is interpreted as an ad valorem tax which is redistributed as lump-sum transfer payments. Allowing for this subsidy changes the equilibrium equation to

$$(1 - \rho)V'(n_t)f(n_t, \ell n_t)/f_1(n_t, \ell n_t)$$
$$= E_t^* f(n_{t+1}, \ell n_{t+1})U'(f(n_{t+1}, \ell n_{t+1})). \tag{4.13}$$

For our earlier specification of production functions and utility functions, and assuming point expectations, this can be written

$$n_t = \mathcal{F}(n_{t+1}^e, \rho),$$

where

$$\mathcal{F}(n, \rho) = (\alpha/(1 - \rho))^{1/(1+\varepsilon)}$$
$$\times \left(An^\alpha \{ \max(I^*, \lambda \ell n/(1 + a\lambda \ell n)) \}^\beta \right)^{(1-\sigma)/(1+\varepsilon)}.$$

For the case $0 < \sigma < 1$, in which $\mathcal{F}(n, \rho)$ is an increasing function of n, an increase in ρ rotates $\mathcal{F}(n_{t+1}^e, \rho)$ counterclockwise. For sufficiently large values of ρ, the graph will be like $\mathcal{F}^a$ in Figure 4.5, with a single (high-activity) interior steady state. For sufficiently low (possibly negative) values of ρ, the graph will be like $\mathcal{F}^b$, with a single (low-activity) interior steady state. A range of intermediate values of ρ will give three interior steady states, as with the graph $\mathcal{F}$.

Changing the value of ρ can have dramatic effects under adaptive learning. Consider slow, gradual changes in ρ such that the learning dynamics are fast relative to changes in ρ. Starting from n_L in Figure 4.5, as ρ is increased the

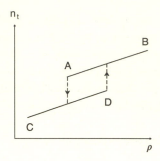

Figure 4.6.

level of economic activity approximately shifts slowly up along the 45-degree line, tracking the increasing value of n_L. However, at a sufficiently high value of ρ, the low steady state disappears and adaptive learning drives economic activity to n_H^a. Thus, in addition to the usual effects, changes in policy can in certain circumstances lead to large discrete changes by shifting the economy between distinct equilibria.

Furthermore, changes in the subsidy rate ρ exhibit irreversibilities over certain ranges. Starting from the high level of ρ associated with the graph $\mathcal{F}^a$ and steady state n_H^a, if the level of ρ is slowly reduced to the original level associated with graph $\mathcal{F}$, the level of economic activity will continue to track the high-activity equilibrium n_H.

The approximate relationship between ρ and n is as shown in Figure 4.6. There are two branches to the relationship, a high-activity branch AB and a low-activity branch CD. Over intermediate ranges of ρ, the level of n depends via the learning dynamics on the history of the variables. Values of ρ outside this intermediate range can be used to shift the two equilibrium branches.

4.6.3   Sunspot Equilibria

The model of increasing returns can be used to illustrate the phenomenon of "sunspot equilibria" which have been much used recently in macroeconomics to model endogenous fluctuations.[6] These rational expectations solutions can be viewed as a modern formulation of a long tradition in economics which emphasizes the possibility of endogenous fluctuations in market economies. The

---

[6]The initial investigations were done in Shell (1977), Azariadis (1981), Azariadis and Guesnerie (1982), and Cass and Shell (1983). See Chiappori and Guesnerie (1991) and Guesnerie and Woodford (1992) for recent surveys.

central idea is that in some models it is possible for the expectations of firms or households to depend on an extraneous random variable in a way which is entirely rational. Shifts in the variable (often called a "sunspot") would then trigger self-fulfilling shifts in expectations, prices, and quantities, creating or amplifying economic fluctuations.[7] We introduce such equilibria in the context of the current model and then take up then issue of whether such equilibria can emerge under adaptive learning.

Assuming rational expectations, equation (4.12) or (4.13) can be written as

$$n_t = \mathcal{W}^{-1}\big(E_t G(n_{t+1})\big), \tag{4.14}$$

where $\mathcal{W}(n_t)$ denotes the left-hand-side function and $G(n_{t+1})$ denotes the right-hand-side function following E_t^*. In the case (4.13) in which the production subsidy is present, ρ is implicit in $\mathcal{W}$. Earlier, when studying steady-state learning, we were able to use the notation $\mathcal{F} = \mathcal{W}^{-1} \circ G$, but we must now drop the assumption of point expectations since in a sunspot equilibrium the economy will be undergoing random shifts.

The definition of a sunspot equilibrium involves the idea that economic agents condition their expectations on some (random) variable s_t which otherwise does not have any influence on the economy. Though different types of sunspot solutions have been considered in the literature, we will focus here on REE that take the form of a finite Markov chain.

We simplify even further by assuming that the extraneous random variable $s_t \in \{1, 2\}$ is a two-state Markov chain with a constant transition matrix $\Pi = (\pi_{ij})$, $0 < \pi_{ij} < 1$, $i, j = 1, 2$. Here π_{ij} denotes the probability that $s_{t+1} = j$ given that $s_t = i$. A two-state Markov chain is specified by probabilities π_{11} and π_{22} since $\pi_{12} = 1 - \pi_{11}$ and $\pi_{21} = 1 - \pi_{22}$. A (two-state) *stationary sunspot equilibrium* (SSE) (n_1^*, n_2^*) is a solution $n_t = n_1^*$ if $s_t = 1$ and $n_t = n_2^*$ if $s_t = 2$ which satisfies equation (4.14).

To show existence of SSEs it is convenient to transform the system, using the monotonic function $y = \mathcal{W}(n)$, into the form

$$y_t = E_t F(y_{t+1}), \tag{4.15}$$

where $F(y) = G(\mathcal{W}^{-1}(y))$. Note that since the transformation $y = \mathcal{W}(n)$ is 1–1, the qualitative features of Figure 4.5 are preserved for the map F. In particular, there are three interior steady states y_L, y_U, y_H.

---

[7]This is one way of modeling the dependence of expectations on "animal spirits," as emphasized, for example, in the title of Howitt and McAfee (1992).

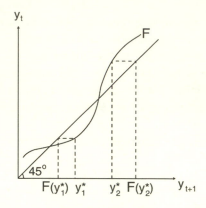

Figure 4.7.

An SSE (n_1^*, n_2^*) can equivalently be represented as an SSE (y_1^*, y_2^*), i.e., a process $y_t = y_1^*$ if $s_t = 1$ and $y_t = y_2^*$ if $s_t = 2$ which satisfies equation (4.15). This is equivalent to the equations

$$y_1^* = \pi_{11} F(y_1^*) + (1 - \pi_{11}) F(y_2^*),$$
$$y_2^* = (1 - \pi_{22}) F(y_1^*) + \pi_{22} F(y_2^*).$$

Note that geometrically an SSE exists if there exist y_1^*, y_2^* in the open interval formed by $F(y_1^*)$ and $F(y_2^*)$. (The transition probabilities must be chosen to correspond to y_1^*, y_2^*.) In particular, it is possible to construct sunspot solutions near a pair of two interior steady states. This is illustrated in Figure 4.7 for an arbitrary mapping $F(y)$ which has two steady states. In a sunspot equilibrium of this kind the economy alternates stochastically between $y_t = y_1^*$ and $y_t = y_2^*$ with transition probabilities π_{ij}.

4.6.4   Learning Sunspot Equilibria

Is it possible that agents in the economy can be led to such an equilibrium if they use a simple learning rule to make their forecasts? We will systematically examine this issue in Chapter 12.[8] Here we briefly take up an example of sunspot equilibria and learning based on the model of increasing social returns.

As shown above, this model can have multiple interior steady states and sunspot equilibria which are near a pair of distinct steady states. For the analysis

---

[8]The seminal work of Woodford (1990) demonstrated that indeed learning can converge to sunspot solutions in the basic OG model.

of learning we return to the formulation in terms of labor supply, n_t. A two-state Markov chain SSE is a process $n_t = n_1^*$ if $s_t = 1$ and $n_t = n_2^*$ if $s_t = 2$ which satisfies equation (4.14), i.e., the equations

$$n_1^* = W^{-1}\big(\pi_{11} G(n_1^*) + (1 - \pi_{11}) G(n_2^*)\big),$$
$$n_2^* = W^{-1}\big((1 - \pi_{22}) G(n_1^*) + \pi_{22} G(n_2^*)\big).$$

If agents try to learn the two values $G(n_1^*)$ and $G(n_2^*)$, a natural estimator for them is the following. Divide a sample of data $G(n_1), G(n_2), \ldots, G(n_t)$ into two groups in accordance with the realization of the sunspot process s_t. That is, for periods t in which $s_t = 1$ one puts the data point $G(n_t)$ into the first group, and for periods in which $s_t = 2$ the data point is put in the second group. Then form the averages of the data points separately for each group, taking into account the number of observations in the group. The average value in each group is the estimate for $G(n_i^*)$, $i = 1, 2$, respectively. That is, $G(n_i^*)$ is estimated, for $i = 1, 2$, by

$$\phi_{i,t} = \big(\#N_i(t - 1)\big)^{-1} \sum_{j \in N_i(t-1)} G(n_j^*),$$

where $N_i(t - 1)$ denotes the set of data points in periods $j \le t - 1$ for which $s_j = i$ and $\#N_i(t - 1)$ denotes the number of these points in periods $1, \ldots, t - 1$. The estimates for a group are then updated using the new data point, provided the realization of s_t corresponds to that group. If it does not, then the estimate is not changed. Finally, given these estimates, the economy evolves according to

$$n_t = W^{-1}\big(\pi_{i1}\phi_{1,t} + \pi_{i2}\phi_{2,t}\big) \quad \text{if } s_t = i.$$

Here $E_t^* G(n_{t+1}) = \pi_{i1}\phi_{1,t} + \pi_{i2}\phi_{2,t}$ when $s_t = i$, because we are assuming that the transition probabilities π_{ij} are known. If they are not known, they can also be estimated.

We will study systematically the convergence of learning based on this type of learning rule in Chapter 12. Here we note the basic result for the above example: a sunspot equilibrium near a pair of distinct steady states is locally stable under learning if it is near two distinct steady states both of which, as steady states, are stable under learning. Applying this result to the model of increasing social returns, we get the result that a sunspot equilibrium (sufficiently) near the steady states (n_L, n_H) is locally stable under learning. Such a pair (n_1^*, n_2^*) is shown for the graph $\mathcal{F}$ in Figure 4.5. In contrast, a sunspot is not stable if it is in the neighborhood of (n_U, n_H), because the "middle" steady state n_U is not stable under learning.

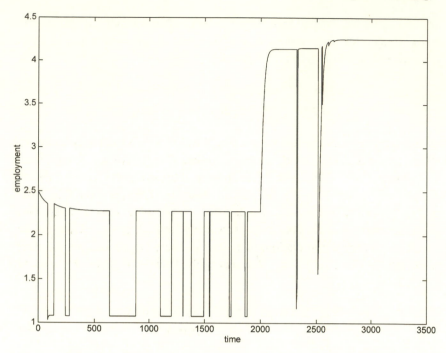

Figure 4.8.

We illustrate learning of sunspot equilibria using a simulation. Assume the production and utility functions given in the previous section. We set the following parameter values: $\sigma = 0.1$, $\varepsilon = 0.25$, $a = 0.025$, $\alpha = 0.9$, $\beta = 1$, $\ell = 40$, $\lambda = 0.5$, $I^* = 14.1935$, $A = 0.0792$, $\pi_{11} = 0.98$, $\pi_{22} = 0.995$. Initially, the subsidy level is set at zero. For these parameter settings the economy has three interior steady states and therefore there exist nearby SSEs. Agents use a recursive version of the above learning rule which conditions expectations on the observed sunspot state. The initial estimates of employment levels for the two states were 1 and 2.5.[9]

Figure 4.8 up to period 2000 illustrates how the economy learns the sunspot equilibrium at $n_1 = 1.020$ and $n_2 = 2.263$. At time $t = 2000$, an unanticipated regime change was made to occur: the subsidy level was raised to $\rho = 0.05$. For

---

[9]We remark that in the simulation we actually used a constant-gain learning rule with gain parameter value equal to 0.5. Constant gain can give convergence in this model since there is no intrinsic noise, and it allows for faster convergence to a new equilibrium following a regime switch. See Evans and Honkapohja (1993b) for further details on the simulations.

this subsidy level only the high-employment steady state exists, and Figure 4.8 shows how, under learning, the economy moves to this steady state.

Although the parameter values in this simulation are extreme, the results qualitatively illustrate an important new role for learning in models of multiple equilibria. Learning is the adjustment mechanism whereby the economy is steered to the new equilibrium after a structural change.

4.7 Other Models

There are numerous other examples of macroeconomic models in which adaptive learning plays an important role. One well-known macroeconomic example of multiple steady states is the seignorage model of inflation in which there are low and high perfect-foresight inflation rates. We will see in Chapter 12 that stability of SSEs in this model is problematic. A model with multiple balanced growth paths is provided in Evans, Honkapohja, and Romer (1998). This is an endogenous growth model with SSEs which switch stochastically between low-growth and high-growth states. It can be shown that these stochastic "growth cycles" can be locally stable under adaptive learning rules.[10]

It is also possible to construct models with perfect-foresight cycles as well as steady states. For the basic OG model this was discussed at length in Grandmont (1985). For such cases there are natural adaptive learning rules which could be employed by agents to forecast the levels of key variables at the different points of the cycle. Since, when equilibrium cycles exist, there are multiple perfect-foresight solutions, this is another case in which stability under learning can provide a useful selection criterion. Chapter 12 develops the relevant conditions for local stability under learning of such models.

Linear stochastic macroeconomic models have been studied extensively and are of considerable importance to applied macroeconomists. Many standard simple examples can be written as univariate stochastic linear models, e.g., the Muth cobweb model, the Cagan model of inflation, asset pricing with risk neutrality, the overlapping contract model, and monetary exchange rate models. It is natural to investigate least squares learning of the REE in such models and the univariate framework is examined in Chapter 8. Although more complex to analyze, there is in principle no barrier to the study of adaptive learning in multivariate linear stochastic models such as the Real Business Cycle model or "irregular" versions with "sunspot" solutions. These are considered in Chapter 10.

---

[10] A simplified steady-state version of this model is developed in Chapter 11.

Finally, although nonlinear models are usually developed in a nonstochastic framework, it is perfectly possible to develop nonlinear models with stochastic productivity, taste, or policy shocks. Such models have REE solutions taking the form of noisy steady states or cycles or noisy SSEs. These solutions can also be investigated for stability under learning. Such models are discussed in Chapters 11 and 12.

4.8 Appendix

We here give results on adaptive learning for the Ramsey and Diamond models. Since the Ramsey and Diamond models are deterministic models, we give direct arguments for stability conditions.

4.8.1 Learning in the Ramsey Model

We log-linearize the model (4.9) with the parametric form used in equation (4.8). (For details of this technique see Chapter 10.) We obtain

$$c_t = \beta\left(1+\alpha\bar{K}^{\alpha-1}\right)E_t^* c_{t+1} - \sigma^{-1}\alpha(\alpha-1)\bar{K}^{\alpha-1}E_t^* k_{t+1},$$
$$k_{t+1} = -(\bar{C}/\bar{K})c_t + \left(1+\alpha\bar{K}^{\alpha-1}\right)k_t.$$

Here $c_t = \log(C_t/\bar{C})$ and $k_t = \log(K_t/\bar{K})$. For notational convenience we write this as

$$c_t = a_c E_t^* c_{t+1} + a_k E_t^* k_{t+1},$$
$$k_{t+1} = d_c c_t + d_k k_t.$$

The REE for this model is given by the saddle path and locally takes the form $c_t = \bar{\phi}k_t$, $k_t = \bar{\lambda}k_{t-1}$. We therefore assume that agents have a PLM of the corresponding form so that $E_t^* k_{t+1} = \lambda_t k_t$ and $E_t^* c_{t+1} = \phi_t E_t^* k_{t+1} = \phi_t \lambda_t k_t$, where λ_t and ϕ_t are the time-t estimates of $\bar{\lambda}$ and $\bar{\phi}$. The estimates are formed using the learning rule

$$\phi_t = \phi_{t-1} + \gamma_t\left((c_{t-1}/k_{t-1}) - \phi_{t-1}\right),$$
$$\lambda_t = \lambda_{t-1} + \gamma_t\left((k_t/k_{t-1}) - \lambda_{t-1}\right).$$

The gain parameter γ_t can be taken to be either a small fixed gain $\gamma > 0$ or a decreasing-gain sequence of the form $\gamma_t = t^{-1}$.

Substituting expectations into the linearized model, we obtain the ALM

$$c_t = (a_c \phi_t + a_k) \lambda_t k_t,$$
$$k_t = \big(d_k + d_c (a_c \phi_{t-1} + a_k) \lambda_{t-1}\big) k_{t-1}.$$

Hence

$$c_{t-1}/k_{t-1} = (a_c \phi_{t-1} + a_k) \lambda_{t-1}$$
$$\equiv T_\phi(\phi_{t-1}, \lambda_{t-1}),$$
$$k_t/k_{t-1} = d_k + d_c(a_c \phi_{t-1} + a_k) \lambda_{t-1}$$
$$\equiv T_\lambda(\phi_{t-1}, \lambda_{t-1}).$$

The REE $(\bar{\phi}, \bar{\lambda})$ is a fixed point of $(T_\phi(\phi, \lambda), T_\lambda(\phi, \lambda))$. The law of motion for the parameter estimates is

$$\begin{pmatrix} \phi_t \\ \lambda_t \end{pmatrix} = \begin{pmatrix} \phi_{t-1} \\ \lambda_{t-1} \end{pmatrix} + \gamma_t \begin{pmatrix} T_\phi(\phi_{t-1}, \lambda_{t-1}) - \phi_{t-1} \\ T_\lambda(\phi_{t-1}, \lambda_{t-1}) - \lambda_{t-1} \end{pmatrix}.$$

Convergence can be verified numerically, e.g., using a fixed gain, and convergence to the REE $(\bar{\phi}, \bar{\lambda})$ values takes place rapidly for the parameter values $\alpha = 0.3$, $\beta = 0.9$ and $\sigma = 0.5$. Since $|\bar{\lambda}| < 1$, this, of course, also implies convergence of (C_t, K_t) to $(\bar{C}, \bar{K})$ as $t \to \infty$.

4.8.2 Learning in the Diamond Model

We now consider learning in the Diamond model as specified in equations (4.10) and (4.11). We first linearize the equation (4.10) and $r_t = f'(K_t)$ at a steady state, which gives

$$K_t = a_k K_{t-1} + a_r r_t^e,$$
$$r_t = b_k K_t,$$

where $a_k = sw'$, $a_r = ws'$, and $b_k = f''$. Here $w = f - Kf'$ and note that $a_k > 0$ and $b_k < 0$. (The functions and the derivatives are evaluated at the steady state under consideration.) For convenience we take here the variables to be deviations from the steady state.

We examine the case of a small constant gain in the learning rule (4.11), so it is written in the form

$$r_{t+1}^e = r_t^e + \gamma (r_t - r_t^e).$$

Using the linearized equations, we can write this in the form

$$K_{t+1} = (1 + a_k + \gamma(a_r b_k - 1))K_t + (\gamma - 1)a_k K_{t-1}$$
$$\equiv \alpha K_t + \beta K_{t-1}.$$

The system is of second order. It is straightforward to show that for small enough values of the gain parameter γ, its eigenvalues are real and both have absolute value less than 1 if and only if $a_k < 1$ and $a_k + a_r b_k < 1$. These are, therefore, the conditions that determine local convergence under learning to the steady state in question.

In order to relate these stability conditions to the steady states shown by the perfect-foresight map in Figure 4.3, we compute the slope of the perfect-foresight map $K_{t+1} = s(f'(K_{t+1}))w(K_t)$. Differentiating, we get the slope

$$\frac{dK_{t+1}}{dK_t} = \frac{sw'}{1 - ws'f''} = \frac{a_k}{1 - a_r b_k}.$$

It is easily verified that the steady state is stable under learning if and only if $0 < (dK_{t+1})/(dK_t)(\bar{K}) < 1$.

Part II

Mathematical Background and Tools

Chapter **5**

The Mathematical Background

5.1 Introduction

This chapter is devoted to a presentation of the mathematical concepts and techniques that are needed for a thorough understanding of the material in this book. Its purpose is to provide a convenient reference of the mathematical concepts and results that appear in different parts of the book. This should make the book essentially self-contained. However, we emphasize that the summary is no substitute for a proper study of these mathematical tools. The references cited in Section 5.8 should be consulted for thorough presentations of the mathematical techniques discussed here. At the same time we wish to point out that most of the presentation in Parts III, IV, and V can be followed with only a quick reading of the key material in Part II. The reader can then refer back to the Part II technical concepts and results as required.

We first consider deterministic dynamics that take the form of a difference or (ordinary) differential equation. Both linear and nonlinear equations will be treated. Stability concepts and results are the most important concepts for the purposes of this book.

The second main part of this chapter focuses on stochastic dynamics, i.e., stochastic processes. Basic notions of stochastic processes and stochastic convergence are introduced, after which relevant results for linear processes, such as ARMA and VAR processes, are presented. After this Markov processes are defined and some of their basic properties are outlined. We will also need the concept of stochastic differential equations and some results for them.

Finally, an appendix outlines some results on matrix algebra and matrix differentials that are needed when reading the book.

5.2   Difference Equations

5.2.1   Introduction

Consider a dynamical system of the form

$$y_t = F(y_{t-1}), \tag{5.1}$$

for $t = 1, 2, 3, \ldots$, with $y_0 = y^0$ given, where $y_t \in \mathbb{R}^m$ and $F\colon \mathbb{R}^m \to \mathbb{R}^m$. This system is traditionally called a "difference equation" in y_t. Let F^n denote the nth iterate of F, i.e., $F^2(y) = F(F(y))$ and $F^n(y) = F(F^{n-1}(y))$). Then it is immediate that equation (5.1) has a solution y_t, $t = 1, 2, 3, \ldots$, and that it is unique and given by $y_t = F^t(y^0)$. In some cases we consider the system (5.1) without imposing an initial condition. In that case the general solution is the set of solutions, indexed by the possible initial condition.

The difference equation (5.1) is said to have an equilibrium $\bar{y}$ if $\bar{y} = F(\bar{y})$. $\bar{y}$ is also referred to as a fixed point or stationary point of F. Clearly, if $y^0 = \bar{y}$, then the solution is $y_t = \bar{y}$ for all t. A question which is often of interest is whether $y_t \to \bar{y}$, or at least remains near $\bar{y}$, as $t \to \infty$, for initial $y_0 \neq \bar{y}$. This is the stability question. Let $B_\varepsilon(y)$ denote an ε-ball (or "ε-neighborhood") of y. We say that $\bar{y}$ is stable if, given $\varepsilon > 0$, there is a $\delta > 0$ such that $y_t \in B_\varepsilon(\bar{y})$ for all t whenever $y^0 \in B_\delta(\bar{y})$. An equilibrium $\bar{y}$ that is not stable is called unstable. If an equilibrium $\bar{y}$ is stable and in addition there exists $\delta > 0$ such that $\lim_{t \to \infty} y_t = \bar{y}$ for all $y^0 \in B_\delta(\bar{y})$, then $\bar{y}$ is said to be asymptotically stable. Because asymptotic stability is a local concept, this aspect is sometimes emphasized by referring to it as local asymptotic stability. If $\bar{y}$ is stable and in addition, for all y^0, solutions are bounded and satisfy $\lim_{t \to \infty} y_t = \bar{y}$, then we say that $\bar{y}$ is globally asymptotically stable.

5.2.2   Linear Systems

We are interested in obtaining stability and instability conditions for equilibria and begin with the linear homogeneous case

$$y_t = Ay_{t-1}. \tag{5.2}$$

First note that $\bar{y} = 0$ is always an equilibrium of equation (5.2) and that if $I - A$ is nonsingular, then this equilibrium is unique. The condition that $I - A$ is nonsingular is equivalent to the condition that A has no roots (eigenvalues) of 1.

The first-order setup (5.2) is more general than may be apparent. Suppose x_t is a scalar which satisfies the pth-order linear difference equation

$$x_t = b_1 x_{t-1} + \cdots + b_p x_{t-p}. \tag{5.3}$$

Defining $y_t' = (x_t, x_{t-1}, \ldots, x_{t-p+1})$, we can rewrite equation (5.3) in the form (5.2) with A the $p \times p$ matrix

$$A = \begin{pmatrix} b_1 & b_2 & \cdots & & b_p \\ 1 & 0 & \cdots & & 0 \\ 0 & 1 & 0 & & 0 \\ & & \vdots & & \\ 0 & 0 & \cdots & 1 & 0 \end{pmatrix}. \tag{5.4}$$

A is known as the "companion" matrix.

Even more generally, if x_t is an $n \times 1$ vector which follows the pth-order difference equation

$$x_t = B_1 x_{t-1} + \cdots + B_p x_{t-p},$$

we can define $y_t' = (x_t', x_{t-1}', \ldots, x_{t-p+1}')$ and

$$A = \begin{pmatrix} B_1 & B_2 & \cdots & & B_p \\ I & 0 & \cdots & & 0 \\ 0 & I & 0 & & 0 \\ & & \vdots & & \\ 0 & 0 & \cdots & I & 0 \end{pmatrix}. \tag{5.5}$$

Then the pth-order equation can again be written as equation (5.2). Here $m = np$ and A is $np \times np$.

The solution to equation (5.2) for initial condition $y_0 = y^0$ is given by $y_t = A^t y^0$. The key to stability is the eigenvalues of the $m \times m$ matrix A. We have the following result, see LaSalle (1992, Theorems 3.11 and 5.1). See also Stokey and Lucas Jr. (1989, Theorem 6.4).

Proposition 5.1. *Suppose $I - A$ is nonsingular. Then $\lim_{t \to \infty} y_t = 0$ for all initial y_0 if and only if all eigenvalues of A are less than 1 in modulus. If A has an eigenvalue with modulus greater than 1, then $\bar{y} = 0$ is unstable.*

In fact $A^t \to 0$ if and only if all eigenvalues of A are less than 1 in modulus. We then also say that A is a stable matrix.[1] The proof of the proposition is particularly simple if we restrict attention to matrices A which are diagonalizable,[2] i.e., such that there exists a representation of the form

$$A = Q \Lambda Q^{-1},$$

where Λ is a diagonal matrix with the eigenvalues of A along the diagonal and Q is a nonsingular matrix. (In this representation some elements of Λ and Q will be complex if some roots of A are complex.) We then have $A^t = Q \Lambda^t Q^{-1}$ and $\Lambda^t = \mathrm{diag}(\lambda_1^t, \dots, \lambda_m^t)$, where $\lambda_1, \dots, \lambda_m$ are the eigenvalues of A. It follows that $\Lambda^t \to 0$ and $A^t \to 0$ if and only if all eigenvalues of A are less than 1 in modulus. If A has a root greater than 1 in modulus, then, writing equation (5.2) as $w_t = \Lambda w_{t-1}$, where $w_t = Q^{-1} y_t$, one can verify that for certain initial w_0 (and hence for corresponding y_0), the solution explodes. For the general case in which A may not be diagonalizable, the proof works in the same way, but the Jordan representation of the matrix is used; see, e.g., LaSalle (1992).

We remark that the condition that all roots have modulus less than 1 is equivalently described as the condition that all roots lie inside the unit circle (in the complex plane).

Next we consider nonhomogeneous linear systems of the form

$$y_t = A y_{t-1} + f(t). \tag{5.6}$$

It is easily shown that the general solution to equation (5.6) is given by the general solution to the corresponding homogeneous equation (5.2) plus any particular solution to equation (5.6). Particular closed-form solutions for specific functions $f(t)$ can be found in the references.

An important and simple special case is $f(t) = a$. A particular solution to

$$y_t = A y_{t-1} + a \tag{5.7}$$

is $\bar{y} = (I - A)^{-1} a$, provided $I - A$ is nonsingular. The general solution to the homogeneous equation $y_t = A y_{t-1}$ is $A^t c$, for arbitrary $m \times 1$ vectors c. Thus

---

[1] In the mathematics literature the term "stable matrix" can also refer to the case where the linear ODE $dx/dt = Ax$ is stable (in a sense discussed later). This should not cause confusion, since it is always apparent whether a discrete- or continuous-time formulation is considered.

[2] It can be shown that if the eigenvalues of A are distinct, then A is diagonalizable. The set of diagonalizable matrices is "generic" in the sense that it contains an open dense subset of the set of all $m \times m$ matrices.

the general solution to equation (5.7) is

$$y_t = \bar{y} + A^t c, \quad \text{where } \bar{y} = (I - A)^{-1} a,$$

for arbitrary c. If an initial condition $y_0 = y^0$ must also be satisfied, then the solution to equation (5.7) is $y_t = \bar{y} + A^t (y^0 - \bar{y})$. Clearly, if A is a stable matrix, then $y_t \to \bar{y}$ as $t \to \infty$.

A special case of interest is the univariate pth-order equation

$$x_t = b_1 x_{t-1} + \cdots + b_p x_{t-p} + k.$$

This can be put in first-order form (5.7) with $p \times p$ companion matrix A given by equation (5.4) and $a' = (k, 0, \ldots, 0)$. It can be shown that the eigenvalues of A are identical to the solutions $\lambda_1, \ldots, \lambda_p$ to the characteristic polynomial

$$\lambda^p - b_1 \lambda^{p-1} - b_2 \lambda^{p-2} - \cdots - b_{p-1} \lambda - b_p = 0.$$

In the case in which the roots $\lambda_1, \ldots, \lambda_p$ are distinct and $b_1 + \cdots + b_p \neq 1$, the general solution is given by

$$x_t = k_1 \lambda_1^t + k_2 \lambda_2^t + \cdots + k_p \lambda_p^t + \bar{x},$$

where $\bar{x} = (1 - b_1 - \cdots - b_p)^{-1} a$, and $k_1, \ldots k_p$ are arbitrary. If initial conditions for $x_0, x_{-1}, \ldots, x_{-p+1}$ are given, then $k_1, \ldots k_p$ can be chosen uniquely to meet these initial conditions. We remark that if some of the roots λ_i are complex, then they come in conjugate pairs and real solutions are generated by choice of the corresponding coefficients k_i to be conjugate pairs: if λ_j, λ_{j+1} are a conjugate pair, written in polar form as $|\lambda_j|(\cos \theta_j \pm i \sin \theta_j)$, then the corresponding terms $k_j \lambda_j^t + k_{j+1} \lambda_{j+1}^t$ can be written as $m_j |\lambda_j|^t \cos(\theta_j t + n_j)$, with m_j, n_j arbitrary real numbers.

Consider the general nonhomogeneous equation

$$y_t = A y_{t-1} + w_t, \tag{5.8}$$

where w_t is some arbitrary specified sequence of $m \times 1$ vectors. w_t is sometimes called the forcing variable. If this equation holds for $t = 1, 2, 3, \ldots$ and there is a given initial condition $y_0 = y^0$, then it follows by recursive substitution that the unique solution is given by

$$y_t = \sum_{i=0}^{t-1} A^i w_{t-i} + A^t y^0.$$

If equation (5.8) holds for $t = 1, 2, 3, \ldots$ but no initial condition is specified, then the general solution is $y_t = \sum_{i=0}^{t-1} A^i w_{t-i} + A^t c$ for c arbitrary, where the sum is interpreted as zero when $t = 0$.

It is sometimes useful to consider solutions which are doubly infinite sequences. That is, we assume that equation (5.8) or (5.1) holds for all $t = \ldots, -1, 0, 1, \ldots$ and we look for solution sequences $\{y_t\}_{t=-\infty}^{\infty}$. We focus here on equation (5.8). A particular solution is given by $y_t = \sum_{i=0}^{\infty} A^i w_{-i}$, provided the sum converges. Convergence is guaranteed, for example, if either $w_t = 0$ for all t sufficiently small or if w_t is uniformly bounded over t and all roots of A have modulus less than 1. The general solution to equation (5.8) is given by

$$y_t = \sum_{i=0}^{\infty} A^i w_{t-i} + A^t c, \tag{5.9}$$

provided the sum converges. If the side condition $y_0 = y^0$ is given, the solution sets $c = y^0 - \sum_{i=0}^{\infty} A^i w_{-i}$.

Sometimes we will be interested in sequences $\{y_t\}_{t=-\infty}^{\infty}$ which solve equation (5.8) subject to a different type of side condition, namely that $\{y_t\}_{t=-\infty}^{\infty}$ be bounded (i.e., there exists M such that $|y_t| \le M$ for all t). Suppose that we are given that the sequence $\{w_t\}_{t=-\infty}^{\infty}$ is bounded. If A is a stable matrix, then

$$y_t = \sum_{i=0}^{\infty} A^i w_{t-i} \tag{5.10}$$

is a well-defined solution since the sum converges. Furthermore, equation (5.10) is bounded and is the unique bounded solution to equation (5.8). The general solution is equation (5.9), but $A^t c$ becomes unbounded as $t \to -\infty$ unless $c = 0$.

5.2.3 Local Stability of Nonlinear Systems

Returning to the in general nonlinear system (5.1), suppose that $\bar{y}$ is an equilibrium. Under appropriate regularity assumptions the local stability of $\bar{y}$ is determined by the stability of the linear approximation to F at $\bar{y}$. We have the following result; see LaSalle (1992, Theorem 7.1). See also Azariadis (1993, Theorem 6.2), and Stokey and Lucas Jr. (1989, Theorems 6.5 and 6.6).

Proposition 5.2. *Suppose that F is continuously differentiable in a neighborhood of $\bar{y}$. Let $A = DF(\bar{y})$ denote the $m \times m$ Jacobian matrix of first derivatives of F at $\bar{y}$. If all eigenvalues of A are less than 1 in modulus, then $\bar{y}$ is locally asymptotically stable. If A has an eigenvalue with modulus greater than 1, then $\bar{y}$ is unstable.*

If A has no eigenvalues with modulus greater than 1, but one or more eigenvalues with modulus equal to 1, then $\bar{y}$ may be (locally) stable, asymptotically stable, or unstable. Such equilibria are called nonhyperbolic. For a discussion of this case see Azariadis (1993).

5.3 Differential Equations

5.3.1 Introduction

We consider first-order vector ordinary differential equations (ODEs)

$$\frac{dy}{dt} = f(y,t), \tag{5.11}$$

where $y \in \mathbb{R}^m$, $t \in \mathbb{R}$, and $f(y,t)$ takes values in $\mathbb{R}^m$. We will often deal with the autonomous special case $dy/dt = f(y)$. Higher-order differential equations can be rewritten as first-order systems. An initial value problem adds the side condition $y(t_0) = y_0$. We start with a result on local existence and uniqueness. These require some conditions on f.

Suppose that f is defined for (y,t) in some set S. We say that y satisfies a Lipschitz condition on S if there exists a constant $K > 0$ such that

$$|f(y,t) - f(x,t)| \leq K|y-x|$$

for all (y,t) and (x,t) in S. It can be shown that if S takes the form $S = \{(y,t) \in \mathbb{R}^{m+1} \mid |y - y_0| \leq b \text{ and } |t - t_0| \leq a\}$ and if f has continuous partial derivatives on S which are bounded on S, i.e., $|\partial f/\partial y_k(y,t)| \leq K$ for some $K > 0$ and all (y,t) in S, then f satisfies a Lipschitz condition on S with Lipschitz constant K. (This result also holds if $|y - y_0| \leq b$ is replaced by $|y| < \infty$.)

We can now state the following result on local existence and uniqueness.

Proposition 5.3. *Suppose that f is a continuous function defined on the set $S = \{(y,t) \in \mathbb{R}^{m+1} \mid |y - y_0| \leq b \text{ and } |t - t_0| \leq a\}$, and that f satisfies a Lipschitz condition on S. Then for some interval containing t_0, there exists a solution to the initial value problem $dy/dt = f(y,t)$, $y(t_0) = y_0$, and this solution is unique.*

We write $y(t \mid t_0, y_0)$ to denote the unique solution to the initial value problem. Under these assumptions it can also be shown that the solutions exhibit continuous dependence on initial conditions. We have the following.

Proposition 5.4. *Under the conditions of the previous proposition, suppose that f satisfies a Lipschitz condition on S with Lipschitz constant K. Suppose that $y(t \mid t_0, y_0)$ and $y(t \mid t_0, y_0')$ are the solutions to $dy/dt = f(y,t)$, with initial conditions $y(t_0) = y_0$ and $y(t_0) = y_0'$, respectively, on some interval I containing t_0, where $|y_0 - y_0'| \leq \delta$. Then $|y(t \mid t_0, y_0) - y(t \mid t_0, y_0')| \leq \delta \exp(K|t - t_0|)$.*

Results on nonlocal existence, i.e., for all t, are also available. For the proofs of the above propositions, further details, and a further discussion of Lipschitz conditions, see Coddington (1961, Sections 6.5 and 6.6 of Chapter 6).

Local stability and instability are defined analogously to their definitions in the case of difference equations. Suppose $f(y,t)\colon \mathbb{R}^m \times [0, \infty) \to \mathbb{R}^m$ satisfies conditions ensuring existence, uniqueness, and continuous dependence of solutions on initial conditions. An equilibrium solution $\bar{y}$ is a solution $y(t) = \bar{y}$ for all $t \geq 0$. Thus the equilibrium $\bar{y}$, also called a rest point or stationary solution, satisfies $f(\bar{y}, t) = 0$ for all $t \geq 0$. We say that $\bar{y}$ is (locally) stable if for every $\varepsilon > 0$, there exists $\delta > 0$ such that $|y_0 - \bar{y}| < \delta$ implies

$$\left| y(t \mid t_0, y_0) - \bar{y} \right| < \varepsilon \quad \text{for all } t \geq t_0.$$

The equilibrium is said to be (locally) asymptotically stable if it is stable and in addition $y(t \mid t_0, y_0) \to \bar{y}$ as $t \to \infty$ for all y_0 in some neighborhood of $\bar{y}$. The domain of attraction is defined as the set of all points (t_0, y_0) with the property that the trajectory $y(t \mid t_0, y_0)$ originating from the point converges to $\bar{y}$.

We are often interested in autonomous systems, i.e., in systems in which $f(y, t)$ does not depend explicitly on time. Definitions of an equilibrium and of stability of the equilibrium for an autonomous differential equation $dy/dt = f(y)$ are obviously special cases. Finally, we will sometimes need a global stability concept. We say that an equilibrium $\bar{y}$ is globally asymptotically stable if it is stable and if the solution $y(t \mid t_0, y_0) \to \bar{y}$ as $t \to \infty$ for all $y_0 \in \mathbb{R}^m$.

The concept of ω-limit set of a trajectory $y(t \mid 0, y_0)$ is defined as the set of points x such that there exists a sequence of times $t_n \to \infty$ such that $y(t_n \mid 0, y_0) \to x$. A set A is an invariant set if for all $x \in A$, the trajectory $y(t \mid 0, x) \in A$ for all t. It can be shown that the ω-limit set is a closed invariant set.

5.3.2   Linear Systems

Consider the linear homogeneous time-invariant system

$$\frac{dy}{dt} = Ay, \tag{5.12}$$

where A is a fixed $m \times m$ matrix. Clearly $y = 0$ is a stationary solution and this is the unique stationary solution if A is nonsingular, i.e., if A has no zero roots. The general solution to system (5.12) is given by

$$y(t) = e^{tA}c, \qquad (5.13)$$

where the vector c is arbitrary. The particular solution that satisfies the initial condition $y(0) = y_0$ is $y(t) = e^{tA}y_0$.

Here $\exp(T) = e^T$, the exponential of a matrix T, is defined by the matrix generalization of the usual exponential series,

$$e^T = \sum_{k=0}^{\infty} \frac{T^k}{k!}.$$

It can be shown that this series is absolutely convergent for every $m \times m$ matrix T. The following properties can be shown to hold: (a) if $Q = PTP^{-1}$, then $e^Q = P(e^T)P^{-1}$, (b) if $ST = TS$, then $e^{S+T} = e^S e^T$, (c) $e^{-S} = (e^S)^{-1}$, and (d) $d/dt(e^{tA}) = Ae^{tA} = e^{tA}A$. See Hirsch and Smale (1974, Chapter 5) for details. The general solution (5.13) to equation (5.12) follows directly from (d).

If the matrix A is diagonalizable, then e^{tA} can be easily computed. In this case $A = Q\Lambda Q^{-1}$. Here $\Lambda = \text{diag}(\lambda_1, \ldots, \lambda_m)$, where λ_i, for $i = 1, \ldots, m$, are the eigenvalues of A and Q is a nonsingular matrix. Then $e^{tA} = Qe^{t\Lambda}Q^{-1}$ and

$$e^{t\Lambda} = \begin{pmatrix} e^{\lambda_1 t} & 0 & \cdots & 0 \\ 0 & e^{\lambda_2 t} & \cdots & 0 \\ \vdots & \vdots & & \vdots \\ 0 & 0 & \cdots & e^{\lambda_m t} \end{pmatrix}.$$

The conditions for stability of the stationary solution $\bar{y} = 0$ are now readily obtained. First note that if λ is real, then $e^{\lambda t} \to 0$ as $t \to \infty$ if and only if $\lambda < 0$. If $\lambda = a + bi$ is complex, then we can write $e^{\lambda t} = e^{at}e^{bti} = e^{at}(\cos(bt) + i\sin(bt))$ so that $e^{\lambda t} \to 0$ as $t \to \infty$ if and only if $a < 0$. Thus, in general $e^{\lambda t} \to 0$ as $t \to \infty$ if and only if $\text{re}(\lambda) < 0$.

To see the implications of the preceding considerations for stability, we transform variables to $x = Q^{-1}y$. The solution $y(t) = e^{tA}y_0$ can then be written $x(t) = e^{t\Lambda}x_0$. It follows that $x(t) \to 0$ for all x_0, and hence $y(t) \to 0$ for all y_0, if all eigenvalues of A have negative real parts. If instead some eigenvalue of A has a positive real part, then for some y_0, including values arbitrarily close to 0, the path $y(t)$ diverges. If A is not diagonalizable, the Jordan form of A can be used and the argument is analogous. We thus have the following result; see Hirsch and Smale (1974, Section 6.5, p. 136).

Proposition 5.5. *Consider the system $dy/dt = Ay$. The equilibrium $\bar{y} = 0$ is globally asymptotically stable if all eigenvalues of A have negative real parts. If A has one or more eigenvalues with a positive real part, then the equilibrium $\bar{y} = 0$ is unstable.*

For the special case of a 2×2 matrix A, it can be shown that the condition that both roots of A have negative real parts is equivalent to the condition that the trace of A is negative and the determinant of A is positive.

Finally, consider the linear nonhomogeneous system

$$\frac{dy}{dt} = Ay + h(t),$$

where $h(t)$ is a continuous function for $a \leq t \leq b$, subject to the initial condition $y(t_0) = y_0$ for $a \leq t_0 \leq b$. The solution is given by

$$y(t) = e^{A(t-t_0)} y_0 + \int_{t_0}^{t} e^{A(t-s)} h(s)\, ds.$$

This can be verified by differentiation.

5.3.3   Local Stability of Nonlinear Systems

Local stability of the autonomous differential equation

$$\frac{dy}{dt} = f(y) \tag{5.14}$$

can be determined by the linearization of $f(y)$ at an equilibrium point. Here $f: W \to \mathbb{R}^m$, where $W \subset \mathbb{R}^m$, W open. $\bar{y} \in W$ is an equilibrium of equation (5.14) if $f(\bar{y}) = 0$. We have the following result; see Hirsch and Smale (1974, Sections 9.1–9.2, p. 181, and p. 187).

Proposition 5.6. *Assume f is continuously differentiable on W. Let $A = Df(\bar{y})$ denote the (Jacobian) derivative of f at $\bar{y}$. If all eigenvalues of A have negative real parts, then $\bar{y}$ is locally asymptotically stable. If A has one or more eigenvalues with positive real parts, then $\bar{y}$ is unstable.*

If A has no eigenvalues with real part greater than zero, but one or more eigenvalues with real part equal to zero, then $\bar{y}$ may be (locally) stable, asymptotically stable, or unstable. For a discussion of this case ("nonhyperbolic" equilibria) see Guckenheimer and Holmes (1983).

5.3.4 Lyapunov's Method for Stability Analysis

There exists a useful method for determining the local stability or instability of an equilibrium $\bar{y}$, known as Lyapunov's direct method. The idea behind this method is to use certain functions to assess the local stability of $\bar{y}$. The basic result is the following; see Brock and Malliaris (1989, Theorem 2.2, p. 94).

Proposition 5.7. *Let $\bar{y} \in W$ be an equilibrium for equation (5.14). If there exists a continuously differentiable function $\mathcal{U} \colon W_1 \to \mathbb{R}$, defined on a neighborhood $W_1 \subset W$ of $\bar{y}$ such that*

(i) $\mathcal{U}(\bar{y}) = 0$ *and* $\mathcal{U}(y) > 0$ *if* $y \neq \bar{y}$,
(ii) $(d/dt)\mathcal{U} < 0$ *on* $W_1 \setminus \{\bar{y}\}$,
   then $\bar{y}$ is locally asymptotically stable.

The function $\mathcal{U}(y)$ in the proposition is called a Lyapunov function. In (ii) of this proposition the derivative is calculated by the chain rule to be

$$\frac{d}{dt}\mathcal{U} = D\mathcal{U}(y)\frac{dy}{dt} = D\mathcal{U}(y)(f(y)),$$

where $D\mathcal{U}(y)$ is the gradient of the real valued function $\mathcal{U}(y)$.

Lyapunov's method is also available for global stability; see Brock and Malliaris (1989, Theorem 4.2, p. 116).

Proposition 5.8. *Suppose that the equilibrium $\bar{y}$ for system (5.14) is unique, $f(y)$ is continuously differentiable on $\mathbb{R}^m$, and let $\mathcal{U} \colon \mathbb{R}^m \to \mathbb{R}$ be a continuously differentiable function such that*

(i) $\mathcal{U}(\bar{y}) = 0$ *and* $\mathcal{U}(y) \geq 0$ *for* $y \neq \bar{y}$,
(ii) $(d/dt)\mathcal{U}(\bar{y}) = 0$, $(d/dt)\mathcal{U}(y) < 0$ *for* $y \neq \bar{y}$,
(iii) $\mathcal{U}(y) \to \infty$ *if* $|y| \to \infty$.

Then all solutions of equation (5.14) exist on $[0, \infty)$, are bounded, and converge to $\bar{y}$ as $t \to \infty$.

We note that there exist alternative slightly different forms of these results with somewhat different conditions on the ODE (5.14). Corresponding results for unstable equilibrium points are also available. The references at the end of this chapter can be consulted for the detailed statements.

Finding a function with the required properties is the main difficulty when applying Lyapunov's method. There is no general way for finding Lyapunov functions, although a number of specific results are available in the literature. Nevertheless, it can be shown that this method is general in the sense that given a locally asymptotically stable equilibrium point for the ODE (5.14), a Lyapunov function can in principle be constructed. This is the general content of the so-called converse Lyapunov theorems and we will make use of these results. We will need the following.

Proposition 5.9. *Suppose that $\bar{y} \in W$ is a locally asymptotically stable equilibrium for system (5.14) with a domain of attraction G. Suppose also that f is continuous in every bounded region of G. Then there exists a function $\mathcal{U}(y)$ with continuous partial derivatives of all orders on every bounded region of G such that*

(i) $\mathcal{U}(\bar{y}) = 0$ *and* $\mathcal{U}(y) > 0$ *for all* $y \in G$, $y \neq \bar{y}$,
(ii) $(d/dt)\mathcal{U}(y) < 0$ *for all* $y \in G$, $y \neq \bar{y}$,
(iii) $\mathcal{U}(y) \to \infty$ *if* $y \to \partial G$ *or* $|y| \to \infty$.

This result is part of Krasovskii (1963, Theorem 5.3, p. 31).

We will also need a more specialized result for the case of exponential stability. First, define an equilibrium point $\bar{y}$ of the ODE (5.11) to be exponentially stable if

$$|y| \le m e^{-\delta(t-t_0)} |y_0| \tag{5.15}$$

for some constants $m > 0$, $\delta > 0$ in some region $G = \{|y| < h, \, 0 < t < \infty\}$. (Here $|y|$ denotes the Euclidean norm of vector y.) The required result is (this is Krasovskii, 1963, Theorem 11.1, p. 60):

Proposition 5.10. *Whenever the solution $y(t \mid y_0, t_0)$ of equation (5.11) satisfies equation (5.15), there exists a function $\mathcal{U}(y, t)$ in region G satisfying*

(i) $c_1 |y|^2 \le \mathcal{U}(y, t) \le c_2 |y|^2$,
(ii) $(d/dt)\mathcal{U}(y, t) = D_y \mathcal{U}(y, t)(f(y, t)) + D_t \mathcal{U}(y, t) \le -c_3 |y|^2$,
(iii) $|D_y \mathcal{U}(y, t)| \le c_4 |y|$,

for some positive constants c_i, $i = 1, 2, 3, 4$.

The notes on the literature at the end of this chapter provide further references for expositions of Lyapunov's method.

5.4   Linear Stochastic Processes

5.4.1   Introduction

A stochastic process is a collection of random variables indexed by time. We focus on infinite or doubly infinite collections of random variables indexed by discrete time, $\{Y_t\}_{t=0}^{\infty} = \{Y_0, Y_1, Y_2, \ldots\}$ or $\{Y_t\}_{t=-\infty}^{\infty} = \{\ldots, Y_{-1}, Y_0, Y_1, \ldots\}$. As an example, if $Y_t \sim \text{IIN}(0, \sigma^2)$, i.e., are identically and independently distributed normal random variables, then $\{Y_t\}_{t=-\infty}^{\infty}$ is a simple stochastic process known as Gaussian white noise. A particular outcome for each of the random variables $\{y_t\}_{t=-\infty}^{\infty} = \{\ldots, y_{-1}, y_0, y_1, \ldots\}$ is known as a realization of the stochastic process.

A more formal definition of stochastic process relies on measure theory and the concept of a probability space. A triple $(\Omega, \mathcal{F}, P)$ is called a probability space if Ω is a given set, $\mathcal{F}$ is a σ-algebra on Ω, and P is a probability measure on $(\Omega, \mathcal{F})$. Here Ω is interpreted as the sample space or set of possible outcomes. A σ-algebra $\mathcal{F}$ on Ω is a collection of subsets of Ω, including Ω and the null set $\varnothing$, which is closed under complementation and countable unions. A probability measure P is a function $P\colon \mathcal{F} \to [0, 1]$ such that $P(\varnothing) = 0$, $P(\Omega) = 1$, and $P(\bigcup_{i=1}^{\infty} A_i) = \sum_{i=1}^{\infty} A_i$ if $A_i \in \mathcal{F}$ and $A_i \cap A_j = \varnothing$ for $i \neq j$. For any set $F \in \mathcal{F}$, $P(F)$ is interpreted as the probability that the event F occurs.

The pair $(\Omega, \mathcal{F})$, where $\mathcal{F}$ is a σ-algebra of subsets of Ω, is also called a measurable space. A real valued function $f\colon \Omega \to \mathbb{R}$ is said to be measurable, or more specifically $\mathcal{F}$-measurable, if $\{\omega \in \Omega\colon f(\omega) \leq a\} \in \mathcal{F}$ for all real a. A vector valued function $f\colon \Omega \to \mathbb{R}^n$ is measurable if $\{\omega \in \Omega\colon f(\omega) \leq a\} \in \mathcal{F}$ for all $a \in \mathbb{R}^n$. [Here $b \leq a$ if $b_i \leq a_i$ for $i = 1, \ldots, n$, where $b' = (b_1, \ldots, b_n)$ and $a' = (a_1, \ldots, a_n)$.]

A random variable Y on $(\Omega, \mathcal{F}, P)$ is then defined as a measurable function $Y\colon \Omega \to \mathbb{R}$. Every random variable Y induces a probability measure μ_Y on $(\mathbb{R}, \mathcal{B})$, where $\mathcal{B}$ is the σ-algebra of Borel sets on $\mathbb{R}$ (the collection formed by a countable number of intersections, unions, or complements of open sets of $\mathbb{R}$). This is given by $\mu_Y(B) = P(Y^{-1}(B))$. The distribution function $F(y)$ of Y is defined by $F(y) = \mu_Y((-\infty, y])$. All of the usual stochastic concepts can be defined in terms of the probability spaces. In particular, the Lebesgue approach can be used to define the integral $\int_{\Omega} f(\omega) P(d\omega)$, also written $\int f \, dP$, of a function f with respect to a probability measure P. (The Lebesgue integral is defined for a broader class of functions than the Riemann integral but coincides with it when the latter exists.)

The expected value $E(Y)$ of a random variable Y is then defined as $E(Y) = \int_{\Omega} Y(\omega) P(d\omega) = \int y \mu_Y(dy)$. When the distribution function $F(y)$ is differentiable, it can be represented by a density function $f(y) = dF/dy$ and we have $E(Y) = \int yf(y)\,dy$.

There are several inequalities for expected values that are often needed. Jensen's inequality states that $f(E(X)) \le Ef(X)$ if f is convex. In particular, $|E(X)| \le E|X|$. The Schwarz inequality states that $E|XY| \le (EX^2)^{1/2} \times (EY^2)^{1/2}$.

A random vector $Y' = (Y_1, \ldots, Y_n)$ on $(\Omega, \mathcal{F}, P)$ is a measurable vector function $Y\colon \Omega \to \mathbb{R}^n$. Again, this induces a probability measure μ_Y on $\mathbb{R}^n$. The distribution function $F(y)$ of a random vector continues to be given by $F(y) = \mu_Y((-\infty, y])$, where $(-\infty, y]$ is interpreted as $\{x \in \mathbb{R}^n\colon x \le y\}$. The expected value of a random vector $E(Y)$ is the n-vector of expectations $E(Y)' = (EY_1, \ldots, EY_n)$.

If $\mathcal{A} \subset \mathcal{F}$ is a σ-algebra and $f\colon \Omega \to \mathbb{R}$ is measurable, the conditional expectation of f relative to $\mathcal{A}$ is an $\mathcal{A}$-measurable function $E(f \mid \mathcal{A})$ such that $\int_C E(f \mid \mathcal{A})(\omega)P(d\omega) = \int_C f(\omega)P(d\omega)$ for all $C \in \mathcal{A}$. One can also define conditional probabilities $P(A \mid B)$, $P(A \mid X)$, and $P(A \mid \mathcal{A})$ with respect to a set $B \subset \Omega$, a random variable X, or a σ-algebra $\mathcal{A}$, respectively. For presentations of measure theory and probability, see the references at the end of this chapter.

A stochastic process can then be formally defined as a parameterized set of random variables $\{Y_t\}_{t \in T}$ defined on a probability space, where $T \subset \mathbb{R}$. If the Y_t are random vectors, then $\{Y_t\}_{t \in T}$ is a multivariate stochastic process. Continuous stochastic processes usually set T to be $[0, \infty)$ or $[a, b]$. Discrete stochastic processes set $T = \{0, 1, 2, \ldots\}$ or $T = \{\ldots, -1, 0, 1, \ldots\}$. Note that for each $t \in T$, $\omega \to Y_t(\omega)$ is a random variable, whereas for fixed $\omega \in \Omega$, $t \to Y_t(\omega)$ is a path or sequence called the realization or path of Y_t.

Until Section 5.6 we now restrict attention to discrete-time stochastic processes. Let $\mu_t = EY_t$ denote the (unconditional) expected value of Y_t, $\gamma_{0t} = E(Y_t - \mu_t)^2$ denote the variance of Y_t, and $\gamma_{jt} = E(Y_t - \mu_t)(Y_{t-j} - \mu_{t-j})$, for $j = 1, 2, 3, \ldots$, denote the autocovariances of Y_t. If for all t we have $\mu_t = \mu < \infty$, $\gamma_{0t} = \gamma_0 < \infty$, and $\gamma_{jt} = \gamma_j < \infty$, for $j = 1, 2, 3, \ldots$, then the process is said to be covariance stationary. More generally, suppose that Y_t is an $m \times 1$ multivariate stochastic process, i.e., sequence of random vectors indexed by time. If the mean $EY_t = \mu < \infty$ is independent of calendar time and if the autocovariances $\Gamma_j = E(Y_t - \mu)(Y_t - \mu)' < \infty$, $j = 0, 1, 2, 3, \ldots$, are independent of calendar time, the vector stochastic process Y_t is said to be covariance stationary.

Other concepts of stationarity, however, are also useful. A stochastic process Y_t is said to be strictly stationary if the joint distribution functions of $(Y_{t_1}, \ldots, Y_{t_k})'$ and $(Y_{t_1+\tau}, \ldots, Y_{t_k+\tau})'$ are the same for all positive integers k, τ and all $t_1, \ldots, t_k \in T$. The term "stationary" can denote either covariance stationary or strictly stationary, depending on the context, and it is common to use the term "stationary" to mean "covariance stationary."

A class of stochastic processes of particular interest is martingales. A stochastic process $Y_t, t \geq 1$, is a martingale if (i) $E|Y_t| < \infty$, and (ii) the conditional expectation $E(Y_{t+1} \mid Y_1, \ldots, Y_t) = Y_t$ for all $t \geq 1$. This conditional expectation should be interpreted as $E(Y_{t+1} \mid \sigma(Y_1, \ldots, Y_t))$, where $\sigma(Y_1, \ldots, Y_t)$ is the σ-algebra generated by the random variables $Y_1, \ldots, Y_t$, i.e., the smallest σ-algebra such that $Y_1, \ldots, Y_t$ are measurable with respect to it. A stochastic process D_t is a martingale difference sequence if $D_t = Y_t - Y_{t-1}$, where Y_t is a martingale. Note that $E(D_t \mid D_{t-1}, \ldots, D_1) = 0$.

5.4.2 Notions of Stochastic Convergence

Consider a sequence of jointly distributed random variables $X_1, X_2, X_3, \ldots$. There are several concepts of stochastic convergence, i.e., several senses in which the sequence $X_1, X_2, X_3, \ldots$ might converge to a random variable X or a constant a. The principal ones are:

1. A sequence of random variables $X_1, X_2, X_3, \ldots$ is said to converge with probability 1 to the random variable X if

$$P\left(\lim_{n \to \infty} X_n = X\right) = 1.$$

Equivalently, in terms of the probability space $(\Omega, \mathcal{F}, P)$, we say that X_n converges to X with probability 1 if there is a set $A \in \mathcal{F}$ with $P(A) = 0$ such that $\lim_{n \to \infty} X_n(\omega) = X(\omega)$ for all $\omega \in A^c$ (where A^c denotes the complement of A). We often write $X_n \to X$ w.p.1. The notion is also called almost sure convergence and is equivalently written $X_n \to X$ almost surely, $X_n \to X$ a.s., or $X_n \overset{\text{a.s.}}{\to} X$. A special case is convergence w.p.1 to a constant a, i.e., X is simply taken to be a constant and we write $X_n \to a$ w.p.1.

2. A sequence of random variables $X_1, X_2, X_3, \ldots$ is said to converge in probability to X if

$$\lim_{n \to \infty} P\{|X_n - X| < \varepsilon\} = 1 \quad \text{for all } \varepsilon > 0.$$

We usually write $X_n \overset{\text{p}}{\to} X$ or $X_n \overset{\text{p}}{\to} a$. Intuitively, convergence in probability means that by choosing n large one can make X_n arbitrarily close to X with arbitrarily high probability.

3. The sequence X_n converges to X in quadratic mean, also called convergence in mean square, if

$$\lim_{n \to \infty} E|X_n - X|^2 = 0.$$

We write $X_n \overset{\text{m.s.}}{\to} X$ (or $X_n \overset{\text{m.s.}}{\to} a$). More generally X_n converges to X in pth mean, for $p \geq 1$, if $\lim_{n \to \infty} E|X_n - X|^p = 0$. These can also be called L_2- and L_p-convergence, respectively, provided one introduces the spaces $L_p = L_p(\Omega, \mathcal{F}, P)$, for $p \geq 1$, consisting of random variables X which satisfy $E|X|^p < \infty$. The L_p norm of a random variable is defined as $\|X\|_p = (E|X|^p)^{1/p}$.

4. Finally, suppose X_n has distribution function F_n and X has distribution function F. Then we say that the sequence X_n converges in distribution to X (or that F_n converges in distribution to F) if

$$\lim_{n \to \infty} F_n(x) = F(x)$$

for all points x at which F is continuous. This concept of convergence is also called convergence in law or weak convergence. We typically write $X_n \overset{\text{d}}{\to} X$ or $X_n \overset{\text{L}}{\to} X$, or sometimes $X_n \overset{\text{d}}{\to} F$ or $X_n \overset{\text{L}}{\to} F$.

All of these convergence concepts can be extended in a straightforward way to sequences of random vectors. It can be shown that convergence a.s. implies convergence in probability, that convergence in mean square implies convergence in probability, and that convergence in probability implies convergence in distribution. There are many other results on the relationships between these concepts and on limits of functions of sequences of random vectors. See, for example, Hamilton (1994, Chapter 7) or Neveu (1965, Chapter 2).

Classic results from the statistics literature concern the sample means of sequences of iid random variables. Suppose $X_1, X_2, X_3, \ldots$ is a sequence of iid random variables with mean μ. Let $\bar{X}_n = n^{-1} \sum_{i=1}^{n} X_i$ denote the sample mean using $X_1, X_2, \ldots, X_n$. Then the Weak Law of Large Numbers states that $\bar{X}_n \overset{\text{P}}{\to} \mu$. Under these assumptions we also have the stronger result, known as the Strong Law of Large Numbers, that $\bar{X}_n \overset{\text{a.s.}}{\to} \mu$. If, in addition, X_n has finite variance σ^2, then the Central Limit Theorem states that $\sqrt{n}(\bar{X}_n - \mu) \overset{\text{d}}{\to} N(0, \sigma^2)$. Here N denotes the normal distribution with mean 0 and variance σ^2. Laws of large numbers and central limit theorems hold under much more general conditions (e.g., for serially dependent sequences) and there are many versions of each. In addition to Hamilton (1994, Chapter 7), good references in the econometrics and economics literature are Davidson (1994), White (1984), and Stokey and Lucas Jr. (1989).

The martingale convergence theorem is an important result behind convergence results in stochastic approximation. We say that a sequence Y_t, $t = 1, 2, \ldots$, is a submartingale relative to a sequence of σ-algebras $\mathcal{F}_t$, where $\mathcal{F}_t \subset \mathcal{F}_{t+1}$ and Y_t is measurable with respect to $\mathcal{F}_t$, if $E(|Y_t|) < \infty$ and $E(Y_{t+1} \mid \mathcal{F}_t) \geq Y_t$ almost surely. The martingale convergence theorem states that for any submartingale Y_t, $t = 1, 2, \ldots$, such that $\sup_t E(|Y_t|) = K < \infty$, we have $Y_t \to Y$ almost surely, where Y is a random variable satisfying $E(|Y|) \leq K$.

5.4.3 ARMA Processes and VARs

For each $t \in T$, suppose that ε_t is a covariance stationary process with mean 0 and autocovariance function $\gamma(0) = \sigma^2$ and $\gamma(h) = 0$ for $h = 1, 2, 3, \ldots$. Here $T = \{0, 1, 2, \ldots\}$ or $T = \{\ldots, -1, 0, 1, \ldots\}$. We say that ε_t is a white noise process.

The autoregressive-moving average (ARMA) class is an important class of discrete-time univariate stochastic processes. Y_t is an ARMA(p, q) process if

$$Y_t - \phi_1 Y_{t-1} - \cdots - \phi_p Y_{t-p} = \varepsilon_t + \theta_1 \varepsilon_{t-1} + \cdots + \theta_q \varepsilon_{t-q}, \qquad (5.16)$$

for each $t \in T$, where ε_t is white noise and p, q are nonnegative integers. If $Y_t - \mu$ is an ARMA(p, q) process, then Y_t is said to be an ARMA(p, q) process with mean μ. Equation (5.16) is a stochastic difference equation, i.e., a nonhomogeneous difference equation in which the exogenous forcing variable $\varepsilon_t + \theta_1 \varepsilon_{t-1} + \cdots + \theta_q \varepsilon_{t-q}$ is stochastic. As with nonstochastic difference equations, it will in general have multiple solutions. If $T = \{0, 1, 2, \ldots\}$ and initial conditions $Y_{-1}, \ldots, Y_{-p}$ are specified, then this will determine a unique solution. If instead $T = \{\ldots, -1, 0, 1, \ldots\}$, then we usually impose the side condition of stationarity.

We initially restrict attention to the case $T = \{\ldots, -1, 0, 1, \ldots\}$. Equation (5.16) is often written as

$$\phi(L)Y_t = \theta(L)\varepsilon_t,$$

where $\phi(z) = 1 - \phi_1 z - \cdots - \phi_p z^p$ and $\theta(z) = 1 + \theta_1 z + \cdots + \theta_q z^q$ and L denotes the lag operator $L^j Y_t = Y_{t-j}$ for $j = \ldots, -1, 0, 1, \ldots$.

A pure moving average process of order q, $Y_t = \theta(L)\varepsilon_t$, known as an MA($q$) process, is easily seen always to be unique and stationary. This is not necessarily true of pure autoregressive processes of order p, defined by

$\phi(L)Y_t = \varepsilon_t$ and known as AR(p) processes, or of ARMA(p, q) processes. Consider the AR(1) process

$$Y_t = \phi Y_{t-1} + \varepsilon_t. \tag{5.17}$$

Applying the results from Section 5.2.2, we see that a particular solution is

$$Y_t = \sum_{i=0}^{\infty} \phi^i \varepsilon_{t-i}, \tag{5.18}$$

provided this sum is well defined, and that the general solution is

$$Y_t = \sum_{i=0}^{\infty} \phi^i \varepsilon_{t-i} + c\phi^t, \tag{5.19}$$

with c arbitrary.

We must therefore consider the convergence of infinite sums such as equation (5.18). This is most conveniently done using the framework of Hilbert spaces, which we now briefly discuss. A good compact reference is Brockwell and Davis (1991, Chapter 2), which we here follow. A vector space on which an inner product is defined is called an inner-product space. Based on this inner product, a vector norm $\|x\|$ can be defined as the square root of the inner product of the vector with itself. For example, the Euclidean space is the set of vectors $(x_1, \dots, x_k)' \in \mathbb{R}^k$ in which the inner product is defined as $\langle x, y \rangle = \sum_{i=1}^{k} x_i y_i$ and the norm of x is its length. Many familiar properties of Euclidean space, such as the Cauchy–Schwarz inequality $|\langle x, y \rangle| \leq \|x\| \|y\|$ and the triangle inequality $\|x + y\| \leq \|x\| + \|y\|$, hold generally for inner-product spaces. A sequence of elements $\{x_n\}$ in the space converges in norm to an element x in the space if $\|x_n - x\| \to 0$ as $n \to \infty$.

A sequence $\{x_n\}$ of elements in an inner-product space is a Cauchy sequence if for all $\varepsilon > 0$, there exists $N > 0$ such that $\|x_n - x_m\| < \varepsilon$ for all $m, n > N$. A Hilbert space is an inner-product space which is complete, i.e., in which every Cauchy sequence $\{x_n\}$ converges in norm to some element of the space. Completeness of the Euclidean space follows from completeness of the real numbers.

We now define the space $L^2(\Omega, \mathcal{F}, P)$. Given a probability space $(\Omega, \mathcal{F}, P)$, consider the collection C of random variables X defined on Ω and satisfying the condition $EX^2 < \infty$. It is easily shown that C is a vector space over the reals. Defining

$$\langle X, Y \rangle = E(XY),$$

it can easily be verified that $\langle X, Y \rangle$ satisfies all of the properties on an inner product, provided that we treat two vectors X and Y as equivalent if $P(X = Y) = 1$. The space L^2, i.e., $L^2(\Omega, \mathcal{F}, P)$, is therefore a normed vector space. Note that norm convergence to $X \in L^2$ of a sequence $\{X_n\}$, where $X_n \in L^2$, means that $E|X_n - X|^2 \to 0$. This is identical to mean square convergence defined earlier, i.e., $X_n \overset{\text{m.s.}}{\to} X$. Finally, it can be shown that L^2 is complete and hence that L^2 is a Hilbert space. In consequence, a sequence $\{X_n\}$ in L^2 converges in mean square to some random variable $X \in L^2$ if and only if it satisfies the Cauchy criterion, i.e., if and only if $E|X_n - X_m|^2 \to 0$ as $m, n \to \infty$.

Returning now to the infinite sum (5.18), the sequence $S_n = \sum_{i=0}^n \phi^i \varepsilon_{t-i}$ satisfies $E(S_n - S_m)^2 = \sigma^2 \sum_{i=m+1}^n \phi^{2i}$, for $n > m$. Clearly, $E(S_n - S_m)^2 \to 0$ provided $|\phi| < 1$. Hence the Cauchy criterion is satisfied and the sum (5.18) converges in mean square if $|\phi| < 1$. It is then easily verified that $Y_t = \sum_{i=0}^\infty \phi^i \varepsilon_{t-i}$ is covariance stationary by direct computation of the first and second moments. Finally, it is easily seen that any other solution (5.19) to equation (5.17), with $c \neq 0$, is nonstationary. Hence when $|\phi| < 1$, there is a unique stationary solution to equation (5.17) given by equation (5.18).

If $|\phi| > 1$, then there is a unique stationary solution of the form $Y_t = -\sum_{i=1}^\infty \phi^{-i} \varepsilon_{t+i}$. This solution is not usually of interest since Y_t is correlated with future white noise shocks ε_{t+i}. Following the terminology of Brockwell and Davis (1991), we say that an ARMA(p, q) process is causal relative to $\{\varepsilon_t\}$ if there exists an absolutely summable sequence ψ_i such that

$$Y_t = \sum_{i=0}^\infty \psi_i \varepsilon_{t-i} \tag{5.20}$$

for $t = \ldots, -1, 0, 1, \ldots$. Here a sequence $\{\psi_i\}_{i=0}^\infty$ is said to be absolutely summable if $\sum_{i=0}^\infty |\psi_i| < \infty$. It can be shown that if $\{\psi_i\}_{i=0}^\infty$ is absolutely summable, then Y_t is stationary. Thus if $|\phi| > 1$, then there are no causal stationary solutions to equation (5.17). Note that the condition $|\phi| < 1$ is equivalent to the condition that the root (zero) ϕ^{-1} of $\phi(z) = 1 - \phi z$ has absolute value greater than 1.

We can now state the central result for ARMA processes (see Brockwell and Davis, 1991, Theorem 3.1.1).

Proposition 5.11. *Let $\{Y_t\}$ be an ARMA(p, q) process for which the polynomials $\phi(\cdot)$ and $\theta(\cdot)$ have no common zeros. Then Y_t is causal if and only if all roots of $\phi(\cdot)$ lie outside the unit circle. The coefficients $\{\psi_i\}$ of the solution (5.20) are* *determined by the relation*

$$\psi(z) = \sum_{i=0}^{\infty} \psi_i z^i = \theta(z)/\phi(z), \qquad |z| \le 1.$$

The process (5.20) is thus the unique stationary solution to equation (5.16) if all roots of $\phi(\cdot)$ lie outside the unit circle.

The stationary solution given in the proposition is often written as $Y_t = (\theta(L)/\phi(L))\varepsilon_t$.

Consider now the ARMA(p,q) process (5.16) for $t = 0, 1, 2, \ldots$, when there are given initial conditions $Y_{-1}, \ldots, Y_{-p}$. Again ε_t is a white noise process for $t = -q, -q+1, -q+2, \ldots$, and it is convenient to set $\varepsilon_t = 0$ for $t < -q$. By recursive substitution, it can be verified that there is a unique solution given the initial conditions.

As an illustration, consider the AR(1) case (5.17). By recursive substitution, we have the solution $Y_t = \sum_{i=0}^{t} \phi^i \varepsilon_{t-i} + \phi^t Y_{-1}$. If $|\phi| \ge 1$, this is a nonstationary and explosive process, e.g., in the sense that var$(Y_t) \to \infty$ as $t \to \infty$. If $|\phi| < 1$, the process is not covariance stationary but it is asymptotically covariance stationary, i.e., for each $k = 0, 1, 2, \ldots$, we have $EY_t \to 0$ and $\gamma_{kt} \to \gamma_k$ as $t \to \infty$. It can also be seen that Y_t converges in mean square to the process $\sum_{i=0}^{\infty} \phi^i \varepsilon_{t-i}$ as $t \to \infty$.

Suppose, as in Proposition 5.11, that $\{Y_t\}$ is an ARMA(p,q) process for which the polynomials $\phi(\cdot)$ and $\theta(\cdot)$ have no common zeros. Then a particular solution is given by $Y_t = (\theta(L)/\phi(L))\varepsilon_t$. [The polynomial $\theta(z)/\phi(z)$ is always well defined for $|z|$ sufficiently small and the sum $(\theta(L)/\phi(L))\varepsilon_t$ always converges since we have set $\varepsilon_t = 0$ for $t < -q$.] The roots of $\phi(z)$ are identical to the inverses of the roots $\lambda_1, \ldots, \lambda_p$ of the complementary polynomial $\lambda^p - \phi_1 \lambda^{p-1} - \phi_2 \lambda^{p-2} - \cdots - \phi_{p-1} \lambda - \phi_p = 0$. Assuming for simplicity that these roots are distinct, the general solution to equation (5.16) is given by

$$Y_t = \left(\theta(L)/\phi(L)\right)\varepsilon_t + k_1 \lambda_1^t + \cdots + k_p \lambda_p^t,$$

where the coefficients $k_1, \ldots, k_p$ are arbitrary. The unique solution to equation (5.16) given the initial conditions is obtained by choosing $k_1, \ldots, k_p$ to meet the given p initial conditions. If all roots of $\phi(\cdot)$ lie outside the unit circle, so that all roots $\lambda_1, \ldots, \lambda_p$ have modulus less than 1, then $Y_t \to (\theta(L)/\phi(L))\varepsilon_t$ in mean square as $t \to \infty$ and the solution is asymptotically covariance stationary. Often in problems with initial conditions, the solution is simply said to be "stationary" when what is meant is "asymptotically covariance stationary."

Consider now multivariate linear stochastic processes. An $n \times 1$ vector stochastic process ε_t is said to be a white noise process if $E\varepsilon_t = 0$, $E\varepsilon_t\varepsilon_s = 0$, for $t \neq s$, and $E\varepsilon_t\varepsilon_t' = \Sigma_\varepsilon$. A vector autoregression of order p, or VAR(p), is a multivariate stochastic process of the form

$$X_t = \Phi_1 X_{t-1} + \cdots + \Phi_p X_{t-p} + \varepsilon_t, \tag{5.21}$$

where ε_t is multivariate white noise. Here Φ_i, for $i = 1, \ldots, p$, are $n \times n$ matrices of constants. If $X_t - \mu$ is a VAR(p) process, then Y_t is said to be a VAR(p) process with mean μ. Using matrix lag polynomials, we can equivalently write equation (5.21) as

$$\Phi(L)X_t = \varepsilon_t, \quad \text{where } \Phi(z) = I - \Phi_1 z - \cdots - \Phi_p z^p,$$

for complex z. As with nonstochastic difference equations, X_t can be rewritten in first-order form

$$Y_t = AY_{t-1} + v_t, \tag{5.22}$$

for $t \in T$, where A is the companion matrix, i.e., the matrix (5.5) with B_i replaced by Φ_i, and where $Y_t' = (X_t', \ldots, X_{t-p+1}')$ and $v_t' = (\varepsilon_t', 0', \ldots 0')$. Here Y_t and v_t are $np \times 1$ and A is $np \times np$.

Suppose $T = \{\ldots, -1, 0, 1, \ldots\}$. Then from equation (5.22) there is a stationary solution $Y_t = \sum_{i=0}^{\infty} A^i \varepsilon_{t-i}$, provided all eigenvalues of A lie inside the unit circle, i.e., have modulus less than 1. Under these conditions the coefficients A^i are absolutely summable and the infinite sum converges in mean square. The stationary solution X_t to equation (5.21) is given by the first component of $Y_t = \sum_{i=0}^{\infty} A^i \varepsilon_{t-i}$. The stationary solution X_t can instead be written as $Y_t = \Phi^{-1}(L)\varepsilon_t$, where of course $\Phi^{-1}(z)$ is defined by the equation $\Phi^{-1}(z)\Phi(z) = I$. It can be shown that the eigenvalues of A are the inverses of the solutions to $\det \Phi(z) = 0$. We have the following result.

Proposition 5.12. *If all solutions to $\det \Phi(z) = 0$ lie outside the unit circle, then equation (5.21) has a unique stationary solution $X_t = \sum_{i=0}^{\infty} \Psi_i \varepsilon_{t-i}$, where the matrices Ψ_i are determined uniquely by $\Psi(z) \equiv \sum_{i=0}^{\infty} \Psi_i z^i = \Phi^{-1}(z)$, $|z| \leq 1$.*

This proposition is a special case of the extension to multivariate ARMA(p, q) processes. See Brockwell and Davis (1991, Chapter 11, Theorem 11.3.1).

If $T = \{0, 1, 2, \ldots\}$ and initial conditions $Y_{-1}, \ldots, Y_{-p}$ are specified, then there is a unique solution to equation (5.21) and, provided all solutions to $\det \Phi(z) = 0$ lie outside the unit circle, the solution is asymptotically covariance stationary.

5.5 Markov Processes

Markov processes form an important class of stochastic processes for many applications. We need some basic concepts and results for Markov processes in discrete time.

The characteristic feature of Markov processes is the notion that the influence of the past comes only through the current state. Thus the probabilities of the possible states of the process next period are a function of only the current state, and Markov processes are usually defined in terms of transition probabilities for moving from one state to another next period.

A transition function for a measurable space $(Z, \mathcal{Z})$ is a function $\Pi\colon Z \times \mathcal{Z} \to [0, 1]$ such that

(i) for each $z \in Z\colon$ $\Pi(z, \cdot)$ is a probability measure on $(Z, \mathcal{Z})$, and
(ii) for each $A \in \mathcal{Z}\colon$ $\Pi(\cdot, A)$ is a $\mathcal{Z}$-measurable function.

Transition functions are interpreted as the probabilities

$$\Pi(z, A) = \Pr\{z_{t+1} \in A \mid z_t = z\},$$

where z_t denotes the random state in period t.

We limit ourselves to the case where the transition probabilities are taken to be independent of time t, so that the transitions are stationary. It can be shown that, given a transition function on a measurable space $(Z, \mathcal{Z})$, there exists a stochastic process on the countable space $(Z^\infty, \mathcal{Z}^\infty)$, where $Z^\infty = Z \times Z \times \cdots$ and $\mathcal{Z}^\infty$ is the σ-algebra generated by the finite unions of finite rectangles of the form $A = A_1 \times A_2 \times \cdots \times A_T \times Z \times Z \times \cdots$.

Given a transition probability Π and a $\mathcal{Z}$-measurable function f, we define the Markov operator Tf associated with Π by the formula

$$(Tf)(z) = \int f(z')\Pi(z, dz'), \quad \text{for all } z \in Z.$$

$(Tf)(z)$ can be interpreted as the conditional expectation of f next period, given z as the current state of the process. It can be shown that operator T maps the space of bounded $\mathcal{Z}$-measurable functions into itself.

For a probability measure on $(Z, \mathcal{Z})$, we define the adjoint operator $T^*\lambda$ by

$$(T^*\lambda)(A) = \int \Pi(z, A)\lambda(dz), \quad \text{for all } A \in \mathcal{Z}.$$

$(T^*\lambda)(A)$ is the probability that the state in the next period lies in set A if the current state is drawn according to the probability measure λ. Operator T^* maps the space of probability measures on $(Z, \mathcal{Z})$ into itself. The connection between T and T^* is that for any bounded $\mathcal{Z}$-measurable function f, we have

$$\int (Tf)(z)\lambda(dz) = \int f(z')(T^*\lambda)(dz')$$

for all probability measures λ.

Example 1: Finite-state Markov chains are a special case of Markov processes. In this case the space Ω is a finite set, say $\{1, \ldots, S\}$, and the process moves between these states in accordance with probabilities $\pi_{ij} = \Pr\{z_{t+1} = j \mid z_t = i\}$. These probabilities form the transition matrix $P = (\pi_{ij})$.

Example 2: Stochastic difference equations of the form

$$z_{t+1} = g(z_t, w_{t+1}),$$

where w_{t+1} is a sequence of iid random shocks on a probability space $(W, \mathcal{W}, \mu)$ and $g\colon Z \times W \to Z$ is a given measurable function, define a transition function on Z by the formula $\Pi(z, A) = \mu([\Gamma(A)]_z)$. Here $\Gamma(A) = \{(z, w) \in Z \times W \mid g(z, w) \in A\}$ and $[C]_z$ denotes the z-section of a set C, i.e., $[C]_z = \{w \mid (z, w) \in C\}$.

If an initial probability measure λ_0 for the initial state of the process is given, the adjoint operator gives the probability measures for the subsequent states, i.e., $\lambda_t = T^*\lambda_{t-1}$. We need the concept of an invariant measure λ^* which has the property that the probabilities of the different states remain unchanged over time. It is given by the fixed point of T^*, that is, $\lambda^* = T^*\lambda^*$.

A variety of sufficient conditions for the existence of an invariant measure and for its uniqueness are available in the literature. The sense of convergence is important in the general case, and there exist results for both almost sure and weak convergence of Markov processes. The references at the end of the chapter may be consulted for details.

It can be shown that a finite Markov chain always has at least one invariant distribution. Here we develop the necessary concepts and conditions for the existence of a unique invariant measure only for the case of finite Markov chains introduced in Example 1 above.

We introduce several definitions. The n-step transition matrix is $P_n = (\pi_{ij}(n))$, where $\pi_{ij}(n) = \Pr(z_{t+n} = j \mid z_t = i)$. According to Chapman–Kolmogorov equations, $P_n = P^n$, the nth power of P. A state i of a Markov chain is transient if $\Pr(z_n = i$ for some $i \geq 1 \mid z_0 = i) < 1$. Otherwise, it is recurrent. Let $T_i = \min\{n \geq 1 \mid z_n = i\}$ and $m_i = E(T_i \mid z_0 = i)$. A recurrent state i is positive recurrent if $m_i < \infty$. The Markov chain is said to be recurrent if all states are positive recurrent.

A set C of states is irreducible if all $i, j \in C$ communicate, i.e., $\pi_{ij}(m) > 0$ for some $m \geq 0$. The Markov chain is said to be irreducible if the set of all states is irreducible. We also say that a state i of the Markov chain is periodic if the greatest common divisor of the set $\{n \mid \pi_{ii}(n) > 0\}$ is bigger than 1.[3] Otherwise, it is said to be aperiodic. The Markov chain is aperiodic if all its states have that property.

We will need the following result for the existence of a unique invariant distribution (see Grimmett and Stirzaker, 1992, theorems on p. 208 and p. 214).

Proposition 5.13. *A finite Markov chain has a unique invariant distribution if it is aperiodic, irreducible, and recurrent. The limits of the n-step transition probabilities are given* $\lim_{n\to\infty} \pi_{ij}(n) = m_j^{-1}$.

5.6   Ito Processes

Some concepts and results for stochastic differential equations are needed for the analysis of constant-gain algorithms and speed of convergence results in Chapter 7.

The basic building block for them is the Wiener process, which can heuristically be thought of as the limit of a discrete-time random walk in intervals.[4] Suppose that the random-walk process is observed at times $t, t + dt, t + 2dt, \ldots$

---

[3] Note that the set $\{n \mid \pi_{ii}(n) > 0\}$ consists of periods n in which the return to state i is possible.

[4] There exist several ways to construct the Wiener process rigorously; see the references at the end of the chapter.

and that it has unit variance over the interval $[t, t+1]$: Consider dt is sufficiently small, so that we can approximate $(dt)^2 = 0$. We write

$$W(t+dt) = W(t) + e(t+dt), \qquad e \overset{iid}{\sim} N(0, dt), \qquad W(0) = 0.$$

Introducing the notation

$$dW(t) \equiv W(t+dt) - W(t), \tag{5.23}$$

we have the limiting continuous-time process $W(t)$ which is called the Wiener process or the Brownian motion. Note that $dW(t)$ is approximately $Z(t)dt^{1/2}$, where $Z(t)$ is a standard normal variate. The rigorous representation of equation (5.23) is the integral form

$$W(t) = W(0) + \int_0^t dW(u). \tag{5.24}$$

This form can be obtained through a limiting operation from discrete time. One should view equation (5.23) as a convenient way of writing the precise expression (5.24).

The Wiener process is a Markov process in continuous time. It has independent increments and the changes of the process over finite intervals are normally distributed. In computations, the following properties are needed:

(i) $E[dW(t)] = 0$,
(ii) $E[dW(t)\,dt] = E[dW(t)]\,dt = 0$,
(iii) $E[dW(t)^2] = dt$.

These follow since the increments dW are iid zero mean random variables with instantaneous variance equal to dt. From these three properties one also has the results $\mathrm{Var}[dW(t)^2] = 0$, $E[(dW(t)\,dt)^2] = 0$, and $\mathrm{Var}[dW(t)\,dt] = 0$, which provide the important multiplication rules

(iv) $dW^2 = dt$,
(v) $dW\,dt = 0$,
(vi) $dt^2 = 0$.

The Wiener process or Brownian motion is continuous in t, but it is nowhere differentiable in t. It is of unbounded variation but bounded in quadratic variation. The distribution of $W(u)$ given $W(t)$, $t < u$, is normal with mean $W(t)$ and variance $(u - t)$.

Quite general continuous-time stochastic processes can be constructed from the Brownian motion. If we allow for generalized drift and heteroscedasticity in the discrete-time random walk, we have the model

$$X(t+1) = X(t) + \alpha(X(t),t) + \sigma(X(t),t)e(t+1),$$
$$X(0) = X_0, e \overset{\text{iid}}{\sim} N(0,1).$$

This has a continuous-time limit of the form

$$dX = \alpha(X,t)\,dt + \sigma(X,t)\,dW, \qquad X(0) = X_0, \qquad (5.25)$$

which is called an Ito process. The mean and variance of the increments are $E(dX) = \alpha(X,t)\,dt$ and $\text{var}(dX) = (\sigma(X,t))^2\,dt$.

Equation (5.25) is a convenient way of writing the integral expression

$$X(t) = X_0 + \int_0^t \alpha(X(s),s)\,ds + \int_0^t \sigma(X(s),s)\,dW(s). \qquad (5.26)$$

Under suitable regularity assumptions the first integral in equation (5.26) has a standard interpretation, while the second one is a stochastic integral whose precise definition and existence requires a lengthy exposition in a rigorous treatment and will be omitted (see the references at the end of the chapter).

The following examples illustrate equation (5.25).

Example 3: Let $dX = \alpha\,dt + \sigma\,dW$, where α and σ are constant. The increment dX has mean $\alpha\,dt$ and variance $\sigma^2\,dt$. This case is known as the *arithmetic Brownian motion*. α is called the drift and σ is called volatility of the process. This process has the following properties: (i) X may be positive or negative, (ii) the distribution of $X(u)$ given $X(t)$, $t < u$, is normal with mean $X(t) + \alpha(u-t)$ and variance $\sigma^2(u-t)$.

Example 4: Let $dX = \alpha X\,dt + \sigma X\,dW$, where α and σ are constant. This process is known as the *geometric Brownian motion*. It has the following properties: (i) if $X(0) > 0$, the process will remain positive; (ii) X has an absorbing barrier at 0: if $X(t)$ hits zero for some t (which is a zero-probability event), then X will remain at 0, (iii) the conditional distribution of $X(u)$, given $X(t)$, $t < u$, is log-normal. Thus $\ln X(u)$ has the conditional mean $\ln(X(t)) + \alpha(u-t) - \frac{1}{2}\sigma^2(u-t)$ and conditional variance $\sigma^2(u-t)$.

5.6.1 Ito's Lemma

We consider a twice continuously differentiable function $f = f(X, t)$ and expand it using Taylor series. If X is an Ito process, we need to take into consideration the second-order term, since dX is a random variable with a positive variance. Thus we have[5]

$$df = f_X \, dX + f_t \, dt + \frac{1}{2} \left[f_{XX} \, dX^2 + 2 f_{Xt} \, dX \, dt + f_{tt} \, dt^2 \right]$$
$$= f_X \, dX + f_t \, dt + \frac{1}{2} f_{XX} \, dt$$

by the above multiplication rules for differentials. Substituting in $dX = \alpha \, dt + \sigma \, dW$ yields

$$df = \left[\alpha f_X + f_t + \frac{1}{2} f_{XX} \right] dt + \sigma f_X \, dW, \qquad (5.27)$$

which is (one-dimensional) Ito's lemma.[6] This result says that if $X(t)$ is an Ito process, then $f(X, t)$ is also an Ito process with differential (5.27).

Suppose that we have two Ito processes

$$dX = \alpha(X, y, t) \, dt + \sigma(X, Y, t) \, dW,$$
$$dY = \beta(X, Y, t) \, dt + v(X, Y, t) \, dZ,$$

where dW and dZ are standard Brownian motions with correlation $dW \, dZ = \rho \, dt$. We consider the differential of the function $f(X, Y, t)$:

$$df = f_X \, dX + f_Y \, dY + f_t \, dt$$
$$+ \frac{1}{2} \left[f_{XX} \, dX^2 + 2 f_{XY} \, dX \, dY + f_{YY} \, dY^2 \right].$$

Since $dX^2 = \sigma^2 \, dt$, $dY^2 = v^2 \, dt$, $dX \, dY = \rho \sigma v \, dt$, we obtain the bivariate Ito's lemma

$$df = \left[\alpha f_X + \beta f_Y + f_t + \frac{1}{2} \sigma^2 f_{XX} + \rho v \sigma f_{XY} + \frac{1}{2} v^2 f_{YY} \right] dt$$
$$+ \sigma f_X \, dW + v f_Y \, dZ.$$

---

[5]The subscripts refer to partial derivatives, e.g., $f_X = \partial f / \partial X$.
[6]Note that α and σ are in general functions of X and t.

In the general n-dimensional case we consider the system

$$dy = g(y,t)\,dt + dv$$
$$= g(y,t)\,dt + S(y,t)\,dz,$$

where dv has the covariance matrix $\Sigma(y,t)\,dt$ and dz is a multidimensional Brownian motion with $\mathrm{cov}(dz) = R\,dt$, so that $SRS' = \Sigma$. We compute the differential of $f(y,t)$, so that

$$df = \left[f_t + f_y g + \frac{1}{2}\,\mathrm{tr}(f_{yy}\Sigma) \right] dt + f_y\,dv,$$

where f_y is the n-vector of partial derivatives of f with respect to y, f_{yy} is the $n \times n$ matrix of second partials, and $\mathrm{tr}\,A$ denotes the trace of matrix A. This is the n-dimensional Ito's lemma. The term

$$E(df) = \left[f_t + f_y g + \frac{1}{2}\,\mathrm{tr}(f_{yy}\Sigma) \right] dt$$

is the generalized drift of the Ito process $f(y(t),t)$, and the term

$$\mathrm{var}(df) = (f_y)'\Sigma f_y$$

is its volatility.

5.6.2   Stochastic Differential Equations

Equation (5.25) can be thought of as a stochastic differential equation when the object is to find explicitly the process satisfying that equation. The initial condition X_0 may be random here.

By a solution to equation (5.25) we mean a stochastic process $X(t)$ on an interval $[0, T]$ such that (i) $X(t)$ satisfies equation (5.26) a.s. on $[0, T]$, (ii) $X(0) = X_0$ a.s.; (iii) $\int_0^T \{|\alpha(X(t),t)| + (\sigma(X(t),t))^2\}\,dt < \infty$ a.s. on $[0, T]$; and (iv) $X(t)$ has certain measurability properties with respect to the sequence of σ-algebras $\mathcal{F}_t$, where $\mathcal{F}_t$ is the smallest σ-algebra such that the variables X_0 and $W(s)$, $s \leq t$, are measurable.

The conditions for the existence and uniqueness of the solution are available in the literature; see, e.g., Karatzas and Shreve (1988, Chapter 5). In this book we need to consider linear equations with time-varying coefficients of the form[7]

$$dX(t) = A(t)X(t)\,dt + B(t)\,dW(t), \qquad X(0) = \xi.$$

---

[7]The discussion is based on Karatzas and Shreve (1988, Chapter 5, Section 6).

Defining $m(t) = EX(t)$, $\rho(s,t) = E[(X(s) - m(s))(X(t) - m(t))']$, and $V(t) = \rho(t,t)$, we have

$$m(t) = \Phi(t)m(0),$$

$$\rho(s,t) = \Phi(s)\left[V(0) + \int_0^{\min(s,t)} \Phi^{-1}(u)B(u)\left(\Phi^{-1}(u)B(u)\right)' du\right]\Phi(t)',$$

$$\frac{dV(t)}{dt} = A(t)V(t) + V(t)A(t)' + B(t)B(t)',$$

where $\Phi(t)$ is a nonsingular matrix solution of the ordinary differential equation $d\zeta/dt = A(t)\zeta(t)$. $\Phi(t)$ is called a fundamental matrix solution (see Brock and Malliaris, 1989, Chapter 2.3 for discussion).

In the case of constant matrices A and B, and provided all the eigenvalues of A have negative real parts, there exists a stationary Gaussian solution with mean zero and covariance function

$$\rho(s,t) = e^{(s-t)A}V \quad \text{for } s \geq t,$$

where

$$V = \int_0^\infty e^{sA}BB'e^{sA'} ds.$$

One can also obtain V from the equation

$$AV + VA' = -BB'.$$

5.7 Appendix on Matrix Algebra

Here we provide some basic matrix algebra definitions, together with several specialized results which will be useful for analyzing matrix differential equations.

Suppose A is an $m \times m$ matrix A. If $Ax = \lambda x$ for an $m \times 1$ (possibly complex) vector $x \neq 0$ and a (possibly complex) number λ, then λ is said to be an eigenvalue or root of A and x is a corresponding eigenvector. The following results should be noted: (i) A is singular if and only if it has a zero eigenvalue. (ii) If A is nonsingular and has eigenvalue λ, then A^{-1} has eigenvalue λ^{-1}. This follows since $Ax = \lambda x$ implies $A^{-1}x = \lambda^{-1}x$. (iii) A real symmetric matrix has only real eigenvalues. (iv) A symmetric matrix A is said to be positive definite (positive semidefinite) if $x'Ax > 0 (\geq 0)$ for all $x \neq 0$. A is positive definite (positive semidefinite) if and only if all its eigenvalues are positive (nonnegative). Similarly, A is said to be negative definite (negative semidefinite) if $x'Ax < 0 (\leq 0)$ for all $x \neq 0$. A is negative definite (negative semidefinite) if and only if all its eigenvalues are negative (nonpositive). A is positive (semi)definite if and only if $-A$ is negative (semi)definite. (v) A matrix of the form $A = BB'$ or $A = B'B$ is positive semidefinite and it is positive definite if it is nonsingular.

A has m eigenvalues, though these may include repeated roots. If A has m distinct eigenvalues $\lambda_1, \ldots, \lambda_m$, then the corresponding eigenvectors $x_1 \ldots, x_m$ are linearly independent. It follows that $AQ = Q\Lambda$, where $\Lambda = \text{diag}(\lambda_1, \ldots, \lambda_m)$, i.e., the $m \times m$ diagonal matrix with elements $\lambda_1, \ldots, \lambda_m$ on the diagonal, and Q is the $m \times m$ matrix $Q = (x_1, \ldots, x_m)$ formed from the corresponding eigenvectors. Since Q is nonsingular, we obtain the diagonalization $A = Q\Lambda Q^{-1}$.

If the eigenvalues of A are not distinct, then it may or may not be possible to diagonalize A. If not, however, there always exists a similar decomposition known as the Jordan decomposition. This takes the form $A = MJM^{-1}$, where J is an $m \times m$ block diagonal matrix $J = \text{diag}(J_1, \ldots, J_s)$ and the Jordan blocks $J_i, i = 1, \ldots, s$, take the form

$$J_i = \begin{pmatrix} \lambda_i & 1 & 0 & \cdots & 0 \\ 0 & \lambda_i & 1 & \cdots & 0 \\ 0 & 0 & \lambda_i & \cdots & 0 \\ \vdots & \vdots & \vdots & & \vdots \\ 0 & 0 & 0 & \cdots & \lambda_i \end{pmatrix}.$$

If A is $m \times n$ and B is $p \times q$, then the Kronecker product of $A = (a_{ij})$ and B is the $mp \times nq$ matrix

$$A \otimes B = \begin{pmatrix} a_{11}B & a_{12}B & \cdots & a_{1n}B \\ a_{21}B & a_{22}B & \cdots & a_{2n}B \\ \vdots & \vdots & & \vdots \\ a_{m1}B & a_{m2}B & \cdots & a_{mn}B \end{pmatrix}.$$

(Here a_{ij} denotes the entry of A in row i and column j.) Suppose that A is $m \times m$ and B is $p \times p$. It is straightforward to show that the mn eigenvalues of $A \otimes B$ are given by the products of the $\lambda_i \mu_j$ of the eigenvalues λ_i of A with the eigenvalues μ_j of B, $i = 1, \ldots, m$, $j = 1, \ldots, p$.

A square matrix $A = (a_{ij})$ is said to be upper triangular if $a_{ij} = 0$ whenever $j < i$ and lower triangular if $a_{ij} = 0$ whenever $i < j$. We say that A is triangular if it is either upper or lower triangular. Using the fact that λ is an eigenvalue of A if and only if $\det(A - \lambda I) = 0$, it follows that the eigenvalues of a triangular matrix are its diagonal elements. If A is a block triangular matrix $A = \begin{pmatrix} A_{11} & A_{12} \\ 0 & A_{22} \end{pmatrix}$, then the eigenvalues of A are the eigenvalues of A_{11} together with the eigenvalues of A_{22}.

Another important result that we will need is that the eigenvalues of a (square) matrix $A = (a_{ij})$ depend continuously on its entries a_{ij}. This follows from the fact that the zeros of a polynomial depend continuously on its coefficients. See Horn and Johnson (1985, Appendix D).

If $f(x)$: $\mathbb{R}^n \to \mathbb{R}$ is a real valued function, then its derivative is the $1 \times n$ vector $\partial f / \partial x' = (\partial f / \partial x_1, \dots, \partial f / \partial x_n)$. The derivative will also be denoted $D_x f$ or Df. Other notations also appear in the literature, and the term gradient is frequently used to denote the corresponding column vector. It is easily verified that

$$\frac{\partial(a'x)}{\partial x'} = a' \quad \text{and} \quad \frac{\partial(x'Ax)}{\partial x'} = x'(A + A'),$$

where a is $n \times 1$ and A is $n \times n$.

If A is the $m \times n$ matrix $A = (a_1, \dots, a_n)$, where a_i, $i = 1, \dots, n$, is an $m \times 1$ vector giving column i of A, then $\text{vec}(A)$ is the $mn \times 1$ vector

$$\text{vec}(A) = \begin{pmatrix} a_1 \\ a_2 \\ \vdots \\ a_m \end{pmatrix}.$$

It can be shown that if A, B, C are matrices such that the product ABC is conformable, then

$$\text{vec}(ABC) = (C' \otimes A) \cdot \text{vec}(B).$$

For this and related results, see Magnus and Neudecker (1988, Chapter 2).

If $f(x)$: $\mathbb{R}^n \to \mathbb{R}^m$ is a vector valued function, then its derivative, or Jacobian matrix, $\partial f / \partial x'$ is the $m \times n$ matrix of partial derivatives, with (i, j) element $\partial f_i / \partial x_j$. We also use the notation Df or $Df(x)$ for the Jacobian matrix. If $f(x) = Ax$, then $Df = A$.

We will encounter matrix differential equations of the form

$$\frac{dX}{dt} = f(X),$$

where X is an $m \times n$ matrix and f is a mapping from the set of $m \times n$ matrices into itself. An equilibrium is a value $\bar{X}$ such that $f(\bar{X}) = 0$. Since X can be regarded as an $mn \times 1$ vector and $f(X)$ can be regarded as a matrix of functions, the matrix differential equation can be vectorized and put into standard form (5.14), $d(\text{vec }X)/dt = \text{vec }f(X)$. Local stability at $\bar{X}$ is then determined using Proposition 5.6, i.e., by checking the roots of the Jacobian $Df = \partial \text{ vec } f(\bar{X})/\partial \text{ vec } X'$ of this vectorized differential equation.

To assess local stability of equilibria of matrix differential equations, one can make use of rules for computing matrix differentials which preserve the information embedded in the matrix structure. The following rules are particularly useful. Let dX stand for the differential of matrix X and dy stand for the differential of the vector y. Then for fixed matrices A and B,

$$d(AYB) = A(dY)B,$$
$$d \text{ vec } y = \text{ vec } dy \quad \text{and} \quad d(\text{vec }X) = \text{vec } dX,$$
$$d(AX + B) = A(dX),$$
$$d(AX^2) = A((dX)X + X\,dX),$$

provided the products are conformable. The Jacobian can be computed using such rules for differentials and the identification rule that if $d(\text{vec } f) = J d(\text{vec } X)$, then the Jacobian $Df = J$. For additional results and discussion, see Magnus and Neudecker (1988, Chapters 8 and 9).

As an example, suppose $f(X) = AX^2$. Then $df = A(dX)X + AX(dX)I$ so that, using the rule for $\text{vec}(ABC)$, we obtain $d \text{ vec } f = ((X' \otimes A) + (I \otimes AX))d \text{ vec } X$. Hence the Jacobian of the map $\text{vec } f(X)$ is $Df = (X' \otimes A) + (I \otimes AX)$.

A further useful result on matrix differentials is the differential of the matrix inverse function. Suppose F is a continuously differentiable map from an open subset of real $p \times q$ matrices into the set of nonsingular $n \times n$ matrices. Then $F^{-1}(X) \equiv (F(X))^{-1}$ is continuously differentiable and its differential is given by

$$dF^{-1} = -F^{-1}(dF)F^{-1}.$$

5.8   References for Mathematical Background

A very basic introduction to difference and differential equations is provided in Chiang (1984). A more advanced treatment of difference equations, with numerous economic examples, is provided in Azariadis (1993). A compact statement of the stability results for difference equations is given in Stokey and Lucas Jr. (1989, Section 6.3). An authoritative mathematical reference on difference equations is LaSalle (1992). There are a number of excellent references for ordinary differential equations, e.g., Coddington (1961), Hirsch and Smale (1974), Brock and Malliaris (1989), and Guckenheimer and Holmes (1983). Lyapunov's method for stability analysis, including the converse theorems, is discussed in Hahn (1963) and Hahn (1967), in addition to Krasovskii (1963).

Treatments of measure and probability are provided in Billingsley (1986), Kingman and Taylor (1973), Neveu (1965), or Stokey and Lucas Jr. (1989, Chapters 7 and 8). For linear stochastic processes, a good introduction is given in Hamilton (1994) and a more advanced treatment is provided in Brockwell and Davis (1991). Stochastic convergence theory is treated in Davidson (1994) and White (1984). Markov processes are extensively treated in many books on stochastic processes; see, e.g., Doob (1953, Chapter 5), or Neveu (1965, Chapter 5), for good rigorous treatments. The presentations in Stokey and Lucas Jr. (1989, Chapters 8, 11, and 12) and in Futia (1982) are geared towards economics. Grimmett and Stirzaker (1992, Chapter 6) contains a readable discussion of the basic concepts and results for finite Markov chains. A good presentation of Ito processes and stochastic differential equations is given in Øksendal (1998). An advanced treatment is given in Karatzas and Shreve (1988).

Good references for matrix algebra are Horn and Johnson (1985), Horn and Johnson (1991), and Hirsch and Smale (1974). For the results on matrix differential calculus see Magnus and Neudecker (1988).

Chapter **6**

Tools: Stochastic Approximation

6.1 Introduction

In Chapter 2 we analyzed in detail the cobweb model and showed how the analysis of least squares learning in that model formally leads to a stochastic recursive algorithm (SRA). Mathematically, such algorithms are dynamical systems consisting of two parts: (i) dynamics for estimating a vector of parameters, and (ii) dynamics for a vector of state variables. These are nonlinear stochastic systems operating in discrete time, but it turns out that their convergence can be studied by using the so-called ordinary differential equation (ODE) approach. The study of the convergence of adaptive learning behavior in macroeconomic models can generally be conducted by means of these systems.

In this chapter our aim is to provide the basic technical tools from the theory of recursive stochastic algorithms, also known as stochastic approximation, in applied mathematics. We provide here rigorous statements of the relevant results, so this chapter can be used as a systematic reference in further economic models. We also give some illustrations of how the application can be accomplished. It should be noted that we will not provide detailed proofs in our treatment. However, the main steps of the arguments will be presented, so that the reader can see the basis for the ordinary differential equation approach to the analysis of stochastic recursive algorithms. We wish to warn the reader that this chapter and the next one are more technical than the rest of the book. Their detailed reading requires some familiarity with advanced probability theory and differential equations. Chapter 5 provides a summary of the necessary background.

Before going to the general analysis, here is an example which studies prediction by means of an instrument variable.

Example 1: **Prediction Using an Instrument Variable.** Consider a simple linear model

$$y_t = \alpha y_t^e + u_t,$$

where y_t is a scalar variable, y_t^e is its (in general nonrational) expectation, and u_t is a disturbance term with $Eu_t = 0$. Suppose that agents cannot directly observe y_t or u_t but instead try to predict y_t using an instrument x_t, assumed to be a scalar for simplicity. We assume that the bivariate process x_t, u_t is identically and independently distributed over time, but that x_t and u_t are correlated with covariance $Ex_t u_t = \sigma_{xu}$. For convenience we also assume that $Ex_t = 0$ and we write $Ex_t^2 = \sigma_x^2$. The prediction rule agents use is

$$y_t^e = x_t a_t,$$

where a_t is formulated using ordinary least squares:

$$a_t = \left[\sum_{i=1}^{t-1} x_i^2 \right]^{-1} \left[\sum_{i=1}^{t-1} x_i y_i \right].$$

Adopting the notation

$$R_{t-1} = \frac{1}{t-1} \sum_{i=1}^{t-1} x_i^2,$$

we have the recursion

$$R_t = R_{t-1} + \frac{1}{t} (x_t^2 - R_{t-1}). \tag{6.1}$$

Note that, if agents use the prediction rule above, the actual value of y_t is given by

$$y_t = \alpha a_t x_t + u_t.$$

For a_t one can compute

$$
\begin{aligned}
a_t &= a_{t-1} + \left[(t-1) R_{t-1} \right]^{-1} \left\{ x_{t-1} y_{t-1} + \left[(t-2) R_{t-2} \right] a_{t-1} \right\} - a_{t-1} \\
&= a_{t-1} + \left[(t-1) R_{t-1} \right]^{-1} \left\{ x_{t-1} y_{t-1} + \left[(t-2) R_{t-2} - (t-1) R_{t-1} \right] a_{t-1} \right\} \\
&= a_{t-1} + \left[(t-1) R_{t-1} \right]^{-1} \left[x_{t-1} (\alpha a_{t-1} x_{t-1} + u_{t-1}) - x_{t-1}^2 a_{t-1} \right],
\end{aligned}
$$

so that

$$a_t = a_{t-1} + \left[(t-1)R_{t-1}\right]^{-1}\left[(\alpha a_{t-1} - a_{t-1})x_{t-1}^2 + x_{t-1}u_{t-1}\right]. \qquad (6.2)$$

To analyze the properties of learning models one studies the system describing the estimation of the parameters, consisting here of equations (6.1) and (6.2) for R_t and a_t. The system for state variables here is simple in this example: It is given by the exogenous processes x_t and u_t.

6.2 Stochastic Recursive Algorithms

6.2.1 General Setup and Assumptions

We now start to discuss in general terms the stochastic recursive algorithms which are the basic tool in the study of models of adaptive learning. The general form of these algorithms is laid out as follows.

Let $\theta_t \in \mathbb{R}^d$ be a vector of parameters. The evolution of its values is described in general form by the difference equation

$$\theta_t = \theta_{t-1} + \gamma_t \mathcal{H}(\theta_{t-1}, X_t) + \gamma_t^2 \rho_t(\theta_{t-1}, X_t). \qquad (6.3)$$

Here γ_t is a sequence of "gains," often something like $\gamma_t = t^{-1}$. $X_t \in \mathbb{R}^k$ is the vector of observable state variables. $\mathcal{H}(\cdot)$ and $\rho_t(\cdot)$ are two functions describing how the vector θ is updated (the second-order term $\rho_t(\cdot)$ is often not present). We remark that in the notation of Chapter 2, equation (2.13), $Q(t, \theta_{t-1}, X_t) = \mathcal{H}(\theta_{t-1}, X_t) + \gamma_t \rho_t(\theta_{t-1}, X_t)$. Both forms appear in the literature and at times it will be convenient for us to revert to the $Q(t, \theta_{t-1}, X_t)$ notation.

In economic models this system is usually the learning rule. In the preceding example, equations (6.1) and (6.2) are the two components of the parameter adjustment equation (6.3).

Next, we come to the dynamics for the vector of state variables. In most (though not all) economic models we can take the state dynamics to be conditionally linear, and we postulate here:

$$X_t = A(\theta_{t-1})X_{t-1} + B(\theta_{t-1})W_t, \qquad (6.4)$$

where W_t is a random disturbance term (with the properties specified later).[1] Without going into details, we note here that it is possible to consider situations

---

[1] Some expositions use an alternative but equivalent timing in which W_t is replaced by W_{t-1}.

where X_t follows a Markov process dependent on θ_{t-1}. This is needed in some applications and the modifications to the analysis will be described in Chapter 7. In the preceding example, equation (6.4) is just the law of the stochastic process for the state variable $X'_t = (x_t, x_{t-1}, u_{t-1})$.

For the precise mathematical analysis it is necessary to formulate the assumptions on the learning rule (6.3) and the state dynamics (6.4). We start with the former.

In local convergence analysis one fixes an open set $D \subset \mathbb{R}^d$ around the equilibrium point of interest. Then postulate the following:

(A.1) γ_t is a positive, nonstochastic, nonincreasing sequence satisfying

$$\sum_{t=1}^{\infty} \gamma_t = \infty \quad \text{and} \quad \sum_{t=1}^{\infty} \gamma_t^2 < \infty.$$

(A.2) For any compact $Q \subset D$, there exist C_1, C_2, q_1, and q_2 such that $\forall \theta \in Q$ and $\forall t$:

    (i) $|\mathcal{H}(\theta, x)| \le C_1(1 + |x|^{q_1})$,
    (ii) $|\rho_t(\theta, x)| \le C_2(1 + |x|^{q_2})$.

(A.3) For any compact $Q \subset D$, the function $\mathcal{H}(\theta, x)$ satisfies, $\forall \theta, \theta' \in Q$ and $x_1, x_2 \in \mathbb{R}^k$:

    (i) $|\partial \mathcal{H}(\theta, x_1)/\partial x - \partial \mathcal{H}(\theta, x_2)/\partial x| \le L_1|x_1 - x_2|$,
    (ii) $|\mathcal{H}(\theta, 0) - \mathcal{H}(\theta', 0)| \le L_2|\theta - \theta'|$,
    (iii) $|\partial \mathcal{H}(\theta, x)/\partial x - \partial \mathcal{H}(\theta', x)/\partial x| \le L_2|\theta - \theta'|$,
    for some constants L_1, L_2.

Note that Assumption (A.1) is clearly satisfied for $\gamma_t = K/t$, K constant. The assumption $\sum_{t=1}^{\infty} \gamma_t = \infty$ is required to avoid convergence of θ_t to a nonequilibrium point, and the assumption $\sum_{t=1}^{\infty} \gamma_t^2 < \infty$ ensures asymptotic elimination of residual fluctuations in θ_t. This last assumption can be weakened to $\sum_{t=1}^{\infty} \gamma_t^{\alpha} < \infty$ for some $\alpha \ge 2$ by strengthening other assumptions. For example, see Ljung (1977) and Benveniste, Metivier, and Priouret (1990, Part II, Chapter 3). We present some results under this assumption in Section 7.3 of Chapter 7.

Assumption (A.2) imposes polynomial bounds on $\mathcal{H}(\cdot)$ and $\rho_t(\cdot)$. Assumption (A.3) holds provided $\mathcal{H}(\theta, x)$ is twice continuously differentiable with bounded second derivatives on every Q. This follows from Coddington (1961,

Chapter 6, Theorem 1):if a function is continuously differentiable with bounded partial derivatives, then the function satisfies a Lipschitz condition with the constant given by the bound on the partial derivatives. Assumption (A.3) can be weakened as indicated by the following remark.

Remark. Assumption (A.3) (i) can be replaced by

$$\left|\partial\mathcal{H}(\theta, x_1)/\partial x - \partial\mathcal{H}(\theta, x_2)/\partial x\right|$$
$$\leq L_1\left|x_1 - x_2\right|\left(1 + |x_1|^{p_1} + |x_2|^{p_1}\right) \quad \text{for some } p_1 \geq 0,$$

and Assumption (A.3) (iii) can be replaced by

$$\left|\partial\mathcal{H}(\theta, x)/\partial x - \partial\mathcal{H}(\theta', x)/\partial x\right|$$
$$\leq L_2|\theta - \theta'|\left(1 + |x|^{p_2}\right) \quad \text{for some } p_2 \geq 0,$$

as shown in Benveniste, Metivier, and Priouret (1990, Theorem 6, p. 262).

For the state dynamics we make the assumptions:

(B.1) W_t is iid with finite absolute moments.

(B.2) For any compact subset $Q \subset D$:

$$\sup_{\theta\in Q} |B(\theta)| \leq M \quad \text{and} \quad \sup_{\theta\in Q} |A(\theta)| \leq \rho < 1,$$

for some matrix norm $|\cdot|$, and $A(\theta)$ and $B(\theta)$ satisfy Lipschitz conditions on Q.

We remark here that in Assumption (B.2) the condition on $A(\theta)$ is a little bit stronger than (asymptotic) stationarity. However, if at some point θ^* the spectral radius (the maximum modulus of eigenvalues) satisfies $r(A(\theta^*)) < 1$, then the condition on $A(\theta)$ in Assumption (B.2) holds in a neighborhood of θ^*.

These are quite general assumptions. In specific models the situation may be a great deal simpler. In some cases, for example, the state dynamics X_t do not depend on the parameter vector θ_{t-1}. An illustration of the independent case is provided by our introductory example above. Another classical special case, first discussed by Robbins and Monro (1951), arises when the distribution of the state variable X_{t+1} can depend on θ_t but is otherwise independent of the history $X_t, X_{t-1}, \ldots, \theta_t, \theta_{t-1}, \ldots$.

As already pointed out, the recursive algorithm consisting of the equations (6.3) and (6.4) for θ_t and X_t, respectively, is a nonlinear, time-varying

stochastic difference scheme. At first sight one might think that the properties of such systems are hard to analyze. It turns out that, due to the special
structure of the equation for the parameter vector, the system can be studied in
terms of an associated ordinary differential equation which is derived as follows:

(i) fix θ and define the corresponding state dynamics

$$\bar{X}_t(\theta) = A(\theta)\bar{X}_{t-1}(\theta) + B(\theta)W_t,$$

(ii) consider the asymptotic behavior of the mean of $\mathcal{H}(\theta, \bar{X}_t(\theta))$, i.e.,

$$h(\theta) = \lim_{t\to\infty} E\mathcal{H}(\theta, \bar{X}_t(\theta)).$$

The *associated ordinary differential equation* (ODE) is then defined as

$$\frac{d\theta}{d\tau} = h(\theta). \tag{6.5}$$

Given Assumptions (A.1)–(A.3) and (B.1)–(B.2), it can be shown that the
function $h(\theta)$ is well defined and locally Lipschitz (see below).

As noted in the introductory discussion of Chapter 2, the essence of the
ODE approach is the result that the locally stable equilibrium points of the associated differential equation are the possible convergence points of the recursive
algorithm.

Example 1 (**Continued**): Continuing with the introductory example of Section 6.1, we first show how to put equations (6.1) and (6.2) into the standard form
(6.3). Here $\theta_t = (a_t, R_t)'$, $\gamma_t = t^{-1}$, and the state vector is $X_t = (x_t, x_{t-1}, u_{t-1})'$
with $W_t = (x_t, u_{t-1})'$. From equation (6.1), the R component of $\mathcal{H}(\theta_{t-1}, X_t)$ is
simply $x_t^2 - R_{t-1}$. The a component of $\mathcal{H}$ and ρ_t can be obtained by rewriting
equation (6.2) as

$$a_t = a_{t-1} + t^{-1}R_{t-1}^{-1}\big[(\alpha-1)a_{t-1}x_{t-1}^2 + x_{t-1}u_{t-1}\big]$$

$$+ t^{-2}\frac{t}{t-1}R_{t-1}^{-1}\big[(\alpha-1)a_{t-1}x_{t-1}^2 + x_{t-1}u_{t-1}\big].$$

We will restrict R_t to positive values, so that the domain for (a_t, R_t) is $D = \mathbb{R} \times (R_L, \infty)$, where R_L is an arbitrarily small positive value. This is natural since R_t is the second sample moment of x_t. The equation for the state vector X_t is

$$X_t = \begin{pmatrix} 0 & 0 & 0 \\ 1 & 0 & 0 \\ 0 & 0 & 0 \end{pmatrix} X_{t-1} + \begin{pmatrix} 1 & 0 \\ 0 & 0 \\ 0 & 1 \end{pmatrix} W_t.$$

The associated differential equation is as follows. Writing $\theta = (a, R)$, the differential equation is simply given by

$$\frac{da}{d\tau} = R^{-1}[(\alpha - 1)a\sigma_x^2 + \sigma_{xu}], \qquad (6.6)$$

$$\frac{dR}{d\tau} = \sigma_x^2 - R.$$

We will conclude discussion of this example after presentation of the main convergence theorems.

6.2.2 Convergence: A Heuristic Discussion

Above, we formulated the general recursive algorithm and derived its associated differential equation. The general idea in the study of (local) convergence of the algorithm will be that, at specific points of time, the trajectories of the differential equation approximate better and better the (discrete-time) trajectories of the algorithm as time gets large. Let us see in heuristic terms why this phenomenon holds.

For the sake of exposition suppose that the gain sequence γ_t is a small constant γ. We can then derive the approximation

$$\theta_{n+N} = \theta_n + \gamma \sum_{i=0}^{N-1} \left[\mathcal{H}(\theta_{n+i}, X_{n+1+i}) + \gamma \rho_{n+1+i}(\theta_{n+i}, X_{n+1+i}) \right]$$

$$\approx \theta_n + \gamma \sum_{i=0}^{N-1} \mathcal{H}(\theta_{n+i}, X_{n+1+i})$$

(since γ is small)

$$\approx \theta_n + \gamma \sum_{i=0}^{N-1} \mathcal{H}(\theta_n, X_{n+1+i})$$

(N is not large and/or γ is very small, so that θ_n does not move much)

$$= \theta_n + (N\gamma)\frac{1}{N}\sum_{i=0}^{N-1}\mathcal{H}(\theta_n, X_{n+1+i})$$

$$\approx \theta_n + N\gamma h(\theta_n)$$

(by the law of large numbers).

This reasoning shows that we are basically close to a standard discretization of an ODE of the form

$$\theta_{n+1} = \theta_n + \gamma h(\theta_n) + \text{perturbation}.$$

This means that $\theta_n \approx \theta(t_n)$, where $\theta(t)$ denotes a trajectory of the ODE and $t_n = n\gamma$. If a small decreasing step size (gain) is used, one has $\theta_n \approx \theta(t_n)$ with $t_n = \sum_{i=1}^{n}\gamma_i$.

The body of the rigorous proof consists of finding and verifying the conditions of validity for the approximately equal signs in the heuristic discussion above.

6.3 Convergence: The Basic Results

6.3.1 Properties of $h(\theta)$

We now return to the general treatment which was interrupted by the last subsections. Consider the state variable process with fixed parameter estimates, i.e., the process

$$\bar{X}_t(\theta) = A(\theta)\bar{X}_{t-1}(\theta) + B(\theta)W_t.$$

Iterating it, one obtains

$$\bar{X}_n(\theta) = A(\theta)^n X_0 + \sum_{k=1}^{n} A(\theta)^{n-k} B(\theta)W_k.$$

Given Assumption (B.2), we have $\lim_{n\to\infty} A(\theta)^n X_0 = 0$, while the second term has the same distribution as the random variable

$$V_n = \sum_{k=1}^{n} A(\theta)^k B(\theta)W_k,$$

which is a martingale (since $E W_k = 0$). Moreover, for the L_p norm,

$$\|V_n\|_p \le \sum_{k=1}^{n} |A(\theta)^k| \|B(\theta)\| \|W_k\|_p \le \sum_{k=1}^{n} \rho^k M \|W_k\|_p.$$

Since the moments of W_k were assumed finite, one has $\|W_k\|_p \le \mu_p < \infty$, and $\rho < 1$ by Assumption (B.2). This shows that $\forall n\colon \|V_n\|_p < C_p$ for some constant C_p. Thus $\forall n, p\colon \|\bar{X}_n(\theta)\|_p \le \tilde{C}_p < \infty$ and one can apply the martingale convergence theorem and conclude:

Lemma 6.1. $\bar{X}_n(\theta)$ *tends in the limit to an L_p-integrable random variable* $\bar{X}_\infty(\theta)$.

Consider next the differential equation (6.5) for which we have:

Lemma 6.2. $h(\theta)$ *is well defined and locally Lipschitz.*

To prove the lemma we consider $E\mathcal{H}(\theta, \bar{X}_t(\theta))$. Using Assumption (A.2)(i),

$$E\big|\mathcal{H}(\theta, \bar{X}_t(\theta))\big| \le C_1\big(1 + E\big(|\bar{X}_t(\theta)|^{q_1}\big)\big) \le \hat{C}$$

for some constant $\hat{C} < \infty$. Lebesgue's dominated convergence theorem then implies that

$$h(\theta) = \lim_{t \to \infty} E\mathcal{H}\big(\theta, \bar{X}_t(\theta)\big)$$

exists. This shows that $h(\theta)$ is well defined.

To prove that $h(\theta)$ is locally Lipschitz we do the following. First, note that Assumption (A.3)(i) implies that

$$\big|\mathcal{H}(\theta, x_1) - \mathcal{H}(\theta, x_2)\big| \le C_1 |x_1 - x_2|\big(1 + |x_1| + |x_2|\big).$$

This can be shown using a variation of Coddington (1961, Chapter 6, proof of Theorem 1).[2] Similarly, Assumption (A.3) (iii) and (A.3) (ii) imply[3]

$$\big|\mathcal{H}(\theta, x) - \mathcal{H}(\theta', x)\big| \le L_2 |\theta - \theta'|(1 + |x|).$$

.

---

[2] If $f'(x)$ is Lipschitz then it is easy to see that $|f'(x)| \le K_1(1 + |x|)$ for some $K_1 > 0$ and the Coddington argument can be used to establish that $|f(x) - f(y)| \le K_2 |x - y|(1 + |x| + |y|)$ for some $K_2 > 0$. Here $|\cdot|$ denotes a vector norm.

[3] Apply the Coddington argument to $f(x) = \mathcal{H}(\theta, x) - \tilde{\mathcal{H}}(\theta', x)$.

Hence

$$\left|\mathcal{H}(\theta, x) - \mathcal{H}(\theta', x')\right| \le \left|\mathcal{H}(\theta, x) - \mathcal{H}(\theta', x)\right| + \left|\mathcal{H}(\theta', x) - \mathcal{H}(\theta', x')\right|$$
$$\le C_1|\theta - \theta'|(1 + |x|) + C_2|x - x'|(1 + |x| + |x'|).$$

Therefore,

$$\left|E\mathcal{H}(\theta, \bar{X}_t(\theta)) - E\mathcal{H}(\theta', \bar{X}_t(\theta'))\right|$$
$$\le E\left|\mathcal{H}(\theta, \bar{X}_t(\theta)) - \mathcal{H}(\theta', \bar{X}_t(\theta'))\right|$$
$$\le E\big[C_1|\theta - \theta'|(1 + |\bar{X}_t(\theta)|)$$
$$+ C_2|\bar{X}_t(\theta) - \bar{X}_t(\theta')|(1 + |\bar{X}_t(\theta)| + |\bar{X}_t(\theta')|)\big]$$
$$\le C_1|\theta - \theta'|E(1 + |\bar{X}_t(\theta)|)$$
$$+ C_2 E|\bar{X}_t(\theta) - \bar{X}_t(\theta')|(1 + E|\bar{X}_t(\theta)| + E|\bar{X}_t(\theta')|).$$

In the last expression, $\lim E(|\bar{X}_t(\theta)|)$ for $\theta \in Q$ is bounded by a constant. Since $A(\theta)$ and $B(\theta)$ are assumed Lipschitz [see Assumption (B.2)], we also have that

$$\lim_{t \to \infty} E|\bar{X}_t(\theta) - \bar{X}_t(\theta')| \le K|\theta - \theta'|$$

for some constant K. These observations show that $h(\theta)$ is Lipschitz.

The importance of Lemma 6.2 is that standard results for differential equations are applicable to the associated ODE. This observation will be used later.

6.3.2   ODE Approximation

The basic idea in this step is to write the algorithm in the form

$$\theta_{n+1} = \theta_n + \gamma_{n+1}h(\theta_n) + \epsilon_n, \quad \text{where}$$
$$\epsilon_n = \gamma_{n+1}\big[\mathcal{H}(\theta_n, X_{n+1}) - h(\theta_n) + \gamma_{n+1}\rho_{n+1}(\theta_n, X_{n+1})\big].$$

Thus, ϵ_n is essentially the approximation error between the algorithm and the associated ODE. We then want bounds on the sums $\sum \epsilon_n$. The precise analysis here is very lengthy indeed and we simply note here the main result that is needed for the next step. [The discussion in Evans and Honkapohja (1998a) fills in many of the details.]

For later use one considers more generally expressions of the form

$$\epsilon_n(\varphi) = \varphi(\theta_{n+1}) - \varphi(\theta_n) - \gamma_{n+1}\varphi'(\theta_n) \cdot h(\theta_n)$$

for certain functions φ. Below, this expression is needed for functions $\varphi \colon \mathbb{R}^d \to \mathbb{R}$ which are twice continuously differentiable with bounded second derivatives. Let now $Q \subset D$ be compact and define the first exit time from Q

$$\tau(Q) = \inf(n; \theta_n \notin Q)$$

and recall the definition of the indicator function $I(A) = 1$ if $\omega \in A$ and 0 otherwise. Elementary but very lengthy arguments lead to the following result.[4]

Lemma 6.3. *For all $x \in \mathbb{R}^k$, $a \in \mathbb{R}^d$: there exists constants B_1 and s such that*

$$E_{x,a}\left\{ \sup I\left(n \le \tau(Q)\right) \left\| \sum_{k=0}^{n-1} \epsilon_k(\varphi) \right\|^2 \right\}$$

$$\le B_1(1 + |x|^s)\left(1 + \sum_{k=1}^{\infty} \gamma_k^2\right) \sum_{k=1}^{\infty} \gamma_k^2$$

and on the set $\{\tau(Q) = \infty\}$ the series $\sum \epsilon_n(\varphi)$ converges almost surely.

Here $E_{x,a}$ is the expectation over the joint distribution of $\{X_n, \theta_n\}_{n \ge 1}$ given starting values (x, a). The interpretation of this interim result is as follows. If φ were the identity map, $\sum \epsilon_n(\varphi)$ would be a measure of the deviation between the standard discretization of the ODE and the time path of the algorithm. The result would then say that the sum of the random deviations remains bounded in mean square as long as the sequence θ_n stays in the set Q. Loosely speaking, conditional on remaining in Q, the individual $\epsilon_n(\varphi)$ have thus a tendency to convergence to zero. In other words, the ODE approximation must get better and better over time.

6.3.3 Asymptotic Analysis

We start the final step by making the assumption that we have an equilibrium point of the ODE θ^* which is locally asymptotically stable for the ODE. It will be shown that, in a particular sense, the time path of θ_t generated by the algorithm will converge to θ^*, provided that at its starting point (x, a), the component a is sufficiently close to θ^*. In doing this the Lyapunov stability theory for ODEs, in particular the so-called converse theorem, is utilized. Section 5.3.4 of Chapter 5 provides a short discussion of this theory and the relevant results.

---

[4]Doob's inequality and the martingale convergence theorem are the central theorems required.

Thus suppose that θ^* is locally asymptotically stable for the associated ODE $d\theta/d\tau = h(\theta(\tau))$. Proposition 5.9 states that on the domain of attraction D of θ^* for the ODE, there exists a twice continuously differentiable Lyapunov function $\mathcal{U}(\theta)$ having the properties:

(a) $\mathcal{U}(\theta^*) = 0, \mathcal{U}(\theta) > 0$ for all $\theta \in D, \theta \neq \theta^*$,
(b) $\mathcal{U}'(\theta)h(\theta) < 0$ for all $\theta \in D, \theta \neq \theta^*$,
(c) $\mathcal{U}(\theta) \to \infty$ if $\theta \to \partial D$ or $|\theta| \to \infty$.

Here ∂D denotes the boundary of D. Next introduce the notation $K(c) = \{\theta; \ \mathcal{U}(\theta) \leq c\}$, $c > 0$ for the contour sets of the Lyapunov function. Also let $\tau(c) = \inf(n; \ \theta_n \notin K(c))$ and let $P_{n,x,a}$ be the probability distribution of $(X_k, \theta_k)_{k \geq n}$ with $X_n = x, \theta_n = a$.

The role of the local asymptotic stability of θ^* is made clear by the following argument. Suppose that $0 < c_1 < c_2$ and $K(c_2) \subset D$. We utilize the result in the preceding subsection with φ chosen to coincide with $\mathcal{U}$ on $K(c_2)$ and such that $\inf_{\theta \notin K(c_2)} \varphi(\theta) = c_2$. If $\tau(c_2) < \infty$, then by the definition of $\epsilon_n(\varphi)$,

$$\varphi(\theta_{\tau(c_2)}) - \varphi(\theta_0) = \sum_{k=0}^{\tau(c_2)-1} \gamma_{k+1} \varphi'(\theta_k) \cdot h(\theta_k) + \sum_{k=0}^{\tau(c_2)-1} \epsilon_k(\varphi).$$

When $a \in K(c_1)$, we have $c_2 - c_1 \leq \varphi(\theta_{\tau(c_2)}) - \varphi(\theta_0)$. Also since φ coincides with $\mathcal{U}$ on $K(c_2)$, we have $\varphi'(\theta_k) \cdot h(\theta_k) \leq 0$. Thus

$$(c_2 - c_1)I(\tau(c_2) < \infty) \leq I(\tau(c_2) < \infty) \left| \sum_{k=0}^{\tau(c_2)-1} \epsilon_k(\varphi) \right|$$

$$\leq \sup_n I\big(n \leq \tau(c_2)\big) \left| \sum_{k=0}^{n-1} \epsilon_k(\varphi) \right|.$$

Hence we get

$$(c_2 - c_1)^2 I(\tau(c_2) < \infty) \leq \left\{ \sup_n I\big(n \leq \tau(c_2)\big) \left| \sum_{k=0}^{n-1} \epsilon_k(\varphi) \right| \right\}^2$$

and

$$(c_2 - c_1)^2 E\big(I(\tau(c_2) < \infty)\big) \leq E \left\{ \sup_n I\big(n \leq \tau(c_2)\big) \left| \sum_{k=0}^{n-1} \epsilon_k(\varphi) \right| \right\}^2.$$

These inequalities imply

$$P[I(\tau(c_2) < \infty)] \le (c_2 - c_1)^{-2} E \left\{ \sup_n I(n \le \tau(c_2)) \left| \sum_{k=0}^{n-1} \epsilon_k(\varphi) \right|^2 \right\}$$

since $P[I(\tau(c_2) < \infty)] = E(I(\tau(c_2) < \infty))$.

Since the conditional distribution of (X_{n+k}, θ_{n+k}) given $X_n = x$, $\theta_n = a$ is equal to the conditional distribution of (X_n, θ_n) with $X_0 = x$, $\theta_0 = a$ and with γ_k and ρ_k replaced by γ_{n+k} and ρ_{n+k}, respectively, the interim Lemma 6.3 in Section 6.3.2 yields the following basic theorem.

Theorem 6.4. *Let θ^* be an asymptotically stable equilibrium point of the ODE $d\theta/d\tau = h(\theta(\tau))$. Suppose Assumptions (A) and (B) are satisfied on $D = \text{int}(K(c))$ for some $c > 0$. Suppose that for $0 < c_1 < c_2$, we have $K(c_2) \subset D$. Then there exist constants B_1 and s such that for all $a \in K(c_1)$, $n \ge 0$, x:*

$$P_{n,x,a}\{\theta_t \text{ leaves } K(c_2) \text{ in finite time}\} \le B_1(1 + |x|^s)J(n),$$

where $J(n)$ is a positive decreasing sequence with $\lim_{n \to \infty} J(n) = 0$. In fact, $J(n) = (1 + \sum_{k=n+1}^{\infty} \gamma_k^2) \sum_{k=n+1}^{\infty} \gamma_k^2$.

The content of this theorem is as follows. Fixing the contour sets $K(c_1) \subset K(c_2)$, we have that if at any time n the parameter vector θ_n remains inside $K(c_1)$, then the probability that θ_t leaves $K(c_2)$ for some $t > n$ is bounded above by an expression which tends to zero as $n \to \infty$. In other words, the probability of divergence outside $K(c_2)$ gets smaller and smaller as the number of steps taken by the algorithm increases.

While this is an important result, there remains the question of convergence to θ^*. To this effect one has the following theorem.

Theorem 6.5. *Under the setup of Theorem 6.4, (i) For all $a \in K(c_1)$, $n \ge 0$, x, one has*

$$P_{n,x,a}\{\theta_t \text{ leaves } K(c_2) \text{ in finite time or } \theta_t \to \theta^*\} = 1,$$

and (ii) for any compact $Q \subset D$, there exist constants B_2 and s such that for all $a \in K(c_1)$, $n \ge 0$, x,

$$P_{n,x,a}\{\theta_t \to \theta^*\} \ge 1 - B_2(1 + |x|^s)J(n),$$

where $J(n)$ is as in Theorem 6.4.

This result states two things. First, the algorithm either converges to θ^* or diverges outside $K(c_2)$. Second, the probability of converging to θ^* is bounded from below by a sequence of numbers tending to 1 as $n \rightarrow \infty$. We omit the proof of Theorem 6.5, which follows fairly easily from Theorem 6.4, see Evans and Honkapohja (1998a) for details.

When applying the results, one proceeds as follows. First, it must be verified that the economic model and the learning algorithm satisfy the basic assumptions (A.1)–(A.3) and (B.1)–(B.2) on a nontrivial open domain containing the equilibrium of interest. Second, a condition guaranteeing local stability of the associated ODE is established. This is usually based on E-stability of the equilibrium, and checking that the linearization of the differential equation yields a stable coefficient matrix (i.e., its eigenvalues have negative real parts). These steps provide a nontrivial domain in which (local) convergence obtains in the sense of Theorem 6.5 or the corollaries below.

6.4 Convergence: Further Discussion

The following two results are special cases yielding convergence when starting at time 0. The first result is an immediate consequence of the second part of Theorem 6.5.

Corollary 6.6. *Suppose* $\gamma_t = \xi \gamma_t'$, *where* γ_t' *satisfies Assumption (A.1). Let the initial value of* θ *belong to some compact* $Q \subset D$. *For all* $\delta > 0$: *there exists* ξ^* *such that,* $\forall 0 < \xi < \xi^*$ *and* $a \in Q$,

$$P_{0,x,a}\{\theta_t \rightarrow \theta^*\} \geq 1 - \delta.$$

Remark 1. Clearly, this result holds more generally for $\gamma_t = \xi \gamma_{t+N}'$, for fixed $0 < \xi < 1$ and nonnegative N. That is, given $\delta > 0$, $P_{0,x,a}\{\theta_t \rightarrow \theta^*\} \geq 1 - \delta$ for any fixed N for all $\xi > 0$ sufficiently small. Similarly, the result holds for every fixed ξ for all N sufficiently large.

The corollary and remark cover various cases of slow adaption. For low enough adaption speeds the probability of convergence can be made "very close" to 1. For general adaption speeds and with additional assumptions one can in some cases obtain convergence with positive probability:

Corollary 6.7. *Assume that* θ^* *is locally asymptotically stable for the ODE and that each component of* W_t *either is a random variable with positive continuous* *density or else is a constant. Fix a compact set $Q \subset D$, such that $\theta^* \in \text{int}(Q)$, and a compact set $J \subset \mathbb{R}^k$. Suppose that for every $\theta_0 \in Q_0$ and $X_0 \in J_0$ in some sets Q_0 and J_0, and for every $n > 0$, there exists a sequence $W_0, \ldots, W_T$, with $T \geq n$, such that $\theta_T \in \text{int}(Q)$ and $X_T \in \text{int}(J)$. Then*

$$P_{0,x,a}\{\theta_t \to \theta^*\} > 0$$

for all $a \in Q_0$ and $x \in J_0$.

Proof. Fix a compact set $Q \subset D$. Using Theorem 6.5, there is $\bar{n}$ such that $P_{n,x,a}\{\theta_t \to \theta^*\} > 0$ for all $n > \bar{n}$, $x \in J$, and $a \in Q$. Substituting recursively in the algorithm, it follows that, for each t, the function $\theta_t = Z_t(\theta_0, W_1, \ldots, W_t, X_0)$ is continuous, because $\mathcal{H}$ and ρ_k are continuous. By the assumptions of the corollary, for some $T \geq \bar{n}$ there exist $W_1, \ldots, W_T$ such that $\theta_T \in \text{int}(Q)$ and $X_T \in \text{int}(J)$. Since $Z_T(\cdot)$ is continuous, and by the assumption of positive density, $P_{0,x,a}\{\theta_T \in \text{int}(Q) \text{ and } X_T \in \text{int}(J)\} > 0$, from which the result follows. □

The example in Evans and Honkapohja (1998b) provides an application of this corollary.

It must be emphasized that it is not in general possible to obtain bounds close to 1 even for the most favorable initial conditions at this level of generality. The reason is that for small values of t, the ODE does not well approximate the algorithm. In particular, for early time periods, sufficiently large shocks may displace θ_t outside the domain of attraction of the ODE.

In the earlier literature, see, e.g., the initial papers Marcet and Sargent (1989c) and Marcet and Sargent (1989b) as well as Evans and Honkapohja (1994b), Evans and Honkapohja (1994c), and Evans and Honkapohja (1995c), this problem was avoided by making an additional assumption on the algorithm, known as the *projection facility* (PF). It is defined as follows: For some $0 < c_1 < c_2$, with $K(c_2) \subset D$, the algorithm is followed provided $\theta_t \in \text{int}(K(c_2))$. Otherwise, it is projected to some point in $K(c_1)$.

An alternative to PF, see, e.g., Ljung (1977), is to introduce the direct boundedness assumption that the algorithm visits a small neighborhood of the equilibrium point infinitely often. Clearly, such a condition can be very hard to verify (and may not hold).

The hypothesis of a PF has been criticized by some as being inappropriate for decentralized markets; see Grandmont and Laroque (1991), Grandmont (1998) and Moreno and Walker (1994). The results above do not invoke the projection facility. However, the above results do have a strong implication when a PF is employed. For algorithms which incorporate a PF, the probability for convergence to a stable equilibrium point can be made equal to 1. This result requires the additional assumption that the state dynamics are bounded in the sense stated below:

Corollary 6.8. *Assume that there exists a random variable Z such that for all t: $|X_t| < Z$ almost surely. Consider the general algorithm augmented by a projection facility. Under the hypotheses of Theorem 6.4, we have for all x, a,*

$$P_{0,x,a}\{\theta_t \to \theta^*\} = 1.$$

Proof. Suppose on the contrary that $P\{\theta_t \to \theta^*\} \le 1 - \varepsilon$ for some $\varepsilon > 0$. Here P denotes $P_{0,x,a}$ for brevity. We first argue that $P\{\text{PF used infinitely often}\} \ge \varepsilon$. Let $N = \{\omega \mid \theta_t(\omega) \nrightarrow \theta^*\}$, $F_t = \{\omega \mid t = \sup_T [\text{PF used at } T], t < \infty\}$, $F_0 = \{\omega \mid \text{PF never used}\}$, and $G = \{\omega \mid \text{PF used infinitely often}\}$. Then $G, \{F_t\}_{t=0}^\infty$ is a partition of Ω and

$$P(N) = P(G \cap N) + \sum_{t=0}^{\infty} P(N \cap F_t).$$

Consider F_t, $t = 0, 1, 2, \ldots$. For $\omega \in F_t$ and $n \ge t$, the algorithm with PF is identical to the algorithm without PF. Applying Theorem 6.5(i), we have, since $\theta_t \in K(c_1)$,

$$P_{t,\theta_t,x}\{\theta_n \text{ leaves } K(c_2) \text{ in finite time or } \theta_n \to \theta^*\} = 1$$

in the algorithm without PF. Hence $P(N \cap F_t) = 0$, so that $P(N) = P(G \cap N) = P(G)$ as $G \subset N$. By assumption, $P(N) \ge \varepsilon$, and thus $P(G) \ge \varepsilon$, as was to be shown.

We now obtain a contradiction by showing that $P(G) < 2\varepsilon/3$. Let $\Omega_z = \{\omega \mid \forall t: \ |X_t| < Z\}$. Fix a constant z sufficiently large so that $P(\Omega_z^c) \le \varepsilon/3$, where Ω_z^c is the set-theoretic complement. Now

$$P(G) = P(G \cap \Omega_z) + P(G \cap \Omega_z^c) \le P(G \cap \Omega_z) + \varepsilon/3.$$

Thus, from now on we can restrict attention to Ω_z. By Theorem 6.4 we have, in an algorithm without a PF, $\exists T_0$ s.t. $\forall T \ge T_0$, $P_{T,a,x}\{\theta_t \notin K(c_2)$ for some $t \ge T\} < \varepsilon/3$ for all $a \in K(c_1)$ and $|x| < z$. Clearly, $G = \{\omega \mid \text{PF used infinitely often after } T_0\}$, and define $B_t = \{\omega \mid t = \inf_{T \ge T_0} \theta_T(\omega) \in K(c_1)\}$. Now $\{G \cap$

$\Omega_z \cap B_t\}_{t=0}^{\infty}$ is a partition of $G \cap \Omega_z$, so that

$$P(G \cap \Omega_z) = \sum_{T=T_0}^{\infty} P(G \cap \Omega_z \cap B_T)$$

$$\leq \sum_{T=T_0}^{\infty} P(\{PF \text{ used after } T\} \cap \Omega_z \cap B_T).$$

However, $P(\{PF \text{ used after } T\} \cap \Omega_z \cap B_T) = \int_{B_T} P(\{PF \text{ used after } T\} \cap \Omega_z \mid \theta_T) \, dP \leq \int_{B_T} (\varepsilon/3) \, dP = (\varepsilon/3) P(B_T)$, since for any $\theta_T \in K(c_1)$ and $x \in \Omega_z$, the probability of $(\{PF \text{ used after } T\})$ for the algorithm with PF is equal to $P_{T,\theta_T,x}\{\theta_t \notin K(c_2) \text{ for some } t \geq T\} < \varepsilon/3$ for the algorithm without PF. Thus,

$$P(G \cap \Omega_z) \leq (\varepsilon/3) \sum_{T=T_0}^{\infty} P(B_T) = \varepsilon/3,$$

so that $P(G) \leq 2\varepsilon/3$.   □

We remark that if, for example, X_t is a stationary VAR driven by a shock with bounded support, then the boundedness condition in the corollary is satisfied.

Finally, we note here [details are in the paper Evans and Honkapohja (1995c)] that in some special models almost sure local convergence can be obtained without a PF, provided that the support of the random shock is sufficiently small. Also, for certain nonstochastic models there is no need to have a PF when one is interested in local stability; see Evans and Honkapohja (2000) and Section 7.2 of Chapter 7 for such results.

Example 1 (**Concluded**): Returning to the introductory example of Section 6.1, equation (6.6) gives the associated ODE in (a, R). Note that from the equation for R we have $\lim_{\tau \to \infty} R(\tau) = \sigma_x^2$, so that the first equation behaves asymptotically like the "small" differential equation

$$\frac{da}{d\tau} = (\alpha - 1)a + \sigma_x^{-2}\sigma_{xu}.$$

This has the unique fixed point $a^* = (1 - \alpha)^{-1}\sigma_x^{-2}\sigma_{xu}$ which is stable if $\alpha < 1$. The theorems of this section thus apply, i.e., $a_t \to a^*$ locally. In particular, from Corollary 6.8 it follows that with a nontrivial projection facility, $(a_t, R_t) \to (a^*, \sigma_x^2)$ with probability 1. It is not hard to show that the projection facility in this example can be made arbitrarily large within the domain D. In fact, for this example with $\alpha < 1$ one can show global convergence without a projection facility using Theorem 6.10 below. (For the detailed method see the treatment of the multivariate cobweb example following that example.)

Finally, if $\alpha > 1$ one can show that a_t converges with probability 0 using results in the following section.

6.5   Instability Results

We will now consider the instability results which will, broadly speaking, state the following: (i) The algorithm cannot converge to a point which is not an equilibrium point of the associated ODE, and (ii) the algorithm will not converge to an unstable equilibrium point of the ODE. The precise meaning and the conditions for validity of these results will be somewhat involved to state, since we will have to adopt a new set of conditions for the results.[5]

Let again $\theta_t \in \mathbb{R}^d$ be a vector of parameters and write the algorithm in the form

$$\begin{aligned} \theta_t &= \theta_{t-1} + \gamma_t \mathcal{H}(\theta_{t-1}, X_t) + \gamma_t^2 \rho_t(\theta_{t-1}, X_t) \\ &\equiv \theta_{t-1} + \gamma_t Q(t, \theta_{t-1}, X_t). \end{aligned}$$

Below, we will impose assumptions directly on $Q(\cdot)$. Again, $X_t \in \mathbb{R}^k$ is the vector of observable state variables with the conditionally linear dynamics

$$X_t = A(\theta_{t-1})X_{t-1} + B(\theta_{t-1})W_t,$$

where W_t is a random disturbance term.

Select now a domain $D^* \subset \mathbb{R}^d$ such that all the eigenvalues of $A(\theta)$ are strictly inside the unit circle. The final domain of interest will be an open and connected set $D \subset D^*$ and the conditions below will be postulated for D. We introduce the following assumptions:

(C.1) W_t is a sequence of independent random variables with $|W_t| < C$ with probability 1 for all t.

(C.2) $Q(t, \theta, x)$ is continuously differentiable in (θ, x) for $\theta \in D$. For fixed (θ, x) the derivatives are bounded in t.

---

[5]The main source for the instability results is Ljung (1977). We will adopt his Assumptions (A). The appendix of Woodford (1990) gives a slightly different version of Ljung's results.

(C.3) The matrices $A(\theta)$ and $B(\theta)$ are Lipschitz on D.

(C.4) The limit $\lim_{t\to\infty} EQ(t,\theta,\bar{X}_t(\theta)) = h(\theta)$ exists for $\theta \in D$, where $\bar{X}_t(\theta) = A(\theta)\bar{X}_{t-1}(\theta) + B(\theta)W_t$.

(C.5) γ_t is a decreasing sequence with the properties $\sum_1^\infty \gamma_t = \infty$, $\sum_1^\infty \gamma_t^\alpha < \infty$ for some α, and $\lim_{t\to\infty} \sup[1/\gamma_t - 1/\gamma_{t-1}] < \infty$.

Ljung (1977) provides an alternative set of assumptions which relaxes Assumption (C.1) at the expense of strengthening other assumptions. We remark that $\gamma_t = K/t$ again satisfies Assumption (C.5).

With these assumptions, the following theorem holds [the long proof will be omitted; see Ljung (1977) for it].

Theorem 6.9. *Consider the algorithm with Assumptions (C). Suppose at some point $\theta^* \in D$, we also have the validity of the conditions (i) $Q(t,\theta^*,\bar{X}_t(\theta^*))$ has a covariance matrix that is bounded below by a positive definite matrix, and (ii) $EQ(t,\theta^*,\bar{X}_t(\theta^*))$ is continuously differentiable in θ in a neighborhood of θ^* and the derivatives converge uniformly in this neighborhood as $t \to \infty$. Then (a) if $h(\theta^*) \neq 0$ (i.e., θ^* is not an equilibrium point of the ODE), or (b) if $\partial h(\theta^*)/\partial\theta$ has an eigenvalue with a positive real part (so that θ^* is not a stable equilibrium point of the ODE), then*

$$\Pr(\theta_t \to \theta^*) = 0.$$

In other words, the possible rest points of the recursive algorithm consist of the locally stable equilibrium points of the associated ODE.[6] It is worth stressing the role of condition (i) in the theorem. It ensures that at even large values of t some random fluctuations remain, and the system cannot stop at an unstable point or nonequilibrium point. For example, if there were no randomness at all, then with an initial value precisely equal to an unstable equilibrium, the algorithm would not move off that point.[7] A similar idea, known as *simulated annealing* in numerical mathematics, is used in algorithms for searching for a global minimum of a function. The idea is to "shake" the system appropriately, so that it does not get stuck at a local minimum.

These instability and the earlier stability results are the main theorems from the theory of recursive algorithms that are used in the analysis of adaptive learning in economics. A global convergence result under rather strong conditions

---

[6] This assumes that the equilibrium points are isolated (and hyperbolic). There are more general statements of the result.

[7] Note that the usual definition of instability for a deterministic dynamical system takes care of this possibility through its definition.

will be discussed later. We turn next to a convenient way of obtaining the convergence condition for adaptive learning and a further example.

6.6   Expectational Stability

The concept of *expectational stability* was introduced in Section 2.9 of Chapter 2. Recall that in its general formulation, a map $\phi \rightarrow T(\phi)$ is constructed from a perceived law of motion to an actual law of motion. If the agents' perceived law of motion nests the rational expectations equilibrium (REE) of interest, then ϕ and $T(\phi)$ are in the same space and the REE is a fixed point of T, i.e., $T(\phi^*) = \phi^*$. The examples in the introductory chapters illustrate this mapping.[8] A given REE ϕ^* is said to be *E-stable (expectationally stable)* if the differential equation

$$\frac{d\phi}{d\tau} = T(\phi) - \phi$$

is locally asymptotically stable at ϕ^*. Here τ denotes "notional" or "virtual" time. For a wide range of models, E-stability of an REE provides the condition for (local) convergence of adaptive learning rules.[9]

The method for establishing the connection between E-stability and convergence of real-time learning rules is naturally dependent on the type of the PLM that agents are presumed to use. For nonlinear models one usually has to be content with specific types of REE, and the connection between E-stability and local convergence of real-time learning is examined for each type of equilibrium. For linear models, the entire set of REE can be given an explicit characterization and the connection between E-stability and real-time learning has been studied more systematically. Immediately below, we provide another example of the connection between E-stability and stability under learning and we explore the connection for different models in later chapters.

The way of parameterizing the REE and the specification of who is learning what (i.e., the perceived law of motion) can in principle affect the stability

---

[8]E-stability can also be used to understand Example 1 of this chapter. Instead of a perceived law of motion, we start directly with a forecast rule $y_t^e = ax_t$ which yields the corresponding actual law of motion $y_t = \alpha a x_t + u_t$. For this law of motion the optimal forecast rule is $y_t = T(a)x_t$, where $T(a) = \alpha a + \sigma_x^{-2}\sigma_{xu}$, yielding the E-stability condition $\alpha < 1$.

[9]Marcet and Sargent (1989c) were the first to note the link between real-time learning and E-stability for a class of models. Their results were generalized in a number of papers.

conditions. In this respect, the situation is not different from other economic models of adjustment outside an equilibrium.[10] However, it is evident that the local stability condition that the eigenvalues of $T(\cdot)$ have real parts less than 1 is invariant to 1–1 transformations $\phi \rightarrow \beta = f(\phi)$, where f and f^{-1} are both continuously differentiable.

Another aspect in parameterizations is the question of overparameterization: Agents may use perceived laws of motion that have more parameters than the REE of interest. This leads to a distinction between *weak* and *strong E-stability*. An REE is said to be *weakly E-stable* if it is E-stable as above and the perceived law of motion takes the same form as the REE. Correspondingly, we say that an REE is *strongly E-stable* if it is locally E-stable even for a specified class of overparameterized perceived laws of motion. (The additional parameters then converge to zero.) It may be remarked that this distinction is not entirely straightforward, since it may be possible to overparameterize solutions in different ways. One should in principle use the concept of E-stability with respect to a given class of perceived laws of motion. However, it turns out that in specific models the distinction can be made precise in natural ways.

Finally, we note the possibility that the perceived law of motion is underparameterized relative to the REE of interest. In such a situation, learning cannot converge to the RE equilibrium, but it may instead converge to some other rest point or not converge at all. Underparameterization was introduced in Chapter 3 and will be discussed further in Chapter 13. The E-stability concept can be extended to cover such cases.

The Multivariate Muth Model

The market model of Muth (1961), known as the cobweb model under naive expectations, assumes that demand is a downward sloping linear function of the market price, while supply depends in an increasing linear fashion on expected price. As noted in Chapter 2, this model was analyzed for learning by Bray and Savin (1986) and Fourgeaud, Gourieroux, and Pradel (1986).

We consider its generalization to simultaneous equations (e.g., to multiple markets):

$$y_t = \mu + A E^*_{t-1} y_t + C w_t, \tag{6.7}$$
$$w_t = B w_{t-1} + v_t.$$

---

[10] A "textbook example" is the standard demand–supply model and the Walrasian adjustment of prices vs. the Marshallian adjustment of quantities.

Here y_t is an $n \times 1$ vector of endogenous variables, w_t is an observed $p \times 1$ vector of exogenous variables, and v_t is a $p \times 1$ vector of white noise shocks with finite moments. The eigenvalues of $B_{p \times p}$ are assumed to lie inside the unit circle. For simplicity, the matrix B is assumed to be known. $E_{t-1}^* y_t$ denotes the expectations of agents held at time $t - 1$ based on their perceived law of motion. Assume also that $I - A$ is invertible.

This model has a unique REE

$$y_t = \bar{a} + \bar{b} w_{t-1} + \eta_t,$$

where $\bar{a} = (I - A)^{-1}\mu$, $\bar{b} = (I - A)^{-1}CB$, and $\eta_t = Cv_t$. Is this REE expectationally stable? Consider perceived laws of motion of the form

$$y_t = a + b w_{t-1} + \eta_t$$

for arbitrary $n \times 1$ vectors a and $n \times p$ matrices b. The corresponding expectation function is $E_{t-1}^* y_t = a + b w_{t-1}$ and one obtains the actual law of motion

$$y_t = (\mu + Aa) + (Ab + CB)w_{t-1} + \eta_t,$$

where $\eta_t = Cv_t$. The T mapping is thus

$$T(a, b) = (\mu + Aa, Ab + CB).$$

E-stability is determined by the differential equation

$$\frac{da}{d\tau} = \mu + (A - I)a,$$
$$\frac{db}{d\tau} = CB + (A - I)b.$$

It can be verified that this system is locally asymptotically stable if and only if all eigenvalues of $A - I$ have negative real parts, i.e., if and only if all eigenvalues of A have real parts less than 1. This is also going to be the convergence condition for real-time learning rules which we now introduce.

In real-time learning the perceived law of motion has the same form but with coefficients (a_t, b_t) which are revised at each time t. Thus expectations are given by

$$E_{t-1}^* y_t = a_{t-1} + b_{t-1} w_{t-1}.$$

We assume that the parameters a_t and b_t are updated running recursive least squares (RLS). Letting $\phi = (a, b)$ and $z'_t = (1, w'_t)$, RLS can be written as

$$\phi'_t = \phi'_{t-1} + t^{-1} R_t^{-1} z_{t-1} (y_t - \phi_{t-1} z_{t-1})',$$
$$R_t = R_{t-1} + t^{-1} (z_{t-1} z'_{t-1} - R_{t-1}).$$

This learning rule is complemented by the short-run determination of the value for y_t which takes the form

$$y_t = T(\phi_{t-1}) z_{t-1} + C v_t,$$

where $T(\phi) = T(a, b)$ as given above.

In order to convert the system into standard form (6.3), it is necessary to make a timing change in the equation governing R_t. Thus set $S_{t-1} = R_t$, so that

$$S_t = S_{t-1} + t^{-1} (z_t z'_t - S_{t-1}) + t^{-2} \left(-\frac{t}{t+1} \right) (z_t z'_t - S_{t-1}).$$

The last term is then of the usual form with $\rho_t(S_{t-1}, z_t) = -[t/(t+1)](z_t z'_t - S_{t-1})$. It is also convenient to substitute in for y_t in the ϕ_t equation to obtain

$$\phi'_t = \phi'_{t-1} + t^{-1} S_{t-1}^{-1} z_{t-1} [(T(\phi_{t-1}) - \phi_{t-1}) z_{t-1} + C v_t]'.$$

The model is now in the form (6.3) with $\theta_t = \text{vec}(\phi_t, S_t)$ and $X'_t = (1, w'_t, w'_{t-1})$.

The dynamics for the state variable are given by equation (6.4) with $W'_t = (1, v'_t)$ and

$$A = \begin{pmatrix} 0 & 0 & 0 \\ 0 & B & 0 \\ 0 & I & 0 \end{pmatrix}, \qquad B = \begin{pmatrix} 1 & 0 \\ 0 & I \\ 0 & 0 \end{pmatrix}.$$

Since w_t is a stationary vector autoregression (VAR), X_t is also a stationary VAR. Since $E z_t z'_t = M_z$ for some positive definite matrix M_z, one can verify that the basic assumptions for the convergence analysis are met. In fact, this model satisfies even stronger assumptions that guarantee global convergence of the learning algorithm to the unique REE. This is discussed in the next section.

The associated ODE is obtained by taking expectations of $S^{-1} z_{t-1} [(T(\phi) - \phi) z_{t-1} + C v_t]'$ and $(z_t z'_t - S)$. Using $E z_t z'_t = M_z$ and $E z_{t-1} v'_t = 0$, this yields the ODE

$$\frac{d\phi'}{d\tau} = S^{-1} M_z (T(\phi) - \phi)',$$

$$\frac{dS}{d\tau} = M_z - S.$$

The second equation is independent of ϕ and it is clearly globally asymptotically stable. Moreover, since $S \to M_z$, the stability of the first equation is governed by the E-stability equation

$$\frac{d\phi}{d\tau} = T(\phi) - \phi.$$

Its local stability condition is that the eigenvalues of A have real parts less than 1; see above. Thus the E-stability condition is the convergence condition for the RLS learning algorithm in this model. In the next section we establish a global result for frameworks with unique equilibria. This general result is also applicable to this particular model.

6.7   Global Convergence

In this section we provide a stronger set of conditions than Assumptions (A) and (B) of Section 6.2.1 that guarantee global convergence of the recursive algorithm

$$\theta_t = \theta_{t-1} + \gamma_t \mathcal{H}(\theta_{t-1}, X_t) + \gamma_t^2 \rho_t (\theta_{t-1}, X_t).$$

The new assumptions are:

(D.1) The functions $\mathcal{H}(\theta, x)$ and $\rho_t(\theta, x)$ satisfy, for all $\theta, \theta' \in \mathbb{R}^d$ and all $x, x' \in \mathbb{R}^k$,

     (i) $|\mathcal{H}(\theta, x_1) - \mathcal{H}(\theta, x_2)| \le L_1 (1 + |\theta|)|x_1 - x_2|(1 + |x_1|^{p_1} + |x_2|^{p_1})$,
    (ii) $|\mathcal{H}(\theta, 0) - \mathcal{H}(\theta', 0)| \le L_2 |\theta - \theta'|$,
    (iii) $|\partial \mathcal{H}(\theta, x)/\partial x - \partial \mathcal{H}(\theta', x)/\partial x| \le L_2 |\theta - \theta'|(1 + |x|^{p_2})$,
    (iv) $|\rho_t(\theta, x)| \le C_2 (1 + |\theta|)(1 + |x|^q)$
    for some constants $L_1, L_2, C_2, p_1, p_2,$ and q.

(D.2) The dynamics for the state variable $X_t \in \mathbb{R}^k$ is independent of θ and satisfies Assumptions (B.1) and (B.2) of Section 2.1.

With these conditions one has the following global result.[11]

Theorem 6.10. *Under Assumptions (A.1), (D.1), and (D.2), assume that there exists a unique equilibrium point $\theta^* \in \mathbb{R}^d$ of the associated ODE. Suppose that there exists a positive twice continuously differentiable function $\mathcal{U}(\theta)$ on $\mathbb{R}^d$ with bounded second derivatives satisfying (i) $\mathcal{U}'(\theta)h(\theta) < 0$ for all $\theta \neq \theta^*$, (ii) $\mathcal{U}(\theta) = 0$ iff $\theta = \theta^*$, (iii) $\mathcal{U}(\theta) \geq \alpha|\theta|^2$ for all θ with $|\theta| \geq \rho_0$ for some $\alpha, \rho_0 > 0$. Then the sequence θ_t converges $P_{0,x,a}$ almost surely to θ^*.*

We now apply this theorem to establish global convergence to the linear simultaneous equation of model (6.7) above.

Multivariate Muth Model (Continued)

Recall that the learning dynamics for model (6.7) are described by the system

$$\phi_t' = \phi_{t-1}' + t^{-1}S_{t-1}^{-1}z_{t-1}\left(T(\phi_{t-1})z_{t-1} + Cv_t - \phi_{t-1}z_{t-1}\right)',$$

$$S_t = S_{t-1} + t^{-1}(z_t z_t' - S_{t-1}) + t^{-2}\left(-\frac{t}{t+1}\right)(z_t z_t' - S_{t-1}).$$

A possible problem is that for some t, the matrix S_t may not be invertible. This happens only a finite number of times with probability 1, and one can then give an arbitrary value for S_t in the equation for ϕ_t. The method of proof is to modify the algorithm, so that it coincides with the original algorithm after a finite time.

Consider first the equation for S_t. It satisfies the conditions for the global convergence theorem with the ODE

$$h_2(S) = M_z - S.$$

The corresponding Lyapunov function is $\mathcal{U}(S) = \|S - M_z\|^2$ and S_t converges almost surely to M_z from any starting point. Now introduce a neighborhood N of M_z such that S^{-1} exists whenever $S \in N$. It is possible to construct a bounded regular function $u(S)$ from the space of $(p+1) \times (p+1)$ matrices to the subspace of positive definite matrices such that $u(S) = S^{-1}$ on N. The modified algorithm is

$$\phi_t' = \phi_{t-1}' + t^{-1}u(S_{t-1})z_{t-1}(T(\phi_{t-1})z_{t-1} + Cv_t - \phi_{t-1}z_{t-1})'.$$

---

[11] The proof follows directly the one in Benveniste, Metivier, and Priouret (1990) as indicated in the remarks in Evans and Honkapohja (1998b).

Assumptions (D.1) and (D.2) are easy to verify, and the associated ODE takes the form

$$\frac{d\theta}{d\tau} = \big(h_1(\phi, S), h_2(S)\big),$$

where $h_1(\phi, S) = u(S)M_z((A - I)(\phi - \bar{\phi}))$, where $\bar{\phi} = (\bar{a}, \bar{b})$ is the REE. This differential equation is globally asymptotically stable when the eigenvalues of $A - I$ have negative real parts. Moreover, the stability is then exponential. By a converse theorem of Lyapunov there exists a twice continuously differentiable Lyapunov function $W(\theta)$ satisfying $W(\theta) \geq \delta_1|\theta|^2$, $\delta_1 > 0$.[12] To ensure a Lyapunov function with bounded second derivatives one sets $\mathcal{U}(\theta) = \psi(W(\theta))$, where ψ is regular with $\psi(0) = 0$, $\psi'(t) > 0$, $\lim_{t\to\infty} \psi(t) = +\infty$, and with derivatives of ψ tending to zero sufficiently rapidly. This $\mathcal{U}(\theta)$ will satisfy all the requirements of Theorem 6.10.

It follows that, provided all eigenvalues of matrix A have real parts less than 1, Theorem 6.10 applies and $\phi_t = (a_t, b_t) \to \bar{\phi} = (\bar{a}, \bar{b})$ globally almost surely. If instead one of the eigenvalues of A has a real part greater than 1, then Theorem 6.9 applies so that $(\phi_t, S_t) \longrightarrow (\bar{\phi}, \bar{S})$ with probability 0. Since by the law of large numbers, $S_t \to \bar{S}$ with probability 1, in this case we have $(a_t, b_t) \to (\bar{a}, \bar{b})$ with probability 0.

---

[12] See Section 5.3.4 for the definition of exponential stability and the relevant converse result, Proposition 5.10.

Chapter 7

Further Topics in Stochastic Approximation

7.1   Introduction

In the preceding chapter we provided the central convergence theorems under the assumption that the dynamics of the state variables follows a stationary vector autoregressive process (that is possibly dependent on the vector of parameters θ_{t-1}). In this chapter we continue with the techniques for analyzing these algorithms and thereby provide some further results that can be useful in the study of econometric learning behavior in different models. We are interested in obtaining several extensions of the basic local convergence results.

First, we present some convergence results of adaptive algorithms that arise from modeling learning in nonstochastic frameworks. Such setups appear in some of the literature, and we also discuss some specific issues that arise in this context. Second, we extend the analysis to situations in which the state variable dynamics follows a Markov process (with, again, possible dependence on θ_{t-1}). Third, we analyze algorithms with a constant gain. In this case we obtain results on the approximate distribution of the parameter estimates. Fourth, for the case of decreasing gain we provide asymptotic distribution results which yield the speed of convergence. Finally, we develop a global convergence result for domains with multiple equilibria. Here we obtain a result stating that there will be convergence to the set of those equilibria satisfying the familiar local stability condition.

7.2   Algorithms for Nonstochastic Frameworks

Convergence conditions for learning of a steady state were already discussed in Chapter 3 for a general framework of type $p_t = F(p_{t+1}^e)$. Other nonstochastic setups encountered so far are the Ramsey and Diamond growth models which were discussed in Chapter 4. Many other examples could be given; the literature studying learning in nonstochastic frameworks is extensively referenced in Grandmont (1998).

Learning in nonstochastic frameworks has been formulated in several ways. One approach is to use fixed finite-memory forecast rules, $p_{t+1}^e = \psi(p_{t-1}, \ldots, p_{t-L})$ or its extension to error learning rules in which the forecast rule is revised depending on the most recent forecast error. The study of finite-memory learning rules in nonstochastic models was initiated in Fuchs (1977), Fuchs (1979), Fuchs and Laroque (1976), and Tillmann (1983). The case of fixed finite-memory rules was examined extensively by Grandmont (1985) and Grandmont and Laroque (1986). They introduce axioms for the forecast function $\psi(\cdot)$ and obtain both stability and instability results. A second approach, used, e.g., in Guesnerie and Woodford (1991), is to postulate a learning algorithm with a constant gain. They obtain stability conditions for steady states and cycles. These models can be viewed as a generalization of adaptive expectations.[1]

Formally, the preceding types of algorithms can be treated using standard techniques for difference equations. Algorithms with decreasing gain have also been used in nonstochastic models. Here we develop local stability and instability results for a general class of algorithms with decreasing gain in the context of nonstochastic setups using the formulation in Evans and Honkapohja (2000). We also develop some applications of these results. Last, we take up some conceptual issues that arise specifically in nonstochastic frameworks.

7.2.1   A General Framework

Consider the algorithm

$$\theta_t = \theta_{t-1} + \gamma_t \big[\mathcal{M}(\theta_{t-1}, \gamma_t) - \theta_{t-1} \big] \tag{7.1}$$

---

[1]Further references of expectation formation and learning in nonstochastic models are Grandmont and Laroque (1990), Grandmont and Laroque (1991), Moore (1993), Böhm and Wenzelburger (1999), and Chatterji and Chattopadhyay (2000).

for $t = 1, 2, 3, \ldots$. Here θ_0 is a given initial condition and $\gamma_t > 0$ is a sequence of gains with the properties

$$0 < \gamma_t < 1, \qquad \lim_{t \to \infty} \gamma_t = 0, \qquad \sum_{i=1}^{\infty} \gamma_i = \infty.$$

The function $\mathcal{M} \colon \mathbb{R}^k \times \mathbb{R} \longrightarrow \mathbb{R}^k$ is assumed to have a fixed point at the origin, i.e., $\mathcal{M}(0, 0) = 0$.

In this section we assume that

(i) $\mathcal{M}(\cdot)$ is continuously differentiable in a neighborhood of $(0, 0)$.
(ii) $\mathcal{M}(0, \gamma_t) = 0$ for all $t = 1, 2, \ldots$.
(iii) $\mathcal{M}(\cdot)$ is continuous in a neighborhood of points $(0, \gamma_t)$.

It follows that $D_2 \mathcal{M}(0, 0) = 0$, where we write $(D_1 \mathcal{M}, D_2 \mathcal{M})$ for the derivative of $\mathcal{M}$. Thus $D_1 \mathcal{M}$ is $k \times k$ and $D_2 \mathcal{M}$ is $k \times 1$. We also impose the *regularity assumption*:

(iv) No eigenvalue of $D_1 \mathcal{M}(0, 0)$ has real part equal to 1.

The following local stability result for the algorithm (7.1) is proved in Evans and Honkapohja (2000).

Theorem 7.1. *Assume that conditions* (i)–(iv) *hold. If in the algorithm (7.1) the real parts of all eigenvalues of $D_1 \mathcal{M}(0, 0)$ are less than 1, then the fixed point is locally asymptotically stable, i.e., there exists a neighborhood U of 0 such that, for all $\theta_0 \in U$, the sequence generated by the algorithm (7.1) converges to 0.*

For the instability result it is necessary to introduce a further assumption:

(v) For all t, $\mathcal{M}(\cdot)$ is continuously differentiable in a neighborhood of $(0, \gamma_t)$ and $D_1 \mathcal{M}(0, \gamma_t)$ has no eigenvalue equal to $-(1 - \gamma_t)/\gamma_t$.

The result for local instability is the following.

Theorem 7.2. *Assume that conditions* (i)–(v) *hold. If in the algorithm (7.1) the matrix $D_1 \mathcal{M}(0, 0)$ has an eigenvalue with real part bigger than 1, then the algorithm (7.1) is locally unstable at $\theta = 0$, i.e., there is a neighborhood U such that, for every neighborhood U_1 of 0 in U, there exist $\theta_0 \in U_1$ such that the sequence generated by the algorithm (7.1) leaves U.*

For a proof see again Evans and Honkapohja (2000). That paper also presents two applications of these propositions, namely the nonlinear multivariate cobweb model and a model of two-cycles for the (univariate) setup $p_t = F(p_{t+1}^e)$.

7.2.2 Applications

Example 1: **Instability of Interest Rate Pegging.** The argument that tight interest rate control is not a feasible monetary policy has recently been reexamined by Howitt (1992) for some alternative economies with learning behavior.

One of the models has both short- and far-sighted agents. The former live for two periods, selling their endowment e when young and consuming only at old age the proceeds $e P_{t-1}$. The latter have a constant endowment y and an objective function $E_t^* \sum_{j=0}^\infty \beta^j u(c_{t+j})$. (Here E_t^* denotes expectations.) They face a finance constraint implying that $M_t = P_t y$, since current consumption and investment in bonds is paid for by initial money, a transfer, and initial bonds (with interest). M_t is end-of-period money holding.

Denoting the nominal interest factor on bonds by R_t, the first-order condition for the far-sighted agent is

$$u'(c_t) = R_{t+1} E_t^* \left[\frac{\beta u'(c_{t+1})}{\pi_{t+1}} \right], \qquad \pi_{t+1} = P_{t+1}/P_t.$$

Market clearing for goods yields $c_t = y + e(1 - 1/\pi_t)$. The finance constraint implies that inflation equals money growth. With a pegged interest factor R, the model has a unique perfect-foresight steady state with inflation factor $\pi^* = R\beta$.

The analysis of this model proceeds by defining the variable

$$x_t = \frac{\beta u'\{y + e[1 - (1/\pi_t)]\}}{\pi_t},$$

so that the first-order condition gives

$$u'[y + e(1 - 1/\pi_t)] = R\hat{x}_{t+1}, \quad \hat{x}_{t+1} \equiv E_t^* x_{t+1}.$$

This equation defines a function $\pi_t = \pi(\hat{x}_{t+1})$. Introducing the notation $h(x) = \beta R/\pi(x)$, the model yields the dynamic equation

$$x_t = \hat{x}_{t+1} h(\hat{x}_{t+1}), \quad \text{where } h, h' > 0, \quad h(x^*) = 1, \tag{7.2}$$

and where $x^* = \pi^{-1}(\pi^*)$.

Given this reduced form (7.2), the formulation of learning of the steady state proceeds along the usual lines. Computing the derivative of $F(\hat{x}_{t+1}) \equiv$

$\hat{x}_{t+1} h(\hat{x}_{t+1})$, we get that $F'(x^*) = h(x^*) + x^* h'(x^*) > 1$ since $h(x^*) = 1$ and $h' > 0$. Thus, the steady state under interest rate pegging is unstable under adaptive learning.[2]

Example 2: **Learning with Contemporaneous Information.** We consider the case of learning a steady state when contemporaneous information is assumed to be available. Let the algorithm be

$$a_t = a_{t-1} + \gamma_t \big[f(a_t) - a_{t-1} \big] \tag{7.3}$$

as discussed in Section 3.4 in Chapter 3. As a normalization we set the fixed point at $a = 0$, so that $f(0) = 0$. We also assume that

(a) $a_t = \gamma_t f(a_t) \Longrightarrow a_t = 0$, $f(a_t) = 0$,
(b) $\gamma_t f'(a_t) \neq 1$.

By (b) it is possible to apply the implicit function theorem to equation (7.3) and obtain the system

$$a_t = H(a_{t-1}, \gamma_t).$$

Defining a function $\mathcal{M}(a_{t-1}, \gamma_t)$ by the formula

$$H(a_{t-1}, \gamma_t) = (1 - \gamma_t) a_{t-1} + \gamma_t \mathcal{M}(a_{t-1}, \gamma_t),$$

this system is in standard form (7.1). Before the theorems above can be applied, it is necessary to verify that $\mathcal{M}(\cdot)$ satisfies the assumptions required in them.

Using the implicit function theorem, we obtain the derivatives

$$D_1 H = \frac{1 - \gamma_t}{1 - \gamma_t f'(a_t)},$$

$$D_2 H = \frac{f(a_t) - a_{t-1}}{1 - \gamma_t f'(a_t)}.$$

We also note that $H(0, \gamma_t) = 0$ for all γ_t using condition (a). The derivatives of $\mathcal{M}(\cdot)$ are

$$D_1 \mathcal{M} = \gamma_t^{-1} \big[D_1 H - (1 - \gamma_t) \big],$$
$$D_2 \mathcal{M} = \gamma_t^{-2} \big[\gamma_t D_2 H - H(a_{t-1}, \gamma_t) + a_{t-1} \big].$$

---

[2]We note here that Howitt (1992) also considers other more general learning rules. This is possible, since the system is one-dimensional and relatively simple.

Clearly, $\mathcal{M}(0, \gamma_t) = 0$ and $D_2\mathcal{M}(0, \gamma_t) = 0$ for all γ_t. Moreover, $D_1\mathcal{M}(0, \gamma_t) = (1 - \gamma_t)[f'(0)/(1 - \gamma_t f'(0))]$, so that

$$\lim_{\gamma_t \to 0} D_1\mathcal{M}(0, \gamma_t) = f'(0).$$

This last result shows that the properties of $f'(0)$ determine the stability of the fixed point 0 under the algorithm (7.3). Thus we have the following.

Proposition 7.3. *If $f'(0) < 1$ (respectively > 1), then 0 is locally stable (respectively unstable) for the algorithm (7.3).*

7.2.3 Discussion

In nonstochastic models the study of learning dynamics is straightforward for the case of learning a steady state using natural classes of learning rules with constant or decreasing gain.[3] Similar techniques can be applied if agents are only trying to learn the slope λ of a first-order process $y_t = \lambda y_{t-1}$. An example is the Ramsey model presented in Chapter 4.

Matters become much more complicated if the perceived law of motion has both an intercept and a slope parameter. Consider, for example, the model

$$y_t = \alpha + \delta y_{t-1} + \beta y_{t+1}^e \tag{7.4}$$

with perfect-foresight solutions of the form

$$y_t = \mu + \lambda y_{t-1},$$

so that normally there are two such solutions. Typically, one is interested in solutions with $|\lambda| < 1$. Under perfect foresight the forecast, with μ and λ known, is given by $y_{t+1} = \mu + \lambda(\mu + \lambda y_{t-1})$, i.e.,

$$y_{t+1}^e = \mu(1 + \lambda) + \lambda^2 y_{t-1},$$

if y_{t-1} is the last available data point. (The case of contemporaneous information can be treated similarly.)

---

[3]The extension to learning rational cycles can be done using essentially the same techniques; see Guesnerie and Woodford (1991) for the case of constant gain. The case of decreasing gain can be treated by our general method; see Evans and Honkapohja (2000).

In such nonstochastic models there is no fully natural way to estimate both μ and λ simultaneously. One might consider using the least squares estimator, which would be natural in the corresponding stochastic framework. We will discuss this approach extensively in the context of stochastic models in Chapter 8.

To see the problems, suppose that forecasts are given by $y^e_{t+1} = a_t(1+b_t) + b^2_t y_{t-1}$, where (a_t, b_t) are the recursive least squares estimates of (μ, λ) at time t. The recursive least squares algorithm can be expressed as

$$\phi_t = \phi_{t-1} + t^{-1} R_t^{-1} z_{t-1} (y_{t-1} - \phi'_{t-1} z_{t-1}),$$

$$R_t = R_{t-1} + t^{-1} (z_{t-1} z'_{t-1} - R_{t-1}),$$

where $\phi'_t = (a_t, b_t)$, $z'_t = (1, y_{t-1})$. From the reduced form (7.4) we get $y_t = T(a, b)' z_t$, with $T(a_t, b_t)' = (\alpha + \beta a_t(1 + b_t), \delta + \beta b^2_t)$. If one attempted to use the stochastic approximation results, the ϕ component of the ODE would be given by

$$h_\phi(\phi, R) = R^{-1} \begin{pmatrix} 1 & \bar{y}(\phi) \\ \bar{y}(\phi) & \bar{y}(\phi)^2 \end{pmatrix} (T(\phi) - \phi)$$

and the R component of the ODE would be given by

$$h_R(\phi, R) = \lim_{t \to \infty} E z_t(\phi) z_t(\phi)' - R$$

$$= \begin{pmatrix} 1 & \bar{y}(\phi) \\ \bar{y}(\phi) & \bar{y}(\phi)^2 \end{pmatrix} - R,$$

where $\bar{y}(\phi) = [\alpha + \beta a(1+b)]/[1 - (\delta + \beta b^2)]$. At the equilibrium, R is singular, so that the ODE is undefined at that point. Thus the stochastic approximation tools cannot be applied.

The econometric intuition for the difficulty is straightforward. Asymptotically, along a rational expectations equilibrium (REE), y_t is converging to a constant. Therefore, the regressors z_t exhibit perfect multicollinearity asymptotically. From an econometric viewpoint, this violates standard assumptions required for consistency, making the procedure questionable. Can such estimates converge even though the standard assumptions fail? This turns out to be an extremely delicate issue and is taken up at length by Grandmont (1998).[4]

It should be noted that these problems disappear in stochastic models. If the model is changed to $y_t = \alpha + \delta y_{t-1} + \beta y_{t+1}^e + u_t$, where u_t is an iid random shock, the RE solution is of the form $y_t = \mu + \lambda y_{t-1} + \eta u_t$, so that in the REE the expected value $E z_t z_t'$ is nonsingular. This point holds even if the shock has a positive but arbitrarily small support. Thus the above problems do not arise in stochastic models and, as emphasized by Evans and Honkapohja (1998b), the stochastic approximation approach can be applied to obtain local stability and instability results under least squares learning. These types of results will be discussed in detail in Part III of this book.

7.3   The Case of Markovian State Dynamics

7.3.1   The Setup and the Assumptions

For the system describing the evolution of the vector of parameters $\theta_t \in \mathbb{R}^d$, we continue with the general form

$$\theta_t = \theta_{t-1} + \gamma_t \mathcal{H}(\theta_{t-1}, X_t) + \gamma_t^2 \rho_t(\theta_{t-1}, X_t). \tag{7.5}$$

Again γ_t is a sequence of "gains" while $X_t \in \mathbb{R}^k$ is the vector of state variables. As before, $\mathcal{H}(\cdot)$ and $\rho_t(\cdot)$ are two functions describing the learning rule. The assumption that is different from Chapter 6 is that the vector of state variables X_t is assumed to follow a Markov process with a transition probability law $\Pi_\theta(x, A)$ which may depend on θ_{t-1}. That is, $\Pr[X_t \in A \mid \theta_{t-1}, X_{t-1}] = \Pi_{\theta_{t-1}}(X_{t-1}, A)$ for Borel sets $A \subset \mathbb{R}^k$. Conditionally linear dynamics is a special case of our formulation, as will be proved below.

For the analysis one again fixes an open set $D \subset \mathbb{R}^d$ which contains the equilibrium point of interest. The assumptions on the algorithm are close to those of Chapter 6. We postulate the following:

(A.1′) γ_t is a nonstochastic nonincreasing sequence satisfying

$$\sum_{t=1}^{\infty} \gamma_t = \infty \quad \text{and} \quad \sum_{t=1}^{\infty} \gamma_t^\alpha < \infty \quad \text{for some } \alpha \geq 2.$$

---

[4]Grandmont and Laroque (1991) consider the problem for least squares with finite memory. Moore (1993) avoids these problems by having agents estimate the slope and the intercepts separately, taking the REE value of the other parameter as given.

(A.2) For any compact $Q \subset D$, there exist C_1, C_2, q_1, and q_2 such that $\forall \theta \in Q$ and $\forall t$,

  (i) $|\mathcal{H}(\theta, x)| \leq C_1(1 + |x|^{q_1})$,
  (ii) $|\rho_t(\theta, x)| \leq C_2(1 + |x|^{q_2})$.

(A.3′) For any compact $Q \subset D$, the function $\mathcal{H}(\theta, x)$ satisfies, $\forall \theta, \theta' \in Q$ and $x_1, x_2 \in \mathbb{R}^k$,

  (i) $|\partial \mathcal{H}(\theta, x_1)/\partial x - \partial \mathcal{H}(\theta, x_2)/\partial x| \leq L_1 |x_1 - x_2|(1 + |x_1|^{p_1} + |x_2|^{p_1})$
      for some $p_1 \geq 0$,
  (ii) $|\mathcal{H}(\theta, 0) - \mathcal{H}(\theta', 0)| \leq L_2 |\theta - \theta'|$,
  (iii) $|\partial \mathcal{H}(\theta, x)/\partial x - \partial \mathcal{H}(\theta', x)/\partial x| \leq L_2 |\theta - \theta'|(1 + |x|^{p_2})$ for some
      $p_2 \geq 0$, for some constants L_1, L_2.

Assumption (A.1′) is more general than Assumption (A.1) of Chapter 6 which sets $\alpha = 2$. Note that Assumption (A.1′) is satisfied for $\gamma_t = K/t^\beta$ for $0 < \beta \leq 1$, $K > 0$ constant.[5] Assumption (A.2) imposes polynomial bounds on $\mathcal{H}(\cdot)$ and $\rho_t(\cdot)$. Assumption (A.3′) generalizes Assumption (A.3) of Chapter 6 in the way pointed out there. We remark that Assumption (A.3′) holds provided $\mathcal{H}(\theta, x)$ is twice continuously differentiable with bounded second derivatives on every Q.

Before stating the assumptions concerned with state dynamics, it is worth introducing the following notation and definitions. For any function, $f(\theta, x)$, we denote by f_θ the mapping $x \to f(\theta, x)$. If $f(\theta, x)$ is differentiable in x, we denote by $f'(\theta, x)$ its derivative with respect to x. Moreover, for any function $g \colon \mathbb{R}^k \to \mathbb{R}^k$, one defines the expression

$$[g]_p = \sup_{x_1 \neq x_2} \frac{|g(x_1) - g(x_2)|}{|x_1 - x_2|(1 + |x_1|^p + |x_2|^p)}$$

and the function space $\mathrm{Li}(p) = \{g \mid [g]_p < \infty\}$.

For the state dynamics one makes the first assumption:

(M.1) For any compact $Q \subset D$ and any $q > 0$, there exists $\mu_q(Q) < \infty$ such that $\forall n, x \in \mathbb{R}^k, a \in \mathbb{R}^d$,

$$E_{x,a}\{I(\theta_k \in Q, k \leq n)(1 + |X_{n+1}|^q)\} \leq \mu_q(Q)(1 + |x|^q).$$

---

[5]Choose $\alpha > \max(2, \beta^{-1})$.

Here $I(A)$ and $E_{x,a}(\cdot)$ denote, respectively, the indicator function of any set A and the conditional expected value given initial conditions $X_0 = x$, $\theta_0 = a$. This assumption states that the conditional moments of X_n, provided θ_k has remained in Q, are uniformly bounded in θ and the bounds are polynomial in the initial state x.

Before stating the next assumption, we introduce the following notation. Let

$$\Pi_\theta^n(x, A) = \Pr\left[X_{t+n} \in A \mid \theta_t = \theta, X_t = x\right]$$

denote the transition probability measure n steps ahead for the Markov process X_t with fixed one-step-ahead transition probability $\Pi_\theta(x, A)$. In addition, denote by $\Pi_\theta^n f_\theta(x)$ or simply by $\Pi_\theta^n f_\theta$ the mapping $x \to \int f(\theta, y)\Pi_\theta^n(x, dy)$, for $n \geq 1$. Thus $\Pi_\theta^n f_\theta(x)$ is the n-step-ahead conditional expectation of $f(\theta, y)$ given the current state x.

We now postulate for any compact $Q \subset D$:

(M.2) For all n, θ, and $m \geq 0$: there exist K such that $\Pi_\theta^n(1 + |y|^m) \leq K(1 + |x|^m)$.

(M.3) For all $p > 0$, there exist K_1, K_2, q_1, and $\rho_1 < 1$ such that for all functions $g \in \mathrm{Li}(p)$, $n \geq 0$, $x_1, x_2 \in \mathbb{R}^k$, $\theta, \theta' \in Q$,

  (i) $|\Pi_\theta^n g(x_1) - \Pi_\theta^n g(x_2)| \leq K_1 \rho_1^n |x_1 - x_2|(1 + |x_1|^p + |x_2|^p)$,
  (ii) $|\Pi_\theta^n g(x) - \Pi_{\theta'}^n g(x)| \leq K_2[g]_p |\theta - \theta'|(1 + |x|^{q_1})$.

(M.4) For all $p > 0$ and for all differentiable functions g with $g' \in \mathrm{Li}(p)$, there exists $K_3(g')$ such that $\forall n \geq 0$, $x_1, x_2 \in \mathbb{R}^k$, $\theta, \theta' \in Q$,

$$\left|\Pi_\theta^n g(x_1) - \Pi_\theta^n g(x_2) - \Pi_{\theta'}^n g(x_1) + \Pi_{\theta'}^n g(x_2)\right|$$
$$\leq K_3(g')\rho_2^n |\theta - \theta'|\left(1 + |x_1|^{q_2} + |x_2|^{q_2}\right)$$

for constants $\rho_2 < 1$ and q_2 independent of g.

We remark that Assumptions (M.1)–(M.4) are identical to the conditions (C.1)–(C.4) in Evans and Honkapohja (1998a), except that Assumptions (M.3) and (M.4) strengthen slightly (C.3) and (C.4), respectively, by the assumption that they hold for all $p > 0$. [This is needed because of the form (A.3′).] In addition we postulate a further assumption:

(M.5) For all $q \geq 1$, there exists an integer r and constants $\bar{\alpha} < 1$, β such that

$$\sup_{\theta \in Q} \int |y|^q \Pi_\theta^r(x, dy) \leq \bar{\alpha}|x|^q + \beta.$$

Assumption (M.5) is necessary to analyze the more general gain sequence permitted in Assumption (A.1′), as well as the constant-gain algorithms that will be discussed later.

These assumptions are sometimes tedious to verify in specific applications. However, in special cases the situation may be simplified. An important case is when the Markov process X_t is independent of θ_{t-1}. Then one only needs to verify Assumptions (M.2), (M.3)(i), and (M.5) in addition to Assumptions (A). Below, we also show that Assumptions (M.1)–(M.5) hold under conditional linear dynamics for the state variable.

Our method of analysis follows that of Chapter 6. One derives an associated ODE whose trajectories, at specific times, approximate the time paths of the algorithm with the approximation becoming sharper for large t. In order to derive the differential equation one needs to show that, for each θ, the state variable X_t has a unique invariant distribution and that the function $\mathcal{H}(\theta, y)$ in the dynamics for the parameter vector is integrable with respect to this distribution. These facts are the content of the following lemma.

Lemma 7.4. *Under Assumptions (M.2) and (M.3)(i) the Markov process X_t, with transition probability $\Pi_\theta(x, A)$ for any fixed θ, has a unique invariant probability distribution Γ_θ, and the function*

$$h(\theta) = \int \mathcal{H}(\theta, y)\Gamma_\theta(dy) \tag{7.6}$$

is well defined and locally Lipschitz for any function $\mathcal{H}(\theta, y)$ satisfying Assumptions (A.2)(i) and (A.3′).

Proof. $\mathcal{H}_\theta(y)$ can be shown to be Li(p) using a modification of the corresponding argument described in the proof of Lemma 6.2, of Chapter 6, to obtain a bound on $|\mathcal{H}(\theta, x_1) - \mathcal{H}(\theta, x_2)|$. The existence of Γ_θ and $h(\theta)$ then follows from Benveniste, Metivier, and Priouret (1990, Proposition 3, p. 255). They also establish that $|\Pi_\theta^n \mathcal{H}_\theta(x) - h(\theta)| \leq K_1 \rho_2^n [\mathcal{H}_\theta]_p (1 + |x|^{p+1})$ for some K_1 and $0 < \rho_2 < 1$. To prove the Lipschitz property of $h(\theta)$ one can modify the argument of the corresponding lemma in Chapter 6 to show that Assumption (A.3′)

implies that

$$\left|\mathcal{H}(\theta, x) - \mathcal{H}(\theta', x)\right| \leq K|\theta - \theta'|\left(1 + |x|^{p_3}\right)$$

for some constants K and $p_3 \geq 0$.

Next, one notes that

$$\left|\Pi_{\theta_1}^n \mathcal{H}_{\theta_1}(x) - \Pi_{\theta_2}^n \mathcal{H}_{\theta_2}(x)\right|$$
$$\leq \left|\Pi_{\theta_1}^n \mathcal{H}_{\theta_1}(x) - \Pi_{\theta_2}^n \mathcal{H}_{\theta_1}(x)\right| + \left|\Pi_{\theta_2}^n \mathcal{H}_{\theta_1}(x) - \Pi_{\theta_2}^n \mathcal{H}_{\theta_2}(x)\right|.$$

Using this, and Assumptions (M.2) and (M.3)(i), we get

$$\begin{aligned} \left|\Pi_{\theta_2}^n \mathcal{H}_{\theta_1}(x) - \Pi_{\theta_2}^n \mathcal{H}_{\theta_2}(x)\right| &\leq \left|\Pi_{\theta_2}^n (\mathcal{H}_{\theta_1}(x) - \mathcal{H}_{\theta_2})(x)\right| \\ &\leq K|\theta_1 - \theta_2|\Pi_{\theta_2}^n \left(1 + |x|^p\right) \\ &\leq K'|\theta_1 - \theta_2|\left(1 + |x|^p\right) \end{aligned}$$

for some K' and p, and

$$\left|\Pi_{\theta_1}^n \mathcal{H}_{\theta_1}(x) - \Pi_{\theta_2}^n \mathcal{H}_{\theta_2}(x)\right| \leq K^*|\theta_1 - \theta_2|\left(1 + |x|^q\right)$$

for some K^* and q. Selecting $x = 0$ and letting $n \to \infty$ yields the Lipschitz condition $|h(\theta_1) - h(\theta_2)| \leq M|\theta_1 - \theta_2|$.   □

The function $h(\theta)$ obtained in the lemma defines the *associated differential equation*

$$\frac{d\theta}{d\tau} = h(\theta)$$

needed for the asymptotic analysis of the time paths of the algorithm. Note that for the conditionally linear state dynamics, this mapping and differential equation were derived through a different but equivalent route. For this important case we establish here that Assumptions (B) of Chapter 6 are a special case of Assumptions (M) above.

Proposition 7.5. *If Assumptions (B) of Chapter 6 hold, then X_t satisfies Conditions (M.1)–(M.5) for any $p > 0$.*

Proof (The main steps)**.** First, define the nth stage

$$U_n(\theta) = \sum_{k=1}^n A^{n-k}(\theta)B(\theta)W_k.$$

It can be shown that for all $p \geq 1$, there are constants K, K^* such that, for all $\theta, \theta' \in Q$, $U_n(\theta)$ satisfies $\|U_n(\theta)\|_p \leq K$ and $\|U_n(\theta) - U_n(\theta')\|_p \leq K^*|\theta - \theta'|$; see Benveniste, Metivier, and Priouret (1990, pp. 266–267). (Here $\|\cdot\|_p$ denotes the L^p norm.) Next, note that by Assumption (B.3) one has $|A^n(\theta)| \leq \rho^n$. Then Condition (M.1) is immediate from Assumptions (B.2) and (B.3).

To prove Condition (M.2) we note that the equation

$$E\big(g(A^n(\theta)x + U_n)\big) = E\big(g(A^n(\theta)x + V_n)\big) \tag{7.7}$$

holds for any bounded and continuous function g satisfying $|g(x)| \leq C(1 + |x|^q)$, where the random variable

$$V_n(\theta) = \sum_{k=1}^{n} A^k(\theta) B(\theta) W_k$$

has the same distribution as U_n and has a limit $V_\infty(\theta) = \lim_{n \to \infty} V_n(\theta)$ almost surely and in L_p for any given θ.[6] Using $g(x) = 1 + |x|^m$ yields Condition (M.2) at once.

To prove Condition (M.3)(i) we use equation (7.7) and the definition of $[g]_p$ in the inequality

$$\big|E\big[g\big(A^n(\theta)x_1 + U_n(\theta)\big) - g\big(A^n(\theta)x_2 + U_n(\theta)\big)\big]\big|$$
$$\leq [g]_p |A^n(\theta)||x_1 - x_2| E\big[1 + \big|A^n(\theta)x_1 + U_n(\theta)\big|^p$$
$$+ \big|A^n(\theta)x_2 + U_n(\theta)\big|^p\big].$$

To prove Condition (M.3)(ii) one notes that

$$\big|E\big[g\big(A^n(\theta)x + U_n(\theta)\big) - g\big(A^n(\theta')x + U_n(\theta')\big)\big]\big|$$
$$\leq [g]_p E\big\{\big[\big|A^n(\theta) - A^n(\theta')\big||x| + \big|U_n(\theta) - U_n(\theta')\big|\big]$$
$$\times \big[1 + \big|A^n(\theta)x_1 + U_n(\theta)\big|^p + \big|A^n(\theta)x_2 + U_n(\theta)\big|^p\big]\big\},$$

to which one applies the Schwarz inequality. Using Assumptions (B.2) and (B.3), the resulting second term is polynomially bounded in $|x|$. The resulting first term is simply the L_2-norm of $|A^n(\theta) - A^n(\theta')||x| + |U_n(\theta) - U_n(\theta')|$. Since U_n, $A(\theta)$ satisfy Lipschitz conditions and $|A^n(\theta)| \leq \rho^n$, the whole expression is bounded by an expression of the form $C|\theta - \theta'|(1 + |x|^q)$ which proves Condition (M.3)(ii).

---

[6]This limit follows from the martingale convergence theorem using the properties of $A(\theta)$ and $B(\theta)$.

We omit the proof of Condition (M.4) for brevity. The lengthy details are given in Benveniste, Metivier, and Priouret (1990, p. 269). Finally, the proof of Condition (M.5) is a straightforward modification of the proof of Condition (M.2).   □

7.3.2   The Convergence Result in the Markovian Case

From this point onwards the analysis proceeds as in the derivation of Theorems 6.4 and 6.5 in Chapter 6. One simply utilizes the new definition of the associated differential equation. Thus assume that θ^* is a locally asymptotically stable equilibrium point for the associated ODE

$$\frac{d\theta}{d\tau} = h(\theta(\tau)),$$

where $h(\theta)$ is given by equation (7.6). By the converse Lyapunov theorem (see Proposition 5.9 of Section 5.3.4 in Chapter 5), there exists a C^2 Lyapunov function $\mathcal{U}(\theta)$ on the domain of attraction D of θ^* having the properties:

(a) $\mathcal{U}(\theta^*) = 0, \mathcal{U}(\theta) > 0$ for all $\theta \in D, \theta \neq \theta^*$,
(b) $\mathcal{U}'(\theta)h(\theta) < 0$ for all $\theta \in D, \theta \neq \theta^*$,
(c) $\mathcal{U}(\theta) \to \infty$ if $\theta \to \partial D$ or $|\theta| \to \infty$.[7]

Again use the notation $K(c) = \{\theta \mid \mathcal{U}(\theta) \leq c\}, c > 0$ for contour sets of the Lyapunov function. Also let $\tau(c) = \inf(n; \theta_n \notin K(c))$ and let $P_{n,x,a}$ be the probability distribution of $(X_k, \theta_k)_{k \geq n}$ with $X_n = x, \theta_n = a$. Following the steps given in Section 6.3.3 of Chapter 6 yields the same results as before. We restate them for completeness and later reference.

Theorem 7.6. *Let θ^* be an asymptotically stable equilibrium point of the ODE $d\theta/d\tau = h(\theta(\tau))$. Suppose Assumptions (A.1'), (A.2), (A.3'), and (M.1)–(M.5) are satisfied on $D = \mathrm{int}(K(c))$ for some $c > 0$. Suppose that for $0 < c_1 < c_2$, we have $K(c_2) \subset D$. Then*

(i) *There exist constants B_1 and s such that, for all $a \in K(c_1), n \geq 0, x$,*

$$P_{n,x,a}\{\theta_k \text{ leaves } K(c_2) \text{ in finite time}\} \leq B_1(1 + |x|^s)J(n),$$

---

[7] ∂D denotes the boundary of D.

where

$$J(n) = \sum_{k=n+1}^{\infty} \gamma_k^{\alpha}.$$

(ii) *For all $a \in K(c_1)$, $n \geq 0$, x, one has*

$$P_{n,x,a}\{\theta_k \text{ leaves } K(c_2) \text{ in finite time or } \theta_k \to \theta^*\} = 1.$$

(iii) *For any compact $Q \subset D$, there exist constants B_2 and s such that, for all $a \in K(c_1)$, $n \geq 0$, x,*

$$P_{n,x,a}\{\theta_k \to \theta^*\} \geq 1 - B_2(1 + |x|^s)J(n),$$

where $J(n)$ is as in (i).

We note that $\lim_{n \to \infty} J(n) = 0$.

Proof (Outline). The key results are Theorem 17 and Corollary 18 of Chapter 3, Part II, of Benveniste, Metivier, and Priouret (1990). The proof for the case $\alpha = 2$ in Assumption (A.1′) is developed in some detail in Evans and Honkapohja (1998a). The strengthened form of Assumptions (M.3) and (M.5) imply that Assumption (A′.5) of Benveniste, Metivier, and Priouret (1990) is satisfied. Assumption (A′.6) of Benveniste, Metivier, and Priouret (1990) is our Assumption (A.1′). Finally, Assumption (A.7) of Benveniste, Metivier, and Priouret (1990) is the existence of the Lyapunov function assumed above. The conditions (M.1) to (M.5) are shown in Evans and Honkapohja (1998a) to imply that Assumptions (A.1)–(A.4) of Benveniste, Metivier, and Priouret (1990) hold. $\qquad\square$

We remark that Corollaries 6.6 and 6.8 of Chapter 6 continue to hold in the Markovian setup. Moreover, the global convergence result, Theorem 6.10 of Chapter 6, can be generalized to the Markovian case for the case $\alpha = 2$. The required assumptions are:

(D.1) The functions $\mathcal{H}(\theta, x)$ and $\rho_t(\theta, x)$ satisfy, for all $\theta, \theta' \in \mathbb{R}^d$ and all $x, x' \in \mathbb{R}^k$,

    (i) $|\mathcal{H}(\theta, x_1) - \mathcal{H}(\theta, x_2)| \leq L_1(1 + |\theta|)|x_1 - x_2|(1 + |x_1|^{p_1} + |x_2|^{p_1})$,

    (ii) $|\mathcal{H}(\theta, 0) - \mathcal{H}(\theta', 0)| \leq L_2|\theta - \theta'|$,

(iii) $|\partial\mathcal{H}(\theta, x)/\partial x - \partial\mathcal{H}(\theta', x)/\partial x| \le L_2|\theta - \theta'|(1 + |x|^{p_2})$,

(iv) $|\rho_t(\theta, x)| \le C_2(1 + |\theta|)(1 + |x|^q)$,

for some constants L_1, L_2, C_2, p_1, p_2, and q.

(D.2′) The transition probability law $\Pi(x, dy)$ of the Markov process $X_t \in \mathbb{R}^k$ is independent of θ and satisfies

(i) for all $n, m \ge 0$, there exists K such that $\int(1 + |y|^m)\Pi^n(x, dy) \le K(1 + |x|^m)$,

(ii) for all $p \ge 0$, there exist K_1 and $\rho < 1$ such that for all functions $g \in \text{Li}(p)$, $n \ge 0$, $x_1, x_2 \in \mathbb{R}^k$,

$$\left| \int g(y)\Pi^n(x_1, dy) - \int g(y)\Pi^n(x_2, dy) \right|$$
$$\le K\rho^n[g]_p|x_1 - x_2|(1 + |x_1|^p + |x_2|^p).$$

Here Assumption (D.1) is exactly the same as in Chapter 6, while Assumption (D.2′) is the analogue of Assumption (D.2) for the more general Markovian setup. The global convergence result can then be stated as follows.

Theorem 7.7. *Under Assumptions (A.1), (D.1), and (D.2′), assume that there exists a unique equilibrium point $\theta^* \in \mathbb{R}^d$ of the associated ODE. Suppose that there exists a positive C^2 function $\mathcal{U}(\theta)$ on $\mathbb{R}^d$ with bounded second derivatives satisfying (i) $\mathcal{U}'(\theta)h(\theta) < 0$ for all $\theta \ne \theta^*$; (ii) $\mathcal{U}(\theta) = 0$ iff $\theta = \theta^*$; (iii) $\mathcal{U}(\theta) \ge \alpha|\theta|^2$ for all θ with $|\theta| \ge \rho_0$ for some $\alpha, \rho_0 > 0$. Then the sequence θ_n converges $P_{0,x,a}$ almost surely to θ^*.*

7.4 Convergence Results for Constant-Gain Algorithms

We now consider algorithms of the form (7.5) where the assumption on the gain sequence (A.1′) is replaced by a constant-gain assumption $\gamma_t = \gamma$, where $0 < \gamma < 1$. We also restrict attention to the case without the complementary term. We thus have

$$\theta_n = \theta_{n-1} + \gamma\mathcal{H}(\theta_{n-1}, X_n), \tag{7.8}$$

$\theta_n \in \mathbb{R}^d$, $X_n \in \mathbb{R}^k$, with a starting point $\theta_0 = a$. Here we use n to denote discrete time so that we can use t below for continuous time. The other assumptions of the preceding section will be retained. We continue to assume that these hold on some open set $D \subset \mathbb{R}^d$.

θ_n cannot now be expected to converge to a nonstochastic point, since the constant gain implies that θ_n is nonnegligibly sensitive to random shocks even asymptotically. However, θ_n may converge to a limiting probability distribution. It turns out that it is possible to obtain the limiting distribution for cases in which γ is small. We begin with some preliminary definitions and additional assumptions.

By the lemma in the preceding section, the Markov process X_n for fixed θ has a unique invariant probability distribution Γ_θ. Let X_n^θ denote this stationary Markov chain with transition probability $\Pi_\theta(x, A)$. Let

$$\mathcal{R}^{ij}(\theta) = \sum_{k=-\infty}^{\infty} \text{cov}[\mathcal{H}^i(\theta, X_k^\theta), \mathcal{H}^j(\theta, X_0^\theta)], \tag{7.9}$$

and let $\mathcal{R}(\theta)$ denote the $d \times d$ matrix with elements $\mathcal{R}^{ij}(\theta)$. We remark that under our assumptions it can be shown that $\mathcal{R}^{ij}(\theta)$ is locally Lipschitz on D.[8] We need to impose an additional assumption on the function $h(\theta)$ used to define the associated ODE of the algorithm.

(H.1) $h(\theta)$ has continuous first and second derivatives on D.

To precisely state the approximation theorem we need further definitions. Let

$$\theta_n^\gamma = \theta_{n-1}^\gamma + \gamma \mathcal{H}(\theta_{n-1}^\gamma, X_n)$$

be the θ_n process, where we make explicit the dependence on the value of the constant-gain parameter γ. We need to construct a corresponding continuous-time process $\theta^\gamma(t)$. Let $t_n^\gamma = n\gamma$ and define $\theta^\gamma(t) = \theta_n^\gamma$ if $t_n^\gamma \le t < t_{n+1}^\gamma$. Finally, let $\tilde{\theta}(t, a)$ denote the solution to the ODE $d\theta/dt = h(\theta)$ with initial condition $\theta(0) = a \in D$.

The first result concerns approximations at finite horizons over which the trajectory $\tilde{\theta}(t, a)$ remains in D. In fact, we shall consider a fixed compact set $Q \subset D$ and a fixed time $T > 0$ such that $\tilde{\theta}(t, a) \in Q$ for all $0 \le t \le T$.

Proposition 7.8. *Assume (A.2), (A.3′), (M.1)–(M.5), and (H.1). Consider the normalized random variables $U^\gamma(t) = \gamma^{-1/2}[\theta^\gamma(t) - \tilde{\theta}(t, a)]$. As $\gamma \to 0$, the*

---

[8]This follows from Benveniste, Metivier, and Priouret (1990, Theorem 5, Chap. 2, Part II) and their formulation of the Poisson equation in (A.8)(ii), p. 321.

process $U^\gamma(t)$, $0 \leq t \leq T$, converges weakly to the solution $U(t)$ of the stochastic differential equation

$$dU(t) = D_\theta h(\tilde{\theta}(t,a))U(t)\,dt + \mathcal{R}^{1/2}(\tilde{\theta}(t,a))\,dW(t),$$

with initial condition $U(0) = 0$, where $W(t)$ is a standard vector Wiener process.

Proof (Outline). The result is essentially that of Theorem 7, Chapter 4, Part II of Benveniste, Metivier, and Priouret (1990). The outline of proof for Theorem 7.6 above indicates how our assumptions imply all the assumptions of Theorem 7 of Benveniste, Metivier, and Priouret (1990), with the exception of their Assumption (A.8). To verify their Assumption (A.8), first note that our Assumption (H.1) postulates the derivative properties of $h(\theta)$. Define the series

$$\nu_\theta(y) = \sum_{k=0}^{\infty}(\Pi_\theta^k \mathcal{H}_\theta - h(\theta))(y).$$

In Evans and Honkapohja (1998a), we show that $\nu_\theta(y)$ is well defined and satisfies certain properties. It can be shown that Theorem 5, Chapter 2, Part II of Benveniste, Metivier, and Priouret (1990) can be applied to the function $\Pi_\theta \nu_\theta^i \nu_\theta^j(y) - \Pi_\theta \nu_\theta^i(y)\Pi_\theta \nu_\theta^j(y)$ to prove that the rest of their Assumption (A.8) is satisfied. The statement of their Theorem 7 is expressed in terms of convergence to a Gaussian diffusion, which can alternatively be described as the solution to the stochastic differential equation above.   □

The definition of weak convergence for stochastic processes in continuous time is given in Billingsley (1968). An implication is weak convergence (convergence of the probability distributions) of the process at any given t as $\gamma \to 0$.

The stochastic differential equation in Proposition 7.8 is linear, though in general it has time-varying coefficients. It can still be analyzed using the methods outlined in Section 5.6.2 of Chapter 5. The results there imply the following. Let $V_U(t) = \text{var}(U(t))$. Then we have

$$EU(t) = 0,$$
$$\frac{dV_U(t)}{dt} = D_\theta h(\tilde{\theta}(t,a))V_U(t) + V_U(t)D_\theta h(\tilde{\theta}(t,a))' + \mathcal{R}(\tilde{\theta}(t,a)),$$

since $U(0) = 0$.

The general results on linear stochastic differential equations suggest that, with additional assumptions, the stochastic differential equation in Proposition

7.8 can have a stationary distribution asymptotically. This can provide an approximation result for large t that can be straightforward to apply. The additional required assumptions on $h(\theta)$ are:

(H.2) θ^* is a globally asymptotically stable equilibrium point of the ODE
$d\theta/dt = h(\theta)$.

(H.3) $D_\theta h(\theta)$ is Lipschitz and all of the eigenvalues of $B = D_\theta h(\theta^*)$ have strictly negative real parts.

We also make the following assumptions that various moments are polynomially bounded in the state variable.

(N.1) There exist $q_1, q_2, q_3 \geq 0$ such that, for all $q > 0$ and all compact sets Q, there is a constant $\mu(q, Q)$ such that for all $x \in \mathbb{R}^d$, $a \in Q$,

(i) $\sup_n E_{x,a}(1 + |X_n|^q) \leq \mu(1 + |x|^q)$,
(ii) $\sup_n E_{x,a}(|\mathcal{H}(\theta_n^\gamma, X_{n+1})|^2) \leq \mu(1 + |x|^{q_1})$,
(iii) $\sup_n E_{x,a}(|v_{\theta_n^\gamma}(X_{n+1})|^2) \leq \mu(1 + |x|^{q_2})$,
    where $v_\theta(y) = \sum_{k=0}^\infty (\Pi_\theta^k \mathcal{H} - h(\theta))(y)$,
(iv) $\sup_n E_{x,a}(|\theta_n^\gamma|^2) \leq \mu(1 + |x|^{q_3})$.

Though clearly strong, in Chapter 14 we will give an example in which these assumptions can be verified. Note that Assumption (N.1)(i) is a strengthening of Assumption (M.1) and that if in Assumption (A.2) the bound on $|\mathcal{H}(\theta, x)|$ is uniform over compact sets Q, then Assumption (N.1)(ii) follows from Assumption (N.1)(i).

Theorem 7.9. *Assume (A.2), (A.3'), (M.1)–(M.5), (H.1)–(H.3), and (N.1). Consider the normalized random variables $U^{\gamma_k}(t) = \gamma_k^{-1/2}[\theta^{\gamma_k}(t) - \theta^*]$. For any sequences $\tau_k \to \infty$, $\gamma_k \to 0$, the sequence of random variables $(U^{\gamma_k}(\tau_k))_{k \geq 0}$ converges in distribution to a normal random variable with zero mean and covariance matrix*

$$C = \int_0^\infty e^{sB} \mathcal{R}(\theta^*) e^{sB'} ds,$$

where B is defined in Assumption (H.3).

Proof (Outline). The result is that of Theorem 15, Chapter 4, Part II of Benveniste, Metivier, and Priouret (1990). Our assumptions (H.2)–(H.3) and (N.1) are the same as their Conditions (A) and (B), pages 334–335. Our conditions

(A.2), (A.3'), (M.1)–(M.5), (H.1) imply that their other assumptions hold as
noted in the preceding proposition.   □

   This theorem gives a simple approximation result for θ_n in the algorithm
(7.8) with constant gain γ. For small γ and large n, the distribution is approximately given by

$$\theta_n \sim N(\theta^*, \gamma C).$$

7.5 Gaussian Approximation for Cases of Decreasing Gain

We return to algorithms with decreasing gain, in particular of the form

$$\theta_n = \theta_{n-1} + \gamma_n \mathcal{H}(\theta_{n-1}, X_n), \tag{7.10}$$

for $n = 1, 2, 3, \ldots$. In this section the complementary term is omitted. In addition to the standard assumptions of Theorem 7.6, we make the following additional assumptions:

(P.1) $\gamma_n = K(n + N)^{-\beta}$, where $0 < \beta \leq 1$, $K, N > 0$, and $0 < \gamma_1 \leq 1$.
(P.2) $\mathrm{Pr}_{x,a}(|\theta_n| > R$ in finite time) is arbitrarily small for R sufficiently large.

Theorem 7.10. *Assume (A.2), (A.3'), (M.1)–(M.5) and (P.1)–(P.2). Consider the
two cases:*

  (i) *$\beta = 1$. Suppose (a) all eigenvalues of $D_\theta h(\theta^*)$ have real parts less than
     $-(2K)^{-1}$ and (b) $(\theta - \theta^*) \cdot h(\theta) \leq -\delta|\theta - \theta^*|^2$ for some $\delta > 0$,
     or*
 (ii) *$0 < \beta < 1$. Suppose all eigenvalues of $D_\theta h(\theta^*)$ have real parts less than
     zero.*

Then the sequence

$$(\theta_n - \theta^*)/\sqrt{\gamma_n}$$

*converges in distribution to a normal random variable with zero mean and co-
variance matrix*

$$C = \int_0^\infty e^{sB} \mathcal{R}(\theta^*) e^{sB'} \, ds.$$

Here $B = D_\theta h(\theta^*) + (2K)^{-1}I$, where I is the identity matrix, in the case $\beta = 1$ and $B = D_\theta h(\theta^*)$ if $0 < \beta < 1$.

This is Theorem 13, Chapter 4, Part II of Benveniste, Metivier, and Priouret (1990) applied to the special case $\gamma_n = K(n + N)^{-\beta}$. As with previous results, our assumptions are adequate to assure that their conditions are satisfied.

This result indicates that the algorithm (7.10) converges at rate $n^{\beta/2}$ under Assumption (P.1). However, note that when $\beta = 1$, an additional condition on the eigenvalues of $D_\theta h(\theta^*)$ is required. In particular for $K = 1$, the requirement is that all eigenvalues of $D_\theta h(\theta^*)$ have real parts less than $-1/2$.

7.6   Global Convergence on Compact Domains

In many economic models the basic assumptions and setup imply that the underlying space for the parameter vector θ can be taken to be compact. With some additional assumptions on the boundary behavior of the learning algorithm, it is possible to prove a global convergence result stating that the time paths of the parameter vector converge to the invariant set of the associated ODE. For such situations it may also be possible to show that the invariant set has a special structure; for example, it may consist only of the equilibrium points of the differential equation. Invoking the local stability and instability results, it is then possible to obtain the result that for some models the learning algorithm converges globally to the set of locally asymptotically stable equilibrium points of the associated ODE.[9]

We adopt the conditionally linear framework of Chapter 6. In particular, let the algorithm take the form

$$\theta_t = \theta_{t-1} + \gamma_t Q(t, \theta_{t-1}, X_t),$$

where $\theta_t \in \mathbb{R}^d$. $X_t \in \mathbb{R}^k$ is the vector of observable state variables with the conditionally linear dynamics

$$X_t = A(\theta_{t-1})X_{t-1} + B(\theta_{t-1})W_t,$$

where W_t is a random disturbance term. As in Chapter 6, select a set $D^* \subset \mathbb{R}^d$ such that all the eigenvalues of $A(\theta)$, for all $\theta \in D^*$, are strictly inside the unit

---

[9]The two papers Woodford (1990) and Evans, Honkapohja, and Marimon (2000) give economic models in which this line of argument can be applied.

circle. The domain of interest will be an open and connected set $D \subset D^*$. We postulate Assumptions (C.1)–(C.5) of Chapter 6 on D. We now state a basic convergence theorem of Ljung (1977).

Theorem 7.11. *Let $\bar{D}$ be a compact subset of D such that the trajectories of $d\theta/d\tau = h(\theta)$ which start in $\bar{D}$ remain in a closed subset of D for all $\tau > 0$. Assume that (a) there is a random variable Υ such that $\theta_t \in \bar{D}$ and $|X_t| < \Upsilon$ infinitely often with probability 1, and (b) the differential equation has an invariant set D_c with domain of attraction $D_A \supset \bar{D}$. Then $\theta_t \rightarrow D_c$ with probability 1 as $t \rightarrow \infty$.*

This theorem states results that generalize (under somewhat different assumptions) the basic convergence results of Chapter 6. The key assumption which makes possible the probability 1 convergence result is the "visiting" condition (a). Note that if by construction the algorithm is defined and remains on a compact set and the state variable is bounded, then this condition is satisfied. (However, otherwise this condition may be difficult to verify.)

In many applications, the invariant set D_c of $d\theta/d\tau = h(\theta)$ consists of isolated equilibrium points. Suppose that this is the case and also that at each equilibrium point θ^* the real parts of the eigenvalues of $D_\theta h(\theta^*)$ are nonzero. In addition we postulate the conditions used in the instability result, Theorem 6.9 of Chapter 6. That is, at each θ^*, (i) $Q(t, \theta^*, \bar{X}_t(\theta^*))$ has a covariance matrix that is bounded below by a positive definite matrix, and (ii) $EQ(t, \theta^*, \bar{X}_t(\theta^*))$ is continuously differentiable in θ in a neighborhood of θ^* and the derivatives converge uniformly in t. With these assumptions we can combine the stability and instability results to obtain a strong global convergence result.

Corollary 7.12. *Suppose that the invariant set D_c of the differential equation $d\theta/d\tau = h(\theta)$ consists of a finite number of isolated equilibrium points and that all of the assumptions made in this section are satisfied. Then θ_t converges with probability 1 to the set of locally asymptotically stable points of the differential equation.*

Finally, we remark that if $Q(t, \theta_{t-1}, X_t)$ is uniformly bounded, then, due to the decreasing-gain assumption, convergence must be to a single point of the set of locally asymptotically stable points.

7.7 Guide to the Technical Literature

The classical theory of stochastic approximation, see Robbins and Monro (1951) and Kiefer and Wolfowitz (1952), was developed for models without full state variable dynamics and feedback from parameter estimates. Recent expositions of stochastic approximation are given, e.g., in Benveniste, Metivier, and Priouret (1990), Ljung, Pflug, and Walk (1992), and Kushner and Yin (1997). A widely cited basic paper is Ljung (1977), which extended stochastic approximation to setups with dynamics and feedback. Ljung's results are extensively discussed in the book Ljung and Söderström (1983). A further generalization of Ljung's techniques is presented in Benveniste, Metivier, and Priouret (1990).

A somewhat different approach, based on Kushner and Clark (1978), is developed in Kuan and White (1994). An extension of the algorithms to infinite-dimensional spaces is given in Chen and White (1998). Stochastic approximation techniques were used by Arthur, Ermoliev, and Kaniovski (1983) and Arthur, Ermoliev, and Kaniovski (1994) to study generalized urn schemes.

The exposition here has followed Evans and Honkapohja (1998b), Evans and Honkapohja (1998a) for the stability results and Ljung (1977) for the instability result. The positive stability results synthesize the results in Benveniste, Metivier, and Priouret (1990). Other useful general formulations are Ljung (1977), Marcet and Sargent (1989c), the appendix of Woodford (1990), and Kuan and White (1994).

Our approach to constant gain algorithms has been based on Chapter 4, Part II of Benveniste, Metivier, and Priouret (1990). Kushner and Yin (1997) also treats extensively these algorithms.

Part **III**
Learning in Linear Models

Chapter **8**

Univariate Linear Models

8.1 Introduction

Many economic applications of rational expectations (RE) use linear models. These may be either exact formulations, for appropriate specifications of technology and preferences, linear approximations around a nonlinear RE solution, or ad hoc specifications which are taken to be linear for convenience. Frequently, the reduced form makes the endogenous variables of interest depend on expected future values of the endogenous variables (as well as on exogenous variables). This is crucial since the dependence on future expectations leads to the possibility of multiple rational expectations equilibria (REEs). This in turn leads to the issue of which solution should be selected by the economic theorist. A variety of "selection criteria" have been proposed. The perspective we will adopt is that the focus should be on those solutions which are stable under an adaptive learning scheme. In other words, the solution should be robust to agents making small forecast errors initially. Of course, stability may be affected by the particular learning scheme adopted. It is therefore also important to determine how sensitive is the stability of any particular REE to the specification of the learning rule. We use the concepts of weak and strong E-stability to analyze this issue. The distinction is introduced in this chapter, but a full discussion is postponed until Chapter 9.

A quite general specification of a linear expectations model is

$$y_t = \alpha + \sum_{i=1}^{d} \delta_i y_{t-i} + \sum_{i=1}^{m} \sum_{j=i}^{n} \beta_{ij} E_{t-i}^* y_{t-i+j} + \kappa w_t + \zeta v_t, \qquad (8.1)$$

$$w_t = \rho w_{t-1} + e_t,$$

173

where y_t is a vector of endogenous variables, $E^*_{t-i}y_{t-i+j}$ denotes the expectation of y_{t-i+j} formed at time $t - i$, w_t is a vector of exogenous observable variables following a vector autoregression, v_t and e_t are white noise shocks, and α, δ_i, β_{ij}, κ, and ζ are conformable matrices. Unfortunately, this model is too general for us in the sense that providing a full characterization of the set of all REEs to this model is itself a formidable task.[1]

Our procedure in this and the following two chapters will therefore be as follows. We start in this chapter with a simple univariate special case, which is nonetheless general enough to illustrate the method of analysis in the presence of multiple equilibria. A number of standard examples in the literature fit this special case. We then go on to consider variations and higher-order univariate models both to illustrate the generality of the techniques and to provide a backdrop for a general discussion of the relationship of learning to other selection criteria. In the next chapter we take up the issues of how to provide a full characterization of the full set of solutions for these simple models and how stability under learning depends on the specification of the learning rule. Chapter 9 also examines some additional topics concerning learning in univariate linear models. Then in Chapter 10 we show how to extend our methods to multivariate linear models. We also apply the techniques to some well-known recent multivariate models.

8.2   A Special Case

Consider the univariate model

$$y_t = \alpha + \beta_0 E^*_{t-1}y_t + \beta_1 E^*_{t-1}y_{t+1} + v_t, \tag{8.2}$$

where v_t is assumed to be an exogenous process satisfying

$$E_{t-1}v_t = 0.$$

Example 1: The Sargent and Wallace (1975) "ad hoc" model introduced in Chapter 4 is of this form, where $y_t = p_t$, the logarithm of the price level, and

---

[1]There is an extensive literature on solution techniques to linear RE models and different possible representations of the solutions. Some central references are Gourieroux, Laffont, and Monfort (1982), Evans and Honkapohja (1986), Broze, Gourieroux, and Szafarz (1990), Whiteman (1983), McCallum (1983), Pesaran (1981), d'Autume (1990), and Taylor (1986).

where v_t is a linear combination of the white noise aggregate supply, IS, and LM curve shocks. Recall that it can be shown that $\beta_1 > 0$ and $\beta_0 + \beta_1 < 1$.

Example 2: The real balance model of Taylor (1977) is a variation of the rational expectations IS-LM model in which a real balance effect enters each equation. His formulation was

$$q_t = a_I + a_m(m - p_t) + u_{1t}, \quad \text{where } a_m > 0,$$
$$q_t = b_I + b_r(r_t - (E^*_{t-1}p_{t+1} - E^*_{t-1}p_t))$$
$$\quad + b_m(m - p_t) + u_{2t}, \quad \text{where } b_r < 0, b_m > 0,$$
$$m = c_I + p_t + q_t + c_r r_t + c_m(m - p_t) + u_{3t},$$
$$\text{where } c_r < 0, \quad \text{and} \quad 0 < c_m < 1.$$

Again, this model can be rewritten as the univariate reduced form (8.2). The reduced form parameters satisfy $\beta_1 = -\beta_0$, where β_0 is given by

$$\beta_0 = b_r(b_m + b_r(1 - a_m - c_m)c_r^{-1} - a_m)^{-1}.$$

Any nonzero value of β_0 is possible for appropriate values of the structural parameters.

8.2.1 The MSV Solution

We start by obtaining the RE solution which is normally recommended in practice. The simplest method of proceeding is to guess the appropriate form of the solution and then to use the method of undetermined coefficients. Here we guess a solution of the form

$$y_t = a + v_t,$$

where a is to be determined. Assuming this guess is correct, we compute

$$E_{t-1}y_t = E_{t-1}y_{t+1} = a,$$

where we have now replaced $E^*_{t-1}y_t$ and $E^*_{t-1}y_{t+1}$ by $E_{t-1}y_t$ and $E_{t-1}y_{t+1}$ to indicate that these expectations are now assumed to be formed rationally. Substituting into equation (8.2), we obtain

$$y_t = \alpha + (\beta_0 + \beta_1)a + v_t.$$

This is consistent with our guess if and only if $a = \alpha + (\beta_0 + \beta_1)a$, i.e., $a = (1 - \beta_0 - \beta_1)^{-1}\alpha$, which yields the REE

$$y_t = (1 - \beta_0 - \beta_1)^{-1}\alpha + v_t. \tag{8.3}$$

The solution (8.3) is often referred to as the minimal state variable (MSV) solution, following McCallum (1983), who introduced the concept for linear rational expectations models. This is a solution which depends linearly on a set of variables (here v_t and the intercept) and which is such that there does not exist a solution which depends linearly on a smaller set of variables.

8.2.2   A Characterization of the Full Set of Solutions

We now list the full set of RE solutions to equation (8.2). Let ε_t denote an arbitrary martingale difference sequence (MDS), i.e., a sequence of random variables satisfying

$$E_{t-1}\varepsilon_t = 0.$$

Here ε_t could be some function of v_t with conditional mean of 0, or it could be an exogenous variable independent of v_t. When ε_t is independent of v_t, it is often referred to as a *sunspot* variable. Then the stochastic process

$$y_t = -\beta_1^{-1}\alpha + \beta_1^{-1}(1 - \beta_0)y_{t-1} + v_t + c_1 v_{t-1} + d_1 \varepsilon_{t-1} \tag{8.4}$$

is an REE for any choice of c_1 and d_1.[2] This can easily be verified by calculating

$$E_{t-1}y_t = -\beta_1^{-1}\alpha + \beta_1^{-1}(1 - \beta_0)y_{t-1} + c_1 v_{t-1} + d_1 \varepsilon_{t-1},$$
$$E_{t-1}y_{t+1} = -\beta_1^{-1}\alpha + \beta_1^{-1}(1 - \beta_0)E_{t-1}y_t,$$

and substituting into equation (8.2). It may be helpful to note that the autoregressive coefficient of equation (8.4) can be obtained from equation (8.2) by replacing $E_{t-1}y_t$ with y_t, $E_{t-1}y_{t+1}$ with y_{t+1}, and solving for y_{t+1} in terms of y_t.

Since, for ε_t white noise, y_t is an ARMA(1,1) process, it is convenient to refer to these as the ARMA(1,1) set of solutions. (When $d_1 \neq 0$ and ε_t is independent of v_t, we refer to these as ARMA(1,1) sunspot solutions, while if

---

[2] If we assume that the model begins at time $t = 0$, then equation (8.4) also contains an arbitrary initial condition y_{-1}.

$d_1 = 0$, they are ARMA(1,1) solutions driven by the fundamental exogenous process.)

In fact, equation (8.4) fully characterizes the set of solutions. That is, every solution can be expressed in the form (8.4) for suitable choices of ε_t and c_1 and d_1. This can be seen as follows. First, taking conditional expectations E_{t-1} of both sides of equation (8.2), it follows that $v_t = y_t - E_{t-1}y_t$. Next, let $\xi_t = E_t y_{t+1} - E_{t-1}y_{t+1}$ and note that ξ_t is an MDS. Note also that $E_{t-1}y_{t+1} = y_{t+1} - (y_{t+1} - E_t y_{t+1}) - (E_t y_{t+1} - E_{t-1}y_{t+1})$. Substituting $E_{t-1}y_t = y_t - v_t$ and $E_{t-1}y_{t+1} = y_{t+1} - v_{t+1} - \xi_t$ into $y_t = \alpha + \beta_0 E_{t-1}y_t + \beta_1 E_{t-1}y_{t+1} + v_t$, we obtain an expression of the form (8.4), where $c_1 = d_1 = 1$ and $\varepsilon_t \equiv \beta_1^{-1}(\beta_0 - 1 - \beta_1)v_t + \xi_t$.

If every solution is of the form (8.4), then the MSV solution (8.3) must have a representation of the form (8.4). To see how this arises, choose $d_1 = 0$ and $c_1 = -\beta_1^{-1}(1 - \beta_0)$. Then the solution can be written

$$(1 - \beta_1^{-1}(1 - \beta_0)L)y_t = -\beta_1^{-1}\alpha + \left(1 - \beta_1^{-1}(1 - \beta_0)L\right)v_t, \qquad (8.5)$$

where L is the lag operator $Lx_t = x_{t-1}$. We have chosen the solution so that there is no dependence on a sunspot variable ε_t and so that the lag polynomials on y_t and v_t are identical. For appropriate choice of the arbitrary initial condition y_{-1}, one can cancel the common lag polynomial to yield equation (8.3).[3] Here, to obtain the constant when multiplying by $(1 - \beta_1^{-1}(1 - \beta_0)L)^{-1}$, we have used the fact that $f(L)c = f(1)c$ for any lag polynomial $f(L)$ and constant c.

Because it can be obtained by deleting a common lag polynomial, the solution (8.3) is often referred to as a *common factor solution*. As we have seen, it is also the minimal state variable solution in McCallum's sense since there is no solution which depends linearly only on the intercept or on v_t but not both. For the model (8.2), it is the MSV solution which practicing macroeconomists typically adopt. Often this choice is argued on the basis of stationarity. For the case at hand the MSV solution is clearly stationary, and in many economic examples it is uniquely so. This is true in Example 1. To see this, note that the ARMA(1,1) solutions can be stationary only if the autoregressive coefficient $\beta_1^{-1}(1 - \beta_0)$

---

[3] For other choices of y_{-1}, it is not legitimate to cancel the common lag polynomial since there is an additional "transient" term associated with the initial condition. This transient term dies out over time if the root $| \beta_1^{-1}(1 - \beta_0) | < 1$. In that case the solutions (8.5) converge to equation (8.3) asymptotically. If this condition is not met, then the term remains nonnegligible for all time. We remark that if attention is restricted to stationary solutions, then the cancellation of common lag polynomials is straightforward since the initial condition is automatically satisfied. However, we do not want to restrict ourselves to the stationary case.

satisfies $|\beta_1^{-1}(1-\beta_0)| < 1$. But the conditions $\beta_1 > 0$ and $\beta_0 + \beta_1 < 1$ imply instead that $\beta_1^{-1}(1-\beta_0) > 1$. Any solution other than the MSV solution is explosive in the sense that $|E_{t-1}y_{t+i}| \to \infty$ as $i \to \infty$. Applied macroeconomists are often prepared to rule out such explosive solutions a priori. (We will later see whether or not they can be attained through a learning process.)

The unique stationarity of the MSV solution in Example 1 is not a general phenomenon. In Example 2 the only restriction is that $\beta_1 = -\beta_0$. In this example it follows that if $\beta_0 > \frac{1}{2}$, then all ARMA(1,1) solutions, and thus the entire set of solutions, are (asymptotically) stationary. It is thus clear that insisting on nonexplosive solutions will not in general be sufficient to guarantee a unique REE.[4]

McCallum (1983) has recommended use of the term "bubble solution" to refer to the other ARMA(1,1) solutions (whether or not they depend on sunspot variables), and the term "fundamental solution" is also frequently used for the MSV solution. The argument for this terminology is that bubble solutions constitute solutions only because agents believe that certain variables matter, eventhough rational agents could also believe that these variables do *not* affect the solution. Thus the "self-fulfilling prophecy" aspect of the solution is salient for the bubble solutions (whether or not they are explosive bubbles). McCallum argues that in practice one should pick the MSV solution unless one is specifically interested in the bubble issue. However, this begs the question of whether bubbles are likely to arise in practice. Our approach will be to see whether this choice can be justified on the basis of stability under adaptive learning.

8.2.3 The Special Case with an Exogenous Observable

It will be useful to consider a somewhat more general version of equation (8.2) which allows for a dependence on an exogenous observable following a stationary AR(1) process:

$$y_t = \alpha + \beta_0 E_{t-1}^* y_t + \beta_1 E_{t-1}^* y_{t+1} + \kappa w_t + v_t, \qquad (8.6)$$
$$w_t = \rho w_{t-1} + e_t,$$

where we assume $|\rho| < 1$. w_t is assumed to be observable at time t.

Again the MSV solution can be obtained by guessing the form of solution

$$y_t = a + bw_{t-1} + ce_t + v_t,$$

[4]Admittedly, we make this point in the context of an ad hoc economic model. However, as is now well recognized, and as will be seen elsewhere in the book, the same point can be made in models with impeccable microfoundations.

and using the method of undetermined coefficients. Calculating $E_{t-1}y_t = a + bw_{t-1}$ and $E_{t-1}y_{t+1} = a + b\rho w_{t-1}$ and substituting into equation (8.6), we obtain

$$y_t = (1 - \beta_0 - \beta_1)^{-1}\alpha + (1 - \beta_0 - \rho\beta_1)^{-1}\kappa\rho w_{t-1} + \kappa e_t + v_t. \qquad (8.7)$$

The full set of solutions can be shown to take the form

$$\begin{aligned} y_t = &-\beta_1^{-1}\alpha + \beta_1^{-1}(1 - \beta_0)y_{t-1} - \beta_1^{-1}\kappa w_{t-1} \\ &+ \kappa e_t + v_t + c_1 v_{t-1} + d_1 \varepsilon_{t-1} + f_1 e_{t-1}, \end{aligned}$$

for arbitrary c_1, d_1, f_1. As in the simple case with no exogenous shock w_t, the MSV solution can be viewed as a common factor solution obtained from the full set of solutions with appropriate choice of $c_1, d_1,$ and f_1.

8.3   E-Stability and Least Squares Learning: MSV Solutions

For the basic model without exogenous variables, we have already considered the stability of the MSV solution under learning in Chapter 4. We briefly review the results and then take up the extension to the case with an exogenous observable. In each case we start with E-stability and then show that this condition governs stability under adaptive learning.

8.3.1   No Exogenous Observables

When no exogenous observable is included, we posit the perceived law of motion (PLM):

$$y_t = a + v_t. \qquad (8.8)$$

Under this PLM we calculate $E_{t-1}y_t = a$ and $E_{t-1}y_{t+1} = a$. Inserting into the model (8.2), we obtain

$$y_t = \alpha + (\beta_0 + \beta_1)a + v_t.$$

This is the actual law of motion (ALM) implied by the PLM (8.8). E-stability is determined by the differential equation

$$\frac{da}{d\tau} = \alpha + (\beta_0 + \beta_1)a - a. \qquad (8.9)$$

The unique equilibrium of $da/d\tau = 0$ is $\bar{a} = \alpha(1 - \beta_0 - \beta_1)^{-1}$, which, when inserted into equation (8.8), yields equation (8.3). This solution is E-stable if $\bar{a}$ is stable under the dynamics of the differential equation. The condition for this is simply

$$\beta_0 + \beta_1 < 1. \tag{8.10}$$

For real-time learning we note that since the MSV solution is an iid process, it is most naturally estimated by the sample mean, i.e.,

$$a_t = t^{-1} \sum_{i=1}^{t} y_{t-i}.$$

An equivalent recursive form is

$$a_t = a_{t-1} + t^{-1}(y_t - a_{t-1}).$$

With expectations $E_{t-1}^* y_t = E_{t-1}^* y_{t+1} = a_{t-1}$, the actual law of motion under learning is given by $y_t = \alpha + (\beta_0 + \beta_1)a_{t-1} + v_t$. Inserting into the recursive equation, we have

$$a_t = a_{t-1} + t^{-1}\big(\alpha + (\beta_0 + \beta_1)a_{t-1} - a_{t-1} + v_t\big). \tag{8.11}$$

Equation (8.11) is a very simple recursive stochastic algorithm of the form (6.3) of Chapter 6. The vector θ_t of equation (8.11) is simply $\theta_t = a_t$ and the state vector X_t is simply $X_t = v_t$. The function $\mathcal{H}(a, v) = \alpha + (\beta_0 + \beta_1 - 1)a + v$. The complementary term ρ_t is absent. Since the state vector is white noise, it follows the conditional linear dynamics (6.4) with $A = 0$ and $B = 1$. It is easy to verify the technical assumptions (A) and (B) for the local stability results of Section 6.2.1 as well as the stronger conditions (D) for the global stability results of Section 6.7. We only need to compute the associated ODE.

Since $Ev_t = 0$, the associated ODE (6.5) of Chapter 6 is

$$\frac{da}{d\tau} = \alpha + (\beta_0 + \beta_1 - 1)a.$$

But this is identical to the E-stability differential equation given above, equation (8.9). If condition (8.10) holds, i.e., $\beta_0 + \beta_1 < 1$, then $\mathcal{U}(a) = (a - \bar{a})^2$ is a Lyapunov function which meets the conditions given in Theorem 6.10. It follows that if $\beta_0 + \beta_1 < 1$, then equation (8.11) will converge to the MSV solution globally with probability 1.

One can also verify that the technical conditions (C) for the instability result of Section 6.5 of Chapter 6 are met provided v_t has bounded support. [This assumption can be relaxed using alternative versions of the instability result given in Ljung (1977)).] It follows that if $\beta_0 + \beta_1 > 1$, then the MSV solution is unstable under equation (8.11), i.e., convergence in that case would occur with probability 0.

Looking at our two examples, we see immediately that the stability condition (8.10) is necessarily satisfied in both examples above.

8.3.2 Learning with an Exogenous Observable

Consider now the case with the exogenous observables w_t. The setup is close to the analysis of the Muth cobweb model in Chapters 2 and 6. Agents now have a PLM of the form

$$y_t = a + bw_{t-1} + \eta_t$$

and they estimate $(a, b)'$ by recursive least squares (RLS). Here η_t is an unobserved iid shock.[5] Let $(a_t, b_t)'$ denote the agents' estimates of (a, b) at time t. Writing

$$\phi_t = \begin{pmatrix} a_t \\ b_t \end{pmatrix} \quad \text{and} \quad z_t = \begin{pmatrix} 1 \\ w_t \end{pmatrix},$$

the RLS formulas are

$$
\begin{aligned}
\phi_t &= \phi_{t-1} + t^{-1} R_t^{-1} z_{t-1} (y_t - \phi_{t-1}' z_{t-1}), \\
R_t &= R_{t-1} + t^{-1} (z_{t-1} z_{t-1}' - R_{t-1}).
\end{aligned}
\tag{8.12}
$$

Expectations are assumed to be formed using the PLM with their most recent parameter estimates. That is,

$$
\begin{aligned}
E_{t-1}^* y_t &= a_{t-1} + b_{t-1} w_{t-1}, \\
E_{t-1}^* y_{t+1} &= a_{t-1} + b_{t-1} \rho w_{t-1}.
\end{aligned}
$$

Note that here we have assumed that ρ is known. If not, it too can be estimated by a separate regression of w_t on w_{t-1}. Finally, we continue to assume that y_t

---

[5] In the MSV solution a and b have the values given earlier and $\eta_t = \kappa e_t + v_t$.

is determined by equation (8.6) using these expectations. It follows that

$$y_t = T(\phi_{t-1})' z_{t-1} + \kappa e_t + v_t, \tag{8.13}$$

where

$$T(\phi) = T\begin{pmatrix} a \\ b \end{pmatrix} = \begin{pmatrix} \alpha + (\beta_0 + \beta_1)a \\ (\beta_0 + \rho\beta_1)b + \kappa\rho \end{pmatrix}.$$

Defining $S_{t-1} = R_t$, equations (8.12) become

$$\phi_t = \phi_{t-1} + t^{-1} S_{t-1}^{-1} z_{t-1} (y_t - \phi_{t-1}' z_{t-1}), \tag{8.14}$$

$$S_t = S_{t-1} + t^{-1}(z_t z_t' - S_{t-1}) + t^{-2}\left(-\frac{t}{t+1}\right)(z_t z_t' - S_{t-1}).$$

Using equation (8.13) to substitute for y_t, we obtain the stochastic recursive algorithm

$$\phi_t = \phi_{t-1} + t^{-1} S_{t-1}^{-1} z_{t-1}\left(z_{t-1}'(T(\phi_{t-1}) - \phi_{t-1}) + \kappa e_t + v_t\right), \tag{8.15}$$

$$S_t = S_{t-1} + t^{-1}\left(z_t z_t' - S_{t-1}\right) + t^{-2}\left(-\frac{t}{t+1}\right)(z_t z_t' - S_{t-1}).$$

This is now written as a recursive stochastic algorithm in the standard form (6.3) of Chapter 6 with $\theta_t = \text{vec}(\phi_t, S_t)$. Since $(-[t/(t+1)])(z_t z_t' - S_{t-1})$ is a second-order complementary term, the associated ODE is easily computed to be

$$\frac{d\phi}{d\tau} = S^{-1} M_z (T(\phi) - \phi),$$

$$\frac{dS}{d\tau} = M_z - S,$$

where

$$M_z = E z_t z_t' = \begin{pmatrix} 1 & 0 \\ 0 & \sigma_e^2/(1 - \rho^2) \end{pmatrix} \quad \text{and} \quad \sigma_e^2 = E e_t^2.$$

Stability of the ODE is determined by the E-stability differential equation

$$\frac{d\phi}{d\tau} = T(\phi) - \phi.$$

Noting that

$$DT = \begin{pmatrix} \beta_0 + \beta_1 & 0 \\ 0 & \beta_0 + \rho\beta_1 \end{pmatrix},$$

we see that stability is determined by the conditions (i) $\beta_0 + \beta_1 < 1$, and (ii) $\beta_0 + \rho\beta_1 < 1$.

Provided both these conditions are met, the global stability results of Chapter 6 can be applied. Verification of the technical assumptions (D) of Section 6.7, and existence of a Lyapunov function of the required form, follow closely the example of the Muth model given in Sections 6.6 and 6.7. It follows that least squares learning converges to the MSV solution with probability 1 from any initial starting point, provided that the E-stability conditions are satisfied. The corresponding instability result is also obtainable using the results of Chapter 6.

We collect the results into the following proposition.

Proposition 8.1. *For the model (8.6):*

(i) *The MSV solution (8.7) is E-stable if $\beta_0 + \beta_1 < 1$ and $\beta_0 + \rho\beta_1 < 1$. The MSV solution is also stable under adaptive learning if it is E-stable.*

(ii) *If instead $\beta_0 + \beta_1 > 1$ or $\beta_0 + \rho\beta_1 > 1$, then there is convergence to the MSV solution or any other point ϕ with probability zero.*

Looking again at our examples, it can be verified that both stability conditions are satisfied for both examples. Thus if agents use the PLM of the same form as the MSV solution, then least squares learning will converge to the MSV solution.

8.4 E-Stability and Learning: The Full Class of Solutions

We now turn to the ARMA(1,1) class of non-MSV solutions. For simplicity we restrict attention to the model (8.2) in which there are no exogenous observables and we are therefore considering the class of solutions (8.4). The central issue is whether it is possible for least squares learning to converge to one of these solutions. Because this class consists of a continuum of solutions, there are technical difficulties with the application of the convergence results from Chapter 6. We therefore develop the analysis in two stages, first considering a setup where a complete answer can be given and then moving to a discussion of the general problem.

8.4.1 Learning a Non-MSV AR(1) Solution

To avoid the technical complications which arise from the continuum of solutions, we here restrict attention to the particular solution from the set (8.4) in which we set $c_1 = d_1 = 0$ in order to obtain

$$y_t = -\beta_1^{-1}\alpha + \beta_1^{-1}(1 - \beta_0)y_{t-1} + v_t. \qquad (8.16)$$

Note that this solution is of the AR(1), i.e., first-order autoregressive, form. In order to keep our analysis straightforward, we also restrict attention to cases in which $|\beta_1^{-1}(1 - \beta_0)| < 1$, so that the solution is (asymptotically) stationary. It should be noted that if the model (8.2) is regarded as defined for $t \geq 1$, then there is also an arbitrary initial condition y_0, the influence of which dies out asymptotically.

We suppose that agents have a PLM of the AR(1) form

$$y_t = a + by_{t-1} + v_t$$

and that they estimate the parameters (a, b) by recursive least squares. We first work out the T-mapping from the PLM, to the ALM. Under the PLM, we compute

$$E_{t-1}^* y_t = a + by_t \quad \text{and} \quad E_{t-1}^* y_{t+1} = a(1+b) + b^2 y_{t-1}.$$

Inserting into equation (8.2), we obtain the ALM

$$y_t = T_a(a, b) + T_b(a, b)y_{t-1} + v_t,$$

where

$$\begin{aligned} T_a(a, b) &= \alpha + \beta_0 a + \beta_1 a(1 + b), \qquad (8.17)\\ T_b(a, b) &= \beta_0 b + \beta_1 b^2. \end{aligned}$$

Note that the solution (8.16) corresponds to a fixed point of $T = (T_a, T_b)$.

Under least squares learning, agents estimate (a, b) by a regression of y_t on an intercept and y_{t-1}. Letting (a_t, b_t) denote the time-t estimates and writing

$$\phi_t = \begin{pmatrix} a_t \\ b_t \end{pmatrix}, \qquad z_{t-1} = \begin{pmatrix} 1 \\ y_{t-1} \end{pmatrix}, \qquad (8.18)$$

the RLS estimates are again given by equations (8.12) or equivalently equations (8.14). Under least squares learning, the agents forecast at $t - 1$ based on their estimated parameters $\phi_{t-1} = (a_{t-1}, b_{t-1})'$ and the observable $z'_{t-1} = (1, y_{t-1})$. Thus $E_{t-1}^* y_t = a_{t-1} + b_{t-1}y_t$ and $E_{t-1}^* y_{t+1} = a_{t-1}(1 + b_{t-1}) +$

$b_{t-1}^2 y_{t-1}$, and inserting into equation (8.2), we obtain the ALM under least squares learning,

$$y_t = T(\phi_{t-1})' z_{t-1} + v_t, \tag{8.19}$$

where

$$T(\phi) = T\begin{pmatrix} a \\ b \end{pmatrix} = \begin{pmatrix} T_a(a,b) \\ T_b(a,b) \end{pmatrix}.$$

The dynamical system under learning is thus defined by equations (8.14), (8.17), (8.18), and (8.19). Combining equations, we again have a recursive stochastic algorithm of the form (6.3) of Chapter 6, with as usual, $\theta_t = \text{vec}(\phi_t, S_t)$ and $\gamma_t = t^{-1}$. This yields a system of the form

$$\phi_t = \phi_{t-1} + t^{-1} S_{t-1}^{-1} z_{t-1} \left(z_{t-1}'(T(\phi_{t-1}) - \phi_{t-1}) + v_t \right), \tag{8.20}$$

$$S_t = S_{t-1} + t^{-1} \left(z_t z_t' - S_{t-1} \right) + t^{-2} \left(-\frac{t}{t+1} \right) \left(z_t z_t' - S_{t-1} \right).$$

The corresponding ODE is

$$\frac{d\phi}{d\tau} = S^{-1} M_z(\phi)(T(\phi) - \phi), \tag{8.21}$$

$$\frac{dS}{d\tau} = M_z(\phi) - S.$$

Here there are two new features, compared to previous examples. First, M_z is replaced by $M_z(\phi)$ which is defined as follows. Let $z_t(\phi)' = (1, y_t(\phi))$, where

$$y_t(\phi) = T(\phi)' z_{t-1}(\phi) + v_t \quad \text{for } \phi' = (a,b),$$
$$= T_a(a,b) + T_b(a,b) y_{t-1}(\phi) + v_t.$$

That is, $y_t(\phi)$ is the stochastic process for y_t that would be followed if agents held a fixed PLM $\phi' = (a,b)$ and followed the corresponding forecast rule. We now define

$$M_z(\phi) = \lim_{t \to \infty} E z_t(\phi) z_t(\phi)'.$$

Since $y_t(\phi)$ is (asymptotically) stationary for values of ϕ near the AR(1) solution $\bar{\phi}' = (-\beta_1^{-1}\alpha, \beta_1^{-1}(1 - \beta_0))$, we know that this limit exists and is finite.

The second new feature is that the state vector X_t includes y_{t-1}. In fact we set $X'_t = (1, y_t, y_{t-1}, v_t)$. Verification of conditions (A) and (B) of Section 6.2.1 of Chapter 6 therefore requires additional care. We discuss this point below.

The local stability of the ODE near the fixed point $\bar{\phi}$, $\bar{S} = M_z(\bar{\phi})$ is again determined by the local stability of $d\phi/d\tau = T(\phi) - \phi$ at $\phi = \bar{\phi}$, i.e., by the E-stability of the AR(1) solutions.[6] Since

$$DT = \begin{bmatrix} \beta_0 + \beta_1(1+b) & \beta_1 a \\ 0 & \beta_0 + 2\beta_1 b \end{bmatrix}, \tag{8.22}$$

the eigenvalues of $DT(\bar{\phi})$ are $\beta_0 + \beta_1(1 + \beta_1^{-1}(1 - \beta_0)) = \beta_1 + 1$ and $\beta_0 + 2\beta_1(\beta_1^{-1}(1 - \beta_0)) = 2 - \beta_0$. The E-stability conditions are that the eigenvalues of $DT(\bar{\phi}) - I$ have negative real parts or, equivalently, that the eigenvalues of $DT(\bar{\phi})$ have real parts less than 1. Thus the conditions for E-stability of the AR(1) solution are that

$$\beta_1 < 0 \quad \text{and} \quad \beta_0 > 1. \tag{8.23}$$

We restrict attention to cases in which $|\beta_1^{-1}(1 - \beta_0)| < 1$, so that the AR(1) solution is asymptotically stationary, and return to the verification of the technical conditions (A) and (B) of Section 6.2.1 of Chapter 6. The regularity conditions (A.2) and (A.3) on $\mathcal{H}(\theta, x)$ and $\rho_t(\theta, x)$ are easily verified. The remaining conditions are on the state dynamics equation (6.4): $X_t = A(\theta_{t-1})X_{t-1} + B(\theta_{t-1})W_t$. Setting $W'_t = (1, v_t)$, it can be seen that

$$A(\theta) = \begin{pmatrix} 0 & 0 & 0 & 0 \\ T_a(\phi) & T_b(\phi) & 0 & 0 \\ 0 & 1 & 0 & 0 \\ 0 & 0 & 0 & 0 \end{pmatrix},$$

$$B(\theta) = \begin{pmatrix} 1 & 0 \\ 0 & 1 \\ 0 & 0 \\ 0 & 1 \end{pmatrix}.$$

$A(\theta)$ and $B(\theta)$ clearly satisfy the Lipschitz conditions and B is bounded. Since v_t is assumed to have bounded moments, condition (B.1) is satisfied. The only

---

[6]It may be checked that the eigenvalues of the linearization of the large ODE (8.21) consist of the eigenvalues of equation (8.22), minus one and (repeatedly) -1.

nonzero root of $A(\theta)$ is $T_b(\phi)$, and at the AR(1) solution, $T_b(\bar{\phi}) = \bar{b}$ is less than 1 in absolute value since we are restricting attention to the stationary solutions. It follows that there is a compact neighborhood Q including the AR(1) solution $\bar{\theta}$ on which the condition that $|A(\theta)|$ is bounded strictly below 1 is satisfied.

Thus the technical conditions for application of the local stability results of Section 6.3.3 of Chapter 6 are satisfied and we conclude that if $|\beta_1^{-1}(1 - \beta_0)| < 1$, $\beta_1 < 0$, and $\beta_0 > 1$, then the AR(1) solution is locally stable under least squares learning. These conditions are equivalent to the conditions $\beta_0 + \beta_1 < 1$, $\beta_0 > 1$. It can also be verified that the conditions (C) of Section 6.5 are satisfied and that conditions (i) and (ii) of Theorem 6.9 hold. It follows that if either $\beta_0 + \beta_1 > 1$ or $\beta_0 < 1$, then there is convergence to the AR(1) solution with probability zero.

Note that the convergence results here are local and have the various interpretations given in Sections 6.3.3 and 6.4 of Chapter 6. In particular, Corollaries 6.6 and 6.8 apply. Thus, for nearby initial ϕ_0 and sufficiently low adaption rates, there will be convergence with probability close to 1. If the learning algorithm is augmented with an appropriate nontrivial projection facility, then there is convergence with probability 1. In contrast, if $|\beta_1^{-1}(1 - \beta_0)| < 1$ but $\beta_1 > 0$ or $\beta_0 < 1$, then there is convergence to the AR(1) solution with probability 0.

If $|\beta_1^{-1}(1 - \beta_0)| > 1$, so that the AR(1) solution is explosive, one can still consider whether the solution is stable under least squares learning. Convergence to explosive AR(1) solutions is one of the topics considered in Chapter 9.

As an illustration, we look at a simulation of equations (8.12), (8.17), (8.18), and (8.19). We set $\beta_0 = 1.5$, $\beta_1 = -1.5$, and $\alpha = 2$, and v_t is iid normal with standard deviation of 0.02. The REE values are $\bar{a} = 4/3$ and $\bar{b} = 1/3$. The dynamic paths are sensitive to initial conditions and to the initial random shocks. (Some dynamic paths are explosive unless a projection facility is imposed, while others converge even without imposing one.) Also, in contrast to the simulation examples of Chapters 2 and 4, the convergence is rather slow. Figure 8.1 shows the first 1000 periods of one simulation run. The values of b_t for this run are $0.5791, 0.3919$, and 0.3247 at $t = 100, 1000$, and $10,000$.

8.4.2 Strong E-Stability of the MSV Solution

In the case of an AR(1) PLM, consider again the map (8.17) from the PLM to the ALM. There are in fact two fixed points of the map. One is the AR(1) solution $(a, b) = (-\beta_1^{-1}\alpha, \beta_1^{-1}(1 - \beta_0))$. The other is the MSV solution $(a, b) = (\alpha(1 - \beta_0 - \beta_1)^{-1}, 0)$. This raises the issue of whether the dynamical system under RLS learning defined by equations (8.12), (8.17), (8.18), and (8.19) could instead

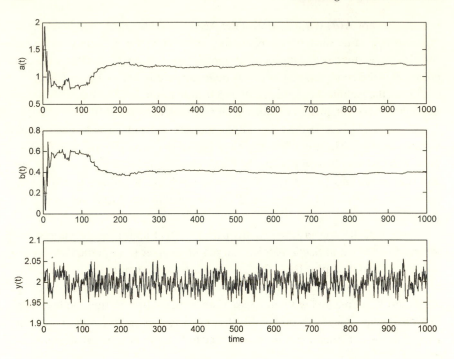

Figure 8.1.

converge to the MSV solution. We are now considering the issue of whether the MSV solution can emerge from an overparameterized learning process. It is overparameterized in the sense that the MSV solution is a constant plus white noise, while the learning rule allows for an additional effect of y_{t-1} on y_t. If this system converges to the MSV solution, agents eventually learn that the value of the parameter on y_{t-1} is 0.

The analysis of this question in fact closely follows the previous section. The only change required is that we evaluate local stability of the ODE, and thus compute E-stability, at the MSV solution instead of the AR(1) solution. Evaluating equation (8.22) at $(a, b) = (\alpha(1 - \beta_0 - \beta_1)^{-1}, 0)$ it can be seen that DT has eigenvalues $\beta_0 + \beta_1$ and β_0. It follows that for PLMs of the AR(1) form, the E-stability conditions of the MSV solution are

$$\beta_0 + \beta_1 < 1 \quad \text{and} \quad \beta_0 < 1. \tag{8.24}$$

Clearly, these conditions are stronger than the condition (8.10) which determines stability under learning when the PLM is of the MSV form.

The stability conditions are thus affected by the precise form of the PLM. We distinguish the two sets of conditions by referring to inequality (8.10) as the *weak E-stability* condition for the MSV solution and to inequalities (8.24) as the *strong E-stability* conditions for the MSV solution. Weak E-stability of the MSV solution governs convergence when the PLM is of the MSV form, while these strong E-stability conditions govern convergence to the MSV solution when the PLM overparameterizes the solution as an AR(1) model. We remark first that, of course, one could consider overparameterizations of the MSV solution that, for example, allowed for additional lags y_{t-i}, and second, that one could also consider overparameterizations of the AR(1) solution. These issues are taken up in Chapter 9.

8.4.3 Discussion of Examples

With these results in hand, we now return to our examples. The Sargent–Wallace example satisfies the restrictions $\beta_1 > 0$ and $\beta_0 + \beta_1 < 1$. This implies $|\beta_1^{-1}(1 - \beta_0)| > 1$ so that the AR(1) solution is nonstationary. The MSV solution always satisfies the weak E-stability condition (8.10) and is globally stable for least squares learning if the perceived law of motion is of the MSV form. It also satisfies the strong E-stability conditions (8.24) and thus is locally stable even when the perceived law of motion is overparameterized as an AR(1) process.

In the Taylor real balance model, the only restrictions are $\beta_1 = -\beta_0$ and $\beta_0 \neq 0$. We can list the cases in terms of the possible values for β_0. Since the MSV solution satisfies the weak E-stability condition (8.10), it is always globally stable for least squares learning if the perceived law of motion is of the MSV form. If $\beta_0 < 1$, it also satisfies the strong E-stability conditions (8.24), and the MSV solution is also locally stable under least squares learning even when it is overparameterized as an AR(1) process. However, if $\beta_0 > 1$, the MSV solution is no longer locally stable under least squares learning when overparameterized as an AR(1) process. That is, when $\beta_0 > 1$, the stability of the MSV solution depends on how the learning is parameterized.

Finally, consider the AR(1) solution in the Taylor real balance model. This is explosive if $\beta_0 < \frac{1}{2}$ and stationary if $\beta_0 > \frac{1}{2}$. Restricting attention to the stationary AR(1) case, we see that the condition for the E-stability condition (8.23) to be satisfied is that $\beta_0 > 1$. If $\frac{1}{2} < \beta_0 < 1$, the AR(1) solution is not locally stable under least squares learning. If $\beta_0 > 1$, then the AR(1) solution is stationary and locally stable under least squares learning.

8.4.4   Learning Sunspot Solutions

Finally, suppose that agents have PLMs which allow for the full class of solutions (8.4). Thus we next consider PLMs of the ARMA(1,1) form

$$y_t = a + by_{t-1} + cv_{t-1} + d\varepsilon_{t-1} + v_t, \tag{8.25}$$

where ε_t is some random variable, observable at t, which satisfies $E_{t-1}\varepsilon_t = 0$.

We obtain E-stability conditions and then discuss stability under least squares learning. Calculating

$$E_{t-1}y_t = a + by_{t-1} + cv_{t-1} + d\varepsilon_{t-1},$$
$$E_{t-1}y_{t+1} = a(1+b) + b^2 y_{t-1} + bcv_{t-1} + bd\varepsilon_{t-1},$$

and inserting into equation (8.2), we obtain the implied ALM

$$y_t = \alpha + \beta_0 a + \beta_1 a(1+b) + (\beta_0 b + \beta_1 b^2)y_{t-1} + (\beta_0 c + \beta_1 bc)v_{t-1}$$
$$+ (\beta_0 d + \beta_1 bd)\varepsilon_{t-1} + v_t.$$

The mapping from PLM to ALM thus takes the form

$$T(a,b,c,d) = \left(\alpha + \beta_0 a + \beta_1 a(1+b), \beta_0 b + \beta_1 b^2, \beta_0 c + \beta_1 bc, \beta_0 d + \beta_1 bd\right).$$

E-stability of the ARMA(1,1) solutions is determined by the stability of the differential equation

$$\frac{d}{d\tau}(a,b,c,d) = T(a,b,c,d) - (a,b,c,d) \tag{8.26}$$

evaluated at the solutions.

First, note that the differential equations in (a,b) do not depend on c or d. To evaluate stability, we linearize the first two components. Letting $T_{ab}(a,b)$ stand for the first two components of T, one sees that DT_{ab} is equal to the value of DT given in equation (8.22). Evaluating the derivative at $a = -\beta_1^{-1}\alpha$ and $b = \beta_1^{-1}(1-\beta_0)$, we obtain the roots $\beta_1 + 1$ and $2 - \beta_0$ as in the case of AR(1) PLMs. The (a,b) subsystem thus leads again to the stability conditions (8.23).

What about the two differential equations involving c and d? The linearization of the last component of (8.26) yields

$$DT_d - 1 = \beta_0 + \beta_1 b - 1. \tag{8.27}$$

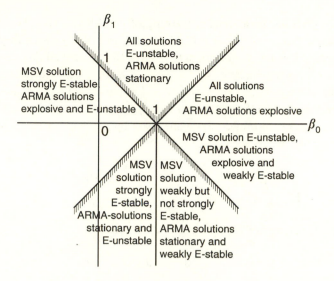

Figure 8.2.

At the ARMA(1,1) solutions, this derivative is zero and thus one must directly examine the nonlinear equation. The equation for d in (8.26) is a linear differential equation with time-varying coefficients via the independently evolving (a, b) and can be directly integrated. Carrying out this integration as in Evans and Honkapohja (1992, p. 6) it can be established that d will converge to some value, provided (a, b) do so. The argument in the case of c is identical. In fact, this result is intuitively clear. The ARMA(1,1) solutions are a continuum with the coefficients c and d arbitrary. This is reflected in the fact that $T(a, b, c, d) = (a, b, c, d)$ for $a = -\beta_1^{-1}\alpha$, $b = \beta_1^{-1}(1 - \beta_0)$, and any c, d. Thus no additional stability condition is required from the equations for c and d.

It follows that, provided equation (8.23) holds, the ARMA(1,1) solutions are E-stable as a set. For nearby values of (a, b), convergence will occur to the ARMA(1,1) REE values of (a, b), and c and d will also converge to some value (determined by the starting point). Because we have not yet considered the possibility of overparameterizing the ARMA(1,1) solutions, we refer to these as the weak E-stability conditions for the ARMA(1,1) solutions. Strong E-stability of the ARMA(1,1) solutions will be considered in the next chapter. The situation for the various solutions to the model (8.2) is illustrated in Figure 8.2.

Returning to the examples, it can be seen that the ARMA(1,1) solutions can never be E-stable in the Sargent–Wallace model. However, if $\beta_0 > 1$, the set of ARMA(1,1) solutions will be weakly E-stable in Taylor's model.

Finally, consider least squares learning of the ARMA(1,1) class of solutions. Suppose that agents have a PLM of the form (8.25) which they use to make forecasts. It is most convenient to assume that v_t as well as ε_t is observable at time t.[7] Agents can then estimate (a, b, c, d) by a least squares regression of y_t on an intercept, y_{t-1}, v_{t-1}, and ε_{t-1}. Letting $\phi_t' = (a_t, b_t, c_t, d_t)$ denote the estimates using data through time t and $z_{t-1}' = (1, y_{t-1}, v_{t-1}, \varepsilon_{t-1})$, the recursive least squares formulas are again given by equation (8.12). Agents are then assumed to forecast according to

$$E_{t-1}^* y_t = a_{t-1} + b_{t-1} y_{t-1} + c v_{t-1} + d \varepsilon_{t-1},$$
$$E_{t-1}^* y_{t+1} = a_{t-1} + b_{t-1} E_{t-1}^* y_t.$$

y_t is of course determined by equation (8.2) so that

$$y_t = T(a_{t-1}, b_{t-1}, c_{t-1} d_{t-1})' z_{t-1} + v_t,$$

where $T(a, b, c, d)$ is given above. This fully defines the dynamical system and the question is: can (a_t, b_t, c_t, d_t) converge to a member of the ARMA(1,1) class of solutions?

Unfortunately, for technical reasons, the formal results of Chapter 6 do not apply and there are no known analytical results. The central technical problem is that we are considering an unbounded continuum of solutions (indexed by c and d) and that such cases are not covered by our convergence theorems. One can still, of course, investigate the stability of real-time learning in such cases using simulations. The limited evidence available suggests that the E-stability conditions do govern the stability of least squares learning, see Evans and Honkapohja (1994b).[8]

In Figure 8.3 we provide a simulation which appears to show convergence to an ARMA(1,1) sunspot solution. In this example the parameters are the same as in Figure 8.1. To reduce the initial volatility of estimates for small t, we use a small constant gain for an initial period of time: $\gamma_t = N^{-1}$ for $t = 1, \ldots, N$ and $\gamma_t = t^{-1}$ for $t > N$, with N set at $N = 20$.[9] Initial settings of parameters were $a = \bar{a}$, $b = \bar{b} + 0.10$, $c = 0.5$, $d = 0.5$, $R = \bar{R}$, and lagged y equal to $\bar{y}$. The sunspot ε_t was generated as an iid standard normal independent of v_t.

---

[7]If v_t is not observable, then v_{t-1} would also need to be estimated at t. See Evans and Honkapohja (1994b) for a discussion and analysis.

[8]However, the results of Heinemann (2000b) suggest that when stochastic gradient learning is used, there may be discrepancies from the E-stability conditions.

[9]Using $\gamma_t = 1/t$ for all t also provided an example with convergence to an ARMA(1,1) sunspot solution.

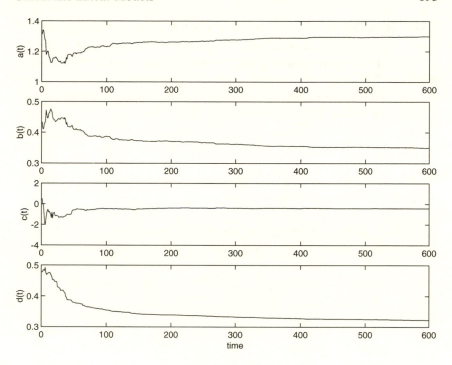

Figure 8.3.

The trajectories of ϕ_t shown in Figure 8.3 do appear clearly to converge to a member of the ARMA(1,1) class. Values of b_t are 0.4333, 0.3867, 0.3436, and 0.3371 at $t = 1$, 100, 1000, and 10,000. The values of the other parameters at $t = 10,000$ are $a = 1.3260$, $c = -0.4085$, and $d = 0.3130$.

Further discussion of sunspot solutions in this model can be found in Chapter 9.

8.5   Extension 1: Lagged Endogenous Variables

We now return to the general class of univariate linear models (8.1) and consider several other cases which arise frequently in macroeconomics. For the remainder of this chapter we will restrict attention to MSV solutions. (The more general class of solutions will for some cases be considered in the following chapter.) We remark that in many cases there are multiple MSV solutions, and that in these cases learning has an important role as a selection criterion.[10] Our objective in this section is to show the wide range of economic examples which fit into the univariate linear framework in which the adaptive learning framework can be readily studied.

We first extend the special case (8.2) to allow direct feedback from y_{t-1}. Thus we consider models of the form

$$y_t = \alpha + \delta y_{t-1} + \beta_0 E^*_{t-1} y_t + \beta_1 E^*_{t-1} y_{t+1} + v_t. \tag{8.28}$$

We will often refer to equation (8.28) as the "extended special case." Models which fit this framework are as follows.

***Example 3:* Taylor's Overlapping Contract Model.** In the model of Taylor (1980), with a contract length of $n = 2$, we have the following system:

$$x_t = \tfrac{1}{2} x_{t-1} + \tfrac{1}{2} E^*_{t-1} x_{t+1} + \tfrac{1}{2} \gamma \left(E^*_{t-1} q_t + E^*_{t-1} q_{t+1} \right) + u_t,$$
$$w_t = \tfrac{1}{2} (x_t + x_{t-1}),$$
$$q_t = k + m_t - w_t + v_t,$$
$$m_t = \bar{m} + (1 - \varphi) w_t,$$

where x_t is the (log of the) contract wage negotiated at time t, w_t is the (log of the) average wage level (equal to the average of the price level plus a constant), q_t is the log of aggregate output, and m_t is the log of the money supply. u_t is an iid supply shock and v_t is an iid supply shock. It is assumed that $0 < \varphi < 1$, and $1 - \varphi$ is a measure of the extent to which the monetary policy rule accommodates price shocks. The reduced form of this equation is

$$x_t = \alpha + \frac{1}{2} \left(1 - \frac{\varphi \gamma}{2} \right) x_{t-1} - \frac{\varphi \gamma}{2} E^*_{t-1} x_t$$
$$+ \frac{1}{2} \left(1 - \frac{\varphi \gamma}{2} \right) E^*_{t-1} x_{t+1} + u_t.$$

***Example 4:* Real Balance Model with Policy Feedback.** Augment Example 2 with a policy feedback $m_t = d_I + d_p p_{t-1} + u_{4t}$. Then the model is of the form (8.28) with β_0 and β_1 determined as in Example 2 and with $\delta = d_p$.

---

[10]Our use of the term "MSV solution" here varies from McCallum (1983), who introduced the term. McCallum provides two principles to define MSV solutions. We adopt his primary but not his subsidiary principle. For a discussion of his subsidiary principle in the context of learning, see Chapter 9.

8.5.1   A Characterization of the Solutions

The MSV solutions are of the AR(1) form and we apply the method of undetermined coefficients. Write the solution as

$$y_t = \bar{a} + \bar{b}_1 y_{t-1} + v_t. \tag{8.29}$$

Computing $E_{t-1} y_t = \bar{a} + \bar{b}_1 y_{t-1}$ and $E_{t-1} y_{t+1} = \bar{a}(1 + \bar{b}_1) + \bar{b}_1^2 y_{t-1}$ and substituting these and equation (8.29) into equation (8.28) and collecting terms, we see that a solution of this form must satisfy

$$\beta_1 \bar{b}_1^2 + (\beta_0 - 1)\bar{b}_1 + \delta = 0, \tag{8.30}$$
$$\alpha(1 - \beta_0 - \beta_1(1 + \bar{b}_1))^{-1} = \bar{a}.$$

Provided $(\beta_0 - 1)^2 - 4\beta_1 \delta > 0$, there are two solutions of the form (8.29). There are thus two MSV solutions if this condition is satisfied. If the discriminant is negative, then there exist no solutions of the AR(1) form.

   In addition to these solutions, there also exists an ARMA(2,1) class of solutions (the method of constructing this complete class of solutions follows the previous lines). We discuss these in Chapter 9.

8.5.2   Stability under Learning of the AR(1) Solutions

We start with E-stability of the two AR(1) solutions. We assume throughout this section that the roots are real and begin with a discussion of weak E-stability. Assume that agents have a PLM of the AR(1) form

$$y_t = a + b_1 y_{t-1} + v_t.$$

Computing $E_{t-1} y_t$ and $E_{t-1} y_{t+1}$ and substituting into equation (8.28), we get the following mapping from PLM to ALM:

$$T_a(a, b_1) = \alpha + (\beta_0 + \beta_1)a + \beta_1 a b_1, \tag{8.31}$$
$$T_{b_1}(a, b_1) = \delta + \beta_0 b_1 + \beta_1 b_1^2.$$

(Weak) E-stability is determined by the usual equation

$$\frac{d\phi}{d\tau} = T(\phi) - \phi, \tag{8.32}$$

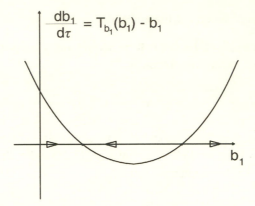

Figure 8.4. *E-stability of the two AR(1) solutions.*

with $\phi' = (a, b_1)$. Linearizing and computing the eigenvalues at an equilibrium $(\bar{a}, \bar{b}_1)$, we obtain the stability conditions

$$\beta_0 + \beta_1 - 1 + \beta_1 \bar{b}_1 < 0, \qquad\qquad (8.33)$$

$$\beta_0 - 1 + 2\beta_1 \bar{b}_1 < 0,$$

which are to be evaluated at the AR(1) solution in question.

It is easily verified that only one of the two AR(1) solutions can be E-stable. This follows immediately from the mapping $T_{b_1}(b_1) \equiv T_{b_1}(a, b_1)$. Figure 8.4 plots $T_{b_1}(b_1) - b_1$ for the case $\beta_1 > 0$. A necessary condition for stability (corresponding to the second condition above) is that

$$\frac{d}{db_1}\left(T_{b_1}(\bar{b}_1) - b_1\right) < 0.$$

Since T_{b_1} is a quadratic in b_1, this condition can be satisfied at only one of the two roots.

We now take up real-time learning when the PLM is of the AR(1) form. At time $t - 1$, the ALM is assumed to be $y_t = a_{t-1} + b_{1,t-1}y_{t-1} + v_t$. Substituting the corresponding expectations into equation (8.28), it can be seen that y_t is determined by the ALM

$$y_t = T_a(a_{t-1}, b_{1,t-1}) + T_{b_1}(a_{t-1}, b_{1,t-1})y_{t-1} + v_t,$$

or

$$y_t = z'_{t-1}T(\phi_{t-1}) + v_t, \tag{8.34}$$

where

$$\phi'_t = (a_t, b_{1,t}), \qquad z'_{t-1} = (1, y_{t-1}),$$

$$T(\phi) = T((a, b_1)') = \left(T_a(a, b_1), T_{b_1}(a, b_1)\right)'.$$

Recursive least squares estimation of ϕ_t as usual takes the form (8.12).

The equations (8.12), (8.31), and (8.34) define the evolution of the system over time under least squares learning. After making the transformation $S_{t-1} = R_t$, we rewrite the system as equation (8.14) and it can be verified that the technical conditions for application of the results in Chapter 6 are satisfied, provided the AR(1) solution being considered is stationary. The argument is virtually identical to that given for the AR(1) solution in Section 8.4.1. Looking at the associated ODE (8.21) and the E-stability equation (8.32), we get the following.

Proposition 8.2. *For model (8.28), assume the characteristic equation (8.30) has a stationary root. Then the stability conditions for the corresponding AR(1) solution (8.29) under least squares learning are given by the E-stability conditions (8.33). If both MSV solutions are stationary, only one can be stable under least squares learning. The other solution will be reached by the learning dynamics with probability zero.*

We will apply these (and other) results to Examples 3 and 4 later in Section 9.4.3 of Chapter 9.

To illustrate numerically the findings of this section, we consider the model (8.28) with $\alpha = 2$, $\beta_0 = 1.5$, $\beta_1 = -1.5$, and $\delta = 0.1$. The two AR(1) solutions have values $\bar{b}_1 = -0.1407$ and $\bar{b}_1 = 0.4740$, respectively. Clearly, both AR(1) solutions are stationary, but the $\bar{b}_1 = -0.1407$ solution is not E-stable, while the other solution is. Figure 8.5 illustrates convergence to the AR(1) solution with $\bar{b}_1 = 0.4740$ for a typical sample path. Figure 8.6 shows a typical simulation which diverges from the unstable AR(1) solution.[11] For this unstable solution, divergence is rapid even though the initial conditions are at the equilibrium.

---

[11] In these simulations we use $\gamma_t = 1/t$.

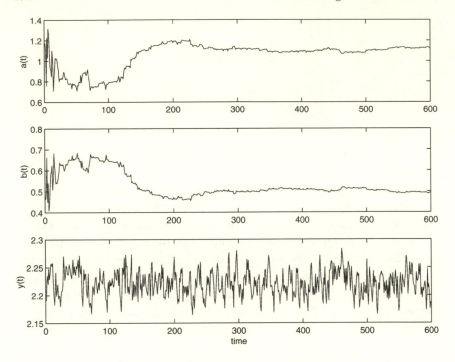

Figure 8.5.

8.6   Extension 2: Models with Time-*t* Dating

8.6.1   Basic Case

In many economic models the variable of interest y_t depends on expectations of future variables which are formed at time t, so that the information set includes y_t itself as well as any exogenous observables dated t or earlier. The simplest setup is

$$y_t = \beta E_t^* y_{t+1} + \kappa w_t + v_t, \qquad (8.35)$$

where w_t is an exogenous stochastic process which is observed at time t and v_t is an unobserved white noise shock. For concreteness we continue to assume that w_t follows a stationary AR(1) process

$$w_t = \alpha + \rho w_{t-1} + u_t, \qquad (8.36)$$

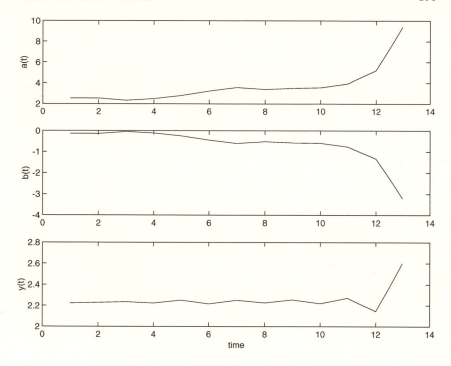

Figure 8.6.

where u_t is white noise and $|\rho| < 1$. The next two examples were already briefly described in Chapter 1.

Example 5: **Cagan Model of Inflation.** The demand for money depends linearly on expected inflation

$$m_t - p_t = -\gamma \left(E_t^* p_{t+1} - p_t \right) + \eta_t, \qquad \gamma > 0,$$

where m_t is the log of the money supply at time t, and p_t is the log of the price level at time t. This can be solved for the above form with $y_t \equiv p_t$, $w_t \equiv m_t$, $\beta = \gamma/(1+\gamma)$, and $\kappa = 1/(1+\gamma)$.

Example 6: **Asset Pricing with Risk Neutrality.** Under risk neutrality and appropriate assumptions, all assets earn expected rate of return $1 + r$, where $r > 0$ is the real net interest rate, assumed constant. If an asset pays dividend d_t at the end of period t, then its price p_t at t is given by

$$p_t = (1+r)^{-1} \left(E_t^* p_{t+1} + d_t \right).$$

We again have the form (8.35), with $y_t \equiv p_t$, $w_t \equiv d_t$, $\beta = \kappa = (1+r)^{-1}$, and $v_t \equiv 0$.

We focus here on the MSV solution to the model, which is unique and given by

$$y_t = \bar{a} + \bar{b}w_t + v_t,$$

where

$$\bar{a} = (1-\beta)^{-1}\alpha\beta\bar{b} \quad \text{and} \quad \bar{b} = (1-\beta\rho)^{-1}\kappa.$$

In the context of the model (8.35) and particularly in the case of the asset pricing application, the MSV solution is often referred to as the *fundamental solution*. Is the MSV solution stable under least squares learning? For PLMs of the form $y_t = a + bw_t$, the map from PLM to ALM is

$$T_a(a,b) = \beta a + \alpha\beta b,$$
$$T_b(a,b) = \beta\rho b + \kappa,$$

and it is easily verified that the fundamental solution is (weakly) E-stable if $\beta < 1$ and $\beta\rho < 1$. We have assumed $|\rho| < 1$ and in the two economic examples above, $0 < \beta < 1$. Thus the E-stability conditions are met.

Under least squares learning, agents at time t estimate the model $y_t = a + bw_t + v_t$ by running a least squares regression of y_t on an intercept and w_t using the data available. Let (a_t, b_t) denote the least squares estimates using data on (w_i, y_i), $i = 1, \ldots, t-1$.[12] Expectations are then given by $E_t^* y_{t+1} = a_t + b_t E_t w_{t+1} = (a_t + b_t \alpha) + b_t \rho w_t$, where for simplicity we treat ρ and α as known, and under learning y_t is given by $y_t = T_a(a_t, b_t) + T_b(a_t, b_t)w_t + v_t$. Applying the standard stochastic approximation results, it follows that the fundamental solution is locally stable under least squares learning provided the E-stability condition above is met. This holds for both of the above economic examples.

---

[12]For technical simplicity we assume that the data point (w_t, y_t) is not available for the least squares estimates at t of the coefficients (a_t, b_t), though we do allow the time-t forecasts to depend on w_t. This avoids simultaneity between y_t and b_t. With additional technical complexity, this simultaneity can be permitted, see, e.g., Marcet and Sargent (1989c).

8.6.2 Models with Lags

Models with one expectational lead and one lag also arise in frameworks, where the expectations are formed at time t. We thus consider models of the form

$$y_t = \alpha + \beta E_t^* y_{t+1} + \delta y_{t-1} + \kappa w_t + v_t, \tag{8.37}$$
$$w_t = \mu + \rho w_{t-1} + e_t,$$

where $|\rho| < 1$.

Example 7: **Investment under Uncertainty.** The Lucas–Prescott model of investment under uncertainty is presented in a linear quadratic framework in Sargent (1987, Chapter XIV). This version also allows for externalities and taxes.

Consider a competitive industry with N identical firms. Output of the representative firm at t is given by

$$x_t = x_0 + f_0 k_t + f_1 K_t + f_2 K_{t-1},$$

where $K_t = N k_t$ denotes the aggregate capital stock. The presence of the two terms in K_t reflect contemporaneous and lagged external effects. These may be positive or negative, so we do not restrict the signs of f_1 or f_2, but $f_0 > 0$ and $x_0 > 0$.

Taxes are levied on firms on capital in place. The rate itself is assumed to depend on current and lagged aggregate capital stock, so that $\tau_t = g_0 + g_1 K_t + g_2 K_{t-1}$. Finally, total output is given by $X_t = N x_t$, and demand for the market is $p_t = D - A X_t + u_t$, where u_t is white noise. We require $p_t \geq 0$.

The firm chooses k_t to maximize

$$E_0 \sum_{t=0}^{\infty} B^t \left\{ p_t (x_0 + f_0 k_t + f_1 K_t + f_2 K_{t-1}) - w_t k_t - \tau_t k_t \right.$$
$$\left. - \frac{C}{2} (k_t - k_{t-1})^2 \right\},$$

where k_{-1} is given and w_t, the one-period-ahead rental on capital goods, is assumed exogenous. We assume that $w_t = \mu + \rho w_{t-1} + e_t$, with $|\rho| < 1$. $C > 0$ reflects quadratic adjustment costs. The Euler equation for this problem can be written

$$p_t f_0 - (w_t + \tau_t) + B C E_t^* k_{t+1} - C(1 + B) k_t + C k_{t-1} = 0$$

for $t \geq 0$. For an optimum solution for the firm, we also require that $k_t \geq 0$,

$x_t \geq 0$, and that the transversality condition is met. These conditions and the nonnegativity of prices rule out explosive paths for k_t.

Substituting the demand curve into the Euler equation, we obtain the form (8.37) with $y_t = K_t$, $\beta = BC\Omega^{-1}$, $\delta = -(f_0 A f_2 N^2 + g_2 N - C)c$, $\kappa = -N\Omega^{-1}$, and $v_t = f_0 N \Omega^{-1} u_t$, where $\Omega = f_0 AN(f_0 + f_1 N) + g_1 N + C(1 + B)$. With no externalities or taxes, there is a unique stationary solution of the form (8.37). However, generally the parameters β and δ are unrestricted.[13]

Example 8: The Cagan model of Example 5 with a monetary policy feedback rule $m_t = m + dp_{t-1} + e_t$.

Returning to the general model (8.37), the MSV solutions are of the form

$$y_t = a + by_{t-1} + cw_t + dv_t, \qquad (8.38)$$

where b is a (real) root of the characteristic equation

$$b^2 - \beta^{-1}b + \beta^{-1}\delta = 0. \qquad (8.39)$$

The roots therefore satisfy $\bar{b} = [1 \pm \sqrt{(1 - 4\beta\delta)}]/2\beta$. Let $\bar{b}_+$ and $\bar{b}_-$ denote the two solutions $\bar{b}$. The values for the other parameters satisfy $\bar{c} = \kappa[1 - \beta(\bar{b} + \rho)]^{-1}$, $\bar{a} = \alpha/(1 - \beta - \beta\bar{b})$, and $\bar{d} = (1 - \beta\bar{b})^{-1}$.

Under least squares learning, agents estimate the parameters (a, b, c) of the appropriate PLM and use estimates (a_t, b_t, c_t) to make forecasts $E_t^* y_{t+1} = a_t + b_t y_t + c_t(\mu + \rho w_t)$. The stability of the MSV solution under learning is again based on the map from the PLM to the implied ALM and is given by

$$T(a, b, c) = \left[(\alpha + \beta a)/(1 - \beta b), \delta/(1 - \beta b), (\kappa + \beta \rho c)/(1 - \beta b)\right]$$

provided $b \neq \beta^{-1}$. This leads to the result:

Proposition 8.3. *For model (8.37), the E-stability conditions for the MSV solutions are $\delta\beta(1 - \beta\bar{b})^{-2} < 1$, $\beta(1 - \beta\bar{b})^{-1} < 1$, and $\rho\beta(1 - \beta\bar{b})^{-1} < 1$, where $\bar{b}$ is a solution to the characteristic equation (8.39). If an MSV solution is stationary and E-stable, then it is locally stable under RLS learning.*

Provided $0 \leq \rho < 1$, the third condition is redundant and for simplicity we make this assumption in the following discussion.

---

[13] Note that the nonnegativity conditions mentioned above will be met in stationary solutions for suitable values of intercepts and with bounded supports for v_t and e_t.

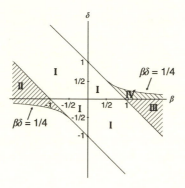

Figure 8.7.

Figure 8.7 shows the possibilities in (β, δ) space. In region I, $|\beta + \delta| < 1$, the solution $\bar{b}_-$ is uniquely stationary, and it is also E-stable and thus locally stable under least squares learning. In regions II, III, and IV, both solutions are stationary (regions II and IV are in part bounded by $\beta\delta = 1/4$). In region II, the $\bar{b}_-$ solution is stable under learning while the $\bar{b}_+$ solution is unstable under learning. In region III, the $\bar{b}_+$ solution is stable under learning while the $\bar{b}_-$ solution is unstable under learning. In region IV, neither solution is stable under learning. (Outside the marked regions, both solutions are explosive or nonreal.) Thus, although multiple stationary solutions to the model can exist, no more than one MSV solution will be locally stable under least squares learning.

It is also possible to introduce somewhat different assumptions about the information available to agents. More specifically, it is sometimes assumed that the current value of the endogenous variable y_t is not available at the time of expectations formation but that the values of the exogenous variables for period t are observable.[14]

To see the implications of this assumption consider the model (8.37) and the PLM of the form (8.38). Iterating forward and using the alternative informational assumption, we have

$$E_t y_{t+1} = a(1 + b) + c\mu + b^2 y_{t-1} + c(b + \rho)w_t + bdv_t,$$

which after substitution into equation (8.37) yields the T-map

$$T(a, b, c, d) = \left[\alpha + \beta(a(1 + b) + c\mu), \delta + \beta b^2, \beta c(b + \rho) + \kappa, 1 + \beta bd\right]'.$$

---

[14]The assumption that current y_t is not observable is made to avoid the simultaneity problem. In the literature on indeterminacy, this assumption is often used.

The E-stability conditions are now different from above. It turns out that $\bar{b}_+$ is always unstable, while the E-stability condition for $\bar{b}_-$ takes the form $-\sqrt{1 - 4\beta\delta} < \min[1 - 2\beta, 1 - 2\beta\rho]$. In particular, if $\beta < 1/2$ and $\beta\rho < 1/2$, this solution is E-stable.

Most of the literature on learning and with t dating of expectations uses the assumption that the current value of the endogenous variable is included in the information set. Nevertheless, it is sometimes convenient to adopt the alternative formulation that the current value of the endogenous variable is not included in the set of available information. We will do so from time to time, and when done this will be clearly indicated.

8.7   Conclusions

This chapter has illustrated a large range of univariate linear examples. Many of the standard workhorses of macroeconomics can be written in this frame-work as our examples illustrate. We have shown that there are readily applicable tools for studying the stability of the RE solutions to these models under least squares learning. Often these models will have a single nonexplosive solution and usually this solution will be stable under learning. However, linear models with multiple stationary solutions do arise and in these situations assessing their local stability under learning is particularly useful.

The solutions to the models of this chapter take various forms. For the MSV solution, the connection between E-stability and real-time learning has been for-mally established. The argument extends to a non-MSV solution which is locally unique relative to the form of solutions allowed. For cases of solutions continua, the connection has not been proven theoretically, though numerical simulations suggest that it holds more generally.

For the economic examples in this chapter, at most one MSV solution is locally stable under learning. This emphasizes the power of adaptive learning as a selection principle. However, in higher-order linear models (and in nonlinear models), there exist cases in which there are multiple stationary MSV solutions that are locally stable under adaptive learning. This will be discussed in the next chapter.

Most of the results and techniques in this chapter are straightforward to use, but we have postponed some issues. For example, models with mixed dates in information sets appear in the literature. We also need to systematically discuss the notion of strong E-stability. In the following chapter we explore these and other issues for univariate linear models. Then in Chapter 10 we take up multi-variate linear models.

Chapter 9

Further Topics in Linear Models

9.1 Introduction

In this chapter we take up a number of further topics in the analysis of learning in univariate linear models. First, we provide an example of learning in a model with a mixture of dates at which expectations are formed. Second, we look at weak and strong stability for the basic "special case" of the previous chapter, as well as for the "extended special case," also considered last chapter, which incorporates a lagged endogenous variable. These cases cover many models in the literature and thus provide a convenient class of models for discussing the literature on alternative selection criteria for choosing among equilibria. Third, we investigate a model with two forward leads present and demonstrate the possibility of a linear model with two distinct AR(1) solutions, each of which is locally stable under learning. Fourth, we show how we examine least squares learning of explosive AR(1) solutions. Fifth, we consider stability of explosive bubbles in the standard asset pricing model. Finally, we allow for certain types of heterogeneity in learning rules.

9.2 Muth's Inventory Model

Models with mixed datings of expectations and with conditional variances arise in various contexts. As an example we consider Muth's inventory model. In addition to the well-known cobweb model, Muth (1961) considered a version in which the good was durable and firms could accumulate inventories. Consider the model

$$C_t = -\delta p_t,$$
$$Q_t = \gamma E_{t-1} p_t + u_t,$$
$$I_t = \alpha(E_t p_{t+1} - p_t),$$
$$C_t + I_t = Q_t + I_{t-1},$$

where Q_t is production at t, C_t is consumption at t, I_t is stock of inventories at t, and p_t is the market price at t. All variables are in deviation from the mean form, so we ignore intercepts.

Muth showed that for small changes in the price, the coefficient in the inventory speculation equation is given by

$$\alpha = K / \operatorname{Var}_t p_{t+1}.$$

Muth took α as fixed but as McCafferty and Driskill (1980) argue, $\operatorname{Var}_t p_{t+1}$ is endogenous and should be solved in terms of the model parameters. Allowing for this and combining equations, we arrive at the following reduced form equation:

$$\left(\delta + K / \operatorname{Var}_t p_{t+1}\right) p_t = \left(K / \operatorname{Var}_{t-1} p_t\right) p_{t-1} - \left(\gamma + K / \operatorname{Var}_{t-1} p_t\right) E_{t-1} p_t$$
$$+ \left(K / \operatorname{Var}_t p_{t+1}\right) E_t p_{t+1} - u_t.$$

There are two minimal state variable (MSV) solutions of the form

$$p_t = b p_{t-1} + \phi u_t.$$

For some choices of parameter values both are stationary, but adaptive learning can be used as a selection criterion. For example, suppose that $\delta = 0.1$, $\gamma = 0.4$, and $\psi = 2.5$. Here ψ denotes $\psi = K / \sigma_u^2$, where $\sigma_u^2 = \operatorname{Var}(u_t)$. Then the two solutions are $b = 0.10$ and $b = 0.66$. The root $b = 0.10$ is strongly E-stable while the root $b = 0.66$ is E-unstable. See Evans (1989) for further discussion of this model.

9.3   Overparameterization in the Special Case

We return to the simple univariate linear model (8.2) introduced in Chapter 8,

$$y_t = \alpha + \beta_0 E_{t-1}^* y_t + \beta_1 E_{t-1}^* y_{t+1} + v_t, \tag{9.1}$$

where v_t is white noise. Recall that there are two types of solution to this model, the MSV solution (8.3)

$$y_t = (1 - \beta_0 - \beta_1)^{-1}\alpha + v_t,$$

and the ARMA(1,1) class (8.4)

$$y_t = -\beta_1^{-1}\alpha + \beta_1^{-1}(1 - \beta_0)y_{t-1} + v_t + c_1 v_{t-1} + d_1 \varepsilon_{t-1},$$

where ε_t is an arbitrary "sunspot" variable satisfying $E_{t-1}\varepsilon_t$.

In Chapter 8 we investigated whether the MSV solution was stable under least squares learning when the perceived law of motion (PLM) was of the same form, and we also investigated whether it was locally stable under least squares learning when overparameterized as an AR(1) process. We saw that the answers were governed, respectively, by the weak E-stability condition (8.10) and the strong E-stability conditions (8.24). For the ARMA(1,1) solution set, we considered whether it was locally stable under learning when correctly specified as an ARMA(1,1) process. There we obtained the weak E-stability conditions (8.23) for the ARMA(1,1) class of solutions.

A question left open was whether the stability conditions [both for the MSV and for the ARMA(1,1) solution set] might be modified if we considered an even larger class of PLMs. This is the question we now take up. We begin with a calculation of the relevant E-stability conditions and then discuss local stability under least squares learning. In Section 9.4 we extend these results to the extended special case with a lagged dependent variable.

9.3.1 Strong E-Stability in the Special Case

To investigate E-stability we postulate a PLM of the general form

$$y_t = a + \sum_{i=1}^{s} b_i y_{t-i} + v_t + \sum_{i=1}^{r} c_i v_{t-i} + \sum_{i=1}^{q} d_i \varepsilon_{t-i}. \tag{9.2}$$

As before, we can compute

$$E_{t-1}y_t = a + \sum_{i=1}^{s} b_i y_{t-i} + \sum_{i=1}^{r} c_i v_{t-i} + \sum_{i=1}^{q} d_i \varepsilon_{t-i}, \tag{9.3}$$

$$E_{t-1}y_{t+1} = a + b_1 E_{t-1}y_t + \sum_{i=2}^{s} b_i y_{t+1-i} + \sum_{i=2}^{r} c_i v_{t+1-i} + \sum_{i=2}^{q} d_i \varepsilon_{t+1-i}.$$

Inserting into equation (9.1), we obtain an ALM of the same form as equation (9.2). Letting $\phi' = (a, b', c', d')$, where $b' = (b_1, \ldots, b_s)$, $c' = (c_1, \ldots, c_r)$, and $d' = (d_1, \ldots, d_q)$, we denote the mapping from the PLM ϕ to the ALM ϕ^* by $\phi^* = T(\phi)$. The explicit T-mapping is stated in the next section for a more general model with a lagged endogenous variable. For the case at hand, set $\delta = 0$ in equation (9.6) below. E-stability of the MSV solution or of the ARMA(1,1) solutions with respect to this general class of PLMs is then determined by local stability of the differential equation

$$\frac{d\phi}{d\tau} = T(\phi) - \phi \tag{9.4}$$

at that solution.

It is possible to demonstrate the following results, see Evans and Honkapohja (1992) for various details. First, the MSV solution is E-stable with respect to PLMs (9.2) provided condition (8.24) holds. Thus our previous "strong E-stability" conditions for the MSV solutions remain sufficient for E-stability with respect to an even larger class of overparameterizations. This result is straightforward to show.

Second, the ARMA(1,1) solutions are *never* strongly E-stable. This result is more difficult to show and somewhat subtle: the roots of the linearization of the differential equation subsystem in $(b_1, \ldots, b_s)$ include 0, so that stability cannot be determined from the linearization. Formally, the center manifold technique must be applied and we find one-sided stability–instability. This result can be shown diagrammatically for the case of $s = 2$. We then have

$$\frac{db_1}{d\tau} = (\beta_0 + \beta_1 b_1 - 1)b_1 + \beta_1 b_2,$$

$$\frac{db_2}{d\tau} = (\beta_0 + \beta_1 b_1 - 1)b_2.$$

Figure 9.1 gives the (b_1, b_2) phase diagram [drawn on the assumption of parameter values consistent with weak E-stability of the ARMA(1,1) class] and shows the failure of the ARMA(1,1) class to be strongly E-stable. For the quadrant northwest of the values $b_1 = \beta_1^{-1}(1 - \beta_0)$, $b_2 = 0$, corresponding to the ARMA(1,1) solutions, there are divergent paths. Of course, there are also convergent paths from other initial points, but the existence of locally divergent paths demonstrates local instability.

Although the ARMA(1,1) solutions are not strongly E-stable, we emphasize that this is a case in which the (non-MSV) equilibrium $b_1 = \beta_1^{-1}(1 - \beta_0)$, $b_1 = 0$ in the differential equation subsystem for b is nonhyperbolic. This is relevant for our discussion of least squares learning.

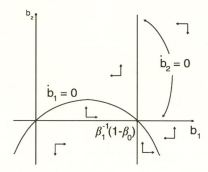

Figure 9.1. *The weakly E-stable ARMA(1,1) solution class is not strongly E-stable.*

9.3.2 Least Squares Learning

Here we examine two questions. First, consider the MSV solution $y_t = \bar{a} + v_t$, where $\bar{a} = \alpha(1 - \beta_0 - \beta_1)^{-1}$. In Sections 8.3.1 and 8.4.2 of Chapter 8 we showed that this solution is stable under learning, when estimated as a constant, if it satisfies the weak stability condition (8.10), and that it is locally stable under least squares learning, when estimated as an AR(1) process, if the strong E-stability conditions (8.24) are satisfied. We can now make an even stronger claim.

Consider now the question of the stability under least squares learning of the MSV solution when agents are assumed to have PLMs of the form (9.2) and to estimate the parameters by recursive least squares, updating their estimates at each point in time. We will assume that the shock v_t and the sunspot ε_t are observable at time t, so that estimation of the parameters (a, b, c, d) can be carried out using the RLS algorithm (8.12) with ϕ_t and z_t augmented to include additional terms. Thus ϕ_t and z_{t-1} are given by

$$\phi_t' = (a_t, b_{1t}, \ldots, b_{st}, c_{1t}, \ldots, c_{rt}, \ldots, d_{1t}, \ldots, d_{qt}),$$
$$z_{t-1}' = (1, y_{t-1}, \ldots, y_{t-s}, v_{t-1}, \ldots, v_{t-r}, \varepsilon_{t-1}, \ldots, \varepsilon_{t-q}),$$

where we will be considering different choices of s, q, and r.

There is a new technical complication which requires discussion. The MSV solution $y_t = \bar{a} + v_t$ is equivalent to a higher-order stationary ARMA process with common factors, i.e., to $g(L)y_t = g(1)\bar{a} + g(L)v_t$ for any finite lag polynomial $g(L)$. The simplest way to avoid this identification problem in the case of the MSV solution is to restrict specifications to $r = 0$, i.e., to specifications in which there are no lagged terms in v_t and ε_t is assumed independent of v_t.

The previous results can now be extended and a strong local stability result stated.

Proposition 9.1. *Under recursive least squares learning in which the regressors include the intercept and s lags of y_t and q lags of ε_t, the MSV solution for model (9.1) is locally stable (in the senses discussed in Section 6.3.3 of Chapter 6) provided the strong E-stability conditions (8.24) are satisfied. If either of the strong E-stability conditions is violated with a strict inequality, then there is convergence with probability 0 to the MSV solution.*

The other question we consider is convergence under least squares learning to the ARMA(1,1) sunspot solutions. Here we are unable to state formal convergence results, for two technical reasons. First, the ARMA(1,1) solutions in general include an unbounded continuum in the form of arbitrary parameters c_1 and d_1. Such cases are not covered by the general stability results stated in Chapter 6. However, even if we set $r = q = 0$ and only include lagged y_t as regressors, there is a difficulty. This can again be seen if we set $s = 2$ and consider the non-MSV AR(1) solution overparameterized as an AR(2) solution. We have shown that the non-MSV AR(1) can be weakly but not strongly E-stable. However, with $s = 2$ the differential equation subsystem in $b' = (b_1, b_2)$ is non-hyperbolic. This carries over into a zero root for the linearized ODE associated with the recursive stochastic algorithm. Inspection of Theorem 6.9 of Chapter 6, however, shows that the case of zero roots is not covered by the instability theorem.

We can, however, consider simulations and we return to the numerical example considered in Section 8.4.4 of Chapter 8. There we considered parameter settings in which the ARMA(1,1) sunspot solutions were weakly E-stable and in Figure 8.3 provided a simulation showing apparent convergence to a sunspot solution. Figure 9.2 shows a simulation for the same parameter values in which $z'_{t-1} = (1, y_{t-1}, y_{t-2}, v_{t-1}, \varepsilon_{t-1})$, i.e., in which we overparameterize by including y_{t-2} as a regressor.

Initial settings of parameters $\phi' = (a, b_1, b_2, c_1, d_1)$ were $a = \bar{a}$, $b_1 = \bar{b}_1 + 0.10$, $c = 0.25$, $d = 0.25$, $b_2 = 0.05$, $R = \bar{R}$, and lagged y equal to $\bar{y}$.[1] It is apparent from Figure 9.2 that there is no longer convergence to the RE ARMA(1,1) sunspot solutions. Over the period shown the parameters diverge, and several periods later explode beyond computational limits.

These simulations suggest that while formal convergence results are not available for such cases, convergence of least squares learning does reflect weak and strong E-stability conditions. However, we remark that relatively little research has been done on these topics and the nonhyperbolic nature of the

---

[1] Again, to reduce the initial volatility of estimates for small t, we use a small constant gain for an initial period of time: $\gamma_t = N^{-1}$ for $t = 1, \ldots, N$ and $\gamma_t = t^{-1}$ for $t > N$, with N set at $N = 20$.

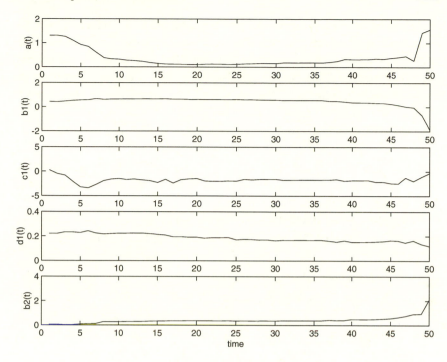

Figure 9.2.

solutions cautions that the situation may be exceedingly complex. The paper by Heinemann (2000b) contains some supporting simulations for this class of models, but also indicates that stochastic gradient learning may have somewhat different stability conditions in nonhyperbolic cases.

9.4 Extended Special Case

9.4.1 E-Stability

We return to the extended special case (8.28) considered in Chapter 8,[2] reproduced here for convenience,

$$y_t = \alpha + \delta y_{t-1} + \beta_0 E^*_{t-1} y_t + \beta_1 E^*_{t-1} y_{t+1} + v_t, \qquad (9.5)$$

[2]For a more detailed discussion of this model, see Evans and Honkapohja (1992).

in which the lagged dependent variable enters the reduced form. Here v_t is assumed to be a white noise process. There are two classes of solution (assuming real roots). The first class contains two distinct AR(1) solutions, taking the form (8.29) of Chapter 8. These are the MSV solutions. The second class is a continuum of ARMA(2,1) sunspot solutions.[3] These take the form

$$y_t = -\beta_1^{-1}\alpha + \beta_1^{-1}(1 - \beta_0)y_{t-1} - \beta_1^{-1}\delta y_{t-2} + v_t + c_1 v_{t-1} + d_1\varepsilon_{t-1},$$

where ε_t is an arbitrary process satisfying $E_{t-1}\varepsilon_t = 0$. In the case of complex roots, in which no real AR(1) solution exists, these ARMA(2,1) "sunspot" solutions remain well defined.

Consider general PLMs of the form (9.2). Inserting equation (9.3) into equation (9.5), we obtain the following mapping to the implied ALM:

$$
\begin{aligned}
a^* &= \alpha + (\beta_0 + \beta_1)a + \beta_1 a b_1, \\
b_1^* &= \delta + \beta_0 b_1 + \beta_1(b_1^2 + b_2), \\
b_i^* &= \beta_0 b_i + \beta_1(b_1 b_i + b_{i+1}), \qquad i = 2, \ldots, s-1, \\
b_s^* &= \beta_0 b_s + \beta_1 b_1 b_s, \qquad\qquad\qquad\qquad\quad (9.6) \\
c_i^* &= \beta_0 c_i + \beta_1(b_1 c_i + c_{i+1}), \qquad i = 1, \ldots, r-1, \\
c_r^* &= \beta_0 c_r + \beta_1 b_1 c_r, \\
d_i^* &= \beta_0 d_i + \beta_1(b_1 d_i + d_{i+1}), \qquad i = 1, \ldots, q-1, \\
d_q^* &= \beta_0 d_q + \beta_1 b_1 d_q.
\end{aligned}
$$

Setting again $\phi' = (a, b', c', d')$, where $b' = (b_1, \ldots, b_s)$, $c' = (c_1, \ldots, c_r)$, and $d' = (d_1, \ldots, d_q)$, we denote the mapping from the PLM ϕ to the ALM ϕ^* by $\phi^* = T(\phi)$. Strong and weak E-stability of the different solutions can then be analyzed according to equation (9.4).

Strong E-stability conditions for the AR(1) solutions can be derived from the linearization of equation (9.4). We obtain the following.

Proposition 9.2. *For model (9.5) an MSV solution with AR(1) coefficient b_1 is strongly E-stable if the weak E-stability conditions (8.33) together with the additional condition $\beta_0 - 1 + \beta_1 b_1 < 0$ are satisfied.*

---

[3] Using the classification sceme of McCallum (1983), these would be called "bubble" solutions, though they need not be explosive. Using his subsidiary principle, McCallum (1983) would also classify one of the AR(1) solutions as a bubble solution.

Weak E-stability of the ARMA(2,1) solutions is obtained by setting $s = 2$ and $r = q = 1$ and computing the roots of the linearized system at the ARMA(2,1) solution. This yields the weak E-stability conditions

$$\delta\beta_1 > 0, \qquad 1 - \beta_0 < 0, \qquad \beta_1 < 0.$$

Strong E-stability of the ARMA(2,1) solutions requires their stability under equation (9.4) for general s, r, q. As with the special case, it turns out that there are zero eigenvalues, so that stability cannot be determined from the linearization. To determine E-stability requires the center manifold technique. This application of the technique to our problem is described in Evans and Honkapohja (1992) and we simply state the result here: The ARMA(2,1) class of solutions is never strongly E-stable.

9.4.2 Least Squares Learning

Under least squares learning with PLMs of the form (9.2), the situation is essentially the same as that discussed for the special case. The analysis of local stability and instability given in Chapter 6 applies to the convergence of least squares learning to stationary MSV solutions which now take the AR(1) form. These MSV solutions are locally stable, provided they are stationary and weakly E-stable, when estimated as an AR(1) process using recursive least squares. For overparameterized learning, there is again potentially a common factor problem when the AR(1) solution is overparameterized as an ARMA process. Again, this can be avoided by setting $r = 0$. An AR(1) solution is locally stable under least squares learning which includes additional lags of y_t and/or lags of the sunspot variable ε_t, provided it is stationary and satisfies the strong E-stability conditions.

For least squares learning of the ARMA(2,1) solutions, the technical difficulties previously mentioned prevent us from obtaining formal results and we are therefore left with the conjecture that E-stability conditions give local stability conditions under least squares learning.

9.4.3 Discussion of Examples

We can now consider our examples from Chapter 8 and consider the possible types of solution that are likely to arise, from the viewpoint of weak and strong E-stability and results on local convergence under least squares learning.

The Taylor overlapping contracts model (Example 3 of Chapter 8) is straightforward. It can be shown that it is saddlepoint stable and therefore one of the MSV solutions is the unique stationary solution. It can also be shown that only this stationary MSV solution can be weakly or strongly E-stable.

The real balance model augmented with a monetary policy feedback (Example 4) is more complicated. As noted earlier, this example has the reduced form

$$p_t = \alpha + dp_{t-1} + hE^*_{t-1}p_t - hE^*_{t-1}p_{t+1} + v_t, \qquad (9.7)$$

where h can take any nonzero value depending on the structural parameters and where d denotes the response parameter of the money supply to the lagged price level. In this example a range of unusual phenomena can occur. In particular, the reader can verify the following.

Proposition 9.3. (i) *If $d < 0$ and $h > 1$, the ARMA(2,1) class of model (9.7) will be (weakly) E-stable and there does not exist a strongly E-stable solution.*

(ii) *For an open set of parameter values, an explosive AR(1) solution can be strongly E-stable. An example is $h = 1.5$, $d = 1.1$. All other solutions are E-unstable.*

(iii) *For an open set of parameter values, all solutions are stationary, with a unique strongly E-stable AR(1) solution and all other solutions E-unstable. An example is $h = 1.5$, $d = 0.1$.*

Note that in these examples of exotic solutions the dependence on $E^*_{t-1}p_t$ is large, and it can be shown that they arise only if $|d|$ or $|h|$ is large. This last point can be made more generally within the context of the extended special case (8.28).

Proposition 9.4. *Consider the model (8.28). If $|\delta|, |\beta_0|, |\beta_1| < \frac{1}{3}$, then there is a unique stationary solution which is strongly E-stable and which is uniquely weakly E-stable.*

For proofs of these propositions see Evans and Honkapohja (1992). Thus, for this class of models the solutions are well behaved when the degree of direct and expectational feedback is not too large: there is a unique stationary solution which is strongly E-stable and thus stable under least squares learning. Only when feedback is large do we find multiple stationary solutions, E-stable explosive solutions, or an E-stable ARMA(2,1) class. Since E-stability governs the local stability under least squares or adaptive learning, we see that in the "well-behaved" case of limited feedback, adaptive learning singles out the standard solution. However, when expectational feedback is large, various exotic possibilities can arise. In these other cases, adaptive learning continues to operate as a selection criterion in the sense that it restricts attention to a smaller set of solutions which are "attainable."

9.5 Linear Model with Two Forward Leads

9.5.1 AR(1) Solutions

We now extend the model further to include a dependence on $E_{t-1}y_{t+2}$. It turns out that this leads to a new phenomenon: multiple MSV solutions which are stable under least squares learning. The reduced form we consider is

$$y_t = \alpha + \delta y_{t-1} + \beta_0 E_{t-1}^* y_t + \beta_1 E_{t-1}^* y_{t+1} + \beta_2 E_{t-1}^* y_{t+2} + v_t, \qquad (9.8)$$

where v_t is white noise. We give an economic example below.

The MSV solutions again take the AR(1) form:

$$y_t = a + b_1 y_{t-1} + v_t. \qquad (9.9)$$

It is straightforward to show that (a, b_1) satisfy

$$\beta_2 b_1^3 + \beta_1 b_1^2 + (\beta_0 - 1)b_1 + \delta = 0,$$
$$a\big(\beta_0 - 1 + \beta_1(1 + b_1) + \beta_2(1 + b_1 + b_1^2)\big) = -\alpha.$$

Generically there are either three or one such solutions. For appropriate parameter values it is possible for there to exist three real stationary solutions.

For this model one can show the following result.

Proposition 9.5. *For model (9.8), we have*

(i) *For an open set of parameter values, two of the AR(1) solutions are stationary and locally stable under least squares learning.*
(ii) *Let* $-1 < \delta < 1$ *be given. Then for all* $\beta_0, \beta_1, \beta_2$ *sufficiently small in magnitude, there is a unique stationary AR(1) solution and it is stable under least squares learning.*

Details of the argument are in Evans and Honkapohja (1994b). The basic idea can be seen from the E-stability conditions. For PLMs of the form (9.9), the map from the PLM to the ALM is given by

$$T_a(a, b_1) = \alpha + \beta_0 a + \beta_1(ab_1 + a) + \beta_2(b_1(b_1 a + a) + a),$$
$$T_{b_1}(a, b_1) = \delta + \beta_0 b_1 + \beta_1 b_1^2 + \beta_2 b_1^3.$$

Stability of the b_1 parameter in the equation $db_1/d\tau = T_{b_1}(b_1)$, where we have written $T_{b_1}(b_1) \equiv T_{b_1}(a, b_1)$, is determined by a cubic which may have two

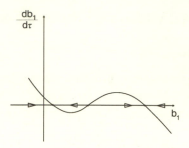

Figure 9.3.   *Model with two forward leads. Example of two E-stable AR(1) solutions.*

stable roots, depending on the parameters. This case is illustrated in Figure 9.3. For appropriate choices of the parameters this will make the (a, b) system locally stable. From Proposition 9.5(ii) we see that this possibility can only arise if the dependence of y_t on expectations is large.

We illustrate the possibility of multiple AR(1) solutions which are locally stable with a simple numerical example. We set $\alpha = 0$, $\beta_0 = -3.53968254$, $\beta_1 = 6.66666667$, $\beta_2 = -3.17460318$, and $\delta = 1$. This leads to three AR(1) solutions with $b_1 = 0.5, 0.7, 0.9$. The solutions $b_1 = 0.5$ and $b_1 = 0.9$ are strongly E-stable and the solution $b_1 = 0.7$ is weakly E-unstable.

Figure 9.4 shows the results of two simulations of recursive least squares learning of an AR(1) process. Both simulations set the initial value of $b_1 = 0.7$. The first simulation suggests convergence to $b_1 = 0.5$. After 20,000 periods the value is 0.4857. The second simulation suggests convergence to $b_1 = 0.9$. After 20,000 periods the value is 0.8728. Although convergence is somewhat slow, the local stability of the two AR(1) solutions appears clear in the simulations. For the AR(1) solutions the local stability and instability results of Chapter 6 do apply, so that formal results on convergence can be demonstrated in the usual way.

An economic example which fits the framework of this section is an open economy model of Dornbusch type with policy feedback. The equations are

$$p_t - p_{t-1} = \pi E_{t-1} d_t,$$
$$d_t = -\gamma (r_t - E_t p_{t+1} + p_t) + \eta (e_t - p_t),$$
$$r_t = \lambda^{-1} (p_t - \vartheta p_{t-1}),$$
$$r_t = E_t e_{t+1} - e_t.$$

Here d_t is (log) aggregate demand, e_t is the (log) exchange rate, p_t is (log) price level, and r_t is the interest rate. The first equation is a Phillips curve, the

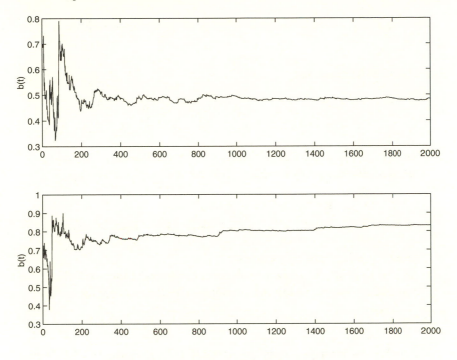

Figure 9.4. *Results for $b_1(t)$ from two simulations.*

second is the IS curve for an open economy, the third is the LM curve in which monetary policy reacts to p_{t-1}, and the last equation is the open parity condition.

It can be shown that the reduced form for p_t is of the required form (9.8); see Evans and Honkapohja (1994b) for details. As an example, suppose $\pi = 1.5$, $\gamma = 1.5, \lambda = 10, \vartheta = 0.5$, and $\eta = 0.2$. Then there is a unique stationary solution with $b_1 = 0.384$. However, if $\pi = 1.5, \gamma = 1.5, \lambda = 10, \vartheta = 1.1$, and $\eta = -0.1$, there are three locally stationary roots $b_1 = 0.716, 0.772$, and 0.989, and the solutions $b_1 = 0.716$ and $b_1 = 0.989$ are both locally stable under least squares learning.

9.5.2 ARMA Solutions

In this section we briefly discuss the full set of solutions in the model with expectations $E_{t-1}y_{t+2}$ included. (The MSV solutions to this model were already discussed in the preceding section.) The reduced form we are considering is equation (9.8).

We can give a complete classification of the solutions, grouped into categories:

(1) The ARMA(3,2) class

$$y_t = -\alpha\beta_2^{-1} - \beta_1\beta_2^{-1}y_{t-1} + (1-\beta_0)\beta_2^{-1}y_{t-2} - \delta\beta_2^{-1}y_{t-3}$$
$$+ v_t + c_1 v_{t-1} + c_2 v_{t-2} + d_1\varepsilon_{t-1} + d_2\varepsilon_{t-2},$$

where c_1, c_2, d_1, and d_2 are arbitrary. Assuming real roots ρ_1, ρ_2, and ρ_3 of the complementary polynomial, this can be written

$$(1-\rho_1 L)(1-\rho_2 L)(1-\rho_3 L)y_t$$
$$= -\alpha\beta_2^{-1} + (1-\mu_1 L)(1-\mu_2 L)v_t + L(d_1 + d_2 L)\varepsilon_t,$$

where μ_1, μ_2, d_1, and d_2 are arbitrary.

(2) ARMA(2,1) classes. These are obtained by choosing the arbitrary coefficients to allow cancellation of a common factor, e.g., $(1-\rho_3 L)$, yielding

$$(1-\rho_1 L)(1-\rho_2 L)y_t = -\alpha\beta_2^{-1}(1-\rho_3)^{-1} + (1-\mu_1 L)v_t + d_1 L\varepsilon_t.$$

If all three roots are real, there are three ARMA(2,1) classes of REE. If only one root is real, then there is only one such class.

(3) AR(1) solutions. For appropriate choices of the remaining free parameters, we can cancel another common factor, yielding, e.g.,

$$(1-\rho_1 L)y_t = -\alpha\beta_2^{-1}(1-\rho_2)^{-1}(1-\rho_3)^{-1} + v_t.$$

Again, there are either three or one such solutions. These are the MSV solutions.

The E-stability results for the AR(1) solutions were discussed above and given fully in Evans and Honkapohja (1994b). For the ARMA classes of solution, Evans and Honkapohja (1994b) show the following result.

Proposition 9.6. *For an open set of parameter values, the ARMA(2,1) and ARMA(3,2) solution classes to model (9.8) can be weakly E-stable. However, they can never be strongly E-stable.*

Again, lack of strong E-stability for the ARMA solution classes is a consequence of the fact that this solution is a nonhyperbolic equilibrium for the ODE defining strong E-stability. Finally, we remark that weakly E-stable ARMA solutions can arise in the Dornbusch-type model with policy feedback.

9.6 Learning Explosive Solutions

So far throughout the book, when considering convergence of adaptive learning to a rational expectations equilibrium, we have made the assumption that the REE was asymptotically stationary. However, as we have seen in the last chapter and this one, there will often also exist (at least as formal solutions) nonstationary processes such as explosive AR(1) processes. We show in this section that it is also possible to analyze the stability under adaptive learning of such explosive solutions.

For concreteness we consider the "extended special case" as discussed in Chapter 8 and earlier in this chapter:

$$y_t = \alpha + \delta y_{t-1} + \beta_0 E^*_{t-1} y_t + \beta_1 E^*_{t-1} y_{t+1} + v_t,$$

and consider the MSV solutions

$$y_t = a + \rho y_{t-1} + v_t,$$

where ρ satisfies $\beta_1 \rho^2 + (\beta_0 - 1)\rho + \delta = 0$.

We are interested in the stability of least squares learning in the case $|\rho| > 1$. There are two complications which now arise when we assume that agents run regressions of y_t on an intercept and on y_{t-1}. First, as t becomes large the intercept will become negligible relative to ρy_{t-1} along an explosive AR(1) path. The simplest way to deal with this point is to assume that agents do not include an intercept in their regression. Second, the error term v_t will also become negligible relative to ρy_{t-1} if its variance is finite and constant over time. This leads to difficulties which can be overcome if we make the assumption that var(v_t) increases over time at an appropriate rate. In particular, we assume that var(v_t) = $\lambda^t \sigma^2$, where $\lambda > \rho^2 > 1$.

The procedure is to transform variables to make them asymptotically stationary. Defining

$$y^*_t = y_t \lambda^{-t/2}, \qquad v^*_t = v_t \lambda^{-t/2}, \qquad \rho^* = \rho \lambda^{-1/2},$$

it is easily verified that along an explosive AR(1) REE path, the process tends to the path

$$y^*_t = \rho^* y^*_{t-1} + v^*_t.$$

We consider recursive least squares based on these transformed variables, i.e., agents estimate ρ^* from a simple regression of y_t^* on y_{t-1}^*. The equations are

$$b_t^* = b_{t-1}^* + t^{-1} R_t^{-1} y_{t-1}^* \left(y_t^* - b_{t-1}^* y_{t-1}^* \right),$$
$$R_t = R_{t-1} + t^{-1} \left(y_{t-1}^{*2} - R_{t-1} \right).$$

These equations can be rewritten in terms of untransformed variables and interpreted as recursive weighted least squares. For details concerning the arguments of this section, see Evans and Honkapohja (1994a).[4]

Agents make time-$(t - 1)$ forecasts based on $y_t^* = b_{t-1}^* y_{t-1}^* + v_t^*$, i.e., $E_{t-1}^* y_t^* = b_{t-1}^* y_{t-1}^*$ and $E_{t-1}^* y_{t+1}^* = b_{t-1}^{*2} y_{t-1}^*$. Equivalently, $E_{t-1}^* y_t = b_{t-1} y_{t-1}$, where $b_{t-1} = \lambda^{1/2} b_{t-1}^*$. Transforming variables in the structural model and inserting these forecasts, we obtain the actual law of motion

$$y_t^* = \alpha \lambda^{-t/2} + \left(\delta \lambda^{-1/2} + \beta_0 b_{t-1}^* + \beta_1 \lambda^{1/2} b_{t-1}^{*2} \right) y_{t-1}^* + v_t^*.$$

Together with the equations for b_t^* and R_t, this now constitutes a stochastic recursive algorithm which can be analyzed in the usual way. It can be shown that, provided the E-stability condition $\beta_0 + 2\beta_1 \rho < 1$ is met, we have locally $b_t^* \to \rho^*$ and hence $b_t \to \rho$. The standard instability result also applies if the E-stability condition fails.

An analogous argument applies to explosive AR(1) solutions to the model $y_t = \alpha + \delta y_{t-1} + \beta_1 E_t^* y_{t+1} + v_t$.

9.7 Bubbles in Asset Prices

The present-value model of asset pricing, according to which the price of a share is equal to the sum of the conditional expectations of the price and dividend next period, leads to the univariate RE model

$$y_t = \alpha E_t^* y_{t+1} + w_t,$$

where y_t is the price of the asset and w_t is the dividend, here assumed to be paid at the beginning of the period. We will assume that w_t is an exogenous stationary (or integrated stationary) AR process. In the risk-neutral asset pricing model, $\alpha = (1+r)^{-1}$, where $r > 0$ is the interest rate which we assume is constant. The

---

[4]For further results on learning of nonstationary solutions, see Zenner (1996).

fundamental or forward solution is given by $\bar{y}_t = \delta \sum_{j=0}^{\infty} \alpha^j E_t w_{t+j}$. If w_t is a stationary AR process, $\bar{y}_t$ coincides with the MSV solution. All other solutions are called bubbles. These are nonstationary if $|\alpha| < 1$.[5] (At the end of the section we briefly comment on the case $|\alpha| > 1$.)

To analyze E-stability, consider for simplicity the special case $w_t = k + u_t$, where u_t is white noise. The fundamentals solution in this case is

$$\bar{y}_t = (1 - \alpha)^{-1} k + u_t. \tag{9.10}$$

The bubble solutions take the form

$$y_t = -\alpha^{-1} k + \alpha^{-1} y_{t-1} - \alpha^{-1} u_{t-1} + \zeta u_t + \epsilon_t, \tag{9.11}$$

where ζ is arbitrary and ϵ_t is an arbitrary (sunspot) process satisfying $E_{t-1} \epsilon_t = 0$.

The next step is to formulate a perceived law of motion which is general enough to include the MSV and the bubbles as special cases. Consider the PLMs of the form

$$y_t = a + b y_{t-1} + c_0 u_t + c_1 u_{t-1} + d \epsilon_t.$$

The corresponding one-step-ahead forecast is $E_t^* y_{t+1} = a + b y_t + c_1 u_t$, or

$$E_t^* y_{t+1} = a(1 + b) + b^2 y_{t-1} + (c_1 + bc_0) u_t + bc_1 u_{t-1} + bd \epsilon_t.$$

Substituting into the structural equation, solving for y_t, and using $w_t = k + u_t$ gives the corresponding actual law of motion[6]

$$y_t = k + \alpha a (1 + b) + \alpha b^2 y_{t-1} + (1 + \alpha(c_1 + bc_0)) u_t + \alpha bc_1 u_{t-1} + \alpha bd \epsilon_t.$$

Thus the T-mapping from PLM to ALM in this example is

$$T(a, b, c_0, c_1, d) = \left(k + \alpha a(1 + b), \alpha b^2, (1 + \alpha(c_1 + bc_0)), \alpha bc_1, \alpha bd \right).$$

Note that the fixed points of the T-mapping are

$$\bar{a} = k(1 - \alpha)^{-1}, \ \bar{b} = \bar{c}_1 = \bar{d} = 0, \ \bar{c}_0 = 1 \quad \text{and}$$
$$\bar{a} = -\alpha^{-1} k, \ \bar{b} = \alpha^{-1}, \ \bar{c}_1 = -\alpha^{-1}, \quad \text{and } \bar{c}_0, \bar{d} \text{ arbitrary}.$$

---

[5] See Salge (1997) for a general discussion of asset bubbles.

[6] In this section we are making the assumption that the time-t information set includes u_t (and y_{t-1}) but not y_t. See the earlier discussion in Section 8.6.2 of Chapter 8.

The first fixed point corresponds to the fundamental solution and the second corresponds to the bubble solutions.

E-stability is, of course, governed by $d\theta/d\tau = T(\theta) - \theta$, where $\theta = (a, b, c_0, c_1, d)$. To determine E-stability of the two types of solutions, we look at the differential equation governing b, which is autonomous:

$$\frac{db}{d\tau} = \alpha b^2 - b.$$

Writing $T_b(b) = \alpha b^2$ we see that $T_b'(\bar{b}) = 2\alpha\bar{b}$ so that $T_b'(0) = 0$ and $T_b'(\alpha^{-1}) = 2$. It follows that the bubble solutions are never E-stable, while the fundamentals value $\bar{b} = 0$ satisfies this E-stability condition. (The ODE dynamics of b closely resembles that shown for b_1 in Figure 8.4 of Chapter 8.) Looking at the remaining equations of the ODE, we see that the fundamentals solution is E-stable provided $\alpha < 1$.

The local stability and instability results of Chapter 6 can be applied in the usual way to show that the fundamentals solution is locally stable under least squares learning. Using also the techniques of the previous section on the local stability under learning of explosive solutions, it can be shown that the bubble solutions are not locally stable under least squares learning.[7] We close with two cautionary remarks on our result that explosive bubbles appear not to be stable under adaptive learning. First, for some initial values of parameter estimates, the paths under learning will not converge to the fundamentals solution but instead follow a nonrational divergent trajectory. Second, more elaborate asset price models may generate explosive bubbles which are stable under learning. Earlier results in this chapter strongly suggest this possibility.

Other economic models of the same form can have $|\alpha| > 1$. We briefly discuss this case. The existence of the forward solution $\bar{y}_t = \delta \sum_{j=0}^{\infty} \alpha^j E_t w_{t+j}$ hinges on the properties of w_t process. For example, if $w_t = k + \rho w_{t-1} + u_t$, this exists iff $|\alpha\rho| < 1$. However, for this w_t the MSV solution exists even if this condition fails. Returning to the special case $w_t = k + u_t$, the fundamentals and bubble solutions still take the form (9.10) and (9.11), respectively. The analysis of learning is unchanged, so that the fundamentals solution is E-stable if $\alpha < -1$, while the bubble solutions are E-unstable.

---

[7] As previously discussed, we cannot give formal convergence results when the agents allow for a continuum of solutions. However, the results will apply, for example, if the agents impose $c_0 = 0$ and $d = 1$.

9.8 Heterogeneous Learning Rules

The analysis has so far mostly been based on the assumption that the economic agents in the model have identical learning rules, though we briefly considered the possibility of heterogeneous expectations in Section 3.2 of Chapter 3. We now allow for heterogeneity and random adjustments in expectations in a model with a continuum [0, 1] of agents. The formulation of heterogeneity in the learning rules is based on the ideas in Evans, Honkapohja, and Marimon (2000), who consider the effects of heterogeneity in a more complex model.

Consider the linear model

$$y_t = \alpha + \beta y_{t+1}^e + \varepsilon_t,$$

where $y_{t+1}^e = \int_0^1 y_{t+1}^{ke} \, dk$, with y_{t+1}^{ke} denoting the expectations of agent $k \in [0, 1]$, and ε_t is an iid random shock. Thus the aggregate endogenous variable depends on the average expectations in the economy. We focus on the steady-state REE $y_t = y^* + \varepsilon_t$ of the model which satisfies $y^* = \alpha(1 - \beta)^{-1}$.

We assume for each agent k the learning rule

$$y_{t+1}^{ke} = \begin{cases} y_t^{ke} & \text{with probability } \rho_{t+1}, \\ y_t^{ke} + \gamma_{k,t+1}(y_{t-1} - y_t^{ke}) & \text{with probability } 1 - \rho_{t+1}. \end{cases}$$

The probability $0 \leq \rho_{t+1} < 1$ captures the degree of inertia. The random gains $\gamma_{k,t+1}$ are taken to be positive and independent of past information and, for each t, $\gamma_{k,t+1}$ are identically and independently distributed across k. Moreover, $\gamma_{t+1} \equiv E\gamma_{k,t+1}$ is assumed to converge to zero as $t \to \infty$.

We assume that $\gamma_t(1 - \rho_t)$ is a positive decreasing sequence satisfying

(i) $\sum_{t=1}^{\infty} \gamma_t(1 - \rho_t) = +\infty$,
(ii) for some $p > 0$, $\sum_{t=1}^{\infty} (\gamma_t(1 - \rho_t))^p < +\infty$,
(iii) $\lim_{t \to \infty} \sup[1/\gamma_t(1 - \rho_t) - 1/\gamma_{t-1}(1 - \rho_{t-1})] < \infty$,
    and that
(iv) for all k, $\gamma_{kt} \leq \bar{\gamma}_t$, where $\bar{\gamma}_t \to 0$ as $t \to \infty$.

A simple special case that satisfies the above assumptions is averaging with inertia: $\gamma_{kt} = t^{-1}$ and $\rho_{t+1} = \rho$ for some constant $0 \leq \rho < 1$.

This class of learning rules is, of course, still restrictive though it generalizes the standard learning rules in a way which admits considerable heterogeneity in learning. Note also that even if *initially* agents have homogeneous expectations, heterogeneous adjustments to forecast errors and/or heterogeneous inertia across agents ensure that heterogeneity of expectations will emerge over time.

We can rewrite the learning rule

$$y_{t+1}^{ke} = y_t^{ke} + \xi_{t+1}^k \gamma_{k,t+1}(y_{t-1} - y_t^{ke}), \tag{9.12}$$

where for each agent k the variable ξ_{t+1}^k is a Bernoulli random variable, independent of past information, and independent across k, which takes the value 0 with probability ρ_{t+1} and 1 with probability $1 - \rho_{t+1}$. In addition, for all j, k, ξ_{t+1}^j are assumed independent of current π_t^{ke} and $\gamma_{k,t+1}$.

Integrating equation (9.12) over k, we get

$$y_{t+1}^e = y_t^e + \int \xi_{t+1}^k \gamma_{k,t+1}(y_{t-1} - y_t^{ke}) \mu(dk).$$

We have

$$\int \xi_{t+1}^k \gamma_{k,t+1} y_t^{ke} \mu(dk)$$

$$= \left(\int \xi_{t+1}^k \mu(dk) \right) \left(\int \gamma_{k,t+1} y_t^{ke} \mu(dk) \right)$$

$$+ \mathrm{Cov}_{\mu(dk)}(\xi_{t+1}^k, \gamma_{k,t+1} y_t^{ke}).$$

Using the law of large numbers for continua of random variables,[8] we have

$$\int \xi_{t+1}^k \mu(dk) = 1 - \rho_{t+1},$$

and from the independence assumption,

$$\mathrm{Cov}_{\mu(dk)}(\xi_{t+1}^k, \gamma_{k,t+1} y_t^{ke}) = 0.$$

Moreover, we get

$$\int \gamma_{k,t+1} y_t^{ke} \mu(dk) = \left(\int \gamma_{k,t+1} \mu(dk) \right) \left(\int y_t^{ke} \mu(dk) \right) = \gamma_{t+1} y_t^e.$$

Analogously, using independence and the law of large numbers, we have

$$\int \xi_{t+1}^k \gamma_{k,t+1} y_{t-1} \mu(dk) = (1 - \rho_{t+1}) \gamma_{t+1} y_{t-1}.$$

[8] See Judd (1985).

These arguments yield that average expectations follow

$$y_{t+1}^e = y_t^e + \gamma_{t+1}(1 - \rho_{t+1})(y_{t-1} - y_t^e). \tag{9.13}$$

With the above assumptions and after substituting in for y_{t-1}, we have a standard setup, so that even with heterogeneous learning rules the average expectations converge to the REE, provided it is E-stable ($\beta < 1$). Coupling the two dynamics (9.12) and (9.13), it is also possible to show that individual expectations y_{t+1}^{ke} also converge to the REE solution, so that heterogeneity disappears asymptotically in this model. We omit the detailed argument, see Evans, Honkapohja, and Marimon (2000) for the formal steps in a somewhat more difficult setup.

This analysis illustrates how it is possible to introduce considerable heterogeneity to the learning behavior of the agents. The aggregation of the individual learning rules was formally the key to the analysis and the result. This is one case where convergence results are obtainable for cases of heterogeneous expectations and learning rules. The stability conditions for the cases of homogeneous and heterogeneous learning rules need not always be identical, as shown by Evans, Honkapohja, and Marimon (2000). The other case that can be analyzed in a similar fashion is the case of n different expectations. This case was illustrated in Section 3.2 of Chapter 3.

Chapter **10**

Multivariate Linear Models

10.1 Introduction

The techniques described in the previous chapter can be generalized to multivariate models, allowing us to analyze most of the models frequently encountered in macroeconomics, including the standard Real Business Cycle model and irregular versions with sunspot solutions, as well as more traditional IS-LM-Phillips curve models. We will present the general formal techniques after first giving an example.

As an introductory example we consider a fairly standard aggregate demand/aggregate supply model with rational expectations and gradual price adjustment.

Example 1: **An IS–LM–Phillips curve model.**

$$p_t - p_{t-1} = a_0 + a_1 q_t + \left(E_{t-1}^* p_{t+1} - E_{t-1}^* p_t \right) + v_{1t},$$
$$q_t = b_0 - b_1 \left(r_t - E_{t-1}^* p_{t+1} + E_{t-1}^* p_t \right) + v_{2t},$$
$$m_t - p_t = c_0 + c_1 q_t - c_2 r_t + v_{3t},$$
$$m_t = d_0 + d_1 p_{t-1} + d_2 q_{t-1} + d_3 r_{t-1} + d_4 m_{t-1} + v_{4t}.$$

The first equation is a Phillips curve in which inflation, $p_t - p_{t-1}$, depends on expected inflation, $E_{t-1}^* p_{t+1} - E_{t-1}^* p_t$, and on aggregate real output, q_t. Under rational expectations, subjective expectations are equal to the true conditional expectation, i.e., $E_{t-1}^* p_{t+1} = E_{t-1} p_{t+1}$ and $E_{t-1}^* p_t = E_{t-1} p_t$. This forward-looking version of the Phillips curve is similar to those found in the new Phillips curve models discussed, for example, in Clarida, Gali, and Gertler (1999). The $t - 1$ dating for expectation formation is often used in the Phillips curve literature. (We discuss below models with expectations dated $E_t^* p_{t+1}$.) The second equation is the IS curve. r_t is the nominal interest rate, and this equation states that q_t depends negatively on the ex ante real interest rate $r_t - E_{t-1}^* p_{t+1} + E_{t-1}^* p_t$. The third equation is the LM curve, equating the supply and demand for money balances $m_t - p_t$. The last equation is a given monetary policy feedback rule, relating the nominal supply of money to lagged prices p_{t-1} and lagged values of the other variables. All variables except r_t are in logarithmic form.

Each equation is also subject to an unobservable iid random shock, v_{it}. We assume $a_1, b_1, c_1, c_2 > 0$.

The previous chapter considered the "ad hoc model" of Sargent and Wallace (1975), which is formally simpler. The Phillips curve equation here introduces a lagged price level into the structure, and the monetary feedback rule also contains a dependence on lagged variables. Although it is possible to solve out for a reduced form in the price level p_t, the resulting equation would incorporate different dates at which expectations are formed as well as moving average disturbances. It is simpler to look at a general multivariate technique which avoids these complications. Also, the standard practice in macroeconomics is to examine solutions represented as a vector autoregression (VAR). Our techniques will allow us to calculate the REE solution, expressed as a VAR, and to examine its stability under adaptive learning.

The first step is to put the model into the form of a multivariate linear expectational difference equation:

$$
\begin{pmatrix} 1 & -a_1 & 0 & 0 \\ 0 & 1 & b_1 & 0 \\ -1 & -c_1 & c_2 & 1 \\ 0 & 0 & 0 & 1 \end{pmatrix} \begin{pmatrix} p_t \\ q_t \\ r_t \\ m_t \end{pmatrix}
$$

$$
= \begin{pmatrix} a_0 \\ b_0 \\ c_0 \\ d_0 \end{pmatrix} + \begin{pmatrix} 1 & 0 & 0 & 0 \\ b_1 & 0 & 0 & 0 \\ 0 & 0 & 0 & 0 \\ 0 & 0 & 0 & 0 \end{pmatrix} \begin{pmatrix} E_{t-1}^* p_{t+1} \\ E_{t-1}^* q_{t+1} \\ E_{t-1}^* r_{t+1} \\ E_{t-1}^* m_{t+1} \end{pmatrix}
$$

$$
+ \begin{pmatrix} -1 & 0 & 0 & 0 \\ -b_1 & 0 & 0 & 0 \\ 0 & 0 & 0 & 0 \\ 0 & 0 & 0 & 0 \end{pmatrix} \begin{pmatrix} E_{t-1}^* p_t \\ E_{t-1}^* q_t \\ E_{t-1}^* r_t \\ E_{t-1}^* m_t \end{pmatrix}
$$

$$
+ \begin{pmatrix} 1 & 0 & 0 & 0 \\ 0 & 0 & 0 & 0 \\ 0 & 0 & 0 & 0 \\ d_1 & d_2 & d_3 & d_4 \end{pmatrix} \begin{pmatrix} p_{t-1} \\ q_{t-1} \\ r_{t-1} \\ m_{t-1} \end{pmatrix} + \begin{pmatrix} v_{1t} \\ v_{2t} \\ v_{3t} \\ v_{4t} \end{pmatrix}.
$$

(10.1)

Multiplying by the inverse of the matrix on the left-hand side, this example can be put into the following general form which we will analyze in this chapter:

$$y_t = \alpha + \beta_0 E_{t-1}^* y_t + \beta_1 E_{t-1}^* y_{t+1} + \delta y_{t-1} + \kappa w_t + \zeta v_t, \qquad (10.2)$$
$$w_t = \varphi w_{t-1} + e_t.$$

Here y_t is an $n \times 1$ vector of endogenous variables and w_t is a vector of exogenous variables which we assume to follow a stationary VAR, so that e_t is white noise and all eigenvalues of φ lie inside the unit circle. Since at some points we will need φ to be invertible, we also allow for a direct dependence of y_t on a white noise disturbance v_t. In the example there is no exogenous variable w_t.

In the discussion of this chapter we will often need to make a distinction between "regular" and "irregular" linear expectations models.[1] A regular linear model is one in which there is a unique stationary REE, whereas in the irregular case there are multiple stationary solutions, in particular solutions that depend on sunspots. There is a straightforward algebraic condition for determining whether models of the form (10.2), or (10.15) below, are regular or irregular, based on the Blanchard–Kahn technique. We discuss this in detail in Appendix 2 of this chapter.

10.2 MSV Solutions and Learning

The general structural model (10.2) is very close to the framework used in the appendix of McCallum (1983) to analyze rational expectations equilibria. The main difference is the dating of expectations. We have chosen here to assume that expectations are conditional on information at time $t - 1$. This avoids a simultaneity between expectations and current values of the endogenous variables which may seem more natural in the context of the analysis of learning. However, we do treat the case in which expectations are based on information at time t in Section 10.3 below.[2]

We follow McCallum and focus on the so-called MSV (minimal state variable) solutions which are of the following form:

$$y_t = a + b y_{t-1} + c w_{t-1} + \kappa e_t + \zeta v_t, \qquad (10.3)$$

---

[1] This terminology follows Farmer (1999) and Pesaran (1987).
[2] Evans and Honkapohja (1998b) also treats the case of time-t information sets.

where a, b, and c are to be determined by the method of undetermined coefficients. One computes

$$E_{t-1}y_t = a + by_{t-1} + cw_{t-1}$$

and

$$\begin{aligned}E_{t-1}y_{t+1} &= a + bE_{t-1}y_t + cE_{t-1}w_t\\ &= (I+b)a + b^2 y_{t-1} + (bc + c\varphi)w_{t-1}.\end{aligned}$$

Inserting these into equation (10.2), one obtains

$$\begin{aligned}y_t &= \alpha + (\beta_0 + \beta_1 + \beta_1 b)a + (\beta_1 b^2 + \beta_0 b + \delta)y_{t-1}\\ &\quad + (\beta_0 c + \beta_1 bc + \beta_1 c\varphi + \kappa\varphi)w_{t-1} + \kappa e_t + \zeta v_t.\end{aligned} \qquad (10.4)$$

It follows that the REE must satisfy the matrix equations

$$(I - \beta_0 - \beta_1 b - \beta_1)a = \alpha, \qquad (10.5)$$
$$\beta_1 b^2 + (\beta_0 - I)b + \delta = 0, \qquad (10.6)$$
$$(I - \beta_0 - \beta_1 b)c - \beta_1 c\varphi = \kappa\varphi. \qquad (10.7)$$

Once b is known, equations (10.5) and (10.7) generically uniquely determine a and c. However, equation (10.6) is a matrix quadratic which will usually have multiple solutions. To our knowledge, there is no straightforward and general method for obtaining the full set of solutions to this equation. Under the assumption that β_1 is invertible, one can adapt the technique of McCallum (1983) to find the solutions. In general, there are up to $2n$ choose n, i.e., $\binom{2n}{n}$, solutions to equation (10.6)[3] and hence up to $\binom{2n}{n}$ distinct MSV solutions to equation (10.2). McCallum (1983) introduced a subsidiary selection criterion to choose among these. We instead examine their stability under learning. If β_1 is not invertible, as in the case of our example 1, there are other procedures for solving equation (10.6). McCallum has extended his technique in McCallum (1998) and McCallum (1999). A related approach together with a toolkit for solving such models using MATLAB programs is provided in Uhlig (1999).[4]

---

[3]In special cases there can be even continua of solutions to the matrix quadratic. Try, e.g., the square roots of the identity matrix.

[4]However, these general techniques usually assume expectations dated as $E_t y_{t+1}$ and so would need to be modified to handle models of the form (10.2).

There are various methods available to obtain solutions of the form (10.3). One well-known method, based on the Blanchard–Kahn technique, we discuss at length in Appendix 2. Another is to use the E-stability equations, which govern the stability of adaptive learning, as an algorithm to obtain the solution.

10.2.1 E-Stability

We consider the stability of the MSV solutions under learning. To derive the conditions for local stability of REE under adaptive learning, one can again use the concept of E-stability.

We now regard equation (10.3) as a perceived law of motion (PLM) for the agents. Computing expectations as before, we obtain the corresponding actual law of motion (ALM) (10.4). Thus the mapping from the PLM to the ALM takes the form

$$T(a, b, c) = \big(\alpha + (\beta_0 + \beta_1 + \beta_1 b)a, \; \beta_1 b^2 + \beta_0 b + \delta,$$
$$\beta_0 c + \beta_1 bc + \beta_1 c\varphi + \kappa\varphi\big). \tag{10.8}$$

Expectational stability is determined by the matrix differential equation

$$\frac{d}{d\tau}(a, b, c) = T(a, b, c) - (a, b, c). \tag{10.9}$$

To analyze the local stability of system (10.9) at an RE solution $\bar{a}, \bar{b}, \bar{c}$, one linearizes the system at that RE solution. Since the equation for b is independent from a and c, we begin with the stability of the differential equation

$$\frac{db}{dt} = \beta_1 b^2 + \beta_0 b + \delta - b$$
$$\equiv T_b(b) - b.$$

To compute the stability conditions, this equation has to be vectorized. For any matrix X, let $\text{vec}\, X$ denote the vector obtained by stacking the columns of X. Using the rule $d(AX^2) = A[(dX)X + X\,dX]$ for matrix differentials [see Magnus and Neudecker (1988, Chapter 9) and the appendix on matrix algebra in Chapter 5 for this and other related matrix formulas used here], we get

$$dT_b = \beta_1(db)b + \beta_1 b(db)I + \beta_0(db)I.$$

The Jacobian of $\text{vec}\, T_b$ is $DT_b = \partial \text{vec}\, T_b/\partial(\text{vec}\, b)'$. Using the rules $d\,\text{vec}\, b = \text{vec}\, db$ and $\text{vec}\, ABC = (C' \otimes A)\,\text{vec}\, B$, we obtain

$$DT_b(b) = b' \otimes \beta_1 + I \otimes (\beta_0 + \beta_1 b).$$

Thus the differential equation for b is locally stable at $\bar{b}$ when all the eigenvalues of $DT_b(\bar{b})$ have real parts less than 1.

Next consider the equation for c in (10.9). Computing the differential of $T_c(b, c) = (\beta_0 + \beta_1 b)c + \beta_1 c\varphi + \kappa\varphi$ and the corresponding Jacobian $DT_c = \partial \operatorname{vec} T_c / \partial (\operatorname{vec} c)'$, we have

$$DT_c(b, c) = \varphi' \otimes \beta_1 + I \otimes (\beta_0 + \beta_1 b).$$

Provided that the motion for b converges to $\bar{b}$, the equation for c is locally stable at $(\bar{b}, \bar{c})$ when the eigenvalues of the matrix $DT_c(\bar{b}, \bar{c})$ have real parts less than 1. Finally, consider the differential equation for a. Provided again that the motion for b converges to $\bar{b}$, the equation for a is locally stable when the eigenvalues of the matrix $\beta_0 + \beta_1 + \beta_1\bar{b}$ have real parts less than 1.

The results of these derivations are summarized in the following proposition.

Proposition 10.1. *An MSV solution $\bar{a}, \bar{b}, \bar{c}$ to equation (10.2) is E-stable if*

  (i) *all the eigenvalues of $DT_b(\bar{b})$ have real parts less than 1,*
 (ii) *all the eigenvalues of $DT_c(\bar{b}, \bar{c})$ have real parts less than 1, and*
(iii) *all the eigenvalues of the matrix $\beta_0 + \beta_1 + \beta_1\bar{b}$ have real parts less than 1.*

Assuming none of the eigenvalues has real part equal to 1, the solution is not E-stable if any of conditions (i), (ii), or (iii) do not hold.

In the next subsection we show that these E-stability conditions govern stability under adaptive learning. Furthermore, implementing the differential equation (10.9) numerically provides a method for computing E-stable MSV solutions. The procedure is simply to iterate the equation

$$(a_{n+1}, b_{n+1}, c_{n+1}) = (a_n, b_n, c_n) + \gamma\big(T(a_n, b_n, c_n) - (a_n, b_n, c_n)\big), \quad (10.10)$$

for $n = 1, 2, 3, \ldots$, where $\gamma > 0$ is a damping factor. For γ sufficiently small, the dynamics (10.10) will converge to an E-stable solution from nearby starting points. We will in fact use this solution method below to obtain the stable solution to Example 1.

10.2.2 Adaptive Learning

In real-time learning, the perceived law of motion is time dependent:

$$y_t = a_{t-1} + b_{t-1}y_{t-1} + c_{t-1}w_{t-1} + \kappa e_t + \zeta v_t,$$

where the parameters a_t, b_t, and c_t are updated running recursive least squares (RLS). Letting

$$\xi' = (a, b, c) \quad \text{and} \quad z'_t = (1, y'_t, w'_t),$$

RLS can be written as

$$\xi_t = \xi_{t-1} + t^{-1} R_t^{-1} z_{t-1} \epsilon'_t, \tag{10.11}$$
$$R_t = R_{t-1} + t^{-1}(z_{t-1} z'_{t-1} - R_{t-1}), \tag{10.12}$$

where

$$\epsilon_t = y_t - \xi'_{t-1} z_{t-1}.$$

Agents use $\xi'_{t-1} = (a_{t-1}, b_{t-1}, c_{t-1})$ and z_{t-1} to form their forecasts $E^*_{t-1} y_t$ and $E^*_{t-1} y_{t+1}$. The realized value for y_t under least squares learning is therefore

$$y_t = T(\xi_{t-1})' z_{t-1} + \kappa e_t + \zeta v_t,$$

where $T(\xi)' = T(a, b, c)$, given in the preceding subsection. Below we use the notation $T_a(\xi)$, $T_b(\xi)$, and $T_c(\xi)$ to denote the a, b, and c components of the T-map given in equation (10.8).

In order to convert the system into the standard form of Chapter 6 it is necessary to make a timing change in the system governing R_t. Thus set $S_{t-1} = R_t$, so that

$$S_t = S_{t-1} + t^{-1}(z_t z'_t - S_{t-1}) + t^{-2}\left(-\frac{t}{t+1}\right)(z_t z'_t - S_{t-1}). \tag{10.13}$$

The last term is then of the usual form with $\rho_t(S_{t-1}, z_t) = -[t/(t+1)](z_t z'_t - S_{t-1})$. Substituting in for ϵ_t and y_t, one obtains for ξ_t

$$\xi_t = \xi_{t-1} + t^{-1} S_{t-1}^{-1} z_{t-1} z'_{t-1}[T(\xi_{t-1}) - \xi_{t-1}]$$
$$+ t^{-1} S_{t-1}^{-1} z_{t-1}(\kappa e_t + \zeta v_t)'. \tag{10.14}$$

The model (10.13), (10.14) is in standard form with $\theta_t = \text{vec}(\xi_t, S_t)$, $X'_t = (1, y'_t, w'_t, y'_{t-1}, w'_{t-1}, e'_t, v'_t)$, and $W'_t = (1, e'_t, v'_t)$. The equation for the state vector X_t takes the form $X_t = A(\xi_{t-1})X_{t-1} + BW_t$, with

$$A(\xi_{t-1}) = \begin{pmatrix} 0 & 0 & 0 & 0\ 0\ 0\ 0 \\ T_a(\xi_{t-1}) & T_b(\xi_{t-1}) & T_c(\xi_{t-1}) & 0\ 0\ 0\ 0 \\ 0 & 0 & \varphi & 0\ 0\ 0\ 0 \\ 0 & I & 0 & 0\ 0\ 0\ 0 \\ 0 & 0 & I & 0\ 0\ 0\ 0 \\ 0 & 0 & 0 & 0\ 0\ 0\ 0 \\ 0 & 0 & 0 & 0\ 0\ 0\ 0 \end{pmatrix},$$

$$B = \begin{pmatrix} 1\ 0\ 0 \\ 0\ \kappa\ \zeta \\ 0\ I\ 0 \\ 0\ 0\ 0 \\ 0\ 0\ 0 \\ 0\ I\ 0 \\ 0\ 0\ I \end{pmatrix}.$$

Consider now an REE corresponding to a fixed point $\bar{\xi}$ of $T(\xi)$. We assume that the eigenvalues of $\bar{b}$ are strictly inside the unit circle, so that the REE is asymptotically stationary. Define $z_t(\xi)' = (1, y_t'(\xi), w_t')$, where $y_t(\xi) = T(\xi)'z_{t-1}(\xi) + \kappa e_t + \zeta v_t$. Then $z_t(\xi)$ is a stationary process for all ξ sufficiently near $\bar{\xi}$. Let $M_z(\xi) = E[z_t(\xi)z_t(\xi)']$ and assume that $\bar{S} = E[z_t(\bar{\xi})z_t(\bar{\xi})']$ is positive definite. Next, choose an open set $\hat{D}$ around $(\bar{\xi}, \bar{S})$ such that, for all $(\xi, S) \in \hat{D}$,

(i) $\bar{\xi}$ is the unique fixed point of T in $\hat{D}$,
(ii) for some $\varepsilon > 0$, $\det(S) \geq \varepsilon$,
(iii) the roots of b are bounded strictly inside the unit circle.

It can now be verified that conditions (A.1)–(A.3) of Chapter 6 hold. Moreover, condition (B.1) holds if the moments of W_t are bounded. Condition (B.2) is satisfied, provided that $\hat{D}$ is sufficiently small.

   The associated ODE can be obtained as follows. Taking expectations and limits based on equations (10.13) and (10.14), one obtains the ODE as

$$\frac{d\xi}{d\tau} = S^{-1}M_z(\xi)[T(\xi) - \xi],$$

$$\frac{dS}{d\tau} = M_z(\xi) - S.$$

Linearizing this system at $(\bar{\xi}, \bar{S})$, it follows that the system is locally stable, provided the eigenvalues of $DT(\bar{\xi})$ have real parts less than 1. Heuristically, this is evident since, when $S \to M_z(\xi)$, the stability of the first equation is essentially governed by the E-stability equation

$$\frac{d\xi}{d\tau} = T(\xi) - \xi,$$

which is equivalent to equation (10.9) since $\xi' = (a, b, c)$.

The local stability condition is the same as the E-stability condition derived in the preceding subsection. Since the basic convergence results of Chapter 6 apply, recursive least squares learning is locally convergent to the RE solution $\bar{\xi}$ when the solution $\bar{\xi}$ is E-stable. We have thus shown the following result.

Proposition 10.2. *Consider the model (10.2) under RLS learning and an MSV solution $\bar{a}, \bar{b}, \bar{c}$ in which all roots of $\bar{b}$ lie inside the unit circle. Then if the solution is E-stable, the learning algorithm converges locally to $\bar{a}, \bar{b}, \bar{c}$.*

Local convergence is here interpreted in the sense of Theorem 6.5 of Section 6.3.3 and its corollaries in Section 6.4 of Chapter 6. In particular, for the case of slow adaption, there is convergence from nearby points with probability close to 1 when the E-stability conditions hold. If the RLS algorithm is augmented with a projection facility, convergence is with probability 1.

Moreover, assuming additionally that e_t and v_t both have bounded supports, conditions (C.1)–(C.5) of Chapter 6 are verified. Thus, provided the additional conditions stated in Theorem 6.9 of Section 6.5, Chapter 6, are met, the recursive least squares algorithm will converge to an E-unstable MSV solution with probability zero.

10.2.3 IS-LM-Phillips Curve Model Continued

We now return to our introductory example. We look at a numerical example with parameter values specified below. Using the method of Blanchard and Kahn, it can be shown that there is a unique stationary solution and that it is of the MSV form. (This solution is sometimes called the "saddle point stable solution.") Details for this example are given in Appendix 2. Since there are no exogenous observables w_t in this example, the MSV solution takes the form

$$y_t = a + by_{t-1} + \zeta v_t, \quad \text{where}$$

$$y_t = \begin{pmatrix} p_t \\ q_t \\ r_t \\ m_t \end{pmatrix} \quad \text{and} \quad v_t = \begin{pmatrix} v_{1t} \\ v_{2t} \\ v_{3t} \\ v_{4t} \end{pmatrix}.$$

To illustrate the technique we select the parameter values $a_1 = 0.5$, $b_1 = 0.1$, $c_1 = 1$, $c_2 = 0.2$, $d_1 = -d_2 = d_3 = 0.1$, $d_4 = 0.2$. The stationary MSV solution can be computed using the Blanchard–Kahn technique given in Appendix 2. The E-stability conditions given in Proposition 10.1 can be verified numerically for this solution. Because the solution is E-stable, one can also obtain the solution by directly implementing the numerical procedure (10.10). For this example this turns out to be a quick and convenient way of obtaining the solution. The numerical results are

$$a = \begin{pmatrix} 3.4606 \\ -0.3124 \\ 15.7408 \\ 1.000 \end{pmatrix} \quad \text{and}$$

$$b = \begin{pmatrix} 0.7117 & -0.0104 & 0.0104 & 0.0209 \\ -0.2159 & -0.0296 & 0.0296 & 0.0591 \\ 1.978 & 0.300 & -0.300 & -0.6001 \\ 0.100 & -0.100 & 0.100 & 0.200 \end{pmatrix}.$$

Based on the arguments of Section 10.2.2, it follows that this solution is locally stable under least squares learning.

10.3   Models with Contemporaneous Expectations

Many macroeconomic models are formulated with a different dating of expectations than used in equation (10.2). Most frequently, expectations are assumed to be formed at time t, i.e., are assumed to include in the information set all variables in the model dated at time t. Then in the structural model (10.2) expectations $E_t y_{t+1}$ appear in place of $E_{t-1} y_t$ and $E_{t-1} y_{t+1}$. This means that the equilibrium values of the endogenous variables y_t and the expectations $E_t y_{t+1}$ are simultaneously determined. A well-known example, the standard RBC model, will be given in the next section.

In this section we redo our analysis using the alternative model

$$y_t = \alpha + \beta E_t^* y_{t+1} + \delta y_{t-1} + \kappa w_t, \tag{10.15}$$
$$w_t = \varphi w_{t-1} + e_t.$$

We remark that any white noise shocks are incorporated into components of w_t. Following the usual convention, we assume that w_t is observable at time t. In this section we also assume that y_t is in the time-t information set. We begin with the MSV solutions and their E-stability conditions. The Blanchard–Kahn technique for calculating solutions is given in the appendix.

Before proceeding, we remark that the E-stability results are sensitive to the precise assumptions made concerning the information set. For the univariate case this point was discussed in Section 8.6.2 of Chapter 8. In this section we make the assumption that in making their forecasts, agents have access to y_t and hence can form $E_t^* y_{t+1}$ as a linear function of $(1, y_t', w_t')'$. This results in a simultaneity between y_t and $E_t^* y_{t+1}$. In Section 10.5 we will instead assume that y_t is not available at t and that $E_t^* y_{t+1}$ is a linear function of $(1, y_{t-1}', w_t')'$, avoiding simultaneity between y_t and $E_t^* y_{t+1}$. Under rational expectations the information sets are equivalent, but this is not the case outside of the REE, i.e., during the learning process. As already observed in the univariate case, this can affect the conditions for stability under learning. Since the detailed information assumptions are part of the specification of the model, we obtain the stability conditions both ways, starting here with the case in which y_t is included in the information set.

The MSV solutions now have the form

$$y_t = a + b y_{t-1} + c w_t, \tag{10.16}$$

with corresponding expectations

$$E_t y_{t+1} = a + b y_t + c \varphi w_t.$$

Inserting into equation (10.15), it follows that the MSV solutions satisfy

$$(I - \beta b - \beta)a = \alpha, \tag{10.17}$$
$$\beta b^2 - b + \delta = 0, \tag{10.18}$$
$$(I - \beta b)c - \beta c \varphi = \kappa. \tag{10.19}$$

To determine E-stability we regard equation (10.16) as a PLM and obtain the mapping from the PLM to the ALM

$$T(a, b, c) = \left((I - \beta b)^{-1}(\alpha + \beta a), \ (I - \beta b)^{-1}\delta, \ (I - \beta b)^{-1}(\kappa + \beta c\varphi)\right).$$

As in Section 10.2.1, we obtain the E-stability conditions based on the linearization of the E-stability differential equation. For example, from $T_b(b) = (I - \beta b)^{-1}\delta$ we use the formula for the differential of the inverse of a matrix function [see Chapter 5 or Magnus and Neudecker (1988, p. 183)] to obtain $dT_b(\bar{b}) = (I - \beta\bar{b})^{-1}\beta(db)(I - \beta\bar{b})^{-1}\delta$. Using the rules for vectorization of matrix products, we compute

$$
\begin{aligned}
DT_a(\bar{a}, \bar{b}) &= (I - \beta\bar{b})^{-1}\beta, \\
DT_b(\bar{b}) &= \left[(I - \beta\bar{b})^{-1}\delta\right]' \otimes \left[(I - \beta\bar{b})^{-1}\beta\right], \\
DT_c(\bar{b}, \bar{c}) &= \varphi' \otimes \left[(I - \beta\bar{b})^{-1}\beta\right].
\end{aligned}
\tag{10.20}
$$

We arrive at the following result.

Proposition 10.3. *Suppose the time-t information set is $(1, y_t', w_t')'$. An MSV solution $\bar{a}, \bar{b}, \bar{c}$ to equation (10.15) is E-stable if all eigenvalues of the matrices $DT_a(\bar{a}, \bar{b}), DT_b(\bar{b}), DT_c(\bar{b}, \bar{c})$, given by equations (10.20), have real parts less than 1. The solution is not E-stable if any of the eigenvalues has real part larger than 1.*

Under least squares learning we have $E_t^* y_{t+1} = a_t + b_t y_t + c_t \varphi w_t$. The recursive least squares equations are given by equations (10.11)–(10.12), where $\xi_t' = (a_t, b_t, c_t)$, $z_t' = (1, y_{t-1}', w_t)$, and $\epsilon_t = y_{t-1} - \xi_{t-1}' z_{t-1}$. Since $y_t = T(\xi_t)' z_t$, we obtain

$$\xi_t = \xi_{t-1} + t^{-1} R_t^{-1} z_{t-1} z_{t-1}' \left(T(\xi_{t-1}) - \xi_{t-1}\right).$$

The analysis of least squares learning, and the link to E-stability, follow essentially the same lines as in Section 10.2.2; see Evans and Honkapohja (1998b) for further details. We thus have the following.

Proposition 10.4. *Consider the model (10.15) under RLS learning and an MSV solution $\bar{a}, \bar{b}, \bar{c}$ in which all roots of $\bar{b}$ lie inside the unit circle. Then if the solution is E-stable, the learning algorithm converges locally to $\bar{a}, \bar{b}, \bar{c}$.*

Again, instability results can also be obtained.

10.4 Real Business Cycle Model

In our next example we apply our methods to a standard Real Business Cycle (RBC) Model.[5] It is convenient to use the formulation presented in Farmer (1999, Chapter 5). This is an infinite-horizon stochastic growth model with a representative agent. The competitive equilibrium is equivalent to the solution to a social planning problem which is more straightforward to formulate. The social planner maximizes

$$\sum_{t=0}^{\infty} E\mathcal{B}^t \left(\log(C_t) - L_t \right)$$

subject to the constraints

$$
\begin{aligned}
C_t + K_{t+1} &\leq Q_t + (1-d)K_t, \\
Q_t &= S_t K_t^{\alpha} (\gamma^t L_t)^{1-\alpha}, \\
K_0 &= \bar{K}_0, \qquad S_0 = \bar{S}_0.
\end{aligned}
$$

Here S_t is a productivity shock that is assumed to follow the process

$$S_t = S_{t-1}^{\rho} V_t.$$

The parameter ρ captures the persistence of the shocks to technology and V_t is an iid innovation with mean 1.

The equilibrium to the economy can be described by the equations

$$
\begin{aligned}
K_{t+1} &= Q_t + (1-d)K_t - C_t, \\
Q_t &= S_t K_t^{\alpha} (\gamma^t L_t)^{1-\alpha}, \\
(1-\alpha)\frac{Q_t}{L_t} &= C_t, \\
\frac{1}{C_t} &= \mathcal{B} E_t \left[\frac{1}{C_{t+1}} \left(1 - d + \alpha \frac{Q_{t+1}}{K_{t+1}} \right) \right], \\
S_t &= S_{t-1}^{\rho} V_t.
\end{aligned}
$$

In Appendix 1 to this chapter we show how to linearize this model around a steady state. The main steps are the following. Using the definitions $\tilde{K}_t =$

---

[5]The RBC model is based on the stochastic formulation of neoclassical growth models by Brock and Mirman (1972). The seminal papers on neoclassical growth theory are Solow (1956) and Solow (1957).

K_t/γ^t, $\tilde{C}_t = C_t/\gamma^t$, etc., these equations are first transformed to equations in terms of asymptotically stationary variables $\tilde{K}_t, \tilde{C}_t, \tilde{Q}_t, L_t$. The resulting model has a unique steady state $\bar{K}, \bar{C}, \bar{Q}, \bar{L}$. Next, we log-linearize around the steady state. Defining the variables $k_t = \log(\tilde{K}_t/\bar{K})$, $c_t = \log(\tilde{C}_t/\bar{C})$, $q_t = \log(\tilde{Q}_t/\bar{Q})$, $\ell_t = \log(L_t/\bar{L})$, $\vartheta_t = \log V_t$, and eliminating ℓ_t and q_t, we obtain the linear equations

$$c_t = \left(1 + (1-\alpha)\mathfrak{B}\gamma^{-1}\left(\frac{\bar{Q}}{\bar{K}}\right)\right)E_t c_{t+1} - \mathfrak{B}\gamma^{-1}\left(\frac{\bar{Q}}{\bar{K}}\right)E_t s_{t+1},$$

$$k_{t+1} = -\gamma^{-1}\left(\left(\frac{\bar{C}}{\bar{K}}\right) + \left(\frac{\bar{Q}}{\bar{K}}\right)\left(\frac{1-\alpha}{\alpha}\right)\right)c_t \qquad (10.21)$$

$$+ \gamma^{-1}\left(1 - d + \left(\frac{\bar{Q}}{\bar{K}}\right)\right)k_t + \gamma^{-1}\left(\frac{\bar{Q}}{\bar{K}}\right)\alpha^{-1}s_t,$$

$$s_t = \rho s_{t-1} + \vartheta_t.$$

Defining $y_t' = (c_t, k_t, s_t)$, this system can be put in the standard form (10.15):

$$\begin{pmatrix} c_t \\ k_t \\ s_t \end{pmatrix} = \begin{pmatrix} \beta_{11} & 0 & \beta_{13} \\ 0 & 0 & 0 \\ 0 & 0 & 0 \end{pmatrix} \begin{pmatrix} E_t c_{t+1} \\ E_t k_{t+1} \\ E_t s_{t+1} \end{pmatrix}$$

$$+ \begin{pmatrix} 0 & 0 & 0 \\ \delta_{21} & \delta_{22} & \delta_{23} \\ 0 & 0 & \rho \end{pmatrix} \begin{pmatrix} c_{t-1} \\ k_{t-1} \\ s_{t-1} \end{pmatrix} + \begin{pmatrix} 0 \\ 0 \\ 1 \end{pmatrix} \vartheta_t,$$

where the coefficients are given implicitly by equations (10.21), i.e., $\beta_{11} = 1 + (1-\alpha)\mathfrak{B}\gamma^{-1}(\bar{Q}/\bar{K})$, etc. Given an MSV solution, this form can be used to analyze its stability under learning using the E-stability result in the preceding section. It is well known that this model is regular. For particular parameter values, the Blanchard–Kahn technique provides one way to compute the unique stationary equilibrium, as discussed in Appendix 2. For example, for the parameter values used in Farmer (1999), the solution in VAR form is

$$\begin{pmatrix} c_t \\ k_t \\ s_t \end{pmatrix} = \begin{pmatrix} -0.1307 & 0.5701 & 0.5907 \\ -0.2458 & 1.0725 & 0.2708 \\ 0 & 0 & 0.95 \end{pmatrix} \begin{pmatrix} c_{t-1} \\ k_{t-1} \\ s_{t-1} \end{pmatrix} + \begin{pmatrix} 0.4703 \\ 0 \\ 1 \end{pmatrix} \vartheta_t.$$

The coefficient matrix b has roots 0, 0.9418, and 0.9500, so this solution is stationary.

To check E-stability of this solution one can apply Proposition 10.3 of the preceding section and compute numerically the eigenvalues of $DT_a(\bar{a}, \bar{b})$ and

$DT_b(\bar{b})$. [As we have set up equation (10.15), all variables are included in y_t, and thus there is no block $DT_c(\bar{b}, \bar{c})$ that needs to be computed.] The roots of $DT_b(\bar{b})$ are $0.8858, 0.8781$, and seven roots equal to zero. $DT_a(\bar{a}, \bar{b})$ has root 0.9324 and two roots equal to zero. This confirms E-stability of the solution. It is also easy to implement the algorithm (10.10) to compute the solution and verify E-stability.

Finally, we consider the stability of REE under least squares learning. Essentially, we follow the framework of Section 10.2.2. However, there is a technical difficulty. To apply the stochastic approximation results, the moment matrix of the regressors $c_{t-1}, k_{t-1}, s_{t-1}$ must be positive definite. This assumption is violated because in the RBC model, c_t is an exact linear combination of k_t and s_t.

There are two ways to overcome this problem. The first and simpler is to introduce an exogenous iid disturbance to consumption. This can be thought of as a deviation from optimizing behavior by the household, and can be assumed to have arbitrarily small variance. With this small modification, the framework of Section 10.3 applies directly and stability of least squares learning is determined by the E-stability conditions verified above. Least squares learning therefore converges to a stochastic process (arbitrarily) close to the REE.

The second approach is to reformulate the perceived law of motion so that c_t depends on the contemporaneous k_t and s_t. Under least squares learning the agents will estimate this equation, together with a VAR of k_t and s_t. The analysis of E-stability must be modified accordingly. Since this complication may arise in other applied models, we now show how to implement this approach. Under this alternative learning scheme, the PLM is

$$c_t = a_1 k_t + a_2 s_t,$$
$$k_t = b_1 k_{t-1} + b_2 s_{t-1}.$$

For simplicity, we assume here that the agents know the stochastic process of the technology shock.

The structural model is still given by

$$c_t = \beta_{11} E_t^* c_{t+1} + \beta_{13} E_t^* s_{t+1},$$
$$k_t = \delta_{21} c_{t-1} + \delta_{22} k_{t-1} + \delta_{23} s_{t-1},$$
$$s_t = \rho s_{t-1} + \vartheta_t.$$

It is easily verified that the T-mapping is given by

$$
\begin{aligned}
T_{a_1}(a_1, a_2, b_1, b_2) &= \beta_{11} a_1 b_1, \\
T_{a_2}(a_1, a_2, b_1, b_2) &= \beta_{11} a_1 b_2 + (\beta_{11} a_2 + \beta_{13}) \rho, \\
T_{b_1}(a_1, a_2, b_1, b_2) &= \delta_{21} \beta_{11} a_1 b_1 + \delta_{22}, \\
T_{b_2}(a_1, a_2, b_1, b_2) &= \delta_{21} \big[\beta_{11} a_1 b_2 + (\beta_{11} a_2 + \beta_{13}) \rho \big] + \delta_{23}.
\end{aligned}
$$

In the differential equation

$$
\frac{d}{d\tau}
\begin{pmatrix} a_1 \\ a_2 \\ b_1 \\ b_2 \end{pmatrix}
= T
\begin{pmatrix} a_1 \\ a_2 \\ b_1 \\ b_2 \end{pmatrix}
-
\begin{pmatrix} a_1 \\ a_2 \\ b_1 \\ b_2 \end{pmatrix},
$$

the first and third equations form an independent bivariate subsystem. This means that the linearized system is block-triangular, and the stability conditions can be verified numerically by checking two trace-determinant stability conditions. For the numerical parameters of the RBC model, these conditions are satisfied.

For least squares learning, let

$$
\xi_t' = \begin{pmatrix} a_{1,t} & a_{2,t} \\ b_{1,t} & b_{2,t} \end{pmatrix}.
$$

Forecasts are given by $E_t^* k_{t+1} = b_{1,t} k_t + b_{2,t} s_t$, $E_t^* s_{t+1} = \rho s_t$, and $E_t^* c_{t+1} = a_{1,t} E_t^* k_{t+1} + a_{2,t} E_t^* s_{t+1}$. RLS learning is as usual given by equations (10.11)–(10.12), where $\epsilon_t = x_t - \xi_{t-1}' z_{t-1}$, with $x_t' = (c_{t-1}, k_t)$ and $z_{t-1}' = (k_{t-1}, s_{t-1})$. Since $x_t = T(\xi_{t-1})' z_{t-1}$, we have

$$
\xi_t = \xi_{t-1} + t^{-1} R_t^{-1} z_{t-1} z_{t-1}' \big(T(\xi_{t-1}) - \xi_{t-1} \big).
$$

Finally, when applying the stochastic approximation we set $\theta_t = \mathrm{vec}(\xi_t, S_t)$, where $S_{t-1} = R_t$, and the state vector is $X_t' = (k_t, s_t, k_{t-1}, s_{t-1})$ with $W_t = \vartheta_t$. The positive definiteness condition of the relevant moment matrix can be verified and the analysis now is analogous to that of Section 10.2.2.

To summarize, under either of these real-time learning schemes, for the numerical specification given, the stationary MSV solution is locally stable under adaptive learning.[6]

---

[6]Packalén (2000) has analytically shown that the RBC model is stable under learning.

10.5 Irregular REE

10.5.1 A General Framework

In the regular case there is a unique stationary solution generated by the fundamental shocks. As in the univariate case, the full set of solutions to equation (10.2) and to equation (10.15) generally includes solutions which depend on extraneous noise or "sunspots." In regular cases these non-saddle point solutions are explosive, but in "irregular" cases there are stationary solutions which depend on sunspots. Irregular versions of the RBC model based on increasing returns have been developed, e.g., in Benhabib and Farmer (1994).

In Appendix 2 we develop an extension of the Blanchard–Kahn technique which provides the full set of stationary solutions in the irregular case. In this section we will restrict attention to sunspot solutions of a particularly simple form that arise in particular cases, including the Farmer and Guo (1994) model. We describe these solutions, which are simple extensions of the MSV solutions, and analyze their stability under learning.

Consider first the model (10.15), with t dating of expectations, reproduced here for convenience

$$y_t = \alpha + \beta E_t^* y_{t+1} + \delta y_{t-1} + \kappa w_t,$$
$$w_t = \varphi w_{t-1} + e_t.$$

Consider solutions of the form

$$y_t = a + b y_{t-1} + c w_t + f \varepsilon_t, \tag{10.22}$$

where ε_t is an arbitrary martingale difference sequence, i.e., a random variable which satisfies $E_{t-1}\varepsilon_t = 0$. Computing $E_t y_{t+1} = a + b y_t + c \varphi w_t$ and inserting into the model, we obtain the following equation which must be satisfied by the ALM:

$$(I - \beta b) y_t = \alpha + \beta a + (\kappa + \beta c \varphi) w_t + \delta y_{t-1}. \tag{10.23}$$

Multiplying the PLM (10.22) by $(I - \beta b)$ and equating to (10.23), we obtain the equations which must be satisfied by any RE solution of the form (10.22). These are given by equations (10.17)–(10.19), together with the additional equation

$$(I - \beta b) f = 0. \tag{10.24}$$

Even restricting attention to stationary solutions, the matrix quadratic (10.18) can in general have multiple solutions $\bar{b}$ in which the roots of $\bar{b}$ lie inside the unit circle. Given $\bar{b}$, if $I - \beta\bar{b}$ is nonsingular, then $f = 0$ and we again arrive at the MSV solution: for this $\bar{b}$, there are no solutions of the form (10.22) which depend on ε_t. However, if $I - \beta\bar{b}$ is singular, then sunspot solutions of the form (10.22) can exist with $f \neq 0$. In this case there is in fact a continuum of solutions in f with the dimension of the solution set for f given by the dimension of the null space of $I - \beta\bar{b}$.

When we look at the stability of these solutions under learning, however, we immediately see that the detailed assumptions about the information set are important. Suppose y_t is in the time-t information set, and consider a sunspot solution $(\bar{a}, \bar{b}, \bar{c}, \bar{f})$, with $\bar{f} \neq 0$ and $I - \beta\bar{b}$ singular. Treating equation (10.22) as a PLM, consider values of b near $\bar{b}$. For all values of b for which $I - \beta b$ is nonsingular, equation (10.23) can be uniquely solved for the ALM in which $T_f(a, b, c, f) = 0$.[7] Thus under the differential equation defining E-stability, the equation for f is independent of the other variables and has $f \to 0$. Therefore these sunspot solutions fail to be E-stable. The E-instability of these solutions to equation (10.15) appears to be due to the contemporaneous dating of the expectations, since ε_t does not appear in $E_t^* y_{t+1}$.

A natural alternative assumption is that y_t is not available when the forecast $E_t^* y_{t+1}$ is formed, so that expectations are a linear function of $(1, y_{t-1}, w_t, \varepsilon_t)$. We now adopt this assumption and obtain the E-stability conditions for the corresponding solutions of the form (10.22).

For PLMs (10.22), expectations are given by

$$E_t^* y_{t+1} = a + b(a + by_{t-1} + cw_t + f\varepsilon_t) + c\varphi w_t$$
$$= (I + b)a + b^2 y_{t-1} + (bc + c\varphi)w_t + bf\varepsilon_t.$$

Inserting into equation (10.15), we obtain the ALM

$$y_t = \alpha + \beta(I + b)a + (\beta b^2 + \delta)y_{t-1} + (\beta bc + \beta c\varphi + \kappa)w_t + \beta bf\varepsilon_t.$$

Hence the mapping from the PLM to the ALM takes the form

$$T(a, b, c, f) = (\alpha + \beta(I + b)a, \beta b^2 + \delta, \beta bc + \beta c\varphi + \kappa, \beta bf).$$

The fixed points of T give the equations for an REE (10.17), (10.18), (10.19), (10.24) above. Consider a $\bar{b}$ that satisfies $\bar{b} = \beta\bar{b}^2 + \delta$ and such that $I - \beta\bar{b}$ is singular, so that there are sunspot solutions of the form (10.22). For convenience

---

[7]Even if $I - \beta b$ is singular, so that there are multiple ALM solutions to equation (10.23), at each of these solutions we have $T_f(a, b, c, f) = 0$. Here T_f denotes the f component of the map from PLM to ALM.

we make the additional assumptions that $a = \alpha + \beta(I + \bar{b})a$ and $c = \beta\bar{b}c + \beta c\varphi + \kappa$ have unique solutions for $\bar{a}$ and $\bar{c}$, but $I - \beta\bar{b}$ singular implies multiple solutions for f. Because there is a continuum of solutions, we need to take care in defining E-stability. As always, we consider the matrix differential equation $d\xi/d\tau = T(\xi) - \xi$, where $\xi = (a, b, c, f)$. Suppose $\bar{b}$ satisfies the preceding conditions and let $S(\bar{b})$ be the set of values of ξ that are fixed points of T with $b = \bar{b}$. We say that the solution set $S(\bar{b})$ is E-stable if, for some neighborhood N of $S(\bar{b})$, the solution $\xi(\tau)$ to the differential equation $d\xi/d\tau = T(\xi) - \xi$ with initial condition $\xi_0 \in N$ satisfies $\xi(\tau) \to \xi^\infty$, where $\xi^\infty \in S(\bar{b})$. Recall that for univariate linear models, we established E-stability for continua of equilibria, according to this definition, in Section 8.4.4 of Chapter 8.

To compute E-stability conditions, we require the following derivatives:

$$DT_a(\bar{a}, \bar{b}) = \beta(I + \bar{b}), \qquad (10.25)$$
$$DT_b(\bar{b}) = \bar{b}' \otimes \beta + I \otimes \beta\bar{b},$$
$$DT_c(\bar{b}, \bar{c}) = \varphi' \otimes \beta + I \otimes \beta\bar{b},$$
$$DT_f(\bar{b}) = \beta\bar{b}.$$

The differential equation $d\xi/d\tau = T(\xi) - \xi$ has an independent subsystem in a, b, and c. If any root of $DT_a(\bar{a}, \bar{b})$, $DT_b(\bar{b})$, or $DT_c(\bar{b}, \bar{c})$ has a real part greater than 1, then this subsystem is locally unstable at $(\bar{a}, \bar{b}, \bar{c})$ and hence the solution set $S(\bar{b})$ is locally unstable. We make the regularity assumption that none of these eigenvalues has real part equal to 1. We can then state the following partial result.

Proposition 10.5. *Suppose the time-t information set is $(1, y'_{t-1}, w'_t)'$. A necessary condition that a solution set $S(\bar{b})$ to the model (10.15) is E-stable is that all eigenvalues of the matrices $DT_a(\bar{a}, \bar{b})$, $DT_b(\bar{b})$, $DT_c(\bar{b}, \bar{c})$, given by equation (10.25), have real parts less than 1. A sufficient condition for E-instability of $S(\bar{b})$ is that at least one eigenvalue of these matrices has a real part greater than 1.*

The preceding proposition gives necessary conditions for stability. We conjecture that additional necessary conditions for E-stability are that all roots of $\beta\bar{b} - I$ have negative real parts, apart from $\dim(\mathfrak{N}(f))$ roots of zero, where $\mathfrak{N}(f)$ is the set of solutions f to $(I - \beta\bar{b})f = 0$. We additionally conjecture that, taken together, these conditions are sufficient for E-stability.

10.5.2   Model with $t - 1$ Dating

Irregular solutions also arise in the model in which expectations are dated at time $t - 1$. Recall the model (10.2)

$$y_t = \alpha + \beta_0 E_{t-1} y_t + \beta_1 E_{t-1} y_{t+1} + \delta y_{t-1} + \kappa w_t + \zeta v_t,$$
$$w_t = \varphi w_{t-1} + e_t.$$

Again, an extension of the Blanchard–Kahn technique can be used to obtain the full set of stationary solutions. These are developed in Appendix 2. We again consider a restricted class of solutions taking the form

$$y_t = a + b y_{t-1} + c w_{t-1} + \kappa e_t + \zeta v_t + f \varepsilon_{t-1}, \tag{10.26}$$

where ε_t is an arbitrary martingale difference sequence. Computing expectations and inserting into equation (10.2), we obtain the ALM

$$y_t = \alpha + (\beta_0 + \beta_1 + \beta_1 b) a + (\beta_1 b^2 + \beta_0 b + \delta) y_{t-1} \tag{10.27}$$
$$+ (\beta_0 c + \beta_1 bc + \beta_1 c\varphi + \kappa\varphi) w_{t-1} + \kappa e_t + \zeta v_t + (\beta_0 + \beta_1 b) f \varepsilon_{t-1}.$$

The mapping from the PLM to the ALM is identical to equation (10.8) plus an additional component for the vector f given by $T_f(a, b, c, f) = (\beta_0 + \beta_1 b) f$. Solutions of the form (10.26) are given by equations (10.5), (10.6), (10.7), and the additional equation

$$(\beta_0 + \beta_1 b - I) f = 0. \tag{10.28}$$

If $I - \beta_0 - \beta_1 \bar{b}$ is nonsingular, then $f = 0$ and the solution does not depend on sunspots. For $I - \beta_0 - \beta_1 \bar{b}$ singular, solutions with $f \neq 0$ can exist. Note that f must lie in the null space of $I - \beta_0 - \beta_1 \bar{b}$ and that if solutions with $f \neq 0$ exist, then a continuum $\mathfrak{N}(f)$ of such solutions exists, corresponding to this null space and indexed by the possible values f.

Turning to E-stability of sunspot solutions of the form (10.26), note that the differential equation defining E-stability is again (10.9), together with the additional equation $df/d\tau = (\beta_0 + \beta_1 b - I) f$. It follows that necessary conditions for E-stability of a solution of the form (10.26) are that the three conditions stated in Proposition 10.1 hold at the solution. In addition, we have a condition from the f differential equation. For f in $\mathfrak{N}(f)$ we have $df/d\tau = 0$, and the E-stability condition is that this set is locally stable. The relevant additional condition is that all roots of $\beta_0 + \beta_1 b - I$ have negative real parts, apart from $\dim(\mathfrak{N}(f))$ roots of zero. We conjecture that these conditions jointly are necessary and sufficient for E-stability.

10.5.3 Real-Time Learning

For the setup of Section 10.5.1, agents can attempt to learn a, b, c, and f by a recursive least squares regression of y_t on $(1, y_{t-1}, w_t, \varepsilon_t)$, where ε_t is an observable sunspot. For the setup of Section 10.5.2, the regressors are instead $(1, y_{t-1}, w_{t-1}, \varepsilon_{t-1})$. In either case the learning algorithm and the law of motion for y_t can be formulated along the lines used for the regular case in Section 10.2.2. Application of the stochastic approximation techniques suggests that a set of sunspot solutions of the form (10.22) or (10.26) will be stable under least squares learning if and only if they are E-stable. Unfortunately, there are technical complications in justifying the stochastic approximation tools because the set of solutions (a, b, c, f) forms an unbounded continuum. This prevents a formal demonstration of the convergence conditions under least squares learning. Simulations in the univariate case appear to support the claim that convergence in these cases is indeed governed by the E-stability conditions, but further work is clearly required to establish the validity of this conjecture.

10.5.4 Learning in the Farmer–Guo Model of Increasing Returns

As an application we consider the Farmer and Guo (1994) model, described also in Farmer (1999, Chapter 7). This is an extension of the RBC model, which can be interpreted either as allowing for externalities or for monopolistic competition. In either interpretation one arrives at structural equations of the form

$$
\begin{aligned}
K_{t+1} &= Q_t + (1-d)K_t - C_t, \\
Q_t &= S_t K_t^\mu (\gamma^t L_t)^\nu, \\
n\frac{Q_t}{L_t} &= C_t, \\
\frac{1}{C_t} &= \mathcal{B}E_t\left[\frac{1}{C_{t+1}}\left(1 - d + m\frac{Q_{t+1}}{K_{t+1}}\right)\right], \\
S_t &= S_{t-1}^\rho V_t.
\end{aligned}
\tag{10.29}
$$

Appendix 1 gives the linearization of this model. Farmer and Guo show that for particular parameter values, this model is irregular, possessing stationary sunspot solutions of the form (10.22).

Farmer and Guo restrict attention to the case $S_t = V_t \equiv 1$ for all t, so that the stochastic shocks in their solution are entirely due to sunspots. In this case we have

$$
\begin{pmatrix} c_t \\ k_t \end{pmatrix} = \begin{pmatrix} \beta_{11} & \beta_{12} \\ 0 & 0 \end{pmatrix} \begin{pmatrix} E_t c_{t+1} \\ E_t k_{t+1} \end{pmatrix} + \begin{pmatrix} 0 & 0 \\ \delta_{21} & \delta_{22} \end{pmatrix} \begin{pmatrix} c_{t-1} \\ k_{t-1} \end{pmatrix}.
$$

This is a special case of the model (10.15) with $w_t \equiv 0$. We look for "sunspot solutions" of the form (10.22), i.e., of the form

$$\begin{pmatrix} c_t \\ k_t \end{pmatrix} = \begin{pmatrix} b_{11} & b_{12} \\ b_{21} & b_{22} \end{pmatrix} \begin{pmatrix} c_{t-1} \\ k_{t-1} \end{pmatrix} + \begin{pmatrix} f_{11} & f_{12} \\ 0 & 0 \end{pmatrix} \begin{pmatrix} \varepsilon_{1t} \\ \varepsilon_{2t} \end{pmatrix}. \qquad (10.30)$$

The coefficients $f_{21} = f_{22} = 0$ since $k_t = E_{t-1} k_t$. Solutions must satisfy both equations (10.18) and (10.24), i.e.,

$$(I - \beta b)b = \delta \quad \text{and} \quad (I - \beta b)f = 0.$$

Using

$$(I - \beta b) = \begin{pmatrix} 1 - \beta_{11} b_{11} - \beta_{12} b_{21} & -\beta_{11} b_{12} - \beta_{12} b_{22} \\ 0 & 1 \end{pmatrix},$$

one can easily verify that $f_{11} = f_{12} = 0$ unless $b = \bar{b}$, where

$$\bar{b} = \begin{pmatrix} \beta_{11}^{-1}(1 - \beta_{12}\delta_{21}) & -\beta_{11}^{-1}\beta_{12}\delta_{22} \\ \delta_{21} & \delta_{22} \end{pmatrix}. \qquad (10.31)$$

This leads to stationary solutions depending on sunspots provided $\bar{b}$ has both roots inside the unit circle. Finally, we note that the solutions can be rewritten

$$\begin{pmatrix} c_t \\ k_t \end{pmatrix} = \bar{b} \begin{pmatrix} c_{t-1} \\ k_{t-1} \end{pmatrix} + \begin{pmatrix} \tilde{\varepsilon}_t \\ 0 \end{pmatrix},$$

where $\tilde{\varepsilon}_t = f_{11}\varepsilon_{1t} + f_{12}\varepsilon_{2t}$ for arbitrary martingale difference sequences $\tilde{\varepsilon}_t$.

We now turn to the stability of these solutions under learning. Farmer and Guo choose the parameter values $m = 0.23, n = 0.7, v = 1.21, \mu = 0.4,$ $\mathcal{B} = 0.99, d = 0.025,$ and $\phi = 1$. This leads to the sunspot solution with

$$\bar{b} = \begin{pmatrix} 1.1555 & -0.0864 \\ 0.7517 & 0.6843 \end{pmatrix}.$$

$\bar{b}$ has roots $0.9199 \pm 0.0971i$ which lie inside the unit circle, so this constitutes a stationary sunspot solution. To check the stability under learning we check the E-stability conditions given in Proposition 10.5. The eigenvalues of $DT_b(\bar{b})$ are two roots of zero and the roots $1.7357 \pm 0.0776i$. Since the latter roots have real parts greater than 1, this sunspot solution is not stable under adaptive learning.

An open question is whether, for other choices of parameter values, the Farmer–Guo model has stationary sunspot solutions which are stable under learning.[8]

10.6 Conclusions

As this chapter shows, it is generally possible to apply stochastic approximation methods to study learning for multivariate linear models. We have treated some of the most common multivariate frameworks, but it is easy to think of extensions, e.g., to models with mixed datings of expectations. For regular models, the local convergence results are essentially complete, but some gaps in the theoretical results remain for irregular models, as was seen in Section 10.5. In these cases it appears that numerical work is needed for the study of stability of the REE under learning.

The extensions in this chapter have allowed us to consider important economic issues. Our result that the sunspot equilibria in the Farmer–Guo model (with their parameter values) are not E-stable leaves open the question whether some variant of the irregular models has sunspot equilibria that are stable under learning for realistic parameter values. Another important line of research would be to consider the stability of REE in other standard macroeconomic models. An example of the latter is the work by Bullard and Mitra (1999) on determinacy and stability of equilibria under different monetary policy rules.

10.7 Appendix 1: Linearizations

Here we describe how to obtain the linearization of the RBC and Farmer–Guo models. (Note that the RBC model is a special case of the Farmer–Guo model with $\mu = m = \alpha$, $\nu = n = 1 - \alpha$.)

We begin by describing a general method for obtaining log-linearizations of nonlinear models. Consider a general framework of the form

$$f(Y_t) + E_t g(Y_{t+1}) = 0, \tag{10.32}$$

---

[8]Packalén (2000) has investigated this issue numerically. There are regions of the parameter space in which stability holds, but the required parameter values are far from the usual calibrations.

where $Y_t = (Y_{1,t}, \ldots, Y_{n,t})'$ is an n-vector. Let $\bar{Y}$ be a steady state of the non-stochastic equation, i.e., $f(\bar{Y}) + g(\bar{Y}) = 0$. Linearizing equation (10.32) around $\bar{Y}$ yields the system

$$\text{constant} + \sum_{i=1}^{n} f_i(\bar{Y}) Y_{i,t} + \sum_{i=1}^{n} g_i(\bar{Y}) E_t Y_{i,t+1} = 0, \tag{10.33}$$

where the expectation has been brought inside using the linearization and where the notation $f_i(\bar{Y}) = (\partial f / \partial Y_i)(\bar{Y})$, $g_i(\bar{Y}) = (\partial g / \partial Y_i)(\bar{Y})$ has been used.

It is often convenient to write the linearization in terms of logarithmic deviations from the steady state. One first writes equation (10.33) as

$$
\begin{aligned}
0 = \text{constant} &+ \sum_{i=1}^{n} \bar{Y}_i f_i(\bar{Y}) \exp\left(\ln\left(\frac{Y_{i,t}}{\bar{Y}_i} \right) \right) \\
&+ \sum_{i=1}^{n} \bar{Y}_i g_i(\bar{Y}) E_t \exp\left(\ln\left(\frac{Y_{i,t+1}}{\bar{Y}_i} \right) \right).
\end{aligned}
$$

Next we define $y_{it} = \ln(Y_{i,t}/\bar{Y}_i)$ and utilize the approximation $\exp(y_i) \approx y_i + 1$. This gives

$$\text{constant} + \sum_{i=1}^{n} \bar{Y}_i f_i(\bar{Y})(y_{it} + 1) + \sum_{i=1}^{n} \bar{Y}_i g_i(\bar{Y}) E_t(y_{i,t+1} + 1) = 0.$$

Finally, since this also holds in the steady state $y_{i,t} = y_{i,t+1} = 0$, the constants can be eliminated and we arrive at the final equation

$$\sum_{i=1}^{n} \bar{Y}_i f_i(\bar{Y}) y_{i,t} + \sum_{i=1}^{n} \bar{Y}_i g_i(\bar{Y}) E_t y_{i,t+1} = 0. \tag{10.34}$$

We now apply this technique to log-linearize the Farmer–Guo model. Let $\phi = \gamma^{\nu/(1-\mu)}$, $\tilde{K}_t = K_t/\phi^t$, $\tilde{C}_t = C_t/\phi^t$, and $\tilde{Q}_t = Q_t/\phi^t$. This transforms the model into one with asymptotically stationary variables. The equations (10.29) become

$$\phi \tilde{K}_{t+1} = Q_t + (1-d)\tilde{K}_t - \tilde{C}_t,$$
$$\tilde{Q}_t = S_t \tilde{K}_t^\mu L_t^\nu,$$
$$\tilde{C}_t = n\frac{\tilde{Q}_t}{L_t},$$
$$\frac{1}{\tilde{C}_t} = \frac{\mathfrak{B}}{\phi} E_t\left(\frac{1}{\tilde{C}_{t+1}}\left(1-d+m\frac{\tilde{Q}_{t+1}}{\tilde{K}_{t+1}}\right)\right),$$
$$S_t = S_{t-1}^\rho V_t.$$

Applying the general method outlined above gives the equations

$$k_{t+1} = \phi^{-1}\left(\frac{\bar{Q}}{\bar{K}}\right)q_t + \phi^{-1}(1-d)k_t - \phi^{-1}\left(\frac{\bar{C}}{\bar{K}}\right)c_t,$$
$$q_t = s_t + \mu k_t + \nu \ell_t,$$
$$q_t = c_t + \ell_t,$$
$$-c_t = -E_t c_{t+1} + \frac{\mathfrak{B}}{\phi}\frac{m\bar{Q}}{\bar{K}}E_t q_{t+1} - \frac{\mathfrak{B}}{\phi}\frac{m\bar{Q}}{\bar{K}}E_t k_{t+1},$$
$$s_t = \rho s_{t-1} + \vartheta_t.$$

Note that we have followed the notation that lowercase letters denote log-deviations from the steady state, i.e., $k_t = \ln(\tilde{K}_t/\bar{K})$, etc.

Finally, eliminating q_t and ℓ_t yields the final equations

$$c_t = \left(1 + \frac{\nu}{1-\nu}\frac{\mathfrak{B}}{\phi}\frac{m\bar{Q}}{\bar{K}}\right)E_t c_{t+1} + \frac{\mathfrak{B}}{\phi}\frac{m\bar{Q}}{\bar{K}}\left(1-\frac{\mu}{1-\nu}\right)E_t k_{t+1},$$
$$-\frac{\mathfrak{B}}{\phi}\frac{m\bar{Q}}{\bar{K}}\frac{1}{1-\nu}E_t s_{t+1}, \qquad\qquad (10.35)$$
$$k_{t+1} = -\phi^{-1}\left(\frac{\bar{C}}{\bar{K}} + \frac{\bar{Q}}{\bar{K}}\frac{\nu}{1-\nu}\right)c_t + \phi^{-1}\left(1-d+\frac{\bar{Q}}{\bar{K}}\frac{\mu}{1-\nu}\right)k_t$$
$$+\phi^{-1}\frac{\bar{Q}}{\bar{K}}\frac{1}{1-\nu}s_t,$$
$$s_t = \rho s_{t-1} + \vartheta_t.$$

Setting $\mu = m = \alpha$, $\nu = n = 1-\alpha$, and $\phi = \gamma$ yields the RBC model (10.21) of Section 10.4. The linearized Farmer–Guo model (10.35) fits the general form

(10.15) and can be written

$$
\begin{pmatrix} c_t \\ k_t \\ s_t \end{pmatrix} = \begin{pmatrix} \beta_{11} & \beta_{12} & \beta_{13} \\ 0 & 0 & 0 \\ 0 & 0 & 0 \end{pmatrix} \begin{pmatrix} E_t c_{t+1} \\ E_t k_{t+1} \\ E_t s_{t+1} \end{pmatrix}
$$

$$
+ \begin{pmatrix} 0 & 0 & 0 \\ \delta_{21} & \delta_{22} & \delta_{23} \\ 0 & 0 & \rho \end{pmatrix} \begin{pmatrix} c_{t-1} \\ k_{t-1} \\ s_{t-1} \end{pmatrix} + \begin{pmatrix} 0 \\ 0 \\ 1 \end{pmatrix} \vartheta_t,
$$

where the coefficients are given in equations (10.35). For the irregular case, Farmer and Guo restrict attention to the case $s_t = \vartheta_t = 0$ so that the system reduces to

$$
\begin{pmatrix} c_t \\ k_t \end{pmatrix} = \begin{pmatrix} \beta_{11} & \beta_{12} \\ 0 & 0 \end{pmatrix} \begin{pmatrix} E_t c_{t+1} \\ E_t k_{t+1} \end{pmatrix} + \begin{pmatrix} 0 & 0 \\ \delta_{21} & \delta_{22} \end{pmatrix} \begin{pmatrix} c_{t-1} \\ k_{t-1} \end{pmatrix}.
$$

10.8   Appendix 2: Solution Techniques

The reduced forms of macroeconomic models are usually expectational difference schemes. The form (10.2) is a general framework in which the available information, used to form the expectations that determine the period-t endogenous variables, includes the values of the different variables up to period $t - 1$. Equation (10.15) differs by the inclusion of the values for variables in period t in the information set.

Different solution techniques have been used to eliminate the expectational variables from the reduced form. The method of undetermined coefficients for obtaining the MSV solution and other solution classes was adopted in this chapter, because it is the most convenient approach for the analysis of learning. However, if one is only interested in obtaining the RE solutions, a widely used approach, known as the Blanchard and Kahn (1980) technique, can be used. In this appendix we show how this technique can be applied in the different frameworks considered in this chapter, and we discuss its relationship to the method of undetermined coefficients. The paper by Blanchard and Kahn (1980) in fact restricted attention to the regular case in a framework in which expectations are formed using information available at time t.

10.8.1 Representing Regular Equilibria

Many macroeconomic models are known to be "saddle point stable" under rational expectations. This refers to a model in which there is a unique stationary (or nonexplosive) solution.

Models with t − 1 Dating of Expectations

We start by considering the framework (10.2) with $t - 1$ dating of the available information. In terms of the MSV solutions, the "saddle point stable" or "regular" case arises when equation (10.6) has a unique solution for b in which the eigenvalues of b all lie inside the unit circle. We now present the alternative solution method in the regular case.

We first rewrite the system (10.2) using a classification of variables into predetermined and nonpredetermined or "free" variables. The former include both exogenous variables and lagged endogenous variables. More generally, we classify as predetermined any variable which does not depend directly on expectations of current or future variables. We thus rewrite equation (10.2), partitioning $y_t' = (\tilde{y}_t', \hat{y}_t')$ into free components $\tilde{y}_t$ and predetermined components $\hat{y}_t$:

$$\begin{pmatrix} \tilde{y}_t \\ \hat{y}_t \end{pmatrix} = \begin{pmatrix} \tilde{\alpha} \\ \hat{\alpha} \end{pmatrix} + \begin{pmatrix} \beta_0^{11} & \beta_0^{12} \\ 0 & 0 \end{pmatrix} E_{t-1} y_t + \begin{pmatrix} \beta_1^{11} & \beta_1^{12} \\ 0 & 0 \end{pmatrix} E_{t-1} y_{t+1}$$
$$+ \begin{pmatrix} \delta^{11} & \delta^{12} \\ \delta^{21} & \delta^{22} \end{pmatrix} \begin{pmatrix} \tilde{y}_{t-1} \\ \hat{y}_{t-1} \end{pmatrix} + \begin{pmatrix} \tilde{\kappa} \\ \hat{\kappa} \end{pmatrix} w_t + \begin{pmatrix} \tilde{\zeta} \\ \hat{\zeta} \end{pmatrix} v_t.$$

We also center the variables by subtracting their means, so that we can now assume that all variables have zero expected values.

The technique, modified for $t - 1$ dating of expectations, starts from the more general form:

$$\begin{aligned} x_t^1 &= B_0 E_{t-1} x_t^1 + B_1 E_{t-1} x_{t+1}^1 + C x_t^2 + u_{1t}, \\ x_t^2 &= R x_{t-1}^1 + S x_{t-1}^2 + u_{2t}. \end{aligned} \tag{10.36}$$

Here x_t^1 is an $n_1 \times 1$ vector of free variables, x_t^2 is a vector of predetermined variables, and $(u_{1t}', u_{2t}')'$ is a white noise process. Note that lags of endogenous variables are incorporated into x_t^2 and will have corresponding zero elements of u_{t2}. x_t^2 can incorporate exogenous variables following a VAR process.[9] x_t^2

---

[9]The seminal paper by Blanchard and Kahn (1980) allows for a more general class of exogenous variables.

can also include variables such as m_t in Example 1 which depend on lags of nonpredetermined variables, but not on their expectations.

Equation (10.2) can always be put in the form[10] (10.36) by defining

$$x_t^1 = \tilde{y}_t \quad \text{and} \quad x_t^2 = \begin{pmatrix} \hat{y}_t \\ \tilde{y}_{t-1} \\ \hat{y}_{t-1} \\ w_t \end{pmatrix}.$$

The matrices in equation (10.36) are given by

$$B_0 = \beta_0^{11} + \beta_0^{12}\delta^{21}, \qquad B_1 = \beta_1^{11},$$

$$C = \begin{pmatrix} \beta_0^{12} + \beta_1^{12}\delta^{22} & \delta^{11} & \delta^{12} & \beta_1^{12}\hat{\kappa} + \tilde{\kappa} \end{pmatrix},$$

$$R = \begin{pmatrix} \delta^{21} \\ I \\ 0 \\ 0 \end{pmatrix}, \qquad S = \begin{pmatrix} \delta^{22} & 0 & 0 & \hat{\kappa}\varphi \\ 0 & 0 & 0 & 0 \\ I & 0 & 0 & 0 \\ 0 & 0 & 0 & \varphi \end{pmatrix},$$

and the white noise processes are given by

$$u_{1t} = -\big(\beta_0^{12} + \beta_1^{12}(\delta^{22} + I)\big)\hat{\kappa}e_t + \big(I - \beta_0^{12} - \beta_1^{12}\delta^{22}\big)\tilde{\xi}v_t,$$

$$u_{2t} = \begin{pmatrix} \hat{\xi}v_t + \hat{\kappa}e_t \\ 0 \\ 0 \\ e_t \end{pmatrix}.$$

Returning to the general formulation (10.36), we show how to obtain the unique stationary RE solution when it exists. To do this we define the innovation

$$\eta_t = E_t x_{t+1}^1 - E_{t-1} x_{t+1}^1.$$

Note that $x_t^1 - E_{t-1}x_t^1 = Cu_{2t} + u_{1t}$. Thus $x_{t+1}^1 - E_{t-1}x_{t+1}^1 = Cu_{2,t+1} +$

---

[10]Before centering the equation, there would also be constants $\tilde{\alpha} + \beta_1^{12}\hat{\alpha}$ in the x_t^1 equation and $(\hat{\alpha}' \ 0 \ 0 \ 0)'$ in the x_t^2 equation.

$u_{1,t+1} + \eta_t$. It follows that equation (10.36) can be written

$$
\begin{pmatrix} I - B_0 & -C \\ R & S \end{pmatrix} \begin{pmatrix} x_t^1 \\ x_t^2 \end{pmatrix}
$$

$$
= \begin{pmatrix} B_1 & 0 \\ 0 & I \end{pmatrix} \begin{pmatrix} x_{t+1}^1 \\ x_{t+1}^2 \end{pmatrix} + \begin{pmatrix} I - B_0 & -B_0 C & -B_1 \\ 0 & 0 & 0 \end{pmatrix} \begin{pmatrix} u_{1t} \\ u_{2t} \\ \eta_t \end{pmatrix}
$$

$$
+ \begin{pmatrix} -B_1 & -B_1 C & 0 \\ 0 & -I & 0 \end{pmatrix} \begin{pmatrix} u_{1,t+1} \\ u_{2,t+1} \\ \eta_{t+1} \end{pmatrix}.
$$

Assuming that the matrix on the left-hand side is invertible, the equation can be put in the form

$$
\begin{pmatrix} x_t^1 \\ x_t^2 \end{pmatrix} = J \begin{pmatrix} x_{t+1}^1 \\ x_{t+1}^2 \end{pmatrix} + \check{K} u_t + \check{L} u_{t+1} + \check{M} \eta_t, \tag{10.37}
$$

where $u_t' = (u_{1t}', u_{2t}')$.

The form (10.37) has been used in Farmer (1999, Chapter 3). Recall that the x_t^2 variables are predetermined. The well-known condition for saddle point stability is that n_1 roots of J lie inside the unit circle. This is known as the "regular" case. The condition for a model to be regular is thus that the number of free variables be equal to the number of "forward stable" roots, i.e., roots of J with modulus less than 1. Making that assumption, and assuming also that J is diagonalizable,[11] we can write $Q^{-1} J Q = \Lambda$ as

$$
\begin{pmatrix} Q^{11} & Q^{12} \\ Q^{21} & Q^{22} \end{pmatrix} J = \begin{pmatrix} \Lambda_1 & 0 \\ 0 & \Lambda_2 \end{pmatrix} \begin{pmatrix} Q^{11} & Q^{12} \\ Q^{21} & Q^{22} \end{pmatrix}, \tag{10.38}
$$

where we have partitioned $Q^{-1} = (Q^{ij})$ and Λ so that Λ_1 contains the roots inside the unit circle. Multiplying equation (10.37) on the left by Q^{-1} and using equation (10.38), we have

$$
\begin{pmatrix} Q^{11} & Q^{12} \\ Q^{21} & Q^{22} \end{pmatrix} \begin{pmatrix} x_t^1 \\ x_t^2 \end{pmatrix} = \begin{pmatrix} \Lambda_1 & 0 \\ 0 & \Lambda_2 \end{pmatrix} \begin{pmatrix} Q^{11} & Q^{12} \\ Q^{21} & Q^{22} \end{pmatrix} \begin{pmatrix} x_{t+1}^1 \\ x_{t+1}^2 \end{pmatrix}
$$
$$
+ K u_t + L u_{t+1} + M \eta_t.
$$

---

[11] If J is not diagonalizable, the Jordan form can be used instead. See Blanchard and Kahn (1980) for details in the case of t dating of expectations.

Letting $p_t = Q^{11}x_t^1 + Q^{12}x_t^2$, the first set of equations can be written

$$p_t = \Lambda_1 p_{t+1} + K_1 u_t + L_1 u_{t+1} + M_1 \eta_t.$$

Taking the ith element of p_t yields $p_{t+1}^i = \lambda_i^{-1} p_t^i - \lambda_i^{-1} K_{1i} u_t - \lambda_i^{-1} L_{1i} u_{t+1} - \lambda_i^{-1} M_{1i} \eta_t$ provided $\lambda_i \neq 0$. This implies $E_t p_{t+1}^i = \lambda_i^{-1} p_t^i - \lambda_i^{-1} K_{1i} u_t - \lambda_i^{-1} M_{1i} \eta_t$ and also $E_t p_{t+s}^i = \lambda_i^{1-s} E_t p_{t+1}^i$ for $s > 1$. Since $|\lambda_i| < 1$, $|E_t p_{t+s}^i| \to \infty$ as $s \to \infty$ unless $E_t p_{t+1}^i = \lambda_i^{-1} p_t^i - \lambda_i^{-1} K_{1i} u_t - \lambda_i^{-1} M_{1i} \eta_t = 0$. Hence the unique stationary solution satisfies $p_t^i = K_{1i} u_t + M_{1i} \eta_t$ for $i = 1, \cdots, n_1$ so that $p_t = K_1 u_t + M_1 \eta_t.$[12]

Using the definition of p_t and assuming Q^{11} is invertible, we obtain

$$x_t^1 = -(Q^{11})^{-1} Q^{12} x_t^2 + (Q^{11})^{-1}(K_1 u_t + M_1 \eta_t). \qquad (10.39)$$

Since from equation (10.36) $x_t^2 = R x_{t-1}^1 + S x_{t-1}^2 + u_{2t}$, this equation can be written $x_t^1 = -(Q^{11})^{-1} Q^{12}(R x_{t-1}^1 + S x_{t-1}^2 + u_{2t}) + (Q^{11})^{-1}(K_1 u_t + M_1 \eta_t)$. Since $x_t^1 - E_{t-1} x_t^1 = C u_{2t} + u_{1t}$, we arrive at the unique stationary solution in VAR form

$$x_t^1 = -(Q^{11})^{-1} Q^{12} R x_{t-1}^1 - (Q^{11})^{-1} Q^{12} S x_{t-1}^2 + C u_{2t} + u_{1t}, \quad (10.40)$$
$$x_t^2 = R x_{t-1}^1 + S x_{t-1}^2 + u_{2t}. \qquad (10.41)$$

Finally, x_t^1 and x_t^2 can be substituted out to obtain a VAR in (y_t, w_t), i.e., in MSV form:

$$\tilde{y}_t = -(Q^{11})^{-1} Q^{12} R \tilde{y}_{t-1} - (Q^{11})^{-1} Q^{12} \begin{pmatrix} \delta^{22} \hat{y}_{t-1} + \hat{\kappa} \varphi w_{t-1} \\ 0 \\ \hat{y}_{t-1} \\ \varphi w_{t-1} \end{pmatrix}$$

$$+ C u_{2t} + u_{1t},$$

$$\hat{y}_t = \delta^{21} \tilde{y}_{t-1} + \delta^{22} \hat{y}_{t-1} + \hat{\kappa} \varphi w_{t-1} + \hat{\zeta} v_t + \hat{\kappa} e_t,$$

$$w_t = \varphi w_{t-1} + e_t.$$

Sticky Price Model Continued

We illustrate how the previous techniques for determining the unique stationary solution work in a concrete model using our introductory example (Example 1).

---

[12] If $\lambda_i = 0$, the same conclusion follows since then $p_t^i = K_{1it} u_t + L_{1i} u_{t+1} + M_{1i} \eta_t$. Operating with E_t on both sides yields $p_t^i = K_{1it} u_t + M_{1i} \eta_t$.

It is convenient to begin by rewriting equation (10.1) directly in the form (10.37). Introduce the notation $p_t^l = p_{t-1}$ and add to the system an equation of the form $p_t = p_{t+1}^l$. Next, move the equation for m_t forward for one time period, replace the expectations in equation (10.1) by their actual values, and add innovations to the equations accordingly.

After these operations, the model can be written as the following matrix system:

$$
\begin{pmatrix}
2 & -a_1 & 0 & 0 & -1 \\
b_1 & 1 & b_1 & 0 & 0 \\
-1 & -c_1 & c_2 & 1 & 0 \\
d_1 & d_2 & d_3 & d_4 & 0 \\
1 & 0 & 0 & 0 & 0
\end{pmatrix}
\begin{pmatrix}
p_t \\ q_t \\ r_t \\ m_t \\ p_t^l
\end{pmatrix}
\tag{10.42}
$$

$$
=
\begin{pmatrix}
1 & 0 & 0 & 0 & 0 \\
b_1 & 0 & 0 & 0 & 0 \\
0 & 0 & 0 & 0 & 0 \\
0 & 0 & 0 & 1 & 0 \\
0 & 0 & 0 & 0 & 1
\end{pmatrix}
\begin{pmatrix}
p_{t+1} \\ q_{t+1} \\ r_{t+1} \\ m_{t+1} \\ p_{t+1}^l
\end{pmatrix}
$$

$$
+
\begin{pmatrix}
v_{1t} \\ v_{2t} \\ v_{3t} \\ 0 \\ 0
\end{pmatrix}
+
\begin{pmatrix}
0 \\ 0 \\ 0 \\ -v_{4,t+1} \\ 0
\end{pmatrix}
+ \mathrm{inn}(t, t+1).
$$

For convenience we drop the intercepts, and $\mathrm{inn}(t, t+1)$ denotes the innovations arising from replacing the expectations in the structural model by their actual values. (We omit their precise form since it is not needed in what follows.) Multiplying through by the inverse of the 5×5 matrix on the left-hand side of equation (10.42), the model is now in standard form (10.37) with

$$
x_t^1 = \begin{pmatrix} p_t \\ q_t \\ r_t \end{pmatrix} \quad \text{and} \quad x_t^2 = \begin{pmatrix} m_t \\ p_t^l \end{pmatrix}.
$$

The methods of the previous section can thus be applied to obtain a VAR in $(x_t^{1\prime}, x_t^{2\prime})'$.

It is more convenient to write the solution as a VAR in $y_t' = (\, p_t \; q_t \; r_t \; m_t \,)'$. This can be done most readily as follows. Equation (10.1) implies that $x_t^1 -$

$E_{t-1}x_t^1 = G^{-1}(\begin{smallmatrix} v_{1t} & v_{2t} & v_{3t} \end{smallmatrix})'$, where

$$G = \begin{pmatrix} 1 & -a_1 & 0 \\ 0 & 1 & b_1 \\ -1 & -c_1 & c_2 \end{pmatrix},$$

and that $x_t^2 - E_{t-1}x_t^2 = (v_{4t}, 0)'$. Thus from equation (10.39), we have

$$x_t^1 = \Pi x_t^2 + G^{-1}(\begin{smallmatrix} v_{1t} & v_{2t} & v_{3t} \end{smallmatrix})' - \Pi(v_{4t}, 0)',$$

where $\Pi = -(Q^{11})^{-1}Q^{12}$ in the general notation developed in the preceding section. In order to obtain a convenient final form, we next note that

$$x_t^2 = \begin{pmatrix} d_1 & d_2 & d_3 & d_4 \\ 1 & 0 & 0 & 0 \end{pmatrix} \begin{pmatrix} p_{t-1} \\ q_{t-1} \\ r_{t-1} \\ m_{t-1} \end{pmatrix} + \begin{pmatrix} v_{4t} \\ 0 \end{pmatrix},$$

or in matrix form,

$$x_t^2 = Dy_{t-1} + \tilde{v}_t,$$

where $y_t = (\begin{smallmatrix} p_t & q_t & r_t & m_t \end{smallmatrix})'$ and $\tilde{v}_t = (\begin{smallmatrix} v_{4t} & 0 \end{smallmatrix})'$. Thus the unique stationary solution can be written as a VAR(1) in y_t with

$$y_t = \begin{pmatrix} \Pi D \\ d \end{pmatrix} y_{t-1} + Hv_t = Ay_{t-1} + Hv_t, \tag{10.43}$$

where $v_t = (\begin{smallmatrix} v_{1t} & v_{2t} & v_{3t} & v_{4t} \end{smallmatrix})'$, $d = (d_1, d_2, d_3, d_4)'$, and H depends on G and Π.

Numerical Example: Select the following parameter values: $a_1 = 0.5$, $b_1 = 0.1$, $c_1 = 1$, $c_2 = 0.2$, $d_1 = -d_2 = d_3 = 0.1$, $d_4 = 0.2$. Using the technique for finding the saddle point stable solution, it can be computed that the coefficient matrix A in equation (10.43) is

$$A = \begin{pmatrix} 0.7117 & -0.0104 & 0.0104 & 0.0209 \\ -0.2159 & -0.0296 & 0.0296 & 0.0591 \\ 1.978 & 0.300 & -0.300 & -0.6001 \\ 0.100 & -0.100 & 0.100 & 0.200 \end{pmatrix}.$$

Models with Contemporaneous Expectations

Here we redo our analysis using the alternative model (10.15) reproduced here for convenience with $E_t^* y_{t+1} = E_t y_{t+1}$ under RE:[13]

$$y_t = \alpha + \beta E_t y_{t+1} + \delta y_{t-1} + \kappa w_t,$$

$$w_t = \varphi w_{t-1} + e_t.$$

$$(10.44)$$

The MSV solutions now have the form

$$y_t = a + b y_{t-1} + c w_t,$$

where the coefficient matrices satisfy equations (10.17)–(10.19). We here consider the saddle point stable case.

The technique introduced in the previous subsection is developed as follows. The relevant general formulation of the reduced form is

$$x_t^1 = B_1 E_t x_{t+1}^1 + C x_t^2,$$

$$x_t^2 = R x_{t-1}^1 + S x_{t-1}^2 + u_t,$$

$$(10.45)$$

where again x_t^1 are the nonpredetermined or free variables and x_t^2 are the predetermined variables.

We next put the reduced form (10.44) into the form (10.45). Divide y_t into free and predetermined variables, so that we have

$$\begin{pmatrix} \tilde{y}_t \\ \hat{y}_t \end{pmatrix} = \begin{pmatrix} \tilde{\alpha} \\ \hat{\alpha} \end{pmatrix} + \begin{pmatrix} \beta^{11} & \beta^{12} \\ 0 & 0 \end{pmatrix} \begin{pmatrix} E_t \tilde{y}_{t+1} \\ E_t \hat{y}_{t+1} \end{pmatrix}$$

$$+ \begin{pmatrix} \delta^{11} & \delta^{12} \\ \delta^{21} & \delta^{22} \end{pmatrix} \begin{pmatrix} \tilde{y}_{t-1} \\ \hat{y}_{t-1} \end{pmatrix} + \begin{pmatrix} \tilde{\kappa} \\ \hat{\kappa} \end{pmatrix} w_t.$$

First, we center the variables (i.e., set $\alpha = 0$) and, without changing notation for convenience, then define

$$x_t^1 = \tilde{y}_t \quad \text{and} \quad x_t^2 = \begin{pmatrix} \hat{y}_t \\ \tilde{y}_{t-1} \\ \hat{y}_{t-1} \\ w_t \end{pmatrix}.$$

---

[13] Note that any iid shocks to the first equation can be included as components of w_t.

Thus we arrive at equation (10.45) with

$$x_t^1 = (I - \beta^{12}\delta^{21})^{-1}[\beta^{11}E_t x_{t+1}^1 + (\beta^{12}\delta^{22}, \delta^{11}, \delta^{12}, \tilde{\kappa} + \hat{\kappa}\varphi)x_t^2],$$

$$x_t^2 = \begin{pmatrix} \delta^{21} \\ I \\ 0 \\ 0 \end{pmatrix} x_{t-1}^1 + \begin{pmatrix} \delta^{22} & 0 & 0 & \hat{\kappa}\varphi \\ 0 & 0 & 0 & 0 \\ I & 0 & 0 & 0 \\ 0 & 0 & 0 & \varphi \end{pmatrix} x_{t-1}^2 + \begin{pmatrix} \hat{\kappa}e_t \\ 0 \\ 0 \\ e_t \end{pmatrix}.$$

Returning to the general formulation and letting $\eta_{t+1} = x_{t+1}^1 - E_t x_{t+1}^1$, we rewrite equation (10.45) as

$$\begin{pmatrix} I & -C \\ R & S \end{pmatrix}\begin{pmatrix} x_t^1 \\ x_t^2 \end{pmatrix} = \begin{pmatrix} B_1 & 0 \\ 0 & I \end{pmatrix}\begin{pmatrix} x_{t+1}^1 \\ x_{t+1}^2 \end{pmatrix} + \begin{pmatrix} 0 & -B_1 \\ -I & 0 \end{pmatrix}\begin{pmatrix} u_{t+1} \\ \eta_{t+1} \end{pmatrix},$$

or

$$\begin{pmatrix} x_t^1 \\ x_t^2 \end{pmatrix} = J\begin{pmatrix} x_{t+1}^1 \\ x_{t+1}^2 \end{pmatrix} + L\vartheta_{t+1}. \tag{10.46}$$

Factoring J as before,

$$\begin{pmatrix} Q^{11} & Q^{12} \\ Q^{21} & Q^{22} \end{pmatrix} J = \begin{pmatrix} \Lambda_1 & 0 \\ 0 & \Lambda_2 \end{pmatrix}\begin{pmatrix} Q^{11} & Q^{12} \\ Q^{21} & Q^{22} \end{pmatrix},$$

and assuming that the number of roots of J inside the unit circle is equal to the dimension of x_t^1, the same arguments as before lead to the restriction $x_t^1 = -(Q^{11})^{-1}Q^{12}x_t^2$. Thus the solution is

$$x_t^1 = -(Q^{11})^{-1}Q^{12}Rx_{t-1}^1 - (Q^{11})^{-1}Q^{12}Sx_{t-1}^2 - (Q^{11})^{-1}Q^{12}u_t$$
$$x_t^2 = Rx_{t-1}^1 + Sx_{t-1}^2 + u_t.$$

10.8.2   Representing Irregular REE

The method of Section 10.8.1 can also be used to calculate the full set of stationary solutions in the irregular case, in which there are multiple stationary solutions. The irregular case corresponds to the condition that the number of free variables be larger than the number of forward stable roots (roots of J inside the unit circle).

Models with $t - 1$ Dating of Expectations

We begin again with the representation of the reduced form (10.36) in terms of predetermined and free variables. After defining innovations as before, we arrive at equation (10.37). We first note that, if J is invertible, then the full set of solutions, including any explosive solutions, can be written in the form

$$\begin{pmatrix} x_t^1 \\ x_t^2 \end{pmatrix} = J^{-1} \begin{pmatrix} x_{t-1}^1 \\ x_{t-1}^2 \end{pmatrix} - J^{-1}\check{L}u_t - J^{-1}\check{K}u_{t-1} - J^{-1}\check{M}\eta_{t-1}.$$

Usually, however, we want to restrict attention to stationary solutions, and in particular to MSV solutions augmented by a sunspot variable.

Assuming that J is diagonalizable, we have $Q^{-1}JQ = \Lambda$, and we conformably partition Q^{-1} and $(x_t^{1\prime}, x_t^{2\prime})'$ as

$$Q^{-1} = \begin{pmatrix} Q^{11}(1,1) & Q^{11}(1,2) & Q^{12}(1) \\ Q^{11}(2,1) & Q^{11}(2,2) & Q^{12}(2) \\ Q^{21}(1) & Q^{21}(2) & Q^{22} \end{pmatrix}$$

and

$$\begin{pmatrix} x_t^1 \\ x_t^2 \end{pmatrix} = \begin{pmatrix} x_t^{1*} \\ x_t^{1\#} \\ x_t^2 \end{pmatrix}.$$

The system becomes

$$Q^{-1}\begin{pmatrix} x_t^{1*} \\ x_t^{1\#} \\ x_t^2 \end{pmatrix} = \begin{pmatrix} \Lambda_1^* & 0 & 0 \\ 0 & \Lambda_1^\# & 0 \\ 0 & 0 & \Lambda_2 \end{pmatrix} Q^{-1}\begin{pmatrix} x_{t+1}^{1*} \\ x_{t+1}^{1\#} \\ x_{t+1}^2 \end{pmatrix} \quad (10.47)$$

$$+ \begin{pmatrix} K_1^* \\ K_1^\# \\ K_2 \end{pmatrix} u_t + \begin{pmatrix} L_1^* \\ L_1^\# \\ L_2 \end{pmatrix} u_{t+1} + \begin{pmatrix} M_1^* \\ M_1^\# \\ M_2 \end{pmatrix} \eta_t.$$

Here Λ_1^* is a diagonal matrix containing the roots of J that lie inside the unit circle and $\Lambda_1^\#$ and Λ_2 are diagonal matrices that contain the roots outside the unit circle (we excluded from consideration cases with roots on the unit circle). In the irregular case, n_1 (the dimension of free variables x_t^1) is larger than s, the number of roots of J inside the unit circle. (The allocation of roots between $\Lambda_1^\#$ and Λ_2 is not unique. A standard procedure is to arrange the eigenvalues in the order of nondecreasing modulus.)

Consideration of the first block of equations from (10.47) leads to the side conditions which rule out explosive solutions. Defining $p_t = Q^{11}(1,1)x_t^{1*} + Q^{11}(1,2)x_t^{1\#} + Q^{12}(1)x_t^2$, we have $p_t = \Lambda_1^* p_{t+1} + K_1^* u_t + L_1^* u_{t+1} + M_1^* \eta_t$.

Following the procedure in Section 10.8.1, we obtain the conditions $p_t = K_1^* u_t + M_1^* \eta_t$, i.e.,

$$Q^{11}(1,1)x_t^{1*} + Q^{11}(1,2)x_t^{1\#} + Q^{12}(1)x_t^2 = K_1^* u_t + M_1^* \eta_t. \qquad (10.48)$$

Turning to the second block of equations from (10.47) leads to the equations

$$Q^{11}(2,1)x_t^{1*} + Q^{11}(2,2)x_t^{1\#} + Q^{12}(2)x_t^2 \qquad (10.49)$$
$$= (\Lambda_1^\#)^{-1}Q^{11}(2,1)x_{t-1}^{1*} + (\Lambda_1^\#)^{-1}Q^{11}(2,2)x_{t-1}^{1\#}$$
$$+ (\Lambda_1^\#)^{-1}Q^{12}(2)x_{t-1}^2 - (\Lambda_1^\#)^{-1}L_1^\# u_t + \zeta_t,$$

where $\zeta_t = -(\Lambda_1^\#)^{-1}K_1^\# u_{t-1} - (\Lambda_1^\#)^{-1}M_1^\# \eta_{t-1}$. Recall that η_t is an arbitrary process satisfying $E_{t-1}\eta_t = 0$. If $M_1^\#$ has full rank, it follows that ζ_t may be taken to be an arbitrary process satisfying $E_{t-1}\zeta_t = 0$. Note that $\dim(\zeta_t) = n_1 - s$.

Assuming that

$$Q^{11} = \begin{pmatrix} Q^{11}(1,1) & Q^{11}(1,2) \\ Q^{11}(2,1) & Q^{11}(2,2) \end{pmatrix}$$

is invertible, equations (10.48) and (10.49) can be solved simultaneously for x_t^{1*} and $x_t^{1\#}$ in terms of $x_t^2, x_{t-1}^{1*}, x_{t-1}^2, u_t$, and ζ_t. From equation (10.36), recall that $x_t^2 = R x_{t-1}^1 + S x_{t-1}^2 + u_{2t}$. Partitioning $R' = ((R^*)' \ (R^\#)')$ and substituting for x_t^2, and also recalling that

$$\begin{pmatrix} x_t^{1*} \\ x_t^{1\#} \end{pmatrix} - E_{t-1}\begin{pmatrix} x_t^{1*} \\ x_t^{1\#} \end{pmatrix} = Cu_{2t} + u_{1t},$$

we obtain

$$\begin{pmatrix} x_t^{1*} \\ x_t^{1\#} \end{pmatrix} = (Q^{11})^{-1}\begin{pmatrix} -Q^{12}(1)S \\ -Q^{12}(2)S + (\Lambda_1^\#)^{-1}Q^{12}(2) \end{pmatrix}x_{t-1}^2$$
$$+ (Q^{11})^{-1}\begin{pmatrix} -Q^{12}(1)R^* & -Q^{12}(1)\hat{R} \\ -Q^{12}(2)R^* + (\Lambda_1^\#)^{-1}Q^{11}(2,1) & -Q^{12}(2)R^\# + (\Lambda_1^\#)^{-1}Q^{11}(2,2) \end{pmatrix}$$
$$\times \begin{pmatrix} x_{t-1}^{1*} \\ x_{t-1}^{1\#} \end{pmatrix} + (Q^{11})^{-1}\begin{pmatrix} 0 \\ \zeta_{t-1} \end{pmatrix} + Cu_{2t} + u_{1t},$$
$$x_t^2 = R^* x_{t-1}^{1*} + R^\# x_{t-1}^{1\#} + S x_{t-1}^2 + u_{2t}.$$

This expression is not in a VAR(1) form in terms of (y_t, w_t) since the right-hand side of the first equation involves x_{t-1}^2 which in turn depends on $\tilde{y}_{t-2}$ and $\hat{y}_{t-2}$. This reflects the fact that, as in univariate models, sunspot solutions are in general higher than first order in the endogenous variables.

Irregular Equilibria, t Dating of Expectations

Finally, we apply the same technique to the reduced form (10.44) which has t dating of expectations. We start from the form (10.46) and, as in the irregular case with $t-1$ dating, factor J as $Q^{-1}JQ = \Lambda$, where

$$
Q^{-1} = \begin{pmatrix} Q^{11}(1,1) & Q^{11}(1,2) & Q^{12}(1) \\ Q^{11}(2,1) & Q^{11}(2,2) & Q^{12}(2) \\ Q^{21}(1) & Q^{21}(2) & Q^{22} \end{pmatrix}.
$$

We also divide the free variables into two sets

$$
x_t^1 = \begin{pmatrix} x_t^{1*} \\ x_t^{1\#} \end{pmatrix}
$$

so that equation (10.46) can be written as

$$
Q^{-1} \begin{pmatrix} x_t^{1*} \\ x_t^{1\#} \\ x_t^2 \end{pmatrix} = \begin{pmatrix} \Lambda_1^* & 0 & 0 \\ 0 & \Lambda_1^\# & 0 \\ 0 & 0 & \Lambda_2 \end{pmatrix} Q^{-1} \begin{pmatrix} x_{t+1}^{1*} \\ x_{t+1}^{1\#} \\ x_{t+1}^2 \end{pmatrix} + \begin{pmatrix} L_1^* \\ L_1^\# \\ L_2 \end{pmatrix} \vartheta_{t+1},
$$

where $\vartheta_{t+1}' = (u_{t+1}', \eta_{t+1}')$. Here the diagonal matrix Λ_1^* contains the eigenvalues with modulus less than 1.

If the matrix $Q^{11} = (Q^{11}(i,j))$ in the top-left corner of Q^{-1} is invertible, we get the solutions

$$
\begin{pmatrix} x_t^{1*} \\ x_t^{1\#} \end{pmatrix} = (Q^{11})^{-1} \begin{pmatrix} -Q^{12}(1)x_t^2 \\ z_t \end{pmatrix},
$$

where

$$
z_t = -Q^{12}(2)x_t^2 + (\Lambda_1^\#)^{-1}Q^{11}(2,1)x_{t-1}^{1*} + (\Lambda_1^\#)^{-1}Q^{11}(2,2)x_{t-1}^{1\#} \\ + (\Lambda_1^\#)^{-1}Q^{12}(2)x_{t-1}^2 - (\Lambda_1^\#)^{-1}L_1^*\vartheta_t,
$$

and

$$
x_t^2 = Rx_{t-1}^1 + Sx_{t-1}^2 + u_t.
$$

These expressions are a VAR(1) in $(x_t^{1\prime}, x_t^{2\prime})'$, but in terms of y_t, w_t they are of higher order. As already noted in the preceding subsection, this is the general case with sunspot solutions. For special models it may be possible to obtain sunspot solutions which are VAR(1) in y_t, w_t. This happens in the application to the Farmer–Guo model.

Part IV
Learning in Nonlinear Models

Chapter **11**

Nonlinear Models: Steady States

11.1 Introduction

In Chapter 4 several nonlinear economic models were introduced for the study of learning dynamics. Some of these models have unique equilibria, while in others multiple equilibria may prevail, as was illustrated in that chapter. The equilibria in nonlinear models can take different forms, such as steady states, cycles, and sunspot equilibria, and the models in Chapter 4 provided examples of these types of equilibria. We now start to analyze systematically adaptive learning in nonlinear models. Our emphasis will be on stochastic models, i.e., models which include intrinsic random shocks such as preference or productivity shocks, though we will briefly consider nonstochastic cases as well. We will develop the stability conditions under learning for these different kinds of REE for certain classes of nonlinear models. A key feature of the analysis is that we do not approximate the model by a linearization around a steady state. Instead, the exact equilibrium solutions are considered for stability. Many of the results concern local stability, but for some specific models global results are also presented.

We consider nonlinear models, e.g., univariate models of the form

$$y_t = F(y_{t+1})^e \quad \text{or} \tag{11.1}$$

$$y_t = F(y_{t+1})^e + v_t, \tag{11.2}$$

where F is a nonlinear function and v_t is an exogenous shock. Throughout this chapter we will assume that v_t is iid with $E(v_t) = 0$. Here $F(y_{t+1})^e$ denotes the expectation of $F(y_{t+1})$ formed at time t. Note that we are distinguishing between deterministic models and models which have intrinsic random shocks.

Recall that the basic overlapping generations (OG) model with production and a constant money stock, described in Chapter 4, yields a nonlinear nonstochastic difference equation of the form (11.1), where the form of F depends on the underlying utility (and production) functions. Below, we see how to incorporate intrinsic noise. In fact, adding productivity shocks into even simple versions of the basic OG model turns out to require the more general reduced form

$$y_t = H\big(G(y_{t+1}, v_{t+1})^e, v_t\big). \tag{11.3}$$

We develop the main results using the general framework (11.3), though the special cases (11.1) and (11.2) are sometimes used for illustrations.

Before developing the results in general, we summarize some central findings. Recall from Section 3.4 of Chapter 3 that for a nonstochastic model of the form $y_t = F(y_{t+1}^e)$, a perfect-foresight steady state $\hat{y} = F(\hat{y})$ is locally stable under adaptive learning if $F'(\hat{y}) < 1$ and locally unstable if $F'(\hat{y}) > 1$. This result holds for decreasing gain or sufficiently small constant gain, and it can be easily verified that this result also holds for models of the form $y_t = F(y_{t+1})^e$. Stochastic models of the form (11.2)–(11.3) do not have perfect-foresight steady states, but they may have rational "noisy steady states," i.e., iid solutions for y_t. In particular, for the model (11.2) there may be solutions of the form $y_t = \bar{y} + v_t$.

The stability results under learning are particularly simple for the model (11.2) if the random shock v_t has sufficiently small support, i.e., if the possible range of values for v_t lies in a sufficiently small interval. It can be shown that in this case there does exist a noisy steady state of the form $y_t = \bar{y} + v_t$, where $\bar{y}$ is close to the perfect-foresight steady state $\hat{y} = F(\hat{y})$ corresponding to $v_t \equiv 0$. Furthermore, we will demonstrate that this noisy steady state is locally stable under adaptive learning when $F'(\hat{y}) < 1$ and locally unstable under adaptive learning when $F'(\hat{y}) > 1$. This result extends to models of the form (11.3) by defining $F(y) = H(G(y, 0), 0)$. For the case in which the support of the noise need not be "small," we develop an extension of this result and interpret it in terms of E-stability. In general, as we shall see, the local stability under adaptive learning of a noisy steady state does depend on the distribution of the stochastic shock.

Throughout this chapter we make the assumption that the mappings F, G, and H are twice continuously differentiable on some open rectangles (possibly infinite). Before taking up the issue of adaptive learning, we first consider some aspects of equilibrium solutions to models of the above forms.

11.2 Equilibria under Perfect Foresight

In models of the form (11.1) the existence of steady states, cycles, and sunspots depends on the shape of F. Recall from Chapter 4 that in the basic OG model with production, the first-order condition for expected utility maximization is

$$E_t^*\left[U'\left(\frac{n_t p_t}{p_{t+1}}\right)\left(\frac{p_t}{p_{t+1}}\right) - V'(n_t)\right] = 0,$$

where n_t is employment and p_t is the money price of goods. With a constant money supply M, the equilibrium condition is $p_t n_t = M$, which implies $p_t/p_{t+1} = n_{t+1}/n_t$, so that $E_t^*[U'(n_{t+1})(n_{t+1}/n_t)] = V'(n_t)$ or

$$n_t V'(n_t) = \left(n_{t+1} U'(n_{t+1})\right)^e,$$

where for convenience we here write $(\bullet)^e$ for $E_t^*[\bullet]$.

Under perfect foresight the equilibrium equation becomes $n_t V'(n_t) = n_{t+1} U'(n_{t+1})$. Since $(d/dn) n V'(n) > 0$, the model can be solved as

$$n_t = \mathcal{F}(n_{t+1}). \tag{11.4}$$

Depending on U and V, the function $\mathcal{F}$ can be either monotonically increasing or hump-shaped; see, e.g., Grandmont (1985) for illustrations. A *steady state* is a solution $n_t = \hat{n}$, where $\hat{n}$ satisfies $\hat{n} = \mathcal{F}(\hat{n})$. A *k-cycle* is defined by a k-tuple $(\hat{n}_1, \ldots, \hat{n}_k)$ and satisfies

$$
\begin{aligned}
n_t &= \hat{n}_i &&\text{if } t \,(\mathrm{mod}\,k) = i, \quad i = 1, \ldots, k-1, \\
n_t &= \hat{n}_k &&\text{if } t \,(\mathrm{mod}\,k) = 0, \quad \text{where} \\
\hat{n}_i &= \mathcal{F}(\hat{n}_{i+1}) &&\text{for } i = 1, \ldots, k-1, \quad \text{and} \\
\hat{n}_k &= \mathcal{F}(\hat{n}_1).
\end{aligned}
$$

Figure 11.1 illustrates steady state, 2-cycle, and 3-cycle solutions. In this chapter we analyze steady-state solutions. k-cycles will be discussed in the next chapter.

11.3 Noisy Steady States

Consider now models with intrinsic noise. These arise, for example, when a stochastic taste or productivity shock is introduced into the basic OG model. We first present some economic examples of nonlinear models with noise and then describe the generalization of the models of perfect-foresight steady states to incorporate this noise (noisy cycles will be treated in the next chapter).

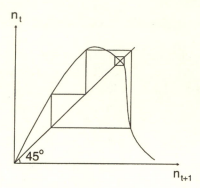

Figure 11.1.

11.3.1   Economic Examples

Example 1: In the basic OG model with production, agents supply labor n_t and produce (perishable) output when young and consume c_{t+1} when old. Output is equal to labor supply and there is a fixed quantity of money M. Holding money is the only mechanism for saving. (See Section 4.2 of Chapter 4 for further details on the model.) We introduce a random taste shock by assuming that the utility function is

$$U(c_{t+1}) - V(n_t) + \epsilon_t \ln(n_t).$$

Here ϵ_t is an iid positive random shock to the disutility of labor and we assume that ϵ_t is known to the agents who are young at time t.[1] The first-order condition for maximizing expected utility thus is $V'(n_t) - \epsilon_t/n_t = E_t^*(p_t/p_{t+1})U'(c_{t+1})$. Combining with the market-clearing condition $c_{t+1} = n_{t+1}$ and using $p_t/p_{t+1} = n_{t+1}/n_t$, we get

$$n_t V'(n_t) - \epsilon_t = \left(n_{t+1} U'(n_{t+1})\right)^e.$$

Finally, if we change variables from n to $y = \vartheta(n)$, where $\vartheta(n) \equiv nV'(n)$ [note that $\vartheta(n)$ is increasing for all $n \geq 0$], we obtain equation (11.2), where $v_t \equiv \epsilon_t - E(\epsilon_t)$.

---

[1]Letting $\tilde{V}(n) = V(n) - \epsilon \ln(n)$, we have $\tilde{V}'(n) = V'(n) - \epsilon/n$ and $\tilde{V}''(n) = V''(n) + \epsilon/n^2$. Under the standard assumptions $V', V'' > 0$, we see that with $\epsilon > 0$ we have $\tilde{V}'(n) > 0$ for n sufficiently large and $\tilde{V}''(n) > 0$ for all $n \geq 0$. Thus, the marginal disutility of labor $\tilde{V}'(n)$ may be negative at small n but we have the required assumptions needed for a well-defined interior solution to the household maximization problem.

Example 2: The technique used in Example 1 to transform the model to the form (11.2) cannot always be used when there are intrinsic shocks. (It should be apparent that the technique requires very special assumptions on utility.) As a result, the more general form (11.3) is usually required when there are intrinsic shocks. As an illustration, consider the case of additive productivity shocks. We return to the assumption that utility is given by

$$U(c_{t+1}) - V(n_t),$$

but now assume that output Q_t is given by

$$Q_t = n_t + \lambda_t,$$

where λ_t is an iid positive productivity shock. The budget constraints are now $p_{t+1}c_{t+1} = M$ and $p_t Q_t = M$, and the first-order condition plus the market-clearing condition $Q_{t+1} = c_{t+1}$ and $p_t/p_{t+1} = Q_{t+1}/Q_t$ yields

$$(n_t + \lambda_t)V'(n_t) = \big((n_{t+1} + \lambda_{t+1})U'(n_{t+1} + \lambda_{t+1})\big)^e.$$

Since $(n + \lambda)V'(n)$ is strictly increasing in n, and letting $v_t \equiv \lambda_t - E(\lambda_t)$, this equation can be solved for n_t and put in the form (11.3) where $y_t \equiv n_t$.

11.3.2   Definition of Noisy Steady States

For the models with intrinsic noise, we now consider the REE (rational expectations equilibria) which are analogs to perfect-foresight steady states. We start with the simplest case: a noisy steady state for the model (11.2). Under rational expectations we have

$$y_t = E_t F(y_{t+1}) + v_t,$$

and we look for a solution of the form

$$y_t = \bar{y} + v_t. \tag{11.5}$$

It follows that $\bar{y}$ must satisfy

$$\bar{y} = EF(\bar{y} + v_t).$$

In general, because F is nonlinear, we cannot be sure that a solution of the form (11.5) exists even if we know that F has a fixed point $\hat{y}$, i.e., if $\hat{y} = F(\hat{y})$.

However, we can state an existence result for the case of "small noise," when there is a perfect-foresight steady state $\hat{y}$ in the nonstochastic model. Informally (we will state the result more precisely in a moment), provided the intrinsic shock is "small" in the sense that it has small bounded support, there exists a noisy steady-state REE of the form (11.5) with $\bar{y}$ near $\hat{y}$.

More generally, consider a noisy steady-state REE for the model (11.3). This is defined by a function $y(v_t)$ such that

$$y(v_t) = H\big(EG(y(v_{t+1}), v_{t+1}), v_t\big).$$

Here the expectation is taken over the distribution of the shocks v_{t+1}. Letting $\bar{\theta} = EG(y(v_{t+1}), v_{t+1})$, note that $y(v_t) = H(\bar{\theta}, v_t)$, so that a noisy steady state is equivalently defined by a value $\bar{\theta}$ satisfying

$$\bar{\theta} = EG\big(H(\bar{\theta}, v_t), v_t\big).$$

As mentioned above, it can be shown that noisy steady states exist near steady states of the corresponding nonstochastic model, provided the noise is sufficiently small. More precisely, defining

$$F(y) \equiv H\big(G(y, 0), 0\big),$$

so that in the nonstochastic case $v_t \equiv 0$ for all t, then under perfect foresight we have

$$y_t = F(y_{t+1}).$$

Suppose $\hat{y}$ constitutes a perfect-foresight steady state for this nonstochastic case. Corresponding to this solution are perfect-foresight expectations

$$\hat{\theta} = G(\hat{y}, 0).$$

Now consider a family of distribution functions for v_t, $W_\alpha(v)$, parameterized continuously by α with $W_\alpha(-\alpha) = 0$ and $W_\alpha(\alpha) = 1$, so that the family converges as $\alpha \to 0$ to the nonstochastic case $W_0(v) = 0$ for $v < 0$, $W_0(v) = 1$ for $v \geq 0$ (i.e., $v = 0$ with probability 1). Then it can be shown that by choosing distributions W_α with α sufficiently small, there exist noisy steady states $\bar{\theta}(\alpha)$ arbitrarily close to $\hat{\theta}$. The proof, which is given in Evans and Honkapohja (1995c), is based on a version of the implicit function theorem (and it also requires appropriate regularity conditions to hold at $\hat{\theta}$).

11.4 Adaptive Learning for Steady States

We now introduce adaptive learning. Suppose agents believe they are in a noisy steady state and at time t have estimates θ_t for the expected values of $G(y_t, v_t)$ in the steady state. In the REE $y_t = y(v_t)$ is iid and hence $G(y_t, v_t) = G(y(v_t), v_t)$ is iid with mean $\theta = EG(y(v_t), v_t)$. A natural estimator of θ is then simply the sample mean

$$\theta_t = t^{-1} \sum_{j=1}^{t} G(y_j, v_j).$$

Somewhat more generally, we consider the recursive version of this algorithm

$$\theta_t = \theta_{t-1} + \gamma_t \big(G(y_t, v_t) - \theta_{t-1} \big), \tag{11.6}$$

where γ_t is a sequence of decreasing-gain parameters satisfying the usual assumptions. (If θ_t is simply the sample mean, then $\gamma_t = t^{-1}$.)

The rest of the dynamic system is then given by equation (11.3) with $G(y_{t+1}, v_{t+1})^e = \theta_{t-1}$, i.e.,

$$y_t = H(\theta_{t-1}, v_t). \tag{11.7}$$

[Here we are making the convenient assumption that only the values of $G(y_i, v_i)$ through time $t - 1$ are used to forecast $G(y_{t+1}, v_{t+1})^e$. This avoids simultaneity between the forecast and y_t which would result in additional technical complications.] Combining equations (11.6) and (11.7), we obtain the following equation which fully describes the system under learning dynamics:

$$\theta_t = \theta_{t-1} + \gamma_t \big(G(H(\theta_{t-1}, v_t), v_t) - \theta_{t-1} \big). \tag{11.8}$$

It is apparent that this equation fits directly into the framework of stochastic recursive algorithms and if, for example, G and H have bounded second derivatives, then equation (11.8) satisfies the basic conditions (A) and (B) of Chapter 6. It is therefore straightforward to analyze convergence of θ_t to an REE steady-state value using the results for recursive stochastic algorithms.

11.5 E-Stability and Learning

Before stating the formal convergence results under adaptive learning, we derive what will turn out to be the appropriate stability condition using the E-stability principle. Recall that under this principle we focus on the mapping from a vector of parameters characterizing the *perceived law of motion* (PLM) to the implied parameter vector characterizing the *actual law of motion* (ALM). Although the noisy steady state is formally defined by a function $y(v_t)$, the agents in the model are only concerned with the expected value of $G(y_{t+1}, v_{t+1})$ in their forecasting and decision making and so learning concerns the equilibrium value of a parameter (and not the whole function).

For learning of a steady state the estimate is $\theta_t = G(y_{t+1}, v_{t+1})^e$. This PLM leads to the ALM $T(\theta) \equiv E(G(H(\theta, v_t), v_t))$, and the definition of E-stability is based on the differential equation

$$d\theta/d\tau = T\big(\theta(\tau)\big) - \theta(\tau), \tag{11.9}$$

where τ denotes notional time. It is easily seen that the fixed points of this T-mapping define a noisy state for this model, and we immediately have the result:

Proposition 11.1. *A noisy steady state $\bar{\theta}$ is E-stable if $T'(\bar{\theta}) < 1$ and it is unstable if $T'(\bar{\theta}) > 1$.*

Clearly, barring exceptional cases, steady states can be divided into stable and unstable fixed points. The stability property alternates as θ is increased in the set of steady states.

We remark that in Chapter 12 we will refer to the condition $T'(\bar{\theta}) < 1$ as the *weak E-stability* condition for a noisy steady state. This is because, as we will there show, a stronger condition must be satisfied to guarantee local stability if the PLM is overparameterized as a regular cycle.

This E-stability condition is also the condition guaranteeing local convergence of θ_t under the learning rule (11.8) since, as noted, the learning rule satisfies the conditions (A) and (B) of Chapter 6. The associated differential equation for the algorithm takes the form

$$\begin{aligned} d\theta/d\tau &= \lim_{t \to \infty} EG\big(H(\theta, v_t), v_t\big) - \theta \\ &= T(\theta) - \theta. \end{aligned}$$

But this is simply the differential equation defining E-stability of a noisy steady state $\bar{\theta}$, and we have proved the following.

Proposition 11.2. *A noisy steady state $\bar{\theta}$ is locally stable under adaptive learning if it is E-stable, i.e., if $T'(\bar{\theta}) < 1$. If $T'(\bar{\theta}) > 1$, then θ_t converges to $\bar{\theta}$ with probability zero.*

By "locally stable" under adaptive learning we mean various more specific statements made explicit in Chapter 6:[2]

(1) Convergence with positive probability for nearby initial points.
(2) Convergence with probability close to 1 for nearby initial points and sufficiently low adaption rates.
(3) Convergence with probability 1 if a sufficiently small projection facility is used.

Finally, consider the nonstochastic case $y_t = H(G(y_{t+1})^e)$. Under perfect foresight, $y_t = F(y_{t+1})$, where $F = H \circ G$. In the nonstochastic case, $T(\theta) = G(H(\theta))$, so that $T'(\bar{\theta}) = G'(H(\bar{\theta}))H'(\bar{\theta})$ and $F'(\bar{y}) = H'(G(\bar{y}))G'(\bar{y})$. Using $\bar{y} = H(\bar{\theta})$ and $\bar{\theta} = G(\bar{y})$, we have $T'(\bar{\theta}) = F'(\bar{y})$. Thus in the nonstochastic case, the stability condition in Proposition 11.2 is simply $F'(\bar{y}) < 1$. In fact, in the nonstochastic case, a stronger version of Proposition 11.2 holds since one can use the results of Section 7.2 of Chapter 7: For all nearby initial values, $\theta_t \to \bar{\theta}$ if $T'(\bar{\theta}) = F'(\bar{y}) < 1$ and θ_t diverges if the reverse inequality is true. No projection facility is required in the nonstochastic case. In the stochastic case with small noise, it follows from continuity of derivatives that $T'(\bar{\theta})$ is close to $F'(\bar{y})$. Thus in Proposition 11.2 the condition $F'(\bar{y}) < 1$ governs local stability of noisy steady states for sufficiently small noise.[3]

***Example 3:* A Model with Small or Large Shocks.** We consider the basic setup (11.3) when the support of the shock v_t may be small or large. Consider Example 2 with the functional forms $U(c) = c^{1-\sigma}/(1 - \sigma)$, $V(n) = n^{1+\varepsilon}/(1 + \varepsilon)$, and a uniform distribution for v_t over $[-\alpha, \alpha]$. Choosing parameter values $\sigma = 4.0, \varepsilon = 1$, and $E(\lambda) = 0.6$ for $\alpha = 0$, then a numerical computation yields the (nonstochastic) steady-state value of $\bar{\theta} = 0.645$ and this steady state is E-stable for learning $[T'(\bar{\theta}) = -0.975]$. Thus for $\alpha > 0$ sufficiently small, the stochastic steady states will also be stable. If in their PLM, agents allow for the possibility that the economy is in a 2-cycle, then the stability of the steady state can be delicate. This issue turns on the distinction between weak and strong E-stability which we take up in the next chapter. We will there return to this example and show that in this case the stability properties of the steady state depend on the size of the support of the random shock. At that point we will also provide numerical results for this example.

---

[2]Statements (2) and (3) are immediate from Corollaries 6.6 and 6.8. We also have result (1) since for this example it is easy to see that the conditions of Corollary 6.7 hold.

[3]In fact, for sufficiently small noise it is possible to obtain local convergence almost surely even if the learning rule has no projection facility; see Evans and Honkapohja (1995c).

11.6 Applications

11.6.1 Increasing Social Returns with Random Shocks

We consider a version of the increasing social returns model of Section 4.6. We make two changes to the earlier model.[4] First, we allow for government consumption financed by seignorage, so that $M_{t+1} = M_t + p_{t+1}g_{t+1}$. In this section we assume that government purchases are a fraction ζ_t of output, i.e., $g_t = \zeta_t Q_t$. Thus from the market-clearing condition $p_t Q_t = M_t$, we obtain

$$p_t/p_{t+1} = (1 - \zeta_{t+1})Q_{t+1}/Q_t.$$

The second modification is that we introduce a random productivity shock, so that

$$Q_t = f(n_t, N_t)v_t,$$

where v_t is a positive iid random productivity shock with mean equal to 1. Here, of course, $N_t = \ell n_t$, where ℓ is the number of agents, captures the positive production externality. As in Section 4.6, we assume the production function takes the form $f(n_t, N_t) = n_t^\alpha \psi(N_t)$ so that $Q_t = n_t^\alpha \psi(N_t)v_t$.

The household's first-order condition is

$$V'(n_t) = E_t^* \left(\frac{p_t}{p_{t+1}} f_1(n_t, N_t)v_t U'(c_{t+1}) \right).$$

Using also $c_{t+1} = p_t Q_t/p_{t+1}$, this can be written as

$$V'(n_t) = E_t^* \left(\frac{p_t}{p_{t+1}} \alpha Q_t n_t^{-1} U'(p_t Q_t/p_{t+1}) \right).$$

Finally, imposing the parametric forms $U(c) = c^{1-\sigma}/(1 - \sigma)$ and $V(n) = n^{1+\varepsilon}/(1 + \varepsilon)$, we obtain

$$\alpha E_t^* (p_t Q_t/p_{t+1})^{1-\sigma} = n_t^{1+\varepsilon}.$$

It is convenient to write this in the form

$$n_t = (\alpha X_{t+1}^e)^{1/(1+\varepsilon)},$$

---

[4]This formulation was first presented in Evans and Honkapohja (1993a).

where $X_{t+1} = (p_t Q_t / p_{t+1})^{1-\sigma}$ is the variable on which the agents are learning, and where the notation $X_{t+1}^e = E_t^* X_{t+1}$ is employed. In a temporary equilibrium we have $X_{t+1} = ((1 - \zeta_{t+1}) f(n_{t+1}, \ell n_{t+1}) v_{t+1})^{1-\sigma}$.

The size of the fraction of government purchases ζ is important for the number of steady-state equilibria. As with the version of the model discussed in Section 4.6 of Chapter 4, in the nonstochastic case with constant ζ, this model can have up to three steady states. In the nonstochastic case with perfect foresight, we can write $n_t = \mathcal{F}(n_{t+1})$, where $\mathcal{F}(n) = \alpha^{1/(1+\varepsilon)}((1-\zeta) f(n, \ell n))^{(1-\sigma)/(1+\varepsilon)}$ and we are restricting attention to the case $0 < \sigma < 1$. A higher value of ζ shifts the graph of $\mathcal{F}(n_{t+1})$ downward in a proportional way. Thus for high enough values of ζ, only the "low-activity" (interior) steady state continues to exist.

The possibility of multiple steady states carries over to the stochastic model. The analysis of the stability under learning of a stochastic steady state is based on the familiar learning rule

$$X_{t+1}^e = X_t^e + \gamma_{t-1}(X_{t-1} - X_t^e),$$

where γ_t is a sequence of decreasing gains with standard properties. Defining $G(n, v) = ((1 - \zeta) f(n, \ell n) v)^{1-\sigma}$, so that $X_t = G(n_t, v_t)$, and $H(X^e) = (\alpha X^e)^{1/(1+\varepsilon)}$, we have $n_t = H(G(n_{t+1}, v_{t+1})^e)$. By setting $\theta_{t-1} = X_{t+1}^e$, the model under learning fits the framework developed earlier in this chapter.[5] Based on Proposition 11.2 and the remarks following, only the high and low steady states are locally stable under this learning rule (assuming that the support of the v_t shocks is not too large). Moreover, using the global convergence theorem in Section 7.6 of Chapter 7, it is evident that there will be convergence with probability 1 to either the low- or the high-activity stochastic steady state.[6]

11.6.2 The Hyperinflation Model

Here we consider the extension of the basic OG production model allowing for government consumption financed by money creation. The government's budget constraint is $g_t = \tau + (M_t - M_{t-1})/p_t$, where g_t is per capita government consumption and τ is per capita lump-sum taxes, assumed fixed. It is convenient (but inessential) to assume that $\tau = 0$, so that

$$g_t = \frac{M_t}{p_t} - \frac{p_{t-1}}{p_t} \frac{M_{t-1}}{p_{t-1}}. \tag{11.10}$$

---

[5]To put the model in the exact form described earlier in the chapter, it is also necessary to rewrite the random shock v_t as $v_t = 1 + \tilde{v}_t$, so that the random term $\tilde{v}_t$ has mean zero.

[6]This follows from the fact that the graph of the mapping $n - [\alpha(1 - \zeta) f(n, \ell n)]^{1/(1+\varepsilon)} \times E(v^{1/(1+\varepsilon)})$ is negative for high enough values of n and low enough positive values of n.

The household's budget constraints are $n_t p_t = M_t$, $M_t = p_{t+1} c_{t+1}$, and the market-clearing condition is now $n_t = c_t + g_t$. In the literature this model has been solved in terms of either the inflation rate or the level of employment. We carry out the analysis in terms of inflation and then comment on the alternative way.

The household's first-order condition

$$V'(n_t) = \left(\frac{p_t}{p_{t+1}} U'(c_{t+1}) \right)^e$$

is unchanged from the basic OG model. Substituting in the budget constraints yields $V'(n_t) = (\pi_{t+1}^{-1} U'(n_t \pi_{t+1}^{-1}))^e$, where $\pi_{t+1} \equiv p_{t+1}/p_t$ denotes the (gross) rate of inflation. We consider the case of point expectation for simplicity. Then it is often possible to solve this equation for n_t to obtain

$$n_t = S(\pi_{t+1}^e).$$

This is the case, e.g., when the offer curve in the basic OG model is upward sloping. $S(\pi_{t+1}^e)$ gives real saving in the economy as a function of expected inflation, as we have $n_t = M_t/p_t$ and money is the only means of saving.

Substituting into equation (11.10) yields the equilibrium equation

$$\pi_t = \frac{S(\pi_t^e)}{S(\pi_{t+1}^e) - g_t} \equiv F(\pi_{t+1}^e, \pi_t^e, g_t) \tag{11.11}$$

for the rate of inflation. For the time being assume for simplicity that real government spending is constant, i.e., $g_t = g$, and that the savings function is linear, i.e., $S(\pi_{t+1}) = a - b\pi_{t+1}$.[7] Under perfect foresight we obtain the difference equation

$$\pi_{t+1} = 1 + \frac{a - g}{b} - \frac{a}{b} \pi_t^{-1}.$$

Figure 11.2 describes the dynamical system in the (π_t, π_{t+1}) space. The two curves are drawn for two different values of g (see below). This model has normally two interior steady states π_A and π_B ($> \pi_A$), and a continuum of dynamic

---

[7]It is formally possible to incorporate first- and second-period endowments to the model by setting $n_t = \omega^1 - c_t^1$ and $c_{t+1} = \omega^2 + M_t/p_{t+1}$, where ω^1 is endowment for the young, c_t^1 denotes leisure, and ω^2 is endowment for the old. If the utility functions are logarithmic, i.e., $V(n_t) = -\ln(\omega^1 - n_t)$ and $U(c_{t+1}) = \ln c_{t+1}$, one obtains the linear labor supply (or savings) function $n_t = \max[0, 2^{-1}(\omega^1 - \omega^2 \pi_{t+1}^e)]$. See Evans, Honkapohja, and Marimon (2000) for further details.

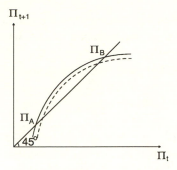

Figure 11.2.

paths which start from any initial point π_0 in the interval (π_A, π_B) or above π_B and converge to π_B under perfect-foresight dynamics. The high-inflation steady state π_B is thus indeterminate under perfect foresight. In contrast, the low-inflation steady state π_A is locally determinate in the sense that any equilibrium path initiating from its neighborhood must eventually leave that neighborhood.

To analyze learning, we begin with the derivation of E-stability conditions for the two steady states. Thus postulate that agents have the PLM (perceived law of motion) of the form $\pi_t^e = \pi_{t+1}^e = \pi$. From equation (11.11), the ALM (actual law of motion) is

$$T(\pi) = \frac{S(\pi)}{S(\pi) - g}.$$

As usual, the differential equation defining E-stability is

$$\frac{d\pi}{d\tau} = T(\pi) - \pi,$$

and the E-stability condition for a steady state π_i, $i = A, B$, is

$$T'(\pi_i) = -gS'(\pi_i)\big[S(\pi_i) - g\big]^{-2} < 1,$$

and normally the low-inflation steady state π_A is E-stable while π_B is not. For example, in the linear case it can be checked that $T'(\pi_A) < 1$ and $T'(\pi_B) > 1$, so that the low-inflation steady state π_A is E-stable while π_B is not.

For the analysis of adaptive learning, there are complications that arise because expectations formed at different periods appear in equation (11.11). This feature must be incorporated in the analysis of learning. We adopt the formulation of Evans, Honkapohja, and Marimon (2000), who consider an extended version of this model in detail.

Agents are assumed to use a standard learning rule

$$\pi_{t+1}^e = \pi_t^e + \gamma_{t+1}\left(\pi_{t-1} - \pi_t^e\right),$$

where again γ_t is a sequence of gains satisfying standard assumptions. (Recall that the sample mean from past data can be written in this form.) Shifting time back one period and substituting for inflation from equation (11.11), we have

$$\pi_t^e = \pi_{t-1}^e + \gamma_t\left(F\left(\pi_{t-1}^e, \pi_{t-2}^e, g_{t-2}\right) - \pi_{t-1}^e\right), \tag{11.12}$$

which is a second-order system in the expectations. In order to have a stochastic model, we assume here that $g_t = g + v_t$, where v_t is iid with $E v_t = 0$ and has a small compact support. (The support may be taken to be arbitrarily small.)

The higher dimensionality can formally be treated by introducing an explicit state variable to the analysis. Thus we write

$$X_t = A\left(\pi_{t-1}^e\right)X_{t-1} + B\left(\pi_{t-1}^e\right)W_t,$$

where $X_t' = (X_{1,t}, X_{2,t}, X_{3,t})$, $W_t = (1, g_{t-2})'$, and

$$A\left(\pi_{t-1}^e\right) = \begin{pmatrix} 0 & 1 & 0 \\ 0 & 0 & 0 \\ 0 & 0 & 0 \end{pmatrix}, \qquad B(\pi_{t-1}^e) = \begin{pmatrix} 0 & 0 \\ \pi_{t-1}^e & 0 \\ 0 & 1 \end{pmatrix}.$$

Then equation (11.12) can be written as

$$\pi_t^e = \pi_{t-1}^e + \gamma_t\left(F\left(\pi_{t-1}^e, X_{1,t}, X_{3,t}\right) - \pi_{t-1}^e\right),$$

and the system is in standard form for recursive stochastic algorithms treated in Chapter 6, where the parameter vector is now $\theta_t = \pi_t^e$. It is easily verified that assumptions (A) and (B) of Chapter 6 are satisfied, so that the convergence theorems can be applied. The associated differential equation is

$$\frac{d\pi}{d\tau} = E F(\pi, \pi, \tilde{g}) - \pi, \tag{11.13}$$

where the expectation is taken with respect to the random variable $\tilde{g}$ which has the same distribution as g_t. In general, this differential equation differs from the equation which above defined E-stability, since the latter was presented for the case of constant $g_t = g$. In the stochastic case, equation (11.13) should be used to define E-stability. However, if the support of the distribution is small, the two E-stability conditions are approximately identical. We can thus state the following result which holds for supports of g_t which are sufficiently small.

Proposition 11.3. *The low-inflation steady state π_A is locally stable under learning, while the high-inflation steady state π_B is unstable under learning in the standard hyperinflation model.*

This proposition suggests that the low-inflation steady state is the plausible equilibrium for the hyperinflation model. A distinct but supportive justification is obtained by looking at comparative static properties. Consider an increase in g. This change shifts the curve downwards in Figure 11.2. One would expect this higher g to be associated with higher inflation. This is true for the stable steady state π_A, whereas the other steady state π_B has the implausible property that higher values of g lower steady-state inflation. From this viewpoint, too, the low-inflation steady state is more natural than the high-inflation steady state.[8]

An alternative analysis of learning can be developed by solving the inflation model in terms of the level of employment. This approach requires the assumption that the market-clearing condition is combined with the agents' optimality conditions. In other words, in this sense agents are assumed to have more information than in the preceding approach.

Using $p_t/p_{t+1} = n_{t+1}/n_t$ and the market-clearing condition, we obtain

$$n_t V'(n_t) = \left((n_{t+1} - g_{t+1})U'(n_{t+1} - g_{t+1})\right)^e. \tag{11.14}$$

Assume again that $g_t = g + v_t$. Then substituting into equation (11.14) and solving for n_t, we have obtained a model of the form (11.3):

$$n_t = H\left(G(n_{t+1}, v_{t+1})^e\right),$$

where the parameter g has been absorbed into the function G. Note that in this formulation the complication of mixed datings of expectations does not arise, and the general analysis of this chapter can be directly applied.

The nonstochastic case with an upward-sloping offer curve is illustrated in Figure 11.3. It is easy to verify that the high-employment steady state $\bar{n}_2$ has a

---

[8]The stability properties under learning can sometimes be reversed. This occurs if agents have access to contemporaneous data in learning and the (constant) gain parameter is sufficiently large. See Lettau and Van Zandt (1999) for a detailed analysis and Section 3.4 of Chapter 3 or Evans and Honkapohja (1999) for summary discussions. Another related paper is Adam (2000a).

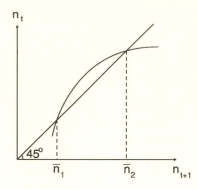

Figure 11.3.

low-inflation rate while the low-employment steady state $\bar{n}_1$ has a high inflation rate. When random expenditure shocks v_t are present, then there will be noisy steady states near $\bar{n}_1$ and near $\bar{n}_2$, provided the shocks are sufficiently "small." The E-stability condition will be determined by the value of the derivative $F'(n)$. Since $F'(\bar{n}_1) > 1$ while $F'(\bar{n}_2) < 1$, the high-employment noisy steady state will be stable under adaptive learning while the low-employment steady state is not stable. Thus, using this alternative formulation of learning does not alter the stability properties of the steady states.

11.6.3   Multiple Equilibria in Growth

In this section we consider a model of innovations and endogenous growth with multiple equilibria, originally developed in Evans, Honkapohja, and Romer (1998). The multiplicity of steady states arises from two central features of the model. First, all (differentiated) capital goods are assumed to be complements, so that the marginal productivity of each capital good depends positively on the amounts of other capital goods. Second, the production technologies for consumption and new capital goods are different and there is a standard convex production possibility set for additions to the stock of capital and consumption. Inventions are modeled as arising from profit-seeking activities of monopolistically competitive entrepreneurs, and there are no externalities in the model. The main features of the model are as follows.

The preference structure in the model is standard; there is a representative consumer who maximizes the discounted expression for utility

$$\sum_{i=0}^{\infty} \beta^{t+i} U(C_{t+i}), \quad \text{where } U(C) = \frac{C^{1-\sigma}}{1-\sigma}.$$

A consumer who is faced with a constant interest rate r will choose to have consumption grow at the constant rate g_C given by

$$g_C = \frac{C_{t+1}}{C_t} = [\beta(1+r_t)]^{1/\sigma}. \tag{11.15}$$

We will characterize our equilibria in terms of two equations in two endogenous variables, the rate of growth and the interest rate. Equation (11.15) gives us one of the two relationships. In the (g, r) space we refer to it as the CC curve.

The second relationship between g and r comes from an arbitrage condition from the production side of the model which involves several technological and market relationships.

The production of final goods from a fixed quantity of labor L and different capital goods $x_t(i)$ takes the form

$$Y_t = L^{1-\alpha} \left(\int_0^{A_t} x_t(i)^\gamma di \right)^\phi.$$

Here $\phi\gamma = \alpha$ and $\alpha \in (0, 1)$, so that constant returns prevail. We assume $\phi > 1$, implying that different capital goods are complements to each other. A_t is the number of differentiated capital goods in existence. In a growth equilibrium, A_t increases over time, as innovations in the form of new capital goods take place.

These capital goods are supplied by monopolistically competitive producers, so that they face the inverse demand functions

$$R_t(j) = \frac{\partial Y}{\partial x_t(j)}$$
$$= L^{1-\alpha} \left(\int_0^{A_t} x_t(i)^\gamma di \right)^{\phi-1} \phi\gamma x_t(j)^{\gamma-1},$$

giving the rental rate $R_t(j)$ as a function of $x_t(j)$ and other variables. The total cost to the capital goods supplier in period t is $r_t x_t(j) p_t^z$.[9] The consumption good is used as the numeraire and p_t^z denotes the price of capital in terms of it. Profit maximization leads to the mark-up rule

$$R_t(j) = r_t p_t^z / \gamma \equiv R(r_t, p_t^z).$$

---

[9]We simplify the original Evans, Honkapohja, and Romer (1998) model by assuming away depreciation of physical capital.

It follows that symmetry $x_t(j) = x_t$ holds, so that

$$Y_t = L^{1-\alpha}(x_t^\gamma A_t)^\phi,$$

where

$$x_t = LA_t^{(\phi-1)/(1-\alpha)}\left[\frac{R_t}{\phi\gamma}\right]^{-1/(1-\alpha)},$$

with R_t given by the mark-up rule.

Profits (at the end of period t) for each type of intermediate good are

$$\pi_t = \Omega A_t^{(\phi-1)/(1-\alpha)}\left(r_t p_t^z\right)^{\alpha/(\alpha-1)},$$

where $\Omega = \phi^{1/(1-\alpha)}(1-\gamma)\gamma^{(1+\alpha)/(1-\alpha)}L$. It is assumed that it takes i^ξ units of foregone output to produce a design for good i, and the parameter restriction $\xi = (\phi-1)/(1-\alpha)$ is imposed. (This is needed to ensure the possibility for balanced growth paths.) In equilibrium with balanced growth, the required zero-profit condition for the marginal good invented at time t (which will have an index $j = A_t$) is given by $p_t^z A_t^\xi = \sum_{s=0}^{\infty}\pi_{t+s}(1+r)^{-(s+1)}$, yielding the relationship

$$g_A^\xi = 1 + r - \Omega(p^z)^{-1/(1-\alpha)}r^{-\alpha/(1-\alpha)},$$

where $g_A = A_{t+1}/A_t$ is the constant growth rate of A_t.

The production possibility frontier between consumption and investment is formulated as

$$C_t = Y_t - Z_t\chi\left(\frac{Z_{t+1}-Z_t}{Z_t}\right). \tag{11.16}$$

$\chi(\cdot)$ is a convex cost function with $\chi(0) = 0$. Total capital is given by

$$Z_t = \int_0^{A_t} x_t(i)\,di + \int_0^{A_t} i^\xi\,di = x_t A_t + \frac{A_t^{1+\xi}}{1+\xi}.$$

It can then be shown that on a balanced growth path, $g_Z = g_A^{1+\xi}$, where $g_Z = Z_{t+1}/Z_t$, so that

$$g_Z = \left[1 + r - \Omega(p^z)^{-1/(1-\alpha)}r^{-\alpha/(1-\alpha)}\right]^{(\phi-\alpha)/(\phi-1)}. \tag{11.17}$$

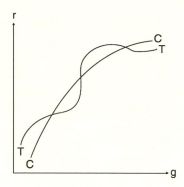

Figure 11.4.

The price of capital is obtained as the marginal trade-off in the production possibility frontier (11.16), so that the price of capital goods in terms of consumption is

$$p^z = \chi'(g_Z - 1), \quad \text{where } g_Z = Z_{t+1}/Z_t. \tag{11.18}$$

Relation (11.18), together with equation (11.17), provide the technology arbitrage relation. It is denoted as the TT curve in (g, r) space. This curve can have both upward and downward sloping segments, depending on the relative strength of the complementarity and price of capital effects; see the detailed discussion in Evans, Honkapohja, and Romer (1998).

On a balanced growth path, $g_C = g_Z = g$. Drawing the TT and CC relations yields the geometric representation of the possible multiple equilibria. Evans, Honkapohja, and Romer (1998) assume a piecewise linear relation for $\chi(\cdot)$ with three linear segments (and corners rounded off to maintain differentiability). Then the TT curve can have two downward sloping portions, and there may be multiple intersections of the CC and TT curves, as illustrated in Figure 11.4.

This model has the property that, under perfect foresight, the economy will immediately be in a steady state from any initial position. Under rational expectations, there is no way to select among the different equilibria. In contrast, modeling dynamics via adaptive learning will narrow down the set of steady states which are locally stable under learning. We now consider the formulation of learning.

In modeling learning, attention is restricted to a simple scheme in which households base their actions on an expected interest rate. Given their beliefs, consumers decide how much to save. Firms observe the current savings behavior of the consumers and project the growth rate of consumption and the implied equal growth rate of total capital Z into the indefinite future. Firms will compete for resources in financial markets. This determines a realized interest rate that is consistent with no-arbitrage on the production side of the market.

After consumers observe the realized rates, they adjust their expectations about future interest rates. For example, if the interest rate that consumers expected was lower than the interest rate that is realized, they will revise their forecasts of interest rates upward.

Formally, given an expected interest rate r^e, we have a temporary equilibrium mapping that takes expected interest rates into realized interest rates:

$$r = T(r^e).$$

To generate an explicit dynamics for the interest rate, we use a standard adaptive learning scheme,

$$r_{t+1}^e = r_t^e + \delta_t (r_t - r_t^e),$$

where $\delta_t = \delta/t$. Together, these equations define a dynamic system which can be analyzed in the vicinity of a fixed point. Such a point is locally stable if $T'(r) < 1$. In Figure 11.4, the stability condition for steady states is characterized by the property that the TT curve cuts the CC curve from above. Thus, in the figure there are two locally stable steady states which are separated by an unstable one.[10]

The number of stable-steady state equilibria depends on the parameter values for the model. In these kinds of models, economic policy can have large effects if it can alter the set of stable equilibria. Honkapohja and Turunen-Red (1999) extend the model to open economies and show how the degree of openness of two identical economies can lead to a favorable growth bifurcation for the two countries. In addition to a standard favorable local effect on a given steady state, the number of steady states can change as a result of the policy change in such a way that only a fast growth state continues to exist. Then the economies can have a large upward change in their growth rates and the learning dynamics will take them towards the high-growth steady state.

---

[10]Evans, Honkapohja, and Romer (1998) show that the existence of multiple steady states which are stable under learning makes it possible to construct stochastic equilibria which shift between two points near the stable steady states. These "growth cycles" are also shown to be locally stable under learning. The argument is similar to that used in Chapter 12 to show stability under learning of Markov sunspot equilibria near a pair of distinct steady states.

Chapter **12**

Cycles and Sunspot Equilibria

12.1 Introduction

In this chapter we will continue the analysis of stochastic nonlinear models of the form

$$y_t = H\big(G(y_{t+1}, v_{t+1})^e, v_t\big). \qquad (12.1)$$

y_t is a scalar variable and v_t denotes a possible iid random shock to, say, preferences or technology, which might be present in the model. Here $G(y_{t+1}, v_{t+1})^e$ denotes the value of $G(y_{t+1}, v_{t+1})$ expected by agents at time t, and under rational expectations, $G(y_{t+1}, v_{t+1})^e = E_t G(y_{t+1}, v_{t+1})$. In the previous chapter this framework was introduced and we studied the stability of rational stochastic steady states under learning. As was there noted, models leading to equation (12.1) can have other types of REE besides steady states. These include both periodic cycles and equilibria which are influenced by extraneous random phenomena, often referred to as "sunspots," in addition to any intrinsic shocks v_t.

In this chapter we first take up the case of periodic cycles. If the random shock v_t is not present, then these solutions take the form of regular perfect-foresight cycles. If intrinsic shocks v_t are present, then the corresponding solutions become "noisy" cycles.

The other type of equilibria we study in this chapter are solutions which depend on a sunspot, i.e., an extraneous random variable which influences the equilibrium only through expectations. These rational expectations equilibria

287

have received a great deal of attention in the literature after the initial investigations by Shell (1977), Azariadis (1981), and Cass and Shell (1983).[1]

These two types of rational solutions can be viewed as a modern formulation of a long tradition in economics, emanating from the work of Kalecki (1935)
and Kaldor (1940), which emphasizes the possibility of endogenous fluctuations
in market economies. The nonlinearity of the economic model is a key element
in generating the possibility of these equilibria, though sunspots can also appear
as part of a rational expectations solution in linear models as well (as discussed
in Part III).

In fact, for much of the chapter we can simplify the presentation and assume
that the preference or technology shocks v_t do not appear in the model. Then we
can focus on the class of models

$$y_t = F(y_{t+1})^e, \tag{12.2}$$

which is a special case of the general class (12.1) above.[2] This class was introduced in Chapter 11. Cyclical equilibria for equation (12.2) exhibit perfect
foresight, so that they satisfy $y_t = F(y_{t+1})$, where y_t is a periodic sequence. In
contrast, sunspot equilibria for equation (12.2) are stochastic processes which
satisfy $y_t = E_t[F(y_{t+1})]$, where E_t denotes the conditional expectation, given
information at time t.

Throughout this chapter we assume that F, G, and H are twice continuously
differentiable.

12.2   Overview of Results

It may be helpful to summarize here some of the most salient results from this
chapter. Consider the nonstochastic model (12.2). Although this model may
have solutions which include perfect-foresight cycles of high order and rational
Markov sunspot solutions with many states, in this section we restrict attention
to perfect-foresight steady states and 2-cycles and to 2-state Markov sunspot
solutions. Recall first from the previous chapter that a steady state $\hat{y} = F(\hat{y})$
is locally stable under adaptive steady-state learning if $F'(\hat{y}) < 1$ and locally
unstable if $F'(\hat{y}) > 1$. The phrase "steady-state learning" means that the agents

---

[1] For recent surveys see Chiappori and Guesnerie (1991) and Guesnerie and Woodford (1992).

[2] Clearly, if there are no shocks v_t and $H()$ is one-to-one, the general model reduces to this
model after a change of variables.

have a PLM in which they model the solution as simply a constant (or as a constant plus unpredictable noise), and therefore follow the adaptive learning rules discussed in the last chapter. The condition $F'(\hat{y}) < 1$ can be interpreted as the E-stability condition for this form of PLM.

A perfect-foresight 2-cycle is defined by $y_t = \hat{y}_1$ if t is odd and by $y_t = \hat{y}_2$ if t is even, where

$$\hat{y}_1 = F(\hat{y}_2) \quad \text{and} \quad \hat{y}_2 = F(\hat{y}_1).$$

We will consider adaptive learning rules appropriate for the case in which the agents have a PLM that allows for a 2-cycle. One simple and natural rule is to estimate separately the values taken by y_t in even and odd periods.[3] Whether this learning rule converges to a perfect-foresight 2-cycle is determined by the E-stability condition for the corresponding PLM. If the PLM is $y_t = y_1$ for t odd and $y_t = y_2$ for t even, then it is easily seen that the corresponding ALM is $y_t = F(y_2)$ for t odd and $y_t = F(y_1)$ for t even. This yields the T-map from PLM to ALM[4]

$$T(y_1, y_2) = \big(F(y_2), F(y_1)\big),$$

with derivative at $(\hat{y}_1, \hat{y}_2)$ given by

$$DT = \begin{pmatrix} 0 & F'(\hat{y}_2) \\ F'(\hat{y}_1) & 0 \end{pmatrix}.$$

It is easily verified that the roots of DT have real parts less than 1 if and only if $F'(\hat{y}_1)F'(\hat{y}_2) < 1$. This provides the E-stability condition for perfect-foresight 2-cycles.

Next consider 2-state Markov sunspot solutions. These were introduced in Section 4.6.3 of Chapter 4, and we first recall the equations defining them. Let $s_t \in \{1, 2\}$ denote an exogenous 2-state Markov process with transition probabilities $0 < \pi_{ij} < 1$, $i, j = 1, 2$. Here π_{ij} is the probability that $s_{t+1} = j$ given that $s_t = i$, and of course $\pi_{12} = 1 - \pi_{11}$ and $\pi_{21} = 1 - \pi_{22}$. A (2-state) stationary sunspot equilibrium (SSE) is a process $y_t = y_1^*$ if $s_t = 1$ and $y_t = y_2^*$ if $s_t = 2$

---

[3] A natural alternative would be to estimate separately the values of $F(y_t)$ in odd and even periods. This rule has the same local stability properties.

[4] For convenience in this chapter we often use row vectors instead of column vectors.

that satisfies equation (12.2), i.e., such that

$$
\begin{aligned}
y_1^* &= \pi_{11} F\left(y_1^*\right) + (1 - \pi_{11}) F\left(y_2^*\right), \\
y_2^* &= (1 - \pi_{22}) F\left(y_1^*\right) + \pi_{22} F\left(y_2^*\right).
\end{aligned}
\tag{12.3}
$$

Using the implicit function theorem, we will show that SSEs exist near certain deterministic solutions. We here emphasize two results, which hold under suitable regularity conditions:

(i) Let $(\hat{y}_1, \hat{y}_2)$ denote a nontrivial 2-cycle, i.e., with $\hat{y}_1 \neq \hat{y}_2$. Then there exist SSEs (y_1^*, y_2^*) near $(\hat{y}_1, \hat{y}_2)$ with transition probabilities π_{11}, π_{22} close to zero.

(ii) Let $\hat{y}_1$ and $\hat{y}_2$ be distinct steady states, i.e., with $\hat{y}_1 \neq \hat{y}_2$. Then there exist SSEs (y_1^*, y_2^*) near $(\hat{y}_1, \hat{y}_2)$ with transition probabilities π_{11}, π_{22} close to 1.

As we later discuss, there may also exist SSEs near a single steady state.

We now consider adaptive learning rules in which the agents have a PLM which allows for the possibility of an SSE. One natural procedure would be for agents to compute separate averages for the values that y_t has taken when $s_t = 1$ and when $s_t = 2$. Again, we will show that whether this learning rule converges to an SSE is determined by the corresponding E-stability conditions. We therefore consider the PLM $y_t = y_1$ if $s_t = 1$ and $y_t = y_2$ if $s_t = 2$. The T-map from the PLM to the ALM is then given by

$$
T(y_1, y_2) = \left(\pi_{11} F(y_1) + (1 - \pi_{11}) F(y_2), (1 - \pi_{22}) F(y_1) + \pi_{22} F(y_2)\right),
$$

and an SSE is E-stable if both roots of $DT(y_1^*, y_2^*)$ have real parts less than 1. From this one can show the following:

(i) an SSE near a 2-cycle is E-stable if $F'(\hat{y}_1) F'(\hat{y}_2) < 1$, and

(ii) an SSE near a pair of distinct steady states is E-stable if both $F'(\hat{y}_1) < 1$ and $F'(\hat{y}_2) < 1$.

Thus SSEs near 2-cycles or a pair of distinct steady states inherit the local stability properties under learning of the corresponding perfect-foresight solutions.

We now turn to a systematic analysis. We first analyze learning for cyclical solutions and then turn to the analysis of learning sunspot equilibria.

12.3 Deterministic Cycles

In the preceding chapter we noted that, besides steady states, simple OG models can exhibit perfect-foresight cycles, and Figure 11.1 of Chapter 11 illustrated the possibility of cycles in the basic Samuelson model.[5] In this model the economic intuition for the possibility of *k-cycles* rests on income and substitution effects. If the income effect is sufficiently large, the function F will be downward sloping over part of the range, and this makes cycles possible. Heuristically, the real wage is p_t/p_{t+1}, since labor is sold at price p_t in year t and goods are bought at price p_{t+1} in year $t + 1$. The budget constraint yields the quantity theory equation $p_{t+1} = M/n_{t+1}$, so that high levels of aggregate employment correspond to years of low prices. In a 2-cycle, employment is, say, a high value $\hat{n}_2$ in even periods and a low value $\hat{n}_1$ in odd periods. Then the real wage is $p_t/p_{t+1} = \hat{n}_1/\hat{n}_2$ if t is even (and the real wage is $p_t/p_{t+1} = \hat{n}_2/\hat{n}_1$ if t is odd). Thus in even (odd) periods, employment is high (low) because the real wage is low (high), inducing more (less) work, given the strong income effect.

The issue of conditions for the existence of k-cycles is one we shall omit; see Grandmont (1985) and Guesnerie and Woodford (1991) for a discussion.

From Figure 11.1, it is apparent that k-cycles can coexist with steady states, so that there are multiple perfect-foresight solutions. This is a general phenomenon, reflecting a well-known mathematical result which we do state.[6]

Sarkovski's Theorem. *Let f be a continuous map of the unit interval into itself. Consider the following ordering of the positive integers:*

$$3 \succ 5 \succ 7 \succ \cdots$$
$$\succ 2 \cdot 3 \succ 2 \cdot 5 \succ 2 \cdot 7 \succ \cdots$$
$$\cdots$$
$$\succ 2^n \cdot 3 \succ 2^n \cdot 5 \succ 2^n \cdot 7 \succ \cdots$$
$$\succ \cdots \succ 2^m \succ \cdots \succ 8 \succ 4 \succ 2 \succ 1.$$

If f has a cycle of period p and $p \succ q$ in the above ordering, then f has a cycle of period q.

In particular, if f has a cycle of period 3, then it has cycles of all orders. It can be shown, see Grandmont (1985), that for appropriate utility functions we

---

[5]Example 1 of Section 12.5.1 repeats some of the details of the model.

[6]For a discussion see Azariadis (1993, p. 107) or Guesnerie and Woodford (1991, p. 357).

can get 3-cycles in the basic OG model, and Figure 11.1 has been drawn for this case. Note that in general, whenever there are cycles in the OG model, there are multiple equilibria, so that the role of learning as a selection criterion becomes important.

To introduce a recursive formulation of learning for cycles, we again consider 2-cycles in the basic nonstochastic model (12.2) of the preceding section. In that section we alluded to learning based on separate averaging of the values of y_t in odd and even periods. However, in order to anticipate learning rules in the more general stochastic model (12.1), we will now instead consider learning based directly on the values of $F(y_t)$, the quantity agents are attempting to forecast. Thus let these forecasts be given by $F(y_{t+1})^e = \theta_{1,t}$ if $t+1$ is odd and $F(y_{t+1})^e = \theta_{2,t}$ if $t+1$ is even. We assume that agents average the past data $F(y_{t-i})$ for even and odd periods separately. To set up the system recursively, we take the data in successive pairs, indexed by s, so that $t = 2s + i$ for $i = 1, 2$. Letting $\theta_s = (\theta_{1,s}, \theta_{2,s})$ for $s = 1, 2, 3, \ldots$, the separate averaging can then be represented as

$$\begin{pmatrix} \theta_{1,s} \\ \theta_{2,s} \end{pmatrix} = \begin{pmatrix} \theta_{1,s-1} \\ \theta_{2,s-1} \end{pmatrix} + \gamma_s \begin{pmatrix} F(y_{2(s-1)+1}) - \theta_{1,s-1} \\ F(y_{2(s-1)+2}) - \theta_{2,s-1} \end{pmatrix}.$$

This algorithm can be analyzed using the techniques in Section 7.2 of Chapter 7. We will show that a 2-cycle $(\hat{y}_1, \hat{y}_2)$ is stable under this learning rule if and only if the previously obtained E-stability condition $F'(\hat{y}_1)F'(\hat{y}_2) < 1$ is satisfied (ruling out the special case where the product is exactly equal to 1).

This analysis can be readily generalized for k-cycles $(\hat{y}_1, \ldots, \hat{y}_k)$. If agents have a PLM which allows for k-cycles, they are assumed to form separate averages of $F(y_{t-i})$ for the k different phases of the cycle. We will see that for $k > 2$, a necessary condition for stability under this learning rule is that

$$F'(\hat{y}_1) \ldots F'(\hat{y}_k) < 1.$$

The formal discussion of this case will be treated as a special case of noisy cycles, to which we now turn. We begin with the definition of stochastic (or noisy) cycles, after which the analysis of stability of such cycles under learning is developed. We then present necessary and sufficient conditions for local stability under learning and interpret these conditions in terms of E-stability.

12.4 Noisy Cycles

We now consider the general class of models (12.1). For this model a rational *noisy k-cycle* is a stochastic process of the form

$$y_t = y_i(v_t) \quad \text{for } t \bmod k = i, \quad i = 1, \dots, k-1, \tag{12.4}$$
$$y_t = y_k(v_t) \quad \text{for } t \bmod k = 0,$$

where the k functions $y_i(v_t)$ satisfy

$$y_i(v_t) = H\big(EG(y_{i+1}(v_{t+1}), v_{t+1}), v_t\big) \quad \text{for } t \bmod k = i,$$
$$i = 1, \dots, k-1,$$
$$y_k(v_t) = H\big(EG(y_1(v_{t+1}), v_{t+1}), v_t\big) \quad \text{for } t \bmod k = 0. \tag{12.5}$$

Since a rational noisy k-cycle is a stochastic process, it will have alternative sample paths. Nevertheless, in a noisy rational k-cycle the *expectations* $G(y_{t+1}, v_{t+1})^e$ follow a deterministic cycle. We will use the notation

$$\bar{\theta}_i = EG\big(y_i(v_t), v_t\big), \qquad i = 1, \dots, k.$$

Thus, in a rational noisy k-cycle,

$$E_t G\big(y_{t+1}(v_{t+1}), v_{t+1}\big) = \begin{cases} \bar{\theta}_{i+1} & \text{if } t \bmod k = i \quad \text{for } i = 1, \dots, k-1, \\ \bar{\theta}_1 & \text{if } t \bmod k = 0. \end{cases}$$

Using the fact that v_t is iid, note that $y_i(v_t) = H(\bar{\theta}_{i+1}, v_t)$ for $i = 1, \dots, k-1$, and $y_k(v_t) = H(\bar{\theta}_1, v_t)$. It follows that a rational noisy k-cycle is equivalently defined by $(\bar{\theta}_1, \dots, \bar{\theta}_k)$ such that

$$\bar{\theta}_i = EG\big(H(\bar{\theta}_{i+1}, v_t), v_t\big) \quad \text{for } i = 1, \dots, k-1, \tag{12.6}$$
$$\bar{\theta}_k = EG\big(H(\bar{\theta}_1, v_t), v_t\big).$$

By setting the noise to zero, we formally obtain the deterministic case:

$$\hat{\theta}_i = G\big(H(\hat{\theta}_{i+1}, 0), 0\big) \quad \text{for } i = 1, \dots, k-1,$$
$$\hat{\theta}_k = G\big(H(\hat{\theta}_1, 0), 0\big).$$

To conclude the definitions, we note here that for the case of small noise, it is possible to prove the existence of these noisy cycles in the same sense as was done in Chapter 11 for stochastic steady states. Evans and Honkapohja (1995c) provide the precise formulation of the result and the required regularity conditions.

To formulate learning for noisy k-cycles, we consider the notion that agents believe they are in a noisy k-cycle and attempt to estimate the mean value of $G(y_t, v_t)$ at the different points in the cycle. Since v_t is iid, in an RE noisy k-cycle, the values of $G(y_t, v_t)$ are independently distributed across time and are identically distributed for the same values of $t \bmod k$. A natural estimator of $(\theta_1, \ldots, \theta_k)$ is then given by separate sample means for each stage of the cycle:

$$\theta_{i,t} = \left(\#N_i(t)\right)^{-1} \sum_{j \in N_i(t)} G(y_j, v_j), \tag{12.7}$$

where

$$N_i(t) = \left\{j = 1, \ldots, t \mid t \bmod k = i\right\} \text{ for } i = 1, \ldots k-1,$$
$$N_k(t) = \left\{j = 1, \ldots, t \mid t \bmod k = 0\right\}.$$

Here, $\#N_i(t)$ denotes the cardinality of the set $N_i(t)$, i.e., the number of elements in the set. Equation (12.7) can also be put into recursive form, though this is less straightforward than for steady states for which $k = 1$. The key is to take the data in k-*tuples*. Thus let

$$t = sk + i, \qquad i = 1, \ldots, k,$$

where s is a nonnegative integer, and for positive s define

$$y_{i,s} = y_{k(s-1)+i} \quad \text{and} \quad v_{i,s} = v_{k(s-1)+i},$$

for $i = 1, \ldots, k$. The recursive form of the learning rule can then be written as

$$\begin{pmatrix} \theta_{1,s} \\ \vdots \\ \theta_{k,s} \end{pmatrix} = \begin{pmatrix} \theta_{1,s-1} \\ \vdots \\ \theta_{k,s-1} \end{pmatrix} + \gamma_s \begin{pmatrix} G(y_{1,s}, v_{1,s}) - \theta_{1,s-1} \\ \vdots \\ G(y_{k,s}, v_{k,s}) - \theta_{k,s-1} \end{pmatrix}, \tag{12.8}$$

$$\theta_{i,s} = G\left(y_{ks+i}, v_{ks+i}\right)^e, \tag{12.9}$$

where γ_s is a positive decreasing-gain sequence with the usual assumptions.[7]

---

[7]Guesnerie and Woodford (1991) consider essentially the same rule for $\gamma_s = \gamma$, a fixed $0 < \gamma \le 1$. (They consider a nonstochastic system.)

The system under learning dynamics[8] is given by equations (12.8), (12.1), and (12.9). It is apparent that these equations define a stochastic recursive algorithm, and it is not hard to show that they can be put into the standard form. Letting $\theta_s = (\theta_{1,s}, \ldots, \theta_{k,s})$ and $v_s = (v_{1,s}, \ldots, v_{k,s})$, this can be written as

$$\theta_s = \theta_{s-1} + \gamma_s \big(M(\theta_{s-1}, \gamma_s, v_s) - \theta_{s-1} \big), \tag{12.10}$$

where

$$M(\theta_{s-1}, \gamma_s, v_s) = \big(M_1(\theta_{s-1}, \gamma_s, v_s), \ldots, M_k(\theta_{s-1}, \gamma_s, v_s) \big),$$

with the components $M_i = G(y_{k(s-1)+i}, v_{k(s-1)+i})$ expressed as functions of $(\theta_{s-1}, \gamma_s, v_s)$. The components are explicitly given as

$$M_i(\theta_{s-1}, \gamma_s, v_s) = G\big(H(\theta_{i+1,s-1}, v_{i,s}), v_{i,s} \big) \quad \text{for } i = 1, \ldots, k-1,$$

$$M_k(\theta_{s-1}, \gamma_s, v_s) = G\big(H\big(\theta_{1,s-1} + \gamma_s \big(G\big(H(\theta_{2,s-1}, v_{1,s}), v_{1,s} \big) - \theta_{1,s-1} \big), v_{k,s} \big), v_{k,s} \big).$$

Here the last component was obtained by substitution for $\theta_{1,s}$ into $G(H(\theta_{1,s}, v_{k,s}), v_{k,s})$ and using $y_{k(s-1)+1} = H(\theta_{2,s-1}, v_{1,s})$. Thus the possible convergence of $(\theta_{1,s}, \ldots, \theta_{k,s})$ to an REE noisy k-cycle can be analyzed using the associated differential equation. We will come back to this issue after defining the concept of E-stability for k-cycles.

The notion of E-stability for cycles is formulated as follows. Although in a noisy k-cycle the solution is given by k functions, $y_i(v_t)$, $i = 1, \ldots, k$, what matters to the agents are only the expected values of $G(y_{t+1}, v_{t+1})$. If agents believe they are in a noisy k-cycle, then their PLM is adequately summarized by a vector $\theta = (\theta_1, \ldots, \theta_k)$, where

$$\theta_i = G(y_t, v_t)^e \quad \text{if } t \bmod k = i, \quad \text{for } i = 1, \ldots, k-1,$$

$$\theta_k = G(y_t, v_t)^e \quad \text{if } t \bmod k = 0.$$

If agents held these (in general nonrational) perceptions fixed, then the economy would follow an actual (generally nonrational) k-cycle

$$y_t = H(\theta_{i+1}, v_t) \quad \text{if } t \bmod k = i, \quad \text{for } i = 1, \ldots, k-1,$$

$$y_t = H(\theta_1, v_t) \quad \text{if } t \bmod k = 0.$$

---

[8] Note that for $k > 1$, the issue of simultaneity between $G(y_{t+1}, v_{t+1})^e$ and y_t does not arise.

The corresponding parameters $\theta^* = (\theta_1^*, \ldots, \theta_k^*)$ of the ALM induced by the PLM are given by the expected values of $G(y_t, v_t)$ under this law of motion:

$$\theta_i^* = EG\big(H(\theta_{i+1}, v_t), v_t\big) \quad \text{if } t \bmod k = i, \quad \text{for } i = 1, \ldots, k-1,$$
$$\theta_k^* = EG\big(H(\theta_1, v_t), v_t\big) \quad \text{if } t \bmod k = 0.$$

In other words, the mapping $\theta^* = T(\theta)$ from the PLM to the ALM is given by

$$T(\theta) = \big(R(\theta_2), \ldots, R(\theta_k), R(\theta_1)\big),$$

where

$$R(\theta_i) = E\big(G(H(\theta_i, v_t), v_t)\big),$$

assuming $k > 1$. The differential equation defining E-stability is

$$d\theta/d\tau = T\big(\theta(\tau)\big) - \theta(\tau). \tag{12.11}$$

It is easily verified using equation (12.6) that fixed points of $T(\theta)$, i.e., zeros of equation (12.11), correspond to REE noisy k-cycles. An REE noisy k-cycle $\bar{\theta}$ is said to be *E-stable* if equation (12.11) is locally asymptotically stable at $\bar{\theta}$. As in other contexts, E-stability is a disequilibrium stability concept which determines whether an REE is stable under a stylized learning rule in which θ is adjusted "slowly" toward the actual θ^* generated by θ. As we show below, E-stability turns out to govern convergence under the real-time adaptive learning rules described in the previous section.

Proposition 12.1. *Consider an REE noisy k-cycle of the model (12.1) with expectation parameters $\bar{\theta} = (\bar{\theta}_1, \ldots, \bar{\theta}_k)$. Let*

$$\xi = \prod_{i=1}^{k} R'(\bar{\theta}_i).$$

Then $\bar{\theta}$ is E-stable if and only if

$$\begin{aligned} \xi &< 1 \quad \text{if } k = 2, \\ -\big(\cos(\pi/k)\big)^{-k} < \xi &< 1 \quad \text{if } k > 2. \end{aligned}$$

Proof. For E-stability we need that the eigenvalues of $DT(\bar{\theta})$ have real parts less than 1. The eigenvalues of

$$
DT(\bar{\theta}) = \begin{bmatrix}
0 & R'(\bar{\theta}_2) & 0 & 0 \cdots & & 0 \\
0 & 0 & R'(\bar{\theta}_3) & 0 \cdots & & 0 \\
& & & \vdots & & \\
0 & & & \cdots & 0 & R'(\bar{\theta}_k) \\
R'(\bar{\theta}_1) & 0 & & & \cdots & 0
\end{bmatrix}
$$

are the kth roots of ξ. If $\xi > 0$, the largest real part is the positive real root $\xi^{1/k}$ yielding the condition $\xi < 1$. If $\xi < 0$, a root with greatest real part is $|\xi|^{1/k} \exp(i\pi/k)$, from which the result follows. [See Evans and Honkapohja (1995c) for some further details of the proof.] □

Recall from Proposition 11.1, Chapter 11, that a noisy steady state $\bar{\theta}$ is E-stable if $T'(\bar{\theta}) < 1$, where $T(\theta) = R(\theta) = E(G(H(\theta), v_t), v_t)$. Then clearly, $\xi = R'(\theta) < 1$ is also the E-stability condition for the case $k = 1$.

In fact, we will refer to the conditions described in Propositions 11.1 and 12.1 more specifically as *weak E-stability* conditions for reasons which we now present.

12.4.1 Weak and Strong E-Stability

E-stability (and stability under adaptive learning) is always defined relative to some specified class of perceived laws of motion. Thus, in general, the stability of an REE can depend on the class of learning rules considered. This often leads to a useful distinction between weak and strong stability, where the latter concept allows for a wider class of perceived laws of motion which overparameterize the REE being considered. In the context of k-cycles, this distinction arises naturally as follows.

A k-cycle can always be regarded as a degenerate nk-cycle for any integer $n > 1$. Thus the 2-cycle $(\bar{\theta}_1, \bar{\theta}_2)$ is also a 4-cycle taking values $(\bar{\theta}_1, \bar{\theta}_2, \bar{\theta}_1, \bar{\theta}_2)$, a 6-cycle taking values $(\bar{\theta}_1, \bar{\theta}_2, \bar{\theta}_1, \bar{\theta}_2, \bar{\theta}_1, \bar{\theta}_2)$, etc. Define k as the primitive period of the cycle if it is not an m-cycle for any order $m < k$ (e.g., the primitive period is 2 in the example just given if $\bar{\theta}_1 \neq \bar{\theta}_2$). Consider now a noisy k-cycle REE of the model (12.1) with primitive period k and expectation parameters $\bar{\theta} = (\bar{\theta}_1, \ldots, \bar{\theta}_k)$. Then we say that $\bar{\theta}$ is *strongly E-stable* if it is E-stable when regarded as an nk-cycle for every positive integer n. $\bar{\theta}_i$ is said to be *weakly E-stable* but not strongly E-stable if it is E-stable when regarded as a k-cycle but not when regarded as an nk-cycle for some integer $n > 1$. Conditions for strong E-stability are given by the following result.

Proposition 12.2. *Consider an REE noisy k-cycle of the model (12.1), with primitive period $k \geq 1$, and with expectation parameters $\bar{\theta} = (\bar{\theta}_1, \ldots, \bar{\theta}_k)$. $\bar{\theta}$ is strongly E-stable if and only if $|\xi| < 1$.*

Proof. Use the results of Proposition 12.1, but now treat the REE as an nk-cycle. The upper inequality of the E-stability condition becomes $\xi^n < 1$, which holds for all positive integer n if and only if $|\xi| < 1$, and the lower inequality in the condition is then automatically satisfied. □

This condition can be compared to the Guesnerie and Woodford (1991) conditions for nonstochastic models and fixed adaption parameter. The strong E-stability condition is identical to their sufficient condition for stability for all constant gains $0 < \gamma \leq 1$.

Returning to Example 3 of Section 11.5, Chapter 11, let the support of the shock be $\alpha = 0.3$. Then numerical computations easily verify that the steady state is now $\bar{\theta} = 0.661$ with $T'(\bar{\theta}) = -1.028$. This means that the steady state is no longer strongly stable under learning, though it continues to be weakly stable. Thus it is stable under learning when regarded as a steady state but not stable under learning when agents use a PLM which allows for a possible 2-cycle. The example shows that for nonlinear models, the probability distribution of the shock term can have an influence on the stability conditions. (Note that this is not the case in linear models of Chapter 8.)

12.4.2 Convergence Results

We can now use the E-stability conditions to state the convergence results for the dynamic system under adaptive learning as specified by equations (12.8), (12.1), and (12.9) if $k > 1$ or simply equation (11.6) if $k = 1$. Because we have set up the system as a stochastic recursive algorithm, we need only verify that the required conditions described in Chapter 6 are met and derive the associated differential equation.

In the case of noisy k-cycles, we consider equation (12.10). Again the technical conditions are fairly straightforward and we need to compute the associated differential equation

$$d\theta/d\tau = \lim_{s \to \infty} EM(\theta, \gamma_s, v_s) - \theta.$$

Taking the individual components in turn (and for the kth component interchanging expectations and limits), one obtains

$$d\theta/d\tau = T(\theta) - \theta,$$

where

$$T(\theta) = \big(R(\theta_2), \dots, R(\theta_k), R(\theta_1)\big) \quad \text{and}$$
$$R(\theta_i) = E\big(G\big(H(\theta_i, v_t), v_t\big)\big).$$

That is, we obtain the differential equation defining E-stability for noisy k-cycles.

Using the results on the convergence of recursive stochastic algorithms from Chapter 6, it is now possible to state various convergence results. For example, we have the following.

Proposition 12.3. *Consider an REE noisy k-cycle of the model (12.1), with primitive period k, and with expectation parameters $\bar\theta = (\bar\theta_1, \dots, \bar\theta_k)$. Suppose that $\bar\theta$ is weakly E-stable. Then $\bar\theta$ is locally stable under adaptive learning. If instead $\bar\theta$ is not weakly E-stable, then θ_s converges to $\bar\theta$ with probability 0.*

As already noted, the deterministic case is formally included by setting $v_t \equiv 0$, and then under perfect-foresight we can define

$$y_t = F(y_{t+1}), \quad \text{where}$$
$$F(y) \equiv H\big(G(y, 0), 0\big).$$

It follows that the E-stability condition for this case is determined in terms of the quantity

$$\xi = F'\big(\hat y_1\big) F'\big(\hat y_2\big) \cdots F'\big(\hat y_k\big)$$

for a perfect-foresight k-cycle $(\hat y_1, \dots, \hat y_k)$.

It was pointed out earlier that noisy k-cycles exist nearby a perfect-foresight k-cycle if the noise is sufficiently "small" in the sense of a sufficiently small support. By continuity, it can be shown that in this case the E-stability conditions are "inherited" from the perfect-foresight case. In other words, if the deterministic k-cycle is E-stable, then noisy k-cycles which are sufficiently near to it are also E-stable. Finally, for small enough noise, it is also possible to show convergence from nearby initial points with probability 1 without a projection facility. The formal details of these results are discussed in Evans and Honkapohja (1995c).

In summary, the results of this section are immediately applicable to both the standard deterministic OG model and to noisy versions allowing for intrinsic shocks. Local stability of steady states or cycles (and of noisy steady states or noisy cycles) is determined by the weak and strong E-stability conditions given by Propositions 11.1, 12.1, and 12.2.

12.5   Existence of Sunspot Equilibria

We now start to analyze the stability of sunspot equilibria under adaptive learning. We first look at the existence of sunspot equilibria by focusing on a few central results in simplified forms. Here our discussion will on purpose be brief, given that extensive treatments are available in the literature.[9] Our main objective is to consider the circumstances in which economic agents might learn to believe in such equilibria. This possibility was first shown by Woodford (1990). In specific models a multitude of these solutions can exist, and we therefore study the selection of equilibria, i.e., derive conditions for the local stability of sunspot solutions under adaptive learning rules.

For simplicity we will use the framework (12.2) without intrinsic noise. This is the most common framework adopted in practice for nonlinear models. We will, however, also provide the stability conditions for the general framework (12.1), which is analyzed formally in Evans and Honkapohja (1998a).

The definition of a sunspot equilibrium involves the basic idea that economic agents in the model condition their expectations on some (random) variable s_t which otherwise does not have any influence on the model economy. Though different types of sunspot solutions have been considered in the literature, we will focus here on REEs that take the form of a finite Markov chain. Clearly, since rational expectations involve conditional expectations, a Markovian setup is in general the most obvious one to consider. Postulating a finite state space is then a further simplification in the analysis.

For most of the analysis, we go even further in this direction by assuming, as in Section 12.2, that the extraneous random variable is a two-state Markov chain with a constant transition matrix $\Pi = (\pi_{ij})$, $0 < \pi_{ij} < 1$, for $i, j = 1, 2$.[10] A (two-state) stationary sunspot equilibrium (SSE) with transition probabilities π_{ij} is then defined by a pair (y_1^*, y_2^*) which satisfies equations (12.3). These equations have the geometric interpretation that the two values (y_1^*, y_2^*) must be convex combinations of $F(y_1^*)$ and $F(y_2^*)$. This observation immediately gives the result:

---

[9]See Chiappori and Guesnerie (1991) and Guesnerie and Woodford (1992) for recent surveys.
[10]Guesnerie and Woodford (1992) discuss possible interpretations of s_t.

Proposition 12.4. *For two points* y_1^* *and* y_2^*, *assume* $F(y_1^*) < F(y_2^*)$. *There exist* $0 < \pi_{ij} < 1$ *such that* (y_1^*, y_2^*) *is an SSE with transition probabilities* π_{ij} *if and only if the points* y_1^* *and* y_2^* *both lie in the open interval* $(F(y_1^*), F(y_2^*))$.

This result can be used to construct examples of SSEs in economic models. It is important to emphasize that two points y_1^* and y_2^* need not in general be near any deterministic equilibria.

A large part of the literature has focused on the existence of SSEs in small neighborhoods around deterministic cycles or steady states for model (12.2). To make this notion precise, we say that an SSE $y = (y_1, y_2)$ is an ϵ-*SSE* relative to $\hat{y} = (\hat{y}_1, \hat{y}_2)$ if y lies in an ϵ-neighborhood of $\hat{y}$. For a local analysis, it is convenient to use the implicit function technique. For this purpose, define the vectors $y = (y_1, y_2)$, $\pi = (\pi_{11}, \pi_{22})$, and the function $g(y, \pi) = (g_1(y, \pi), g_2(y, \pi))$, where

$$g_1(y, \pi) = \pi_{11}F(y_1) + (1 - \pi_{11})F(y_2) - y_1,$$
$$g_2(y, \pi) = (1 - \pi_{22})F(y_1) + \pi_{22}F(y_2) - y_2.$$

The equations (12.3) can then be written compactly as the vector equation

$$g(y, \pi) = 0.$$

To be able to use the implicit function theorem, we need $\det(g_y) \neq 0$, where

$$g_y = \begin{pmatrix} \pi_{11}F'(y_1) - 1 & (1 - \pi_{11})F'(y_2) \\ (1 - \pi_{22})F'(y_1) & \pi_{22}F'(y_2) - 1 \end{pmatrix},$$

for the existence of ϵ-SSEs near deterministic equilibria.

A deterministic equilibrium 2-cycle is a limiting case of an SSE when $\pi_{11}, \pi_{22} \to 0$. Consider thus the case of an equilibrium 2-cycle $(\hat{y}_1, \hat{y}_2)$ such that $\hat{y}_1 = F(\hat{y}_2)$ and $\hat{y}_2 = F(\hat{y}_1)$. Evaluating $\det(g_y)$ at $(\hat{y}_1, \hat{y}_2)$, $\pi = (0, 0)$, it is easy to check that SSEs exist in a neighborhood of the 2-cycle, provided $F'(\hat{y}_1)F'(\hat{y}_2) \neq 1$. Similarly, a pair of distinct steady states, i.e., a pair $(\hat{y}_1, \hat{y}_2)$ satisfying $\hat{y}_1 \neq \hat{y}_2$, $\hat{y}_1 = F(\hat{y}_1)$ and $\hat{y}_2 = F(\hat{y}_2)$ is a limiting case of SSEs with $\pi_{11}, \pi_{22} \to 1$. One evaluates $\det(g_y)$ at $(\hat{y}_1, \hat{y}_2)$, $\pi = (1, 1)$. A quick computation yields the existence of ϵ-SSEs in a neighborhood of a pair of distinct steady states if $F'(\hat{y}_1) \neq 1$ and $F'(\hat{y}_2) \neq 1$ at $(\hat{y}_1, \hat{y}_2)$. We collect these results into the following.

Proposition 12.5. (i) *If* $F'(\hat{y}_1)F'(\hat{y}_2) \neq 1$ *holds for a 2-cycle* $(\hat{y}_1, \hat{y}_2)$, *there is an* $\epsilon > 0$ *such that, for all* $0 < \epsilon' < \epsilon$, *there exists an* ϵ'-*SSE relative to* $(\hat{y}_1, \hat{y}_2)$.

(ii) *If $F'(\hat{y}_1) \neq 1$ and $F'(\hat{y}_2) \neq 1$ at a pair of distinct steady states $(\hat{y}_1, \hat{y}_2)$, there is an ϵ such that, for all $0 < \epsilon' < \epsilon$, there exists an ϵ'-SSE relative to $(\hat{y}_1, \hat{y}_2)$.*

For an illustration of an SSE near a pair of distinct steady states, see Figure 4.7 of Chapter 4. SSEs can also exist near a single steady state $\hat{y} = F(\hat{y})$ under some conditions. The implicit function technique is unhelpful in this case as $g_\pi = 0$. One can nevertheless use a direct argument based on Proposition 12.4; see Evans and Honkapohja (1994c) for details of the proof. This yields the result:

Proposition 12.6. *There is an $\epsilon > 0$ such that, for all $0 < \epsilon' < \epsilon$, there exists an ϵ'-SSE relative to a single steady state $\hat{y}$ if and only if $|F'(\hat{y})| > 1$.*

To conclude the general discussion on the existence of SSEs, we remark here that for fully specified models it is sometimes possible to utilize arguments based on global analysis (such as the index theorem of Poincare and Hopf) to prove the existence of SSEs. This argument was developed in Azariadis and Guesnerie (1982), Azariadis and Guesnerie (1986), and Spear (1984). We do not go into details here.

We next provide several examples of SSEs in various versions of the overlapping generations (OG) model.

12.5.1   Examples: OG Models

Example 1. **The Basic OG Model.** The basic building blocks for this model were developed in Section 4.2 of Chapter 4. As before, the economy consists of identical generations of identical agents who live each for two periods. Agents work when they are young and consume when old. The utility function of an agent in generation t takes the form $U(c_{t+1}) - V(n_t)$, where c_{t+1} is consumption at old age and n_t is labor supply. There is a constant stock of money M and money is the only means of saving the revenue obtained from working. The budget constraints are $p_t n_t = m_t = p_{t+1} c_{t+1}$, where m_t is nominal saving by the representative agent of generation t.

Letting p_t denote the price of the good and assuming an interior solution, the first-order condition for utility maximization takes the form

$$E_t^* \left[U'\left(\frac{p_t n_t}{p_{t+1}}\right)\left(\frac{p_t}{p_{t+1}}\right) - V'(n_t) \right] = 0,$$

where E_t^* denotes the subjective expectation over (the random variable) p_{t+1} by the agent.

An REE is achieved by requiring that (i) desired savings are equal to the existing amount of money, $\forall t: m_t = M$, and (ii) the subjective expectations of the agents are true conditional expectations of future prices given information at time t, i.e., $\forall t: E_t^*(\cdot) = E_t(\cdot)$. The information set is assumed to include current values of the endogenous variables. For simplicity we formulate the analysis in terms of employment n_t. Noting that the equilibrium condition $p_t n_t = M$ implies $p_t/p_{t+1} = n_{t+1}/n_t$, an REE can be defined as a (possibly random) sequence of labor inputs $\{n_t\}$ satisfying

$$E_t\big(U'(n_{t+1})n_{t+1}\big) - V'(n_t)n_t = 0.$$

If agents do not necessarily have rational expectations but it is known that prices will clear markets each period, we obtain a corresponding equation characterizing the temporary equilibrium in any period t, given subjective expectations, namely,

$$V'(n_t)n_t = E_t^*\big(U'(n_{t+1})n_{t+1}\big).$$

This equation states that current labor supply depends on the expectations of the (marginal utility) value of labor supply/output next period. Given the properties of $V(\cdot)$, this equation can be solved for n_t to yield

$$n_t = \mathcal{W}^{-1}\big[E_t^*\big(G(n_{t+1})\big)\big], \tag{12.12}$$

where $\mathcal{W}(n) = V'(n)n$ and $G(n) = U'(n)n$. Alternatively, defining $y = V'(n)n$, we can write the equation for a temporary equilibrium in the form $y_t = E_t^*(F(y_{t+1}))$, where $F = G \circ \mathcal{W}^{-1}$.

Depending on the specification of the utility of consumption $U(\cdot)$ and disutility of labor $V(\cdot)$, the mapping $F(\cdot)$ can take various forms, and different types of REE are possible, including stationary sunspot equilibria. Using the existence results above, it is easy to construct examples of SSEs near a steady state and a deterministic cycle. The situation is best described with the aid of the offer curve

$$n_t = \mathcal{W}^{-1}\big(G(n_{t+1})\big) \equiv \mathcal{F}(n_{t+1}), \tag{12.13}$$

which characterizes the possible perfect-foresight (nonstochastic) time paths in the (n_{t+1}, n_t)-space. Suppose now that in the Samuelson model the offer curve is downward sloping at the interior steady state $\bar{n}$ with $\mathcal{F}'(\bar{n}) < -1$. (In this case the steady state is called locally indeterminate, since there exists a continuum of dynamic paths converging to it.) Then by Proposition 12.6 above, there exist ϵ-SSEs in the vicinity of $\hat{n}$.

After the work of Grandmont (1985), the existence of deterministic cycles has been much studied in the case of utility functions $U(c) = (c + \tilde{c})^{\alpha_1}$ and $V(n) = -(\tilde{n} - n)^{\alpha_2}$, where $\tilde{n}$ is the initial endowment of labor and $\tilde{c}$ is a consumption good endowment of the old. With suitable values for the parameters α_1 and α_2, this case can lead to the existence of cycles of different order. Proposition 12.5(i) above then yields the existence of ϵ-SSEs near such deterministic cycles.

Example 2. **Money-Financed Government Deficits.** In Section 11.6.2 of Chapter 11, we developed the extension of the basic OG model, where it is assumed that the government buys a positive constant amount g of output from the young and finances its purchases by printing money.[11] The equation for the offer curve can be written in the form (11.14), which with constant government purchases is

$$n_t V'(n_t) = U'(n_{t+1} - g)(n_{t+1} - g). \tag{12.14}$$

This offer curve was graphed in Figure 11.3 in Chapter 11. If we suppose that with $g = 0$ the offer curve is upward sloping, a steady state with autarky (no trade) exists in addition to an interior steady state. Then the effect of $g > 0$ is to shift the offer curve (12.14) downward. This shift creates two interior steady states as was illustrated in Figure 11.3. Using Proposition 12.5(ii), it is evident that with two interior steady states, sunspot equilibria near them, i.e., ϵ-SSEs, are possible near the distinct steady states.

Example 3. **The Model with Increasing Social Returns.** A different generalization of the basic OG model incorporating increasing social returns to production was developed in Section 4.6 of Chapter 4. This model often has three interior steady states, so that by Proposition 12.5(ii), there exist sunspot solutions, i.e., ϵ-SSEs, near any pair of distinct steady states, verifying the earlier discussion of such equilibria in Chapter 4.

12.6 Learning SSEs

12.6.1 Formulation of the Learning Rule

We now start to model learning rules that can in principle enable agents' expectations to converge to an SSE. If agents believe that the economy is in an SSE,

---

[11] This is a special case of the models studied by Grandmont (1986).

a natural estimator for the value of y_t in the two different sunspot states is the computation, for each state of the sunspot process in the past, of the average of the observations of y_t that have arisen in that state of the sunspot s_t. Throughout our discussion we are assuming that the state is observed at t. We remark that alternatively learning could be formulated in terms of estimating the values of $F(y_t)$ in the two different states, as was done in Section 4.6.4 of Chapter 4. Although these procedures are not identical, they have the same local stability properties.

Thus let $\phi_t = (\phi_{1t}, \phi_{2t})$ be the estimates of the values that y_t takes in states 1 and 2 of the sunspot. Let also $\psi_{jt} = 1$ if $s_t = j$ and 0 otherwise be the indicator function for state j of the sunspot. Clearly, $\psi_{2t} = 1 - \psi_{1t}$. Then we can write the learning rules based on state-contingent averaging in the following form:

$$\phi_{jt} = \phi_{j,t-1} + t^{-1}\psi_{j,t-1}q_{j,t-1}^{-1}(y_{t-1} - \phi_{j,t-1} + \varepsilon_{t-1}), \qquad (12.15)$$
$$q_{jt} = q_{j,t-1} + t^{-1}(\psi_{j,t-1} - q_{j,t-1}),$$
$$y_t = \psi_{1t}[\pi_{11}F(\phi_{1t}) + (1 - \pi_{11})F(\phi_{2t})]$$
$$+ \psi_{2t}[(1 - \pi_{22})F(\phi_{1t}) + \pi_{22}F(\phi_{2t})],$$

for $j = 1, 2$. We note here that in the learning rules, agents are assumed to use observations only through period $t - 1$. This is to avoid a simultaneity between y_t and expectations $F(y_{t+1})^e$.

Equations (12.15) are interpreted as follows. $tq_{j,t-1}$ is the number of times state j has occurred up to time $t - 1$. The recursion for the fraction of observations of state j is the second equation in (12.15). The first equation is then a recursive form for the state averages, with one modification to be discussed shortly. Finally, the third equation in (12.15) gives the temporary equilibrium for the model, since the right-hand side is the expectation of the value of $F(y_{t+1})$ given the forecasts ϕ_{jt}. In this formulation we implicitly assume that the agents know the transition probabilities π_{ij}.

The modification in the learning rule mentioned above is that we have included a random disturbance ε_t to the algorithm. It can be interpreted as a measurement or observation error, and it is assumed to be iid with mean zero and bounded support ($|\varepsilon_t| < C, C > 0$, with probability 1).[12]

12.6.2   Analysis of Convergence

We now show that, under a stability condition developed below, the learning rule (12.15) above converges locally to an SSE. We utilize the local conver-

---

[12]The observation error is needed only for the instability result. $C > 0$ can be arbitrarily small.

gence results in Chapters 6 and 7. The key stability condition will, as usual, be interpreted as E-stability conditions. First introduce the variables

$$\theta_t' = (\phi_{1t}, \phi_{2t}, q_{1t}, q_{2t}),$$
$$X_t' = (\psi_{1,t-1}, \psi_{2,t-1}, \varepsilon_{t-1}),$$

and the functions

$$H_j(\theta_{t-1}, X_t) = \psi_{j,t-1} q_{j,t-1}^{-1}(y_{t-1} - \phi_{j,t-1} + \varepsilon_{t-1}), \qquad j = 1, 2,$$
$$H_{2+i}(\theta_{t-1}, X_t) = \psi_{i,t-1} - q_{i,t-1}, \qquad\qquad\qquad i = 1, 2.$$

For state dynamics, we note simply that X_t is a Markov process independent of θ_t. The system is then in the standard form (6.3) for recursive algorithms. [Note that the complementary term $\rho_t(\theta_{t-1}, X_t) \equiv 0$.] For the formal analysis, this requires an extension of the basic conditionally linear framework of Chapter 6 to non-iid shocks or alternatively to Markovian state dynamics treated in Chapter 7. The formal details are given in Evans and Honkapohja (1994c) for the former approach and Evans and Honkapohja (1998a) for the latter.

The associated ODE governing local convergence is $d\theta/d\tau = h(\theta)$, where

$$h_1(\theta) = \bar{\pi}_1 q_1 \big[\pi_{11} F(\phi_1) + (1 - \pi_{11}) F(\phi_2) - \phi_1 \big],$$
$$h_2(\theta) = \bar{\pi}_2 q_2 \big[(1 - \pi_{22}) F(\phi_1) + \pi_{22} F(\phi_2) - \phi_2 \big],$$
$$h_3(\theta) = \bar{\pi}_1 - q_1,$$
$$h_4(\theta) = \bar{\pi}_2 - q_2.$$

Here $(\bar{\pi}_1, \bar{\pi}_2)$ is the limiting distribution of the states of the Markov chain. Clearly, at the equilibrium point $q_1 = \bar{\pi}_1$, $q_2 = \bar{\pi}_2$, and (ϕ_1, ϕ_2) is an SSE. In the ODE $\dot{\theta} = h(\theta)$, the subsystem consisting of the last two components of $h(\theta)$ is independent of (ϕ_1, ϕ_2) and it is globally stable in the domain $q_i \in (0, 1)$, $i = 1, 2$. It follows that the entire ODE is locally stable provided $DT(\phi_1, \phi_2)$ has all eigenvalues with real parts less than 1, where

$$T(\phi_1, \phi_2) = \big(\pi_{11} F(\phi_1) + (1 - \pi_{11}) F(\phi_2),$$
$$\qquad\qquad (1 - \pi_{22}) F(\phi_1) + \pi_{22} F(\phi_2) \big). \tag{12.16}$$

Note that the function $T(\phi_1, \phi_2) = [T_1(\phi_1, \phi_2), T_2(\phi_1, \phi_2)]$ defines the mapping from the perceived law of motion $[y_{t+1} = \phi_1$ if $s_{t+1} = 1$, $y_{t+1} = \phi_2$ if $s_{t+1} = 2]$ to the actual law of motion $[y_{t+1} = \phi_1^*$ if $s_{t+1} = 1$, $y_{t+1} = \phi_2^*$ if $s_{t+1} = 2]$, where $(\phi_1^*, \phi_2^*) = T(\phi_1, \phi_2)$. The condition on the eigenvalues can thus be used to define the concept of E-stability for sunspot equilibria.

We have completed the proof of the result:

Proposition 12.7. *The learning rule (12.15) converges locally to an SSE* (y_1^*, y_2^*) *provided it is weakly E-stable, i.e., the eigenvalues of* $DT(y_1^*, y_2^*)$ *have real parts less than* 1.

Remark. The notion of convergence is that of Chapter 6, Theorem 6.5. If the algorithm is augmented with a projection facility, almost sure convergence obtains.

It is also possible to derive an instability result along the lines of Evans and Honkapohja (1994c) for SSEs which are not weakly E-stable:

Proposition 12.8. *Suppose that an SSE* (y_1^*, y_2^*) *is weakly E-unstable, i.e.,* $DT(y_1^*, y_2^*)$ *has an eigenvalue with real part greater than* 1. *Then the learning dynamics (12.15) converges to* (y_1^*, y_2^*) *with probability zero.*

The stability result can also be developed for the general model (12.1) mentioned in the beginning of this chapter. We can at the same time extend our analysis to the case of a K-state Markov chain specified by an s_t with transition probabilities π_{ij} and states $j = 1, \ldots, K$. A *noisy sunspot equilibrium* is an RE solution to equation (12.1) which is of the form $y_t = y_i(v_t)$ if $s_t = i$, for $i = 1, \ldots, K$, where $y_i(\cdot)$ are functions defined as follows:

$$y_i(v) = H\left(\sum_{j=1}^{K} \pi_{ij}\lambda_j, v\right), \qquad \lambda_j = EG(y_j(w), w).$$

Here w is a random variable having the same distribution as the shock v_t and E denotes the expectation over w.

To analyze stability under learning, the corresponding T-mapping is constructed as follows. Let λ_{jt} denote the expectations of agents at time t of the mean value of $G(y, v)$ when the sunspot is in state j. Define $T(\lambda) = (T_1(\lambda), \ldots, T_K(\lambda))$, where

$$T_i(\lambda) = EG\left(H\left(\sum_{j=1}^{K} \pi_{ij}\lambda_j, w\right), w\right).$$

The E-stability condition is then that all the eigenvalues of the matrix

$$DT(\lambda) = \left[\partial T_i(\lambda)/\partial\lambda_j\right]$$

have real parts less than 1. As before, the E-stability condition governs the local convergence under adaptive learning.[13]

12.6.3   Stability of SSEs near Deterministic Solutions

We return to the case of two-state Markov SSEs in the model (12.2). The results from the preceding section show that local convergence to SSEs can be studied using E-stability based on equation (12.16). Computing DT, we have

$$DT(y) = \begin{pmatrix} \pi_{11} F'(y_1) & (1 - \pi_{11}) F'(y_2) \\ (1 - \pi_{22}) F'(y_1) & \pi_{22} F'(y_2) \end{pmatrix}.$$

The analysis of E-stability of SSEs near deterministic solutions (ϵ-SSEs) is based on two observations. First, $DT(y)$ can be computed for the deterministic solutions, which are limiting cases for ϵ−SSEs. Second, under a regularity condition, the continuity of eigenvalues provides corresponding E-stability conditions for ϵ-SSEs in a neighborhood of the deterministic solution. This approach yields the following result.

Proposition 12.9. *(i) Given a 2-cycle $\hat{y} = (\hat{y}_1, \hat{y}_2)$ with $F'(\hat{y}_1) F'(\hat{y}_2) \neq 0$, there is an $\epsilon > 0$ such that, for all $0 < \epsilon' < \epsilon$, all ϵ'-SSEs relative to $\hat{y}$ are weakly E-stable if and only if $\hat{y}$ is weakly E-stable, i.e., it satisfies $F'(\hat{y}_1) F'(\hat{y}_2) < 1$.*

(ii) Given two distinct steady states $\hat{y}_1 \neq \hat{y}_2$, there is an $\epsilon > 0$ such that, for all $0 < \epsilon' < \epsilon$, all ϵ'-SSEs relative to $\hat{y} = (\hat{y}_1, \hat{y}_2)$ are weakly E-stable if and only if both steady states are weakly E-stable, i.e., $F'(\hat{y}_1) < 1$ and $F'(\hat{y}_2) < 1$.

Proof. (i) Computing DT at the 2-cycle $(\hat{y}_1, \hat{y}_2)$, one obtains

$$DT(\hat{y}_1, \hat{y}_2) = \begin{pmatrix} 0 & F'(\hat{y}_1) \\ F'(\hat{y}_2) & 0 \end{pmatrix},$$

since the 2-cycle is the limiting case $\pi_{11} = \pi_{22} = 0$. The eigenvalues are given by the equation $\lambda^2 - F'(\hat{y}_1) F'(\hat{y}_2) = 0$. The 2-cycle is weakly E-stable if and only if $\text{Re}\{[F'(\hat{y}_1) F'(\hat{y}_2)]^{0.5}\} < 1$, which is equivalent to $F'(\hat{y}_1) F'(\hat{y}_2) < 1$. The rest of the proof is based on the continuity of eigenvalues and on Proposition 12.5(i); see Evans and Honkapohja (1994c) for details.

---

[13]This result is due to Evans and Honkapohja (1998a), which may be consulted for details on both the existence of such equilibria and the proof of the convergence result.

(ii) The pair of distinct steady states is a limiting case $\pi_{11} = \pi_{22} = 1$ for SSEs. *DT* becomes

$$DT = \begin{pmatrix} F'(\hat{y}_1) & 0 \\ 0 & F'(\hat{y}_2) \end{pmatrix}.$$

The rest of the proof again follows from a continuity of eigenvalues argument.□

We remark that analogous results are available when the 2-cycle or the distinct steady states are strongly E-stable; see Evans and Honkapohja (1994c) for the definition of strong E-stability and other details.

For the case of a single steady state the situation is more complex, but the following partial result can be established.

Proposition 12.10. *Let $\hat{y}$ be a weakly E-unstable steady state, i.e., $F'(\hat{y}) > 1$. Then there exists an $\epsilon > 0$ such that, for all $0 < \epsilon' < \epsilon$, all ϵ'-SSEs relative to $\hat{y}$ are weakly E-unstable.*

Proof. By continuity, the eigenvalues of *DT* are in a small neighborhood of the eigenvalues of the matrix

$$F'(\hat{y}) \begin{pmatrix} \pi_{11} & 1 - \pi_{11} \\ 1 - \pi_{22} & \pi_{22} \end{pmatrix} = F'(\hat{y})\Pi.$$

The eigenvalues of Π are 1 and $\pi_{11} + \pi_{22} - 1$. Thus the roots of $F'(\hat{y})\Pi$ include $F'(\hat{y}) > 1$ and we have instability.   □

One may recall from Proposition 12.6 that SSEs near a single steady state $\hat{y}$ also exist when $F'(\hat{y}) < -1$. For this case, it appears that both E-stable and E-unstable ϵ-SSEs relative to $\hat{y}$ may exist. However, it can be shown that there is a neighborhood of $\hat{y}$ such that SSEs in the neighborhood are E-unstable in a strong sense; see Evans and Honkapohja (1994c), Proposition 4.3 for details.

12.6.4 Stability in Overlapping Generations Models

In Section 12.5.1 we sketched three OG models which had steady-state and periodic REEs. We now consider each of these models for stability of SSEs.

Example 1 (Continued): **The Basic OG Model.** The perfect-foresight equilibria in the basic model satisfy equation (12.13) and this model has both steady-state and periodic REEs. It was also noted that if the steady-state solution is locally indeterminate, i.e., it satisfies $F'(\hat{n}) < -1$, there exist SSEs near $\hat{n}$. We can now apply Proposition 12.7 and the remarks after Proposition 12.10 and note that there is a neighborhood, i.e., $\epsilon > 0$, such that, for all $0 < \epsilon' < \epsilon$, all ϵ'-SSEs relative to $\hat{n}$ are strongly unstable under adaptive learning. These equilibria may, however, sometimes be weakly stable.

Consider next the equilibrium 2-cycle $(\hat{n}_1, \hat{n}_2)$ for the same model. If the 2-cycle satisfies $F'(\hat{n}_1)F'(\hat{n}_2) < 1$, all SSEs sufficiently near $(\hat{n}_1, \hat{n}_2)$ are weakly stable under adaptive learning by Propositions 12.7 and Proposition 12.9(i).

***Example 2 (Continued)*: Model with Money-Financed Deficits.** We recall that in the (n_{t+1}, n_t) space there are two interior steady-state equilibria $\hat{n}_1$ and $\hat{n}_2$ given by the intersection of the offer curve (12.14) and the 45° line (assuming an upward-sloping curve). Of these, the low steady state is locally indeterminate under perfect-foresight dynamics, but it is unstable under adaptive learning, since the offer curve cuts the 45° line from below (i.e., the derivative of the offer curve at $\hat{n}_1$ is greater than 1). For SSEs sufficiently near $\hat{n}_1$, we also have that these SSEs are weakly unstable under adaptive learning.

The high steady state $\hat{n}_2$ is stable under learning under the assumption that agents perceive the economy to be in a steady-state law in their learning. We can note that there are no SSEs in the neighborhood of $\hat{n}_2$. However, since the model has two interior steady states, there also exist SSEs that alternate between points near $\hat{n}_1$ and $\hat{n}_2$. Nevertheless, these SSEs are not stable under learning, since the low steady state $\hat{n}_1$ is not E-stable.

***Example 3 (Continued)*: OG Model with Increasing Social Returns.** As a third application of the stability results, consider the extension of the basic OG model to include increasing social returns. The formulation of learning for this model was developed in Section 4.6.4 of Chapter 4. As was noted above, with an upward-sloping offer curve, there can be three intersections with the 45° line in the (n_{t+1}, n_t) space and so three interior steady-state solutions can exist. The low and high steady states are both E-stable, since the derivative of the offer curve at these points is between 0 and 1. By Propositions 12.7 and 12.9(ii), all SSEs in a neighborhood of this pair are stable under learning. In addition, SSEs near the middle steady state also exist, but all SSEs sufficiently near it are unstable since the slope of the offer curve at that steady state is greater than 1. Similarly, SSEs near a pair of steady states, which includes the middle steady state, are unstable under learning.

12.7 Global Analysis of Learning Dynamics

The previous section focused exclusively on the local convergence of learning dynamics to SSEs. For some fully specified models, such as the overlapping generations model, it is also possible to derive results about the global convergence of the learning algorithms. This was done in Woodford (1990). Formally, such results require a careful specification of the model at the boundaries of the state space, so that the technique in Section 7.6 of Chapter 7 can be employed. This is usually best done in the context of a specific economic model, but it is possible to develop the following somewhat more general approach which is suitable for models of the form (12.2). We consider only two-state SSEs.

Assume now for concreteness that the mapping $F(y)$ in equation (12.2) is nonnegative and it is defined in some interval $[0, \infty)$.[14] For the boundary behavior, $F(y)$, it is assumed that

(A.1) There exists a point $\tilde{y}$ such that for all $y \geq \tilde{y}$, $F(y) \leq \tilde{F}$, a constant.

(A.2) There exists a $\check{y}$ such that $F(y)$ is increasing for all $y \leq \check{y}$ and $\lim_{y \to 0} F(y)/y > 1$.

Let us now adopt the vector notation $y = (y_1, y_2)$ when convenient. A basic implication of these two assumptions is the following.

Lemma 12.11. *Assume (A.1) and (A.2) hold. Then for each k, the functions* $m_k(y) = \sum_{j=1}^{2} \pi_{kj} F(y_j) - y_k$ *have the following boundary behavior:*

(i) *There exists a y^1 such that $y_k \leq y^1$, $y^1 \geq y_j \geq y_k$, $j \neq k$ implies $m_k(y) > 0$.*

(ii) *There exists a y^2 such that $y_k \geq y^2$, $y^2 \leq y_j \leq y_k$, $j \neq k$ implies $m_k(y) < 0$.*

Proof. To prove part (i), one notes that when $y_j \leq \check{y}$, one has $m_k(y) \geq F(y_k) - y_k$, since $\sum \pi_{kj} = 1$. Then Assumption (A.2) implies the result. To prove (ii), note that Assumption (A.2) implies that $m_k(y) \leq \tilde{F} - y_k$ for all y large enough. Then making y_k sufficiently large yields the result. $\square$

This lemma has the important consequences that in some compact domain $[y_L, y_H]^2$, the vector field $\dot{y} = m(y) \equiv (m_1(y), m_2(y))$ is inward pointing in the boundaries of that domain, and that it has no critical points outside that domain [except possibly at $(0, 0)$]. These zeroes, of course, constitute the SSEs of the system, together with the possible steady state $\hat{y} = F(\hat{y})$. At this stage we also introduce the following regularity assumption:

(A.3) At the critical points $\check{y}$ of $m(y)$, no eigenvalue of $Dm(\check{y})$ has a zero real part.

---

[14]If $F(y)$ is defined on a finite domain, Assumption (A.1) below needs to be strengthened somewhat.

We reconsider the learning rule (12.15). Using the functions $m_k(\cdot)$ introduced in the lemma, it is seen that, provided $\psi_{j,t-1} = 1$, the evolution of ϕ_{jt} is determined by

$$\phi_{jt} = \phi_{j,t-1} + t^{-1} q_{j,t-1}^{-1} \left(m_j(\phi_{1,t-1}, \phi_{j,t-1}) + \varepsilon_{t-1} \right).$$

In view of the lemma above, it then appears natural to limit the parameter estimates ϕ_{jt} to a compact set $[y_L, y_H]$ implied by the lemma. If the learning agents are endowed with this knowledge, it is also evident that the learning rule (12.15) itself must be modified in order to ensure that ϕ_{jt} remain inside $[y_L, y_H]$. Thus we postulate that

$$\phi_{jt} = \phi_{j,t-1} + t^{-1} \psi_{j,t-1} q_{j,t-1}^{-1} \left(y_{t-1} - \phi_{j,t-1} + \varepsilon_{t-1} \right)$$

$$\text{if RHS} \in [y_L, y_H],$$

$$\phi_{jt} = y_L \quad \text{if RHS} < y_L,$$

$$\phi_{jt} = y_H \quad \text{if RHS} > y_H,$$

while we retain the other parts of the system

$$q_{jt} = q_{j,t-1} + t^{-1} (\psi_{j,t-1} - q_{j,t-1})$$
$$y_t = \psi_{1t} \left[\pi_{11} F(\phi_{1t}) + (1 - \pi_{11}) F(\phi_{2t}) \right]$$
$$\quad + \psi_{2t} \left[(1 - \pi_{22}) F(\phi_{1t}) + \pi_{22} F(\phi_{2t}) \right].$$

The analysis of the modified algorithm proceeds along the same lines as before. One derives the associated differential equation $d\theta/d\tau = h(\theta)$, which is the same as before in Section 12.6.2. Using the notation in the lemma, it can be written in the form

$$h_1(\theta) = \bar{\pi}_1 q_1 m_1(\phi_1, \phi_2), \qquad (12.17)$$
$$h_2(\theta) = \bar{\pi}_2 q_2 m_2(\phi_1, \phi_2),$$
$$h_3(\theta) = \bar{\pi}_1 - q_1,$$
$$h_4(\theta) = \bar{\pi}_2 - q_2.$$

We note here that for some $q^* > 0$ small enough, the independent subsystem consisting of the last two components of equation (12.17) is inward pointing in the cube $[q^*, 1]^2$. Moreover, by Assumption (A.3), no eigenvalue of $Dh(\theta)$ has a zero real part at the zeroes of $d\theta/d\tau = h(\theta)$. Using a "nonlocal" version of the convergence theorem for recursive algorithms [e.g., Ljung (1977, Theorem 1) or Theorem 7.11 in Section 7.6 of Chapter 7], one obtains the following result.

Proposition 12.12. *(i) Assume that the associated differential equation* $d\theta/d\tau = h(\theta)$*, where* $h(\theta)$ *is given by equation (12.17), has an invariant set* I *whose domain of attraction includes the compact set* $D = [y_L, y_H]^2 \times [q^*, 1]^2$. *Then all the trajectories of the modified learning algorithm converge to* I.

(ii) Any point $(\phi_1, \phi_2, q_1, q_2)$ *is either a fixed point of the differential equation such that the eigenvalues of* $Dh(\theta)$ *have negative real parts, or the point has a neighborhood* N *such that, under the learning dynamics, the probability of* $\theta_t \to N$ *is zero.*

This proposition is important, since it shows that, under the assumptions made in this section, the learning algorithm will converge globally to the invariant set of the associated differential equation. Moreover, the possible convergence points consist of those that are locally stable for the differential equation. Taking into account the fact that the last two components of $h(\theta)$ form an independent subsystem with a unique zero at $(\bar{\pi}_1, \bar{\pi}_2)$, it is evident that the invariant set takes the form $I = J \times (\bar{\pi}_1, \bar{\pi}_2)$, where J is the union of ω-limit sets in $[y_L, y_H]$ of the "small" differential equation

$$\frac{d\phi}{d\tau} = T(\phi_1, \phi_2) - (\phi_1, \phi_2),$$

which just defines E-stability. Under some additional assumptions, it is possible to rule out ω-limit sets that are not fixed points of $T(\cdot)$.[15] When this is possible, then the result says that the learning dynamics converges globally to the set of E-stable REEs. If more than one REE is E-stable, the eventual point of convergence depends on the learning rule, the starting points, and the values of shocks during the adjustment.

12.8 Conclusions

The analysis in this chapter shows that the theory of local stability under learning is essentially complete for rational cycles and finite-state Markov sunspot equilibria. The E-stability conditions are straightforward to compute and they provide the local convergence condition under the real-time learning rule considered. One gap in the theory concerns the weak stability of sunspot solutions near a single steady state.

---

[15] See Woodford (1990) for a detailed example of how this can be done in the context of the standard OG model. Note that Woodford specifies the learning somewhat differently from our formulation in Section 3.

The reason for these tight results is that the REEs are locally unique in the space of functional forms permitted. For example, when considering two-state sunspot equilibria, we treat the exogenous sunspot as given with fixed transition probabilities. This assumption typically ensures local uniqueness. However, in many cases, if we were to allow a small perturbation in the transition probabilities (together with the corresponding change in the value of the endogenous variable), another "nearby" sunspot equilibrium can often be found. Obtaining a functional form with a finite number of parameters for the full set of Markov sunspot solutions is not straightforward. The corresponding analysis of learning would be evidently more difficult.

Throughout this chapter we have maintained the nonlinear form of the model. Another approach is to linearize the model in a neighborhood of the steady state. One can then analyze the various solutions for stability under learning using the techniques in Part III. When linearized, the models (12.1) and (12.2) are of the univariate form with expectations conditional on information dated at t. Applying the analysis of Section 9.7 of Chapter 9, it can be seen that the sunspot solutions are E-unstable. However, for multivariate frameworks, there is the possibility of E-stable sunspot solutions as discussed in Chapter 10.

Part **V**

Further Topics

Chapter **13**

Misspecification and Learning

13.1 Learning in Misspecified Models

In Section 3.6 of Chapter 3 we briefly considered the possibility of agents using a misspecified model. We take up this issue here at greater length. We will focus on two examples using models that have been previously analyzed under the assumption that their perceived laws of motion (PLMs) are correctly specified asymptotically. We will show that the same convergence tools used for correctly specified models can be used to show convergence to a restricted perceptions equilibrium in a misspecified model. Depending on the model and the nature of the misspecification, the relevant E-stability conditions which govern convergence may need to be altered, but the required analytical techniques are unchanged.

Before proceeding, we remark that when we say "misspecified model," we use the term to mean that the estimated PLMs cannot possibly converge to an REE, because the class of PLMs considered does not nest an REE. We remind the reader that even when this kind of misspecification is absent, there will still be econometric misspecification during the learning process. This is because, as econometricians, the agents act as if they are estimating a fixed process which is in fact time varying due to the self-referential feature of learning. This point was made in Chapter 2, Section 2.5. However, when the class of PLMs nest the REE of interest and estimates converge, the econometric misspecification vanishes asymptotically. The new feature in this chapter is that agents converge to a misspecified model over time.

317

13.1.1   Cobweb Model

Consider, again, the Muth cobweb model with reduced form

$$p_t = \mu + \alpha E_{t-1}^* p_t + \gamma' w_{t-1} + \eta_t, \tag{13.1}$$

where w_{t-1} is a vector of observable exogenous variables and η_t is an unobservable white noise shock independent of the w_t process. We assume that w_t follows a stationary VAR. For convenience and without loss of generality, we assume that w_t has zero mean. Instead of assuming that agents have a PLM of the form $p_t = a + b' w_{t-1} + \eta_t$, corresponding to the REE, we assume their PLM is (even asymptotically) misspecified. Clearly, there are many ways in which the model can be misspecified. Here we assume that the PLM takes the form of omitting a subset of the variables w_t. More specifically, write $w_t' = (w_{1,t}', w_{2,t}')$ and assume that the PLM takes the form

$$p_t = a + c' w_{1,t-1} + \varepsilon_t,$$

where ε_t is believed to be white noise. The agents' estimates $\phi_t' = (a_t, c_t')$ of ϕ are updated by recursive least squares (RLS) as usual. Let $x_t' = (1, w_{1,t}')$. The system can now be described as follows. Under RLS, parameter estimates are updated according to

$$\phi_t = \phi_{t-1} + t^{-1} R_t^{-1} x_{t-1} (p_t - \phi_{t-1}' x_{t-1}), \tag{13.2}$$

$$R_t = R_{t-1} + t^{-1} (x_{t-1} x_{t-1}' - R_{t-1}). \tag{13.3}$$

Expectations are given by $E_{t-1}^* p_t = \phi_{t-1} x_{t-1} = a_{t-1} + c_{t-1}' w_{1,t-1}$, so that the realized price p_t is given by

$$p_t = (\mu + \alpha a_{t-1}) + (\gamma_1 + \alpha c_{t-1})' w_{1,t-1} + \gamma_2' w_{2,t-1} + \eta_t,$$

where $\gamma' = (\gamma_1', \gamma_2')$. The updating equation for ϕ_t can thus be written as

$$\phi_t = \phi_{t-1} + t^{-1} R_t^{-1} x_{t-1} \left(x_{t-1}' \ \ w_{2,t-1}' \right) \begin{pmatrix} \mu + (\alpha - 1) a_{t-1} \\ \gamma_1 + (\alpha - 1) c_{t-1} \\ \gamma_2 \end{pmatrix}$$

$$+ t^{-1} R_t^{-1} x_{t-1} \eta_t.$$

To compute the associated differential equation for this stochastic recursive algorithm (SRA), note that

$$ER^{-1}x_{t-1}\big(x'_{t-1} \ w'_{2,t-1}\big)\begin{pmatrix} \mu + (\alpha - 1)a \\ \gamma_1 + (\alpha - 1)c \\ \gamma_2 \end{pmatrix}$$

$$= R^{-1}\left((Ex_{t-1}x'_{t-1})\begin{pmatrix} \mu + (\alpha - 1)a \\ \gamma_1 + (\alpha - 1)c \end{pmatrix}\right.$$

$$\left. +\begin{pmatrix} 0 \\ (Ew_{1,t-1}w'_{2,t-1})\gamma_2 \end{pmatrix}\right)$$

$$= R^{-1}(Ex_{t-1}x'_{t-1})\left(\begin{pmatrix} \mu + (\alpha - 1)a \\ \gamma_1 + (\alpha - 1)c \end{pmatrix}\right.$$

$$\left. +\begin{pmatrix} 0 \\ (Ew_{1,t-1}w'_{1,t-1})^{-1}(Ew_{1,t-1}w'_{2,t-1})\gamma_2 \end{pmatrix}\right).$$

Letting $Exx' = \lim_t Ex_t x'_t$, we thus obtain the ODE

$$d\phi/d\tau = R^{-1}(Exx')\big(T(\phi) - \phi\big),$$
$$dR/d\tau = Exx' - R,$$

where

$$T(\phi) = \begin{pmatrix} T_a(a, c) \\ T_c(a, c) \end{pmatrix} = \begin{pmatrix} \mu + \alpha a \\ \gamma_1 + \Omega_{11}^{-1}\Omega_{12}\gamma_2 + \alpha c \end{pmatrix}$$

and

$$E\begin{pmatrix} w_{1t} \\ w_{2t} \end{pmatrix}\big(w_{1t} \ w_{2t} \big)' = \begin{pmatrix} \Omega_{11} & \Omega_{12} \\ \Omega_{21} & \Omega_{22} \end{pmatrix}.$$

Since R converges globally to Exx' under the ODE, it follows as usual that stability of the ODE is determined by stability of the smaller differential equation $d\phi/d\tau = T(\phi) - \phi$. It is easily seen that this differential equation has the unique equilibrium

$$\bar{\phi} = \begin{pmatrix} \bar{a} \\ \bar{c} \end{pmatrix} = \begin{pmatrix} (1 - \alpha)^{-1}\mu \\ (1 - \alpha)^{-1}(\gamma_1 + \Omega_{11}^{-1}\Omega_{12}\gamma_2) \end{pmatrix}, \tag{13.4}$$

and that it is globally stable if and only if $\alpha < 1$. Applying the stochastic approximation results of Chapter 6, it follows that ϕ_t converges to $\bar{\phi}$ with probability 1. We have the following.

Proposition 13.1. *Consider the cobweb model (13.1) under the misspecified recursive least squares learning rule (13.2)–(13.3). Provided $\alpha < 1$, the estimates ϕ_t converge with probability 1 to the restricted perceptions equilibrium (13.4).*

The T-map above has a natural interpretation. For a given PLM with fixed parameters $\phi = (a, c')'$, the parameters $T(\phi)$ give the coefficients of the best linear forecast of p_t (in the mean square error sense) using the information set $x_{t-1} = (1, w'_{1,t-1})'$. That is, a PLM $p_t = \phi' x_{t-1} + \varepsilon_t$, where ε_t is white noise uncorrelated with x_{t-1}, generates the actual law of motion (ALM) $p_t = (\mu + \alpha a) + (\gamma_1 + \alpha c)' w_{1,t-1} + \gamma'_2 w_{2,t-1} + \eta_t$. For this ALM, the best model in the permitted class of PLMs is the "projected ALM" obtained by computing $E(p_t \mid x_{t-1}) = T(\phi)' x_{t-1}$. The fixed point $\bar{\phi}$ of $T(\phi)$ does not provide the coefficients of an REE, because a larger information set is available, namely $(x'_{t-1}, w'_{2,t-1})$. However, the forecasts are optimal relative to the restricted information set actually used by agents, and we therefore call this solution a *restricted perceptions equilibrium*.

We have shown that, provided the differential equation $d\phi/d\tau = T(\phi) - \phi$ is stable, a condition which we will call the "modified E-stability condition" for the misspecified model, there will be convergence of least squares learning to the restricted perceptions equilibrium $\bar{\phi}$. For the cobweb model, this condition is in fact identical to the familiar E-stability condition for the correctly specified model, $\alpha < 1$.[1]

13.1.2 Underparameterized Dynamics

In some cases misspecification can alter the stability condition for the resulting equilibrium. An interesting example is from Section 8.6.2 of Chapter 8, equation (8.37), which we reproduce here in simplified form:

$$y_t = \alpha + \beta E_t^* y_{t+1} + \delta y_{t-1} + v_t. \tag{13.5}$$

Here v_t is an unobserved white noise shock (we consider the case in which there are no observable exogenous shocks). Recall that under RE, there are two minimal state variable (MSV) solutions of the form $y_t = a + b y_{t-1} + d v_t$, where b is a root of the associated quadratic (this assumes two real roots). Section 8.6.2, Chapter 8, considered the local stability of these solutions under least squares learning.

---

[1] The related concepts of "limited information REE" and "reduced order limited information REE" were developed in Marcet and Sargent (1989b) and Sargent (1991), respectively.

We consider the case where agents estimate a simple underparameterized model, $y_t = a + \varepsilon_t$, where ε_t is white noise. A recursive estimate a_t of the mean is given by

$$a_t = a_{t-1} + t^{-1}(y_{t-1} - a_{t-1}), \tag{13.6}$$

so that the PLM at time t is $y_t = a_t + \varepsilon_t$ with corresponding forecasts

$$E_t^* y_{t+1} = a_t. \tag{13.7}$$

From the reduced form (13.5), it follows that y_t will actually follow the process

$$y_t = \alpha + \beta a_t + \delta y_{t-1} + v_t. \tag{13.8}$$

Equations (13.6) and (13.8) form an SRA in standard form. To obtain the associated ODE $da/d\tau = h(a)$, we need to calculate

$$h(a) = \lim_{t \to \infty} E(y_t(a) - a),$$

where

$$y_t(a) = \alpha + \beta a + \delta y_{t-1}(a) + v_t,$$

for fixed a. It is easily seen that

$$h(a) = \frac{\alpha + \beta a}{1 - \delta} - a,$$

provided $|\delta| < 1$, which ensures that the process $y_t(a)$ is asymptotically stationary. The ODE has a unique fixed point at $\bar{a} = (1 - \beta - \delta)^{-1}\alpha$. Furthermore, the ODE is globally stable if and only if $\beta(1 - \delta)^{-1} - 1 < 0$, which is equivalent (given $|\delta| < 1$) to the condition $\beta + \delta < 1$. The global stability results of Chapter 6 can be applied, yielding the following result.

Proposition 13.2. *Consider the model (13.5) with adaptive learning rule (13.6)–(13.7). Then a_t converges almost surely to the restricted perceptions equilibrium $\bar{a} = (1 - \beta - \delta)^{-1}\alpha$ provided $|\delta| < 1$ and $\beta + \delta < 1$.*

Again, there is a straightforward interpretation in terms of E-stability. For the PLM $y_t = a + \varepsilon_t$ with fixed a, the actual law of motion (ALM) is $y_t(a) = \alpha + \beta a + \delta y_{t-1}(a) + v_t$. This does not belong to the same parametric class as the PLM, so we project the ALM onto the space of permitted PLMs to find the best forecaster from this class (in the sense of mean square forecast error). This gives

$y_t = T(a) + \varepsilon_t$, where $T(a) = Ey_t(a) = (\alpha + \beta a)/(1 - \delta)$, provided $|\delta| < 1$. Because of the misspecified class of PLMs, agents ignore the serial correlation present in the y_t process, which is evident from writing the ALM as $y_t(a) = T(a) + (1 - \delta L)^{-1}v_t$ (here L is the lag operator). The "projected ALM" $y_t = T(a) + \varepsilon_t$ is the best description of the y_t process (for fixed a) within the class of PLMs considered, because it has the correct mean $T(a)$.[2] E-stability is then defined in terms of the equation $da/d\tau = T(a) - a$, which of course gives the stability conditions provided in Proposition 13.2.

Two important features of the results of this section should be noted. First, the assumed misspecification has radically altered the nature of the equilibria. Under rational expectations, there are two distinct solutions of the AR(1) form (assuming real roots). Under our simple misspecified model, there is a unique equilibrium. Second, the E-stability conditions are not the same for the correctly specified and the misspecified model. For the correctly specified model, the E-stability conditions for local convergence are shown in Figure 8.6 of Chapter 8. As we showed in that chapter, the conditions differed for the two distinct AR(1) solutions and it is clear that they in general differ from the modified E-stability conditions $|\delta| < 1$ and $\beta + \delta < 1$ for the misspecified model. However, we note that if $|\delta| < 1$ and $|\beta + \delta| < 1$, then both the $\bar{b}_-$ AR(1) REE and the underparameterized equilibrium are locally stable under learning.

13.1.3   Consistent Expectations Equilibria

In the above examples we have seen that, provided the modified E-stability conditions are met, adaptive learning can converge to a restricted perceptions equilibrium in which expectations are optimal within a limited class of PLMs. The basic idea of a restricted perceptions equilibrium is that we permit agents to fall short of rationality specifically in failing to recognize certain patterns or correlations in the data. Clearly, for this concept to be "reasonable" in a particular application, the unrecognized pattern or correlation should not be obvious. Hommes and Sorger (1997) have proposed the related, but distinct, concept of *consistent expectations equilibria*. This requires that agents correctly perceive all autocorrelations of the process.

It is worth reconsidering the above examples from this perspective. In the example of the preceding section, the dynamics are underparameterized. Consequently, in the restricted perceptions equilibrium, agents fail to notice the first-order serial correlation in the data and the equilibrium is not a consistent expectations equilibrium. If agents did notice this pattern and attempted to deal with

---

[2]In the case $|\delta| \geq 1$, the process is nonstationary and the mean is undefined.

it by including y_{t-1} as a regressor in their forecast rule, this would lead them to a class of PLMs that includes the AR(1) REE.

However, consider the Muth cobweb model. Here the specification error is the omission of variables $w_{2,t-1}$ which can help to forecast prices. Whether or not the restricted perceptions equilibrium fails to capture the serial correlation properties of the data depends on the stochastic process followed by the exogenous observable process $w_t' = (w_{1,t}', w_{2,t}')$. It is straightforward to calculate that at the restricted perceptions equilibrium $(\bar{a}, \bar{c})$ given by equation (13.4), the forecast errors are given by

$$\epsilon_t \equiv p_t - E_{t-1}^* p_t = -\left(\Omega_{11}^{-1}\Omega_{12}\gamma_2\right)' w_{1,t-1} + \gamma_2' w_{2,t-1} + \eta_t.$$

In general, this will not be a consistent expectations equilibrium since ϵ_t may be serially correlated. It remains a restricted perceptions equilibrium because $E(\epsilon_t \mid w_{1,t-1}) = 0$. However, in special cases the restricted perceptions equilibrium will also be a consistent expectations equilibrium. The most obvious case arises when w_t is an iid process. In this case there is no time-series structure in ϵ_t to exploit. The deviation from REE arises solely from the failure of agents to take direct account of the correlation with the observables $w_{2,t-1}$.[3]

13.1.4 Deterministic Cycles Misperceived as Random Fluctuations

Although they did not take up the issue of learning, Evans, Honkapohja, and Sargent (1993) present another interesting example of a restricted perceptions equilibrium. The basic idea is as follows. As is well known, and was discussed in Chapter 12, the standard overlapping generations (OG) model can have perfect-foresight equilibria that follow regular k-cycles or even exhibit chaotic trajectories. This raises the question of whether actual business cycle fluctuations could be the result of complex nonlinear dynamics rather than, as commonly assumed, due to random shocks. This viewpoint would require a dichotomy in which the agents in the model have perfect foresight, while the outside observers, i.e., econometricians, misperceive the fluctuations as random. This dichotomy appears too drastic, and Evans, Honkapohja, and Sargent (1993) raise the question of whether complex nonlinear dynamics could still be obtained in an economy in which the agents themselves, or at least a nonnegligible fraction of them, misperceive those dynamics as random fluctuations.

---

[3]If ϵ_t is serially correlated due to the serial correlation of w_t, agents may attempt to allow for this by including p_{t-1} as an additional regressor. In certain cases this may lead to a consistent expectations equilibrium.

Consider the standard OG model with production in which the utility of an agent from generation j is given by $U(c_{j+1}) - V(n_j)$, where n_j is labor supply when young and c_{j+1} is consumption when old. The budget constraints are $p_j n_j = m_j$ and $m_j = p_{j+1} c_{j+1}$, where m_j is the quantity of money held when young. We will be looking for periodic equilibria, i.e., k-cycles with price sequences $(p_1, \ldots, p_k)$. It is assumed that there are two types of agents. In each generation a fraction $1 - \mu$ has perfect foresight and a fraction μ has limited knowledge. The perfect-foresight agents solve the problem

$$\max_{n_j} U(p_j n_j / p_{j+1}) - V(n_j). \tag{13.9}$$

The agents with limited knowledge (who are called "econometricians") are assumed to know the unconditional distribution of prices, but to be ignorant of the serial correlation pattern. (Clearly, this assumption is plausible only if k is large and the pattern is complex.) They therefore use the unconditional distribution and assume that in each period each price $p_1, \ldots, p_k$ occurs with probability $1/k$, so that they solve the problem

$$\max_{n_j} (1/k) \sum_{i=1}^{k} U(p_j n_j / p_i) - V(n_j). \tag{13.10}$$

There is a fixed nominal stock of money M. We therefore define an equilibrium k-cycle to be a $3k$-tuple $\{(p_1, \ldots, p_k), (n_1^d, \ldots, n_k^d), (n_1^w, \ldots, n_k^w)\}$ such that, for all $j = 1, \ldots, k$,

(i) $M/p_j = \mu n_j^d + (1 - \mu) n_j^w$,

(ii) n_j^d solves equation (13.10), and

(iii) n_j^w solves equation (13.9).

Such an equilibrium is clearly a restricted perceptions equilibrium as long as $\mu > 0$ and the k-cycle is nontrivial, i.e., $k \geq 2$.

It is easily seen that, for $\mu = 1$, there are in fact no equilibrium k-cycles for any $k \geq 2$. This follows since then (i) implies $p_j / p_i = n_i / n_j$. Substituting this into the first-order condition for equations (13.10) implies that n_j is independent of j. Evans, Honkapohja, and Sargent (1993) show that, under some additional mild assumptions about preferences, we can obtain the following result: for every $k \geq 2$, there exists $\mu_k < 1$ such that there are no nontrivial k-cycles if $\mu > \mu_k$.

These results show that, for this specific model, equilibrium complex nonlinear dynamics which exist under perfect foresight are no longer possible when all or almost all agents misperceive them as an independently, identically distributed random process with the correct unconditional distribution.[4] This analysis can be criticized, since the agent-econometricians as modeled here are perhaps not sufficiently smart.[5] However, the example is a special case of a more general approach in which the agent-econometricians model the equilibrium as a stochastic process and where in equilibrium we impose that the "actual dynamic process be consistent with the forecasting rule." Evans, Honkapohja, and Sargent (1993) suggest in particular that it would be worth investigating whether, if the agent-econometricians perceive the data as following an AR(k) process, there exists an equilibrium p-cycle, with $p > k + 1$. As part of our restricted perceptions equilibrium concept, we would impose that the perceived AR(k) process be the one that best fit the p-cycle.

13.2 Misspecified Policy Learning

Although we have focused on models in which private agents are learning adaptively, similar considerations can be applied to optimizing policy makers. This point is developed extensively by Sargent (1999) and Cho and Sargent (1999), based on an earlier model by Sims (1988) and Chung (1990). In this work, the government is assumed to be estimating a popular but misspecified model of the inflation process. Here we present the simplest (static) version of Sargent's model. We focus on the case of decreasing gain, leaving the constant-gain case for the next chapter.

The government (falsely) believes that there is a Phillips curve trade-off between the time-t unemployment rate u_t and the time-t inflation rate, given by

$$u_t = \beta_0 + \beta_1 y_t + \varepsilon_t, \tag{13.11}$$

where ε_t is a white noise disturbance assumed uncorrelated with y_t.

Through monetary policy, the government sets a target inflation x_t, which determines inflation subject to a white noise shock v_{2t}:

$$y_t = x_t + v_{2t}. \tag{13.12}$$

---

[4]Evans, Honkapohja, and Sargent (1993) do show, however, that even with $\mu = 1$, equilibrium 2-cycles can arise in the classical version of the OG model.

[5]In Chapter 12 we allow the agents to estimate a k-cycle of appropriate order and we find that they can locally "learn" the k-cycle if the equilibrium cycle is E-stable.

The objective function of the government is to minimize the expected squared loss function $E(u_t^2 + x_t^2)$. For given β this would be minimized, given the above constraints, by

$$x_t = g(\beta), \tag{13.13}$$

where

$$g(\beta) = -(1 + \beta_1^2)^{-1}\beta_0\beta_1.$$

The true relationship between u_t and y_t is assumed to be given by an expectational Phillips curve

$$u_t = u^* - \varphi(y_t - \hat{x}_t) + v_{1t},$$

where $\hat{x}_t$ denotes expected inflation. v_{1t} is a white noise shock uncorrelated with v_{2t} and the parameters satisfy $u^*, \varphi > 0$. Let $Ev_{1t}^2 = \sigma_1^2$ and $Ev_{2t}^2 = \sigma_2^2$. Various assumptions are possible for $\hat{x}_t$ [and are explored in Sargent (1999)], but to focus on learning by the policy makers we assume rational expectations on the part of private agents: $\hat{x}_t = x_t$. This would be appropriate if a fully credible monetary authority simply announced its policy. We therefore have

$$u_t = u^* - \varphi(y_t - x_t) + v_{1t}. \tag{13.14}$$

The government thus has a PLM for the relationship between u_t and y_t given by equation (13.11) and parameterized by β. The ALM for (u_t, y_t, x_t) is instead given by equations (13.14), (13.12), and (13.13). Is the resulting ALM consistent with the government's PLM? Under the PLM β, the values for u_t and y_t are given by

$$u_t = \left(u^* + g(\beta)\varphi\right) - \varphi y_t + v_{1t}, \tag{13.15}$$
$$y_t = g(\beta) + v_{2t}. \tag{13.16}$$

Hence the ALM for the relationship between u_t and y_t takes the same form as equation (13.11) but with parameters $(\beta_0^*, \beta_1^*) = T(\beta_0, \beta_1)$, where

$$T(\beta) = \begin{pmatrix} u^* + g(\beta)\varphi \\ -\varphi \end{pmatrix}. \tag{13.17}$$

The ALM is consistent with the PLM if and only if $\beta = T(\beta)$. This is easily shown to imply that

$$\beta_0 = u^*(1 + \varphi^2), \qquad \beta_1 = -\varphi,$$

and hence $x_t = \varphi u^*$.

The value $\bar{\beta}$ such that $\bar{\beta} = T(\bar{\beta})$ is called by Sargent a "self-confirming equilibrium." Clearly, it is an example of what we have termed a "restricted perceptions equilibrium": given the restricted class of models envisioned by the government, parameter values $\bar{\beta}$ generate a stochastic process which is consistent with their PLM. We note that Sargent shows that this equilibrium corresponds to the time-consistent high-inflation Nash equilibrium identified by Kydland and Prescott (1977).

We next consider whether the equilibrium is stable under adaptive learning. We now assume that β is unknown by the government and estimated by a recursive least squares type regression of u_i on an intercept and y_i. The time-t estimate of β, obtained using data through time t, is given by

$$\begin{aligned} \beta_t &= \beta_{t-1} + \gamma_t R_{t-1}^{-1} z_t \left(u_t - \beta_{t-1}' z_t \right), \\ R_t &= R_{t-1} + \gamma_t \left(z_t z_t' - R_{t-1} \right), \end{aligned}$$

where $z_t' = (1, y_t)$. In the standard recursive least squares formulation we have $\gamma_t = t^{-1}$, and more generally we might consider $\gamma_t = \xi(t + N)^{-1}$ for $\xi > 0, N \geq 0.$[6] At time t, the government's perceptions are described by the parameters β_{t-1}, since data are not yet available on y_t and u_t, so policy sets the inflation target to $x_t = g(\beta_{t-1})$ and $y_t = g(\beta_{t-1}) + v_{2t}$. From equations (13.15) and (13.17) we have

$$u_t = T(\beta_{t-1})' z_t + v_{1t}.$$

Since from equations (13.14) and (13.12) we have $u_t = u^* - \varphi v_{2t} + v_{1t}$, and from equation (13.16) we have $y_t = g(\beta) + v_{2t}$, we arrive at the system

$$\begin{aligned} \beta_t &= \beta_{t-1} + \gamma_t R_{t-1}^{-1} z_t \left((T(\beta_{t-1}) - \beta_{t-1})' z_t + v_{1t} \right), \\ R_t &= R_{t-1} + \gamma_t \left(z_t z_t' - R_{t-1} \right), \\ z_t' &= \left(1, \ g(\beta_{t-1}) + v_{2t} \right). \end{aligned} \qquad (13.18)$$

---

[6]For simplicity, following Cho and Sargent (1999), in the β_t equation we use R_{t-1}^{-1} in place of the usual R_t^{-1}. This facilitates putting the algorithm in standard form.

The system (13.18) is in the form of a standard stochastic recursive algorithm. Convergence will therefore be governed by the associated differential equation. Using standard methods, we compute the ODE

$$d\beta/d\tau = R^{-1}M_z(\beta)\big(T(\beta) - \beta\big),$$
$$dR/d\tau = M_z(\beta) - R,$$

where

$$M_z(\beta) = \begin{pmatrix} 1 & g(\beta) \\ g(\beta) & (g(\beta))^2 + \sigma_2^2 \end{pmatrix}.$$

Clearly, there is a unique equilibrium of the ODE, i.e., $\beta = \bar{\beta}$ and

$$\bar{R} = M_z(\bar{\beta}) = \begin{pmatrix} 1 & u^*\varphi \\ u^*\varphi & (u^*\varphi)^2 + \sigma_2^2 \end{pmatrix}.$$

Local stability is easily examined since it is governed by the E-stability equation

$$d\beta/d\tau = T(\beta) - \beta,$$

where

$$T(\beta)' = \big(u^* - (1 + \beta_1^2)^{-1}\beta_0\beta_1\varphi, -\varphi\big), \tag{13.19}$$

so that

$$DT(\beta) = \begin{pmatrix} -(1 + \beta_1^2)^{-1}\beta_1\varphi & -(1 + \beta_1^2)^{-2}(1 - \beta_1^2)\beta_0\varphi \\ 0 & 0 \end{pmatrix}$$

and

$$DT(\bar{\beta}) - I = \begin{pmatrix} -(1 + \varphi^2)^{-1} & -u^*(1 + \varphi^2)^{-1}(1 - \varphi^2)\varphi \\ 0 & -1 \end{pmatrix}.$$

Clearly, both roots of $DT(\bar{\beta}) - I$ are real and negative, so that the ODE is locally stable. It follows that under the decreasing-gain sequence $\gamma_t = 1/t$, the stochastic approximation convergence results of Chapter 6 apply, so that there is local convergence to the self-confirming equilibrium $\bar{\beta}$ in the various senses discussed in that chapter. For example, under the gain sequence $\gamma_t = \xi(t + N)^{-1}$, for ξ sufficiently small or N sufficiently large (slow adaption), there will be convergence from initial nearby points with probability arbitrarily close to 1.

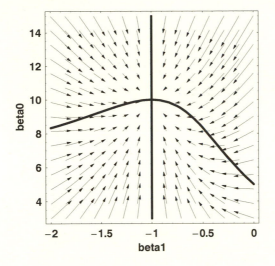

Figure 13.1.

The dynamics for E-stability (13.19) can be easily illustrated using a phase diagram. This is given in Figure 13.1 for the parameter values $u^* = 5$ and $\varphi = 1$ used by Sargent. The vertical line is the set of points for which $d\beta_1/d\tau = 0$, and the curve is the locus $d\beta_0/d\tau = 0$. It is evident from the figure that the system is in fact globally stable. This suggests that the real-time learning under decreasing gain is globally stable (though this would need to be investigated in detail).

Sargent considers the behavior of learning when the algorithm has constant gain $\gamma_t = \gamma$. This turns out to alter the dynamics substantially, because occasional large shocks can push the system far away from $\bar{\beta}$ for a substantial period of time. We take up this possibility in the next chapter.

13.3 Conclusions

When agents have a misspecified PLM and estimate the parameters by recursive least squares, the techniques of stochastic approximation can often still be applied. Convergence, when it occurs, is now to a restricted perceptions equilibrium instead of an REE. The number of such equilibrium points may depend on the form of misspecification. In the examples presented, the stability conditions are given by the E-stability principle modified to take account of the misspecification.

Chapter **14**

Persistent Learning Dynamics

14.1 Introduction

Throughout most of the book we have focused on the conditions under which adaptive learning rules converge in the limit to an REE. We have seen that this is usually governed, at least locally, by E-stability conditions and that, when there are multiple equilibria, these impose a substantive selection criterion. The previous chapter altered the framework to permit asymptotic misspecification of the law of motion followed by the economy. We saw that under appropriate stability conditions, the parameter estimates of the learning rule still converge asymptotically, but now to a forecast rule which is not fully rational, and which we called a "restricted perceptions equilibrium." Although the forecast rules in these equilibria are not fully rational, they are still rational in a weaker sense. It is well known that conditional expectations give the minimum MSE (mean square error) forecasts. In an REE the forecast rule is thus fully optimal in the sense of giving the minimum MSE over all forecast rules which are functions of the full information set.[1] In a restricted perceptions equilibrium, the forecast rule is optimal in the more limited sense of having the minimum MSE over forecast rules chosen within some class, e.g., linear rules which are a function of a specified subset of the full information set.

In this chapter we continue to depart from fully rational expectations, but do so in a different way. When agents estimate a misspecified model with a

---

[1] Since our models are typically self-referential, some care must be taken in interpreting the statement. In an REE the forecast rule is optimal given that the variables follow the stochastic process of that RE solution. Thus if there are multiple REE, a different forecast rule would be optimal in another REE and the MSE in that REE may be higher or lower.

decreasing-gain sequence, they are attempting to find the parameter value within some set which gives the optimal forecast rule. Suppose, however, that agents recognize that the class of forecast rules they are considering is misspecified. It is then no longer necessarily the case that a single forecast rule, with fixed parameters, is optimal at all times. In particular, if there is structural change in the sense that the economy follows a stochastic process within the set of models considered by agents, but with parameter values that evolve over time, then a more appropriate learning rule will attempt to track the evolution of the parameters.

Thus, structural change provides a motivation for using gain sequences which do not decrease to zero but instead remain bounded above zero. The simplest examples of this are constant-gain estimators in which $\gamma_t = \gamma$ for some $0 < \gamma \leq 1$. The use of constant-gain estimators to deal with structural change is well known from the statistics and engineering literature, as discussed, for example, in Benveniste, Metivier, and Priouret (1990, Part I, Chapters 1 and 4). In choosing the size of the gain parameter, there is a trade-off which is familiar from the statistics literature: a larger gain is better at tracking changes but at the cost of a larger variance. We discuss this issue below in connection with self-referential models in our analysis of the increasing social returns model with constant-gain learning.

Within self-referential models there is actually a second rationale for using constant- (or nondecreasing) gain estimators, namely the possibility of nonconvergence to RE. If, for whatever reason, the model under learning is not converging to an REE, then the actual stochastic process followed by the economy may best be modeled, given the PLMs employed by agents, as undergoing structural change over time. The use of a constant-gain estimator thus has aspects of a self-fulfilling prophecy, as we note in Section 14.3.4.

Because constant-gain estimators do not in general converge even to forecast rules that are rational in a restricted sense, they can give rise to additional learning dynamics not found in an REE, i.e., to "persistent learning dynamics." Such models thus have the potential to explain phenomena that cannot arise under REE, a point emphasized in Sargent (1993) and Sargent (1999). Formal analysis of learning with constant-gain algorithms is still possible using versions of the technical results given in Chapter 7, as we demonstrate below.

Before turning to the analysis, we remark that the division between the "misspecified learning" of the preceding chapter and the "persistent learning dynamics" of the current chapter is not necessarily clear-cut, since it depends on the class of PLMs used by the agent. As a simple example, suppose that y_t follows some stationary exogenous process, while agents incorrectly believe that y_t follows an IMA(1,1) process $\Delta y_t = \varepsilon_t - (1 - \gamma)\varepsilon_{t-1}$. If agents also believe they know the value of γ, then they will form forecasts of y_t at time $t - 1$ according to $y_t^e = \gamma \sum_{i=0}^{\infty} (1 - \gamma)^i y_{t-1-i}$. This is the minimum mean square error forecast given their mistaken beliefs, and it is an example of a (fixed) misspecified forecast rule.[2] On the other hand, suppose that agents model the process as a mean plus white noise, where the mean is subject to structural shifts. In this case they might use the simple constant-gain learning rule $y_t^e = a_t$, with $a_t = a_{t-1} + \gamma (y_{t-1} - a_{t-1})$, and we would say that the system exhibits persistent learning dynamics. Yet of course these two forecast rules are identical.

The same point holds if y_t is generated by a self-referential model such as the cobweb model. From the point of view of the evolution of the economy, it is arbitrary in this case whether to regard the deviation from REE dynamics as due to a misspecified model with a fixed forecast rule or as the result of persistent learning dynamics arising from changing parameter estimates. The distinction rests in the class of PLMs considered by the agents and the learning rule they adopt. Nonetheless, the distinction will prove useful, and the technical analysis of this chapter uses somewhat different tools.

14.2 Constant-Gain Learning in the Cobweb Model

The techniques of Section 7.4 of Chapter 7 can be applied to analyze the cobweb model when recursive least squares is modified to have constant gain. We focus on a special case of the model is which there is a single iid observed exogenous variable and in which there is no intercept, so that only the slope coefficient is estimated. The model is thus

$$p_t = \alpha p_t^e + \delta z_{t-1} + \eta_t,$$

where z_{t-1} is an iid exogenous variable observed at time $t - 1$ and η_t is unobserved white noise independent of the z_t process. Agents are assumed to forecast prices according to

$$p_t^e = \phi_{t-1} z_{t-1},$$

---

[2]If agents treat γ as unknown, they might update estimates of it over time using a decreasing-gain estimator, such as recursive nonlinear least squares, and asymptotically obtain the optimal value within the IMA(1,1) class.

where ϕ_{t-1} is their time-$(t-1)$ estimate of the slope coefficient of a regression of p_t on z_{t-1}. The algorithm for updating ϕ_{t-1} is

$$\begin{aligned} \phi_t &= \phi_{t-1} + \gamma R_t^{-1} z_{t-1}(p_t - \phi_{t-1} z_{t-1}), \\ R_t &= R_{t-1} + \gamma(z_{t-1}^2 - R_{t-1}). \end{aligned}$$

Using $p_t = (\delta + \alpha\phi_{t-1})z_{t-1} + \eta_t$ and writing $S_{t-1} = R_t$, we can rewrite the algorithm in the form

$$\begin{aligned} \phi_t &= \phi_{t-1} + \gamma\big(S_{t-1}^{-1} z_{t-1}^2(\delta + (\alpha-1)\phi_{t-1}) + S_{t-1}^{-1} z_{t-1}\eta_t\big), \\ S_t &= S_{t-1} + \gamma(z_t^2 - S_{t-1}). \end{aligned}$$

This is thus in the standard form

$$\theta_t = \theta_{t-1} + \gamma \mathcal{H}(\theta_{t-1}, X_t),$$

where

$$\theta_t = \begin{pmatrix} \phi_t \\ S_t \end{pmatrix}, \qquad \mathcal{H}(\theta_{t-1}, X) = \begin{pmatrix} \mathcal{H}_\phi(\theta_{t-1}, X_t) \\ \mathcal{H}_S(\theta_{t-1}, X_t) \end{pmatrix}, \qquad X_t = \begin{pmatrix} z_t \\ z_{t-1} \\ \eta_t \end{pmatrix},$$

and

$$\begin{aligned} \mathcal{H}_\phi(\theta_{t-1}, X_t) &= S_{t-1}^{-1} z_{t-1}^2(\delta + (\alpha-1)\phi_{t-1}) + S_{t-1}^{-1} z_{t-1}\eta_t, \\ \mathcal{H}_S(\theta_{t-1}, X_t) &= z_t^2 - S_{t-1}. \end{aligned}$$

We focus on the infinite-horizon asymptotic results. The basic result is that, under the additional assumptions stated in Theorem 7.9 of Chapter 7, the distribution of θ_t can be approximated, for small γ and large t, by

$$\theta_t \sim N(\theta^*, \gamma C),$$

where

$$\begin{aligned} \theta^* &= \big(\delta(1-\alpha)^{-1}, E z_t^2\big)', \\ C &= \int_0^\infty e^{sB} \mathcal{R}^* e^{sB'}\, ds. \end{aligned}$$

We need to establish that the required assumptions are met and then to calculate C. Let $D = \{(\phi, S) \mid \phi \in \mathbb{R},\ S \in (\zeta, \infty)\}$ for some fixed arbitrarily small $\zeta > 0$.

Assume that z_t has support on some closed interval $[z_L, z_H]$ and let $m_2^z = E z_t^2 > 0$. Assume also that η_t has compact support.

We show that Assumptions (A.2), (A.3), (M.1)–(M.5), (H.1)–(H.3), and (N.1) hold on the set D. From the form of $\mathcal{H}$, it is easily verified that the polynomial bound and Lipschitz conditions (A.2)–(A.3) on $\mathcal{H}$ and $\partial \mathcal{H}/\partial x$ are met for compact sets $Q \subset D$. Conditions (M.1)–(M.5) follow immediately from the assumptions that z_t and η_t are iid exogenous processes with bounded support. The function $h(\theta)$ which defines the ODE $d\theta/d\tau = h(\theta)$ is easily calculated to be

$$
\begin{aligned}
h_\phi(\phi, S) &= S^{-1} m_2^z (\delta + (\alpha - 1)\phi), \\
h_S(\phi, S) &= m_2^z - S.
\end{aligned}
$$

Here $\theta = (\phi, S)'$. Clearly, $h(\theta)$ has continuous first and second derivatives on D. From the theorem of Coddington (1961, p. 248), it follows that $D_\theta h(\theta)$ is Lipschitz on D. It is easily verified that $\theta^* = (\delta(1 - \alpha)^{-1}, m_2^z)'$ is the unique equilibrium point of $d\theta/d\tau = h(\theta)$, that the eigenvalues of $B = D_\theta h(\theta^*)$ are $\alpha - 1$ and -1, and that θ^* is a globally asymptotically stable equilibrium point of the ODE if $\alpha < 1$. Hence Assumptions (H.1)–(H.3) are met.

There remains to check Assumption (N.1). Assumption (N.1)(i) again is immediate from the assumptions on z_t and η_t. Assumption (N.1)(iv) requires that $\sup_t E_{x,a}(|\theta_t|^2) \le \mu(Q)(1 + |x|^{q_3})$ for $a = \theta_0 \in Q$ compact. Consider first the component $S_t = (1 - \gamma)S_{t-1} + \gamma z_t^2$. Clearly,

$$
\min(z_L^2, S_0) \le S_t \le \max(z_H^2, S_0).
$$

It follows that S_t^2 is uniformly bounded.

Next consider the component ϕ_t. We can write

$$
\phi_t = A_{t-1}\phi_{t-1} + B_{t-1},
$$

where

$$
\begin{aligned}
A_{t-1} &= \left(1 + \gamma S_{t-1}^{-1} z_{t-1}^2 (\alpha - 1)\right), \\
B_{t-1} &= \gamma \left(S_{t-1}^{-1} z_{t-1}^2 \delta + S_{t-1}^{-1} z_{t-1} \eta_t\right).
\end{aligned}
$$

Since $S_{t-1}^{-1} z_{t-1}^2 > 0$ has a uniform upper bound, for $\alpha < 1$ there exists $\gamma > 0$ sufficiently small so that $0 < A_{t-1} < \rho$ for all t for some $\rho < 1$. Clearly also $|B_{t-1}|$ has an upper bound, i.e., $|B_{t-1}| \le \bar{B}$ for all t for some $\bar{B} > 0$. Since

$$
\phi_t = \left(\prod_{i=0}^{t-1} A_i\right)\phi_0 + \sum_{k=0}^{t-2}\left(\prod_{i=k+1}^{t-1} A_i\right) B_k + B_{t-1},
$$

we have

$$|\phi_t| \le \rho^t \phi_0 + \bar{B} \sum_{i=0}^{t-1} \rho^i \le \phi_0 + \bar{B}(1-\rho)^{-1}.$$

Hence $|\phi_t|^2$ is bounded. By Cauchy–Schwartz, $|\phi_t S_t|$ is also bounded, so that $|\theta_t|^2$ is uniformly bounded over t. Condition (N.1)(iv) is therefore satisfied. Since $\mathcal{H}(\theta, x)$ is continuous on D, and since $|\theta_t|$ and $|X_t|$ are bounded, condition (N.1)(ii) also follows. Finally, from Evans and Honkapohja (1998a, property (i), p. 77), we have that $|v_\theta(y)| \le C(1 + |y|^{q_3})$ for some C, q_3 which may depend on θ. Since $|\theta_t|$ is bounded, there is some uniform constant $\bar{C}$ such that $|v_{\theta_t}(y)| \le \bar{C}(1 + |y|^{q_3})$. Since also $|X_t|$ is bounded, we have that $|v_{\theta_t}(X_{t+1})|$ and hence $|v_{\theta_t}(X_{t+1})|^2$ is bounded by some constant. Condition (N.1)(iii) follows.

In summary, provided $\alpha < 1$, the conditions required for Theorem 7.9 are met. Assuming $\alpha < 1$, we now turn to the calculation of $B = D_\theta h(\theta^*)$, R^*, and C. Computing $D_\theta h$ and evaluating it at $\theta^* = (\delta(1-\alpha)^{-1}, m_2^z)'$, we obtain

$$B = \begin{pmatrix} \alpha - 1 & 0 \\ 0 & -1 \end{pmatrix}.$$

From equation (7.9) of Chapter 7 we have the formula

$$\mathcal{R}^{ij}(\theta) = \sum_{k=-\infty}^{\infty} \mathrm{cov}\big[\mathcal{H}^i(\theta, X_k^\theta), \mathcal{H}^j(\theta, X_0^\theta)\big].$$

Since z_t and η_t are iid, it is straightforward to calculate $\mathcal{R}$ from the above equations for $\mathcal{H}(\phi, S)$. Evaluating at θ^*, we obtain

$$\mathcal{R}(\theta^*) = \begin{pmatrix} \left(m_2^z\right)^{-1}\sigma_\eta^2 & 0 \\ 0 & m_4^z - \left(m_2^z\right)^2 \end{pmatrix},$$

where $m_4^z = E z_t^4$. Thus,

$$e^{sB}\mathcal{R}^* e^{sB'} = \begin{pmatrix} \left(m_2^z\right)^{-1}\sigma_\eta^2 e^{2(\alpha-1)s} & 0 \\ 0 & \left(m_4^z - \left(m_2^z\right)^2\right)e^{-2s} \end{pmatrix},$$

and

$$C = \begin{pmatrix} \sigma_\eta^2 \left(2m_2^z(1-\alpha)\right)^{-1} & 0 \\ 0 & \left(m_4^z - \left(m_2^z\right)^2\right)/2 \end{pmatrix}.$$

It follows that for large t and small γ, we have that ϕ_t is approximately distributed as

$$\phi_t \sim N(\bar{\phi}, \gamma C_{11}),$$

where

$$\bar{\phi} = \delta(1-\alpha)^{-1}, \qquad C_{11} = \sigma_\eta^2 \left(2m_{\bar{z}}^2(1-\alpha)\right)^{-1}.$$

We remark that the condition $\alpha < 1$ required for this result is the familiar E-stability condition. Results presented in the early chapters showed that, for appropriate decreasing-gain sequences γ_t, we had $\phi_t \to \bar{\phi}$ with probability 1 provided the E-stability condition is met. With constant-gain algorithms, we instead obtain the results that, provided the E-stability condition holds, (i) the estimates are unbiased asymptotically, i.e., $E(\phi_t) \approx \bar{\phi}$ for t large, and (ii) ϕ_t approaches a limiting distribution which is tight around $\bar{\phi}$, for small γ, in the sense that the mean square deviation from $\bar{\phi}$ is small.

14.3 Increasing Social Returns and Endogenous Fluctuations

In Section 11.6.1 of Chapter 11, we introduced random production shocks and government consumption into the increasing social returns (ISR) model of Chapter 4. We reproduce here the basic structure for convenience. Employment is given by

$$n_t = H\left(G(n_{t+1}, v_{t+1})^e\right),$$

where

$$X_t = G(n_t, v_t) = \left((1-\zeta)f(n_t, \ell n_t)v_t\right)^{1-\sigma}$$

and

$$H(X) = (\alpha X)^{1/(1+\varepsilon)}$$

are appropriate functions, depending on preference and production parameters, which arise from the first-order condition. $f(n_t, \ell n_t)v_t$ is the production function, with the dependence on $N_t = \ell n_t$ representing a positive production externality associated with aggregate output, and v_t is a white noise positive productivity shock with mean 1. ζ gives government purchases as a proportion of output, assumed financed by seignorage. σ and ε are preference parameters, α is a production parameter, and we assume $0 < \alpha, \sigma < 1$ and $\varepsilon > 0$ throughout. For a range of parameters there are multiple stochastic steady-state REE, as illustrated for the nonstochastic case in Figure 4.5.

Under adaptive learning we write

$$\theta_{t-1} = G\left(n_{t+1}, v_{t+1}\right)^e,$$

and assume that expectations are updated according to the rule

$$\theta_t = \theta_{t-1} + \gamma_t (X_t - \theta_{t-1}).$$

In Chapter 11 we showed that, under standard decreasing-gain assumptions such as $\gamma_t = t^{-1}$, the low and high activity states are locally stable and that there is global convergence to one of these stochastic steady states, depending on the initial position and the sequence of shocks.

14.3.1 Constant-Gain Learning

We now turn to the question of how the dynamics of the model are affected by replacing the decreasing-gain assumption by the assumption of constant gain $\gamma_t = \gamma$ for some $0 < \gamma < 1$. Our discussion here follows and extends Evans and Honkapohja (1993a), where this question was taken up. The key difference from the decreasing-gain case is that, under constant-gain algorithms, there is the possibility of endogenous fluctuations, as the economy occasionally escapes from the basin of attraction of one stochastic steady state to the basin of attraction of another stochastic steady state.

We have previously noted that rational Markov sunspot equilibria can arise in this model and that they can be locally stable under an appropriate learning rule which allows for the possibility that agents condition their estimates on an observable sunspot. However, here we see that even if agents do not condition their estimates on an extraneous exogenous variable, but estimate a steady state using a constant-gain algorithm, then endogenous fluctuations can arise in which the economy shifts between high and low activity levels in a random way.

Recall from Chapter 11 that, for the specification of the production function $f(n_t, \ell n_t)$ given in Chapter 4, Section 4.6.1, there will generically be one or three steady states. Nonstochastic perfect-foresight steady states, when $v_t = 1$ with probability 1, are given by

$$n = \mathcal{F}(n) \equiv \alpha^{1/(1+\varepsilon)}\left((1-\zeta)f(n,\ell n)\right)^{(1-\sigma)/(1+\varepsilon)} = H\left(G(n,1)\right).$$

When there are three steady states we label them as $n_L < n_U < n_H$. Increases in the proportion of government purchases ζ rotate $\mathcal{F}$ downward, lowering both n_L and n_H. Sufficiently large increases in ζ can bifurcate the system, eliminating n_H. Similarly, sufficiently low values of ζ may also bifurcate the system, eliminating n_L. The following properties follow from $0 < \alpha, \sigma < 1$, $\varepsilon > 0$, and the form of $f(n, \ell n)$ given in Chapter 4, and will be used below:

(i) $\mathcal{F}(n)$ is continuous and strictly increasing with $\mathcal{F}(0) = 0$.

(ii) If there is a single interior steady state $\bar{n}$, then $\mathcal{F}(n) - n > 0$ for $0 < n < \bar{n}$ and $\mathcal{F}(n) - n < 0$ for $n > \bar{n}$. If there are three distinct steady states $n_L < n_U < n_H$, then $\mathcal{F}(n) - n > 0$ for $0 < n < n_L$ or $n_U < n < n_H$, and $\mathcal{F}(n) - n < 0$ for $n_L < n < n_U$ or $n > n_H$. Furthermore, $\mathcal{F}(n) - n \to -\infty$ as $n \to \infty$.

(iii) $\mathcal{F}(n)$ is differentiable almost everywhere and $\mathcal{F}'(0) = +\infty$, $0 < \mathcal{F}'(n_L)$, $\mathcal{F}'(n_H) < 1 < \mathcal{F}'(n_U)$.

These properties are illustrated in Figure 4.5.

The "size" of the productivity shock v_t plays a key role under constant-gain learning. This is seen most acutely by restricting attention to distributions with compact support. In particular, we assume that the support of v_t is the interval $I_v = [\bar{v}_1, \bar{v}_2]$, where $\bar{v}_1 < 1 < \bar{v}_2$, and that v_t has continuous positive density over $[\bar{v}_1, \bar{v}_2]$. Our first result is that if the support of v_t is sufficiently small, then n_t will become trapped in a small region of either n_L or n_H. Throughout this section we hold the gain parameter γ fixed at some value $0 < \gamma < 1$. (The choice of γ is considered later in the chapter.) We focus on the case in which three steady states exist. Let $\theta_L = G(n_L, 1)$, $\theta_U = G(n_U, 1)$, and $\theta_H = G(n_H, 1)$ be the values of $X = G(n, 1)$ corresponding to n_L, n_U, and n_H, respectively.

Proposition 14.1. *Suppose there are three steady states. There exist $\hat{v}_1 < 1 < \hat{v}_2$ so that, for all $\bar{v}_1, \bar{v}_2$ satisfying $\hat{v}_1 < \bar{v}_1 < 1 < \bar{v}_2 < \hat{v}_2$, there are neighborhoods $N(\theta_L) = (a_1, a_2)$ and $N(\theta_H) = (b_1, b_2)$, with $0 < a_1 < \theta_L < a_2 < \theta_U < b_1 < \theta_H < b_2$, such that $\theta_{t-1} \in N(\theta_L)$ implies $\theta_t \in N(\theta_L)$ and $\theta_{t-1} \in N(\theta_H)$ implies $\theta_t \in N(\theta_H)$.*

Proof. Combining equations, we have

$$\theta_t = \theta_{t-1} + \gamma \mathcal{H}(\theta_{t-1}, v_t), \tag{14.1}$$

where

$$\mathcal{H}(\theta, v) = G\big(H(\theta), v\big) - \theta.$$

From the forms for G and H, it can be seen that $G(H(\theta), v)$ is increasing and continuous in θ and v and that for any given $\theta > 0$, we have $\mathcal{H}(\theta, v) > 0$ for v sufficiently large and $\mathcal{H}(\theta, v) < 0$ for $v > 0$ sufficiently small. The above assumptions also guarantee that $\mathcal{H}(\theta_L, 1) = \mathcal{H}(\theta_U, 1) = \mathcal{H}(\theta_H, 1) = 0$, that $\mathcal{H}(\theta, 1) > 0$ for $0 < \theta < \theta_L$ or $\theta_U < \theta < \theta_H$, that $\mathcal{H}(\theta, 1) < 0$ for $\theta_L < \theta < \theta_U$ or $\theta > \theta_H$, and that $\partial \mathcal{H}(\theta_L, 1)/\partial \theta$, $\partial \mathcal{H}(\theta_H, 1)/\partial \theta < 0$ and $\partial \mathcal{H}(\theta_U, 1)/\partial \theta > 0$.

There is a critical value $\hat{v}_2 > 1$ of v such that $\mathcal{H}(\tilde{\theta}, \hat{v}_2) = 0$ for some $\tilde{\theta}$ satisfying $\theta_L < \tilde{\theta} < \theta_U$ and $\mathcal{H}(\theta, v) > 0$ for all $0 < \theta \leq \theta_H$ with $\theta \neq \tilde{\theta}$. Choose $1 < \bar{v}_2 < \hat{v}_2$. Then there exist $\theta_L < \hat{\theta}_1 < \hat{\theta}_2 < \theta_U$ such that $\mathcal{H}(\theta, \bar{v}_2) < 0$ for $\hat{\theta}_1 < \theta < \hat{\theta}_2$. Choose $\hat{\theta}_1 < a_2 < \hat{\theta}_2$. For any $0 < \bar{v}_1 < 1$, choose $0 < a_1 < \theta_L$ such that $\mathcal{H}(a_1, \bar{v}_1) > 0$. The function $\theta + \gamma \mathcal{H}(\theta, v) = (1 - \gamma)\theta + \gamma G(H(\theta), v)$ is continuous and increasing in θ and v. Since $\mathcal{H}(a_1, \bar{v}_1) > 0$ and $\mathcal{H}(a_2, \bar{v}_2) < 0$, the function $\theta + \gamma \mathcal{H}(\theta, v)$ maps the interval (a_1, a_2) into itself for every v satisfying $\bar{v}_1 \leq v \leq \bar{v}_2$. Thus from equation (14.1), $\theta_t \in N(\theta_L)$ if $\theta_{t-1} \in N(\theta_L)$.

The argument is analogous for $N(\theta_H)$. There is a critical value $0 < \hat{v}_1 < 1$ such that $\mathcal{H}(\tilde{\theta}, \hat{v}_1) = 0$ for some $\tilde{\theta}$ satisfying $\theta_U < \tilde{\theta} < \theta_H$ and $\mathcal{H}(\theta, v) < 0$ for all $\theta > \theta_L$ with $\theta \neq \tilde{\theta}$. One can then pick $\hat{v}_1 < \bar{v}_1 < 1 < \bar{v}_2$, and the rest of the argument is analogous. Clearly, by choosing $(\bar{v}_1, \bar{v}_2)$ so that $\hat{v}_1 < \bar{v}_1 < 1 < \bar{v}_2 < \hat{v}_2$, the arguments used to construct $N(\theta_L)$ and $N(\theta_H)$ can be simultaneously satisfied.   □

Thus, for a sufficiently small support for the productivity shock v_t, expectations will remain trapped in a neighborhood of θ_L or θ_H if they start in (or enter) that neighborhood. Note that since $n_t = H(\theta_{t-1})$, this also implies that n_t will be confined to a neighborhood of n_L or n_H. For initial expectations within the appropriate neighborhood, the arguments from Chapter 7, Theorem 7.9, can also be applied to obtain the limiting distribution of θ_t for small γ.[3] We note that the E-stability of θ_L and θ_H plays a critical role in this proposition.

Next we consider what happens if the support of v_t is increased.

Proposition 14.2. *Suppose there are three steady states. Suppose* $\bar{v}_1 < \hat{v}_1$ *and* $\bar{v}_2 > \hat{v}_2$.[4] *Then for every interval* $J = (\bar{\theta}_1, \bar{\theta}_2)$, $0 < \bar{\theta}_1 < \bar{\theta}_2$, *and for all neighborhoods* $N(\theta_H)$ *of* θ_H *and* $N(\theta_L)$ *of* θ_L, *there is a positive integer* T *such that if* $\theta_t \in J$, *then, for all* $s > t + T$, $\theta_s \in N(\theta_H)$ *with positive probability and* $\theta_s \in N(\theta_L)$ *with positive probability.*

---

[3] Even if γ is not small, an adaptation of the arguments of Honkapohja and Mitra (1999) can be used to show that θ_t converges to some limiting distribution.

[4] $\hat{v}_1$ and $\hat{v}_2$ are formally defined in the proof of the preceding proposition.

Proof. Pick any $0 < \bar{\theta}_1 < \theta_L$. From the proof of the preceding proposition, it follows that $\mathcal{H}(\theta, v) > 0$ for all $v > \hat{v}_2$ and $\bar{\theta}_1 \leq \theta \leq \theta_H$. Pick $\hat{v}_2 < v_2^* < \bar{v}_2$. Since $\mathcal{H}(\theta, v_2^*)$ is continuous in θ, it has a minimum on $\bar{\theta}_1 \leq \theta \leq \theta_H$ and $\Delta = \min_{\bar{\theta}_1 \leq \theta \leq \theta_H} \mathcal{H}(\theta, v_2^*) > 0$.

Given θ_t, consider paths $\tilde{\theta}_{t+i}$, $i = 1, 2, 3, \ldots$, generated by equation (14.1) with $v_{t+i} = v_2^*$, i.e., $\tilde{\theta}_{t+i} = \gamma \mathcal{H}(\tilde{\theta}_{t+i-1}, v_2^*)$ and $\tilde{\theta}_t = \theta_t$. For every $\bar{\theta}_1 \leq \theta_t \leq \theta_H$, there is such a path $\tilde{\theta}_{t+i}$ with $\theta_H < \tilde{\theta}_{t+K} < \theta_H + \gamma \Delta$ for some finite integer $K \leq 1 + (\theta_H - \bar{\theta}_1)/\gamma \Delta$. There is a continuation path $\tilde{\theta}_{t+i}$, $i = K + 1, \ldots$, starting from $\tilde{\theta}_{t+K}$ and generated by $v_{t+i} = 1$, i.e., $\tilde{\theta}_{t+i} = \gamma \mathcal{H}(\tilde{\theta}_{t+i-1}, 1)$, which converges to θ_H. Hence the path $\tilde{\theta}_{t+i}$ enters $N(\theta_H)$ in a finite number of steps L depending on $N(\theta_H)$. Let $T = K + L$. Thus there is a path $\theta_{t+i} = \tilde{\theta}_{t+i}$, starting from θ_t, which obeys (14.1) and with $\theta_{t+T} \in N(\theta_H)$ which is generated by a sequence $v_t, v_{t+1}, \ldots, v_{t+T}$ which lies within the support of the shocks. Because v_t is iid with positive density on the support, continuity of $\mathcal{H}(\theta, v)$ implies that the set of paths with $\theta_{t+T} \in N(\theta_H)$ has positive probability. Because continuation paths $\tilde{\theta}_{t+i}$, for $i \geq T + 1$ with $v_{t+i} = 1$, remain in $N(\theta_H)$, it also follows that for all $s > t + T$, $\theta_s \in N(\theta_H)$ with positive probability.

The argument presented assumes $\bar{\theta}_1 \leq \theta_t \leq \theta_H$, but clearly it also holds for $\theta_H < \theta_t \leq \bar{\theta}_2$, where T depends also on $\bar{\theta}_2$. The argument that for all $s > t + T$, $\theta_s \in N(\theta_L)$ with positive probability, is analogous. $\qquad\square$

This proposition shows that for a given constant gain γ, there is a critical size of the support of the exogenous shock v_t which prevents θ_t (and hence n_t) from remaining trapped forever in a neighborhood of the low-level state or in a neighborhood of the high-level steady state. Occasional sequences of large shocks can lead to paths which "escape" the ODE basin of attraction of θ_L to a neighborhood of θ_H for a period of time. Similarly, an occasional sequence of shocks can lead θ_t to escape the ODE basin of attraction of θ_H and return toward θ_L. Simulations illustrating this phenomenon are presented in Evans and Honkapohja (1993a) and below.

These "endogenous fluctuations" are induced by the learning rule in conjunction with the random shocks and depend on the constant-gain assumption. Under decreasing gain, such escape paths occur only with probability zero because the weight placed on current data shrinks to zero at an appropriate rate. By bounding the gain parameter γ_t away from zero, we obtain persistent learning dynamics dramatically different from either REE stochastic steady state.

14.3.2 Endogenous Fluctuations

To illustrate the possibility of endogenous fluctuations under constant-gain learning, we provide some results of a simulation in which the parameter values

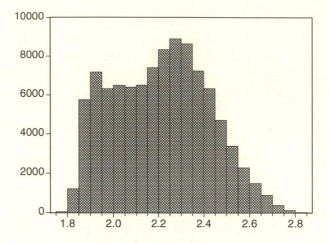

Figure 14.1. *Histogram for* $n(t)$.

are set so that there are three interior steady states, as illustrated in Figure 4.5, and in which there is constant-gain learning and a support for the productivity shock that is not "too small." For the simulation we use the production function developed in Evans and Honkapohja (1995b):

$$f(n, N) = An^\alpha \{\max(I^*, \lambda N(1 + \alpha\lambda N)^{-1})\}^\beta,$$

with parameters $A = 0.0805$, $\alpha = 0.025$, $\lambda = 0.5$, $\ell = 40$, $\beta = 1.007$, and $I^* = 19.5$. The other model parameters are set at $\varepsilon = 0.25$, $\sigma = 0.1$, and $\zeta = 0.04$. The random productivity shock is distributed as an iid lognormal random variable, i.e., $\ln \nu_t$ is normal with mean 1 and standard deviation 0.0577.[5] We choose the gain parameter $\gamma = 0.15$.

Figure 14.1 provides a histogram of the employment values n_t over a simulation of 100,000 periods. With the fixed-gain learning rule, the values of employment are concentrated around the two E-stable steady states, leading to a bimodal distribution. For these parameter values, $n_L \approx 1.9$, $n_U \approx 1.95$, and $n_H \approx 2.3$. There is nonetheless a wide range of n_t values as a result of the stochastic shocks in connection with the fixed-gain estimator.

Figure 14.2 exhibits the same data using a line graph of n_t plotted against n_{t-1} for a representative sequence of 2500 periods. This shows a very simple

---

[5] In Evans and Honkapohja (1993a), a uniformly distributed shock was used instead. Very similar results to those shown in Figures 14.1 and 14.2 are obtained for uniform shocks with an appropriate variance.

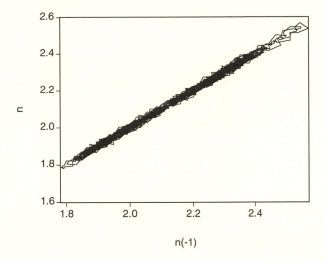

Figure 14.2.

example of the "escape route" phenomenon discussed in Sargent (1999) and in Cho and Sargent (1999). The path from a neighborhood of one steady state to a neighborhood of the other steady state takes a very specific form of a series of positive or negative productivity shocks by which estimates move from one regime to the other. We conjecture that further details about these paths for small gains could be obtained using the "large deviation theory" techniques described, for example, in Dupuis and Ellis (1997). Sargent (1999) and Cho and Sargent (1999) provide a general discussion and apply such techniques to analyze the Phillips curve policy model discussed in Chapter 13. We take this up in Section 14.4

14.3.3 Hysteresis with Time-Varying Policy

One motivation for use of fixed-gain learning rules is to deal with structural change. In nonlinear models such as the ISR model, changes in structural parameters can in some cases lead to a system bifurcation which changes the number of perfect-foresight steady states. For example, for appropriate parameter values, changes in the fiscal policy parameter ζ can alter the $\mathcal{F}(n)$ map as shown in Figure 14.3, so that for high values of ζ only the low-level (interior) steady state n_L exists, for low-levels of ζ only the high-level (interior) steady state n_H exists, and for intermediate levels there are the three interior steady states n_L, n_U, and n_H.

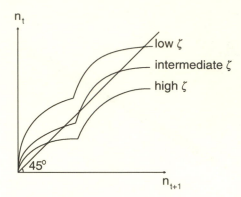

Figure 14.3. $n_t = \mathcal{F}(n_{t+1})$.

We have seen above that n_L and n_H are locally stable under adaptive steady-state learning (for decreasing or small gain). A change in the policy parameter leads to a shift in the system dynamics which is tracked better by a constant-gain estimator than by a decreasing-gain estimator, though at the cost of increased asymptotic variability when the structure is stable. If a change in ζ bifurcates the system, then this provides an additional advantage to the use of a fixed-gain learning rule when there is a large shift to a new steady state.

We illustrate this with the following example, which is based on Evans and Honkapohja (1993a). Suppose that fiscal policy changes slowly relative to the "learning speed," indexed by the fixed-gain parameter γ. Specifically, we choose a time-varying policy rule which follows a cosine function of time with a low frequency and an amplitude large enough to include each of the three regimes shown in Figure 14.3. Agents are assumed not to know the law of motion of this "structural change" resulting from the policy shifts, but to be aware that there are shifts and to use a fixed-gain rule to track the continually shifting mean value of the variable they are forecasting.

Figure 14.4 shows the path over time of a stochastic simulation with the ISR model for this setup. The amplitude of ζ is chosen so that it varies from $\zeta = 0$ to $\zeta = 0.12$ with a frequency of $\omega = 0.0005$. The fixed-gain parameter is set at $\gamma = 0.20$.[6] For this simulation, the productivity shock is distributed as an iid uniform random variable with support $1 \pm \tau$ with $\tau = 0.20$. The stochastic simulation is taken over 314,159 periods, giving 25 complete cycles of ζ.

---

[6]Other parameters are $\varepsilon = 0.25$, $\sigma = 0.1$, $A = 0.085$, $a = 0.025$, $\alpha = 0.9$, $\lambda = 0.5$, $K = 40$, $I^* = 14.1935$, $\beta = 1$, $\tau = 0.25$.

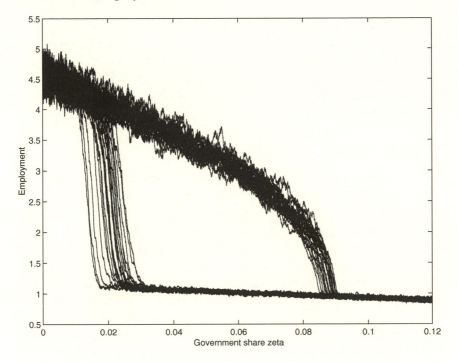

Figure 14.4.

The most dramatic aspect of Figure 14.4 is the strong hysteresis effects over intermediate ranges of ζ. Starting from high values of ζ, employment levels track fairly closely the low-level steady state as ζ moves through the high and intermediate ranges. For values of ζ somewhere in the 0.02 to 0.03 interval, the system bifurcation leads to a rapid revision upward of expectations and corresponding increases in employment. As ζ moves through the low range and back through the intermediate range, employment levels stay high until another system bifurcation occurs as ζ nears and goes beyond 0.09.

The parameters ω and γ are set so that there is relatively "fast learning" of the ever-shifting equilibrium. However, because of the stochastic productivity shocks v_t, there is significant random variation in the path for n_t. On the one hand, the conditional distribution in n_t for each value of ζ above 0.09 is quite tight around the mean, and for values in between 0.035 and 0.08 the distribution is bimodal but tight around each mode. On the other hand, for values of ζ between 0.02 and 0.03 or near 0.085, there is a large range of the distribution of n_t reflecting the uncertainty at which the "regime shift" will occur.

Policy effects in this type of model can therefore be highly nonlinear. In addition to the usual comparative statics type effects, in certain circumstances a change in ζ can exhibit threshold effects at critical levels, in which small changes induce large changes in n_t by shifting the economy between equilibria. Note that these effects are a joint result of the model and the form of adaptive learning behavior posited.

14.3.4 Equilibria in Learning Rules

With constant-gain learning rules there is a further issue which requires consideration: what determines the choice of the gain parameter γ? So far we have examined the effects on economic dynamics of a particular choice of γ by the agents. This naturally leads to the question: which gain parameter γ would be optimal from the point of view of an individual agent? This issue does not arise with the same force when agents use decreasing gains, provided parameters converge to their rational expectations values. If there is convergence to rational expectations, then asymptotically agents are using a fully optimal method of forming expectations. However, with constant-gain learning there typically is convergence to a stationary stochastic process in which agents are not forming expectations optimally even in the limit. It may then be possible for an individual agent to improve their forecast accuracy by altering their choice of gain parameter.

This line of thought suggests the concept of an equilibrium in learning rules, following Evans and Honkapohja (1993a). We continue to develop this within the context of the ISR model. Recall that under constant-gain learning with fixed gain γ_0, we have $n_t = H(G(n_{t+1}, v_{t+1})^e)$, where $G(n_{t+1}, v_{t+1})^e = \theta_{t-1}$ and $\theta_t = \theta_{t-1} + \gamma_0(G(n_t, v_t) - \theta_{t-1})$. This defines a Markov process in $n_t^{(\gamma_0)}$ and $\theta_t^{(\gamma_0)}$, where we use the superscript (γ_0) to denote the stochastic process induced by a particular choice γ_0. Consider now the optimal choice of γ given the economic equilibrium just defined. Let $\theta_t^{(\gamma_0)}(\gamma)$ be defined by the recursive algorithm

$$\theta_t^{(\gamma_0)}(\gamma) = \theta_{t-1}^{(\gamma_0)}(\gamma) + \gamma\left(G(n_t^{(\gamma_0)}, v_t) - \theta_{t-1}\right).$$

That is, $\theta_{t-1}^{(\gamma_0)}(\gamma)$ is the sequence of forecasts $G(n_{t+1}, v_{t+1})^e$ that would be obtained from using the fixed-gain parameter γ when the other agents in the economy are actually using gain γ_0. Let

$$MSE^{(\gamma_0)}(\gamma) = \lim_{t \to \infty} E\left(G(n_{t+1}, v_{t+1}) - \theta_{t-1}^{(\gamma_0)}(\gamma)\right)^2,$$

Table 14.1.

γ	$\widehat{MSE}^{(\gamma_0=0.15)}(\gamma)$
0.05	0.0276
0.10	0.0256
0.15	0.0253
0.20	0.0255
0.25	0.0259
0.30	0.0265
0.40	0.0278
0.50	0.0295
0.60	0.0314
0.70	0.0336
0.90	0.0395

provided this limit exists, be the asymptotic mean square error from using the fixed-gain rule γ when the other agents are in fact using γ_0. If

$$\gamma_0 = \arg\min_{\gamma} MSE^{(\gamma_0)}(\gamma),$$

then we say that we have an *equilibrium in learning rules*. Clearly, this is a Nash equilibrium in the sense that in such an equilibrium, no agent has an incentive to change to an alternative value of γ. (We assume that there is a large number of agents and each agent treats its actions as having negligible effects.)

For the ISR model, this equilibrium was investigated numerically in Evans and Honkapohja (1993a). Table 14.1 gives $\widehat{MSE}^{(\gamma_0)}(\gamma)$, the estimated values of $MSE^{(\gamma_0)}(\gamma)$ obtained as[7]

$$\widehat{MSE}^{(\gamma_0)}(\gamma) = T^{-1} \sum_{t=1}^{T} \left(G(n_{t+1}, v_{t+1}) - \theta_{t-1}^{(\gamma_0)}(\gamma)\right)^2,$$

using a stochastic simulation with $T = 100{,}000$.

From Table 14.1 it can be seen that $\gamma = 0.15$ is an approximate equilibrium in learning rules. These parameter values give rise to endogenous fluctuations in

---

[7]For this table the model parameters are those used in generating Figures 14.1 and 14.2, with the lognormal shock and $\zeta = 0.04$. In Evans and Honkapohja (1993a), a similar analysis was done using a uniformly distributed shock.

the sense defined above: the path of n_t periodically shifts between regions near the high- and low-level steady states. Note that there is a self-fulfilling prophecy operating here, but it is at the metalevel of learning rules. If all agents used a decreasing-gain sequence, this would also be individually optimal in the limit, but would converge to one of the two stable rational stochastic steady states.

For a treatment of equilibrium in learning rules within the context of the asset pricing model, see the discussion of "Optimal Misspecified Beliefs" in Sargent (1999, Chapter 6). A treatment within the context of an underparameterized model is given in Evans and Ramey (1998a).

14.4   Sargent's Inflation Model

We return to the model of inflation introduced by Sims (1988), Chung (1990), and Sargent (1999), discussed earlier in Section 13.2 of Chapter 13. In that section we showed that under decreasing-gain learning, there is convergence to the "high-inflation equilibrium" in which the Phillips curve parameters are perceived by the government to be

$$\bar{\beta}_0 = u^*(1 + \varphi^2), \qquad \bar{\beta}_1 = -\varphi.$$

We now consider the effects of altering the adaptive learning rule employed by the policy makers to employ a small constant gain in place of decreasing gain. This turns out to have a dramatic effect, as discussed at length in Sargent (1999) using an extended version of the model. Cho and Sargent (1999) consider the simplified version discussed in Chapter 13.

Using stochastic simulations, they show that while the paths still tend to converge toward $\bar{\beta}' = (\bar{\beta}_0, \bar{\beta}_1)$, with constant gain the parameter estimates follow a stochastic process that remains noisy in the limit. The paths tend to stay for a long period of time in a neighborhood of $\bar{\beta}$. However, the time paths occasionally deviate far from the equilibrium $\bar{\beta}$. These deviations, called "escape routes," appear almost always to go specifically in the direction of the "Ramsey" point $(\beta_0, \beta_1) = (u^*, 0)$.[8] This point corresponds to the fully optimal but time-inconsistent "low-inflation" policy since the inflation target x_t is zero at this value of β. Intriguingly, the escape routes to the Ramsey point always follow a narrowly circumscribed band in the parameter space. The Ramsey point,

---

[8]See Barro and Gordon (1983a) and Barro and Gordon (1983b) for further discussion of the significance of the Ramsey point.

however, is not an equilibrium: eventually the mean dynamics drive β back to a neighborhood of $\bar{\beta}$, the unique equilibrium.

Cho and Sargent (1999) provide a theoretical analysis of these escape route dynamics for the special case of discrete multinomial shocks. Our intention here is to provide an intuition for the appearance of escape routes in the model, based on the results from Chapter 7 on constant-gain algorithms and simulations of the mean ODE. As commented below, our treatment here is heuristic and we do not attempt to present a full analysis.

Under constant-gain learning, we now have

$$\begin{aligned}
\beta_n &= \beta_{n-1} + \gamma R_{n-1}^{-1} z_n (u_n - \beta_{n-1}' z_n), \\
R_n &= R_{n-1} + \gamma (z_n z_n' - R_{n-1}),
\end{aligned}$$

where $\beta_n' = (\beta_{0,n}, \beta_{1,n})$ are the time-n estimates of β and $z_n' = (1, y_n)$. Note that here we use n to denote real (discrete) time, so that we can later use t for corresponding fictitious (continuous) time. At time n, the government's perceptions of the Phillips curve parameters are described by the parameters β_{n-1}, since data are not yet available on inflation, y_n, and unemployment, u_n. Policy sets the inflation target to $x_n = g(\beta_{n-1})$ and $y_n = g(\beta_{n-1}) + v_{2n}$, with $g(\beta) = -(1 + \beta_1^2)^{-1} \beta_0 \beta_1$. From equations (13.15) and (13.17), we have

$$u_n = T(\beta_{n-1})' z_n + v_{1n},$$

where

$$T(\beta) = \begin{pmatrix} u^* + g(\beta)\varphi \\ -\varphi \end{pmatrix}.$$

Following the steps in Section 13.2 of Chapter 13, we arrive at the system

$$\begin{aligned}
\beta_n &= \beta_{n-1} + \gamma R_{n-1}^{-1} z_n ((T(\beta_{n-1}) - \beta_{n-1})' z_n + v_{1n}), \\
R_n &= R_{n-1} + \gamma (z_n z_n' - R_{n-1}), \\
z_n' &= (1, g(\beta_{n-1}) + v_{2n}).
\end{aligned} \tag{14.2}$$

We will analyze this system using Proposition 7.8 of Chapter 7. Let θ_n be the 6×1 vector $\theta_n' = (\beta_n', \text{vec}(R_n)')$. The components of the associated ODE $d\theta/dt = h(\theta)$ are given by

$$\begin{aligned}
h_\beta(\beta, R) &= R^{-1} M_z(\beta)(T(\beta) - \beta), \\
h_R(\beta, R) &= M_z(\beta) - R,
\end{aligned} \tag{14.3}$$

where

$$M_z(\beta) = \begin{pmatrix} 1 & g(\beta) \\ g(\beta) & (g(\beta))^2 + \sigma_2^2 \end{pmatrix}.$$

Using Proposition 7.8 of Chapter 7, we can approximate the time paths of the constant-gain learning dynamics using stochastic differential equations as follows. For clarity in this paragraph, we make the dependence of the algorithm on γ explicit by writing θ_n^γ for θ_n. Define the continuous-time interpolation $\theta^\gamma(t)$ of the real-time process θ_n^γ by

$$\theta^\gamma(t) = \theta_n^\gamma \quad \text{if} \quad n\gamma \le t < (n+1)\gamma.$$

We assume the initial condition $\theta_0^\gamma = a$. Let

$$U^\gamma(t) = \gamma^{-1/2}[\theta^\gamma(t) - \tilde{\theta}(t, a)],$$

where $\tilde{\theta}(t, a)$ is the solution to the ODE $d\theta/dt = h(\theta)$ with initial condition $\theta(0) = a$. Then for γ small, the probability distribution of $U^\gamma(t)$ converges to the probability distribution of the solution $U(t)$ to the stochastic differential equation

$$dU(t) = D_\theta h\big(\tilde{\theta}(t, a)\big) U(t)\, dt + \mathcal{R}^{1/2}\big(\tilde{\theta}(t, a)\big)\, dW(t), \qquad (14.4)$$

where $U(0) = 0$ and $W(t)$ is a standard Wiener process. Note that since $EU(t) = 0$ for all t, it follows that in the (small γ), limit $E\theta^\gamma(t) = \tilde{\theta}(t, a)$ for starting points $\theta(0) = a$. This implies that the estimates are asymptotically unbiased when $\lim_{t \to \infty} \tilde{\theta}(t, a) = \bar{\theta}$.[9] (This result is an approximation since it is based on Proposition 7.8.)

This is a high-dimensional system which in principle could be used to obtain an approximation for the algorithm from any starting point. A detailed study is beyond the scope of this book, but the key aspects of the dynamics can in fact be illustrated by (i) considering the stationary distribution of $\beta(t)$ for initial points at the equilibrium, and (ii) by considering the mean dynamics of β generated by the associated ODE for arbitrary starting points.

---

[9] Since $\bar{\theta}$ is E-stable, there will necessarily be convergence from nearby starting points. Simulations suggest that global convergence also obtains.

We start by calculating the 6×6 Jacobian $D_\theta h(\theta)$. Taking matrix differentials of h_β with respect to β, we have

$$dh_\beta = R^{-1}\big(dM(T-\beta) + M(dT - d\beta)\big)$$
$$= \text{vec } R^{-1} dM(T-\beta) + R^{-1}M\,dT - R^{-1}M\,d\beta.$$

Hence,

$$d \text{ vec } h_\beta = (T-\beta)' \otimes R^{-1} d \text{ vec } M + R^{-1}M(d \text{ vec } T - d \text{ vec } \beta),$$

so that

$$D_\beta h_\beta = \big((T-\beta)' \otimes R^{-1}\big)\frac{\partial \text{ vec } M}{\partial \text{ vec } \beta} + R^{-1}M(DT - I_2),$$

where $DT = \partial \text{ vec } T / \partial \text{ vec } \beta$.

Similarly, taking matrix differentials of h_β with respect to R, we have

$$dh_\beta = -R^{-1}(dR)R^{-1}M_z(\beta)\big(T(\beta) - \beta\big)$$
$$= -\big(T(\beta) - \beta\big)'M_z(\beta)'R'^{-1} \otimes R^{-1}d \text{ vec } R,$$

so that

$$D_R h(\beta) = -\big(T(\beta) - \beta\big)'M_z(\beta)'R'^{-1} \otimes R^{-1}.$$

Finally, since $dh_R(\beta, R) = dM_z(\beta) - dR$, we have

$$D_\beta h_R = \frac{\partial \text{ vec } M}{\partial \text{ vec } \beta} \quad \text{and} \quad D_\beta h_R = -I_4.$$

$\partial \text{ vec } M / \partial \text{ vec } \beta$ can be calculated explicitly from $M_z(\beta)$ and $g(\beta)$, but this will not be needed.

Evaluating the derivatives at the self-confirming equilibrium $\theta = \bar\theta$, i.e., at $\beta = \bar\beta$ and $R = \bar R$, we obtain

$$D_\theta h(\bar\theta) = \begin{pmatrix} DT(\bar\beta) - I_2 & 0 \\ \dfrac{\partial \text{ vec } M}{\partial \text{ vec } \beta}(\bar\beta) & -I_4 \end{pmatrix}. \tag{14.5}$$

Note that this matrix is block-triangular at $\bar\theta$ (though this does not hold elsewhere).

Next we need to calculate $\mathcal{R}(\bar\theta)$ from equation (7.9) of Chapter 7, i.e., $\mathcal{R}^{ij}(\theta) = \sum_{k=-\infty}^{\infty} \text{cov}[\mathcal{H}^i, \mathcal{H}^j]$. For this model, the components $\mathcal{H}_\beta$ and $\mathcal{H}_R$

of $\mathcal{H}(\theta, v_{1n}, v_{2n})$ are given by

$$\mathcal{H}_\beta = R^{-1}\left(\frac{1}{g(\beta)+v_{2n}}\right)\left((T(\beta)-\beta)'\left(\frac{1}{g(\beta)+v_{2n}}\right)+v_{1n}\right),$$

$$\mathcal{H}_R = \left(\frac{1}{g(\beta)+v_{2n}} \quad \frac{g(\beta)+v_{2n}}{(g(\beta)+v_{2n})^2}\right) - R.$$

Evaluating these expressions at $\beta = \bar{\beta}$ and $R = \bar{R} = M_z(\bar{\beta})$, we obtain

$$\mathcal{H}(\bar{\theta}, v_{1n}, v_{2n}) = \begin{pmatrix} \mathcal{H}_\beta \\ \mathrm{vec}\,\mathcal{H}_R \end{pmatrix}$$

$$= \begin{pmatrix} v_{1n} - (\varphi u^*/\sigma_2^2)v_{1n}v_{2n} \\ v_{1n}v_{2n}/\sigma_2^2 \\ 0 \\ v_{2n} \\ v_{2n} \\ 2\varphi u^* v_{2n} + v_{2n}^2 - \sigma_2^2 \end{pmatrix}.$$

Because v_{1n} and v_{2n} are white noise, it follows that

$$\mathcal{R}(\bar{\theta}) = E\mathcal{H}(\bar{\theta}, v_{1n}, v_{2n})\mathcal{H}(\bar{\theta}, v_{1n}, v_{2n})'.$$

Using the assumption that $Ev_{1n}v_{2n} = 0$, we obtain that $\mathcal{R}(\bar{\theta})$ takes the form

$$\mathcal{R}(\bar{\theta}) = \begin{pmatrix} \mathcal{R}_\beta(\bar{\theta}) & 0 \\ 0 & \mathcal{R}_R(\bar{\theta}) \end{pmatrix}, \tag{14.6}$$

where

$$\mathcal{R}_\beta(\bar{\theta}) = \begin{pmatrix} \sigma_1^2 + \sigma_1^2(\varphi u^*)^2/\sigma_2^2 & -\varphi u^* \sigma_1^2/\sigma_2^2 \\ -\varphi u^* \sigma_1^2/\sigma_2^2 & \sigma_1^2/\sigma_2^2 \end{pmatrix}.$$

For the initial condition $\theta(0) = \bar{\theta}$, we see from equations (14.5) and (14.6) that the process $U(t)$ in equation (14.4) is block-triangular and that the first two components $U_\beta(t)$ form an exogenous block. Attention can thus be focused on the small two-dimensional subsystem

$$dU_\beta(t) = D_\beta h(\bar{\theta})U_\beta(t)\,dt + \mathcal{R}_\beta^{1/2}(\bar{\theta})\,d\hat{W}(t), \tag{14.7}$$

where $U_\beta(t) = \gamma^{-1/2}\beta^\gamma(t)$, $\hat{W}(t)$ is a two-dimensional standard Wiener process, and $\beta^\gamma(t)$ are the first two components of $\theta^\gamma(t)$. In equation (14.7) we have

$$D_\beta h(\bar\theta) = DT(\bar\beta) - I_2$$
$$= \begin{pmatrix} -(1+\varphi^2)^{-1} & -u^*(1+\varphi^2)^{-1}(1-\varphi^2)\varphi \\ 0 & -1 \end{pmatrix}.$$

Using the results in Section 7.4 of Chapter 7 and Section 5.6.2 of Chapter 5, it follows that the stationary Gaussian solution to equation (14.7) has mean zero and a covariance function

$$\rho(k) = e^{kD_\beta h(\bar\theta)} V, \quad \text{where } k = s - t,$$

where the 2×2 matrix $V = (\mathcal{V}_{ij})$ satisfies the matrix equation

$$D_\beta h(\bar\theta) V + V \left(D_\beta h(\bar\theta)\right)' = -\mathcal{R}_\beta(\bar\theta). \tag{14.8}$$

The solution to equation (14.8) is given by

$$\mathcal{V}_{22} = \frac{\sigma_1^2}{2\sigma_2^2},$$

$$\mathcal{V}_{12} = \mathcal{V}_{21} = -u^*(2+\varphi^2)^{-1}\frac{\sigma_1^2}{\sigma_2^2}\left[\frac{(1-\varphi^2)\varphi}{2} + \varphi(1+\varphi^2)\right],$$

$$\mathcal{V}_{11} = -u^*(1-\varphi^2)\varphi v_{12} + \left(\frac{1+\varphi^2}{2}\right)\left[\sigma_1^2 + \frac{(u^*\varphi)^2\sigma_1^2}{\sigma_2^2}\right].$$

Adopting the numerical values $\varphi = 1$, $u^* = 5$, $\sigma_1 = \sigma_2 = 0.3$ utilized in Cho and Sargent (1999), one has

$$V = \begin{pmatrix} 29.09 & -10/3 \\ -10/3 & 1/2 \end{pmatrix}.$$

Our first task is to illustrate the approximate stationary distribution β_∞ for β_n, given the initial condition $\beta_0 = \bar\beta$. Note that $(\beta_\infty - \bar\beta) \sim \sqrt{\gamma} U_\infty$, so that $\text{var}\,\beta_n \approx \gamma V$ for large n. Moreover, the limiting distribution is Gaussian so that $\beta_n \sim N(\bar\beta, \gamma V)$ holds approximately for small γ and large n. For our numerical work we choose $\gamma = 0.05$ and compute the concentration ellipses for β_∞. Figure 14.5 gives the 50- and 95-percent concentration ellipses for the numerical example. Note that the first principal axis has a negative slope and the distribution is heavily concentrated near the principal axis. Under constant-gain learning, starting from the self-confirming equilibrium, one would expect to see many realizations in the directions indicated by the ellipses.

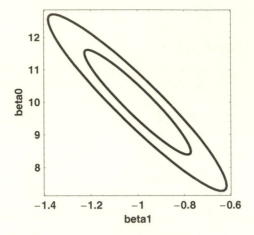

Figure 14.5.

Our other task is to study numerically the mean dynamics $E\theta^\gamma(t) = \tilde{\theta}(t, a)$ given by the associated ODE $d\theta/dt = h(\theta)$, where $h(\cdot)$ is given by equation (14.3). We consider a number of starting points using various initial values for β chosen from various regions in the 50-percent confidence ellipse. For R we choose the initial value equal to the equilibrium value $\bar{R}$.

Figure 14.6 illustrates the time paths for mean dynamics $\tilde{\beta}$ for β from the ODE for starting points chosen as follows: $\beta_0 = 10.75$, $\beta_1 = -1.1$ for panel a, $\beta_0 = 9.25$, $\beta_1 = -0.9$ for panel b, $\beta_0 = 9.85$, $\beta_1 = -1.025$ for panel c and $\beta_0 = 10.15$, $\beta_1 = -0.975$ for panel d. These points are (approximately) on the 50-percent concentration ellipse in the directions of the two principal axes. Note that for three of the four starting points, the time paths of β show a rapid transitory movement towards the Ramsey outcome $\beta_0 = 5$, $\beta_1 = 0$ before ultimately converging to the self-confirming equilibrium. These paths behave like the escape routes discovered by Sargent (1999) and analyzed further by Cho and Sargent (1999).[10]

Since the self-confirming equilibrium $\bar{\beta}$ is E-stable, starting points sufficiently close to $\bar{\beta}$ should not exhibit escape routes in the mean dynamics. In Figure 14.7 we provide a second set of numerical solutions to the ODE giving the mean dynamics for starting points which are placed as in the preceding figure but at half the distance from $\bar{\beta}$. Thus $\beta_0 = 10.375$, $\beta_1 = -1.05$ for panel a,

---

[10]The phenomenon of escape routes appears to be sensitive to the choice of the learning rule. Preliminary simulations with the mean dynamics corresponding to stochastic gradient learning under constant gain have not turned up escape paths.

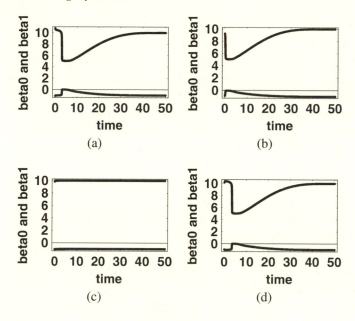

Figure 14.6.

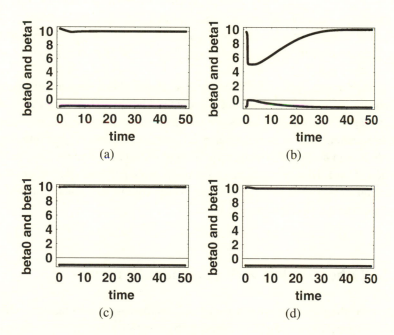

Figure 14.7.

$\beta_0 = 9.625$, $\beta_1 = -0.95$ for panel b, $\beta_0 = 9.925$, $\beta_1 = -1.0125$ for panel c, and $\beta_0 = 10.075$, $\beta_1 = -0.9825$ for panel d. The initial value of R is still set at $\bar{R}$. Now the paths do not exhibit escape routes except for panel b. In simulations (not presented here) in which the initial conditions are chosen even closer to $\bar{\beta}$, the phenomenon of escape routes for the ODE does not arise.

This shows the importance of the constant-gain assumption for obtaining recurring escape routes. Under decreasing gain, the parameter estimates will track the mean dynamics increasingly over time. Thus although for some initial conditions an escape route can arise en route, there is ultimately convergence to $\bar{\beta}$. In contrast, under constant-gain learning there will be occasional random displacements far from the mean dynamics. One can think of these as occasionally resetting the initial conditions sufficiently far from $\bar{\beta}$ to generate recurrent escape routes in the stochastic dynamics.

It should be emphasized that this analysis is illustrative in that we have not rigorously derived the existence and properties of the random escape routes discovered by Sargent (1999). Since the escape routes of the constant-gain algorithm (14.2) are a "rare event," i.e., arise with draws from the tails of the distribution of the shocks, the $\gamma \to 0$ limit of the constant-gain algorithm in the sense of weak convergence, given by the stochastic differential equation (14.4), may not provide a sufficiently good approximation to the paths of the original algorithm (14.2). As a further analysis, Cho and Sargent (1999) introduce the concept of a "dominant escape path" and study its properties for the special case of multinomially distributed shocks. Williams (2000) provides additional theoretical results.

In his book, Sargent (1999) shows that similar phenomena arise if policy makers are assumed to estimate an augmented Phillips curve including a distributed lag of past inflation terms. Occasionally the parameters escape along a path in which the sum of the distributed lag coefficients supports the natural rate hypothesis and leads policy makers to follow low-inflation Ramsey policies for a period of time. However, the mean dynamics eventually push the system back toward the self-confirming high-inflation Nash equilibrium where the system stays until the next escape episode arises.

14.5   Other Models with Persistent Dynamics

In the preceding sections we have analyzed and discussed a number of models with persistent learning dynamics arising from agents adopting a learning procedure which can account for possible structural changes but which cannot fully converge to an REE. All these models have the feature that full convergence of parameter estimates fails for all possible structural parameter configurations of the model. *Learning is incomplete* in the terminology of Honkapohja and Mitra (1999).

Persistent learning dynamics can also arise in situations in which the learning is (potentially) *complete*, but where the REE outcome is unstable for learning for particular configurations of the parameters of the economic model. Indeed, the chapters in this book contain a number of instability results. If a given REE is unstable under learning, it is important to consider the resulting dynamics further. One possibility is that there may exist stable solutions, besides the unstable one, and the dynamics may then converge to such outcomes asymptotically. We have seen examples of this phenomenon in earlier parts of the book. Another possibility is that the model has only a unique unstable REE, so that the dynamics do not settle down but nevertheless exhibit a great deal of regularity asymptotically.[11] A prominent example of this possibility is the "learning equilibria" suggested by Bullard (1994).

The model of Bullard (1994) is a modification of the hyperinflation model, discussed in Section 11.6.2 in Chapter 11. Bullard replaced the assumption of constant (real) government spending by constant nominal money growth $\theta = M_t/M_{t-1}$. Government spending is then made endogenous, so that the budget constraint is satisfied.

Bullard's model can be described in terms of the savings (or money demand) function $M_t/P_t = S(P_t/E_t^* P_{t+1})$ and forecasting of the inflation rate $\beta_t = E_t^* P_{t+1}/P_t$. Given forecasts, the temporary equilibrium is

$$P_t = \theta \, \frac{S(\beta_{t-2}^{-1})}{S(\beta_{t-1}^{-1})} \, P_{t-1}.$$

It is easy to see that the mapping from the PLM with fixed β to the ALM is $T(\beta) = \theta$, so that the steady state $\beta = \theta$ is always E-stable.

For real-time learning, Bullard postulates that agents estimate β by running a first-order autoregression of prices on lagged prices using data through $t - 1$. This system can be written as a system of three nonlinear difference

---

[11] The asymptotic outcome need not show any regular behavior; see, e.g., Brock and Hommes (1997a) and (1997b) .

equations:

$$\beta_t = \beta_{t-1} + g_{t-1} \left[\theta \, \frac{S(\beta_{t-2}^{-1})}{S(\beta_{t-1}^{-1})} - \beta_{t-1} \right],$$

$$\beta_{t-1} = \beta_{t-1},$$

$$g_t = \left[g_{t-1}^{-1} \left(\frac{S(\beta_{t-2}^{-1})}{S(\beta_{t-1}^{-1})} \right)^{-2} + 1 \right]^{-1}.$$

Bullard shows that if the money growth rate θ is not too large, this system is stable with inflation given by $\beta^* = \theta$. However, if θ is increased beyond a critical value, the steady state becomes unstable and the learning dynamics converge to a limit cycle.[12] There is a multiplicity of these learning equilibria depending on the starting point.

This result might appear to contradict the E-stability principle. However, the reconciliation is straightforward. The key point is that the regressor, the past price level, is a nonstationary variable, in the steady state, when $\theta > 1$. Thus the standard recursive least squares algorithm would include an explosive state variable. In such cases the stochastic approximation technique is not applicable. (The above formulation of least squares as a difference equation is not in standard SRA form.) A natural alternative assumption is that agents estimate β by computing the mean of past inflation rates. It can be verified that the steady state is always stable under this learning rule.

A possible objection to the notion of learning equilibria is that when parameter estimates converge to a (nonrational) limit cycle, forecasting errors may become large and exhibit some regularities. If such a regularity is found, then agents would try to exploit it and hence would stop using the previous learning rule. However, Bullard shows that for carefully chosen savings functions, the forecast errors can exhibit a complex pattern, so that agents do not necessarily find regularities that they could exploit.[13]

There are several other examples of persistent learning dynamics in the literature. Franke (2000) shows that complex cyclical dynamics can arise in a complementarities model if agents use a mixture of adaptive and extrapolative forecast rules. Adam (2000b) shows that convergence to a nonrational equilibrium is possible when agents have a choice between two classes of model, even when one of the models is rational. Another way to generate persistent learning

---

[12] In fact, the system undergoes a Hopf bifurcation.

[13] Schönhofer (1999) examines this issue further and shows that the forecast errors can even be chaotic.

dynamics is to replace the decreasing-gain or constant-gain assumption with an endogenous gain sequence or some alternative assumption. Models with alternative gain sequences are discussed in Section 15.2 of Chapter 15.

14.6   Conclusions

In this chapter we have looked at learning rules for which the estimators do not converge to REE solutions and in fact continue to evolve over time. The estimators nevertheless appear to be "reasonable" in the sense that they tend to track the parameters of interest using fairly standard statistical methods. Furthermore, in many cases the estimators are unbiased asymptotically. In some cases, such as the cobweb model, the distribution of the estimators is tightly concentrated around the REE value. In other cases, there may be periods where estimates are relatively far from any REE as they attempt to track the evolving dynamics.

A possible drawback of these approaches is that, since the estimates do not converge to REE values, there are potential regularities in the forecast errors which could be exploited. Whether this criticism is telling depends upon how large and obvious are such patterns in the forecast errors. In some ways this is like the issue of whether an econometrician can be expected to eventually learn the true model or whether some misspecification will always be present. The gain from these approaches is that they can provide frameworks generating new forms of dynamics that can be taken to the data.

Chapter **15**
Extensions and Other Approaches

The main body of this book has been devoted to statistical or econometric learning, since the greatest concentration of research has probably been in this approach. In recent years other approaches have also been introduced to model learning behavior in macroeconomic models, and the literature has also considered some topics that we have not covered in the earlier chapters. We rectify these omissions here by providing an overview of other approaches and some further topics.

15.1 Models from Computational Intelligence

Several strands of alternative learning models have their origins in computational intelligence. The basic idea is that certain artificial devices have capabilities to memorize and reproduce patterns of behavior. Other structures can be used as approximate representations of nonlinear behavior rules, and their parameters can be updated adaptively. The different setups include genetic algorithms, classifier systems, and neural networks. These have recently found some applications in economics.

15.1.1 Genetic Algorithms

Basic Description

Genetic algorithms (GAs) were initially designed for finding optima in non-smooth optimization problems. GAs are essentially a specific way for finding increasing values of some objective functions. The system is subjected to random perturbations by the GA and this helps in avoiding getting stuck at local extrema.

We describe the main features of GAs using the Muth market model, which is one of the very first applications of GAs to economics. The exposition follows Arifovic (1994).

Consider a market with n firms with quadratic cost functions $C_{it} = xq_{it} + \frac{1}{2}ynq_{it}^2$, where q_{it} is the production by firm i and x and y are parameters. Given price expectations p_t^e, the expected profit of firm i is $\Pi_{it}^e = p_t^e q_{it} - xq_{it} - \frac{1}{2}ynq_{it}^2$, and one obtains the supply function for firm i as $q_{it} = (yn)^{-1}(p_t^e - x)$. The demand function is taken to be $p_t = A - B\sum_{i=1}^n q_{it}$, and the RE solution $p_t = p_t^e$ yields $q_{it} = q_t = (A-x)/[n(B+y)]$.

Arifovic (1994) considers some alternative GAs. We outline here her "single-population" algorithm. Formally, there is a population A_t of "chromosomes" A_{it} which are strings of length ℓ of binary characters 0, 1:

$$A_{it} = (a_{it}^1, \ldots, a_{it}^\ell), \quad \text{where } a_{it}^k = 0 \text{ or } 1.$$

To each chromosome A_{it} one associates a production decision by firm i by the formula

$$q_{it} = x_{it}/\bar{K}, \quad \text{where } x_{it} = \sum_{k=1}^\ell a_{it}^k 2^{k-1}.$$

Here $\bar{K}$ is a norming factor. Note that for large ℓ, the expressions x_{it} can approximate any real number over the range of interest. Short-run profits $\mu_{it} = \Pi_{it} = p_t q_{it} - C_{it}$ provide a measure of a "fitness" for alternative chromosomes (production decisions). Here p_t is the short-run equilibrium price, given a configuration of n chromosomes.

The basic idea in a genetic algorithm is to apply certain genetic operators to different chromosomes in order to produce new chromosomes. In these operators, the fitness measure provides a criterion of success, so that chromosomes with higher fitness have a better chance of producing offspring to the population. The following operators are used by Arifovic (1994):

(1) *Reproduction*: Each chromosome A_{it} produces copies with a probability which depends on its fitness. The probability of a copy c_{it} is given by $P(c_{it}) = \mu_{it}/(\sum_{i=1}^n \mu_{it})$. The resulting n copies constitute a "mating pool."

(2) *Crossover*: Two strings are selected randomly from the pool. Next, one selects a random cutoff point, and the tails of the selected chromosomes are interchanged to obtain new chromosome strings.

Example: If there are two strings [110101111] and [001010010], and tails of length 4 are interchanged, then the new strings are [110100010] and [001011111]. Altogether $n/2$ pairs are selected (assume that n is even, for simplicity).

(3) *Mutation*: For each string created in step (2), in each position 0 and 1 are changed to the alternative value with a small probability.

These are standard genetic operations. In her analysis, Arifovic (1994) adds another operator which is not present in standard GAs.

(4) *Election*: The new "offspring" strings created by the preceding three operators are tested against their "parent" strings using profit measured at the previous price as the fitness criterion. The two offspring and two parents are ranked based on the actual fitness value of the parents and the potential fitness values of the offspring. The two strings with highest fitness values are chosen to be placed into the population of the next generation.

It turns out that the election operator is crucial for the results: the market model does not converge when it is absent. Since mutation is always occurring, unless it is made to die off asymptotically, something like the election operator must be utilized to get convergence.

These four operations determine a new population of size n and, given this configuration, a new short-run equilibrium price is determined by the equality of demand and output. After this, the genetic operators are applied again using the new market price and profits as the fitness measure. Arifovic (1994) shows by simulations that this algorithm converges to the RE solution irrespective of the model parameter values.[1] This result is remarkable, since it happens in spite of the myopia in the fitness criterion. (The system, however, has no stochastic shocks.) For some specifications, it also turns out that the time paths of the GA correspond reasonably well with certain experimental results for the market model.

These genetic operations can be given broad interpretations in terms of economic behavior. First, reproduction corresponds to imitation of those who have done well. Second, crossover and mutation are like testing new ideas and making experiments. Finally, election means that only promising ideas are in fact utilized.

---

[1] This finding is consistent with the E-stability condition and corresponds to the least squares learning results: downward-sloping demand and upward-sloping supply is sufficient for global convergence.

To conclude this discussion, we remark that as a model of learning, the genetic algorithm is probably best interpreted as a framework of social rather than individual learning; cf. Sargent (1993). Indeed, individual firms are like individual chromosomes that are replaced by new ones according to the rules of the algorithm.

Recent Applications of Genetic Algorithms

The seminal paper by Arifovic (1994) demonstrated the potential of GAs to converge to the REE. A natural question is whether such convergence occurs in other models, and whether, when there are multiple equilibria, there is a one-to-one correspondence between solutions which are stable under statistical or econometric learning rules and solutions which are stable under GAs. The expectational stability principle, which states that there is a close connection between stability under adaptive learning rules and expectational stability, would argue for a tight correspondence between stability under econometric learning and under GAs.

One setup in which this question can be investigated is the OG model with seignorage, in which a fixed real deficit is financed by printing money. Recall that, provided the level of the deficit is not too large, there are two REE monetary steady states. Under small-gain adaptive learning of the inflation rate, the low-inflation steady state is locally stable while the high-inflation steady state is locally unstable, and these results are consistent with the E-stability conditions of the two steady states. Learning in this model was actually first investigated under least squares learning by Marcet and Sargent (1989a). They assumed that agents forecast inflation according to the perceived law of motion $p_{t+1} = \beta_t p_t$, where β_t is given by the least squares regression (without intercept) of prices on lagged prices. They showed that there could be convergence only to the low-inflation steady state, never to the high-inflation steady state. In addition, in simulations they found some cases with unstable paths leading to expected inflation rates at which there did not exist a temporary equilibrium (i.e., at which it was impossible to finance the deficit through money creation).

Arifovic (1995) sets up the GA so that the chromosome level represents the first-period consumption of the young. Using GA simulations (with an election operator), she also finds convergence to the low-inflation steady state and never to the high-inflation steady state. There are some differences in detail from least squares learning. From some starting points which lead to unstable paths under (Marcet–Sargent) least squares learning, there was convergence under GA learning. It is possible that some of these apparent discrepancies arise from the particular least squares learning scheme followed. Since the price level in either steady state is a trended series, whereas the inflation rate is not, it would be more natural to an econometrician to estimate the inflation rate by its sample mean rather than by a regression of prices on past prices.[2] In any case, there does appear to be a close connection in this model between the local stability properties of statistical and GA learning, and key features of learning dynamics are revealed by E-stability.

In Bullard and Duffy (1998a), GAs are used to look at the issue of convergence to cycles in the standard deterministic OG endowment model with money. One may recall that Grandmont (1985) showed that, for appropriate utility functions, it is straightforward to construct models in which there are regular perfect-foresight cycles. Recall also that Guesnerie and Woodford (1991) and Evans and Honkapohja (1995c) provide local stability conditions for the convergence of adaptive and statistical learning rules to particular RE k-cycles. For "decreasing gain" rules, these are the E-stability conditions which are given in Chapter 12. It is therefore of interest to know whether GAs exhibit the same stability conditions.

In Bullard and Duffy (1998a), agent, i uses the following simple rule for forecasting next period's price: $F_t^i[P(t+1)] = P(t - k_i - 1)$. Different values of k_i are consistent with different perfect-foresight cycles. (Note that every value of k_i is consistent with learning steady states.) The value of k_i used by agent i is coded as a bit string of length 8, so that the learning rule is in principle capable of learning cycles up to order 39. Given their price forecast, each agent chooses its optimal level of saving when young, and total saving determines the price level. A GA is used to determine the values of k_i used in each generation. Note that in this setup [in contrast to the approach in Arifovic (1994) and Arifovic (1995)], the GA operates on a forecast rule used by the agent, rather than directly on its decision variable.[3]

The question they ask is: starting from a random assignment of bit strings, will the GA converge to cycles? To answer this question, they conduct GA simulations for a grid of values of the parameter specifying the relative risk-aversion parameter of the old. Their central finding is that, with only a handful of exceptions, there is convergence either to steady states or 2-cycles, but not to higher-order cycles. This finding raises the possibility that GAs may have somewhat different stability properties than other learning rules. However, the results are

---

[2] Section 11.6.2 of Chapter 11 gives the local stability results in this model when expected inflation is equal to the mean of.past inflation rates.

[3] This makes GA learning closer in spirit to least squares and other adaptive learning of forecast rules. Using GAs to determine forecast rules was introduced in Bullard and Duffy (2000). Bullard and Duffy (1998b) show how to use GAs to directly determine consumption plans in n-period OG endowment economies.

based on simulations using a GA with a particular specification of the initial conditions and the forecast rule. Thus many issues concerning stability under GAs remain to be resolved.[4]

We close this section with a brief description of two other papers which use GAs in macroeconomic learning models. Arifovic (1996) considers an OG model with two currencies. This model possesses a continuum of stationary perfect-foresight solutions indexed by the exchange rate. In the GA setup, each agent has a bit string which determines the consumption level and the portfolio fractions devoted to the two currencies. Fitness of string i used by a member of generation $t - 1$ is measured by its ex post utility and is used to determine the proportion of bit strings in use in $t + 1$ according to genetic operator updating rules. The central finding is that the GA does not settle down to a nonstochastic stationary perfect-foresight equilibrium, but instead exhibits persistent fluctuations in the exchange rate driven by fluctuations in portfolio fractions. Arifovic, Bullard, and Duffy (1997) incorporate GA learning in a model of economic development based on Azariadis and Drazen (1990). This model, which emphasizes the roles of human capital and threshold externalities, has two perfect-foresight steady states: a low-income zero-growth steady state and a high-income positive-growth steady state. In the GA setup, the bit strings encode the fraction of their time young agents spend in training and the proportion of their income they save.[5] The central finding, based on simulations, is that, starting from the low-income steady state, economies eventually make a transition to the high-income steady state after a long, but unpredictable length of time.

These examples illustrate that GAs can be readily adapted to investigate a wide range of macroeconomic models. An advantage of GAs in economics is that they automatically allow for heterogeneity. A disadvantage is that there are no formal convergence results. Although in some cases there are supporting theoretical arguments, the findings in economics to date rely primarily on simulations. This literature is growing fast. Dawid (1996) provides an overview of GAs and discusses their applications to both economic models and evolutionary games. Lettau (1997) considers the effects of learning via genetic algorithms in a model of portfolio choice.

15.1.2   Classifier Systems

Classifier systems provide a different variety of learning algorithms which can be made more akin to thought processes of individuals than a GA. This allows a

---

[4]GA learning of 2-cycles has also recently been investigated in Arifovic (1998).

[5]In this model all of the standard genetic operators are used except the election operator.

direct behavioral interpretation with individual economic agents doing the learning.

A classifier system consists of an evolving collection of "condition–action statements" (i.e., decision rules) which compete with each other in certain specified ways. The winners become the active decisions in the different stages. The strengths (or utility and costs) of the possible classifiers are a central part of the system and accounts are kept of these strengths. When a "message" indicating current conditions arrives, one or more classifiers are activated as the possible decisions given the signal. Next, the competition stage starts to select the active classifier. The strengths are updated according to the performance of the active classifier. (As will be illustrated below, the updating rules mimic the updating of parameter estimates in stochastic approximation.) Typically, there are also ways for introducing new classifiers.[6]

Lettau and Uhlig (1999) have proposed that rules-of-thumb behavior, which is modeled as a classifier system, can account for some observed anomalies in dynamic decision problems. We use their analysis as an illustration of classifier systems.

Consider the following standard dynamic programming problem:

$$v(s) = \max_{a \in \mathcal{A}} \big[u(s, a) + \beta E_{\Pi_{s,a}} v(s') \big],$$

where $\mathcal{A} = \{a_1, \ldots, a_m\}$ is the set of alternative actions, $\mathcal{S} = \{s_1, \ldots, s_n\}$ is the set of states, and $\Pi_{s,a}$ is a probability distribution on the set of states (which is dependent on the actions). A standard argument can be used to show that there is a unique value v^* solving the problem, though the optimal decision function $h^* \colon \mathcal{S} \to \mathcal{A}$ may not be unique.

The alternative model as a classifier system is formulated as follows. First, let $\mathcal{A}_0 = \mathcal{A} \cup a_0$, where a_0 is the decision of no action. Rules of thumb are functions $r \colon \mathcal{S} \to \mathcal{A}_0$ with $r(\mathcal{S}) \neq \{a_0\}$. Let also $z \in \mathbb{R}$ denote the strength of a rule, so that the pair $c = (r, z)$ is a classifier. It is said to be applicable for state s if $r(s) \neq a_0$. A classifier system is a list of classifiers $\mathcal{C} = \{c_1, \ldots, c_K\}$ so that for each state there is at least one applicable classifier.

We also choose an initial classifier system $\mathcal{C}_0$, an initial state s_0, and a decreasing sequence $\{\gamma_t\}$ of gains such that $\sum_{t=1}^{\infty} \gamma_t = \infty$ and $\sum_{t=1}^{\infty} \gamma_t^p < \infty$ for some $p \geq 2$. Classifier system learning is described by sequences of states $(s_t)_{t=0}^{\infty}$, indices of classifiers $(k_t)_{t=0}^{\infty}$, and classifier systems $(\mathcal{C}_t)_{t=0}^{\infty}$ with the following steps:

---

[6]Sargent (1993, pp. 77–81) and Dawid (1996, pp. 13–17) provide more detailed general descriptions. Holland (1992) is a treatise on classifier systems.

(i) In each date t, the classifier $c_t \in C_t$ with the highest strength among all classifiers applicable in state s_t is selected (with random choice in case of a tie). k_t denotes the index of the winning classifier.

(ii) The action $a_t = r(s_t)$ according to the winning classifier is executed and this generates instantaneous utility $u(s_t, a_t)$.

(iii) In date $t + 1$, the state changes in accordance with the probability distribution Π_{s_t, a_t}. In this date, the index $k' = k(s_{t+1}, C_t)$ of the strongest classifier in C_t which is applicable in s_{t+1} is determined, and let the strength be z'. Update the strength of the classifier with index k_t to

$$\tilde{z} = z - \gamma_{t+1}(z - u_t - \beta z'). \tag{15.1}$$

The classifier system C_{t+1} for $t + 1$ is given by C_t with c_t replaced by $\tilde{c} = (r, \tilde{z})$.[7]

Suppose that there has been convergence in the dynamics (15.1), so that $z = u_t + \beta z'$. This equation is formally similar to the dynamic programming equation with expectations dropped. One can think of equation (15.1) as a stochastic approximation scheme. It is also called a bucket brigade. The activated classifier gives up some of its current strength but it also receives the instantaneous reward and the discount payment of the classifier in C_t that would have been strongest given s_{t+1}.

Lettau and Uhlig (1999) study the asymptotic behavior of this classifier system and show that it can lead to decision making which is different from that coming from dynamic programming. In particular, they suggest that this kind of behavior can account for the "good state" bias, i.e., bad decisions in good states of nature, which are said to describe the inability to distinguish between good luck and smart decisions. In the model of consumption and saving, this phenomenon is a possible explanation for the puzzle of excess sensitivity of consumption to current income.

A well-known economic application of classifier systems is Marimon, McGrattan, and Sargent (1989). They introduce classifier system learning into the model of money and matching due to Kiyotaki and Wright (1989). Using simulations, Marimon, McGrattan, and Sargent show that learning converges to a stationary Nash equilibrium in the Kiyotaki–Wright model, and that, when there are multiple equilibria, learning selects the fundamental low-cost solution.

---

[7]We note here that new classifiers are sometimes generated by other means, for example, by using a genetic algorithm.

15.1.3 Neural Networks

Another recent approach to learning models based on computational intelligence has been the use of neural networks.[8] The basic idea in neural networks is to represent an unknown functional relationship between inputs and outputs in terms of a network structure. In general, the networks can consist of several layers of nodes, called *neurons*, and connections between these neurons. The simplest example of a network is the *perceptron*, which is a single neuron receiving several input signals and sending out a scalar output. In *feedforward networks*, information flows only forward from one layer of neurons to a subsequent one. Such a network usually has several layers of neurons, organized so that neurons at the same layer are not connected to each other, and neurons in later layers do not feed information back to earlier layers in the structure.

In network structures, signals are passed along specified connections between the different neurons. In each neuron, a weighted sum of input signals is processed through an activation function for that neuron. The processed signal is outputted from the neuron, and either is sent to further neurons connected to it or, if it is at the terminal layer, becomes a component of the output of the whole network.

An important property of these networks is that they can provide good approximations of the unknown functional relation between the inputs and the outputs. To achieve this the networks must be "trained": the weights for inputs at each neuron must be determined so that, given the training data, the network approximates well the functional relation present in the input and output data. This training is often based on numerical techniques such as the gradient method, and in fact many training schemes can be represented as stochastic approximation algorithms. The training can be done with a fixed data set, so that it is then an "off-line" algorithm, or it may be done "on-line" as a recursive scheme. In the latter case the basic setup corresponds closely to adaptive learning.

In economic theory, neural networks have very recently been utilized as representations of approximate functional forms, as computational devices, and as an approach to bounded rationality and learning. One use of neural networks has been the computation of (approximate) solutions to economic models; see, e.g., Beltratti, Margarita, and Terna (1996) for various illustrations from economics and finance.

Another use of neural networks has been in modeling bounded rationality and learning. Cho (1995) uses perceptrons in the repeated prisoner's dilemma

---

[8]The use of neural networks in economics is discussed, e.g., in Beltratti, Margarita, and Terna (1996), Cho and Sargent (1996b), and Sargent (1993). White (1992) is an advanced treatise discussing the relationship of neural networks to statistics and econometrics.

game, so that the perceptrons classify the past data and, through a threshold, this leads to a decision in accordance with the output of the perceptron. Such strategies are quite simple, and thus the modeled behavior is very much boundedly rational. Nevertheless, the efficient outcomes of the game can be recovered by use of these simple strategies. Cho and Sargent (1996a) apply this approach to study reputation issues in monetary policy.

Some other papers using neural networks as a learning device in macroeconomic models are Barucci and Landi (1995) and Salmon (1995). Heinemann (2000a) and Packalén (1998) have shown that convergence of neural network learning is connected to E-stability conditions in the Muth model. Packalén (1998) also simulates such learning rules for some versions of the Cagan inflation model and shows the connection between convergence and E-stability of the RE equilibria.

15.2   Alternative Gain Sequences

The speed of convergence for learning algorithms is evidently an important issue for the study of learning behavior. An analytic result on asymptotic speed of convergence for stochastic approximation algorithms, based on Theorem 13, Chapter 3, Part II of Benveniste, Metivier, and Priouret (1990), was presented in Section 7.5 of Chapter 7. For gain sequences of the form $\gamma_t = t^{-1}$, and under appropriate assumptions, the asymptotic speed of convergence is the usual rate of $\sqrt{t}$ provided the real parts of all eigenvalues of the derivative of the associated ODE are less than -0.5. No analytic results are available if the eigenvalue condition fails. Marcet and Sargent (1995) have applied this result to adaptive learning in a version of the Cagan inflation model. They also carried out Monte Carlo simulations. The numerical results appear to accord with the analytics if the model satisfies the eigenvalue condition. However, the speed of convergence can be very slow when the eigenvalue condition fails.[9] For gain sequences of the form $\gamma_t = t^{-\beta}$ for $0 < \beta < 1$, the speed of convergence is asymptotically $t^{\beta/2}$.

We have emphasized two main choices for the gain sequence in adaptive learning algorithms. (i) Decreasing-gain sequences such as $\gamma_t = t^{-\beta}$ or, more generally, $\gamma_t = K(t + N)^{-\beta}$, where $0 < \beta \le 1$ and $K, N > 0$, which decrease toward zero at a rate which can give convergence in the limit to an REE if the PLM is correctly specified. We have frequently chosen $\gamma_t = t^{-1}$ in line with

---

[9]Vives (1993) has established a similar asymptotic speed of convergence result for Bayesian learning.

standard recursive least squares algorithms. (ii) Constant-gain algorithms with $\gamma_t = \gamma$, with $0 < \gamma \leq 1$, which will not converge to REE in stochastic models for correctly specified PLMs, though they may do so in nonstochastic models. However, in stochastic models, a gain which is bounded above zero has the advantage of being able more effectively to track the quantity being forecasted when the structure is subject to structural change or, more generally, when the economy does not converge to an REE. We have seen in the previous chapter that constant-gain learning can give rise to persistent learning dynamics not found in an REE.

These two classes for gain sequences do not exhaust the set of natural choices. There are several natural ways to combine constant and decreasing gain. One could use constant gain for a fixed period of time T_0 and then switch to gains which decrease toward zero at one of the usual rates. This has the advantage of being more responsive to the data at the initial stages, but asymptotically behaves like a decreasing-gain estimator. Alternatively, one could use a decreasing-gain estimator up to time T_1, at which point the gain is fixed at a small positive value. This ensures that the estimates remain sensitive to new data in the limit and might be appropriate if the economic structure is assumed to undergo recurrent small structural changes. Clearly, asymptotically this choice behaves like constant-gain estimators. Barucci (1999, 2000) proposes "exponentially fading memory learning," in which the gain is time varying but asymptotically similar to a constant gain.

Another possibility is to make the gain sequence endogenous. The *restarting-gain* method was discussed in Timmermann (1995) in connection with an asset pricing model. Suppose that the economic structure undergoes occasional large shifts, which alters the equilibrium values of the parameter estimates. If the times at which these shifts occur are known, then it would be natural to "restart" the gain sequence whenever a structural shift occurs. This corresponds to the econometric practice of discarding data before events such as world wars, presumed to mark major changes in structure.

If such shifts are believed to occur, but are unobservable, there are several natural possibilities. One is to make the gain contingent on recent forecast errors. A number of such *endogenous-gain* sequences are possible, e.g., one might increase the size of the gain when recent forecast errors have been large, on the assumption that this indicates a shift in structure. In Marcet and Nicolini (1998), the gain sequence is switched to constant gain if the forecast errors exceed some threshold. Another possibility is to use econometric misspecification tests (such as a breakpoint test or forecast error test) to determine whether gains should be restarted or switched to constant gain.

Another alternative is to use finite-memory rules. This is most easily set up in a nonrecursive way. Recursive algorithms with constant-gain estimators effectively use exponentially declining weights on observed data. Recursive algorithms with gains $\gamma_t = t^{-1}$ effectively weight each data point equally. An alternative would be to use rolling least squares, which runs least squares using the last T data points for some fixed horizon T. Honkapohja and Mitra (1999) consider this *bounded-memory* estimator for the special case of sample means.

15.3   Nonparametric Learning

In the discussion of statistical learning procedures, it is a standard assumption that the PLM can be specified parametrically. However, just as an econometrician may not know the appropriate functional form, it may be reasonable to assume that agents face the same difficulty. In this case a natural procedure is to use nonparametric techniques. This is discussed in Chen and White (1998).

As an illustration, consider learning a noisy steady state in a nonlinear model $y_t = H(E_t^* G(y_{t+1}, v_{t+1}), v_t)$. This model was analyzed in detail in Chapter 11 under the assumption that the shock is iid. In this case a noisy steady state $y(v_t)$ could be described in terms of a scalar parameter $\theta^* = EG(y(v), v)$. (Here the expectation is taken with respect to the distribution of v.) Chen and White (1998) instead consider the case where v_t is an exogenous, stationary, and possibly nonlinear AR(1)-process. A natural PLM is now of the form $E_t^* G(y_{t+1}, v_{t+1}) = \theta(v_t)$, and under appropriate assumptions there exists an REE $\bar{\theta}(v_t)$ in this class. Agents are assumed to update their PLM using recursive kernel methods of the form

$$\theta_t(v) = \theta_{t-1}(v) + t^{-1}\big[G(y_t, v_t) - \theta_{t-1}(v)\big]\Re\big((v - v_{t-1})/h_t\big)/h_t,$$

where $\Re(\cdot)$ is a kernel function (i.e., a density which is symmetric around zero) and $\{h_t\}$ is a sequence of band widths (i.e., a sequence of positive numbers decreasing to zero). Chen and White establish that under a number of technical assumptions and an E-stability–like condition, the learning mechanism converges to $\bar{\theta}(v_t)$ almost surely, provided a version of the projection facility is employed.

15.4   Eductive Learning

Some discussions of learning are "eductive" in spirit, i.e., they investigate whether the coordination of expectations on an REE can be attained by a mental process of reasoning.[10] Some of the early discussions of expectational stability, based on iterations of expectation functions, had an eductive flavor, in accordance with the following argument.

Consider the reduced form of the univariate cobweb model discussed in Chapter 2:

$$p_t = \mu + \alpha p_t^e + \eta_t, \tag{15.2}$$

where for convenience we include only a white noise exogenous shock η_t. Recall that for the market model, we have $\alpha < 0$, and that this is also the reduced form of the Lucas aggregate supply model, in which case $0 < \alpha < 1$. Suppose that initially all agents contemplate using some (nonrational) forecast rule

$$p_t^e(0) = a^0. \tag{15.3}$$

Inserting these expectations into equation (15.2), we obtain the actual law of motion which would be followed under this forecast rule:

$$p_t = \left(\mu + \alpha a^0\right) + \eta_t,$$

and the true conditional expectation under this law of motion:

$$p_t^e(1) = \left(\mu + \alpha a^0\right).$$

Thus if agents conjecture that other agents form expectations according to equation (15.3), then it would instead be rational to form expectations according to $p_t^e(1) = a^1$, where $a^1 = \mu + \alpha a^0$.

Continuing in this way, if agents conjecture that all other agents form expectations according to the rule $p_t^e(N) = a^N$, then it would be rational to instead form expectations according to $p_t^e(N+1) = \mu + \alpha a^N$. We therefore consider the recursion

$$a^{N+1} = \mu + \alpha a^N,$$

and we then say that the REE is iteratively expectationally stable (or iteratively E-stable) if $\lim_{N \to \infty} a^N = \bar{a} = (1 - \alpha)^{-1}\mu$. [Using the notation of Section 2.9 of Chapter 2, we are iterating on the map $a^{N+1} = T(a^N)$, where $T(a^N) = \mu + \alpha a^N$.]

---

[10]The term "eductive" is due to Binmore (1987).

The interpretation is that if this stability condition is satisfied, then agents can be expected to coordinate, through a process of reasoning, on the REE.[11] Clearly, for the problem at hand, the stability condition is $|\alpha| < 1$. For the Lucas supply model, this condition is always satisfied, and for the cobweb model, with $\alpha < 0$, satisfaction of the stability condition depends on the relative slopes of the supply and demand curves and is satisfied when $\alpha > -1$. Note that the condition $|\alpha| < 1$ is stricter than the condition for stability under adaptive learning, $\alpha < 1$, obtained in Chapter 2.

An apparent weakness of the argument just given is that it implicitly assumes homogeneous expectations of the agents. A more elaborate eductive argument, which at the same time is based on a rigorous common-knowledge argument, allows for heterogeneity of expectations. The idea is closely related to the concepts of rationalizability and iterated elimination of dominated strategies familiar from game theory, and a careful eductive argument for the cobweb model was given by Guesnerie (1992). The cobweb model can be readily reformulated as a producers' game in which the strategy of each firm is its output and the optimal choice of output depends on expected price. The equilibrium market price is given by $p_t = \mu + \alpha \int p_t^e(\omega)\, d\omega + \eta_t$, where we now assume a continuum of agents indexed by ω and that $p_t^e(\omega)$ is the market price held by agent ω. Let $S(\bar{a})$ denote a neighborhood of $\bar{a}$. Suppose it is common knowledge (CK) that $p_t^e(\omega) \in S(\bar{a})$ for all ω. Then it follows that it is CK that $E p_t \in |\alpha| S(\bar{a})$. Hence, assuming individual rationality, it follows that it is CK that $p_t^e(\omega) \in |\alpha| S(\bar{a})$ for all ω. If $|\alpha| < 1$, then this reinforces and tightens the CK assumption. Iterating this argument, it follows that $p_t^e(\omega) \in |\alpha|^N S(\bar{a})$ for all $N = 0, 1, 2, \ldots$, and hence the REE $E p_t = \bar{a}$ is itself CK. Guesnerie calls such an REE "strongly rational."

This argument can be extended in various ways. One can allow for heterogeneity in the structure, e.g., a different supply curve for each agent, due to different cost functions, so that the reduced form is $p_t = \mu + \int \alpha(\omega) p_t^e(\omega)\, d\omega + \eta_t$. Evans and Guesnerie (1993) extend the argument to cover the multivariate cobweb model with a possibly heterogeneous struc-

---

[11] Interpreting convergence of iterations of the T-map as a process of learning the REE was introduced in DeCanio (1979) and was one of the learning rules considered in Bray (1982). [Lucas (1978, Section 6) also considered convergence of such iterations.] DeCanio (1979) and Bray (1982) give an interpretation based on real-time adaptive learning. The eductive argument presented here was given in Evans (1983), where the term "expectational stability" was introduced, and in Evans (1985), where the iterative form of E-stability was used as a selection criterion. Related papers include Champsaur (1983) and Gottfries (1985).

ture,

$$y_t = k + \int A(\omega) y_t^e(\omega)\, d\omega + \eta_t,$$

where now y_t is $n \times 1$ and $A(\omega)$ is $n \times n$, and investigate the connections between iterative E-stability and strong rationality. If the model is homogeneous in structure, so that $A(\omega) = A$ for all ω, then (even allowing for heterogeneity in beliefs) an REE is strongly rational if and only if it meets the iterative E-stability condition that all roots of A lie inside the unit circle. However, if heterogeneity in the structure is permitted, then iterative E-stability is a necessary but not sufficient condition for strong rationality of the REE.

The argument can also be extended to cases with multiple REE by making the argument local—one posits a (nontrivial) initial set of CK in a neighborhood of an REE. In Evans and Guesnerie (1999), eductive arguments are considered in dynamic models with multiple rational expectations equilibria. They again find that iterative E-stability is a necessary condition for local strong rationality of an REE. For a general presentation of the eductive point of view, additional analysis, and references to further work, see Guesnerie (1999).

We conclude this section by discussing the relationship between the eductive arguments and the conditions for convergence to REE of adaptive learning schemes. Iterative E-stability appears to be a necessary condition for strong rationality, and E-stability, based on the corresponding differential equation, is clearly a necessary condition for iterative E-stability (see Section 2.9 of Chapter 2). Since we have argued that E-stability governs local convergence of adaptive learning schemes, it follows that local strong rationality appears in general to be a stricter requirement than local stability under adaptive learning. (This claim should be treated as a hypothesis whose general validity remains to be established.)

A plausible conjecture for empirical and experimental work is that when an REE is strongly rational, then convergence of the economy to that REE in real time will occur more quickly than under econometric or adaptive learning, because the latter can be supplemented with direct reasoning of an eductive nature. However, when strong rationality does not obtain, so that eductive reasoning fails, adaptive learning results should provide guidance on the paths which can arise in the economy. Agents must make forecasts in order to formulate their decisions. As emphasized in Chapter 1, a major advantage of the adaptive learning approach is that it models agents as forming expectations and making forecasts in the same way that econometricians do, by estimating statistical time-series models and using them to forecast key variables. Thus local stability under adaptive learning provides a natural criterion in many economic frameworks for assessing the likelihood of observing a particular REE.

15.5   Calculation Equilibria

The "expectation calculation" approach of Evans and Ramey (1992) goes beyond the adaptive learning approach in two ways. First, it introduces the costs and benefits of alternative forecasts. Second, it introduces the possibility of agents using an explicit model to calculate expectations. The model considers a continuum of firms ω, with total mass 1, who must make forecasts of the (logarithm of the) price level $p_t^e(\omega)$. The logarithm of aggregate output y_t (measured as a deviation from the natural rate) is given by an aggregate supply function $y_t = \gamma(p_t - \int p_t^e(\omega)\,d\omega)$, where $\gamma > 0$. Aggregate demand is given by the quantity theory equation, $m_t - p_t = y_t + v_t$, where m_t is the logarithm of the money stock, and money supply rules are assumed to take the form $m_t = p_{t-1} + g + \mu_t$. Combining equations and writing $\beta_t(\omega) = p_t^e(\omega) - p_{t-1}$, we have the temporary equilibrium mapping

$$\Delta p_t = T\big(\beta_t(\bullet)\big)$$
$$\equiv \gamma(1+\gamma)^{-1}\int \beta_t(\omega)\,d\omega + (1+\gamma)^{-1}(g+u_t),$$

where $u_t = \mu_t - v_t$ is assumed white noise. The unique REE is given by $\beta_t(\omega) = g$, $\Delta p_t = g + (1+\gamma)^{-1}u_t$, and $y_t = \gamma(1+\gamma)^{-1}u_t$.

The structure $T(\beta(\bullet))$ is assumed known and can be used to calculate expectation revisions. In making their inflation forecasts $\beta_t(\omega)$, each firm is permitted two choices. It can form expectations statically, not calculating and continuing to use the forecast $\beta_t(\omega) = \beta_{t-1}(\omega)$. This is assumed to cost nothing. Alternatively, it can update by performing one calculation, at real cost $c \geq 0$, using the T-map and information on last period's average expectation, revising its expectation to $\beta_t(\omega) = T(\beta_{t-1}(\bullet))$. Although simple and stylized, this model captures both the resource and time costs of expectation revision. Finally, the real cost of expectational errors is assumed to be quadratic, i.e., $k(\Delta p_t - \beta_t(\omega))^2$ for $k > 0$, and firms are assumed to be expected to form expectations optimally, i.e., to choose via optimization whether or not to calculate an expectation revision.

The main results of the basic model are the following. Suppose for convenience that all firms initially have homogeneous expectations, $\beta_t(\omega) = \beta_{t-1}$. Evans and Ramey (1992) study "calculation equilibria" for this model, i.e.,

Nash equilibria in which each firm optimally chooses whether or not to calculate, at each point in time, given the decisions of other firms. They show that, with a fixed policy and economic structure, for each initial β_0 there exist two-stage equilibrium paths (TEP) in which firms calculate at t if and only if $\beta_{t-1} \geq g + \sqrt{\kappa}$ or $\beta_{t-1} \leq g - \sqrt{\kappa}$. The value of κ is not unique but must lie between bounds which depend positively on c and γ and negatively on k. Along a TEP, if β_0 is sufficiently far from the REE value, all agents calculate each period until some later time τ which depends on κ. For $t \geq \tau$, no firms calculate because, with expectations close enough to rational expectations, the costs of further calculation outweigh the benefits.

These results imply that there is a long-run Phillips curve trade-off despite the natural rate structure of the supply side. Suppose the economy is initially in the REE and then policy makers change the monetary policy parameter g by Δg. If, say, $|\Delta g|$ is large, agents will calculate for a period of time, but will cease calculation before convergence to the new REE is reached, with a long-run effect on output. Furthermore, there can be hysteresis effects: if (once terminal expectations are reached) the policy parameter is returned to its original value, optimal calculation will move the system back toward the original REE but will stop short of the old REE. Thus monetary policy is not fully reversible.

Clearly, this line of thought can be developed in various ways. Evans and Ramey (1995) allow agents multiple calculations per period, with an associated cost function. Evans and Ramey (1992) also consider two natural extensions. First, suppose the environment is more complex, e.g., because monetary policy periodically shifts in a known stochastic way, with a current policy depending also on a variable z_t which is observable with a lag. The forecast rules and the corresponding calculation algorithm T are more complex, but calculation equilibria still exhibit a business cycle bias induced by incomplete calculation. Second, one can allow for heterogeneous calculation capabilities of the agents, e.g., by allowing a subset of ("fast") firms to make a second calculation each period at additional cost. The presence of fast firms turns out to affect the optimal calculation behavior of the slow firms through a calculation externality.

Evans and Ramey (1998b) consider two substantial extensions to the expectation calculation approach. First, the default (no calculation) forecast can be more sophisticated and might be given, for example, by least squares learning. Second, the (Nash equilibrium) assumption that agents optimally choose the intensity of their calculation each period is replaced by a calculation decision rule in which agents estimate the benefits of improved forecasts relative to calculation costs. This framework is used in an asset pricing model to show how more rapid adjustment and forward-looking behavior arise when there are large anticipated structural or policy shifts. Illustrative applications show how the severity of asset price bubbles and the intensity of hyperinflationary episodes depend on the cognitive ability of the agents.

15.6 Adaptively Rational Expectations Equilibria

The paper by Brock and Hommes (1997b) applies, in the context of the cobweb model, the discrete-choice models of Manski and McFadden (1981) and Anderson, De Palma, and Thisse (1993) to the prediction problem. Agents are assumed to have a finite set of predictors or expectation functions for predicting price. Each predictor has a fitness measure associated with it, based on past performance, as well as a cost of using that predictor. The discrete-choice models dictate that the proportion of agents who select a predictor depends on its performance or fitness, which is an estimate of the profits net of costs for that predictor. The implied forecasts determine prices which, in turn, alter the performance measures and hence the predictor proportions in the following period. Brock and Hommes (1997b) study the resulting "adaptively rational expectations dynamics."

   In related work, Sethi and Franke (1995) look at the implications, within the Haltiwanger and Waldman (1989) complementarities model, of the coexistence of two forecast rules: costly perfect foresight and costless adaptive expectations. The proportions of agents using the alternative forecast rules evolve according to their relative payoffs, and in the long run are shown to depend on the degree of exogenous variability as well as the cost of using the perfect-foresight predictor.

   The presentation here follows Brock and Hommes (1997b), and we develop the details in the context of their main example, the cobweb model with two predictors: rational and naive forecasts. The model is nonstochastic, so that rational expectations is equivalent to perfect foresight. Markets are perfectly competitive and demand is assumed to take the linear form $D(p_t) = A - Bp_t$. Firms have a quadratic cost function $c(q) = q^2/2b$ and thus a supply curve which depends linearly on expected price, $S(p_t^e) = bp_t^e$. There are two predictors available, the perfect-foresight predictor $p_t^e = p_t$, which costs $C \geq 0$, and the naive predictor $p_t^e = p_{t-1}$, which is free. Letting n_{1t} and n_{2t} denote the proportion of agents using the perfect-foresight and naive predictors, respectively, market equilibrium at t is given by

$$D(p_t) = n_{1,t-1}S(p_t) + n_{2,t-1}S(p_{t-1}).$$

To provide a simple dynamic system, the performance measure for the predictors is taken to be the net realized profit in the last period. Since profits in period t are

$\pi_t = p_t S(p_t^e) - c(S(p_t^e))$, we have realized time-$t$ profits, net of forecast costs, given by

$$\pi_{1t} = \frac{b}{2} p_t^2 - C \quad \text{and} \quad \pi_{2t} = \frac{b}{2} p_{t-1}(2p_t - p_{t-1}).$$

In the discrete-choice literature, if there are $j = 1, \ldots, K$ choices, with performance measures U_j, the proportion of agents using the jth predictor is given by $n_{j,t} = (\exp(\beta U_{j,t})) / \sum_{j=1}^{K} \exp(\beta U_{j,t})$. For the case at hand, we have

$$n_{1,t} = \exp(\beta \pi_{1,t}) / \big(\exp(\beta \pi_{1,t}) + \exp(\beta \pi_{2,t})\big) \quad \text{and} \quad n_{2,t} = 1 - n_{1,t}.$$

The parameter β governs the intensity of choice and measures the intensity with which agents choose higher performance predictors. For $\beta = +\infty$, all agents choose the highest performance predictor.

These equations fully define the adaptively rational equilibrium dynamics. Combining equations, setting $A = 0$ to normalize the system so that the steady-state price is at the origin, and defining $m_t = n_{1,t} - n_{2,t}$, it can be shown that the system reduces to

$$p_t = \frac{-b(1 - m_{t-1})p_{t-1}}{2B + b(1 + m_{t-1})},$$

$$m_t = \tanh\left(\frac{\beta}{2}\left(\frac{b}{2}\left(\frac{b(1 - m_{t-1})}{2B + b(1 + m_{t-1})} + 1\right)^2 p_{t-1}^2 - C\right)\right).$$

This is a two-dimensional system of nonlinear difference equations $(p_t, m_t) = F_\beta(p_{t-1}, m_{t-1})$, parameterized by β. It is easily seen to have a unique steady state $E = (0, \bar{m}(\beta))$. Brock and Hommes (1997b) focus on the case $b/B > 1$, in which the model is locally unstable under naive expectations because of explosive overshooting, and investigate how the dynamics depend on β.

Assume, therefore, that $b/B > 1$. If $C = 0$, the steady state $E = (0, 0)$ is globally stable. However, if $C > 0$, the dynamics depend crucially on the intensity of choice parameter β. There exist critical values $0 < \beta_1 < \beta_2$ such that the following hold:

(i) for $0 \le \beta < \beta_1$, the steady state is globally stable,
(ii) for $\beta > \beta_1$, the steady state E is an unstable saddlepoint, and
(iii) for $\beta_1 < \beta < \beta_2$, there is a locally unique stable two-period orbit.

Stable higher-order cycles, the coexistence of low periodic attractors, and chaotic attractors appear as β increases. Brock and Hommes call the resulting complicated dynamical phenomena a "rational route to randomness."

The economic mechanisms generating the complex dynamics are straight-forward. When agents use the cheapest predictor (here static expectations), the steady state is unstable (when $b/B > 1$), whereas the costly sophisticated predictor is stabilizing. Near the steady state, it pays to use the cheap predictor, but this pushes the economy away from the steady state. For a high enough intensity of choice, this tension leads to local instability and complex global dynamics. This line of research has been extended to asset pricing models in Brock and Hommes (1997a).[12]

15.7 Experimental Work

Since adaptive learning can have strong implications for economic dynamics, experimental evidence in dynamic expectations models is of considerable interest. However, to date only a relatively small number of experiments have been undertaken. The limited evidence available seems to show that, when convergent, time paths from experimental data converge towards steady states which are stable under small-gain adaptive learning.

Perhaps the clearest results are from experiments based on the hyperinflation (seignorage) OG model. Recall that in this model the high real balance/low-inflation steady state is E-stable, and thus stable under adaptive learning, whereas the low real balance/high-inflation steady state is unstable (provided the gain is sufficiently small). This theoretical result is strongly supported by the experiments described in Marimon and Sunder (1993): convergence is always to the high real balance steady state and never to the low real balance steady state.[13]

Marimon, Spear, and Sunder (1993) consider endogenous fluctuations (2-cycles and sunspot equilibria) in the basic OG model. Their results are mixed: persistent, belief-driven cycles can emerge, but only after the pattern has been induced by corresponding fundamental shocks. These papers also consider some aspects of transitional learning dynamics. One aspect that clearly emerges is that heterogeneity of expectations is important: individual data show considerable variability.

Arifovic (1996) conducts experiments in the two-currency OG model in which there is a continuum of equilibrium exchange rates. These experiments

---

[12] Branch (1999) examines the implications of introducing adaptive expectations into this framework as a third predictor.

[13] Related experiments are reported in Arifovic (1995).

exhibit persistent exchange rate fluctuations, which are consistent with GA learning. For the same model, using a Newton method for learning decision rules, simulations by Sargent (1993, pp. 107–112) suggest path-dependent convergence to a nonstochastic REE. These results raise several issues. First, it would be useful to simulate learning rules such as the Newton method with heterogeneous agents and alternative gain sequences. Second, given the existence of sunspot equilibria in models of this type, one should also investigate whether such solutions are stable under adaptive learning.

Experimental results for policy changes in OG economies with seignorage are analyzed in Marimon and Sunder (1994) and Evans, Honkapohja, and Marimon (2000). The former paper considers the effects of preannounced policy changes. The results are difficult to reconcile with rational expectations, but the data are more consistent with an adaptive learning process. The latter paper introduces a constitutional constraint on seignorage which can lead to three steady states, two of which are stable under learning. The experiments appear to confirm that these are the attractors. The learning rules in this paper incorporate heterogeneity with random gain sequences and inertia. This generates considerable diversity and variability during the learning transition, with the potential to match many aspects of experimental data.

Coordination games are another area in which there has been a considerable amount of experimental work. Van Huyck, Cook, and Battalio (1994) consider a version of the coordination game outlined in Section 3.4.1 of Chapter 3 in which the utilities of agents depend on their own and the median action:

$$U(x_i, M(x)) = c_1 - c_2 |x_i - \omega M(x)(1 - M(x))|.$$

Here $M(x)$ is the median of all the actions $x = (x_1, \ldots, x_I)$, and $c_1, c_2 > 0$ and $\omega \in (1, 4]$ are constants. The best response to the median is $b(M) = \omega M(1 - M)$. They analyze both the myopic best response dynamics

$$M_{t+1} = b(M_t) \tag{15.4}$$

and the (by now familiar) adaptive dynamics

$$M_t = b(M_t^e), \tag{15.5}$$
$$M_t^e = M_{t-1}^e + \gamma_{t-1}(M_{t-1} - M_{t-1}^e).$$

Given that $b(M)$ is quadratic, it is evident that the properties of the best response dynamics (15.4) depend critically on the value of ω. For values $\omega > 3.86957$, the dynamics exhibit chaotic behavior. In contrast, the interior equilibrium is always stable under adaptive dynamics with decreasing gain (15.5) using the results from Section 7.2 of Chapter 7.[14] Van Huyck, Cook, and Battalio (1994) present experimental evidence for this game for different values of ω. The stability of the interior equilibrium is consistent with the adaptive dynamics (15.5), whereas the experimental results are inconsistent with the best response dynamics (15.4).

Crawford (1995) analyzes adaptive learning dynamics of the form

$$x_{it} = x_{i,t-1} + \gamma_{it}(y_{t-1} - x_{i,t-1}) + a_{it} \qquad (15.6)$$

in a coordination game, where x_{it} is the action of agent i and $y_t = f(x_{1t}, \dots, x_{It})$ is an aggregate statistic of the actions. Here a_{it} and γ_{it} are exogenous coefficients representing trends and responses to new information. Note that this framework in fact fits the stochastic approximation setup in which γ_{it} are agent-specific gain parameters. If certain assumptions are made, it turns out that x_{it} and y_t converge to a common limit under the adaptive dynamics (15.6). Using the data of Van Huyck, Battalio, and Beil (1990) and Van Huyck, Battalio, and Beil (1991), Crawford estimates the means and covariances of a_{it} and γ_{it}. He finds that this kind of learning scheme is able to provide a "simple, unified explanation for the complex patterns of history-dependence and discrimination among equilibria" in the experimental data.

15.8   Some Empirical Applications

So far there has been only a handful of studies that use adaptive learning frameworks to explain empirical findings in macroeconomics and finance. We briefly describe four major projects in this line of work.

Currie, Garratt, and Hall (1993), Garratt and Hall (1997), and Hall and Garratt (1995) model the formation of exchange rate expectations as a learning process using the London Business School large-scale macroeconomic model. A key feature of these studies is that the model parameters become time dependent as a result of the learning dynamics. Several different learning rules are considered, and the notion of model-consistent learning is formulated. The focus of these studies is directed at the implications of learning for dynamics after various structural changes, such as oil shocks or shifts in exchange rate policy.

Learning dynamics can be used to explain anomalies in the asset price literature. Timmermann (1993) and Timmermann (1996) argue that adaptive learning

---

[14] The derivative $b'(\bar{M}) = 2 - \omega < 1$ at the interior equilibrium $\bar{M}$, while $b'(0) = \omega > 1$.

can explain the apparent predictability of stock returns and the excess volatility found in the data. The framework is in line with present-value models, but, in contrast to the rational expectations setup, it is postulated that the agents know the form but not the true parameter values of the dividend process and estimate the parameters by least squares. During the learning transition there will be effects on asset prices. In the kinds of sample sizes which are empirically relevant, the learning effects can be important in explaining asset price volatility and the predictability of excess returns, in particular the ability of the dividend yield to forecast stock market returns.

Marcet and Nicolini (1998) set forth an open-economy version of the monetary inflation model to analyze the inflation and exchange rate experiences of Latin-American economies. In their model, learning has two regimes with different gain sequences. Agents use a decreasing-gain rule, provided it does not lead to forecast errors above some threshold level. When the threshold is exceeded, agents switch to a constant-gain rule, since it has the ability to track changing circumstances better. This kind of learning dynamics can account for the periodic bouts of inflation and subsequent stabilizations by means of exchange rate pegs. In contrast, these features of the data would be difficult to explain using a framework based on continuous rational expectations.

Sargent (1999) uses the constant-gain version of his inflation model, discussed in Section 13.2 of Chapter 13 and Section 14.4 of Chapter 14, to provide a possible explanation of the dramatic reduction in inflation in the United States from the 1980s to the present. As we have already seen, the constant-gain version exhibits occasional "escape routes" from the high-inflation Nash equilibrium to a neighborhood of zero inflation. Sargent shows the potential of this account to explain the recent U.S. historical experience using an estimated version of the model for the post-war period. This analysis provides an intriguing interpretation of the policy makers' behavior: as a result of misspecified learning, their perceived unemployment–inflation trade-off shifted so as to induce a more aggressive stand against inflation.

Chapter 16
Conclusions

This book has focused on macroeconomic models in which expectations of current or future variables play a central role. We have treated a large range of models which are in current use in macroeconomics. These include standard linear setups, such as the cobweb, Cagan, overlapping contracts, and IS-LM-Phillips-curve models, and linearized multivariate structures, such as the Real Business Cycle and Farmer–Guo models. Several nonlinear frameworks, including various versions of overlapping generations models and economies with complementarities and coordination failure, have also been analyzed at some length.

Our approach has been to treat the forecasting agents as statisticians or econometricians who have a model of the data-generating process, i.e., a perceived law of motion (PLM), and who estimate its unknown parameters by standard techniques and then use the estimated model to make the forecasts needed in economic decision making. This is a form of bounded rationality, since the agents treat the data generation as exogenous, while the evolution of data in fact depends on the forecast rules actually employed by the agents. From an econometric point of view, agents are using a temporarily misspecified model, but we have seen that, nonetheless, the economy often converges to a rational expectations equilibrium (REE). This convergence implies that the misspecification vanishes asymptotically.

In the bulk of the book we have followed the literature and postulated that agents use least squares or closely related econometric learning schemes. The key question has been the formulation of the conditions under which this kind of learning behavior converges to an REE. As we have seen, for these learning rules the convergence results, which can be precisely stated using stochastic approximation techniques, are quite generally given by the corresponding expectational stability (E-stability) conditions.

385

Many aspects of the theory are essentially complete. In linear economic models the stability results can be fully described for RE solutions if they are locally unique fixed points in the agent's class of PLMs. In particular, this is the case for minimal state variable (MSV) solutions, which are the most commonly used REE in applied work. If there are multiple MSV solutions, only a subset of them are E-stable, so that learning operates as a selection criterion. For non-linear economic models the theory is also complete for certain specific classes of solutions, in particular for steady states, cycles, and finite Markov sunspot solutions. The E-stability conditions for these particular types of REE are easily obtained, the connection between E-stability and convergence of statistical learning rules can be demonstrated, and equilibria can be classified into locally stable and unstable REE.

There remain some gaps in the theory. For univariate linear models the complete class of solutions can be listed, and these include ARMA-type continua of solutions as well as the MSV solutions. We have shown how to obtain E-stability conditions for the ARMA-type solution classes. However, the assumptions needed to apply established stochastic approximation results do not hold in these cases. The link with least squares learning for the ARMA-type solutions has thus not been formally established, although simulations appear to support the connection with E-stability in these cases as well. In multivariate linear models, while the theory is complete for MSV solutions, we have only partial E-stability results for the continua of "sunspot solutions" (when these exist), and no formal convergence results for econometric learning rules are available in these cases.

For nonlinear models our treatment has covered only univariate models with iid shocks and without lags. While the extension to the corresponding multivariate framework would seem to be straightforward, nonlinear models with non-iid shocks, or with lags, present problems in obtaining closed-form RE solutions. Even for the nonlinear models that we have examined, there can exist other types of REE which have not been studied under adaptive learning. These include, in particular, Markov sunspot equilibria with an infinite number of states for the sunspot. Of course, if one is prepared to linearly approximate a multivariate nonlinear model in a neighborhood of a steady state, then the methods in Chapter 10 for multivariate models can be applied even when non-iid shocks and lags are present. For many applied models, this approach may be satisfactory.

E-stability is an important unifying theme in the basic theory presented in Parts I–IV. E-stability determines whether an RE equilibrium is locally learnable under least squares and closely related learning schemes, provided the variables remain bounded and the gain sequence of the algorithm tends to zero in the usual way. Stability does depend on the precise PLMs entertained by the agents.

The distinction between weak and strong E-stability has been used to allow for possible overparameterization of the PLM relative to the REE.

The theory in Parts I–IV focused on the benchmark case, where the form of the PLM used by the agents includes the RE solution of interest. Chapters 13 and 14 in Part V analyze some central cases where this does not hold. If agents are acting like econometricians, they will be subject to the same challenges as are economists when formulating applied forecasting models. It would thus not be surprising if agents sometimes use PLMs which fail to nest any REE. We present examples in which agents omit relevant variables, and clearly other forms of misspecification might arise. In the cases examined, a form of the E-stability principle continues to hold, despite underparameterization of the PLM. Because the misspecification prevails even asymptotically, convergence is to a restricted perceptions equilibrium rather than an REE.

Another possibility is that agents themselves recognize the possibility of misspecification and believe that this takes the form of frequent or occasional structural shifts. This suggests using algorithms in which the gain sequence remains bounded above zero, and indeed, constant-gain algorithms have been used to deal with potential structural change. Such algorithms have the advantage of tracking shifting parameters, though at the cost of higher variance of the estimated parameters. We have shown how to analyze several models under learning with constant gain. Again E-stability underlies the analysis of the dynamics. These models exhibit persistent learning dynamics which can be quite different from any REE dynamics. The advantage of this approach is that it can potentially explain a greater range of empirical phenomena. The plausibility of such equilibria depends on whether there are apparent regularities in the forecast errors which agents can readily exploit.

The statistical approach we have adopted is an appealing form of inductive behavior in which, at each moment of time, agents have a view or model of the relevant aspects of the economy, make decisions on that basis, and then, for the next period, adjust their view or model in the light of experience. Procedures from computational intelligence discussed in Chapter 15 provide some alternative adaptive approaches. A common principle is that agents attempt to optimize some criterion function. In the case of statistical learning, least squares, for example, aims to minimize the mean square forecast error, and agents choose optimal decisions given the forecasts. In many of the computational models, the trial-and-error process assesses alternative actions or forecasts directly in terms of the utility or profit of the agents. We have also discussed how adaptive approaches can be extended to incorporate costs of making forecasts or decisions.

Adaptive approaches to learning can be contrasted with the eductive approaches in which agents take explicit account of the reasoning abilities of other agents. Eductive learning requires strong assumptions about common knowledge available to all the agents. In circumstances where these assumptions hold, it might be possible and desirable to combine the two approaches.

Least squares learning is a particular form of bounded rationality, which can, however, converge to full rationality over time. As is always the case when bounded rationality is employed, one can instead assume more or less rationality on the part of agents. The use of least squares learning implicitly assumes that agents know how to act optimally, given forecasts, and that these econometric forecasting procedures have minimal cost.

In some cases one might want to treat agents as having a different level of econometric sophistication. Indeed, the technical skills postulated should depend in part on the existing state of the art in econometrics. The assumption that agents use multiple regressions would have been ridiculous before the 1950s. Even now, the assumption that all agents use least squares forecasting may be too strong, and one may want to replace this with a simpler forecast rule for some agents. On the other hand, as econometric practice progresses, e.g., in the availability of specification tests or the development of time-varying parameter models, the standard of econometrics employed by some agents might be assumed to rise. We think that least squares learning provides a natural benchmark.

The techniques presented here should prove valuable in the study of least-squares learning in a large variety of economic models, particularly when these models have multiple REE. The approach of this book should also be of use in the analysis of alternative econometric learning methods. We anticipate that some version of E-stability will continue to play a central role in the general study of learning dynamics.

Bibliography

Adam, K. (2000a): "Adaptive Expectations and Equilibrium Selection," mimeo, European University Institute.

——— (2000b): "Learning and Business Cycles," mimeo, European University Institute.

Amman, H. M., D. A. Kendrick, and J. Rust, eds. (1996): *Handbook of Computational Economics*, Vol. 1. Elsevier, Amsterdam.

Anderson, S. A., A. De Palma, and J. Thisse (1993): *Discrete Choice Theory of Product Differentiation*. MIT Press, Cambridge, MA.

Arifovic, J. (1994): "Genetic Algorithm Learning and the Cobweb Model," *Journal of Economic Dynamics and Control*, 18, 3–28.

——— (1995): "Genetic Algorithms and Inflationary Economies," *Journal of Monetary Economics*, 36, 219–243.

——— (1996): "The Behavior of the Exchange Rate in the Genetic Algorithm and Experimental Economies," *Journal of Political Economy*, 104, 510–541.

——— (1998): "Stability of Equilibria under Genetic Algorithm Adaption: An Analysis," *Macroeconomic Dynamics*, 2, 1–21.

Arifovic, J., J. Bullard, and J. Duffy (1997): "The Transition from Stagnation to Growth: An Adaptive Learning Approach," *Journal of Economic Growth*, 2, 185–209.

Arrow, K. J. (1986): "Rationality of Self and Others in an Economic System," *Journal of Business, Supplement*, 59, S385–S449.

Arthur, W. B. (1994): *Increasing Returns and Path Dependence in the Economy*. The University of Michigan Press, Ann Arbor.

Arthur, W. B., Y. M. Ermoliev, and Y. M. Kaniovski (1983): "On Generalized Urn Schemes of the Polya Kind," *Kibernetika*, 19, 49–56.

——— (1994): "Strong Laws for a Class of Path-Dependent Stochastic Processes with Applications." In *Increasing Returns and Path Dependence in the Economy*, ed. W. B. Arthur, The University of Michigan Press, Ann Arbor, 185–201.

Azariadis, C. (1981): "Self-Fulfilling Prophecies," *Journal of Economic Theory*, 25, 380–396.

——— (1993): *Intertemporal Macroeconomics*. Blackwell, Oxford.

Azariadis, C., and A. Drazen (1990): "Threshold Externalities in Economic Development," *Quarterly Journal of Economics*, 104, 501–526.

Azariadis, C., and R. Guesnerie (1982): "Propheties Creatrices et Persistence des Theories," *Revue Economique*, 33, 787–806.

——— (1986): "Sunspots and Cycles," *Review of Economic Studies*, 53, 725–737.

Barnett, W., B. Cornet, C. D'Aspremont, J. Gabszewicz, and A. Mas-Colell, eds. (1991): *Equilibrium Theory and Applications, Proceedings of the Sixth International Symposium in Economic Theory and Econometrics*. Cambridge University Press, Cambridge.

Barnett, W., J. Geweke, and K. Shell, eds. (1989): *Economic Complexity: Chaos, Sunspots, Bubbles, and Nonlinearity*. Cambridge University Press, Cambridge.

Barro, R. J., and D. B. Gordon (1983a): "A Positive Theory of Monetary Policy in a Natural Rate Model," *Journal of Political Economy*, 91, 589–610.

——— (1983b): "Rules, Discretion and Reputation in a Model of Monetary Policy," *Journal of Monetary Economics*, 12, 101–121.

Barucci, E. (1999): "Heterogeneous Beliefs and Learning in Forward-Looking Models," *Journal of Evolutionary Economics*, 9, 453–464.

——— (2000): "Exponentially Fading Memory Learning in Forward-Looking Models," *Journal of Economic Dynamics and Control*, 24, 1027–1046.

Barucci, E., and L. Landi (1995): "Non-Parametric versus Linear Learning Devices: A Procedural Perspective," Working paper.

——— (1997): "Least Mean Squares Learning in Self-Referential Stochastic Models," *Economics Letters*, 57, 313–317.

Beltratti, A., S. Margarita, and P. Terna (1996): *Neural Networks for Economic and Financial Modelling*. International Thompson Computer Press, London.

Benhabib, J., and R. A. Farmer (1994): "Indeterminacy and Increasing Returns," *Journal of Economic Theory*, 63, 19–41.

Benveniste, A., M. Metivier, and P. Priouret (1990): *Adaptive Algorithms and Stochastic Approximations*. Springer-Verlag, Berlin.

Bertocchi, G., and W. Yong (1996): "Imperfect Information, Bayesian Learning and Capital Accumulation," *Journal of Economic Growth*, 1, 487–503.

Billingsley, P. (1968): *Convergence of Probability Measures*. John Wiley and Sons, New York.

——— (1986): *Probability and Measure*, second edition. John Wiley and Sons, New York.

Binmore, K. (1987): "Modeling Rational Players," *Economics and Philosophy*, 3, 179–214.

Blanchard, O., and C. Kahn (1980): "The Solution of Linear Difference Models under Rational Expectations," *Econometrica*, 48, 1305–1311.

Blanchard, O. J., and S. Fischer (1989): *Lectures on Macroeconomics*. MIT Press, Cambridge, MA.

Blume, L., M. Bray, and D. Easley (1982): "Introduction to Stability of Rational Expectations Equilibrium," *Journal of Economic Theory*, 26, 313–317.

Böhm, V., and J. Wenzelburger (1999): "Expectations, Forecasting, and Perfect Foresight—A Dynamical Systems Approach," *Macroeconomic Dynamics*, 3, 167–186.

Branch, W. (1999): "Local Convergence Properties of a Cobweb Model with Rational Heterogeneous Expectations," Working paper, University of Oregon.

Bray, M. (1982): "Learning, Estimation, and the Stability of Rational Expectations Equilibria," *Journal of Economic Theory*, 26, 318–339.

Bray, M., and D. M. Kreps (1987): "Rational Learning and Rational Expectations." In *Arrow and the Ascent of Modern Economic Theory*, ed. G. R. Feiwel, New York University Press, New York, 597–625.

Bray, M., and N. Savin (1986): "Rational Expectations Equilibria, Learning, and Model Specification," *Econometrica*, 54, 1129–1160.

Brock, W. A., and C. H. Hommes (1997a): "Models of Complexity in Economics and Finance." In *System Dynamics in Economic and Financial Models*, eds. B. Hanzon, C. Heij, C. Praagman, and J. Schumacher, John Wiley and Sons, New York, 3–41.

——— (1997b): "A Rational Route to Randomness," *Econometrica*, 65, 1059–1095.

Brock, W. A., and A. Malliaris (1989): *Differential Equations, Stability and Chaos in Dynamic Economics*. North-Holland, Amsterdam.

Brock, W. A., and L. J. Mirman (1972): "Optimal Growth under Uncertainty: The Discounted Case," *Journal of Economic Theory*, 4, 497–513.

Brockwell, P. J., and R. A. Davis (1991): *Time Series: Theory and Methods*, second edition. Springer-Verlag, New York.

Broze, L., C. Gourieroux, and A. Szafarz (1990): *Reduced Forms of Rational, Expectations Models, Fundamentals of Pure and Applied Economics*. Harwood Academic Publishers, Chur, Switzerland.

Bryant, J. (1983): "A Simple Rational Expectations Keynes-Type Model," *Quarterly Journal of Economics*, 98, 525–528.

——— (1987): "The Paradox of Thrift, Liquidity Preference and Animal Spirits," *Econometrica*, 55, 1231–1236.

Bullard, J. (1992): "Time-Varying Parameters and Nonconvergence to Rational Expectations under Least Squares Learning," *Economics Letters*, 40, 159–166.

——— (1994): "Learning Equilibria," *Journal of Economic Theory*, 64, 468–485.

Bullard, J., and J. Duffy (1998a): "Learning and the Stability of Cycles," *Macroeconomic Dynamics*, 2, 22–48.

——— (1998b): "A Model of Learning and Emulation with Artificial Adaptive Agents," *Journal of Economic Dynamics and Control*, 22, 179–207.

——— (2000): "Using Genetic Algorithms to Model the Evolution of Heterogeneous Beliefs," *Computational Economics*, forthcoming.

Bullard, J., and K. Mitra (1999): "Learning About Monetary Policy Rules," mimeo.

Cagan, P. (1956): "The Monetary Dynamics of Hyper-Inflation." In *Studies in the Quantity Theory of Money*, ed. M. Friedman, University of Chicago Press, Chicago.

Carton, J. (1999): "Replicator Dynamics Learning in Muth's Model of Price Movements," Working paper, University of Oregon.

Cass, D., and K. Shell (1983): "Do Sunspots Matter?," *Journal of Political Economy*, 91, 193–227.

Champsaur, P. (1983): "On the Stability of Rational Expectations Equilibria," Working paper 8324, Centre for Operations Research in Economics (CORE).

Champsaur, P., et al., eds. (1990): *Essays in Honor of Edmond Malinvaud*, Vol. 1. *Microeconomics*. MIT Press, Cambridge, MA.

Chatterji, S., and S. K. Chattopadhyay (2000): "Global Stability in Spite of 'Local Instability' with Learning in General Equilibrium Models," *Journal of Mathematical Economics*, 33, 155–165.

Chen, X., and H. White (1998): "Nonparametric Adaptive Learning with Feedback," *Journal of Economic Theory*, 82, 190–222.

Cheysson, E. (1887): "La Statistique Geometrique: Ses Applications Industrielles et Commeriales," *Le Genie Civil, Jan. 29 and Feb. 5*, 10, 206–210 and 224–228.

Chiang, A. C. (1984): *Fundamental Methods of Mathematical Economics*, third edition. McGraw-Hill, New York.

Chiappori, P., and R. Guesnerie (1991): "Sunspot Equilibria in Sequential Market Models." In *Handbook of Mathematical Economics*, ed. W. Hildenbrand and H. Sonnenschein, North-Holland, Amsterdam, 1683–1762.

Cho, I.-K. (1995): "Perceptrons Play the Repeated Prisoner's Dilemma," *Journal of Economic Theory*, 67, 266–284.

Cho, I.-K., and T. J. Sargent (1996a): "Learning to be Credible," Working paper.

———— (1996b): "Neural Networks for Encoding and Adapting in Dynamic Economies." In *Handbook of Computational Economics*, ed. H. M. Amman, D. A. Kendrick, and J. Rust, 441–470.

———— (1999): "Escaping Nash Inflation," Working paper.

Chung, H. (1990): "Did Policy Makers Really Believe in the Phillips Curve? An Econometrics Test," Ph.D. dissertation, University of Minnesota.

Clarida, R., J. Gali, and M. Gertler (1999): "The Science of Monetary Policy: A New Keynesian Perspective," *Journal of Economic Literature*, 37, 1661–1707.

Coddington, E. A. (1961): *An Introduction to Ordinary Differential Equations*. Prentice-Hall, Englewood Cliffs, NJ.

Cooper, R. (1999): *Cooperation Games: Complementarities and Macroeconomics*. Cambridge University Press, Cambridge.

Cooper, R., and A. John (1988): "Coordinating Coordination Failures in Keynesian Models," *Quarterly Journal of Economics*, 113, 441–464.

Crawford, V. P. (1995): "Adaptive Dynamics in Coordination Games," *Econometrica*, 63, 103–143.

Currie, D., A. Garratt, and S. Hall (1993): "Consistent Expectations and Learning in Large Scale Macroeconometric Models." In *Macroeconomic Modeling and Policy Implications*, eds. S. Honkapohja and M. Ingberg, North-Holland, Amsterdam, 21–42.

d'Autume, A. (1990): "On The Solution of Linear Difference Equations with Rational Expectations," *Review of Economic Studies*, 57, 677–688.

Davidson, J. (1994): *Stochastic Limit Theory*. Oxford University Press, Oxford.

Dawid, H. (1996): *Adaptive Learning by Genetic Algorithms: Analytical Results and Applications to Economic Models*. Springer-Verlag, Berlin.

DeCanio, S. (1979): "Rational Expectations and Learning from Experience," *Quarterly Journal of Economics*, 94, 47–57.

Diamond, P. A. (1982): "Aggregate Demand Management in Search Equilibrium," *Journal of Political Economy*, 90, 881–894.

Dixon, H., and N. Rankin, eds. (1995): *The New Macroeconomics: Imperfect Markets and Policy Effectiveness*. Cambridge University Press, Cambridge.

Doob, J. L. (1953): *Stochastic Processes*. Wiley, New York.

Dupuis, P., and R. S. Ellis (1997): *A Weak Convergence Approach to the Theory of Large Deviations*. Wiley, New York.

Ellison, G., and D. Fudenberg (1995): "Word-of-Mouth Communication and Social Learning," *Quarterly Journal of Economics*, 110, 93–125.

Evans, G. W. (1983): "The Stability of Rational Expectations in Macroeconomic Models." In *Individual Forecasting and Aggregate Outcomes*, "*Rational Ex-*

pectations" Reexamined, eds. R. Frydman and E. E. Phelps, Cambridge University Press, Cambridge, 67–94.

——— (1985): "Expectational Stability and the Multiple Equilibria Problem in Linear Rational Expectations Models," *Quarterly Journal of Economics*, 100, 1217–1233.

——— (1989): "The Fragility of Sunspots and Bubbles," *Journal of Monetary Economics*, 23, 297–317.

Evans, G. W., and R. Guesnerie (1993): "Rationalizability, Strong Rationality, and Expectational Stability," *Games and Economic Behaviour*, 5, 632–646.

——— (1999): "Coordination on Saddle Path Solutions: The Eductive Viewpoint. 1—Linear Univariate Models," Working paper.

Evans, G. W., and S. Honkapohja (1986): "A Complete Characterization of ARMA Solutions to Linear Rational Expectations Models," *Review of Economic Studies*, 53, 227–239.

——— (1992): "On the Robustness of Bubbles in Linear RE Models," *International Economic Review*, 33, 1–14.

——— (1993a): "Adaptive Forecasts, Hysteresis and Endogenous Fluctuations," *Federal Reserve Bank of San Francisco Economic Review*, 1993(1), 3–13.

——— (1993b): "Learning and Economic Fluctuations: Using Fiscal Policy to Steer Expectations," *European Economic Review*, 37, 595–602.

——— (1994a): "Convergence of Least Squares Learning to a Nonstationary Equilibrium," *Economic Letters*, 46, 131–136.

——— (1994b): "Learning, Convergence, and Stability with Multiple Rational Expectations Equilibria," *European Economic Review*, 38, 1071–1098.

——— (1994c): "On the Local Stability of Sunspot Equilibria under Adaptive Learning Rules," *Journal of Economic Theory*, 64, 142–161.

——— (1995a): "Adaptive Learning and Expectational Stability: An Introduction." In *Learning and Rationality in Economics*, eds. A. Kirman and M. Salmon, Basil Blackwood, Oxford, 102–126.

——— (1995b): "Increasing Social Returns, Learning and Bifurcation Phenomena." In *Learning and Rationality in Economics*, eds. A. Kirman and M. Salmon, Basil Blackwood, Oxford, 216–235.

——— (1995c): "Local Convergence of Recursive Learning to Steady States and Cycles in Stochastic Nonlinear Models," *Econometrica*, 63, 195–206.

——— (1997): "Least Squares Learning with Heterogeneous Expectations," *Economic Letters*, 52, 197–201.

——— (1998a): "Convergence of Learning Algorithms without a Projection Facility," *Journal of Mathematical Economics*, 30, 59–86.

——— (1998b): "Economic Dynamics with Learning: New Stability Results," *Review of Economic Studies*, 65, 23–44.

——— (1998c): "Stochastic Gradient Learning in the Cobweb Model," *Economic Letters*, 61, 333–337.

——— (1999): "Learning Dynamics." In *Handbook of Macroeconomics*, eds. J. Taylor and M. Woodford, Elsevier, Amsterdam, Vol. 1, 449–542.

——— (2000): "Convergence for Difference Equations with Vanishing Time Dependence, with Applications to Adaptive Learning," *Economic Theory*, 15, 717–725.

Evans, G. W., S. Honkapohja, and R. Marimon (2000): "Convergence in Monetary Inflation Models with Heterogeneous Learning Rules," *Macroeconomic Dynamics*, forthcoming.

Evans, G. W., S. Honkapohja, and P. Romer (1998): "Growth Cycles," *American Economic Review*, 88, 495–515.

Evans, G. W., S. Honkapohja, and T. J. Sargent (1993): "On the Preservation of Deterministic Cycles When Some Agents Perceive Them to be Random Fluctuations," *Journal of Economic Dynamics and Control*, 17, 705–721.

Evans, G. W., and G. Ramey (1992): "Expectations Calculation and Currency Collapse," *American Economic Review*, 82, 207–224.

——— (1995): "Expectation Calculation, Hyperinflation and Currency Collapse." In *The New Macroeconomics*: *Imperfect Markets and Policy Effectiveness*, eds. H. Dixon and N. Rankin, Cambridge University Press, Cambridge, 307–336.

Evans, G. W., and G. Ramey (1998a): "Adaptive Expectations, Underparameterization and the Lucas Critique," mimeo.

——— (1998b): "Calculation, Adaptation and Rational Expectations," *Macroeconomic Dynamics*, 2, 156–182.

Ezekiel, M. (1938): "The Cobweb Theorem," *Quarterly Journal of Economics*, 52, 255–280.

Farmer, R. E. (1999): *The Economics of Self-Fulfilling Prophecies*, second edition. MIT Press, Cambridge, MA.

Farmer, R. E., and J.-T. Guo (1994): "Real Business Cycles and the Animal Spirits Hypothesis," *Journal of Economic Theory*, 63, 42–72.

Feiwel, G. R., ed. (1987): *Arrow and the Ascent of Modern Economic Theory*. New York University Press, New York.

Feldman, M. (1987a): "Bayesian Learning and Convergence to Rational Expectations," *Journal of Mathematical Economics*, 16, 297–313.

——— (1987b): "An Example of Convergence to Rational Expectations with Heterogeneous Beliefs," *International Economic Review*, 28, 635–650.

Fisher, I. (1930): *Theory of Interest*. Macmillan, New York.

Fourgeaud, C., C. Gourieroux, and J. Pradel (1986): "Learning Procedures and Convergence to Rationality," *Econometrica*, 54, 845–868.

Franke, R. (2000): "Equilibrium Selection Under Cyclical Disequilibrium Dynamics," *Oxford Economic Papers*, forthcoming.

Friedman, B. M. (1979): "Optimal Expectations and the Extreme Information Assumptions of 'Rational Expectations' Macromodels," *Journal of Monetary Economics*, 5, 63–41.

Friedman, M., ed. (1956): *Studies in the Quantity Theory of Money*. University of Chicago Press, Chicago.

——— (1957): *Theory of the Consumption Function*. Princeton University Press, Princeton.

Frydman, R., and E. S. Phelps (1983): *Individual Forecasting and Aggregate Outcomes, "Rational Expectations" Reexamined*. Cambridge University Press, Cambridge.

Fuchs, G. (1977): "Formation of Expectations: A Model in Temporary General Equilibrium Theory," *Journal of Mathematical Economics*, 4, 167–187.

——— (1979): "Is Error Learning Behavior Stabilizing?," *Journal of Economic Theory*, 20, 300–317.

Fuchs, G., and G. Laroque (1976): "Dynamics of Temporary Equilibria and Expectations," *Econometrica*, 44, 1157–1178.

Fudenberg, D., and D. K. Levine (1998): *Theory of Learning in Games*. MIT Press, Cambridge, MA.

Futia, C. (1982): "Invariant Distributions and the Limiting Behavior of Markovian Economic Models," *Econometrica*, 50, 377–408.

Gale, D. (1996): "What Have We Learned from Social Learning?," *European Economic Review*, 40, 617–628.

Garratt, A., and S. Hall (1997): "E-Equilibria and Adaptive Expectations: Output and Inflation in the LBS Model," *Journal of Economic Dynamics and Control*, 21, 1149–1171.

Gottfries, N. (1985): "Multiple Perfect Foresight Equilibriums and Convergence of Learning Processes," *Journal of Money, Credit, and Banking*, 17, 111–117.

Gourieroux, C., J. Laffont, and A. Monfort (1982): "Rational Expectations in Dynamic Linear Models: Analysis of the Solutions," *Econometrica*, 50, 409–425.

Grandmont, J.-M. (1985): "On Endogenous Competitive Business Cycles," *Econometrica*, 53, 995–1045.

——— (1986): "Stabilizing Competitive Business Cycles," *Journal of Economic Theory*, 40, 57–76.

Grandmont, J.-M., ed. (1988): *Temporary Equilibrium: Selected Readings*. Academic Press, New York.

Grandmont, J.-M. (1998): "Expectations Formation and Stability of Large Socioeconomic Systems," *Econometrica*, 66, 741–781.

Grandmont, J.-M., and G. Laroque (1986): "Stability of Cycles and Expectations," *Journal of Economic Theory*, 40, 138–151.

——— (1990): "Stability, Expectations, and Predetermined Variables." In *Essays in Honor of Edmond Malinvaud*, eds. P. Champsaur et al., MIT Press, Cambridge, MA, 71–92.

——— (1991): "Economic Dynamics with Learning: Some Instability Examples." In *Equilibrium Theory and Applications, Proceedings of the Sixth International Symposium in Economic Theory and Econometrics*, eds. W. Barnett et al., Cambridge University Press, Cambridge, 247–273.

Griliches, Z., and M. Intriligator (1986): *Handbook of Econometrics*, Vol. 3. North-Holland, Amsterdam.

Grimmett, G., and D. Stirzaker (1992): *Probability and Random Processes*. Oxford University Press, Oxford.

Guckenheimer, J., and P. Holmes (1983): *Nonlinear Oscillations, Dynamical Systems and Bifurcations of Vector Fields*. Springer-Verlag, New York.

Guesnerie, R. (1992): "An Exploration of the Eductive Justifications of the Rational-Expectations Hypothesis," *American Economic Review*, 82, 1254–1278.

——— (1999): "Anchoring Economic Predictions in Common Knowledge," Working paper, DELTA, Paris.

Guesnerie, R., and M. Woodford (1991): "Stability of Cycles with Adaptive Learning Rules." In *Equilibrium Theory and Applications, Proceedings of the Sixth International Symposium in Economic Theory and Econometrics*, eds. W. Barnett et al., Cambridge University Press, Cambridge, 111–134.

——— (1992): "Endogenous Fluctuations." In *Advances in Economic Theory: Sixth World Congress*, ed. J.-J. Laffont, Cambridge University Press, Cambridge, 289–412.

Hahn, W. (1963): *Theory and Application of Liapunov's Direct Method*. Prentice-Hall, Englewood Cliffs, NJ.

——— (1967): *Stability of Motion*. Springler-Verlag, Berlin.

Hall, S., and A. Garratt (1995): "Model Consistent Learning and Regime Switching in the London Business School Model," *Economic Modelling*, 12, 87–96.

Haltiwanger, J., and M. Waldman (1989): "Limited Rationality and Strategic Complements: The Implications for Macroeconomics," *Quarterly Journal of Economics*, 104, 463–483.

Hamilton, J. D. (1994): *Time Series Analysis*. Princeton University Press, Princeton, NJ.

Hanzon, B., C. Heij, C. Praagman, and J. Schumacher, eds. (1997): *System Dynamics in Economic and Financial Models*. John Wiley and Sons, New York.

Hart, O. D. (1982): "A Model of Imperfect Competition with Keynesian Features," *Quarterly Journal of Economics*, 97, 109–138.

Harvey, A. C. (1981): *Time Series Models*. Philip Allan Publishers Ltd., Oxford.

Hebert, R. F. (1973): "Wage Cobwebs and Cobweb-Type Phenomena: An Early French Formulation," *Western Economic Journal*, 11, 394–403.

Heinemann, M. (2000a): "Adaptive Learning of Rational Expectations Using Neural Networks," *Journal of Economic Dynamics and Control*, 24, 1007–1026.

——— (2000b): "Convergence of Adaptive Learning and Expectational Stability: The Case of Multiple Rational Expectations Equilibria," *Macroeconomic Dynamics*, forthcoming.

Hicks, J. R. (1939): *Value and Capital*. Oxford University Press, Oxford.

——— (1965): *Capital and Growth*. Oxford University Press, Oxford.

Hildenbrand, W., and H. Sonnenschein, eds. (1991): *Handbook of Mathematical Economics*, Vol. IV. North-Holland, Amsterdam.

Hirsch, M. W., and S. Smale (1974): *Differential Equations, Dynamic Systems and Linear Algebra*. Academic Press, Orlando, FL.

Holland, J. H. (1992): *Adaptation in Natural and Artificial Systems*. MIT Press, Cambridge, MA.

Hommes, C. H., and G. Sorger (1997): "Consistent Expectations Equilibria," *Macroeconomic Dynamics*, 2, 287–321.

Honkapohja, S., and M. Ingberg, eds. (1993): *Macroeconomic Modeling and Policy Implications*. North-Holland, Amsterdam.

Honkapohja, S., and K. Mitra (1999): "Learning with Bounded Memory in Stochastic Models," Working paper, University of Helsinki.

Honkapohja, S., and A. Turunen-Red (1999): "Complementarity, Growth and Trade," Working paper, University of Helsinki.

Horn, R., and C. Johnson (1985): *Matrix Analysis*. Cambridge University Press, Cambridge.

——— (1991): *Topics in Matrix Analysis*. Cambridge University Press, Cambridge.

Howitt, P. (1992): "Interest Rate Control and Nonconvergence to Rational Expectations," *Journal of Political Economy*, 100, 776–800.

Howitt, P., and R. P. McAfee (1992): "Animal Spirits," *American Economic Review*, 82, 493–507.

Hurwicz, L. (1946): "Theory of the Firm and of Investment," *Econometrica*, 14, 109–136.

Judd, K. (1985): "The Law of Large Numbers with a Continuum of IID Random Variables," *Journal of Economic Theory*, 35, 19–25.

Jun, B., and X. Vives (1996): "Learning and Convergence to a Full-Information Expectations are not Equivalent," *Review of Economic Studies*, 63, 653–674.

Kaldor, N. (1940): "A Model of the Trade Cycle," *Economic Journal*, 50, 78–92.

Kalecki, M. (1935): "A Macrodynamic Theory of Business Cycles," *Econometrica*, 3, 327–344.

Karatzas, I., and S. E. Shreve (1988): *Brownian Motion and Stochastic Calculus*. Springer-Verlag, Berlin.

Keynes, J. M. (1936): *The General Theory of Employment, Interest and Money*. Macmillan, London.

——— (1937): "The General Theory of Employment," *Quarterly Journal of Economics*, 51, 209–223.

Kiefer, J., and J. Wolfowitz (1952): "Stochastic Estimation of the Modulus of a Regression Function," *Annals of Mathematical Statistics*, 23, 462–466.

Kingman, J. F. C., and S. J. Taylor (1973): *Introduction to Measure and Probability*. Cambridge University Press, Cambridge.

Kirman, A., and M. Salmon, eds. (1995): *Learning and Rationality in Economics*. Basil Blackwell, Oxford.

Kirman, A. P. (1995): "Learning in Oligopoly: Theory, Simulation, and Experimental Evidence." In *Learning and Rationality in Economics*, eds. A. Kirman and M. Salmon, Basil Blackwell, Oxford, 127–178.

Kiyotaki, N., and R. Wright (1989): "On Money as a Medium of Exhange," *Journal of Political Economy*, 97, 927–954.

Krasovskii, N. (1963): *Stability of Motion*. Stanford University Press, Stanford, CA.

Kreps, D., and K. Wallis, eds. (1997): *Advances in Economics and Econometrics: Theory and Applications*, Vol. I. Cambridge University Press, Cambridge.

Kuan, C.-M., and H. White (1994): "Adaptive Learning with Nonlinear Dynamics Driven by Dependent Processes," *Econometrica*, 62, 1087–1114.

Kurz, M., ed. (1997): *Endogenous Economic Fluctuations. Studies in the Theory of Rational Beliefs*. Springer-Verlag, Berlin.

Kushner, H., and D. Clark (1978): *Stochastic Approximation Methods for Constrained and Unconstrained Systems*. Springer-Verlag, Berlin.

Kushner, H. J., and G. G. Yin (1997): *Stochastic Approximation Algorithms and Applications*. Springer-Verlag, Berlin.

Kydland, F. E., and E. C. Prescott (1977): "Rules Rather Than Discretion: The Inconsistency of Optimal Plans," *Journal of Political Economy*, 85, 473–491.

Laffont, J.-J., ed. (1992): *Advances in Economic Theory: Sixth World Congress*, Vol. 2. Cambridge University Press, Cambridge.

LaSalle, J. P. (1992): *The Stability and Control of Discrete Processes*. Springer-Verlag, New York.

Lettau, M. (1997): "Explaining the Facts with Adaptive Agents: The Case of Mutual Funds Flows," *Journal of Economic Dynamics and Control*, 21, 1117–1147.

Lettau, M., and H. Uhlig (1999): "Rules of Thumb and Dynamic Programming," *American Economic Review*, 89, 148–174.

Lettau, M., and T. Van Zandt (1999): "Robustness of Adaptive Expectations as an Equilibrium Selection Device," Working paper.

Lindahl, E. (1939): *Studies in the Theory of Money and Capital*. Allen and Unwin, London.

Ljung, L. (1977): "Analysis of Recursive Stochastic Algorithms," *IEEE Transactions on Automatic Control*, 22, 551–575.

Ljung, L., G. Pflug, and H. Walk (1992): *Stochastic Approximation and Optimization of Random Systems*. Birkhauser, Basel.

Ljung, L., and T. Söderström (1983): *Theory and Practice of Recursive Identification*. MIT Press, Cambridge, MA.

Loasby, B. (1976): *Choice, Complexity and Ignorance*. Cambridge University Press, Cambridge.

Lucas, Jr., R. E. (1972): "Expectations and the Neutrality of Money," *Journal of Economic Theory*, 4, 103–124.

——— (1973): "Some International Evidence on Output–Inflation Trade-offs," *American Economic Review*, 63, 326–334.

——— (1978): "Asset Prices in an Exchange Economy," *Econometrica*, 46, 1429–1445.

——— (1981): *Studies in Business Cycle Theory*. MIT Press, Cambridge, MA.

——— (1986): "Adaptive Behavior and Economic Theory," *Journal of Business, Supplement*, 59, S401–S426.

Lucas, Jr., R. E., and T. J. Sargent, eds. (1981): *Rational Expectations and Econometric Practice*. University of Minnesota Press, Minneapolis.

Magnus, J., and H. Neudecker (1988): *Matrix Differential Calculus*. Wiley, New York.

Manski, C., and D. McFadden, eds. (1981): *Structural Analysis of Discrete Data with Econometric Applications*. MIT Press, Cambridge, MA.

Marcet, A., and J. P. Nicolini (1998): "Recurrent Hyperinflations and Learning," Working paper 1875, CEPR.

Marcet, A., and T. J. Sargent (1989a): "Convergence of Least Squares Learning and the Dynamic of Hyperinflation." In *Economic Complexity: Chaos,*

Sunspots, Bubbles, and Nonlinearity, eds. W. Barnett, J. Geweke, and K. Shell, Cambridge University Press, Cambridge, 119–137.

———— (1989b): "Convergence of Least-Squares Learning in Environments with Hidden State Variables and Private Information," *Journal of Political Economy*, 97, 1306–1322.

———— (1989c): "Convergence of Least-Squares Learning Mechanisms in Self-Referential Linear Stochastic Models," *Journal of Economic Theory*, 48, 337–368.

———— (1995): "Speed of Convergence of Recursive Least Squares: Learning with Autoregressive Moving-Average Perceptions." In *Learning and Rationality in Economics*, eds. A. Kirman and M. Salmon, Basil Blackwell, Oxford, 179–215.

Margaritis, D. (1987): "Strong Convergence of Least Squares Learning to Rational Expectations," *Economics Letters*, 23, 157–161.

———— (1990): "A Time Varying Model of Rational Learning," *Economics Letters*, 33, 309–314.

Marimon, R. (1997): "Learning from Learning in Economics." In *Advances in Economics and Econometrics: Theory and Applications*, eds. D. Kreps and K. Wallis, Cambridge University Press, Cambridge, 278–315.

Marimon, R., E. McGrattan, and T. Sargent (1989): "Money as Medium of Exchange with Artificially Intelligent Agents," *Journal of Economic Dynamics and Control*, 14, 329–373.

Marimon, R., and A. Scott, eds. (1999): *Computational Methods for the Study of Dynamic Economies*. Oxford University Press, Oxford.

Marimon, R., S. E. Spear, and S. Sunder (1993): "Expectationally Driven Market Volatility: An Experimental Study," *Journal of Economic Theory*, 61, 74–103.

Marimon, R., and S. Sunder (1993): "Indeterminacy of Equilibria in a Hyperinflationary World: Experimental Evidence," *Econometrica*, 61, 1073–1107.

———— (1994): "Expectations and Learning under Alternative Monetary Regimes: An Experimental Approach," *Economic Theory*, 4, 131–162.

McCafferty, S., and R. Driskill (1980): "Problems of Existence and Uniqueness in Nonlinear Rational Expectations Models," *Econometrica*, 48, 1313–1317.

McCallum, B. T. (1983): "On Nonuniqueness in Linear Rational Expectations Models: An Attempt at Perspective," *Journal of Monetary Economics*, 11, 134–168.

———— (1998): "Solutions to Linear Rational Expectations Models: A Compact Exposition," *Economics Letters*, 61, 143–147.

———— (1999): "Role of Minimal State Variable Criterion in Rational Expectations Models," *International Tax and Public Finance*, 6, 621–639.

McGough, B. (1999): "Statistical Learning and Time Varying Parameters," Working paper, University of Oregon.

McLennan, A. (1984): "Price Dispersion and Incomplete Learning in the Long Run," *Journal of Economic Dynamics and Control*, 7, 331–347.

Moore, B. J. (1993): "Least-Squares Learning and the Stability of Equilibria with Externalities," *Review of Economic Studies*, 60, 197–208.

Moreno, D., and M. Walker (1994): "Two Problems in Applying Ljung's 'Projection Algorithms' to the Analysis of Decentralized Learning," *Journal of Economic Theory*, 62, 420–427.

Muth, J. F. (1961): "Rational Expectations and the Theory of Price Movements," *Econometrica*, 29, 315–335.

Nerlove, M. (1958): *The Dynamics of Supply: Estimation of the Farmers' Response to Price*. Johns Hopkins University Press, Baltimore.

Neveu, J. (1965): *Mathematical Foundations of the Calculus of Probability*. Holden-Day, San Francisco.

Nyarko, Y. (1991): "Learning in Mis-Specified Models and the Possibility of Cycles," *Journal of Economic Theory*, 55, 416–427.

——— (1997): "Convergence in Economic Models with Bayesian Hierarchies of Beliefs," *Journal of Economic Theory*, 74, 266–296.

Øksendal, B. (1998): *Stochastic Differential Equations: An Introduction with Applications*. Springer-Verlag, Berlin.

Packalén, M. (1998): "Adaptive Learning of Rational Expectations: A Neural Network Approach," mimeo, University of Helsinki.

——— (2000): "On the Learnability of Rational Expectations Equilibria in Three Business Cycle Models," Research report no. 87, University of Helsinki.

Pesaran, M. H. (1981): "Identification of Rational Expectations Models," *Journal of Econometrics*, 16, 375–398.

——— (1987): *The Limits to Rational Expectations*. Blackwell, Oxford.

Robbins, H., and S. Monro (1951): "A Stochastic Approximation Method," *Annals of Mathematical Statistics*, 22, 400–407.

Romer, D. (1995): *Advanced Macroeconomics*. McGraw-Hill, New York.

Salge, M. (1997): *Rational Bubbles. Theoretical Basis, Economic Relevance and Empirical Evidence with Special Emphasis on the German Stock Market*. Springer-Verlag, Berlin.

Salmon, M. (1995): "Bounded Rationality and Learning; Procedural Learning." In *Learning and Rationality in Economics*, eds. A. Kirman and M. Salmon, Basil Blackwell, Oxford, 236–275.

Sargent, T. J. (1973): "Rational Expectations, the Real Rate of Interest and the Natural Rate of Unemployment," *Brookings Papers on Economic Activity*, 2, 429–472.

——— (1987): *Macroeconomic Theory*, second edition. Academic Press, New York.

——— (1991): "Equilibrium with Signal Extraction from Endogenous Variables," *Journal of Economic Dynamics and Control*, 15, 245–273.

——— (1993): *Bounded Rationality in Macroeconomics*. Oxford University Press, Oxford.

——— (1999): *The Conquest of American Inflation*. Princeton University Press, Princeton, NJ.

Sargent, T. J., and N. Wallace (1975): "'Rational Expectations,' the Optimal Monetary Instrument and the Optimal Money Supply Rule," *Journal of Political Economy*, 83, 241–254.

Schleifer, A. (1986): "Implementation Cycles," *Journal of Political Economy*, 94, 1163–1190.

Schönhofer, M. (1999): "Chaotic Learning Equilibria," *Journal of Economic Theory*, 89, 1–20.

Schumpeter, J. A. (1954): *History of Economic Analysis*. Allen and Unwin, London.

Sethi, R., and R. Franke (1995): "Behavioral Heterogeneity under Evolutionary Pressure: Macroeconomic Implications of Costly Optimization," *Economic Journal*, 105, 583–600.

Shell, K. (1977): "Monnaie et Allocation Intertemporelle," Working paper, CNRS Seminaire de E. Malinvaud, Paris.

Sims, C. A. (1988): "Projecting Policy Effects with Statistical Models," *Revista de Analisis Economico*, 3, 9–20.

Solow, R. (1956): "A Contribution to the Theory of Economic Growth," *Quarterly Journal of Economics*, 70, 65–94.

——— (1957): "Technical Change and the Aggregate Production Function," *Review of Economics and Statistics*, 39, 312–320.

Spear, S. E. (1984): "Sufficient Conditions for the Existence of Sunspot Equilibria," *Journal of Economic Theory*, 34, 360–370.

Stokey, N., and R. E. Lucas Jr. (1989): *Recursive Methods in Economic Dynamics*. Harvard University Press, Cambridge, MA.

Taylor, J. (1975): "Monetary Policy during a Transition to Rational Expectations," *Journal of Political Economy*, 83, 1009–1021.

——— (1977): "Conditions for Unique Solutions in Stochastic Macroeconomic Models with Rational Expectations," *Econometrica*, 45, 1377–1386.

—— (1980): "Aggregate Dynamics and Staggered Contracts," *Journal of Political Economy*, 88, 1–23.

—— (1986): "New Approaches to Stabilization Policy in Stochastic Models of Macroeconomic Fluctuations." In *Handbook of Econometrics*, eds. Z. Griliches and M. Intriligator, North-Holland, Amsterdam, 1997–2055.

Taylor, J., and M. Woodford, eds. (1999): *Handbook of Macroeconomics*, Vol. 1. Elsevier, Amsterdam.

Thornton, H. (1939): *An Enquiry into the Nature and Effects of the Paper Credit of Great Britain*. Allen and Unwin, London.

Tillmann, G. (1983): "Stability in a Simple Pure Consumption Loan Model," *Journal of Economic Theory*, 30, 315–329.

Timmermann, A. G. (1993): "How Learning in Financial Markets Generates Excess Volatility and Predictability in Stock Prices," *Quarterly Journal of Economics*, 108, 1135–1145.

—— (1995): "Volatility Clustering and Mean Reversion of Stock Returns in an Asset Pricing Model with Incomplete Learning," Working paper.

—— (1996): "Excessive Volatility and Predictability of Stock Prices in Autoregressive Dividend Models with Learning," *Review of Economic Studies*, 63, 523–557.

Townsend, R. M. (1978): "Market Anticipations, Rational Expectations, and Bayesian Analysis," *International Economic Review*, 19, 481–494.

—— (1983): "Forecasting the Forecasts of Others," *Journal of Political Economy*, 91, 546–588.

Turnovsky, S. (1969): "A Bayesian Approach to the Theory of Expectations," *Journal of Economic Theory*, 1, 220–227.

Uhlig, H. (1999): "A Toolkit for Analyzing Nonlinear Dynamic Rational Expectations Models Easily." In *Computational Methods for the Study of Dynamic Economies*, eds. R. Marimon and A. Scott, Oxford University Press, Oxford, 150–200.

Van Huyck, J. B., R. C. Battalio, and R. Beil (1990): "Tacit Coordination Games, Strategic Uncertainty, and Coordination Failure," *American Economic Review*, 80, 234–248.

—— (1991): "Strategic Uncertainty, Equilibrium Selection Principles, and Coordination Failure in Average Opinion Games," *Quarterly Journal of Economics*, 106, 885–910.

Van Huyck, J. B., J. P. Cook, and R. C. Battalio (1994): "Selection Dynamics, Asymptotic Stability, and Adaptive Behaviour," *Journal of Political Economy*, 102, 975–1005.

Vives, X. (1993): "How Fast do Rational Agents Learn?," *Review of Economic Studies*, 60, 329–347.

Weitzman, M. (1982): "Increasing Returns and the Foundations of Unemployment Theory," *Economic Journal*, 92, 787–804.

White, H. (1984): *Asymptotic Theory for Econometricians*. Academic Press, Orlando, FL.

White, H. (1992): *Artificial Neural Networks: Approximation and Learning Theory*. Basil Blackwell, Oxford.

Whiteman, C. (1983): *Linear Rational Expectations Models*. University of Minnesota Press, Minneapolis.

Williams, N. (2000): "Convergence and Escape: Learning Dynamics and the Time Paths of Inflation in a Model of Monetary Policy," mimeo, University of Chicago.

Woodford, M. (1990): "Learning to Believe in Sunspots," *Econometrica*, 58, 277–307.

Zenner, M. (1996): *Learning to Become Rational. The Case of Self-Referential Autoregressive and Non-Stationary Models*. Springer-Verlag, Berlin.

Author Index

Subject Index

411